C000226248

Doors of Possibility
The life of Dame Emmeline Tanner
1876-1955

Doors of Possibility

The life of Dame Emmeline Tanner
1876-1955

Susan Major

The Lutterworth Press
Cambridge

The Lutterworth Press

PO Box 60
Cambridge
CB1 2NT

British Library Cataloguing in Publication Data:
A catalogue record is available from the British Library.

ISBN 0 7188 2922 0

Printed in Great Britain by
St Edmundsbury Press

Contents

List of illustrations
appearing between pages 182-183

Acknowledgments

When my mother, Mrs Pamela Kirton, asked me to help set in order the extant personal papers of her aunt Emmeline Tanner I did not expect this book to result; it took shape as I realised how Emmeline's life and work charted much of the terrain of girls' educational history over a period of important development, in some of which she herself had a hand. From that time Pam Kirton gave me free access not only to these papers but to her own knowledge, and supplied unstinting patient encouragement. So my first thanks are to her.

It is pleasant now to remember with how much kindness my further inquiries and requests for material concerning Emmeline Tanner were so often received. Each of her surviving nephews and nieces, and sometimes great-nephews and great-nieces, offered sympathy and often helpful detail; in particular I am grateful to Mrs Margaret Fox-Andrews and her husband for their hospitality in Bath, their local knowledge and some illuminating conversations, and to Mrs Ruth Cousins for answering a formidable questionnaire on her school days in the Second World War (a period on which the late Miss Jacqueline Tanner was also informative). My warm thanks go also to Emmeline's godson Mr J. J. Crofts, and to her goddaughter Mrs Ida Sobey for their help on her personal friendships.

I profited also from letters or conversations with many individuals who knew Emmeline and am grateful to all, but especially to those whose words I have quoted: Mrs J. Anderson, Mrs E. Atkinson, Mrs J. Baker, Mrs M. C. Baker, the Rev. J. Barbour, Mrs J. Beaver, Miss M. Boyd, Miss B. S. Briggs, Miss P. Burnaby, Miss C. Chovil, Mrs M. Cruse, Mrs E. Edwards, Dr B. Evans, Mrs R. Forsyth, Mrs F. Gater (and her daughter Mrs J. Babbage), Mrs S. Grice, Mrs P. Halcrow, Mrs K. E. Harries, Mrs J. Harrison, Mrs P. Haselhurst, Mrs J. Houghton, Mrs M. Hudson, Mrs R. Huebener, Mrs H. M. Humphrey-Smith, Mrs Y. Johnston, Mrs D. Jordan, Mrs A. Leakey, Miss A. Lightfoot, Miss L. Lowndes, Miss M. Middleton, Mrs H. J. Miller, Miss R. Newbolt, Miss B. Patterson, Sister M. Popper, Miss C. Smith and her amanuensis Miss M. Reeves, Miss E. M. E. Sprent, Mrs E. Thom-Postlethwaite, Miss E. M. Waddy, and Miss N. B. Woodcock. Mr Henry Blyth was himself helpful, and also introduced me to Mrs B. Tyler who kindly lent some letters of Beatrice Lawrence. But thanks to all who responded to my inquiries.

In addition to the staffs of the library and record departments named on p. 397, and the resources of the British Library and the London Library, I am greatly indebted to the schools directly concerned with phases of Emmeline Tanner's career. So my thanks go to Sherborne School for Girls, to Mrs J. M. Taylor, Headmistress, and to Mr B. Williams for his assistance there; to Mr D. O. Prior, Head Teacher of Etone School, Nuneaton, and to the office and maintenance staff at the school for their help with records of its predecessor, Nuneaton High School. At Bedford the Clerk of the Bedford Charity (the Harpur Trust) kindly allowed access to relevant material on Bedford High School, where the Headmistress, Mrs D. Willis, introduced me to Miss P. Burnaby, whose hospitality and store of personal and school knowledge enriched the records she showed me. I am most grateful to Roedean Council, and especially Dr J. Peacey, for access to Roedean's records. Dr Peacey was also kind enough to provide valuable and stimulating personal memories. Thanks too to the Headmistress, Mrs A. Longley, and to Mr R. Castleden for their assistance at Roedean School, and to Miss V. Kent, Miss N. Frith and Mrs V. Allen of the Old Roedeanians Association who helped me trace many ORs.

For help with elucidating some aspects of Emmeline Tanner's early life I am very grateful to the Library and Documents Committee at Swedenborg House, especially to Mr H. W. Turner, and to Miss R. Holmes of the New Christian Church, Combe Down, Bath. The staff of the Modern Records Centre at the University of Warwick Library were helpful in uncovering material on some educational associations; and I am also grateful to the Secondary Heads Association for use of the Reports of the Association of Head Mistresses. Mr W. Hetherington of the Peace Pledge Union checked some of their records on my behalf.

Crown Copyright material in the Public Record Office is reproduced by permission of the Controller of Her Majesty's Stationery Office.

To none do I owe more than to my husband Christopher Major, in too many ways to enumerate.

List of abbreviations

AAM	Association of Assistant Mistresses
AHM	Association of Head Mistresses
AHMBS	Association of Head Mistresses of Boarding Schools
AHMIDG	Association of Head Mistresses of Independent and Direct Grant Schools
ARP	Air Raid Precautions
ESU	English-Speaking Union
FAU	Friends' Ambulance Unit
GBA	Governing Bodies Association
GBGSA	Association of Governing Bodies of Girls' Schools
GPDSC	Girls' Public Day School Company (to 1906)
GPDST	Girls' Public Day School Trust (GPDSC reconstituted from 1906)
HMC	Head Masters' Conference
IAAM	Incorporated Association of Assistant Masters
IAHM	Incorporated Association of Head Masters
Joint Four	Joint Committee of Four Secondary Associations (AHM, IAHM, AAM, IAAM)
LEA	Local Education Authority
LNU	League of Nations Union
MAHM	Midlands Association of Head Mistresses
NUT	National Union of Teachers
ORA	Old Roedeanians Association
WEA	Workers' Educational Association
YMCA, YWCA	Young Men's Christian Association, Young Women's Christian Association

Chapter 1
First things first

Halfway through writing a letter to her mother on the evening of 27 February 1924 Emmeline Tanner was interrupted by knocking at her cottage door: 'a visit from the *Daily Mail* man, out here in the dark in a bad snowstorm, poor wretch!' The journalist saw a woman of forty-seven, tall and deep-bosomed, but his wait was ill repaid for 'I had no photograph to give him and I did not interview well' – here she added the wavy vertical line which was her symbol for a chuckle. But the snowstorm won more of her sympathy for the representative of the *Daily Mail* than for the *Sketch* journalist who 'hid round the corner and snapped me as I went off on my bicycle' earlier that day.[1]

The minor ripple Emmeline sent through the Press that week was due, not to her minimal photogenic qualities but to the reputation of Roedean School and of the three Lawrence sisters who were its founders. Emmeline had just been appointed headmistress to Roedean , and in her letter to her mother she was describing her meeting with two of these ladies and with the school's Council. Two days earlier she had sat in the Grosvenor Hotel in London with the eldest and most formidable sister, Penelope Lawrence, now in her late sixties and as weighty in body as in personality; her sisters' ill-health rather than her own had precipitated their joint retirement. But she was still Chairman of Roedean Council and her voice had been the most influential in overtures to Emmeline.

Penelope Lawrence wanted no pliable tool, yet 'it seemed so unnatural', Emmeline heard, 'to be handing their life-work over to someone of whose private life they knew nothing, that she didn't know where I was born, who my father was ... They had already asked Lady Ampthill about my parentage and the breadth of my religious views and she had said that she knew nothing definite about either but she felt sure they were both all right and I couldn't be such a success in Bedford if they weren't', and again the chuckle symbol follows. 'I said that could soon be remedied so I gave her full information about my birth, etc.' Penelope Lawrence digested the information, and then said valiantly that 'of course they all knew a great deal about the reputation and position I had made for myself'.

For power or prestige in Bath in the 1870s Emmeline was born into the wrong class, the wrong religion and the wrong sex. If her family were 'respectable', that is, far from the extremes of poverty that hopelessly handicapped the slum-dwellers of Dolemeads, and further from the atheism that rendered a teacher almost unemployable, they were also outside the Anglican establishment of gentry, higher professionals and substantial merchants, who set the tone and ran the affairs of a city developed to minister to gentry comforts.

When they married in 1875, Emmeline's parents had had plenty of opportunity to observe this process, Sam Tanner in the office of a coal-factor, Nettie as assistant in a high-class draper's in fashionable Milsom Street. They did not seek to emulate those who thought themselves their betters; rather they deliberately and conscientiously made choices that separated them from the powers-that-were, in pursuit of a better future both here, and, as they saw it, in the life to come. They did not expect it to be easy.

Probably neither would have claimed to have had a hard life before marriage, using Victorian standards. Very little is known, however. Samuel was a local man, born the fifth of eight children in 1849 at Weston, then just outside Bath. His father Edward Tanner at that time gave his address as 'Weston Lock' and his occupation as carpenter – perhaps he was lock-keeper too – but by 1875 he was described as a 'contractor' and seems to have been involved in building projects. One grandson thought Edward had had engineering skills and had worked in Canada; if so, this might account for the long gaps between the births of his children, Jane (born 1835) being more than twenty years older than her youngest brother, Fred. Fred was drowned at seventeen, swimming in the River Avon, but the other four sons of the artisan Edward Tanner entered modest white-collar jobs, Sam starting as an adolescent clerk. His sisters, Jane, Adelaide and Julia, took up the equally characteristic options available to such a family's daughters. Jane seems always to have stayed at home, Adelaide became housekeeper to a country clergyman (and developed into the perfect aunt), and Julia married a railway official.

There were many such families in that precarious and unheroic area known, for convenience, as the lower middle class. Precarious, because some were on their way up towards the comfortable region in which dwelt the Victorian professional middle classes with cook, parlourmaid, nanny, gardener and 'leisured' wife, while others, through ill-luck or incompetence, were drifting down to the sad squalor of the unskilled poor. Their energy was fuelled by hope and fear.

Nettie Fry was a suitable wife for Sam Tanner. She had been brought up in Lynton on the coast of North Devon, even then a noted beauty spot admired by honeymooners and lovers of the picturesque, and all her life Nettie craved the splendours of flowers and trees, hills and sea. The cliffs and the steep wooded valleys of Lynton remained her yardstick for natural beauty. There her father, George Fry, had also been born, apparently becoming almost a factotum in Lynton: in 1866 a directory lists him as 'farmer and Post-horse proprietor', a later edition puts him in the Post Office, and perhaps he combined this with the grocer's trade assigned to him in another directory. His image, though, survived in the memory of his grandson Herbert as an entrepreneur with trading ship and postal service, and in that of his granddaughter Beatrice as a noted local wrestler.

Nettie, the daughter of his second wife, was named Jeanetta Jane after two infants who died before her birth, and was some years younger than her half-brother and sisters. The family was completed by her younger brother George, these two youngest being brought up by their father's third wife, his third Mary, after their own mother died when Nettie was six. It must have been the third Mary Fry who taught Nettie to speak without a regional accent, to sit and stand straight, to know the forms of behaviour and appearance that were considered 'correct'; she was in her forties when she married George Fry and is thought previously to have been some kind of nursery-governess to one of the 'good' Devonshire families.

At any rate, when Nettie left home to support herself in Bath she had the ladylike manners necessary for an assistant in an élite retailing establishment. The rewards were usually meagre – long hours, low pay, compulsory board-lodging over the shop. From her lodging at 7 Milsom Street she wrote the earliest letter to Sam which survives, a letter vividly evidencing an ardent nature and a passionate religious faith. Nettie may indeed have met Sam Tanner through shared attendance at a Nonconformist chapel, or perhaps through their common and equally wholehearted commitment to teetotalism, for temperance zeal blossomed in social activities of many kinds. When they married, in 1875 – probably as soon as Sam had been promoted to be manager at the office of George Benjamin, Coal Factor, and (as the phrase went) could support a wife – the ceremony was held in the Baptist Chapel at Redland, Bristol, witnessed by friends from their working lives rather than family members.

The pair went to live in a small end-of-terrace house at 1 Locksbrook Place in Weston, now rapidly developing as a suburb of Bath after the Midland Railway linked through, running parallel to the Great Western Railway on the other side of the river. For all of the five years they lived in that house they must have been within sight and sound of building operations as little villas grew and spread in ribbons along the roads westward. Sam's father Edward was apparently engaged in some of these building works, for Nettie noted in her diary a visit to the 'houses Sam's father built' there.

Sam could support a wife, but not in a style which afforded tedious leisure. Usually the Tanners had one general servant, typically a teenager, who did 'the rough' of scrubbing floors, laying and clearing fires, cleaning gas-lamps, fuelling the stove (naturally the coal merchant's family always cooked on coal even when gas became a viable fuel), the heavier washing chores – the maintenance of a Victorian home was a full-time job – while Nettie cooked, made beds, sewed, and produced babies.

By the end of 1876 the birth of her first child was imminent. The rigours of confinement were endured at home, as was normal, and though a 'monthly' (residential) nurse was too expensive a doctor and nurse were at hand for the birth and immediately after, rather than the 'handywoman' employed by poorer people before midwives required registration in 1911.

On 28 December Sam was able to write notes to family and friends that Nettie was safely delivered of a fine daughter.

'You were lucky to get your Christmas dinner first,' Nettie's sister Lizzie added to her more high-flown comment that 'that new feeling of mother love is the sweetest thing on earth'. Other responses also show stock attitudes to childbirth, divided between relief that 'your trial' or 'your great trouble' was safely accomplished and heavy-handed jokes asking 'how many times has Sam made his arms ache already nursing his firstborn?' As Sam's sister Jane pointed out, 'Of course you won't be able to go to Lodge much now ... when you do go to Lodge again they will offer you a congratulatory address'; she was referring to the meetings of the Independent Order of Good Templars, a temperance organisation whose group solidarity was expressed in ritual and in social activities and philanthropic efforts. Despite family responsibilities the Tanners remained keen members.

The infant daughter was indeed received with all the welcome anticipated by family and friends, and Nettie was probably already disposed to join her stepmother in her prayer to 'our heavenly Father to give you health and grace to bring up your little offspring for His own child'; soon she began to jot odd notes in a small diary, clearly revealing the pride and delight she and Sam took in their first child. No doubt the baby was a more enjoyable focus for their thoughts than were their parents. Mary Fry had added anxiously to her letter that trade was bad and 'your father cannot get rid of his cough', and Edward Tanner sent an awkward appeal from Brighton, where he had just lost a job through a downturn in business: 'I have been expecting that before, and as I have been paid 30/- and the other man 20/- a week I could not expect to stop, I a stranger and the other last year's man.' Now he was returning to Bath where his wife Pamela had remained – 'she have had her own way so long that it will seem very hard to her to have a master, no doubt,' said Edward, but asked his son to look out for another job for him: 'splitting wood, etc. will do better than nothing at all.' Sam, it seems, was already one of the rocks on which his family leant.

His brother Sylvanus, or Sill, raised a more cheerful issue, even if the flippant and sarcastic tone of his letter was hardly sympathetic. What should the child be named? Others had assumed Jane, or referred to 'your Geraldine', but Sill urged as 'a most appropriate and delicate compliment to our maternal ancestors' the use of mother's and grandmothers' names, Pamela Catherine Esther, or one of a list of thirty 'noted for their rarity, antiquity and euphonism', with 'Temperance' heavily underscored. Taken with Jane's reference to 'Lodge' this implies Sam's teetotalism was sometimes mocked by his family. The discrepancy between the literary facility of Sill (and the other children) and his father's style also suggests that Tanner social strivings and skills may have derived from their mother Pamela, born Ridler, a West Country name.

As for the baby's name all suggestions were rejected in favour of Emmeline Mary. Hardly, however, were the parents through the flutters aroused by the firstborn than Nettie was pregnant again. Within ten years of Emmeline's birth Nettie and Sam had completed their family of seven children, the first four arriving at yearly intervals, the last three biennially, and so the eldest had little opportunity to loiter about the business of childishness or dependence. Until she was eleven or so Emmeline scarcely knew her mother not to be expecting or nursing a new child, and thus she formed her image of family life.

By the age of eighteen months she had a baby sister, Eva, whose name Sam decided on the way to the register office, and after Eva's birth came Beatrice's, leaving Nettie unwell and 'very very thankful' when her sister-in-law Adelaide arrived to look after the elder two. But Nettie was soon in charge again and, as soon as the baby was weaned at eight months, pregnant again. Frederick emerged before doctor or nurse arrived, his birth attended only by Sam and his sister Jane; nevertheless 'I was only poorly for about 1½ hours' and a day later Nettie was dashing off 'two sheets to Polly about "Parturition without Pain" and did not feel at all tired', but delighted with the large handsome child who soon 'had a smile for everybody'. The physical impact told on Nettie's teeth, however, and she now acquired a false set.

It was just two years before the next child, Herbert, seemingly sickly but a survivor, and two more before Winifred, in her turn two years older than the youngest, Arthur. At his birth in 1886 Sam and Nettie had seven children under ten years, not unusual though family size was by then falling, the upper classes leading the way. When Winifred herself married, her mother gave her – probably was able to give – no advice on birth control, and inbred reticence about sexual matters discouraged enquiry.

The parents on whom her eyes had opened, set standards and formed principles Emmeline retained, sometimes deliberately. Though her life was spent in education and at the end of it she declared that the greatest gift a school could give its pupils was a standard of values, yet she refused to set school influence above that of home: the former was more malleable but less fundamental or authoritative. That was a judgement of experience. Sometimes, however, Sam and Nettie seem to have established terms for life which Emmeline absorbed unawares. They set a value on success, and she wanted success, she knew she wanted success, but the concept fused contradictory elements deriving from the conditions of her parents' lives. Aware of poverty and the iron grip of class prejudice they valued material prosperity and social esteem as liberators, but, insisting as earnest Christians on the prior needs of others and the duty to lay up treasures especially in heaven, they assessed success also in terms of public utility, the practice of generosity and self-abnegation. Very often Emmeline's decisions could bear interpretations in both sets of terms. To put it another way, the Tanners conceived of well-being in personal terms of individuals' qualities, aspirations and activities, not as a function of their location in the socio-economic structure.

The infant Emmeline was certainly not apprehensive about abstracts, however. She was a healthy baby and gratified her mother with smiles as she became aware of Nettie as a separate being, and grew to recognise her mother's deepset eyes gazing directly, piercingly, from a strongly-boned face, her straight and not small nose, firm chin and firm mouth, naturally down-curved but habitually disciplined by her self-imposed rule 'Keep the corners up'. Nettie was not, it seems, a cuddling woman, even if the late Victorian style of fitting stiff fabrics tightly over boning had encouraged cuddling, but her maternal care suffuses her diary notes.

She observed her children's characteristics ('Emmie is a very particular child about having clean things ... Eva hides all sorts of things, such as her doll in ashes'), cared for their ailments, and imposed her own forms of discipline. When Emmeline was rude to the young servant 'I had to put her to bed. She begged pardon after', but bribery was another technique: 'I have promised Em, Eva and Bee presents if they will not quarrel – Em has improved during the year in that respect since I gave her a large book.' Em was then four years old. Nettie could also smack when exasperated, but since Em's brothers Fred and Herbert were both slightly surprised and disgusted to find the cane in use at school, corporal punishment cannot have been frequent. Indeed, just before Herbert's birth Nettie noted sadly, as if to score it in her mind, that 'Mr Pitman preached and begged Mothers not to be irritable, impatient or unkind but quite patient and loving, for the sake of example'.

Though less immediate Sam was no less significant. He was fond of small children, and good at playing with them, though his usual adult style was one of quiet dignity, enhanced by the beard he wore, like most of his contemporaries, and his hooded eyes. 'More remote' than their mother, thought Herbert, and 'we took no "liberties"',[2] but lines etched only by humour edge Sam's eyes in photographs. Rarely did he raise his voice – only, his children said, at boot menders' bills, and then Nettie would fling wide the windows to shame him in the neighbours' ears – but his decisions were final and his word the more potent because day-to-day discipline was Nettie's affair. So was child care in general, though when Nettie was visiting her sister or in bed with the latest child responsibility might often be entrusted to a relative. But it was Sam, as Nettie's diary shows, who often got up at night for a crying child, and when Emmeline was just two he was her sole escort first on a coach journey to Lynton, then on a train to Bournemouth where a branch of Benjamin's firm was being established, with Sam's father and brother in charge. So he must have been both able and willing to cope with a small child's physical needs.

Nettie's diary treasured up each tiny development. At six months Emmeline could say 'Pa' and 'Ma' and 'shake her hands for ta-ta'; just after her first birthday 'Emmie can say a great many words and has six teeth through'; at sixteen months 'Emmie is so fond of a doll; puts it to sleep, sings to it', and at eighteen months 'Emmie repeated the alphabet after Pa, also the last word of lines of nursery rhymes from memory': such are just a few examples. At eighteen months also, in June 1878, Emmeline was taken on her first visit to Bournemouth for Sam's exploration of business prospects. 'Sam met us at the station and took us to Mrs Joy's – very nice apartments – Emmie had on her white Princess and we went to the sands ... Emmie is afraid to paddle in the sea.'

This fear she rapidly overcame and on subsequent seaside visits learnt to love swimming, though later she ruefully recalled the requirements of modesty. 'When I think [in 1938] of the petticoats I wore in my youth, of the length of the skirts in which I played games, of the sort of bathing-dress in which I cautiously stepped out of the bathing-machine already discreetly wheeled right up to the water's edge if not actually into the water while I was undressing inside', then the adult Emmeline linked their restrictive clothes not only to the internal sense of restriction she detected in her contemporaries, but also to the formality of adult-child relationships in late Victorian England. In 1938 she welcomed 'easy familiarity' between parent and child, and its extension to 'the relationship between the sexes. Girls go almost anywhere unchaperoned nowadays; they read anything, they talk about anything; they are absolutely frank in talking about sex with their contemporaries of either sex if not always with their elders. And I believe that is all to the good.' And a contrast to her youth.

Even Victorian infants had their romps, of course. There were still summer hayfields round Weston where 'Emmie enjoys being covered over', and in September they went blackberrying, while the swing in the garden 'is a great source of amusement', though Emmeline was in her teens before the younger children found a new thrill in 'the Tricycle' of adult size which Nettie rode as well as they. But the code was there: Nettie would rebuke a grandchild for tickling even a baby above the knee. These were respectable circles, where Emmie was praised for saying 'Little Jack Horner' 'quite perfectly without any help, and some of "Bo-Peep"' before she was two, and where no swear-words were heard at home, but also circles where mothers took their babies to tea with each other, not where visits were paid with calling-cards; the Tanners ate dinner at midday not in the evening. Such details were class signposts.

The Tanners' house welcomed visitors almost daily for tea or supper or overnight, usually their numerous relations or friends from before marriage at first, or Mrs Benjamin, the wife of Sam's employer, who brought a nursemaid along with her child (but Nettie was not above noticing that Emmie was half a head taller and talked more distinctly than little Daisy), or soon the friends they were making from the new little villas that rose along Newbridge Road as suburbs formed at the edge of Weston. They met through temperance activities, through their church and through politics. Sam's loyalty to the Liberal Party was sufficiently established for him to act as Secretary to the Weston Liberal Association and unpaid agent at election times, and to be listed as such in the local directory. Emmeline absorbed early the lesson that to favour a cause entailed action and responsibility but not necessarily remuneration – more often contributions squeezed from the tight Tanner budget.

Extravagance was a matter for guilt. When Nettie had recovered her figure after Eva's birth she had a new dress made up, and knew it 'too elaborate for a poor woman, consequently I'm sure it will be three times too expensive. I like it awfully – sinner that I am', and then added her elder daughter's consolation: 'Nedder mind, ma.' Emmeline learnt to mind, though, about wasting money or provisions – when she made that note Nettie was between pickling vegetable marrows and pickling onions to preserve them – and even in her late forties, when Emmeline was well paid for a woman, she could not spend money on herself without painstaking justification. The purchase of Zeiss field-glasses in 1923 she rationalised with four separate reasons, and thought it necessary to disclose these to her family.

What of the wider environment on which Emmeline opened her eyes? Weston was not incorporated into the city of Bath till 1911, and though by the 1870s the old village with its summer fair for livestock and cheese from local pastures was fast developing into a suburb with its own small industries of woollen mills, sawmills, gasworks and malthouses, the countryside lay open to the north and west, and Kelston Round Hill was visible at the end of Newbridge Road. The south was hemmed by the railways and the river. Bath was not a city of heavy industry, and the hot springs which had attracted the Romans and, with other social amusements, had drawn the Georgian gentry who built their elegant and dignified houses up the slopes of the Avon, had given rise to a prosperity resting predominantly on lighter service trades, on retailers and builders, cabinet- and carriage-makers, dressmakers and milliners. A comparatively high proportion of the labour force were employed in domestic service. On such a base the city's fortunes fluctuated, but revived in this second half of the 19th century as the tourist trade picked up again and as more effective management developed after the local authority was reformed by statutes from 1834.

So in the mid-19th century public works were undertaken – gas lighting, a new water supply and sewage system, road and bridge improvements. The hospitals, however, the general United Hospital as well as the specialist Eye and Ear, Nose and Throat institutions, were funded by charitable subscription. Private charity aided innumerable causes but the chief public relief of the poor was by the parish rate and the workhouse, a building of 1838 at Odd Down to the south, managed by the locally elected Board of Guardians. In the 1890s the young daughter of one Guardian was impressed by the old women's 'white muslin caps and cotton frocks', 'the tables scrubbed white' and the strong odour of Lifebuoy soap, and she played young hostess at the Christmas parties given for the pauper children, but it was a destination few welcomed.[3] Visiting an aged acquaintance at the workhouse in the 1880s Nettie may have reflected on the imperative need to provide for old age, nor did she need to be aware of the exact statistics to observe how common were unmarried women, with the marriage rate at its lowest and the problem of 'surplus women' – a sufficiently slighting phrase – bruited about the Press. In 1871, women outnumbered men nationally by 600,000 in a total population of 22,712,000, and in Bath the ratio was more marked.

For those who might more freely choose their pleasures, Victoria Park had opened in 1830 as a respectable pleasure-ground for middle-class families, but the older Sydney Gardens also offered agreeable promenades and bandstands, as well as the annual Flower Show. The excitement of 1877, when Emmeline was just six months, was the great Centenary Show of the Bath and West of England Society, agricultural in origin: the city was *en fête* with illuminations and distinguished visitors. But the Great Western Railway had advertised the Widcombe footbridge as the quickest way from the station, and the tolls were taken on the further side. As two or three hundred crowded on to the bridge it collapsed, killing eight. 'Mr Child preached about Accident,' noted Nettie the next Sunday. The Tanners were not among the victims. They held a family party with Nettie's father and her sister Polly, Sam's mother and his sister Jane, and several friends – 'They all say what a dear good child Emmeline is' – and went to see the illuminations. When they visited the Show itself next day 'it was uncomfortably wet and muddy; we lost Father – he came home shortly after us.' Possibly George Fry did not care for restriction to soft drinks.

Not till 1880, though, were the Roman Baths uncovered, and by the time the Concert Hall extension was added to the Pump Room, Emmeline was twenty and had left the city. The Literary and Philosophical Society, like the other societies of high culture, was dominated by the upper middle classes, the professional, ex-military and ex-colonial families and wealthier tradesmen who were numerous in Bath, and Isaac Pitman's attempts to induce the city to start a Free Library were rejected by ratepayers, who thought the private subscription libraries provided adequate reading matter. There was always cricket, though, even if the County Ground was a 1/3d train journey away at Bristol. Somerset-born Sam Tanner developed a partisan loyalty to Gloucestershire, joining the County Club in the 1890s and taking his daughters as well as his sons to watch W. G. Grace and other stalwarts whenever he could. At thirteen or fourteen his eldest son was sufficiently inspired to form a cricket and hockey club in Weston itself and to keep it going for some years.

Without such self-help there was little enough for teenagers save the Band of Hope and the diverse philanthropies towards the sick, aged, orphaned and otherwise unfortunate. So middle-class women eased their consciences and filled their time: 'The closest the Victorians came to having an apparatus of social service,' says one social historian, was not legislative but 'the consequence of the largely unsystematised efforts of vast numbers of individuals and voluntary associations, mainly inspired by religious motives, and sustained by the work of vast armies of middle-class women.'[4]

The relationship of giver and receiver did not necessarily break down the prejudices of either, though it might afford opportunities for observation by youthful middlemen. 'When we collected for the hospital, on Hospital Saturday,' wrote Eva in a schoolgirl essay, 'when we asked many to give, they said, "Well, we must draw the line somewhere," and so left us as poor as we were before, only wishing they had not thought of doing so just then ... Rich people often like heading Charity lists, but when asked to give a poor crossing-sweeper a penny, often refuse.'

Not that Nettie was troubled by empty time in the 1870s and 1880s. The load of children was spread by exploiting the family network, reciprocally where necessary. Frequently one or other of the young Tanners was staying with one of the aunts, with Adelaide as she kept house for the Rector of Sherrington, or with Julia and her railway-employed husband in Reading, or Polly in Salisbury, or Uncle Charles and his wife in Bournemouth, and such visits could last several months. Adelaide took Eva for three months when she was three, and in the same year Emmeline spent three months in Reading. Beatrice stayed more or less permanently at Sherrington for several years, to return home at about the age of ten to meet some disagreeable shocks: no cream on her porridge, and cold baths. Furthermore, she was smacked when she objected. Learning adaptability could be a bitter process.

Friends and relations were at hand when Nettie spent an occasional week or so at Lynton with her father and stepmother. The newest baby might accompany her, still needing the breast, but not normally the older children. George Fry's health was declining, as were his fortunes, and by 1881 he was supplementing trade as a beerhouse keeper with a lodger, a mason from Porlock. The Tradesman's Arms, his home, may not have been suitable, or spacious enough, for Nettie's children, however beautiful the surroundings of Lynton. Quiet Sherrington in Wiltshire, with its watercress beds and the mound of an ancient castle, was the place for country holidays, housed safely in the benevolent Rev. Mr Heard's thatched stone Rectory, wrapped in creepers and climbing roses, and watched over by Adelaide, the perfect aunt who sewed crimson pelisses for the girls and spent her holidays helping in Weston. At Sherrington children could hang over the bridge to watch for trout in the clear chalk-filtered water of the Wylye, and play croquet in the Rectory garden. At Bournemouth were the more formal entertainments of the beach, the Punch and Judy stand and 'nigger minstrels'.

To all these they travelled by train, since the Tanners kept no horse or carriage, and it was to Sam that they turned to unravel the intricacies of private lines' separate timetabling and changes. Emmeline's father taught her, deliberately or otherwise, an appetite for precise times, distances, heights, temperatures, and a capacity for infinite and accurate detail. Later, when she attempted description, she turned often to cataloguing flowers or animals or mountain peaks, but skill at inventory was to be a professional asset and passionate precision may hunger after truth not pedantry.

As yet Emmeline had no need to describe unfamiliar scenes, for this south-western circuit bounded her youth, with occasional excursions to Bristol or the seaside at Weston-super-Mare, with its donkey-rides and cliffs and its harbour for the steamers to Minehead and Lynton. Absence did not entail forgetfulness for the children's well-being. Eminently characteristic was a letter Nettie wrote to eight-year-old Emmeline in Bournemouth.

My precious Emmie, I've just left Winnie and Bertie upstairs with pencils and paper and have stolen away on tiptoe to come and write to you. Bert has already been out and shouted 'Ma, Ma, where are you?' I've told him to go back, and shall be up to him presently ... Have you heard Butcher has lost a little girl? She was thirteen, but such a good kind child always to her little brothers and sisters. Must it not be much nicer for her parents to think of her as such instead of a cross irritable girl? They say they will miss her so much, especially her mother whom she used to help a great deal. (Bert is calling again – he is going to write you now.)

Well, my dear little girl, it seems a long time since we had a chat. You will try not to forget what Mother wants you to be – a little Christian. You know to be that – you must never speak ill of others, no matter who or what they are. You must always be gentle and kind as Jesus was, and if anybody makes you vexed you must try to give 'the soft answer that turneth away wrath'. Oh, if I could only impress on you the necessity of never saying anything behind a person's back, what you would not say in their hearing – I should be so thankful. We know not the misery we should save ourselves and others if we could do that. I shall send down a book for you to learn a piece of poetry on 'Words'. I learnt it years ago ...

If this suggests Emmeline tended to be impatient and critical she had learnt to be tolerant of her relations by the time she was twelve, at least in letters to her mother. By then she could travel alone by train to Reading, changing at Didcot, and like a well-trained daughter sent home an account of her doings:

Saturday it was raining all day. Sunday morning I went to the station with Uncle at quarter past ten and came back at quarter past one. In the afternoon I was going to Chapel ... Monday morning I went out for Auntie to the baker's and helped her a little in the afternoon. The two Miss Warrens came and stayed to tea and supper, and in the evening I played my 'Sonatina' and 'Sweet Seventeen', and a game of Bezique with Auntie Burt, and then we all played Pope Joan (not for money).

Today I just went into the Queen's Road for Auntie and read a little, and this afternoon a little girl named Florrie Gooding is coming to tea. I am enjoying myself very much. Auntie Jue has been very poorly and was in bed till after dinner yesterday and is in bed now. Uncle is very busy and will not be home till five or six tomorrow morning. Auntie Burt wants to know if you had a second honeymoon yesterday, and Auntie Jue wouldn't have a honeymoon next time but a treacle one because that's sweeter ... Auntie Jue sends her love, and so would Auntie Burt only she is afraid it would fall out a cabbage leaf.

The rest of the programme for such a visit, unenlivened by the family friend 'Auntie Burt', would otherwise have been much as Winifred described a few years later. Win practised on her aunt's new sewing-machine, making some tea-cloths and a sheet ('They didn't look bad'), went to tea with some friends of her parents, and went to Chapel. Aunt Julia remained invalidish, her permanent condition, but enjoyed the Beverley buns Nettie sent and would like 'just a taste of our Christmas pudding'. Otherwise:

When I am dressed I dust Auntie's bedroom and do her flowers and other little things, look after the drawing-room and dust the dining-room on cleaning day. Then I take my work [the standard term for any needlework], stockings or something, and do with Auntie. In the afternoon Auntie lies down so I write letters and then go out and do some shopping for her. Sometimes I go to meet Uncle and after supper he likes to play cards. I thought I would tell you so that you should not think I was lazy. Auntie has had the piano tuned so I have practised, but I have hurt my hand by running into the lock of the door.

It was forty years since the Grossmith brothers had started to publish *The Diary of a Nobody* in *Punch* but not a very different world for some of the Tanners' family. They provided one support network; so did another institution, one which sharply distinguished Sam and Nettie Tanner from Charles Pooter and his wife.

Chapter 2
'Awake our souls!'

At the beginning of 1878 Sam and Nettie had made a deeply serious commitment: on 9 January they were both formally proposed as members of the Bath Society of the Church of the New Jerusalem, the New Church, as it was known, and they were duly elected by members' votes in April. It may have been his anxiety about the Trinity, a problem he and Nettie had discussed before they married, that first drew Sam to investigate the New Church, the first of whose tenets of belief stated: 'I believe that God is One, in whom there is a Divine Trinity, and that He is the Lord God and Saviour Jesus Christ.'[1] This formulation had been decisive at least in the conversion of the then Treasurer of the Bath group, David Chivers.[2]

On closer acquaintance the democratic organisation of the group would certainly have appealed to Sam's liberal principles. The Church was formally a society, founded in the late 18th century to study, honour and live by the doctrines of Emanuel Swedenborg, the Swedish scientist, engineer and visionary prophet whose experiences and insights inspired voluminous writings and an international following. The mainstream of his British adherents was loyal to the annual Conference, attended by representatives of local societies, cells in the honeycomb, varying in size but normally organised independently by committees elected by members. Rarely could the local society in Bath, established in 1829, muster more than seventy or eighty members in the later 19th century, though its annual returns to Conference indicate a rather larger number of non-subscribing attenders.

They were attracted by low-key tactics of quiet conversation with neighbours and work contacts, and any of the several members living in Weston may first have brought the Tanners to attend the handsome chapel in Bath's Henry Street. To embark on membership, however, displayed an energy of moral decision, for to belong entailed not only subscription payments but possible suspicion as 'sectarian', for New Churchmen had long noted sadly that in Bath new ideas were 'looked on with distrust and aversion', and that was not the path to social or political advancement in the city then.[3] One of the Bath group's more prominent members, Isaac Pitman, had indeed been expelled from his Gloucestershire post as a schoolteacher in the 1830s when he embraced Swedenborgian beliefs. Sam and Nettie's membership, however, required no drastic changes in their way of life; they proceeded on Sundays to the service in Henry Street and perhaps on Thursdays attended some of the tea-meetings started in 1878 for a prayer, a hymn and a paper 'on some point of spiritual experience or doctrine'. In his *Culture and Anarchy* (1869) Matthew Arnold seized on these tea-meetings, so characteristic of Nonconformist churches, as a particular object of scorn, archetypal expression of the middle-class philistinism which mistook complacent earnestness for 'sweetness and light'.

For children a Sunday school was held, exhilarated by the harmonium, but this the young Tanners did not attend until Emmeline was ten, old enough to shepherd her little troop into the city. Her religious education was not, of course, neglected. If sectarian, Sam and Nettie displayed no excess of rigidity here: their children attended the Sunday school held closer to home by the wife of the Congregationalist minister Edwin Simon. Possibly the Tanners admired Edwin and Fanny Simon for their wide sympathies and austere principles – many did. And Fanny Simon played her part in inculcating a sense of responsibility in Emmeline, telling her on her seventh birthday:

> I know this morning you have been saying thank you to God for another birthday and for another year of happy life. How beautiful that your birthday comes so near to that of the dear Jesus! May you, my little woman, grow every year more and more like Him, then you will indeed have happy years and make them for all about you. I hope you will like this card. The pretty wild flowers make us think of the Spring days we love so much and are just like your life now. They will fade, but they always leave seed behind them to make flowers for other Springtimes, do they not?
>
> Let your life, my Emmie, be such that when it is ended the memory of you and faithful work you did in it will be seed for other flowers to grow out of. Eva and Beatie and the brothers will all copy you more or less; so that you have a great deal of seed sowing before you.

It was the New Church, however, that signified most in the lives of the young family, as various other churches did for so many of Emmeline's contemporaries. The church furnished social life and friendships so that more and more through the 1880s the non-family names mentioned in Nettie's diary were those of stalwarts of the Henry Street society, on the committee, on lists for social outings and tea-meetings and 'ladies' visiting' (a social work rota), and the chapel building provided facilities for meetings and weddings. The New Church offered an outlet both for the Tanners' ingrained idealistic impulses and aspirations, shaped in terms of Christian charity (expressed as widows' pensions, orphans' support, care of the sick and elderly) and Christian worship (justifying such impulses), and for their democratic activism, thwarted in the secular world.

The structure of the society afforded practice in elections, committee work, decision making. From 1895 the right of women to appear on lists of committee candidates was canvassed; in 1897 female names appeared; in 1898 the first woman served. Nettie stood, but she was not elected. Sam, however, had been consistently elected since 1880, and frequently served on subcommittees too, achieving one of the central seats of power, if arduous and thankless, as Treasurer from 1906. The Bath society cherished its self-supporting status and financial independence, and though its income was always precarious and its capital – other than the chapel building – tiny, members regularly refused a grant from the central Conference's Augmentation and Sustentation Fund.[4]

In their hands too they kept the duty to choose their minister, by committee vote, and pay him for his theological expertise and pastoral skills, though ordination was through the Conference superstructure. Thus when in 1885 discontent with the minister's 'activities and attitudes' boiled to a head, leading to a stormy scene at the quarterly meeting of January 1886 and his resignation, the committee heard several potential candidates preach before they recommended one, and the Rev. John Martin was chosen, at £150 a year plus a house. The committee took the precaution of listing in writing the minister's duties, and more Bible classes, 'Mutual Improvement' meetings, lectures, 'soirées and entertainments', and so on stud the records subsequently.

The New Church reinforced the Tanners' social as well as political values. Its family base was strong, for among the core members both husband and wife were usually active, if in separate spheres. Visiting the needy, taking Sunday school classes, providing refreshment at meetings were women's work, but decisions on finance, building repairs, the library and forms of service were for men, by habit and expectation not formal rule. Swedenborg's writings gave unusual prominence to the marital relationship as a progressive union of minds whereby the wife transmitted the Creator's love to her husband, but 19th century interpretations tended to mute more radical implications within more familiar patterns. Nevertheless the young Tanner girls were not reared to suppose proper Christian behaviour required a diffident retreat into silence or circumscribed their duties to the hearth and nursery. Their church legitimated their parents' ambitions.

Several strongly held Tanner views were, if not inscribed in doctrine, congruent with those of other members, sometimes influencing, sometimes influenced by them. Probably one major influence was that of the society's most significant member, Sir Isaac Pitman. He had established a small private school in Bath in the 1830s when his original job had been sacrificed to his beliefs, but his abundant energies were poured into diverse channels as time went on. Pitman's enthusiasms, disciplined by regular and long hours of work, extended far beyond the system of phonetic shorthand to which he gave his name, to teetotalism, vegetarianism, the New Church, the struggle against compulsory vaccination, the peace movement, Liberal politics, spelling reform, opposition to tobacco and to vivisection. The bright-eyed health and vigour he maintained into his eighties seemed to justify his mode of life.

The Tanners looked up to Pitman, asked his advice on Arthur's learning difficulties or Fred's career, and felt honoured to receive notes inviting himself to 'taik a kup ov tee' with the family. And the principles and practices Sam and Nettie held or developed were – except for spelling reform – identical with his.

The teetotalism issue, however, nearly caused dissent within the society in the spring of 1882. Sam seconded Pitman's motion to allow the Total Abstinence Society to use the chapel's Library and harmonium once a week; another leading member, William Harbutt, argued against the implicit endorsement of abstention from alcohol as distinct from moderation. Within a month Harbutt had backed down, persuaded by pamphlets and arguments that Swedenborg did indeed teach that 'intoxicating drinks are *evil*', and was apparently himself converted to abstinence on this ground. Exactly at this time Nettie's diary shows a change in the Tanner diet, perhaps even the effect of Harbutt's persuasion in his turn. The previous winter they had entertained Sam's brother Sill and his family to a dinner of chicken, bread sauce and beef pies; a month after the abstinence argument they were dining on new potatoes, green peas and wild asparagus, and Nettie was soon attending Food Reform (vegetarian) meetings at the Harbutts' address and Sam was applying successfully for use of the New Church tea service for monthly Food Reform meetings. The cost of meat may have assisted this decision but ideology must have been its base: meat was not even a treat for high days or an indulgence of more prosperous times.

William Harbutt and his wife enjoyed the Tanners' respect as well as friendship, and had artistic gifts the Tanners lacked: she painted elegant portraits on ivory between her welfare activities, and he taught at the School of Science and Art, with a particular bent to the applied arts. There he developed a new modelling material he christened 'Plasticine', publicising it in *Harbutt's plastic method and the use of Plasticine* (1897), and establishing a plant in Bath to produce it – too late for Emmeline's childhood play, however.

Through church membership the Tanners gained a network of acquaintance much farther afield than Bath. Just as they themselves regularly offered hospitality to New Church visitors to Bath, so they could call for advice and support on Swedenborgians far and wide, some known personally through Sam's frequent service as Bath representative at the annual Conference – and they were to do so.

What the New Church as a satisfying secular resource could not offer was civic authority or social advantage. In 1903 Sam mourned their alienation not only from the Church of England, with its paramount grip on the municipal authorities of Bath, but even from the Council of the Free (Nonconformist) Churches. They 'were much misunderstood', he said, though 'people who depreciated the details of the New Church belief know very little about them.'[5] Two years earlier he himself had tried to persuade other Free Church ministers to attend a special service but only three turned up, one being the Congregationalist Edwin Simon. At the service the New Church minister spoke of a 'growing recognition of the fact that men and women differed one from the other in matters of religious opinions and communion and did not cease to be brothers ... this broadening movement meant an increase in charity and goodwill', but the call to brotherly love and tolerance was largely ignored.[6]

Sam, unusually, extended this embryonic ecumenicism to Roman Catholicism. On an Irish holiday with his sons in 1903 he told his wife how he

> looked in at eight o'clock to the Catholic church [in Enniskillen], a beautiful building, and saw the people coming in to their morning devotions. They may be mistaken, as I believe they are, but one cannot but be struck with the fact of poor working men and women, together with others, coming into the building and kneeling down for a few moments in silent prayer. They do at least spend a slight portion of time each day in what they believe to be worship, whereas with many of us it consists in going to church on Sundays only. I know we can worship God wherever we may be and at all times but still these people think they must go to church to do so, and they do it. I must not stay to moralise ...

That Sam Tanner should make these personal efforts to reach outwards, shows how aware he was that to belong to a closely knit and distinctive group ran the risk of a parochialism of the mind and heart, the philistinism criticised by Matthew Arnold, and he taught his children to abhor it.

A more subtle risk arose from the New Church as a spiritual resource, especially perhaps for one of Nettie's ardent enthusiasms. Though the forms of service included few emotional embellishments of vestments, music and ritual and were the essence of restraint, the content was potent with the presence of spiritual beings in mundane lives. All human things had correspondences with spiritual things; the Divine order was imaged in man. Nettie had immortal longings in her – so much is sure – but she conceived of daily life as a struggle between the nobler and the baser impulses, the bad angels of anger, envy, sloth and malice and more, which blocked the open way to God and which quite literally created hell on earth and in the heart. This habit of casting the quotidian in moral terms became deeply ingrained. When heaven and hell are perceived as present internal states personal individual responsibility becomes very great.

At four Emmeline speculated cheerfully on whether the moon was God's gas-lamp or Jesus put the little children to bed in heaven, but at five she encountered a central problem of the religious life. 'Emmie naughty,' noted Nettie. 'In going to bed she told me she could not get the good angels to come in. She asked Jesus, but she didn't feel any better. Would I ask Jesus? – I did so after that ... she said her prayers and was quite bright: may I get more fit to train her.'

Nettie's Swedenborgianism was not, as far as can be told, doctrinally profound; rather, her equivalent to Sam's deliberate breadth of mind was an eclectic gathering of sentiments and teachings, tempered by a robust horse-sense and a streak of Evangelical social conscience. When she had time she read widely, for enjoyment and in fiction as well as ideas, but especially in devotional verse. Emmeline said her mother tried to learn some lines every day, and certainly she was free with verses and fragments in her letters. Her tastes ranged from the Anglican George Herbert to the Baptist journalist Marianne Farningham, taking in such popular verse of the day as she required her children to recite at entertainments in the Jubilee Hall, the home of temperance activities in Weston. Their pieces included not only 'Murdered by Drink' but 'The Factory Chimney' by J. Makins and 'Try Again', sixteen quatrains on Robert the Bruce by the best-selling Eliza Cook, and once 'Beatie was to have recited King Alfred dividing his loaf with the beggarman but she had chickenpox the day before'. Sense was what Nettie read for, and she liked best a book she agreed with. Sam preferred the newspapers.

Nettie's ethical values of simplicity and sincerity co-operated with a practical business sense. When she drilled her children to stand and sit straight ('as though the top of your head were drawn up by a string'), to develop speaking voices free of both affectation and regional idiosyncrasy, neither shrill nor mumbling, and to adopt a simple and unjarring style of clothes and manners, she was certainly aware that these were vital assets to an ambitious working woman, outward signs of behavioural standards, as well as – transposed into a more ideal key – expressive of an inner discipline: as Emmeline once quoted in private notes, 'Let thy mind's sweetness have its operation upon thy body, clothes and habitation' (slightly adapted from a passage of George Herbert). The traces of the West Country that lingered in Emmeline's voice were not intrinsically ugly. Nettie was ready with aphorisms too, such as 'Punctuality is the soul of business', and reckoned it absurd of a young visitor to go for interview as a milliner's assistant in her second-best hat – she should have trimmed a 'stylish' one herself to show her talent. The economic calculus, in fact, counterbalanced the moral overreach, yet did not render it hypocritical: both were aspects of striving to do well.

The more her family responsibilities enlarged, and it is clear that domestic affairs were considered her terrain, the greater Nettie's anxiety to learn and practise modes of doing well. Vegetarianism she took seriously, reading pamphlets and Dr Allinson's newspaper column on health, struggling for variety and balance without refrigeration and when seasons dictated supplies. Her eldest son could recall, fifty years later, more than a hundred lines of verse listing and praising fruits, vegetables and pulses; the Tanners did not repudiate cheese and eggs, however. Nettie was confident enough of her regime to deliver a paper on 'The Common Good Uncommonly Developed' at the 1896 Congress of the Vegetarian Union.

At first when childhood ailments struck she preferred older herbal methods to expensive doctors and a half-pennyworth of saffron reduced the fever of measles for Emmeline at three, but a decade later Nettie treated young Herbert's scarlet fever, a child killer, with the advice of Professor Kirk of Edinburgh's *Papers on Health*, wrapping the child in blankets soaked in cold water. So they avoided the opium- and alcohol-based medicines so often prescribed and so freely sold. Abstinence from alcohol commanded more passion than care for health: the crusade against the demon that impoverished and brutalised was assisted by the regular meetings of local members of the Women's Total Abstinence Union in Nettie's drawing-room, giving the young Tanners more practice in organisational skills.

So her parents built up, in the early years of Emmeline's life, a body of beliefs powered by varying degrees of moral fervour, decidedly at a tangent to mainstream bourgeois habits but parallel with those of many other petit-bourgeois Nonconformists and – often vigorously disdainful of their co-believers – radical intellectuals, especially as the century closed. Teetotal, vegetarian, non-smoking, in favour of peace and the female parliamentary vote, against vivisection and vaccination ... of James Joyce's 'brutish Empire' the Tanners rejected all of 'beer, beef, business, bibles, bulldogs, battleships, buggery and bishops' save the third and fourth, but if one were not a poet, a playwright, a peer or a priest, one was considered a vulgar crank and rather ridiculous.

The vaccination issue is a case in point. An Act of 1871 obliged local authorities to appoint vaccination officers to police the vaccination of infants against smallpox, compulsory since an Act of 1851, and to impose a fine of 25/- for non-compliance, with prison as a last resort. For those who thought liberty worthy of vigilance this was tyranny: information and advice were acceptable but here was interference with personal freedom, the dictatorship of the state. Moral as well as political principle might be at stake: to inject impurities into the blood violated the human body. Sam and Nettie may have been swayed by either argument or both, and Emmeline herself was later heard to fulminate against 'putting filth into children's bodies', but they apparently paid the fines, at least when the bailiffs called, their youngest daughter remembered. Not till 1898 did a new Vaccination Act permit magistrates to grant exemption certificates to conscientious objectors, and by then Emmeline was twenty-one and still unvaccinated.

Yet those who knew Sam thought him a quiet man, averse to public histrionics, preferring reconciliation to antagonism. Certainly a man who later reckoned his highest honour his acceptance as a Justice of the Peace for Somerset, can hardly have been a temperamental rebel against established orders. But the integration of unorthodox views into the mainstream of English national life required a society liberal enough to accept diversity, free trade in ideas, individualism. Thus the dominant Liberal ideologies of the time, and the political philosophy of T. H. Green, were perfectly shaped to suit Sam's needs, including from the 1890s his economic needs as a small capitalist. That came when George Benjamin died and Sam joined forces with the firm's accountant to buy the business, reconstitute it as a limited company, and himself take on the roles of chairman and managing director. Chief among the assets were some exclusive colliery contracts and a number of private railway wagons, and several members of the family, including Emmeline were in due course to have small packets of shares, but the fundamental shift in Sam's relation to the mode of production affected the Tanners' way of life and thought not at all, to outward appearances – except that at the turn of the century Sam's children clubbed together to give him a top hat for his birthday.

By that time the family had long left Locksbrook Place. In early 1880 Sam and Nettie had walked the short distance to Newbridge Road with three-year-old Emmeline 'to see the new house. We like it very much.' They saw a newly built house, three-storeyed and terraced in a block of four, with a baker conveniently two doors away and other shops nearby for basic provisions. Down from its entry path led steps to the basement 'area' and the door to the basement floor, but the path itself led directly to the front door edged by fluted pilasters with detailed capitals. Indeed the builder had adorned the whole most elegantly, with decorative brickwork, a metal awning over the first floor, and bow windows. True, each floor held only two or three rooms but these included a bathroom, properly plumbed, and Sam eventually added a small extension upwards to accommodate his growing family and their frequent visitors. Behind stretched a long narrow garden where they might hope for flowers and vegetables and where the children could play. They called the house Fern Bank, and were installed by the time of the Census of April 1881, with now four children and a seventeen-year-old servant, Emma. On one side lived a schoolmaster with his wife, sister-in-law and two adult children, on the other a surveyor for the sanitary authority with his wife and mother-in-law, while surrounding houses held families of similar status, a 'master tailor employing men', a clerk, a market gardener. The Tanners settled in happily, and stayed for forty years.

Further along Newbridge Road was the family of George Benjamin, the coal factor and Sam's employer, and soon the Simon family settled into a house named Trecarrol, where the young Tanners attended Fanny Simon's Sunday school. And soon, one after another, the children trotted up the road to Somerset Villa. There, in what Emmeline later called a 'dame school', their formal education began.

It was not only convenient but also seemed an obvious choice for the Tanners. Such schools were not registered but a survey of 1871 estimated that of the 9287 children between three and thirteen in Bath (eligible for schooling under the 1870 Education Act) 22.9 per cent attended such private schools, the cheapest charging as little as 2d a week but most 1/- or 1/6d. A detailed examination of educational provision in Bath finds that from the 1850s 'children of ambitious artisans and skilled craftsmen' were joining those of 'lower middle-class tradesmen, shopkeepers and clerks' who preferred 'middling' (a class, not quality, term) private schools to the publicly provided elementary schools – the domain of the working classes.[7]

Social, educational and religious pressures may have combined to persuade Sam and Nettie that the homely little private establishment down the road was more appropriate at this stage than one of Weston's two elementary schools, both provided by the Church of England. Most schools for the 'common people' were church-provided, aided by government grants, and in Bath the School Board established under the Education Act of 1870 to fill gaps in such 'voluntary' provision found it cheaper to assist the enlargement of existing voluntary schools (predominantly Church of England and teaching Anglican beliefs) than to open their own 'Board schools' (statutorily non-denominational), funded by local rates. In some newly developing areas such as Twerton, contiguous to Weston, there was no alternative, however, but Board schools too could and did charge fees – not till 1891 was the right to free education granted by law – and Bath's teachers were poorly paid by standards elsewhere.[8]

In Weston the older of the two elementary schools held in 1889 an average of 183 under three teachers and the other 130 children and one mistress.[9] Even with the assistance of pupil-teachers, classes must have been dauntingly large, and though little evidence is available for this area examination of school logbooks in Bath suggests a narrow curriculum, ultra-formal teaching methods and minimal equipment. To obtain government grant voluntary schools obeyed the Code for Public Elementary Schools, but narrowly interpreted this meant that to the end of the century 'reading, writing, spelling and arithmetic continued to form the basis of the curriculum of the Bath elementary school, together with religious and moral instruction', singing and physical exercises, with sewing for girls.[10] Educational provision in Bath lacked zeal; in 1902 a Board of Education report commented caustically that 'The people of the West of England are still many years behind the Midlands and the northern counties in their ideas as to education.'[11]

So the young Tanners started lessons at the little private school run by the widowed Mrs Fanny Straub in her own house. But here Sam and Nettie allowed gender to determine educational courses. For their boys they used Mrs Straub's establishment merely as a kindergarten, a word which, whether they knew it or not, was heard increasingly as Froebel's methods were disseminated with growing vigour by the Froebel Society (founded 1874) and the training it fostered. When Fred and Herbert could walk as far as Twerton, clutching their season tickets for the river's bridge toll and 6d a week for the fee, they learnt their 'elements' at the Twerton Board School, and when the pressure of Twerton's growing population forced out non-locals they transferred to the Bathforum School, the most respected of the elementary schools in Bath provided by the Nonconformist churches, and also non-denominational in its religious teaching.

Such public elementary schools had departments for both sexes, but the Tanner girls never joined their brothers. Emmeline remained at Mrs Straub's school until, as she said, 'I was a big girl' – that is, a tall and well-developed twelve – 'and started to do some teaching.' Some doubted that those who acquired their 'elements' privately were thereby privileged. The author of one handbook published in 1879 argued that, in contrast to the Board school which 'takes nothing for granted', the typical girls' private school 'at once launches her into what are vaguely called "the usual branches of English".

It makes no systematic attempt to promote the simultaneous development of the moral, intellectual and physical powers of the little one, who is mostly jerked from spelling to English grammar, from English grammar to outlines of geography, before, perhaps, she can read without misgiving the words pronoun and promontory.'[12] He had in mind precisely such modest establishments as Mrs Fanny Straub's in Newbridge Road. They varied, of course. But no 'average' school can be identified, no scales calculated of their 'efficiency', no local patterns grouped, for no public authority interfered to register or inspect, and most have left few traces in public records.

Perhaps Mrs Straub and her daughters Franziska and Amelia were skilled and thorough teachers; at least Sam and Nettie clearly had confidence in them and they retained the family's respect even when Emmeline at least had developed standards of comparison. All that remains directly of Emmeline's own experience though, is, first, a letter in a fluent if careful round hand on faintly pencilled lines, to inform her parents of the date 'our vacation will commence' for the Christmas of her seventh birthday, and to hope 'the progress I have made will meet with your approbation ... our Holidays will be all the more pleasant on account of our application to our studies during the past year'. The second piece of evidence is a memorandum of daily work made apparently about the same time: 'Prayers. 3 sums, copy capital letters from blackboard. Dictation, learn words off blackboard spelt wrongly. Sums, copies. Finish sums. Read testament. Grammar. Say lessons. Fold arms – the best leave first ...' and more of the same for other days of the week.

Emmeline mastered basic arithmetic thoroughly and could later awe colleagues with her speed in summing columns of figures and in identifying errors and anomalies in accounts – mental arithmetic practice, she considered, fostered mental agility – and as she grew older 'Prayers, orothography [sic], Bible history, sums' clearly did not fill the whole day since in her seventies she could still quote 'the *Child's Guide to Knowledge* of my youth' on the 'baobab or breadfruit tree', and visualise the empty spaces in the atlas depiction of Central Africa, still largely unknown land to Europeans.

What next, in the Christmas of 1889, when she was nearly thirteen and a 'big girl'? Emmeline's contemporaries at elementary schools usually left at that age, if not earlier, for the minimum leaving age was set at eleven in 1893, at twelve in 1899, and children who stayed to thirteen or so found little to do. In 1892 the Chairman of the Bath Liberals, the draper W. C. Jolly, attacked the Bath School Board's slackness and its hostility to providing a 'higher grade' school for adolescents who had exhausted the possibilities of the elementary 'standards' but only an evening continuation school, mainly for mechanics and book-keeping, became available in that year. A few elementary pupils were identified as potential teachers and paid a tiny maintenance sum to remain as pupil-teachers, teaching by day and studying under the head teacher after school, eventually to take the Queen's

Scholarship examination to qualify for one of the forty-nine training colleges, though even the successful might find no place available. At college the student gained a certificate, and would then return to an elementary school, where the uncertificated were already at work: it was a closed and rather inbred circle. In 1895 Bath was to follow the example of most major cities and arranged central classes for pupil-teachers' own studies.

Others of Emmeline's contemporaries, those born to the professional middle and upper classes, might expect 'secondary' education, an undefined term denoting something different from elementary and technical forms. Three factors governed decisions on a girl's education for the interested parent: money, educational goals, and knowledge of what was available.

By the end of the 1880s financial pressures weighed on Sam and Nettie, the weight of seven children (and after Nettie's father died in 1890 her elderly stepmother also joined the household). They were conscientious about paying their subscriptions to the New Church and various societies; they took seriously their duty of almsgiving; and their children suspected that the various relations who sought occasional help were not turned away. Much depended on Sam, and Nettie was sharply reminded of the fate of a family without a breadwinner when she heard of her brother George's death and eventually found his children in an orphanage. Almost certainly the Tanners knew the truth of a sentence in a report Emmeline signed thirty-six years later:

> It is only too true that a large number of parents, especially when there are several children in the family, are liable to be faced by a genuine and cruel dilemma. They wish to do the right thing by all their children, but they know that, if the eldest boy or girl continues at school instead of going to work, the youngest brothers or sisters may suffer, and they hesitate to expose them to a sacrifice from which they would not shrink themselves.[13]

Though Nettie admired the learned and Sam's friendships show he enjoyed the company of educated men, for their children they apparently saw as more urgent the need for a good job, and deemed education the means to this end. As Nettie confided to her stepmother, she had hoped to give Emmeline 'a good education to have taken a superior governess's engagement'. Governesses had a respectable lady-like image, and to live in a home and nurture children seemed 'naturally' womanly; besides, a well-qualified one might easily be employed by a 'good' family, and was especially in demand on the Continent, in Germany and Russia. Less obvious was that many faced a lonely tiring progress towards a destitute old age. 'But,' Nettie added, 'we cannot have all we want', and this must refer to lack of money.

Probably Nettie's notions on how a lady might earn a living were drawn only from her acquaintances' experience. In a schoolgirl essay Eva was to sum up the possibilities that occurred to her at fourteen:

> Some young ladies never get on in life because they have [a] restless

nature ... When they leave school they think they would like to serve in a shop, but after a little experience thinks a governess's life much easier, so therefore becomes a governess. After a while she takes an insane idea to change her situation and even her present employment, and become a hospital nurse or ladies' companion. Therefore in the end she can do nothing thoroughly.

Eva, like Nettie, was probably not even aware that nationwide some 19,000 women were clerks (still only 5.1 per cent of clerks employed), for when Nettie had been twenty the figure had been only 400, and Eva forgot or disdained the needle trades or hotel service which most commonly occupied women in Bath. Teaching of some sort offered 'prospects' too, even one day a school of one's own. Emmeline did briefly take some shorthand lessons from Pitman himself that winter of 1893, but presumably for its general utility; she did not keep it up. To become adept at such desirable skills as French, music and literature, the staples of traditional education for girls of the middle and upper classes, one required secondary education, not the technical skills taught at the School of Science and Art in Bath.

So much the Tanners knew, but what, without much money, could they find? The old Free Grammar School, now named King Edward's School, was for boys only, and the only endowed school for girls in Bath, the Royal School, was for daughters and granddaughters of military officers. For nearly fifteen years, however, Bath High School GPDSC had brought a new wave of education for girls to the city, through what was termed a 'proprietary' (shareholding) company, the Girls' Public Day School Company (later Trust) which now maintained a score of similar schools throughout England. At the moderate rate of four to five guineas a term, plus the cost of books and stationery, Bath High School attracted chiefly the daughters of tradesmen, through the broad range of the aspiring middle classes – the GPDSC was proud of a social range which unnerved some parents – and taught them English, classical and modern languages, mathematics, history, some sciences and 'elements of moral science and logic', with some physical training and singing.[14] One day the principles and practices represented by the GPDSC, and the ideals of the founders of the 'high school' movement, would matter very much to Emmeline, but that day was not yet and the work of the 'pioneers' was irrelevant to her. Although the Tanners certainly knew of Bath High School, for Edwin and Fanny Simon sent their daughter there before they moved north, they had four daughters to the Simons' one and this was not only an unfamiliar pattern to them but dauntingly incalculable in costs and benefits.

Otherwise, for girls especially, the words of C. H. Stanton of the Schools Inquiry Commission twenty-one years earlier still rang true: 'a great want in Bath ... of a school which could afford to the many residents there whose means did not permit them to make use of the existing upper schools in the city ... the advantages of obtaining at a cheaper rate a liberal education.' As far as the quality of 'upper schools' was concerned Stanton complained that his investigations were hampered by the schools' resentment at intrusion, their refusal to allow access or answer enquiries, particularly those for girls.[15] Directories list about forty-seven privately owned schools for girls in Bath in 1892, most apparently catering to the profitable end of the market, the better-off businessmen and professionals who could pay twenty to thirty guineas a year for a day girl. But details of what and how they taught are very scarce. If the Royal Commission for which Stanton acted could gather little information in 1868, it is unlikely that Sam and Nettie could act on an informed judgement of private schools in 1889.

In the end they negotiated with the establishment of Henry Kendall MA, at the top of Devonshire Buildings in Bath for Emmeline to attend as a student-teacher, teaching the little ones and learning with the big girls, but more cheaply than they and acquiring 'training'. This arrangement was akin to the system for elementary teacher training, except that in elementary schools HM Inspectors annually examined the young pupil-teachers: no external expert was to evaluate Emmeline's skills. Devonshire Place School fell into the most common pattern of the four general types described by a witness to the Royal Commission on Secondary Education, chaired by Sir James Bryce, in 1895, as a small school, of about forty or fifty pupils including a few boarders, dealing particularly in preparatory work for both sexes, with the boys often leaving at thirteen or fourteen for a 'higher' school or a technical training.

So in January 1890, three weeks after her thirteenth birthday and deeply conscious of the constraints of money, Emmeline faced a class of eight-year-old boys. What they saw is shown in a family photograph of the time – a tall, long-legged girl, with the developing bosom of maturity and a neat waist, blue eyes shrewdly watchful and a slight, demure flicker of smile which may hide the desire to laugh she admitted photographers induced; only the fair hair, short on top and tied behind, baby-fine and never as luxuriant as Victorians desired, still advertises youth. In the classroom the next year they may also have seen spectacles, for in October 1891 Emmeline took Herbert to the Eye Infirmary. 'We had to wait an hour and three quarters then was ordered spectals [sic]'; in adult life she preferred pince-nez.

How much guidance was given to these early teaching efforts with the junior members of the Boys' Department at Devonshire Place School is unknown, but at the end of term Kendall encouraged her parents with the report 'Shews much ability both as a "student" and "teacher"', and she had at least established a pattern of long hard hours of work. Two and a half miles each way on foot, and an hour's piano practice before or after school, cut into any spare time for keeping up with the work of the girls' class she attended in alternate weeks. The comment 'Wants perseverance' in July 1891 stung.

The classes were very much smaller than those of an elementary school. A surviving prospectus of 1891 lists only twenty-three in the Boys'

Department, eighteen (including Emmeline) in the Girls', a not unusual size for a middle-class private school, and with a wide age range, probably from about eight to sixteen. For learning Emmeline took her place in the senior class of ten or eleven girls and tackled in time the full range of the curriculum advertised in the prospectus, 'English subjects', French, music and drawing in her first year, with mathematics and Latin the next year. Eva had joined her then, as a full-time pupil (reduced fees for sisters were common), and from an exercise book she used for 'English subjects' comes the only evidence for the content of the lessons. Revealingly, the umbrella of 'English' sheltered not only grammar and composition but also history, geography and Scripture – and brought the diverse disciplines to one dead level, and though roughly yoked not integrated or related.

A stilted and turgid style of written work on Cardinal Wolsey or the poet Cowper suggests dictation or textbook copying, and lists of geographical features such as ports in the Eastern USA hardly relieve the tedium of dictated sentences defining geographical terms; some tabulated analyses of grammar and syntax show mistaken correction as well as original error. What brings the book to life are the 'compositions', for here the pupil freely composed her own descriptions and reflections, usually on proverbial tags, and practised letter writing. Undoubtedly Eva wrote what she thought was acceptable, but, released from the pomposities of dictation, she unselfconsciously gave sprightly form to her very second-hand musings on manners and morals, and gained good marks. Everything was marked, including 'conduct', in numbers totalled at the term's end to discover a pupil's 'place'. Devonshire Place was innocent of the charge made against such schools a quarter-century earlier by Frances Mary Buss, of providing an 'almost entirely showy and superficial [education] – a little music, a little singing, a little French, a little ornamental work, and nothing else',[16] and innocent too of the opposite fault of diffused fire at every appealing subject from astronomy to logic and political economy, but both acquittals argue its limited goals, on the one hand social, on the other intellectual.

However handicapped by her teaching duties Emmeline kept good marks in her lessons, except for her vulnerable point, her piano playing – 'music' was interpreted primarily as instrumental performance. She gained the London College of Music's 'Practical Piano' certificate at both junior and senior levels only because full points for 'Questions on rudiments of music' counteracted very moderate solo performances, that is, for memory not musicality. Rare were opportunities to understand what musicality might mean, few were the professional or even skilled musicians she heard save for the military and German bands of the parks and the barrel-organs of the streets, and of the two or three permanent orchestras in Britain she probably knew nothing at all. 'We forget what a bad state music was in,' said the composer William Walton, born in 1902 and recalling that he was fifteen or more before he heard an orchestra play, although he – unlike Emmeline – came of a musical family.[17] So, too, Emmeline copied out pages of

Shakespeare but the theatre was a luxury so remote and exotic that she never entirely outgrew the extreme thrill of mere attendance. Paintings at least could be reproduced, tinted appropriately – if one could afford the books – and to live in Bath might be, if one were interested, an architectural education, but there is no record that the school exploited the local resources for its teaching of history or anything else.

One of the recent changes in girls' education did affect her. No longer was a girl's an unexamined life necessarily: Emily Davies and others had struggled to win in 1865 girls' formal admission to the Cambridge Local Examinations ('The idea almost takes one's breath away,' said the *Saturday Review*), and Oxford and Durham Universities followed suit with their examinations for schools. In 1879 London University offered boys and girls alike the same Matriculation papers to qualify them for entrance to degree study, and soon became the first English university to grant degrees to women. At secondary levels, however, the examination popular with modest schools was the very modest set of papers administered by an association of private teachers, the College of Preceptors, and in this Emmeline duly passed, second class, just before her fourteenth birthday.

The College of Preceptors examination marked the limit of her brothers' academic qualifications. Elementary schools did not take examinations, but the Tanners' ambitions sent their sons after the end of their elementary schooling to a small private school in Weston which offered 'commercial subjects' such as book-keeping and business correspondence as well as 'English subjects', algebra, trigonometry and extras of French or German. This school was owned by James Knight, an ex-elementary schoolteacher and probably already an acquaintance of the Tanners for he and his daughters lived just along Newbridge Road. Sam and Nettie may have felt comfortable, too, with the familiar organisation of small numbers, with a few boarders, a usual leaving age of fifteen or sixteen, and respectable 'black-coated' careers as a destination. In contrast Edwin Simon's son John was sent to acquire Latin and Greek at the grammar school and rapidly took the scholarship route to Fettes School in Scotland and Wadham College, Oxford, despite Simon's puny ministerial stipend.

Inasmuch as Knight and his wife, also an ex-elementary teacher, prepared their boys not only for the general test of the College of Preceptors but for such preliminary professional examinations as parents desired, for the Civil Service, the Law Society or the Pharmaceutical Society, his school exemplified a second common type found by the Bryce Commission, described by their witness as 'suited to the less well-to-do and lower middle classes'.[18] Few of these thought of university, any more than they thought of the public schools like Monkton Combe on the edge of Bath, though they knew that these were the gateway to the universities, the learned professions, and civil and colonial administration. Money and expectations alike curtailed opportunities, or – in some cases – directed able boys to the invigoration of business and the industrial muscles of the economy.

So when, just before she reached sixteen, Emmeline entered for the Cambridge Senior Local examination, she outstripped her brothers academically because she was a girl and her mother wanted her to teach. The choice must have been the Tanners': the examination results paraded on the school's prospectus show no regular triumphs here. Emmeline offered papers in English language and arithmetic (both compulsory), English history with geography and Shakespeare, French, religious knowledge and music. 'Poor child,' thought her mother, 'I do pity her, altho' she seems to rather enjoy it. I hope she will pass. She seems to have her doubts about it.' There would be no second chance. 'She leaves Mr Kendall's this term. Eva takes her place as pupil-teacher.'

Whatever Emmeline's doubts it is certain she intended to pass, and privately she admitted years later that 'from nursery days' she had wanted to climb to 'the top of the ladder'. She may not yet have been encouraged to regard education in the idealistic terms of Dorothea Beale as 'the perfection of the individual and the good of the community ... the cultivated mind, the power of work, the disciplined will',[19] nor even as the transmission over generations of a cultural stock, but the whole bias of her upbringing induced a belief in its instrumental value, that is, in the crudest terms, its job-seeking utility.

Of the 1825 candidates for the Cambridge Senior Local in 1893, 1261 were girls and 895 of these passed. Emmeline passed, of course. Any glance at typical papers shows that accurate memory, succinct expression and speedy focus on essentials was vital, and those could be won to some extent by effort and practice; reasoned thought or connected ideas would have been wasted, even if the school had cared to develop or prize these. But Devonshire Place could offer her no more, for few if any of her contemporaries reached this level, and at fifteen or sixteen most had left, as, for example, her friend Edie Andrews who had departed with her mother for a *pension* in Paris to take 'lessons three times a week from a lady' – she told Emmeline, to improve the French that was so highly, if oddly, valued in an often insular nation. Edie was more impressed, though, by memories of the Siege of 1870 when 'they had bread which had human bones in it, with horse-flesh, and were ordered to live in the cellars'.

There could be no Paris for Emmeline, and Nettie fretted: 'I don't know what we shall do with her.' But she, and Emmeline, were not without plans.

Chapter 3
Opening windows

Emmeline had discovered that by recent regulation the Cambridge Senior Local certificate now enabled its holder to become, after two years' service, a certificated teacher in an elementary school, that there was, in the words of the elementary teachers' leader J. H. Yoxall, 'an avenue to the work of the Public Elementary School from the private schools'.[1] 'We have been writing to Birmingham,' Nettie told her stepmother in the week Emmeline took that examination. 'If she passes this exam she will be able to attain an Assistant Mistress-ship in a Board School with not less than £40 p.a. We have two friends there who are interesting themselves on her behalf.'

The friends may be tentatively identified, and both stemmed from the New Church. In 1891 Sam helped to organise supply clergy for the Bath Society during a six-month visit of their own minister, Martin, to the USA; one of those he invited was Thomas Lowe from Birmingham, already an acquaintance from times he and Sam had represented their respective societies at the annual Conference. Now, when Lowe visited the Tanners at home, he was impressed by the lively intelligence of their eldest daughter and is said to have discussed educational problems with Nettie. The second friend was probably John Bragg, of a family with an illustrious New Church history for a Mr and Mrs Bragg had been present at the opening in Birmingham in 1791 of the first English New Church, and it was their son who had introduced Pitman to Swedenborg's teachings. The Tanners had known the widow of his son, an active Bath member, and Braggs still based in Birmingham were received by the Bath society as honoured guests when they visited, to the extent of a special social meeting in 1890. Emmeline decided Mr John Bragg was 'nice'. She thought Mr Lowe was 'nice', too.

If experience of the laodicean attitudes of the Bath School Board might have rendered Board school service unattractive, Lowe and Bragg would have been able to paint a different picture of the Birmingham School Board, even to echo the praise offered by heads of two of the most respected Birmingham secondary schools in 1895 to a Royal Commission on Secondary Education ('the Bryce Commission'). Birmingham education, the Commissioners found, was distinguished in two ways. As regards elementary schools, the School Board was 'enlightened', and in addition the city and its suburbs were uncommonly amply supplied with good secondary schools, particularly the nine endowed by the King Edward VI Foundation and the two proprietary girls' high schools in Edgbaston.[2]

For Emmeline an ambition to work for the Birmingham School Board may be seen as both intelligible and intelligent. In contrast to Bath, Birmingham made of its elementary schools objects of pride, symbolic of its municipal reform programme, and from the 1870s built them promptly and soundly. Moreover, the School Board's training and payment of teachers, and the size and rate of growth of its city, opened rosy prospects of joining the élite 13 per cent of elementary heads who earned over £300 a year (if male) – a figure principals of privately-owned schools claimed they envied from afar.[3] Birmingham Board schools charged no fees, and the city awarded scholarships to the secondary schools for picked elementary children; from 1888 the School Board itself began to develop higher grade schools in addition to the technical and commercial classes provided by the Midland Institute.

Of the secondary schools Emmeline would learn more later, but from their mere existence flowed two consequences for the elementary schools, and for the private schools. First, an unusually high proportion of the lower middle classes sent their children to elementary schools, in the hopes of a King Edward's school scholarship – enough to diffuse their ethos significantly, or 'raise the tone', as the Bryce Commission was told – and, second, the standard curriculum was interpreted with sufficient generosity and flexibility to afford an adequate foundation for development to a higher level. Elsewhere in the county of Warwickshire, said the headmistress of Edgbaston High School sardonically, 'it runs in grooves'.[4]

The Christmas of 1892 and Emmeline's sixteenth birthday could, therefore, be celebrated with some hope. While her career still hung in doubt, in January 1893 she was sent off to Reading to be cheerful company for the sickly Aunt Julia, and Nettie set off to visit a cousin in Liverpool, travelling via Birmingham. She had her own devices for maintaining order among those left at home: 'I've offered three prizes for work [crocheting on this occasion] done during my absence – the one who does most gets biggest prize. I did it to keep them out of mischief.' From Liverpool she returned straight to Birmingham, where Sam met her on the 28th to stay over the weekend at the Great Western Temperance Hotel.

The Birmingham School Board might attract Emmeline; there was, however, little reason why a sixteen-year-old from Bath should be of interest to the Board, especially since she was, contrary to their rules, unvaccinated. Perhaps Nettie, still hankering after the 'superior governess's engagement', was not wholly sorry. Nor was she without other resources, for Thomas Lowe himself owned a private school in Handsworth, just outside the city proper. By the end of that weekend a new plan had emerged, and she dashed off a note to Emmeline in Reading:

We have spent a very pleasant day – went to the New Church in the morning and to dinner and tea with Mr Lowe. You will, I know, be glad to hear we have almost arranged for you to go with Miss Lowe as Governess Student – as they are wanting one *at once* Father thinks you had better arrange to come home as soon as possible *not later than Wednesday*, as you will probably have to go early next week, say, after the Sunday school party, and there will be a great many things to see to. *I shall be sorry if you are disappointed about the 'Board School', dear*, but these things have to be borne – and you know what I always say, 'All things work together for good', etc.

Emmeline's reaction is not recorded. But by the end of the first week in February she had packed her boxes and set off for Birmingham, or rather for a private school in Handsworth. Never again did she live permanently with her family, and never did she choose a job immediately in their vicinity. Often she visited in holidays, always she kept in the closest touch, but against a manifest desire to be at the heart of the family was insistence on a firm control of her own plans and decisions. In Birmingham she ceased to be defined as daughter or sister.

The arrangement was that she should teach in exchange for her own further tuition and board; thus her education continued, and in a city with much to teach. Birmingham was Joseph Chamberlain's city, 'Radical Joe', whose 'gas-and-water' collectivism was transforming the huddle of varied manufactories, the heartland of the Industrial Revolution and home of steam-power. In 1876, the year he was elected a Liberal Member of Parliament, the year Emmeline was born, Chamberlain wrote that 'The Town will be parked, paved, assized, marketed, Gas-and-Watered and Improved – all as the result of three years' active work'.[5] There was need enough for all these projects in a city whose history of industrial initiative and scientific energy had generated a myriad small businesses, many highly skilled and many poorly paid, whose humblest workers clung to life in some of the most squalid of British slums, dark and dank little courts and back-to-back houses still in 1900 home to 200,000. Despite the Council's publicised reforms the pace of growth constantly outstripped that of improvement.[6]

Chamberlain's Unionist views were now, in the 1890s, splitting the Liberal Party, but Birmingham men backed him, and the artisans, businessmen and professionals maintained the active responsibility for urban reform they had developed as Liberals even as they followed Chamberlain to Conservative Unionism, proclaiming their care for their neighbour and for urban development as the motor of progress – towards civic welfare and prosperity – where urban meant, especially, the metal and engineering industries. To many of the small masters characteristic of Birmingham the city offered opportunities for individual growth, so that among the multiplicity of small and specialised industries radical union-based forms of socialism grew with more difficulty than in Bradford or Manchester. Instead, pressed by the demons of epidemic and civil chaos, Birmingham men often preferred to seek social and moral development by means of slum clearance, clean water for all, sewage disposal, hospitals, art galleries and public parks, with continued progress guaranteed by elementary schools teaching the values of orderly living and sober industry as well as skills. As Emmeline arrived in 1893, and two years after civic leaders expressed their pride and order with the great redbrick and terracotta Arts-and-Crafts decorated Victoria Law Courts, George Cadbury embarked on his personal dream of social engineering at Bournville, a model housing development with gardens and trees and varied styles (and baths), 'for the amelioration of the condition of the working-class and labouring population'.[7] No alert visitor could miss the vision of progress achieved by practical effort.

Cadbury had moved his business out of the city in 1874, following a trend set much earlier in the 1760s by Matthew Boulton, who established the Soho Manufactory to develop James Watt's steam technology two and a half miles to the north-west, to turn Handsworth into one of the most important industrial centres of his time. It was to Handsworth, still formally a part of West Bromwich, that Emmeline was now travelling. The Soho Works had been demolished in the 1860s, to leave only a few older buildings, St Mary's Church, Boulton's own house and some moderately-sized dwellings, detached or in small terraces, to remind of the days when Handsworth had been a scattered parish or an industrial development described in 1801 as 'of picturesque beauty'.[8] But although a closely woven matting of working-class houses was by the 1890s spreading over an increasing area, still to the north, along Handsworth Wood Road towards the River Tame, farms hemmed the middle-class houses whose masters commuted from the country air by the convenient railways to their Birmingham businesses as engraver and printer, wholesale draper and manufacturing goldsmith, die-striker and stamper, and here stood the substantial building where the Lowe family kept their school. Typical of their neighbours was their Swedenborgian friend John Bragg, himself now a widower and retired, living with the family of his jeweller son and their two servants in a house on Hamstead Road, leafier and more spacious than the city – and cleaner.

What Emmeline might first have noticed, like others, as she arrived at Snow Hill station in central Birmingham was the yellow, stinking cloud that shadowed it, eddying and oozing among the thousand chimneys that constantly renewed it, trickling black dirt on to clothes and down throats. As she travelled by local train to Handsworth she passed through acres of foundries, metal-shops, factories, houses and warehouses. Later she could inspect Birmingham's Art Gallery, famous for its Pre-Raphaelite collection, the Midland Institute, the Library with its notable Shakespeare Room, the Chamberlain Memorial built while Chamberlain yet lived, and all the monuments which civic pride had piled in brick and stone, and she could peer into the murk of more miles of canals than Venice boasted, busy with barges whose children talked strangely and lived differently and went to no school at all for the most part. But most of Birmingham's voices sounded strange to her ears, with flat vowels and a nasal twang – not like Bath.

In the bitter cold of February 1893, however, she was eager to meet first those among whom she would live, all strangers except Mr Lowe himself and one of his boarders, Frank Martin, the son of the New Church minister in Bath and about her own age. At first she was nervous and uncertain, and rather homesick, looking out at every post, she said, for a letter from home. 'I like it here as much as I could at any *boarding* school,' she told her sister

Beatrice. 'It is much, much nicer at home, and seeing nearly all the people you know and like at least once a week. Mrs Lowe is very nice but not, as Mother thought, quite as nice as Mr Bragg. I like Mr Lowe still more, but see very little of him.'

Of his daughters, aged nineteen to thirty, she saw more, except for the second, Lilian, who was in Berlin. The eldest, Jessie, was in charge of the 'Young Ladies' Department' in which Emmeline taught, and the youngest, Kathleen, took care of the Kindergarten with two students to help her – as momentum built in the Froebel movement it was becoming common for private schools to prepare student assistants for Froebel examinations, though the absent Lilian herself had attended the Kindergarten Training College in Tavistock Place, London, in the 1880s. The third daughter in age, Janet, seems also to have done some teaching at this time, though subsequently she was to develop her own business making dolls' clothes. In the household too was their brother Lockhart (a medical student), an assistant master or two for the 'Boys' Department', and a handful of boarders of both sexes. For a private house Hamstead Hill School was large, of 'about thirty rooms', Emmeline reported, but she shared her bedroom with the Kindergarten students and the work was done by 'four servants, two laundresses, a man and a boy'. Round the house spread a garden, enough to allow 'the children [to] simply revel' when summer came, and for a hammock to be suspended between trees, but unmistakably garden and not sports field, organised exercise taking the form of walks or evening dancing, as Emmeline described on her arrival:

> After tea we dressed, and dancing began at 6.30. Miss Jessie played most of the time, and Mrs Lowe a little while. I danced the polka, Circassian Circle, and Ninepins (a sort of game). We had the Quadrilles afterwards slowly for the benefit of the new boys and myself. Mrs Lowe gave me Frank as a partner. He dances very well, and was very nice about it, telling me everything to do. Then we had supper and afterwards a game of whist.

In these first few days, though she taught classes and 'did some Latin and practised' on the piano on free evenings, 'the only lesson I have had so far' was when Jessie heard her read some French, only to be interrupted by tea though not before 'Miss Jessie was surprised at my bad pronunciation'. Despite her pronunciation, however, Emmeline taught (as Jessie later recorded) 'a junior class all the usual English subjects and French. She has also taken some of the work of the higher classes ... Latin, Algebra and Euclid.'

But Emmeline must soon have realised how the growth of the King Edward's and proprietary (corporate-owned) high schools had affected Birmingham schools owned by private individuals, by eroding their competitive ability and reducing almost all to mere preparatory feeders to themselves and higher schools elsewhere, and by setting the standards – the 'private schools adjust themselves to our standards', said the secondary heads. Even 'an extremely good private school', the Handsworth Ladies'

College, 'has gone on under difficulties', according to the headmistress of Edgbaston High School, and was in fact given up just about this time; 'superior private schools have dwindled very much' since the girls' schools endowed by the King Edward VI Foundation had opened.[9]

The Bryce Commissioner investigating Warwickshire doggedly tried to include private schools in his survey but found it a frustrating and exasperating task. Very numerous were the small ones but his enquiries elicited little as to their efficiency, 'my letters being sometimes ignored and my questions often vaguely handled', while parental opinions were almost worthless.[10] As one outspoken London headmistress remarked, 'Many parents consider a flaming advertisement to be quite a sufficient gauge of the efficiency of a school and its teachers.'[11]

The Commissioner's persistence did, however, win information on about fifty or so in the greater Birmingham area, and Mr Lowe's school is at once in the superior minority as being conducted by a graduate, for Thomas Lowe was a London BA. Otherwise it fits perfectly the general picture of schools, for the most part preparatory, 'kept by ladies ... in ordinary private houses, not originally built for school purposes and neither adapted nor adaptable to such purposes', and often with unsatisfactory sanitation. Such schools' orientation was evident in their claims, for only six of these fifty 'refrain from distinctly claiming successes at the examinations for entrance to King Edward's Foundation schools or the Oxford and Cambridge Locals', but since virtually none entered whole classes the odd success might be attributable to concentration on a few promising pupils and was no sure guide.[12] This is the context in which Emmeline was gratified by a letter of 1895: 'you will be very glad to know that your old pupil has won a scholarship at King Edward's High School for Girls ... There were about 150 sat for the exam, but only 54 vacancies and six scholarships to be given and I am one of those six (thanks to your good teaching in "History" and "Grammar", nobody has ever taught them me so well ...).' In general, the secondary heads told the Bryce Commission, 'the mass of the pupils who come to the schools from these sources give no particular signs of having been taught methodically'.[13]

At their best, such schools as the Lowes' could construct a simulacrum of civilised and cultured family life, the interaction of animated minds with literature and ideas, music and arts which broadened outlook and enabled critical appreciation. Certainly the Lowes themselves struck the Tanners as 'intellectual and musical', though criteria for assessment are peculiarly inexact and subjective, as the Bryce Commissioners found. The New Church continued to be very much part of Emmeline's life since the Lowes were active members themselves, but the school was in no sense exclusive nor could it have afforded to be, and the light of a less provincial world, derived from the widely-read Lowe sisters (at least two of whom had studied in France and Germany, when none of Emmeline's family had even crossed the Channel), was not dimmed.

When the Froebel-trained Lilian returned from Berlin she brought a range of new ideas, pursued with quiet determination: she was, for example, one of those women active in philanthropic work who joined the National Union of Women Workers later renamed the National Council of Women. Never strongly feminist, though in 1902 it espoused women's suffrage, the group expressed Lilian's energy of conscience as well as her refined dignity – a child would not lick the honey spoon in her presence, it was said. But Lilian, like the gentle Janet, the nurse of invalids and sympathetic correspondent with Nettie when Emmeline's future was again debated, and like the merrier Kathleen, who enjoyed a walk to the top of the Mendips and 'a yellow-backed novel' alike, cared enough for their young student's friendship to sustain it lifelong. And from now on Emmeline looked to wider horizons.

But no such culture could, for educational purposes, substitute wholly for the laboratories and gymnasia now being built into more ambitious schools or compensate for haphazard assemblages of libraries and specialised subject materials. As a testing ground of community skills, however, the school itself was metaphorically both laboratory and gymnasium, facilitating observation and experiment, demanding agility and poise. Emmeline was somewhat precariously situated, subordinate to the family patriarchally headed by Thomas Lowe, organised domestically by Mrs Lowe and academically by 'Miss Jessie' (Emmeline used, but did not receive, the prefix 'Miss' for the other sisters too), but in authority over those she taught, and distinguished from the Kindergarten students because she pursued a full academic range while they learnt only French and music. But Emmeline was detached from the senior boarders like Frank Martin or Annie Gauntlett who learned with her, by the duties which drove her into more independent, self-managed study. Since she subsequently maintained friendships with members of each of those groups, and was even receiving pages of confiding chatter from ex-pupils years later, she must have developed some of the elastic skills applicable to other hazardous networks of relationships.

Illustrative of the hazards encountered was the backwash from a financial crisis in the Bath New Church in 1894. Emmeline's father led the committee's retrenchment campaign with a proposal to cut the salary of the minister, Frank Martin's father. Negotiations and resentment were briefly muted by the Bath Society's jubilee celebrations in October, but these failed to restore the group's finances or its attendance level; a 'change in the ministry would be desirable', concluded Harbutt in committee, but beyond the committee storms brewed.[14]

'Frank has told Mr Lowe about Mr Martin,' wrote Emmeline carefully to her father. 'He gave a fairly impartial account, and mentioned that you were rather hot and that Mother seemed to try to keep you back a little. He says that Mr Martin intends to resign in any case but that he would rather resign with a majority in his favour than be under a cloud as at present. He feels sure of getting a majority.' Sam called a special meeting of all members, analysed the society's difficulties and proposed acceptance of Martin's resignation, with a gloss of regret at the 'loss of a worthy pastor'. Yet no rancour subsisted between their children, now working together for Matriculation and later keeping up a friendly correspondence.

Some friendships were not only preserved but spread through families like sap through branches, as with that with Annie Gauntlett, the senior boarder and the tenth of a farmer's thirteen children; the eleventh, Edwin, also boarded with the Lowes until he was about fourteen and, offered the choice, abandoned school to work on his father's farm in Wiltshire. Through Emmeline both groups of brothers and sisters were brought into contact, and the future of two determined. Among the staff likewise relationships were personal rather than professional, though Emmeline was later to find some of the assistants who came from time to time could pass on information about schools elsewhere in a scanty grapevine. So it was the dress sense of the Kindergarten student Minnie that she particularly observed, and especially Minnie's facility for elegance on small means, for Emmeline was still as fastidious as in childhood about her clothes. Conveniently the Tanner girls had been taught to identify elegance with simplicity, so that Eva remarked at fourteen:

Ladies should not over dress, they look much nicer and more ladylike if they are dressed simply. There is no need of so many colours as some wear, or of such a lot of jewellery which showy people think so pretty ... Generally common people, if they have money to spend on anything but the necessaries of life, spend it on a lot of cheap, showy things; they will have common dresses so that they may get ribbons, laces and cheap jewellery to wear on top of it.

Emmeline did not phrase her preference for simple styles in such openly class-based terms but she maintained it more consistently than Eva herself. So Emmeline learnt informally as well as studying the subjects expected of senior schoolgirls, but what was no part of the Tanners' agreement with the Lowes was that she should receive formal teacher training. In the eyes of consciously 'progressive' secondary headmistresses this now meant systematic instruction in educational psychology, history and philosophy, and in techniques of lesson preparation and class observation with evaluative analysis; in 1894 the Principal of the Cambridge Training College levelled damaging criticism against the casual apprenticeship of Emmeline's experience, saying pupils were at risk from the 'prentice hand', that experience, unless subjected to 'a thoughtful habit of analysing and understanding it, is apt to degenerate into a routine, which is likely to remain uncriticised so far as it may be comfortable. Experience may confirm error instead of correcting it.'[15] 'Such 'error' accounted for the inadequate grounding so many secondary heads found in entrants from privately-owned preparatory schools, according to Dorothea Beale: 'small schools cannot pay their teachers properly. Then good teachers do not like to go to private schools and they cannot get a proper staff ... They have seldom had a good general education or any training in the art of teaching, I think.'[16]

Training for secondary teaching had emerged as a visible desideratum, as long before for elementary teaching, and a problem of ways and means. Facilities for training existed, in one-year courses at some specialised colleges like the Maria Grey College, and a few larger schools, notably Cheltenham Ladies' College and the Mary Datchelor School, included professional training departments – but all cost money. All were also categorically distinct from the elementary training colleges – indeed, when the Cheltenham Training head invited an elementary lecturer to speak she was appalled at the mechanical repetitious methods he taught – and so the growth of training tended to widen the gulf between the elementary and secondary professions. No more mention is now heard of Board schools in Emmeline's plans for the future as she began to grasp how much more freely a secondary teacher could range, how much more deeply penetrate. It widened too the gulf between the sexes, for few men were interested in professional diplomas for secondary teaching, arguing that a degree assured competence, or experience for those without a degree, or simply 'character' for those as yet without experience. Women were far more enthusiastic, their university aspirations having dawned in desire for professional advancement as much as intellectual extension but with graduates still few.

As Harriett Morant Jones, head of a GPDSC high school, pointed out, 'the profession is so overstocked' that, other things being equal, the teacher with systematic training would be preferred; training 'certainly does facilitate their getting work', and this was apparent in the 'situations' lists of the educational journals.[17] Yet trained teachers remained a small minority through the 1890s, and Emmeline represented three overlapping groups, of those lacking money, those lacking guidance towards facilities, and those who deemed a university education superseded the need.

For as she reached eighteen the idea of university was taking shape among the formless swell of ambitious images that surged within her. The years surrounding her own birth had seen the infancy of women's colleges in Cambridge and Oxford; from 1878 London University granted them degrees on equal terms with men; since 1881 women had been admitted to Cambridge University's Tripos examinations. Through the 1880s and 1890s women entered the Victoria University (newly federated from the colleges of Leeds, Manchester and Liverpool), the ancient Scottish universities, the federal University of Wales. Of them all, London was the most accessible, not for any lack of rigour but because no specific lecture course need be followed and no institutional residence was demanded, only the examination entry fee. Justly H. G. Wells claimed that 'London University with its hard examinations to all-comers has been difficult but a possible and encouraging way from down below there to a position as teacher, journalist, or what not, to a breathing-space wherein a young man of this type may find his possibilities.'[18] Or a woman.

Cartoonists might drift from the rocks of ridicule to the sandbanks of soggy sentiment over 'sweet girl graduates', but for an idealistic girl the perilous seas and faery lands of scholarship were viewed through magic casements. This is not an idle image, for Emmeline, who was to insist always that children approached history most readily through stories, was herself kindled by the images of heroic romance, the literary qualities of history which force its student into the alien experience of Saxon king or Sedgemoor rebel, the narrative and figurative power brilliantly exploited by Carlyle and Macaulay, writers Emmeline now encountered. Her intellectual ship was not yet well fitted, and college principals like Elizabeth Wordsworth or Anne Jemima Clough, who had always moved among scholars and poets and wits, would have pitied the scanty stimuli of a provincial preparatory school. But the less charted the seas the more boundless their possibilities.

A hinge on which those magic casements swung was, mundanely disciplining fancy, the Matriculation examination of London University, not yet (as later) regarded as a school-leaving certificate but the preliminary rung on the ladder for a London degree, the first of those 'hard examinations to all-comers'. All one needed was to be over sixteen and pay a fee of £2 plus an extra pound or two if the papers were taken at a local centre such as Birmingham. Most found them 'hard'. In five days, in January or June, the candidate sat through twenty-three hours of written papers on Latin, another language (French for Emmeline), English language with English history and relevant geography, mathematics, mechanics, and a chosen science – all these were compulsory. With no laboratory to hand Emmeline probably made her choice of the sciences on offer as a correspondence college advised: 'the candidate ... will do well to take Heat and Light, as he can get a more intelligent knowledge of this subject than he can of the others without the aid of practical work.'[19]

'You know that if you fail in one subject you fail altogether, don't you?' she wrote uneasily but accurately to her parents. Still it seemed enough to remember daisy-chains of facts, to develop a facility for calculation and a command of grammar, when, for instance, 'English' meant sentences for analysis with questions on historical grammar and etymology. Perhaps only through her own efforts to light enthusiastic fires in pupils' minds rather than cram them with inert data did Emmeline then dimly apprehend why Professor Henry Sidgwick and others warned that methods 'well adapted to secure success in examination are not so well adapted for the communication of solid knowledge and the development of intellectual faculty'.[20]

Life was not all work. She was thrilled when her father spared an evening from his attendance at the New Church Conference in Birmingham to take her to the opera – it was Gounod's *Faust* – while on another musical evening she decided of Plunket Greene that 'I liked him more than any other singer', and there were plays too, and lectures, in Birmingham's vigorous urban culture. Once Emmeline met her mother at Stratford and visited Anne Hathaway's cottage, a child beggar hovering outside, and perhaps the other Shakespeare sites along with the Gothic towered theatre erected in the 1870s;

such excursions fed an appetite to hear, to see, to partake – it was all so *interesting*, she found. But as June 1895 approached, with the Matriculation examination boding, she was fretting at time and rising at five to con her books, for her days were still spent teaching. 'Don't think I am wasting my time doing this,' she implored her parents to excuse a letter. 'I am doing it in lunch-time.'

She was now looking ahead of this final term, knowing that now she was eighteen she must begin not only to contribute by her work to the expense of her maintenance but to support herself, yet longing to glut that appetite for experience. Specifically she wanted to stay in Germany, as Lilian Lowe had and as many girls went, *en pension*, to learn the language and absorb the rich scholarship, poetry and music inherited from Germany's Romantic flowering. There were practical arguments too: 'We have been looking at advertisements,' she wrote, 'and so many of them mention Germany and France', while the linguistic knowledge would be an asset because 'Of course the headmistress must understand what the others are teaching or she cannot tell whether they are doing it properly.'

It was a dream, distracting Emmeline not only from the examination but from the pain in her back and shoulder. Some months earlier, from her seat among a group huddling round the drawing-room fire in the bitter winter of 1894-5 she had leapt up, with her accustomed energy, to catch her neck and shoulder on the heavy marble overmantel. One did not fuss about such aches, and she could not bear to be treated as an invalid and perhaps have her studies curtailed, so she gritted her teeth and got on with her work. But two weeks after she had revealed her dreams of travel, and sat the examination, she was writing to her parents in a different vein:

I know I ought to write you a nice long letter but I don't think I ever felt so utterly tired as I do today. I suppose it is because it is all over and I don't feel obliged to keep up. We had very nice English Language and History papers on Thursday; but oh! the Mechanics! They were awful. They have done for us entirely, I'm afraid. Mr Lowe says it is a most unfair paper for Matric. Frank Martin showed it to a man who has passed Intermediate and he said that his paper was not so difficult and that he never [saw] such a one for Matriculation.

It seemed so strange to wake at five this morning and not to feel obliged to begin working ... I really feel too tired to write any more now. You won't forget to write to me tomorrow, will you? Miss Jan is only waiting for a letter to begin to teach Annie and me German.

There were no German lessons. Emmeline had collapsed, almost certainly with the first of the migraine headaches that were periodically to devastate her for the rest of her life. They could last three days, often involving nausea and visual disturbance. The Lowes were extremely anxious, and it was Janet who cared for her and kept her family in touch:

I don't think the exam is the real reason of Emmie's breakdown. If she had been in her usual good health the work would not have hurt her, but having been poorly for so many weeks before with her back made her unfit for her work. I think if we had known how bad her back really was, she would not have gone in, but she is so abominably uncomplaining and was so determined to keep up, that she put us all off as to how she really felt. Her back is much better now.

While Emmeline recovered she contemplated a new and somewhat drab plan, of a post in a private school in Southampton. Janet Lowe pressed its advantages to the Tanners:

Lilian ... is most probably going to Southampton as KG teacher and she wants Emmie to go there as well. Of course we have talked the subject over and Emmie has come to the conclusion that she would like to go. At first she did not think the salary was enough but Father says considering her age, it is as much as she will get ... You see, although she looks so much older than she really is, and although she is to all intents and purposes older, people who don't know her won't take that into consideration. Then again, if she has failed, she would arrange to have time to work up for Matric again, and if she has passed, to have time to work into a higher exam. Altogether it would be as well for her to get into an easy position for a year or two till she has worked up to something higher. It would be so nice for Lilian and Emmie to be together. It will be a fearful break-up next term ... Emmie will write to the lady in Southampton tomorrow for all particulars, but would like to hear your opinion on the subject as soon as possible.

Sam's opinion was favourable. 'I think it would be capital if you could secure it upon satisfactory terms, especially if Miss Lilian is likely to go there,' he told Emmeline. 'Of course I take it that Miss Lil has made enquiries as to the status and character of Mrs Hoare and her school and is satisfied upon those points which are most important. Southampton is a very nice town and I could run over from Bournemouth occasionally to see you.'

The salary can be guessed only from Emmeline's reckoning two years later that £35 a year would better her position; £25 a year for a residential post was not unusual, for board and lodging were included. Her father's words carried great weight, and he was plainly anxious to see her settled in a steady job rather than pursue mirages. She was still waiting, rather anxiously, for her results, so he added a few paternal words: 'We all hope you may have passed your Matric exam but shall not be surprised to find you have not done so as it appears to have been an exceptionally stiff one in certain subjects. It will be a disappointment but you must not let it trouble you too much as you have done your best and could not do more.'

Both parents now wanted her home, but though she knew as well as the Lowes that she was still, at eighteen, under their authority she was reluctant. Mrs Lowe wrote for her:

Emmie has shown me your letter, and asked what she had better do about going home, with such pleading eyes, asking to stay, that I really could not find it in my heart to say 'You had better go' – and I am writing entirely unknown to her, to ask you to permit her to stay on till the end, or at least till nearer the end than Thursday of this week.

Of course Emmie will love to see you all, and be at home when the others have to go, but I can feel how it is, she thinks her going from here closes the chapter of her free and happy girlhood and that it will never return. When she is a full-fledged mistress at Southampton she will be in a rather different position, with more responsibilities, and she does not want to leave her girlhood sooner than she needs ... she is evidently upset at finding her own desires are somewhat contrary to yours. I feel this – she is so quiet – and we love to see her happy.

Just such a shrinking, or sometimes desire to escape, can occasionally be detected later when a demanding change was in prospect, a moment when strength had to be gathered and the will to freedom disciplined – in the terminology Emmeline inherited and habitually used. So in 1908 and 1924 she was again incapacitated by illness in the course of a crisis of effort when her professional advancement was at stake.

Now she was permitted to enjoy the last summer days of term at the school in Handsworth, and there she received her Matriculation results. Of the 3420 candidates in 1895, 1710 passed, graded as Honours, First, and Second Class; Emmeline gained the First Class, but both her fellow-candidates at the Lowes' failed. Her mother, busy making Arthur a suit, wrote briefly, mingling commiseration for Annie and Frank with advice to impart the news to Emmeline's future headmistress, but others were more effusive, and none in the flood of congratulations implied anything unfeminine in academic success. In the words of Aunt Adelaide, 'I am very proud of my niece. And I am sure your Father is prouder than ever of his eldest daughter. I am sure, dear, you *must* have worked very hard and great credit is due to you.'

The letter from John Bragg, the Swedenborgian friend and neighbour in Handsworth, hints that Emmeline may have confided ambitions other than schoolmistressing in his hope that 'sometime you will most fully realise all the success of a literary kind that now seems possible for you', but of this nothing definite is known. Most practical was her father's enclosure of a guinea for her fare home, and 'the balance you may look on as pocket money to do as you please with. You may perhaps be wanting to make a little present or two as a slight acknowledgement for kindness rendered.' Sam's formula for advice ('you may want to ...') was often utilised later by Emmeline.

So she went home, wreathed in glorious laurel, to find she shared attention with the aftermath of a parliamentary election and wrangles over the Liberal political machine. Sam had earlier resigned his unpaid secretaryship in Weston to a Quaker newcomer, George Gales, a paid full-time agent, but not his commitment or the political education of his family. Beatrice was eager to tell her sister how she had heard Lord Weymouth, the Conservative candidate, at a pre-election meeting, and how she and her father had joined the thousands to hear that he had won in their constituency of Frome: 'Mr

Bertie thinks the district visitors should be drowned!' At the next by-election the seat was gained by the Liberals, with the enthusiastic voluntary help of young Tanners still at home.

So Emmeline found her family intact and busy. But time persistently destabilises, and while Winnie and Arthur (known as 'the children') still thought themselves 'in a state of bliss – i.e. riding donkeys' on a seaside excursion to Weston-super-Mare, and Fred and Herbert were as yet still schoolboys on holiday, Eva and Beatrice had reached the problematic ages of seventeen and sixteen.

Unlike Emmeline, Eva did not continue teaching after her spell as a pupil-teacher at Devonshire Place; instead she was informed she was to stay at home to help with the household, especially with the piles of sewing. Ready-made clothes were appearing in the shops but rarely as yet acceptable in both quality and price, and the boys needed shirts, the girls blouses and skirts and all the layers of a Victorian wardrobe. No evidence remains of Eva's attitude to this (save for her claim in old age that she longed to be an actress), but from the 1890s scattered records suggest reluctance to be confined at home: occasionally she visited London, frequently Bristol, and more and more she took a hand in charitable bazaars and meetings, until by the 1900s Eva was herself organising meetings and functions for the Anti-Vivisection Society and others and at times used the New Church premises.

Such characteristically middle-class activities contrast both with Emmeline's adult assumption of self-support and with Beatrice's nascent intention to become a nurse, a trained 'hospital nurse' in distinction from a domestic childcarer, though teaching hospitals did not accept recruits in their teens and Bee knew she must wait. 'In the 19th century,' said Emmeline in 1938, a nursing career 'was either a vocation or a release from the narrowness, dullness and restraint of home life; for many it was both', but it was not, as by 1938 she thought it had become, one of a range of potential careers to be weighed on its advantages; and Bee was the nurse of that time Emmeline knew best.

In September 1895 Emmeline was packing again, to spend a few days at Sherrington where the Rev. Mr Heard had suggested 'you may rest on your oar' before taking up work in Southampton, at St Winifred's School.

Private girls' schools were fortunately placed in Southampton with no other choice for the middle classes save to send their daughters away, and at this time St Winifred's took boarders too (fifteen were counted in the 1891 Census), a significant financial asset for the owner, Elizabeth Hoare, wife of an assistant warehouse keeper at the Docks. Southampton itself was comparatively small, of about 65,000 people in 1891, but as in Bath its western suburbs increased schools' catchment areas. Like Bath too it clothed itself in architectural history, so that the Victorian infill on the old estates surrounding such mansions as Bevois Mount or Banisters Court extended beyond Regency terraces in the upper part of Above Bar, themselves beyond the Georgian houses of Gloucester Square, and so back through time to the port's ancient roots and the Roman fragments to the east. As a port Southampton was profiting from redevelopment in the 1890s. From there one might embark for almost any other port in the world, and there in 1895 was built the largest dry dock in the world.

Within the town municipal projects were taking shape, somewhat on Birmingham's pattern, with public bath-houses, a Free Library, some slum clearance, but not till later in the 1890s a municipal electricity scheme, and Bills for municipal water were repeatedly delayed in Parliament. The water that dominated, however, was that of the sea, so that when Lilian Lowe gave her Kindergarten children an outing she took them to the pier, and when Emmeline's father visited her in her first year the two of them explored the docks and boats together, quickening each other's curiosity about productive processes of all kinds. 'I have not enjoyed myself so much for ages,' said Emmeline.

The school buildings, as at Handsworth, were converted from domestic use, and like many private-school staff Emmeline lived in, sharing a bedroom, an arrangement more economical for school authorities than paying non-residential salaries, with the advantage of fuller control over assistants. The principal, Mrs Elizabeth Hoare, seems to have been a remote figure and the staff was large enough for Emmeline's humble appointment to be that of 'third English governess' – specialists were employed only for French and music – though she was also responsible for a form, apparently of about a dozen girls. The term 'governess' was becoming obsolete, replaced by 'mistress' in schools developed on 'high school' principles, but though within a year or two St Winifred's was also styling itself High School, when Emmeline started it retained features characteristic of 19th-century private schools. So Emmeline took her girls for walks for their exercise, in a 'crocodile' if numerous, and in the evenings they might dance or do 'fancy-work', for which occupation Emmeline sent an urgent appeal home for 'a pair of white or black lace mittens' since bare hands were unacceptable.

In direct authority over her was Miss Jarvis. 'Miss Jarvis is a new governess for Form IV (the one above mine). She lives in the house, but she and one of the governess-pupils have to have a bedroom out. She has been a missionary in South Africa, is tall and thin, and talks through her nose. She is second English governess ... I am awfully afraid she will be coming for the walks and then I shall never be able to walk with the girls.' Emmeline's role as form mistress was perhaps the most notable aspect of her two years in Southampton, involving her not only in substantial teaching duties, with a wide range of subject, but in oversight of the girls' attendance, health and behaviour, as well as their amusements, and she was first refuge for any academic or personal problems they might confide. The principle behind this long-established office was that of teaching a child not a subject but to wheel around the circle of knowledge in a unified process of learning, co-ordinating all aspects of a child's life; in practice schools found it a cheap and practical way to maximise use of staff.

It was on the pastoral side that Miss Jarvis laid most stress when compiling a leaving reference for Emmeline in 1897, in the glowing terms appropriate to the genre:

Throughout this period she has shown unusual ability in the management of her class, and has combined a firm discipline with good judgement and gentleness. Her influence on her class was most marked and beneficial, and she impressed upon them her own earnestness and industry. Miss Tanner's personal appearance is greatly in her favour. Her physique is splendid and she has exceptionally good health. She has been leader in the school games; her robust health, cheerful temperament, and readiness to enter into the amusements of the girls, have made her a general favourite with them. Miss Tanner possesses a great capacity for work. She seems untiring both in regard to her own study and also her school duties.

'But can she teach?' a prospective employer might have asked. It is obvious, however, that health was regarded as a priority, and Emmeline managed to sustain a general reputation for 'exceptionally good health' by resolutely ignoring ailments: to be able to work through a migraine is a rare achievement. Here too is the only indication that Emmeline attempted to continue 'her own study', for she made no attempt to climb the next rung of the London degree ladder, the Intermediate examination, and perhaps was solitarily exploring the seas of knowledge with only clouded stars to guide her. Certainly she had little opportunity to obtain tuition in the required levels of mathematics, Latin, and now Greek as well. She may have attended some lectures or evening classes at one of Southampton's most notable institutions, once the Hartley Institute and later the University College, but she is not recorded as having joined any of the more systematic courses now being established there. In 1896-7 courses leading to the London BA and BSc degrees were started, with the first BA gained in 1898, but these were full-time and day-time, impracticable for Emmeline, and most evening classes concentrated on such technical subjects as naval architecture and joinery. The frustrations were familiar to many in the provinces. Guidance was one problem, time another, money a third, and books limited by the pitiful salary of an assistant mistress to what could be borrowed – and Emmeline knew few with scholarly libraries.

She was no worse off than many others; her hardships, indeed, probably less than for many in the same field. To be 'underpaid, overworked and badly fed' was a common fate for assistant mistresses, especially at the crowded lower end.[21] Those who wrote of their experiences recalled cold and insanitary conditions, severe scrutiny of everything they read or did, with the pettiest of faults noted, supervision of children at all hours, no free periods, and lights out at 10.00 pm. The food at St Winifred's may not have been above average if, as is thought, it was at this time that Emmeline abandoned vegetarianism, not on ideological grounds but out of hunger. But she was at least allowed some free time. Then the expanses of the New

Forest drew her on a borrowed bicycle, or the wide horizons of the sea, so that when she and Lilian went down to the Docks to wish their Handsworth colleague Minnie good sailing as she emigrated to South Africa Emmeline felt that 'for some reasons I would have liked to be going for a voyage'.

This period strengthened her friendship with Lilian Lowe, but otherwise the quality of personal relationships, the most critical of all factors to an assistant's happiness, remain unknown. Few other friendships can be firmly dated to these years, and the conventionally hollow phrases ('every satisfaction ... most conscientious') condensed into three lines of frigidity in Mrs Hoare's parting reference do not imply much warmth of sympathy. After two years Emmeline was happily excited by her decision to leave, and unworried that she thereby flouted her father's 'prudent paternal advice' to persevere in her post, as she told her mother, giving as one reason that 'Mrs Hoare has not asked me to'.

Sam's advice can probably be best understood in the light of his greater familiarity with the qualitatively different prospects available to Emmeline's brothers. In July 1896 Fred left school, aged fifteen. One option he considered was the slow but steady career structure of the Civil Service, for boy clerkships (the lowest of the low) were available by competitive scholarship, about one in ten candidates gaining one. The Tanners turned to the venerable Sir Isaac Pitman for advice. As the pioneer of the technological software of stenography he urged its advantages to the enterprising, the greater as the developing hardware of typewriters and telephones promised speedier office work. With three hours' work a day, he said, Fred could be proficient at shorthand within two months, and to ensure this the old man himself corrected the week's exercises after Sunday morning services at Henry Street.

Soon the Civil Service idea faded before the attractions of free enterprise and, after a month or two in the office of a local clothing factory, Fred took the train to Bristol and trudged round promising businesses. In his own account lurk the contours of Dick Whittington's story, as, about to return fruitlessly home, the tired boy paid a last call at the paper and packaging manufacturers E. S. & A. Robinson, was seen by a director, passed a test triumphantly and was engaged as a clerk. He started in the Estimate Department at a salary of 5/- a week, still dependent on his parents for a home but at least, unlike contemporaries who took articles with solicitors and accountants, taking money home and not himself paying a premium. That he chose a business with the promise of expansion yet still small enough for a clerk to learn all its aspects and adapt to different roles, and to be himself known to the directors, was fortunate, or shrewd.

Thus Fred's potential career structure could be fitted into the framework Sam Tanner understood, of gradual promotion through increasing responsibility within the same establishment. On the shadow side prowled the danger that if a job were lost the knowledge appropriate to one office or business might be useless elsewhere; no one sank in the economic scale faster than the jobless clerk with neither mobile artisanal skills nor the

developed physical strength to compete in the unskilled market. If one did
not rise it was best to be doggedly loyal. So Sam may have found it hard to
appreciate the different dynamic of a teaching career within a still dimly
adumbrated professional structure. Plenty of mythic roles were available
here but they were those of the missionary, the mother, the gardener or the
lantern, and offered no clear path of advancement as Dick Whittington did,
or more emphatically the Industrious Apprentice, the buried theme of
Herbert's account of himself. After Fred had been at Robinsons' a year
another young clerk was needed: had young Tanner a brother? Herbert
was not yet fifteen and still at school, but Herbert was not one to miss an
opportunity, though his parents agreed only 'rather reluctantly', he thought,
and he began work the week he was interviewed, rapidly identifying himself
with the business and their interests as his.

But for an ambitious teacher in a private school, without capital to buy
out an owner and so with no prospect of headship, hope of professional
progress lay instead in taking her subject knowledge and teaching skills on
angled steps between different institutions. Now Emmeline turned not only
the advertisement pages of journals but to a firm of 'Tutorial Agents',
Griffith, Smith, Powell & Smith in the Strand, London, and she found them
productive but not flawlessly efficient:

> On Saturday at 10.30 am I received a notice from Griffiths & Co
> requesting me to be at their offices, Strand, at noon that day as Miss
> Skeel of the Nottingham High School, to whom I had applied for a
> post from £80-90 non-res., wanted a personal interview and had come
> expressly to engage a teacher. Of course I wired and said I couldn't be
> there in time but would come by the next train. She wired back to me
> not to come, and wrote to say she was very sorry Griffiths had not sent
> in time ... It is one of Girls' Public Day School Co.'s schools and they
> pay 2nd class return railway fare, so I should have made something
> on that little biz. Unfortunately it didn't come off.

The coarsening sensibility hinted by the final phrases here may suggest
the road not taken: later Emmeline would not have used such an expression
as 'that little biz.' and shunned, if she could, the vulgarity of the thought.
At present she replaced regret with consideration of the offers of lesser
calibre that came, but with no sign that she was calculating either long-
term interest or any idealistic aspiration. 'Today I have received two more
offers, both in London, N and SW, one £35 the first year and £40 the second;
the other at £40.'

She took the best of the week, not waiting for more: 'Miss Roebuck of the
Ladies' College, Halifax, has offered me £45 a year, resident, to be the Head
English Mistress in her school.' Though Emmeline had seen neither the
school nor Miss Roebuck she assured her parents that both were reported,
at second or third hand, to be 'very nice indeed'. 'Ask Father to let me know
what the railway fare is. Not much under 17/6d, I expect. I shall go through
Birmingham, shan't I?'

Chapter 4
Halifax

Travelling northwards Emmeline carried little baggage of elaborately embroidered ideas on Education, and journeyed, it seems, with no sense of mission, only with personal hopes of development. The very title 'Head English Mistress' was excitingly full of scope for choice and ordering of her work, and at twenty a new job in a strange district must always hold the possibilities of the yet-to-be-explored, however familiar the framework of a small private school after seven years of learning and teaching. At Halifax Emmeline was to serve seven more years, having won as yet, like Jacob, a Leah, not the Rachel of desire. That desire of intellectual expansion was to hold her there, but in those years she not only grew to intellectual maturity, but began to grope towards a more just view of the possibilities of girls' education.

Its pretentious name was the most aspiring feature of Halifax Ladies' College, a second-grade school in the classification of the Bryce Commission, where girls left at sixteen or so, with a curriculum restricted by the brevity of their stay, the capacity of the staff and the facilities of the premises. Emmeline found only two or three colleagues other than the visiting music and drawing staff, but it is doubtful that there were ever more than about thirty pupils, in age from eight to sixteen, though the house was handsome and its situation 'splendid', said Emmeline, healthily on the hill above the town itself and close to Savile Park.

Mary Roebuck had taken it over some twelve years earlier, and for her Emmeline developed a considerable respect. Perhaps she was connected to the same extensive Yorkshire-based family as was J. A. Roebuck, the fiery Liberal MP for Bath and later Sheffield whose name Emmeline may have heard not only as a thorn in government flesh but for the anti-Swedenborgian tract he wrote in Bath in the 1880s. Perhaps Mary Roebuck was the headmistress friend Emmeline later described as learning Sanscrit in retirement to keep her mind lively and full; she was vigorous enough in 1912 to spend a few days walking in Wales with Emmeline and seems to have been alert to ideas and possessed of some breadth of knowledge. Proofs are lacking. But soon after she had appointed Emmeline she apparently gave up active teaching to content herself with domestic and financial management, and Emmeline was very happy that in her hands now lay the arrangement of lessons and class organisation, with full command of the syllabus she taught. First, however, Mary Roebuck had to assess Emmeline, and Emmeline to assimilate her new terrain.

She thought she was coming to a foreign land, she said later, as the train steamed into the West Riding where the names of the stations, 'particularly

Mytholmroyd and Luddenden Foot, sounded even stranger than they looked on the boards', an allusion to the Yorkshire vowels and downright final syllables of local voices, an articulation so much at variance with southern English that in some rural areas educational inspectors were dismayed to find pupils and masters in grammar schools failing altogether to understand each other. The difficulty was less acute with the middle-class urban girls who were Emmeline's pupils but her ear had to become accustomed outside school. Those voices spoke of a different culture, a strong tradition of valuing independence, directness, the well-kept household, a practical approach to practical ends, the combination of self-sufficiency and powerful will with pithy humour and blunt speech of which Elizabeth Gaskell had written, setting the scene for her *Life of Charlotte Brontë*. Not herself a woman of the West Riding Mrs Gaskell found that 'even now [1857] a stranger can hardly ask a question without receiving some crusty reply, if, indeed, he receive any at all. Sometimes the sour rudeness amounts to positive insult. Yet if the "foreigner" takes all this churlishness good-humouredly, or as a matter of course, and makes good any claim upon their latent kindliness and hospitality, they are faithful and generous, and thoroughly to be relied upon.'[1] Emmeline too reckoned she 'had never known a more hospitable and warm-hearted people'.

Their proverbial independence reacted paradoxically on girls' education, as the Bryce Commission of 1895 found. Their Assistant Commissioner Miss C. L. Kennedy, herself an ex-headmistress, concluded: 'I fear that on the whole there is a widespread apathy throughout the West Riding with regard to the intellectual education of girls.' Parents, she thought, rarely saw any practical advantages in a secondary school for daughters because their 'love of independence ... takes the form of a strong repugnance to allowing them to become the recipients of salaries and wages' – 'it is pride which makes people keep their children at home', she was told, though at home she observed that they were expected to do more of the household work with fewer or no servants than in comparable households elsewhere, and deal with the baking and laundry and other tasks habitually sent out in the south.[2] High domestic standards were traditional. So when she asked five headmistresses for details of parental occupations and school-leavers' activities she discovered a constant level of 60-70 per cent of girls remained at home, whether they were daughters of professional men and manufacturers educated at a leading city high school, or lower middle-class leavers from a rate-supported 9d-a-week higher grade school, whose parents, like those of pupils of Halifax Higher Grade school, worked as carpenters, plasterers and shoemakers, as publicans, grocers, upholsterers and coal merchants, as clerks, book-keepers and commercial travellers, and as lower managers in all the branches of the wool trade, worsted spinning, dyeing, wool stapling, cloth pressing, that was the town's great business.

Many of those parents who were prepared to pay secondary fees of five to twelve guineas a year sought, Miss Kennedy concluded after visiting nearly a hundred schools, not intellectual training but the individual attention, the contact with 'cultured' lady teachers, and the social advantages unobtainable in the top classes of an elementary school.[3] Particularly the lower middle classes utilised elementary schools initially before sending their daughters to secondary schools for a year or two 'to finish' – too late, according to the Bryce Commissioners, to repair earlier defects, too brief for substantial educational gain, and preventing coherent course design in schools. Such attitudes did not facilitate the growth of schools with a demanding intellectual curriculum except in the largest cities: Leeds' and Sheffield's GPDSC high schools were reverently praised by the Commission.

Halifax High School demonstrated this. Founded in 1877 by a company formed of prominent and public-spirited local citizens on the pattern of the GPDSC schools, it was heading into financial trouble even when Miss Kennedy visited it in 1895, though it possessed an excellent site with adequate premises at Savile Hall. In 1897 it failed financially, the company dissolved, and the school was taken over as a private establishment by an able assistant mistress, Ellen Bolton, dedicated to the 'best High School ideal', according to HM Inspectors in 1907, and well-qualified, well-skilled and devoted to an 'efficient standard of work' at the expense of any financial profit to herself.[4] Yet by 1907 the school was depending on pupil-teachers and scholars sent by the local authority to maintain a viable size, and its future was uncertain if these were to be drained away into a new municipal school. When Emmeline arrived in Halifax in 1897, however, she may have observed Ellen Bolton's exertions and aspirations rather than foreseen the frustrations of the next decade.

For boys the case was different. For them the Bryce Commission found that the revival since the 1860s of the old endowed grammar schools, plentiful in the West Riding, 'has crushed or is crushing the private day schools out of existence', but not only were there a mere nine endowed girls' schools, and four proprietary high schools, but 'the same parents who are quite willing to allow their boys to mix with boys from all classes, are not willing to do so in the case of their girls'.[5] The urban working classes could rarely pay any fees – too often many of their children became 'half-timers' at an early age, struggling daily to remain awake through a long day divided between factory and elementary school – so that, with prevailing attitudes, a survey in 1897 found only 389 girls receiving secondary education in Halifax, of whom 99 were boarders at the Crossley and Porter Orphan Home and School and not necessarily native to the town. Two mixed-sex schools and the mixed higher grade school accounted for 143 more, leaving a total of 147 divided between the other three girls' secondary schools, all listed as 'private', in a town of 90,000 people.[6]

The market for Mary Roebuck lay perforce among parents who prized social selectness or the home-like intimacy of small classes and close relationships with staff from whom girls might acquire desirable *mores*, and in whom they might confide the problems and anxieties they were too shy to tell at home, in the course of a genteel education biased towards literary rather than scientific subjects (the higher grade school was oriented to science and technology). Parents approved unstressful school days, with afternoon hours usually devoted to music, art, sewing or gymnastic exercise in the form of 'drill'. Against the 'high school ideal' of specialist teaching and intellectual challenge smaller private schools competed with social and psychological advantages. Most were small: of the 2886 private all-girls' schools submitting returns to the Department of Education in 1897 (91 per cent of girls' secondary schools of all types) only 2.5 per cent held over a hundred pupils, and the average number was just over thirty, less than a quarter of the average number of girls at an endowed or proprietary school.

Rather imperfectly realised, then, two models of girls' education were embodied in the majority of private schools and high schools. One was domestic in its ethos, characterised by satisfaction with literacy, useful skills such as arithmetic for account-keeping and needlework, social skills such as music and conversation, and oriented to feeling; the other was fiercely emulous of the knowledge transmitted to boys, characterised by desire, replacing the subjective approach via feeling and data with the objective way of observation and inquiry. What synthesis might emerge, and the effect of powerful influences like that of Cheltenham Ladies' College which constructed its own model, was debated in the 1890s, stimulated by discussion at the 1890 Conference of the Association of Head Mistresses. The debate was not neutral. The Association formed in 1874 was for heads of endowed and proprietary girls' schools, those of privately-owned ones being barred, and as a body it threw in its lot with the high school ideal, fostering it in influential circles including the Bryce Commission.

Thus their Assistant Commissioner for the West Riding noted how resources and parental prejudices encouraged sexual differentiation in schooling. Girls' schools very frequently lacked money for suitable equipment for science teaching (a problem at Halifax High School), and usually lacked playing fields and outdoor games organisation, partly because parents often preferred girls to come home earlier and feared the social mixing more probable in games than in lessons. In all types of girls' schools a shorter school day than for boys was customary, leaving less time for thorough teaching, and Miss Kennedy often found that in private schools more of the remaining hours were devoted to music and drawing, both usually ignored in boys' schools, than to languages and mathematics. She could have added to this list a shortage of classical language teaching, both because few women could teach Greek and Latin for lack of learning themselves and because few parents saw any use in these save for university entrance (where they were often mandatory) and had little interest in them for daughters.

The very picturesque geography of Halifax typified the wedge between social classes which reinforced social prejudices. The early site of a wool industry town was often the river-bank in the bottom of a valley, rising steeply to the open moors, so that as mills rose and spewed their smoke and dirt those who made money moved to higher ground up the valley sides. Though Halifax's River Calder ran to the south of the town so that the mills pushed up their chimneys on steep streets up windy hills, the better-off preferred the yet higher areas of the irregular uplands, abutting on the moors themselves – and wanted their daughters at school nearby. Schools like Mary Roebuck's thus depended on the immediate neighbourhood and the preferences of parents, spelling insecurity financially in a limited market and enslavement academically, unless boarders could be attracted in sufficient numbers. In boarding fees there was profit. But those who could pay boarding fees tended to shrink from the grime of a manufacturing town and forget the airiness of the heights and the beauty of the situation, to distrust chill winds off the moors and favour some noted health resort. The three Halifax private girls' schools reporting in 1897 could muster only one boarder between them.

Uncommitted as yet in educational sympathies but wholehearted in her loyalties, Emmeline supported Mary Roebuck's efforts to attract boarders, to the extent that by her second term she was begging her parents for her own youngest sister, Winifred, for schools commonly built a magnetic core with a few girls at unobtrusively reduced fees. Her letter reveals the curriculum she found:

Miss Roebuck's terms are £50 a year for board and English, then Laundry, Pew-rent, Music, French, Drawing, Painting, Gymnasium and Dancing are all extras, also Class-singing, I believe. She says she will take Winnie for £14 a term inclusive of French, Music (under a mistress), Class-singing, Drawing (Painting I am not sure of), Gymnasium. She says she could not arrange for Mr Sharpe to teach her music as he charges Miss Roebuck 2 guineas a term for each pupil, and the dancing mistress 25/- for ten lessons.

Be sure and tell me what you think about it when you write. It would be a very good thing for Winnie, and it is a good deal of reduction. With the subjects she has put in, her terms are about £24 a term ... All the teaching is very good, French, Music, Gymnasium and everything, and the girls are very well looked after in the house.

This optimistic assessment persuaded Nettie – the financial outlook was brighter now than a decade earlier, as Sam made his way – and she sent Mary Roebuck some Bath buns ('as nice as any I have ever tasted, if not nicer,' said Emmeline) and her youngest daughter, now nearly fourteen.

By now, it is clear, Mary Roebuck was developing a personal liking for the warm, vital young assistant who lived in her house, introducing her to a Halifax society dominated by the manufacturers, often Liberal and Nonconformist, who sat on the Town Council, donated to charities and lived in solid stone houses hardly protected from the moorland winds by the shrubberies approved by fashion. To some of these Emmeline went to teas and to tennis parties as these became popular, though Miss Roebuck's household, Winnie recalled, attended Church of England services at the new St Jude's Church rather than Nonconformist chapel; the Tanners focused on the spirit rather than the letter of worship, and went with the rest where 'pew-rent' was paid though Emmeline's allegiance was still to the New Church, as affirmed by her application for and admission into senior membership of the Society in Henry Street, Bath, in 1897. Swedenborgian friends were discoverable locally, especially Cunnington Goldsack, a minister in Bradford who had several times already been a guest of the Tanners in Bath. Religion was not to be a bone of contention, however.

So Emmeline was acquiring a social training more – whatever term is applied, polished, genteel, smart or elegant, necessarily reeks of class distinction – formal, at least, than she had customarily known. When, for instance, she was asked to dine with Mary Roebuck's respected guests, it was 'the first time I had dined properly like that', in evening dress and gloves and proper forms. 'We had dinner at seven and they stayed till nearly eleven. Everything was very nice and the table looked lovely; we had five courses.' And she was taken to concerts, to hear Plunket Greene again, singing Brahms and 'simply splendid', and to the Halifax Choral Society, though their production of *The Spectre's Bride* and *The First Walpurgis Night* was marred by the guest soprano's failure to appear.

By the turn of the century Halifax had two theatres, but ladies did not care for the one in poorer surroundings, though they might occasionally patronise the musical comedies of the other, varied occasionally by visiting companies playing Shakespeare rather than anything more commercially risky. These were social as well as aesthetic occasions. For Plunket Greene Emmeline wore 'my evening dress' (a significant singular), and for other entertainments 'my blue silk blouse' or 'my blue with the chiffon'. Blue was always a favourite colour, answering to her blue eyes and considered suitable for a schoolmistress as neither garish nor dowdy. An eye for visual arts was not easily developed in non-sartorial ways in what contemporary guidebooks called a 'busy smoky town' whose principal tourist attraction was its long-repealed 'gibbet law' – the legalised lynching of those caught red-handed in certain forms of theft – and the old parish church filled with sombre black oak.

The beauties of Halifax lay most of all in its surroundings, in the rugged and wooded Ripponden Valley, at Hardcastle Crags, or along the valley of the Calder towards Hebden Bridge. In the valleys was sometimes shelter, welcome when 'it has been almost impossible to stand on the moor the last few days', as Emmeline wrote in the February of 1898, and 'people who don't live in Halifax don't know what wind is'. Though she thought the weather of her first northern winter 'perfectly appalling', she found too that a vigorous young woman could walk expansive miles on the moors and even, if one took the train through Luddenden Foot and Mytholmroyd to Hebden Bridge, strike north on foot through the tough grass locally called 'bents', and over Oxenhope Moor by a mountain road eight miles past

Peckett Well to Haworth, to join the steady stream of Brontë-reverencing pilgrims. They came to inspect the 'weedy confusion' of the sisters' graveyard, the outside of the Parsonage (open inside to 'introduced visitors' only, the guidebooks warned) and the tiny museum opened in 1895 in two rooms above the village's Penny Bank.[7] Emily Brontë had written of the wildness and storms round Wuthering Heights but also of 'a west wind blowing, and bright, white clouds flitting rapidly above; and not only larks but throstles, and blackbirds, and linnets, and cuckoos pouring out music on every side, and the moors seen at a distance, broken into cool dusky dells';[8] in seven years Emmeline met both.

Increasingly as maturity ripened the limitations and narrowness of her experience became obvious to her, never, so far as can be detected, to be conceived by her merely in terms of gender restrictions, and her appetite for exploration was whetted. Some she owed to Mary Roebuck. After term ended in Emmeline's first Halifax spring, for instance, Mary Roebuck took her for her first visit to London. Even before she arrived at their hotel in Eccleston Square (where she had 'a nice little room to myself, with a wardrobe') Emmeline was enchanted that in Park Lane 'the air all the way is scented with hyacinths' and she found it 'quite exciting crossing over the road in Piccadilly Circus, Regent Street or anywhere like that ... I think the London streets are delightful, they are so busy and so full of life ... the shops are exceedingly gay and hundreds of pretty things in them.'

Some errands were school-related, ordering desks in the Strand and other materials at Whiteley's in Queen's Road, but when Mary Roebuck was confined to bed by a cold Emmeline went over the Houses of Parliament and spent a morning at the National Gallery where, inevitably, 'I think you want to go there dozens of times to take in all the pictures', to Westminster Abbey on Sunday morning and in the evening to St George's, Albemarle Street, 'where the music is most perfect'. For other evenings there were *The Liars* at the Criterion Theatre with Mary Moore, admired by Miss Roebuck, and a 'charming piece' called *The Little Minister* which persuaded Emmeline to prefer the acting of Winifred Emery. She acquired tickets for Tussaud's and the Zoo, and for a recital by Rosenthal at St James's Hall, to which she took a resident in the hotel who had earlier responded affably to her frank friendliness. It was the mixed catalogue typical of tourists, in fact; Emmeline discovered delight even in 'lovely William pears and grapes for dessert', and cheerfully answered her mother's teasing about the traffic: 'Your imagination leads you astray, Mother dear, when you think of my smiling on the policemen, as I depend entirely on my own presence of mind to get me safely over the road.'

This is typical of the buoyancy, and independence, of her self-presentation. It did not preclude concern with serious issues but it did mask any anxieties she may have felt and renders these hard to detect. A brief reference years later discloses that she considered the Boer War one of the two external events that made a major impact on her in her seven years in Halifax, but all evidence of what she said or thought or did during that war is lost. Emotions ran high, so that Joshua Rowntree, the Quaker Mayor of the Yorkshire town of Scarborough, with Quaker views on war, had his house stoned and his windows smashed, and in Bath Emmeline's brother Herbert withdrew his application for membership of the New Church Society after long discussions with the minister on the inconsistency with the teachings of Christ of the minister's apparent support for the war.

In the 1890s too, American tariff laws bit deeply into the export trade of Halifax and the other wool towns and manufacturers foundered, their mills ceasing to ooze oily smoke, so that workless men haunted the streets, provoking questions. Old questions, responding to what Charlotte Brontë had put into Robert Moore's mouth: 'I saw many originally low, and to whom lack of education left scarcely anything but animal wants, disappointed in those wants, ahungered, athirst, and desperate as famished animals ... Something there is to be looked to, Yorke, beyond a man's personal interest ...'[9] The answers had long roots too, embittered by the struggles Brontë's *Shirley* dramatised, as the growing labour movement organised in trade unions while Joseph Chamberlain, once of Birmingham, argued for UK tariff reform and Protection. But the old Liberal instinct was for Free Trade, and valiantly Emmeline tried to assess the arguments for herself, to understand protectionists' hopes and fears: she attended lectures, read the papers, sought out the texts on economics in the great mansion which housed the Halifax Free Library. It was, she said, 'the duty of every intelligent citizen to make up his mind on the question' and she 'sat down and studied it, becoming an absolutely convinced Free Trader', the more convinced through listening at Tariff Reform meetings to arguments that 'seemed spurious and fallacious' to her. Politically, of course, Emmeline's views were irrelevant: she had no parliamentary vote and no influence. But her conviction was a fruit not only of earnest thought but of a deep hunger for opportunity, and not just for herself.

Despite the refurbishing of the school organised in the visit to London, and despite Winifred's arrival the next term, boarders remained worryingly scanty, in twos and threes only. Emmeline thought 'Poor Lilian' when she heard there were now eight Kindergarten boarders in the school at Southampton, but an influx of older girls would have been welcome on the slopes above Halifax. Winnie made her friends among the day girls, and a year or so later she and Emmeline both furthered an intimacy with Kathleen Lowe when she joined to teach the juniors, enhancing the family atmosphere. It was with Kathleen that Emmeline took oranges to an elderly Swedenborgian and shared in a birthday gift of *The Ingoldsby Legends*, illustrated by Cruikshank, for Mary Roebuck, and with Kathleen both sisters went to tea parties with neighbours and friends.

Winifred was to look back happily enough on her school days under her sister's tutelage, but as an inadequate magnet had to accept a partial *quid pro quo* for reduced fees, to do light dusting of Miss Roebuck's drawing-room and – far more abhorrent – to clean out her birdcage; neither task cherished her self-respect. She leant on Emmeline but the eight-year gulf in age and wider gulf in confidence kept the relationship uneven, even if that of teacher and pupil had not imposed inequality. 'She works very well for me always,' Emmeline assured their mother, and Winnie took pride in the two little silver medals she won 'for perseverance', though their inscription *Labor omnia vincit* was all she learnt of Virgil at Halifax Ladies' College. Winnie remained eager for Emmeline's advice, admiring and respectful to a sister ready to give everything except her private thoughts and who was never quite to lose the elder sister in the friend.

At this time Emmeline seems to have been only sporadically alert to the dangers in pupils' reliance on her for cheerful strength (as one told her, 'You can always say the right thing and courage is pumped into me just by your mere presence') and more rarely than later to have urged mental independence as vital for her pupils, as for herself. Winifred was certainly not Emmeline's only admiring pupil, and certainly did not develop the exaggerated form of the schoolgirl infatuation. But to others Emmeline was an obvious idol, young, lively, kind, and prepared to listen attentively and sympathetically; and she devised her response, it seems, at this time if not earlier.

That plenty of girls lavished on their seniors or teachers an excess of emotion was a well-recognised hazard, and Emmeline coped, like many others, with kindness suspended on braces. Thus the injunction 'Don't fuss', applied impartially to all affectation and excitability, to be taken as the cap fitted and to be remembered by her pupils as characteristic, was used as her check on the emotional displays she called 'demonstrative', though by the light rein of humour. 'Do you remember once saying, "I wonder what you'll do when you get a husband if he isn't demonstrative"?' teased one Halifax pupil when she found an openly affectionate fiancé. Another tactic was to keep minds busy and bodies active. The pioneer of organised games for schoolgirls, Penelope Lawrence, in a paper written for the Department of Education in 1897, included among their several beneficial effects that games became a topic of interest, of 'healthy impersonal conversation' distracting girls from silly gossip, an attitude neatly summarised by Blanche Clough of Newnham College: 'they occupy the vacant space and they also produce an antiseptic atmosphere'.[10] Perhaps there were reasons other than physical health why Emmeline not only took her girls for walks but introduced hockey in 1900.

By indirect means, then, she could avoid inflating the consequentiality of passing phases of adolescence, as attitudes like those of one contemporary headmistress might: 'No words were strong enough to express her condemnation of the morbid kind of sentimental affection not worthy of the name of friendship which tends to sap the spiritual life and lower the spiritual standard ...'[11] Don't fuss, Emmeline might have said to this. Her fresh-air standpoint might be read as part of a larger muting of sexuality, or more correctly perhaps as its sublimation or conversion to supra-personal ends, but also as part of the education of feeling, a necessary and appropriate aspect of the education of the adolescent.

The privacy of her own feelings she kept inviolate, deflecting such speculation as inevitably leeched itself to a vital young woman with a ready smile. In posed photographs Emmeline is statuesque, erect and calmly dignified; in the snapshots now feasible even poor exposure and wavering focus cannot fade a springing energy and the beam of a smile reaching every muscle of her face. That face lacks the prominent bones of Nettie's, the masterful nose and deep eye-sockets, but while its framework is softened by more rounded bones its surface has firmed now to the confidence of authority, a growing power defined in every line of expression as in stance – direct without aggression, candid without coyness – in her own control. At twenty-three in 1900 the verve that took her for long walks on the moors kept her what her contemporaries deemed a 'fine figure', a comely woman, never meagre but yet compactly shaped to her long limbs, and so one who drew men's eyes despite the 'surplus' of women, if they did not fear the strength.

Sometimes rumour reached her parents' ears, to be deflected with mockery. 'I was interested to hear of my engagement,' Emmeline wrote ironically in 1900 when gossip had hit on Lockhart Lowe's name at the time of Lilian Lowe's engagement. Writing in the room she shared with Kathleen she continued: 'Kath sends her love; she says that she and Winnie have arranged that there shall be a double wedding – Andrew and Lil, Lockhart and I – and Winnie and she are going to be the bridesmaids. They are now practising walking up and down our bedroom. "Would that it were true!" says Kath' – and here another hand seized the pen to insert 'and Tannie agrees! So does little Tannie.' Emmeline recovered her pen – 'No!' – and moved to another topic. The unemphatic shift of focus away from her personal feelings was habitual and characteristic.

Emmeline was at ease in men's company, enjoyed it often. Exuberance rings, for example, through her account of a holiday in the summer of 1903 with Lilian and Andrew Eadie, now married, at their home in Argyllshire, and chimes nine times in the name of a young doctor, Jim Eadie: 'Jim and I walked to Dunoon and back', 'Jim and I went out in the *Findhorn*', and when a group sailed to the head of Loch Long and walked to Loch Lomond 'Jim and I did about five miles in the hour and a quarter but the others did not get as far', and so on. He addressed her by the affectionate nickname 'Tannie' and seven years later could mock himself for arguing with her logic; they stayed friends and no more.

Many such friends invigorated her life, and she remained, by desire or default, her own woman. Yet only the crass could suppose her preference inclined to her own sex. At no time can any one woman be found who takes priority over other friends, and the fashion for 'demonstrative' displays Emmeline rejected. At least so far as concerned herself she seems always, like many of her contemporaries, to have recognised sexuality in an exclusively heterosexual framework, the commitment to marriage welded to it as tightly as the notion of family and domesticity to marriage, and with the same liberal equanimity as informed her overt attitude to religious or political difference she respected what diversity she observed in others, even while her educational modes tacitly assumed her pupils would not only observe but be swayed by her values.

At Halifax Emmeline was not formally the headmistress and the school's atmosphere, serenely ordered or feverish and fretting, was the responsibility of Mary Roebuck. But that lady was soon satisfied to hand over to Emmeline 'the responsibility and arranging of all the school work', in the words of her subsequent reference, though her permission must have been necessary for innovations, hockey for example, and to approve decisions about the prime way to keep youthful minds busy – examinations. Throughout girls' secondary schools at this time examinations were on the increase, approved by some for their stimulus to thought-out directions and exacting standards, distrusted by others like Dorothea Beale for their competitive essence, and unpopular among Yorkshire parents for their irrelevance to domestic life, as the Bryce Commission found.

Organising examination candidatures, even for the minority of girls who hoped or needed to work outside the home, enlarged Emmeline's experience of further aspects of school management, planning syllabuses, co-ordinating staff, and dealing with parents. True, academic staff were few: names of only three or four can be elicited, and these remain shadowy figures save for Kathleen Lowe who worked with the younger children. But surviving result forms for Cambridge Locals at Preliminary, Junior and Senior levels for 1899 and 1901 for a total of eleven girls provide one source for information on Halifax Ladies' College's curriculum, and notes on these disclose that of the subjects taken the only ones not taught by Emmeline herself were French, drawing, music, and the lowest level of history, geography and arithmetic. The last three she dealt with at Junior and Senior levels, just as she taught throughout for papers on religious knowledge, English grammar, composition and Shakespeare, and probably Euclid and algebra.

The result forms also show that no candidate listed took any of the several science papers available or a foreign language other than French, and so were left with barely more than the minimum number necessary to achieve a pass certificate in the examination as a whole, and subjects listed on a termly report of 1900 confirm the examined subjects as the full standard menu. Uniformly the girls achieved 'good' or 'moderately good' for papers taught by Emmeline, 'weak' or 'failure' for French; in drawing and music they varied widely. Simply to assimilate this small part of the high school ethos, its response to external standards, therefore exposed the problems of compromise at a level deeper than a shortage of facilities: the curriculum of the private school was incongruous with examination requirements and the burden on the generalist teacher too great.

The ideal curriculum drawn up in 1897 by Sophie Bryant, head of the archetypal high school, the North London Collegiate School, stood on four rather unequal legs. The first leg, the 'Humanities', supported 'knowledge of the world and the history of humanity' (geography and history) and 'letters' (English language and literature) with the languages and literatures of a Romance (French) and Teutonic (German) modern language as well as the 'educated currency' of Greek and Latin language and literature. Second came 'Science', as many branches as possible and taught as experimentally as possible, never as 'dogmatic enunciation', including mathematics, natural and physical sciences. On the third leg stood 'Arts', the doing or achieving of some end by the use of eye (drawing), hand (any handicraft, including needlework), vocal organs (singing), ear (music generally) and the limbs (games). The fourth propped up 'Religion and morality', but not in a controversial spirit: Mrs Bryant wanted Scripture taught as history and literature with the 'central and simple truths' of Christianity (she was not afraid to identify these as God's Fatherhood and universal love, His call to men, the brotherhood of men, repentance, faith and grace), with some practical everyday applications. Less able girls and those who must leave at sixteen could manage, Mrs Bryant believed, only a less detailed and more limited version – one or two foreign languages, say, and only arithmetic and geometry, botany and hygiene from the science group – but still they should attempt a course designed to develop all faculties.[12]

The radical thinking behind this scheme and its assumption that a course extending over four years was viable can hardly be detected in the curriculum found at Halifax Ladies' College; but when it is compared with a discussion more accessible than Mrs Bryant's paper for the Department of Education, *Work and play in girls' schools*, published in 1898 and largely written by Dorothea Beale of Cheltenham Ladies' College with contributions by Lucy Soulsby, ex-headmistress of Oxford High School, and Frances Dove, founder of Wycombe Abbey, a common core of thought is obvious. Here are five divisions – the Humanities, Mathematics, Science, Aesthetics, and Exercise – with moral education pervasive through staff example and attitudes, backed up by regular Bible study and the exploration of philosophy and religion as part of the Humanities category, but the scope is the same, as are the assumptions.

At the turn of the century Halifax Ladies' College had neither the staff, the facilities for specialised work nor the number of pupils even to contemplate these balanced curricula, and the radically different demands of parents of private-school pupils held the purse-strings. Yet there were compensations. When, fifty years later, Emmeline recalled 'those prehistoric times when one mistress taught a number of subjects' she remembered how 'I have myself experienced the real satisfaction of watching the unfolding of a girl's mind and her unconscious discovery of the unity of knowledge when she finds again and again how one subject dovetails into another'. Here her phrasing refers the process to an impersonal or pupil-generated operation, as of leaves opening, and displaces the teacher's centrality; and she went on to throw the weight on the importance of teaching '*how* to learn' and mental habits of critical analysis rather than the feeding in of information; the significance of this must have impressed her in her own generalist days at Halifax. But the teacher's real omnipresence in the process described strengthened, if she were liked, the personal element of the smaller school.

Generalist teaching and permanent presence were reinforced by the sharing of non-class activities, sporting, artistic, dramatic, whatever, in the less formal organisation possible for small numbers. Personalities loomed large here. But it was typical of such a school that if contact were perpetuated it was in personal relationships rather than in formal old-girl networks, and extended to whole families. For Emmeline several friendships with pupils persisted, for example with Jessie Appleyard, only a year or so older than Winifred and one of the daughters of a hospitable family living nearby on her father's 'own means', as the 1891 Census records, and whose own life was to reflect many of the changes of her times. The Tanner sisters were welcomed to her family's house, and Jessie visited the Tanners in Bath; Emmeline encouraged her to develop vocationally her quick responsiveness to natural beauty by studying horticulture at Studley, received and wrote letters through Jessie's years in Southern Rhodesia before 1920, stood godmother to one of her daughters, and in old age admitted her to the select group of non-family members to whom her circular family letters were sent. Through such friends, unconnected with professional educational concerns and living in different ways, Emmeline could keep her own balance and a broad-based vantage.

What is not detectable is any inclination to project her own hopes and aims on to her pupils. By 1900 her hopes were invested in a new plan, to reach for the golden fruit of more advanced intellectual life than afforded by a petty school round or even omnivorous reading. But all that is clear is that the plan ended in something worse than disappointment.

The end of the summer term of 1900 found Emmeline ebullient. She had been in touch with Dr Stewart, the Principal of the Hartley College in Southampton and responsible for implementing its development towards university college status with courses leading to London University's BA and BSc degrees; she could even refer lightly to 'my going to the Hartley' as a settled expectation. Indeed, she was planning where to lodge, weighing the advantages of the women's hostel, or hall of residence, with its moderate fee for board and 'the advantage of a study for work, although it is a common one', against the offer of lodging in a private house 'on the same terms. I am to have a bedroom for myself and as there are two sitting-rooms downstairs I am to have one always alone to work in. If by any chance both are occupied there is to be a fire in my bedroom and Mrs Findlow is going to put a writing-table there; there is a bookcase already.' *Somehow*, therefore, she believed the costs of tuition and board in Southampton could be met.

But, and again *somehow*, within a month she was thwarted. Extant Hartley College records leave no clue as to how, and nor did she. Only her mother's response allows conjecture:

My dear darling Child ... My heart aches for you this morning, dear child. I only wish you could see (as you will some day) *that it is for a wise purpose*. My darling, read the chapter on Duty and Interest in your *Pathway of Promise*. That chapter made me do my Duty once when apparent Interest would have kept me where I was, with a probable chance of marrying an old rich nasty man who was making love to me. We must be so thankful, darling, that the alteration of your plans that were made has not been through death, or disgrace. Hard as it will be to bear, we must thank God for that. I too wished Dr S.'s reply might have been in the affirmative if it was God's will in the wishing tree.

The BA *I* don't trouble about a bit. I would rather have a healthy bright daughter, which I am so thankful for now. Don't trouble about what other people say, dearie, remember God knows, and feel strengthened. I know only too well what a disappointment it is to you and I feel for you as only a Mother can. I also can see the discipline which sometimes makes character.

Much as I should have loved to have seen you I don't wish you here, because we have to study other people before ourselves. Mary Cholmondeley says those who shirk will have a loveless old age. I glance at Aunt J. and Miss W. and think it must be true. Let us put ourselves and pleasures *last*, dearie.

Money may have been the problem. Since Emmeline did not apparently apply to the several other institutions that offered teaching for the London BA for which her Matriculation qualified her to try, she may have hoped to subsidise herself by concurrent teaching at Southampton where she already had acquaintance. Perhaps the fact that Dr Stewart, frustrated by economies forced on him, was to leave Southampton at this time has some bearing. Whatever the facts this episode illustrates again how precarious were academic chances without the securities of money and connections.

Whatever bitter fruits Emmeline tasted then she did not let them sour her mouth visibly. She remained at Halifax, and by the next spring was contemplating a new scheme, for in the new century Mary Roebuck had announced her intention to retire and sell her school.

Chapter 5
The turning point

The most potent symbol of the passing of the 19th century was the death of Queen Victoria in January 1901. Drapers were consoled by the enormous demand for black cloth though Winifred was so repelled by being thrust into black cast-offs thriftily and hastily altered that she announced her conversion to republicanism and maintained it ever after in complete inconsistency with loyalties she took for granted. The memorial service at St Jude's to which the school trooped in a body interrupted the working week, and with the rest of the people of Britain and her Empire the Tanners became Edwardians. The Census of 1901 found 32,525,716 of these living in England and Wales, 3.5 million more than in 1891, and so, it might be reckoned, there would be a need for more school places. But Mary Roebuck was retiring.

So Emmeline looked to the future. Here it is useful to compare the parallel lives of her sisters. Beatrice would not wait until she was twenty-three, the minimum age for probationers to begin training at most general hospitals, but in June 1899 left home for Manchester where the seventy-bed Clinical Hospital for Women and Children would accept girls of twenty if they provided references as to 'character, education, health and physique', for a two-year training leading, after examination, to a certificate. As in all respected hospitals places were vastly exceeded by applications, at this time averaging 150. Unpaid for the first six months, probationers received £6 in the next six, and in the second year £15, though uniform and laundry were provided as well as board and lodging.[1] Generalisations are hazardous, for a comprehensive directory of 1900 shows how various was probationers' training in hundreds of hospitals, some with as few as fifteen beds, some specialising in maternity, orthopaedic or fever work, but, as described by Sir Henry Burdett, the typical day for a probationer nurse meant that she rose at 6.30 am or so, to scrub lockers, window-sills and patients' backs under the direction of a staff nurse until about 9.45 pm when chapel preceded bed. About two hours off duty was allowed daily (and at the Manchester Women's and Children's Hospital one day and night a month was free) and class instruction by the Matron, with lectures on anatomy and physiology by the medical staff, varied a Sister's teaching on the ward. Little is known of Beatrice's experience, but she would have learnt some practical skills with instruments and some principles, such as antiseptic treatment.

Manchester was a mere hour or so by train from Halifax, so that occasionally Emmeline could visit Bee, on a Wednesday or Saturday afternoon when she had some free time, and she was vexed that Mary

Roebuck should object to this when Bee was ill with 'two attacks of influenza and dry pleurisy' in an epidemic of February 1900. 'I couldn't bring it back to anyone, of course,' said Emmeline airily, 'but I suppose it is possible, though not at all probable, that I might have it myself.' But she learnt that every school was terrified of the spread of infectious disease. After her Manchester training Bee transferred to St Mary's Hospital, Paddington, to join the eighteen staff nurses who oversaw fifty-four probationers (figures for 1900), under the Matron and sisters.

With Winifred's future Emmeline had a more direct concern. By December 1900 Win at sixteen was just about to take the Cambridge Senior Local examination which all assumed would mark the end of her formal schooling. Unlike the bad egg she was given for breakfast the day of her first paper, Emmeline's optimism supported her: 'She has worked splendidly this term and my only fear about the exam is that she might not get a large enough total number of marks as she only has just enough subjects. It won't be her fault, though, if she fails and we'll hope she won't ... We are going to Louie's on the Saturday because I think it'll be much better for her to have a thorough change than to look up then.' As to what would come next Win had her own ideas, as Emmeline reported to their father:

Miss Roebuck is very anxious for me to ask if Winnie can come back as governess-pupil next term. She would take her for £15 a year and would give her good French lessons – separate ones from the new French mistress – music, and any other subjects she might want to take up. Winnie has an idea that she would like to go in for type-writing and shorthand. What do you think of that idea? Is there any opening for girls like that? I suppose there is. I know girls in Southampton who are learning but they haven't begun to look for posts yet. Will you please give it your serious consideration?

I told Miss Roebuck that that was what Winnie thought of, and she said why couldn't she learn at the Technical School here ... but perhaps you will think £15 is only a little less than you pay now, but what she is paying is really the ordinary pupil-governess fee. She would take the Third Class – three or four little girls – for two hours a day and would have the rest of the time for her own work. Personally I think teaching would be better for her in the end ... She would do very well, I think, and if she were going to teach this would be about as good a beginning as any. She could be prepared for either Matric. or Cambridge Higher Local.

That Emmeline should underrate the growth in office employment is not surprising; that Sam, involved in the business world, should is less likely, and perhaps, like many, he thought that a commercial atmosphere was inappropriate to a half-grown girl. Win's wishes were overridden but though she stayed at Halifax through the next year she took no higher examinations, and was persuaded by her mother into accepting first one job, then another, as a private governess on the nursery level. Sam put his foot down on one 'lady-companion' post in a household without servants, pointing out that 'she will have to do the general work of the house, which I do not think will suit her when there are fires to light and floors to be scrubbed, etc., neither should I like to feel she had to do it.' But in the governessing jobs she did take Win was bitterly unhappy. What was involved is revealed by one employer:

I am requiring an experienced nursery governess for my three children. The eldest, a girl of twelve, goes to school but requires some supervision with her homework, etc., then the next child is nine, a boy, for whom I require some teaching; he has been to school but is rather delicate so I wish him taught at home. The youngest is a boy of four, he requires a good deal of attention. There would be their bathing, etc., their wardrobes to be kept in repair. Are you competent to teach the usual English subjects and Music? Harold has begun Latin, of course it is very elementary – I do not know if you have learnt it or not?

Terrified, Win told her mother that 'I most certainly do not feel competent to teach such old children, especially boys', but Nettie's draft answer was positive to the extent of suggesting that though 'she does not know Latin ... I think it would be quite possible to keep a few lessons in advance of your little boy (without his knowing it)', and that after ten years' learning music Win 'would be quite capable to teach although not a brilliant player herself.' Certainly Win never claimed any musical ability.

So it was not till 1904 that Win's misery and isolation in these child-minding jobs impelled her parents to consider her wishes, and she learnt to type at classes started in Bath by Remington, the UK licensee of the most advanced typewriters patented in the USA, for work in a Bristol office. There, with regulated hours and freedom outside, with duties for which she had the technical skills, her happiness allowed her organisational competence to flower so that over the next five years she was promoted to become personal secretary to the manager (with five girls under her, she remembered) at a salary of £75 a year. Her job survived a crisis over a new regulation demanding employees be vaccinated or face dismissal when she offered on principle to resign, but when she was exempted she refused to exempt herself from typing the admonitory letters. That, she said, was her job, with a decisive independence lacking in her adolescence.

So the Tanner sisters did not suffer the frustration that 'it was "not done" for a girl of a family like ours, in Halifax at any rate, to take paid work', the words of Phyllis Bentley, writing of 1912 and echoed by many of the better-off middle class.[2] But nor were such material opportunities offered to the teacher, the nurse or the secretary as to their brothers.

In May 1901 Fred brought his parents the news that Robinsons' had asked him to go to South Africa as their first export representative there, to build up business in the expectation that the Boer War would soon end. He had been 'travelling' for the firm in the UK for some time but was still only twenty when he sailed from Southampton to Cape Town in June, to find that the prosperity brought to manufacturers and tradesmen by British Army expenditure swelled his markets as he worked round the major towns, 'pioneer work in an unknown country, with the Boer War still being fought', as Herbert rather romantically envisaged it. Until the end of 1906 Fred was to spend most of his time in South Africa, developing the markets he opened, and he brought back stories, of how he was stranded on the open veldt with a drunken ox-driver one night; scrambled over recent battlefields; met exotic personalities; of the strangeness and beauty of the wide wild landscape and of the commercial energy of the settlers in what seemed a promised land. For his sisters South Africa became both more immediately real and more glamorous than from newspaper reports veiled in moral indignation or pugnacity.

The flow of settlers to clear and farm new land, land of their own, absorbed a number of the Tanners' acquaintance, but Fred had no interest in farming and returned to join the management of his firm. Emmeline herself, though she never ceased to be fascinated by the pioneers' efforts and problems, rejected a settler friend's notion that 'I should have made a good pioneer because I accept all kinds of different conditions cheerfully and appear to enjoy and adapt myself quickly. I do that easily enough but I should *not* have made a good pioneer because I am not skilful enough with my hands and I have not the physical courage or the agility to run up a tree if faced by wild animals, or to shoot them for that matter.'

Fortunately no leopards roamed the gardens of Halifax Ladies' College. A private school was a business, however, with chances of expansion: the Education Department's returns of 1897 found 49 girls' private schools with over 100 pupils, a mere 2.5 per cent of the privately-owned total but the iceberg's visible peak – though larger ones must offer something more than homely intimacy. Baffled in her hopes for further education at a time when in endowed and proprietary schools (that is, not owned by private individuals nor run for profit) a quarter of women teachers and most heads were graduates, Emmeline contemplated a change of direction.

Mary Roebuck had put the school's sale into the hands of Griffiths', the London agency she dealt with for teaching staff, but simultaneously she negotiated with her head English mistress. The block advertisement Griffiths' put in the school sales category of the *Journal of Education* includes only one in Yorkshire, repeated from March to November in 1901, and it is hardly enlightening: 'Superior Day School for young ladies. About 28 pupils at good fees. Splendid premises. Reasonable terms of sale.' Other less veiled advertisers enable the northern price for 'goodwill' at comparable schools to be gauged at between £170 and £400, depending on the fee income claimed (from £400 to £1,200 for about thirty pupils); buildings seem usually to be rented and the school furniture sold separately. Since calls on that income included rent, staff salaries, rates, insurance and maintenance, and normal domestic outgoings such as food and fuel, as an investment a private school was not especially attractive. In 1905 it was calculated that with twenty pupils to a full-time teacher the cost for staffing in a secondary school worked out at £15 per pupil in a school of 100 girls, at £9/10/- in a school of 200; this correlates with evidence to the Bryce Commission of 1895 that the cost to a school whose girls left at about sixteen averaged about £10 a year per pupil.[3] No profit started until such costs were covered. But there were always cheering examples of success from slight beginnings, such as the school owned and run by the three Lawrence sisters which had recently moved into an impressive building, designed for them to house 200 boarding girls, at Roedean just outside Brighton. Emmeline brooded:

I think a great deal must depend upon whether I can get some boarders to begin with or not. Even if they paid lower fees it would be a great thing to have them as it would make an impression here and people would begin to think the school was looking up at once. Do you think there is any chance of my getting the two Eyres? ... I shall have *all* really good teachers and the girls will be well looked after as well as having a nice time. It is really much better to send away sooner than Winifred went – it gives them more chance. I would take the two for £70 a year including Laundry, French, Music, Drawing and Painting, besides the ordinary subjects ... Would Mrs George let Gwen come? I would take her for £25 or perhaps even £20 if no one else ever heard about it. Halifax is a *most healthy* place and our situation is splendid.

What does Father think ought to be the rent of a house valued at £1,600 taken on a repairing lease for 7 or 14 years? £80? It is in very good condition now. Miss Roebuck will probably have the lecture-hall re-papered. I might have to do the music-room. All other rooms have been done since I came, I think. Miss Roebuck very much wants to have the money in one sum and not in instalments but she *might* be persuaded to take half in July and the other half in December 1902 with interest. She is most anxious to do all that is fair to whoever buys it. I have told her to go on with her communications with Griffiths'.

Again she was thwarted. Some old friends, including Mr Heard of Sherrington, were apparently willing to advance small sums but the figures would not balance, and at the end of 1901 the school was sold to Miss Esther Pannett and her sister. Very soon, however, Emmeline realised that her judgment in even making the attempt had been at fault.

The impact on Emmeline of the Education Act (1902) at this time was from its consequences for small private schools, later from the impetus it gave for new municipal secondary schools, and still later from its enshrinement in education of parallel tracks for children over about eleven. Probably it contributed to her decision now to leave the world of private schools, when she could grind out the key to the door of that possibility. So a brief glance at its significant provisions is necessary.

That national educational changes were imminent had been obvious for several years, signalled by, for instance, the appointment of the Bryce Commission and by the Act of 1899 to unite functions previously scattered round several agencies in a single Board of Education charged with the 'superintendence of matters relating to education in England and Wales'. That cleared the way for major reorganisation at local level. Duly, in March 1902, an Education Bill was introduced, designed to tackle increasing problems of funding and control of elementary schools and to address the inadequacy of secondary provision uncovered by Bryce.

The vast majority of children attended elementary schools, either Board schools provided by 2,568 locally-elected School Boards and funded by a rate levied by the local authority, or 'voluntary' schools provided mainly by religious bodies and run by 14,238 boards of managers with some governmental grant aid but now facing a rapidly worsening financial crisis. The Bill's solution was to create 318 new Local Education Authorities (LEAs) which would replace the old School Boards, directly controlling the schools provided, and provide rate aid for voluntary schools in exchange for minority representation on their boards of managers and some extra rights over secular instruction. With these LEAs, not with thousands of tiny boards, the Board of Education would now deal; they were identified as 63 County Councils, 82 County Borough Councils, and 173 Borough and Urban District Councils of areas with populations over 10,000 and 20,000 respectively in 1901. Thus, like sanitation, policing and highways, education was recognised as a service provided by the normal mechanisms of local government, through each LEA's new Education Committee of Council representatives and nominees.

The Bill took nine stormy months to be enacted, and more parliamentary argument than for any previous Act as well as massive public protest – 80,000 gathered in Leeds, for instance, to demonstrate – so battering the government that no other dared face major administrative change until 1944. Chiefly the blast blew on the proposal to aid voluntary schools from the rates, seen as the use of rates paid by Nonconformists to inculcate Anglican or Roman Catholic doctrine, and on the proposal to abolish School Boards. Nor did resistance, mainly by the Liberals, vanish with enactment and when a Liberal government was elected in 1906 various attempts at drastic revision (especially to pass voluntary schools altogether into the power of LEAs) were drafted and killed. So the 'Dual Control' structure of 'provided' and 'voluntary' schools remained. To one of these schools any child whose parents had not arranged for her to learn the 'elements' of education elsewhere would go. No other form of education was legally compulsory. So too remained the distinction – made wholly for administrative and not educational ends – between elementary and secondary schooling.

As the minimum leaving age rose, the upper classes of elementary schools therefore overlapped with the lower classes of secondary schools whose pupils usually entered at about 11 to 13 years, though the position was complicated by several forms of technical and higher elementary schools established here and there. These structural tram-lines were held in parallel by the enabling powers the 1902 Act gave to 145 of the LEAs, those of County

Councils and County Borough Councils, in a directive to 'consider the educational needs of the area and to take such steps as seem to them desirable, after consultation with the Board of Education, to supply or aid the supply of education other than elementary'. Not a duty, then, but a permission was granted to some LEAs to use their own initiative in non-elementary education, an initiative extending over the area of smaller LEAs confined to elementary duties, creating a double-level system.

'Other than elementary' – splendidly unspecific – might include many forms of adult and specialised education, and also allowed for the first time local rates to be levied for the provision of secondary schools, though no definition of 'secondary' was available in the Act and the laws compelling children to be educated referred only to instruction in 'elements'. Nor did the Act make many local residents more enthusiastic about paying rates, and since the minimum cost of secondary education was reckoned at about £9/10/- for a girl (more for a boy since male teachers were paid more), excluding the capital cost of building, considerable spending would be involved if an LEA chose to embark on secondary schooling. Fees paid by pupils looked necessary.

In 1902-3, while the representatives of endowed and proprietary schools, with serene self-confidence, officially welcomed the LEAs' accession to responsibility for secondary schooling and focused on practical problems in the Act's provision for inspection, teacher registration and teacher representation on the new Education Committees, the private schools were struck with panic, at least those who smelt a 'dangerous rival'.[4] The most sensible and detached voice was that of Michael Sadler, once on the Education Department's senior staff, a member of the Bryce Commission and now holding a Chair in Education at Manchester University. He pointed out that rate-supported schools must have large classes to hold costs down; would not parents of means prefer 'the study of individual character and idiosyncrasies ... the special bent of a pupil cannot be discovered, nor can his special qualities be developed, when he can command only the thirtieth or fortieth part of a master's attention'?[5] Private schools were quick to pick up this line and it became for many years their first line of defence, shielding the social exclusivity that also shepherded girls especially into their folds, and obscuring the difficulties of attracting able staff when teaching opportunities were expanding. But they were right to feel threatened, as experience in Halifax showed.

The County Borough of Halifax took up the chance offered by the Act. In 1905 the Council Secondary School (Girls) was opened; by 1908 the headmistress, Celia Greenwood, had 269 girls and 14 assistant staff in her care. The school did not spring fully formed, an Athena from the Council's head, but was in fact developed out of the Higher Grade school, with a brother school for boys. However, it now operated according to the outline *Regulations for secondary schools* published by the Board of Education in 1904. What these amounted to will be seen later when Emmeline herself had to study a version. What the end of the Higher Grade school and the start of the Secondary school meant was that private schools faced a competitor that charged £3 a year.

This might well deter the poorer parents who had managed to find 6d a week for the Higher Grade school but it was a powerful argument to the middle classes, as is shown by HM Inspectors' analysis of the 'class in life' from which girls of the Halifax Secondary School were drawn in 1908: parents of 76 of the 269 pupils belonged to the upper categories of professional and independent men, merchants and manufacturers.[6] Within a few years Ellen Bolton sacrificed independence to her standards and handed her High School into the LEA's care, to be amalgamated with the municipal school; she herself became the second headmistress of the school subsequently known as the Princess Mary High School. The whole story was typical of many.

Before the Education Bill struggled into law in 1902, however, Emmeline was concentrating much of her attention on the circle of knowledge demanded by London University for its BA (Hons) degree. As her last cast she decided on an independent effort, while earning her living and without the teaching support, library and chances of discussion and argument afforded by an institution but thankful that London had retained a Council for External Students and examined External and Internal on, by its statutes, 'the same standard of knowledge and attainments'. To work alone was not unique: 188, or about half, the external BA and BSc degrees gained in 1904 were achieved through 'private study' rather than an institution. The majority were Pass degrees, though since 1858 additional papers for Honours in particular fields might be offered. However, until 1904 specialised Honours papers were additional to the full Pass range, not alternative.

What then was Emmeline facing? First she must tackle the Intermediate Arts examination, the middle rung between Matriculation and the Final BA examination, with its papers in Latin with Roman history, Greek, French or German, English language with literature and history, and Mathematics (Honours papers were available in most of these subjects). When the Ladies' College finally changed hands in December 1901 she bargained with the new owner:

> Miss Pannett is very anxious indeed for me to come back, and she has offered to see that I have all the time free each day except from 9 to 12 and such time as I shall need for the preparation of lessons and correction of books, and she will give me £25 for the year, and of course board and laundry. She says she will guarantee not to infringe on my time in any way, and will see that there is a room free for me during afternoon school time but in the evenings I should work as usual where the others were sitting. I think I ought to be able to do the exam if I work hard during the time and it will be much better to be earning a little money and my own board all through, won't it?

I should not have any responsibility for the school, of course, only for the particular subjects in the particular classes that I took during the three hours, and in those I should not be interfered with at all. At present I arrange and superintend all the work of all the classes but Miss Pannett would do that herself. She means to work awfully hard – I don't know if she'll be able to do all she wants to ... It is very hard on her beginning without any boarders now that Mary has left.

So Emmeline remained head English mistress, at a reduced salary and with reduced duties, officially at least. At about the time she finally left, nearly three years later, to the school came the future novelist Phyllis Bentley, then a child of eight or nine. In her autobiography she recorded, alongside her debt to Miss Pannett's love of literature and gift for communicating it, some censorious observation of that lady – 'thoroughly a "lady" in manners', she said – for her careless dressing, with belt turned wrongly, and for her weak insight into girls' characters, a charge substantiated by young Phyllis's sufferings at the hands of an undetected bully.[7] But the real energy of her description is poured into the housekeeping of Miss Pannett's sister Kate, the burnt porridge, the scrappy mess called hash, the mouse in the marmalade.

Both were 'kind and good women', Phyllis Bentley assures her reader, but Emmeline, always quick to notice the least litter on a classroom floor, the book wedged upside-down in a shelf, yesterday's water in flower vases (an insult to the flowers that had been alive and beautiful, she said), was perhaps compelled to hone her tact, to discipline her tendency to manage. Her views on the housekeeping are not recorded.

Phyllis Bentley was also to attempt an external London BA, at home in Halifax in 1912, and her attempt exemplifies the problems. For English and history she was confident of her independent powers, and Greek was by then no longer compulsory, but she baulked at the hurdles of Latin and mathematics without tuition: she visited a local headmaster, inquired at the technical college, found 'nowhere – we knew nothing of Leeds – could my requirements be accommodated', and abandoned the scheme until she could scrape together fees for the BA teaching at Cheltenham Ladies' College.[8] One of the resorts she had considered was a correspondence course; so did Emmeline, turning to the leader in its field, a commercial venture dignifying itself as the 'University Correspondence College', with its own textbook publishing business. Weekly lessons were posted out, detailing textbook pages to study, with 'Hints' and 'Notes on difficult and salient portions' and tests for the student to post back for correction by one of over forty 'tutors'. This service Emmeline may have used for only one or two subjects, Greek perhaps, where the lessons' utilitarian skill at cramming the essential minimum appeared a priority. Whatever her procedure she sat the Intermediate papers after less than a year, in July 1902, and she tried for Honours in history, the newest of the Honours subjects.

When results were published she betrayed some nervous tension, making 'a muddle' of scanning the lists and for a day believing she had failed. But no – if Third Class Honours were a relief, no more. Technically only a year need elapse before the Final BA examination, but prudently Emmeline took two to cope with the full Pass range of papers in Latin and Greek (both with relevant history), English or another modern language, mathematics (pure or mixed) or 'mental and moral science', all still compulsory in addition to her three papers for history Honours. Occasionally she found local lecture courses, it seems, probably organised by University Extension workers, to supplement the correspondence course but the bulk of the work was solitary.

The school was not developing as Miss Pannett had hoped, with numbers barely rising (an average of six to a class) and never more than five boarders. Sometimes some advanced teaching was tried and Emmeline prepared one or two girls successfully for Matriculation and Cambridge Higher Local, but as Halifax's new LEA meditated its secondary school the outlook bleakened. Emmeline had no intention of staying now as she ripened her understanding of intellectual modes, with growing suspicion of the processed, pre-digested cramming of a correspondence course. Now in history she explored as it suited her, and ever after conceived her Honours special period, the mid-15th to 16th-century European Renaissance and Reformation, in terms of 'a passionate interest in man ... The right of the individual to think for himself.' Attempting briefly to characterise 'the spirit of these men of the Renaissance', she wrote that 'Their curiosity was aroused; they had an insatiable craving for knowledge; they realised the beauty and interest of the world, and felt they had a right to use and enjoy the earth in which they lived'; these particular emphases must surely be rooted in her first immersion in it, the temper in which she tackled her reading.[9]

At the end of the spring term in 1904 she formally resigned, filed with previous testimonials Miss Pannett's eulogy of her classwork, discipline, organising power and co-operative loyalty, and returned to Bath. Within five years the Pannetts also abandoned Halifax in favour of a boarding school in the more propitious Sussex resort of Seaford. Emmeline had the summer of 1904 free for work, and when an essay of hers was returned with probing comments by Professor Hearnshaw of Hartley College, temporarily covering a 'tutor's' holiday, she recognised their quality and seized the chance of contact with his university-trained mind, begging him to continue to read her essays. Less than two months now remained.

She did not wait to know what academic qualifications she might claim before applying for another job; she would soon be twenty-seven and had no time to waste. Only a few days before the examination began she travelled to the little Dorset town of Sherborne for an interview. To those who sent their sons to public schools the name of Sherborne School evoked one of the most ancient foundations, housed in ex-Abbey buildings, but Sherborne School for Girls was new. 'This school is mainly a boarding school and has grown very rapidly since it was founded in September 1899,' wrote the headmistress in answer to Emmeline's application. 'I have now over a hundred pupils excluding the Kindergarten. Most of these are boarders, although we have a few day girls from Sherborne.'

Such rapid growth was impressive, but the headmistress concentrated on two other points. One was the careful statement: 'Most of our girls are high-spirited and many come from homes in which they have been allowed to do always as they like, so that they require careful and tactful management.' The other was cast as an urgent question: 'Would you feel able to work in a school founded on Evangelical Church of England lines?... The school is founded on distinctly Evangelical principle and I do not think that a High Church woman would be really in sympathy with us ... I am very anxious to find a colleague who will be in sympathy with our aims, and will help us to build up what we hope will be a great school.' 'Evangelical', as Emmeline knew, was the term applied to those Protestants who held to the doctrine of salvation by grace through faith in Christ's atoning death, and not by good works or sacraments, though faith was expected to express itself in good works, to shun frivolities, to abide by conscience guided by the Gospels' unique authority.

Just before the westward train enters Sherborne through the pastoral and wooded edge of Thomas Hardy's Wessex, the traveller's eye is caught by the stark ruins of the Old Castle on its small hill, then by the imposing pile of the New Castle, begun by Sir Walter Raleigh, elaborated after the Stuart Restoration, elegantly emparked, and long home to the Digby family. Present Digbys mattered not only as lords of much of their prospect, but also as prime movers in originating Sherborne School for Girls, having underwritten a share issue and given land for buildings. Now they served as vigorous members of the small Governing Body chaired by the Headmaster of Sherborne School, Canon Westcott, and operating under the articles of association of a limited company. This school therefore ranked as a proprietary school in the terms of the day, with Mr and Mrs Wingfield Digby as benevolent godparents and Mrs Digby's Evangelical fervour a driving force for many years after Kenelm Digby's death in 1904; their daughter was one of its early pupils.

Whether or not Emmeline yet knew such details she certainly appreciated the visual appeal of their town: 'I feel a little thrill directly the train brings me into sight of the castle grounds, and to walk up the Digby Road till one comes to the beautiful Abbey and the Almshouses, the School dining-hall, the Lady Chapel, or go up the Yeatman Road and peep through the gateway towards the boys' studies, chapel, library, is pure joy.' So in 1904 she walked up the hill to the new buildings on the road to Bradford Abbas, a wide green view stretching behind them over Dorset and Somerset, to meet the headmistress, Beatrice Mulliner MA, and Kathleen Moore BA, her second-in-command from the start in 1899 though only two years older than Emmeline herself.

The problem of discipline recurred in the interview, Emmeline told her mother in amusement, but what else was discussed is not known. She returned home to her revision but was not too busy with it to respond to an encouraging telegram from Sherborne with shrewd questions, eliciting from Beatrice Mulliner a reply poised, not atypically for headmistresses of her era, between the high-minded and hard-headed:

I am so sorry that I did not make it clear when I saw you that in a new school like this we have to be careful about finances just at present. We shall only be too glad to raise the salaries of those who are proved to be really what we want, and in a school whose numbers have gone up nearly every term since it was opened, there is of course an excellent prospect of becoming head of a department, as it were. I have, I think, secured my probable Head Mathematics Mistress, and also my Head Science Mistress. I am looking for one who will do for the History side and be able to work that up and the Library, that is to say advise me about the latest historical authorities and so on. At the same time I do not think we are justified in giving quite the high salaries next term, especially to anyone before they have attempted quite the kind of work it would be here.

I engage my Mistresses always (as does the Girls' Public Day School Co.) for a term on trial, so that I do not think this next term of offering more than *at most* £75 or £80 [per year] the next term if she proves herself to be what we want, and to be capable of filling such a really important post in a school which, with God's blessing, we mean to be a *great* one ... the matter is far too serious both for you and for us for me to act hastily. I do so much feel the *imperative* necessity of securing the right person who shall come to us to help build up a really noble school, and I know you too feel what a serious thing it is to go into a new life and take up new work. I believe we shall both be guided rightly in the matter.

But now the examination timetable governed Emmeline, through the last week of October and the first of November, with the history Honours papers last in the sequence, demanding ebbing energy. She sat them in Bristol and then returned to Halifax to stay with friends there. So it was Winifred who left her Bristol office to scan the lists when they were posted up on 2 December, and Winifred who sent the telegrams to Emmeline in Halifax and her parents in Bath: 'Hurrah – First Class – heartiest congratulations', read Emmeline in the early afternoon. Within ten minutes a second telegram was delivered, from her mother, a simple 'Thank God'.

Chapter 6
Sherborne

'We wondered what we were getting,' Kathleen Moore was heard to say later. 'An external degree – and she'd never been at a proper school!' But Emmeline learnt fast, and at Sherborne she learnt much: she saw how a transient assortment of individuals could be blandished, manipulated, coerced to operate as a coherent community and how at its best this might fructify and fortify a school's educative force; she enlarged her stock of ideas among stimulating colleagues; she appreciated and exploited the escape of history from the mantle of 'English subjects' to a distinct discipline. Sherborne showed Emmeline a definite ethos and its daily practical expression led her to a new vision of what a school might be, and at last to a new opportunity to shape one herself.

First to the school, where she found herself expected not only to reorganise the history teaching but to cover geography too, as well as some English. Beatrice Mulliner might have been slightly disingenuous as to Emmeline's salary and duties – other instances can be found where her zeal for the school obscured inconvenient details – but she was exact in her claims of the school's growth. When Emmeline started work in early 1905 Sherborne School for Girls held 105 pupils; the next year 111 came, then 115, 128, 146, and in 1910, 163, though with those in the lowest forms she would have little to do as the Preparatory work was separately organised and located. It is not hard to understand Sherborne's growth: its advantages were visibly embodied not only in the district's attractions but in the Governors' sedulous care.

Their Chairman, Canon Westcott, for example, personally taught the first girls hockey, lent his Sherborne School masters for cricket and music lessons, brightened an autumn evening with a 'Lantern lecture on Cambridge', composed the school song, preached at services. The Governing Body not only organised capital funding but also spread the word through a sturdy web of social and clerical connections, just as one of Kathleen Moore's non-teaching assets was her pull on her father's parishioners in Wimbledon. So in 1902 when Mr and Mrs Wingfield Digby met in London an Indian Christian, Sir Harnam Singh, they promptly asked him to stay at Sherborne Castle and urged the merits of the new girls' school for his 13-year-old daughter. There the young Amrit Kaur went, and there she stayed until 1906, Mrs Digby keeping an anxious eye on the sprains and strains of a girl reared to the enclosed sedateness of a nobly-born Indian when she discovered that she both enjoyed and excelled at games.

Eight other girls from overseas, most of British stock, were at the school when Emmeline came, with others from all over the UK, but geographical heterogeneity was masked by broad social similarity: four-fifths were daughters of 'professional and independent men' or 'merchants, bankers, etc.', not surprisingly, since to the basic boarding and tuition fees of £69/6/- to £91/7/- (varied by age) were added 'extras' for most musical, artistic and gymnastic activities, conversational French and German, dancing, stationery, a single bedroom.[1] The curricula envisaged by Sophie Bryant and Dorothea Beale included aesthetic and physical education and without these most girls would have been conscious of inferiority.

As in social class so in age. Emmeline's first problem in planning her work was already familiar and was to continue to plague many girls' schools for years. Over half the girls at Sherborne in 1905 were over 15 but only seven over 18; so many arrived at 14 or 15 with no common body of knowledge (for they came from private schools or governesses) and stayed only two years or so, making classwork in such subjects as mathematics and languages hard to organise, and progressive courses over several years were impossible. Constant experiments in subdivisions of groups were needed, particularly as new girls were accommodated in new classes, with much individual timetabling, patiently worked out by Kathleen Moore, instilling in Emmeline's receptive mind the value of flexibility and the importance of a younger entry to secondary education.

Emmeline soon found her own quarters at a house on Cornhill used for staff, a few minutes' walk from the main school, but in 1905 most girls lived under Beatrice Mulliner's eye and guidance, in Aldhelmsted, a new boarding house beside the newly extended school buildings, arranged as Senior and Junior Floors each with its own housekeeper – well-read ladies, not domestics. A few stayed in the school's original house, renamed Wingfield, with Kathleen Moore and (according to HM Inspectors) inadequate bathrooms. The fire-conscious Inspectors fretted too at the rooms in which domestic servants slept, up a 'steep and narrow' staircase at the top of Aldhelmsted. But growth was the keynote of these years, physically contained by constant building work for a gymnasium, a new boarding house (Dun Holme) and then an enlarged hall, and nothing was static.

Emmeline came as the sixth full-time assistant for the Upper School, including Kathleen Moore, and several others 'visited' for extras like music, but as the permanent staff nearly doubled in the next five years Beatrice Mulliner's departmental plans took more realistic shape. So too the school grew as a community with the beginnings of school societies, a magazine, an Old Girls' Union, and an annual Commemoration service. Less tangibly – but more vitally – growth marked also the school's intellectual life, as described by two reports of HM Inspectors.[2] The first of these reports took place in Emmeline's first term, by the Governors' request since the Board of Education did not inspect schools not receiving public money unless they sought 'recognised' status, and the report plainly shows how HMIs saw their role as advisory and constructive.

Two and a half foolscap pages, for example, are devoted to ideas on how to improve the teaching of science, although the HMIs did not expect science to 'form a fundamental subject' in more than the most elementary sense but to encourage practical learning by observation and experiment, for use in everyday affairs, and a further two pages deal with proposals for improving art teaching. In general they were happy with the humanities-based curriculum, regretting only that all music, even class singing, was an 'extra' and that needlework was limited to basic mending. Plain needlework, they say unequivocally, is 'good for all girls', and why should not the more skilful take up art needlework with its potential for learning design principles? They also remarked on the defects of the gymnastic facilities, demonstrated 'rather forcibly' in an apparatus lesson. But the HMIs of 1905 found much to praise, especially the use of English literature to provide 'backward girls with a stock of ideas' and the wherewithal to express them.

To all this the Governors and headmistress listened with care, and in 1910 the next Inspection found all pupils given some class singing, a well-equipped gymnasium, needlework taught to all boarders, a small laboratory fitted up and some promising basic science work. The Governors had also apparently responded to severe strictures on low staff salaries. But now HMIs' standards had risen, so that they observed too little intellectual rigour, with only the staff and not the girls working earnestly and energetically. Beatrice Mulliner could have pointed out that parents tended to remove daughters who grumbled at working hard. The HMIs were also baffled to find Greek now taught to the whole Sixth Form, even to those with no Latin and surely too late for a firm grasp; perhaps they did not realise the point was purely to enable the study of the New Testament stripped of its veil of translation. Religious teaching was excluded from their remit, somewhat skewing their view of the school.

First in the practical suggestions of the 1905 report, however, had been to relieve the strain on the 'clearly overworked' history mistress, perhaps by diminishing her geography and English responsibilities. In front of class after class through the two days they spent in the school the HMIs found Emmeline – and enjoyed her 'bright, vigorous and stimulating' teaching – and they found her too in charge of the library, consisting as yet of assorted gifts reportedly more 'curious and valuable' than helpful to schoolgirls. Emmeline's overworked appearance was in fact probably due largely to her start-of-term efforts to plan syllabuses and revise methods: she jettisoned the previous practice of dictated notes, for example, and she used Sixth Form essay work for general reviews of such subjects as 'Growth of the principle of popular representation'. At the same time she was planning ambitious middle school work in general European history, and she was getting to know the girls themselves, a school full of strangers. Despite defining a need for a specialist geography teacher the HMIs approved Emmeline's correlation of geography with history, obvious especially in the lessons they heard 'on the introduction of free trade' and 'on the consequences in Afghanistan of the English fear of aggression in India'.

History received a fortuitous boost in 1905 from the Sherborne Pageant, devised by a Sherborne master of dramatic talent to present a great panorama of Dorset-centred history from the Ancient Britons on. The open-air performance, acted by amateurs, was a strikingly successful community venture, drawing visitors even from overseas, and it set a fashion for pageants: Bath produced its own in 1909, Nettie impersonating an Elizabethan court lady in purple velvet and gold-embroidered stomacher, Winifred draped in white as a Roman lady.

Nor was life at Sherborne School for Girls all work, and the Inspectors' reservation on girls' intellectual energy was balanced if not outweighed by their marked approval of a regime geared to develop girls without stress and with time for 'quieter occupations'. At such a time the box Brownie might be brought out to catch Emmeline on a grassy bank, girls lying at her feet, their skirts half-hiding a tennis racquet, or with parasols raised to watch a cricket match. Or they might walk and talk, for school was a term-time home for the staff as much as for boarders:

It is a gorgeous morning – I would like to be going for a walk with you this afternoon. Yes – rather. I remember hunting for the stream so well. I believe it was my very first walk with you and you told me I went about looking miserable and would never do as a Head unless I cheered up! It was that one, wasn't it? I didn't know you at all hardly then, and was quite embarrassed when you asked me to come!! I remember so well.

So wrote Amrit Kaur, Head Girl in her last year. In the summer of 1906 her English education ended for, though Emmeline would have liked her to go to university, her parents wanted her home, but until November Amrit stayed in Wimbledon, taking singing lessons, attending occasional lectures, missing Sherborne:

These people here are so amazed at my wanting to go back to school!! They all hated school – but they never went to a boarding one and I don't think you get nearly such a good time as a day-girl at a High School, do you? They tell me school friends never remain friends – they always chuck you! I had quite a heated argument about it – so they ended by saying perhaps mine would be exceptions! They aren't a bit my style – I mean the girls – but still they aren't bad to talk to ordinarily ...

Amrit wrote a spate of letters to Emmeline, her style for the most part pure stream of consciousness, the stream sparkling with a high and swiftly responsive intelligence, original, with strong feelings tensely strung in a conflict of emotions over her return to India, and they spell out a youthful need not only for sympathy and understanding, but for a mind to challenge hers, argue, advise and reprove: '... but you understand, don't you? Yes – I don't mind how much you lecture me, I am sure it does me good because I need it – but you do *always* understand, and that is the chief thing.' For fifty years she and Emmeline kept up the friendship, but few letters now survive, only the earliest, telling of Amrit's journey home, escorted by an elderly missionary, overland to Marseilles, then by sea via Port Said, Suez, Aden, Bombay and then by train again north to Jullundur City, to re-establish her in the life of a high-caste Indian Christian, to tell how she chafed at its restrictions. Amrit was not the only girl to find a friend in Emmeline, nor the only source for Emmeline of vicarious experience.

Among the staff too she made permanent alliances, with Kathleen Moore perhaps most of all, who had the merit of being an adult companion with no need for what she called Emmeline's readiness to 'help, when we meet them, lame dogs over stiles'.[3] Instead Emmeline could catch from her an enthusiasm for Italian art, for Dante and St Francis, and a sympathy with the spirit of France and the French nation that the HMIs observed in Kathleen Moore's lessons. And at times Kathleen Moore could show a dry humour, if not to the girls who called her 'Fuss Buss'. Her pre-Sherborne experience could stand for that of many women secondary teachers of her time: after early parish duties as the eldest child of a conscientious clergyman and education at a GPDSC high school, a spell at a Swiss-French school, and Westfield College, London, secondary teaching looked an obvious form of work at the turn of the century.

So staff and girls laid the personal bricks of a community structure by explorations of personalities and ideas – were forced to if they were to avoid personal isolation – but little outward exploration took them from Sherborne. The occasional picnic via horse-drawn charabancs to Chanctonbury Rings or other beauty spots kept girls inside an invisible protective wall of care. Only once in the early records does there seem to have been an attempt at an educational and more ambitious excursion of a whole day, described officially for the school magazine by Emmeline and also probably promoted by her.

Glastonbury served literary and geographical ends as well as the historical ones Emmeline emphasised. On 4 July 1906 the party of sixty stopped for lemonade and biscuits at Ilchester (to be reminded of its ladies' welcome to Monmouth in 1680), lunched at the inn built for 14th-century guests at Glastonbury Abbey (to cobweb their hats visiting the dark cellar for wine, prisoners and penitents), admired the evocative ruins (Emmeline catalogued here Joseph of Arimathea, Dunstan and St Patrick, Arthur and Guinevere, before the dissolving hand of Thomas Cromwell), and climbed the Tor for a topographical survey. Emmeline mourned the lack of time for the newly excavated Lake Village – 'a great disappointment to some of us' – but they could study a few artifacts in the museum. The experiment, however, was not apparently repeated; perhaps there were problems untold in the magazine account.

The school's own grounds were the girls' normal bounds, most effectively varied by the exploitation of games. From the start organised games were an accepted non-intellectual priority. Beatrice Mulliner had absorbed the message of their utility and followed Penelope Lawrence's recommendations on management by a committee of elder girls and one or two staff, for, as

Penelope Lawrence shrewdly pointed out, pressure on the reluctant to take part was far more effectively applied by peers than by official authority.[4] In these early improvisatory days matches with outsiders fell victim sometimes to the ever-lurking fear of infection and sometimes to erratic organisation: 'The match against Parkstone was scratched – I suppose they couldn't get a good enough XI, so we played the Staff and Sixth v. the rest of the school' and 'It was simply sickening those wretched Salisbury ladies sent a card to say they couldn't get an XI and so they had to scratch the match' was the tale told Emmeline the term after she left.

Experiment marked the growth of games. 'I hope the Basket Ball will appeal to the girls,' commented a 1906 leaver. 'It is inclined to be rather rough, isn't it? I remember trying to play it two years ago and it was an awful scrimmage, but perhaps we played it all wrong.' Experiment likewise discovered other amusements by trial and error, and with growth the winters' evening parlour-games and fancy-dress parties gave way to House-based activities. For the school as a whole, or at least for seniors, recitals developed, usually by the part-time music staff, and lectures were given, illustrated with lantern slides. 'Aren't you looking forward to the musical lecture? I think it will be absolutely ripping,' wrote an absentee to Emmeline.

All such activities stayed within the magic circle of school buildings and some tended to be passive. So other experiments tried to encourage participation, and a Debating Society was formed, Emmeline taking a 'leading part', according to Beatrice Mulliner. Again management was by a joint committee of staff and girls, but the tasks of proposing and opposing motions were given to girls, and they were expected to prepare seriously, except in 'sharp practice' debates when several motions were drawn from a hat in rapid succession to elicit sharp thinking. Non-platform speakers would be scolded, too, when they relied on notes instead of responding to points raised. Soon a Natural History Society followed and the society habit was established; a Glee Competition was organised in 1909 and an orchestra was already assembled.

By 1907 society activities could be reported in the school magazine, another experiment in corporate action. Tentative at first, a slight wrapper of 'local news' bound round a journal issued by an Evangelical philanthropic group in London, the magazine was the subject of 'heated discussion' at the first (1906) business meeting of the Old Girls' Union (another innovation), between proponents of a full-scale independent magazine and conservatives nervous of printing costs; a year later only details of frequency and format had to be settled and the first free-standing issue appeared in October 1907. The articles, competitions and reports of activities contained derived from staff and Old Girls, at whom it was partly aimed, not from present girls, and 'Don't write and ask me to do anything for *Encaenia*!' was more than once the postscript to an Old Girl's letter to Emmeline.

The name *Encaenia* points to the magazine's commemorative function, recalling the Oxford ceremony honouring founders and benefactors. As another gesture of school solidarity from May 1906, Beatrice Mulliner adopted an annual custom of a Commemoration Service shared with parents, friends and Old Girls as well as present girls. As the focus for an ever-larger array of social events it prospered, and the central religious service with a guest preacher was soon hedged about with a concert in the flower-decked hall, a tennis tournament, a garden party, a 'sale of work' for charity, a Kindergarten entertainment, and the Old Girls' business discussion of group charitable activities.

Willingness to try all these enterprises, none original to Sherborne, all relatively novel for girls' schools, argues an adventurous spirit. In 1940 Cyril Norwood described Beatrice Mulliner as quintessentially Victorian but underrated the essentially pioneering force common to late-Victorian headmistresses of the new generation of girls' schools, for without improvisation and experiment growth in numbers might have swamped organisation and drowned the ideals they sought to realise.[5] The organised visible activities within the school were not, however, the only mode of growth for these.

On the quotidian and petty plane the enclosed life bred its rituals and traditions to be handed down and elaborated, from the braid sewn on games skirts before House matches and retained by the winner, to the things 'done' and 'not done'. 'It is rather a trial to have a cousin here,' sighed one girl to Emmeline, 'specially as she is very proper indeed and has never been away to school before ... It was awful the first morning, she came running up to me in the passage upstairs and *kissed* me good-morning with lots of people watching. I was wrathful!' These superimposed themselves on the official rules and practices Beatrice Mulliner inherited chiefly from her earlier experience at Cheltenham Ladies' College under Dorothea Beale. So Sherborne ordained silence within school buildings, its headmistress sat in on weekly mark-reading for every form, a prefect system was developed (negligible in power, heavy with responsibilities), white coats and skirts were prescribed for Sundays, and the form of morning prayers was established. Then all assembled in the hall for hymn and reading and prayers, led by the headmistress with any subjoined remarks she thought necessary. To Emmeline all this was new.

All expressed the central ethic, the Cheltenham ethic refracted through Beatrice Mulliner's Evangelical lens, a code of honour and duty. Its solid basis lay in the two central Christian commandments, to love God (as regular religious services and the Sunday Scripture essay reminded and taught) and to love one's neighbour, defined as a commitment to others' well-being and effected for a schoolgirl in a strict unwritten code. One did not lie or cheat or tell tales, conceal one's guilts or flaunt one's woes and triumphs; a girl with honour was neat, decorous in speech, punctual, public-spirited, self-forgetful, mounting (to quote one admirer) 'the stairway to the Shrine of Beauty, and it was the Beauty of Holiness that we worshipped, both in its essence and by reflection in the human character'.[6]

This was a fair assessment of Beatrice Mulliner's constant endeavour, though over the years the strain of her 'ascetic idealism' stiffened her endearing kindness into repressiveness, particularly after Kathleen Moore's astringent sense and humour were removed in 1917 on her appointment to the headship of Queen Anne's, Caversham, and the Great War mimicked too shockingly the 'last, dim, weird battle' which ended Arthur's Christian kingdom in Tennyson's *Idylls of the King*, a favourite lecture subject of Beatrice Mulliner. By 1919 her rigidity caused one staff member to explode bitterly in Emmeline's private ear: 'B.C.M. is unspeakable – and there is *no one* to stand up to her. It is nothing short of a tragedy when one thinks of what the School might be ... B.C.M. grates!' That was the time of the unhappy school days E. Arnot Robertson avenged in an essay of 1934, days she spent resenting enthusiastic games-playing – the enthusiasm artificial, she thought – the code geared to produce 'thorough-going prigs'. 'Everything affected one's "honour", the hardest worked word in our narrow world', and 'if one broke a rule one was expected to confess it to a prefect and have a nice spiritual wallow together', and most of all she resented the majority's acceptance, even endorsement of the code – they were so suggestible, she thought.[7] Writing of similar demands at Cheltenham the far-from-suggestible Phyllis Bentley reckoned 'honour' admirably designed to produce women of incorruptible rectitude, capable and useful wives for civil servants and bishops, excellent doctors and missionaries, 'not perhaps warm lovers or original artists'.[8]

In the school's early days the code was still in tender bud but already it was clear that the private school's unspoken fetishes of market and profit, geared to parental demand, were here replaced by religious paradigms of mission and vocation. What Emmeline brought to an ethos congruent but not identical with her parents' ideology was a belief that dedication was best suffused with cheerfulness – hence woebegone assurances from girls who missed her when she left that 'I'm awfully sorry to be so grumbly', 'I will try *awfully* hard to be cheerful' – and wholehearted enjoyment of whatever life offered, and what could be reached for. Even Beatrice Mulliner would tell Emmeline how her letters 'often cheer me up', and go on to reiterate her faith:

It is sometimes to me an extraordinary paradox – that life is *such* a fight – and then just when one feels no more *can* be done – there seems to come that strange but immensely strong help out of the Unseen – and we conquer and prosper, and the world says 'how successful' – and *I know* what it is ... your life and mine will always be that, I think, but if we are really building even a small part of that 'Spiritual City' we shall feel it abundantly worth while, shall we not...

In the 'many talks we have had' Beatrice Mulliner had possibly elaborated these themes.

Cheltenham was not the only source, though Beatrice Mulliner was often heard to quote Dorothea Beale's sayings and practices, nor was the strand of Victorian idealism that Ruskin popularised in his lecture 'Of Queens' Gardens', that women ought to inspire and exalt men to active virtue, provide a place of peace and serious wisdom, and so should be educated to 'the same advantages that you give their brothers – appeal to the same grand instincts of virtue in them; teach *them* also that courage and truth are the pillars of their being': Dante's Beatrice, Spenser's Una, Homer's Penelope all rolled into one.[9] That strand was present: Canon Westcott echoed it in a stanza of Sherborne's school song, referring to 'high-born maids' (an embarrassing phrase, soon discarded) 'trained as their brothers were, trained to be their peers', and Beatrice Mulliner herself celebrated it in a parable for the school magazine when she contrasted Tennyson's Lynette – the type of the women who 'mistake shadow for substance, who mock the Aspirant to Reality' – and the Greek girl Balaustion, mentioned by Browning, exemplary of the inspirational nobility which raises men spiritually.

Intellectual underpinnings, however, were furnished by Beatrice Mulliner's interpretation of J. F. Herbart's educational theories, part psychological, part philosophical. Herbart (1776-1841) had lived and lectured in Germany at the beginning of the 19th century but his greatest impact on England came at that century's end and the start of the 20th, fostered in part by translations such as Beatrice Mulliner's own, published in 1898, and by debate in journals and academic circles where the theoretical study of education was gaining ground.

In her long explanatory introduction to her translation of Herbart's letters, called *The application of psychology to the science of education*, Beatrice Mulliner stressed Herbart's suggestive rather than dogmatic value, freeing herself to analyse with a modernising, interpretative slant; what she says represents her views, therefore, at least as much as her authority's.[10] The aim of education is to 'lead the pupil to realise his own free personality in choosing the good and refusing the evil' – that is, an ethical aim – and 'the good' was to be identified in a modified Kantian concept of principle not relative to an end (briskly she discarded the alternatives of good as what tends either to individual or to social happiness) and recognised as imperative rightness. Music and mathematics provide analogies. Since such recognitions have no force in themselves to compel action in response to their claims, the personality, the *will*, must establish them as imperatives to act by, and the *willing* personality can be achieved only cognitively, by the formation of clusters of ideas fully and appropriately organised. An 'idea' here is what the mind makes of knowledge presented by experience or formally.

Beatrice Mulliner examined theoretical issues and analysed, as Herbart himself had, procedures to be followed in actual instruction and discipline, including a specimen lesson on part of Spenser's *Faerie Queene*. There is no space to discuss these here, but only to note that in this work Beatrice Mulliner's every emphasis at Sherborne can be traced, if with a more overtly Christian slant justified by her identification of good as the will of God. Three consequences are significant. First, the theory justified Sherborne's decided bias towards literature and history, not seen as less rigorous disciplines than the empirical and speculative knowledge of mathematics and the sciences, but as offering a richer, more vivid source of vicarious experience of moral problems and their potential negotiation.

Second, here is theoretical justification for an emphasis on will and its real efficacy, on concentration (to attain clear percepts) and reflection (to deduce accurate general notions), on the teacher's need to stir both cognitive and sympathetic interest, and to ensure the new data presented by daily experience or formally were co-ordinated properly with related data already in the child's mind. The will was centrally important because it was believed subjectively to modify new conceptions as it fitted these to existing idea clusters: thus a constant dynamic interplay was set up between ideas acting on the ego and the ego acting on ideas. This was perhaps Herbart's most significant legacy; and so, in the early 20th century, the notion strengthened that education comes from within, not from without, is guided by the teacher and not spoon-fed. As Beatrice Mulliner wrote to Emmeline in 1911, concerning 'the need of arousing more activity in the *girls*, rather than telling too much', 'I am profoundly conscious of its truth – and I am sure we ought to do it in literature and Scripture a *great* deal. It is very hard to do it well but it is *psychologically* the right thing, and the *best* – in fact the only – method.'

Third, this dynamic interplay between ideas and the mind, which starts with the baby's first breath, was held to generate the patterns of thought and action collectively known as character. So Herbart made character training, or more accurately character construction, an intellectually respectable objective for education, linked it to the cognitive faculties, and demonstrated that knowledge is not morally neutral.

Had his been the only voice advocating character formation in schooling it might have carried little weight. But of course it was not. The ideology of Thomas Arnold, disseminated by the headmasters harvested from his Rugby seeds, was received not only into public schools but into elementary schools, in a form suitably adapted to followers rather than leaders, through the new Board of Education's newly revised *Code of regulations for public elementary schools*, introduced by a statement of objectives: 'The purpose of the Public Elementary School is to form and strengthen the character and to develop the intelligence of the children entrusted to it ...' Even 'progressive' Bedales, founded in 1893 to break with the formulae of boys' public schools, was intended to train character, though its definition of leadership and responsibility, its view of what mental, moral and physical training should be, was different, according to its head J. H. Badley.[11]

Desirable character traits, then, were those legitimated by accepted values and cultural habits, as was admirably demonstrated by Sherborne's declension from Christian-mediated Herbartian theory to the code of honour. Emmeline could not escape, if she had wished, so pervasive a doctrine as that of character-building, yet she herself remained reticent on ultimate aims as represented in educational theory, reluctant to assent to and even suspicious of dogmas; instead she approached the question 'how to live?' inductively, through exploring particulars and the variety of possible lives.

From her work at Sherborne the shapes of her own 'clusters of ideas' emerge far more distinctly than before. Passionately attentive to particulars, she stored innumerable details of individuals in her capacious mind, surprising pupils and ex-pupils frequently, building a mental library of experiential diversity – though none thought her uncommitted or ambivalent about moral values. As a subordinate she was still discovering and testing these, examining in new contexts the values her parents had instilled, or her various milieux had suggested, or her reading had yielded, and, in the same way as in history or geography she turned often to maps and charts, so she was trying to chart different human goods, things valued, and to respond as openly as possible to each set of particulars so as to understand it in relation to other sets of all kinds. Evidence for this interpretation can be found, for example, in the character of the longest personal letters surviving from this time, describing her first venture across the Channel.

It seems a timid enough adventure, four weeks in Brittany with a friend of her Bath school days, Edie Andrews, staying with a Mme Guilloux in Fougères, at a time when educational journals were detailing cheap travel all over Belgium, Italy, Germany, as well as France, in articles designed for women elementary teachers. But to Emmeline it was immensely exciting, and she was glad to find her French adequate for conversation even if 'I don't know how to say nearly everything I want', for she talked to everyone. She talked in cafés, and to village women washing clothes in the river at Pontorsan, and to *sabotiers* in their tree-trunk huts in the Forest, and she won sufficient trust from 'a lady here in Fougères' to be sent to arrange with a farmer's wife for the wet-nursing of the lady's baby. Emmeline, who took it for granted that children as young as eight or nine might be sent away to school, had to adjust:

> Just imagine sending one's baby to be nursed in a place one had never seen by people one had only casually heard of! It is quite an ordinary thing here. The house had one room in it with four beds round the room, and the family live and sleep there, and yet they take an extra infant to add to the number; it is considered quite a desirable place. There were many beautiful brass and copper pans, etc. hanging up and they were brilliantly polished, but the woman (like all country-women) wore on her feet only wooden 'sabots', no stockings and her feet looked horribly dirty, but Mai assured us it was only through walking (probably without even the sabots) through the mud to look after the cows.

So observation struggles with judgment, and wins priority. So it does when Emmeline attended the only available religious service, the Latin Mass:

> ... we found it rather difficult to follow the service as it is all in Latin and there is such a lot of getting up and sitting and kneeling down

again. It was a very picturesque scene – lots of real Breton women with different kinds of white caps (according to the place they come from), work-women, who never wear hats on weekdays, with their Sunday hats and dresses, men in ordinary dress, as well as the priests, some in white surplices and some in very gorgeous raiment. The prayer-books were printed so that the prayers in one column are French and in the other Latin (I suppose most of the people don't understand the Latin). One thing they did there that Mai says they only do in country places was to pass round huge baskets full of pieces of bread which had been blessed (nothing to do with the Sacrament) for each person to take a piece to show they are all brethren. Edie and Miss Waddell did not take any but I took a piece ... I expect, though, they had already decided we were heathen.

She describes Breton food and natural history, the legend of the *Saut de Roland* and the banner-filled pilgrimage honouring a vision of the Virgin at Pontmain, with breathless zest for every un-English aspect of life, whether in art-filled châteaux or in a third-class railway carriage. But she became slightly impatient with Edie's lesser enthusiasm. Poor Edie did not feel well, was inclined to take the train home from Dompierre rather than walk the seven miles, as Emmeline preferred, and she rather resented Emmeline's speedy amity with Mme Guilloux's daughter Mai and with Winnie Waddell, a Holloway College student also staying. Differences were patched up, and Emmeline dissuaded Edie from leaving earlier than planned, but the next time she travelled abroad her companion was Kathleen Moore, equally prepared to walk miles among Swiss mountains, investigate every object or custom or person or manufacturing process of interest, and ask about agricultural practices or historical origins or geological formations.

This openness and appetite for particulars in all their particularity was habitual to Emmeline, not merely a visitor's curiosity, but survives most clearly in letters from holidays because she was trying to share these novel experiences with her parents and they carefully hoarded the reports. Certainly, because these were letters they were intended to interest and not disquiet, to describe phenomena, not to analyse her personal responses; she remained reticent about herself. Yet there is no evidence that responsive attention to particulars was a strategy evolved consciously, or that Emmeline sought friendships, sights, books, or whatever, for any end beyond themselves. Often she did indeed turn them to adventitious use, as the Brittany holiday, for instance, provided extra material for a Saturday lecture at Sherborne on the French Revolution, or as friends were pressed into service: 'Oh, Miss Tanner, don't say *you* will be disappointed if I don't write for the Mag., because it makes me feel a beast and I really feel I cannot write, but I will try and think of a subject,' wrote Amrit Kaur from India. Amrit found a subject suited to the school magazine in two able and independent Indian queens of the 16th and 18th centuries, though in the same letter she had discussed for Emmeline's own eyes the deportation of the political activist Lajpat Rai and described the hill station of Simla. But Emmeline's curiosity was too all-embracing and too ingrained a habit to be written off as instrumental only.

Nor was attention alone enough: to be useful it must yield responsible action, even within the small but time-absorbing world of a school, a conclusion Beatrice Mulliner had also reached by her Evangelical route.

Chapter 7
'An excellent chance'

In a school debate at Sherborne on the motion 'That the man of action has been more beneficial to the world than the man of thought', Emmeline spoke in support; in another she opposed the view 'That the progress of the world is due to the man of one idea'. Progress was defined as 'the movements ... which ameliorate the conditions social, moral and intellectual of the greatest number of individuals'; accepting this, Emmeline argued that 'progress was due rather to something inherent in the people which caused a gradual development of their minds and ideas, and that the individuals to whom the world was chiefly indebted were those who brought it into such a condition of law and order as to make this development more easy.' Her examples were Justinian and Charlemagne, who 'by the variety of their culture' became, she thought, the civilisers of Europe.[1] The notion that development originated in the people's activity, not in their rulers' command, and that it was facilitated by freedom from the tyrannies of violence and theft and injustice, the ideal, that is, of the open society, was one which governed much of Emmeline's subsequent work.

The call to action encouraged the school's own more outward-reaching activities, and so for a while Emmeline became chief correspondent with the missionary in charge of a girls' school in Western China, originally brought to Sherborne's attention by Mrs Digby's missionary sister. Emmeline asked how Sherborne's donations (raised partly by the annual 'sale of work') were spent and about the most pressing needs; and she gained an assurance that the mission school did not aim to 'foreignise' the Chinese children. Through a Saturday lecture on 'Life in Western China' by a missionary clergyman philanthropy and education were closely knit.

Another lecture, by Kathleen Moore's sister Evelyn, in 1909 brought life among Bermondsey factory girls to Sherborne's notice, and prompted further enquiry. Kathleen Moore uncovered necessary facts on the Federation of Working Girls' Clubs, helped by her sister's knowledge of girls' clubs, and the Welcome Club in Jewin Street was chosen as Sherborne's focus. Since Thring of Uppingham had established in 1864 the principle that 'the rich boys must learn to help the poor boys', public schools had engaged in forms of social work, ranging from helping with boys' clubs to full-scale settlement work in depressed areas, and equivalent girls' schools such as Cheltenham as they arose followed suit. Philanthropic activities suited an ethic of service but it would be wrong to link this too closely to notions of femininity since the impetus was given by boys' schools; the case here is one of class not gender.

Originally designed to provide cheap nourishing lunches for working women, the Welcome Club had developed as a social and educational centre, the only club in the City of London run in girls' interests, and its organiser, Eleanor Seton-Karr, was found to exercise the 'human sympathy, understanding and service' to meet Sherborne criteria. When details were given to the Old Girls' Union at their meeting in 1910 'Miss Tanner took the matter up warmly' and 'with delicious practicality. She almost forced each one of us to undertake something definite for a Factory Girls' Club', mostly very minor, a promise to supply blouses or shoes, for example.[2] By then Emmeline had left Sherborne but through Evelyn Moore and Eleanor Seton-Karr she developed further and more personal contact with other social workers in London.

But teaching was her most immediate responsibility, and it was now she began to attend conferences and holiday courses designed to provide both new knowledge and fresh stimuli. At Oxford, for example, were summer courses run by the Oxford Society for the Religious Instruction of Women Teachers in Secondary Schools, planned to give 'young mistresses the stimulus of personal contact with university teachers' and held at Lady Margaret Hall with strong support from the Principal, still the small, vital Elizabeth Wordsworth, coruscating with ideas and wit.[3] Emmeline's gratification in 1907 at dining there was not due solely to the intellectual interest of the course, however; she was no Jude the Obscure but a glamour gleamed round Oxford.

In school itself she wrestled with the teaching of history. In general, history teaching was bedevilled by at least three nagging if protean bogies, the question of purpose, the problem of content, and the demands of examinations which could, as the Inspectors of 1905 found at Sherborne, break up attempts at continuous courses. The Sixth Form essays Emmeline set surely reflect the purpose of history as a moral study, as Dorothea Beale saw it when she argued that experience was broadened by observing men organised in institutions or set in unfamiliar situations or in moments of crisis, so that more rational and less emotional judgments could be practised than might be made of present figures and policies.[4] In addition general questions could be raised, such as what form of government is best, and the complexity of moral issues discussed, for example the relationship of intentions to means and consequences. The helpful Professor Hearnshaw of Southampton also identified, in a series of articles for *School World* in 1904, education's 'ultimate aim' as to develop mental force and moral character, with history as the instrument to this; the notion was widespread.

It could be transposed into political terms, as when Edith Major, headmistress of King Edward's High School, Birmingham, advanced the idea in 1911 that through the study of 19th-century history the embryo citizen might best learn something of her country's role in the world and the duties and responsibilities in store,[5] and this too Emmeline may have considered when in 1905 the Inspectors found her teaching the period 1815-71 (in varying degrees of detail) to the third and fourth forms, and to VB also –

unless this served the yet more utilitarian end of enabling girls to move easily between forms, as often happened in a school with numerous late entries.

In an address to the elementary teachers of an NUT branch in 1912 she herself limited her claims for history teaching. Then, when 'the details of the campaigns of the Wars of the Roses may still be found in textbooks', as Edith Major noted in 1911,[6] Emmeline urged that it was far more important to cultivate the imagination and train powers of reasoning than merely to deliver a load of facts, to encourage a sense of sequence and cause and effect, to develop an ability to think developmentally and to appreciate evidence and achieve perspective, and that the teacher worked best with a broad sweep that helped significant foci to be identified. So she used time charts, remembered by Sherborne girls, a visual aid Emmeline credited to Dorothea Beale. For lower forms she drew a large one as a bird's-eye view of the 'whole field of human endeavour and achievement in Britain', and experimented with smaller charts displaying individual lives or themes such as scientific discovery and inventions. Based on grids of squares representing years, these charts were filled with symbols, driving home sequence and perspective – the relative length of the Roman occupation, for instance – and arousing interest and participation in choosing effective symbols.

All these motives could have contributed to Emmeline's determination to teach European history at least to older girls, a project made technically feasible, as other large-scale historical arenas were not, by the subject's status as examinable for Oxford Locals. Few took the paper, offered in response to both subject- and child-based arguments of the 1900s: English history was fundamentally affected by events in Europe; insularity was unbecoming to citizens of a worldwide Empire; wider knowledge encouraged wider sympathies. 'English children are brought up in hopeless confusion or blank ignorance about the other countries – and become, when grown up, narrow of sympathy and unable to understand the lessons of history,' roundly declared the historian Kitchin to Beatrice Mulliner in 1908, in approval of Emmeline's own efforts.[7]

One problem, she realised, was a dearth of textbooks of adequate scope and suitable level for older schoolgirls. Some historians' works assumed too much knowledge, some were too detailed, some confined to particular topics. Moreover Sherborne's library remained underfunded and inadequate. Emmeline discussed the difficulty with her headmistress, who listened and remembered. Staying with her mother in Oxford in January 1907, Beatrice Mulliner 'had a very interesting talk with Mr Gerrans, the Secretary of the Oxford Locals':

> He was most sympathetic ... His suggestion was that you should study the questions last given on European History and the length of period, and that you should *choose* your own period (which will of course be a certain part of your Honours) – the most picturesque, I should suggest – then, if you draw up a really good textbook and submit it to the

Oxford Press, we may by dint of influence get *this period* set for 1909. The textbook would of course have to be quite ready by the summer of 1908. This seems to me to give you an excellent chance, provided you, can turn out something really good ... Of course your MS would in any case have to pass a somewhat severe criticism before it is accepted, but the point is that thanks to influence and Mr Gerrans' courtesy we thus get it looked at, and of course if the Oxford Locals set this period the publishers will be quite ready to accept the textbook, if it is up to their standard ... Mr Gerrans seemed to know a good deal about us. He is specially interested in the new English syllabus, and was disappointed at so few taking European History throughout the country.

Emmeline was excited – perhaps those hopes for 'success of a literary kind' confided to old Mr Bragg still lay dormant – and plunged for Renaissance and Reformation Europe, at first dating her period 1453 to 1598, then revising this to 1494 to 1610. 'Influence' had given her the opportunity, and it set the terms: obviously the textbook envisaged would not be original historical work, the sort of research she admitted to Kathleen Moore she yearned to attempt for an MA thesis but could not combine with earning a living. It must be a synthesis of secondary sources, so shaped and proportioned that main points emerged clearly and accurately yet not superficially or over-simplified, and it should deal, she decided, with the whole of Europe from the Scandinavian countries of the north to the South Mediterranean, from the eastern fringes of the Holy Roman Empire (with an excursus on Russia) to Britain in the West.

She told Professor Hearnshaw, and he responded with a reading list; as 1907 progressed she set to work in what free time she had. There was a great deal of reading, and such checking as she could manage in available English and French sources to reconcile variant accounts, control biases, and correct out-of-date interpretations in the light of fresh evidence. 'Never waste time reading,' was her own advice, 'but read a book as though you'll never have a chance to see it again', and all her powers of concentration were called on now.

Beatrice Mulliner busied herself with publishers, and by winter had set up a meeting with Humphrey Milford, recently transferred to the London office of Oxford University Press but still closely co-operating with the Oxford-based Clarendon Press. Already Emmeline had established an outline and drafted some chapters; she should get these typed, she was told, to show as a specimen, and 'I will try and see Mr Gerrans again, and get him to write to Mr Milford explaining this is only the beginning as it were, and we intend a grander whole! ... you should put down what the complete book will have – index, questions [for school essays], maps, tables, summaries, etc.'

Emmeline met a slightly-built, athletic man of her own age with the solid Winchester-and-Oxford classical education OUP favoured, and shortly afterwards heard that 'Miss Tanner's specimen is approved' and that 'all that is now necessary is for Miss Tanner to work twenty-four hours a day for two months'. The deadline made both women anxious. Beatrice Mulliner urged Emmeline to think over 'what can possibly be done to help you for next term – i.e. what class or corrections can possibly be taken off for six weeks, without injuring the Examination work'. Her priority was always the school.

Emmeline worked and worked. By May Milford was asking for sketches for the maps she insisted on; within ten days she supplied the first batch of beautifully neat, accurate sketches, carefully coloured to distinguish the complexities of political divisions. As she sent these off she collapsed. Organic causes of her illness are not now known, only that it was serious and the doctor blamed overwork; the episode, recalling her illness after Matriculation, reinforced the migraine tendency. When, after a couple of days, she was well enough to be moved to the school's sanatorium she asked her mother to join her, saying:

I am so much better today that I think with you there I shall be well in three days, or at any rate by Monday ... there is a beautiful garden in which we can have all our meals when the sun shines. The caretaker cooks very well and would do everything for us, and we should just be peaceful ... Can you come by the train leaving Bath about 2.30 tomorrow, take the bus at the station to the Girls' School Sanatorium at Castleton (fare 6d) and Miss Mulliner says she shall take me over in a carriage in the afternoon ... I think it will be lovely especially if it is fine.

Optimistic, finding pleasant features in an undesired situation, tending to organise – Emmeline was clearly recovering herself. Nettie stayed several days, for the doctor would sanction no return to work for Emmeline before the start of June, and then her thoughts were with her examination candidates, now close to their delivery.

In mid-June she wrote to Milford again with the news, humiliating to her, that her manuscript could not be delivered until mid-August; he replied that mid-September publication might be just possible if all the mapwork were done by mid-July. Between the promise and the threat Emmeline accomplished her part and supplied on demand manuscript sections for specimen typesetting and advance publicity. By the end of July the text was complete enough for her to ask Hearnshaw to cast a critical eye over it, and he spared enough time from his multifarious commitments to offer a few suggestions and general reassurance, a kindness she did not forget. Milford kept up the pressure, reporting how 'the Oxford people' could keep to dates only if proof-correction were minimal, and how he feared that ragged style as a result of pressure might militate against this. He threatened postponement but Emmeline knew she must synchronise with examination syllabuses.

The manuscript once delivered, responsibility was transferred to the

Clarendon Press and to Robert Chapman, at twenty-six Assistant Secretary to the OUP Delegates and another classicist, a Scot later distinguished for scholarly work on Samuel Johnson and others. Writing almost daily with advice on proof-correction technicalities as batches of proofs flowed between Emmeline and Oxford, he appeared to be giving her book the attention it needed. Then befell what Milford was to call 'the cartographic catastrophe'. Chapman sent Emmeline the mapmaker's drawings, ready for the press, with warnings not to crease or mark, a plea to return them speedily, and an apology for limiting the colours to blue and red. 'But the maps will *look* coloured, and the vigorous shading ought to prove very attractive.'

Emmeline looked at the maps and was appalled. Somehow meaningful distinctions of land tenure had been converted to meaningless decoration. The 'mapmaker', given (she was told necessarily) a free hand, had proved more artist than cartographer, and Chapman's swift glance had observed outlines and labels rather than colour; his training perhaps alerted him to words rather than graphics, for he confessed he thought Emmeline's stress on colour 'mainly for the sake of a picturesque appearance'. Her use of colour in her later maps was indeed more complex than in her first batch, to cope with complex areas, and she knew nothing of the printing problems involved. Apologies over, Chapman proved resourceful at clarifying the political values of the maps, and compromises were evolved as September began.

The heartening feature of the summer holidays for Emmeline was the news of what Beatrice Mulliner called 'peculiarly successful examination results. We are very proud of having the first and third places in History Distinction', and Emmeline's proof correction continued, from galley to paged proof. Milford suggested a price of 4/6d; she demurred; he agreed to 3/6d, to compensate for the map problems, he said. With 'slips' for paged proofs trickling in she started to index, and now it was she who pressed the publisher. On 23 September Charles Cannan, Secretary to the Delegates, explained firmly that 'The type of 16 pages of your book weighs more than a hundredweight, and it takes time to incorporate corrections in the slips, put headings, make up, read and dispatch proofs'.

By 1 October Cannan was able to say: 'We have corrected p. 248 and have received the last of the Index ... The maps are at machine.' On 29 October Emmeline was sent 'by Passenger train, with the Compliments of the Delegates of the Press, ten copies of *The Renaissance and the Reformation*', a compact volume of 308 pages and eight maps. It was regrettable that on some copies the spine was lettered *The Reformation and the Renaissance*, but Emmeline was grateful for her publishers' efforts and relations remained cordial enough for her to be asked two years later to compile another work on 'General (or only European) History' – 'Everyone is crying out for a book ... teachers want it to be in one volume, but perhaps you will say that it is impossible.' By 1910 Emmeline knew that it was impossible for her as she poured all her energy into a different enterprise, and she wrote no more books.

What of this one? Its firm organisation groups chapters in five major parts; its ordered layout and apparatus (summary chapter headings, marginal headings, footnotes, chronological chart, genealogical table, index, maps and so on) assure the reader that historical discourse is logical and analytical, however slippery its object and narrative its form, not persuasively oratorical or poetically self-expressive. Historiography has its fashions, as it has its guarantors in theology, philosophy, the social sciences or political theory, and Emmeline used the fashion of the late 19th and early 20th centuries, looking for validation to a blend of psychology and documentary archaeology, for the factors revolutionising 19th-century historical work and its offspring (her principal sources) included the use of archival material.

She named the book after 'movements' but carried these general concepts on the backs of people, a chessboard with fresh pieces set out constantly. She does not shrink from character assessment, but here they are rarely sweeping and always explained in terms of action: hagiography and vilification are improper genres. She represents individual action as part of wider cultural and social systems, offering her psychological readings in terms of such systems, but she also regards individual consciousness as an analytical object, implying the experience of an individual is not a flat 'given' but depends on how the human subject organises its understanding (a Herbartian notion), and so she presents a Maximilian or a Luther as innovative, actively contributing to the continuity and transformation of institutions. The rise of individualism is indeed a major underlying message.

Oxford did its part in sending out review copies, principally to educational journals, and *The Renaissance and the Reformation* was generally approved as a 'graphic and succinct' account with 'superb thumb-nail sketches' (*Education Times*), 'exceptionally able ... planned so admirably and written so well' (*Liverpool Post*), a task accomplished 'skilfully and impartially' (*Westminster Review*), and so on. Beatrice Mulliner shrewdly sent copies to such historians as Oxford's J. A. R. Marriott, who was involved in University Extension work and whose praise for excellent proportions was valuable. Most valuable, perhaps, was the wide-ranging response from another Oxford historian, Charles Firth, then Regius Professor of Modern History.

Of particular interest to Emmeline was not the vigorous condemnation of the narrow and scrappy teaching of history found, he thought, in most girls' schools, nor his criticism of detailed period or subject-bound teaching, but his observation that her book was well suited to the scheme he favoured. Her scope, her clarity, her subordination of detail and the way she looked at British history in a European persepective, all fitted for upper forms what Firth proposed, that is, an overview of national history followed by a general course of European history in its development as a whole. He put this in the context of a liberal education: such a course should help to enlarge ideas, extend horizons, he said.[8]

On the practical level, he promised to suggest inclusion of Emmeline's book in the next European bibliography to be issued by the Historical Association, mentioned that the Association was shortly to discuss school teaching of European history and asked for exact details of the Sherborne syllabus. Though Firth's inaugural lecture in 1904 and his ideas for historical study at university level had stirred disagreement, such notice can only have been welcome, and a prop to Emmeline's own developing ideas.

Firth was President of the young Historical Association, formed in 1906 by a group of teachers at all levels from elementary to university, to advance the teaching of history and promote communication between the various teaching interests, not without hope that they might exert pressure on examination boards and school authorities as well as propagate publications and materials. They were careful not to trespass on the more scholarly terrain of the Royal Historical Society but paralleled the 'subject' associations already in existence for Mathematics, Classics, Modern Languages, and Geography. Local branches were envisaged as the chief means to bring together teachers, and later others interested, but as yet the Association was more a seedling than a branched tree.

Emmeline was beginning to take an interest in professional organisations, and the Historical Association was one she now joined, one of 800 members by the AGM of January 1909 when they officially welcomed the Board of Education's Circular 599 on 'Teaching of history in secondary schools'. This leaflet suggested a progress from stories for the under-12s, chosen widely (the Siege of Troy, Alexander, early Christian history, Columbus, William the Silent, Garibaldi were all mentioned) so as to fund general notions of 'the nature of the great nations and stages in civilisation ... in chronological sequence', followed by at least three years covering English history from the Romans to the present day, also chronologically, with more detailed study of some aspects as understandings matured, and including local history for concrete illustration. Foreign history, however, was advised only when, as in the case of the Crusades, it was essential to Anglo-centred affairs.

Hardly surprisingly in this official climate international history was explored only by the more ambitious schools, some GPDST high schools, for instance, and others with substantial Sixth Forms, and the guidelines of Circular 599 satisfied most. Other non-English-centred history received even shorter shrift. Although the ancient history of Mesopotamia, Egypt, Greece and Rome was the normal fare of the youngest secondary children, under 12 years, only the lands of Britain's Empire in the times of British power otherwise intruded on a version of 'our island story' which minimised Scotland and Wales. Even Europe continued to fare badly as economic and social history demanded more time and attention, and, as Emmeline was to discover, shifting political patterns brought new subjects to the fore so that by 1943 a *Report on the curriculum and examinations in secondary schools* (the Norwood Report) ignored Western Europe to assert the claims of the Commonwealth, the USA and Russia. The Board of Education's *Handbook* for elementary teachers quailed altogether, so vast the field of history, so brief the school life, and in 1927, for example, specified only that 'what should be known by the end of the course' was 'the story in connected and definite outline of Britain and the British Commonwealth of Nations'.[9]

A tangible result from *The Renaissance and the Reformation* was a trickle of royalties, thin but steady, for the rest of Emmeline's life. The best year in the first decade was the year of publication, with £7/4/- paid to her, but reprints after the first print run of 2,000 were issued every few years into the 1950s, though all colour in the maps was replaced by complicated patterns of dots and crosses.

Publication pleased Emmeline's family, though Nettie's thanks for her copy evaded any claim to reading it and was mingled with family news: Emmeline's passionate interest in her family was permanent and important to her, and Sam and Nettie's home functioned as clearing-house for news and centre for meetings as increasingly the brothers and sisters pursued independent lives. She sent a copy too to her first niece, and heard from the infant's father, Herbert, that 'we have great difficulty in preventing her devouring it'. He was the only member of Emmeline's family to show evidence of reading her work: it was not, as he added to his remarks on Luther and Calvin, 'like a novel which can be skipped'. Most of all he was surprised that the miner's son Luther had been educated to university level – 'even today such a thing would be most unusual'.

The lives of her family continued to provide their parallels and contrasts to Emmeline's. As a boy clerk the second Tanner brother had proved as satisfactory to E. S. & A. Robinson as the first, and at twenty-six Herbert was organising the firm's Scottish sales, living in a five-room Glasgow flat on a salary of £300 a year, and he was a married man. 'All the girls fell in love with Herbert,' observed his sister Winifred, 'but he never looked at anyone except Agatha' after, at nineteen, he met Agatha Gales, the Quaker daughter of the Liberal Party agent in his home constituency. She taught and worked in embossed leather for bookbinding, a very Quaker combination of beauty with utility in the service of literacy, but when she finally agreed to marry him neither expected her to be employed outside the home in other than voluntary service, although Herbert was to write of marriage as a partnership of equals.

For the birth of their first child, Barbara, they summoned Herbert's sister Beatrice, and called her in again for the arrival of their son Tom in 1910. Bee's career had taken an unplanned turn, perhaps one of the few family events unknown to Emmeline for it was more than half a century before Bee talked of it to a niece. As a staff nurse at St Mary's Hospital, Paddington, she gained a spread of qualifications and was able to register with the Central Midwives Board, formed under the Midwives Act of 1902 to seal off from childbirth assistance all who were not doctors or registered midwives, and she continued her general nursing with some district work in London. Good reports of her work duly led to promotion to Sister, and a few days' leave, spent at home in Bath, spread the news, as Nettie preened herself on her children.

On her return to St Mary's Bee was told to report immediately to Matron, not to pause even to remove her outdoor clothes. The Matron received her icily. *Nurse* Tanner had been seen, socially and in public, in the company of a doctor. She had broken the rules. She was to leave, at once. From Matron there was no appeal, and Bee left, unemployed, homeless, humiliated and furious. She telegraphed her parents and returned to Bath, to find a brief, hidden asylum at Sherrington with Aunt Adelaide and Mr Heard while a face-saving story was concocted. So she told it. It was no consolation that the doctor concerned, under no such disciplines, continued to write what she called 'three hundred' letters, and she refused to marry him.

But a competent trained nurse needed never be out of work long in the 1900s, when over 60 per cent were engaged in private work, for few but 'the poor' had recourse to hospitals (mainly funded by charity, apart from the rate-supported Poor Law infirmaries), and a private nurse was called in when families could not or would not provide invalid care themselves, or for the births and deaths woven into the normal web of home life. Such was the demand that many hospitals hired out their own nurses for private work, another source of hospital funds. Freelance nurses worked through agencies, or through doctors' or ex-patients' recommendations, and they enjoyed more freedom to travel and to choose in exchange for the loss of the hierarchical career structure of a hospital in which the top women wielded considerable power.

So Bee became a private nurse and seems never to have lacked work. While Emmeline was negotiating with Humphrey Milford in early 1908 Bee had escorted one patient to Menton to convalesce on the Riviera, and found another:

My patient is an American girl of 26, with a cold in her head. Isn't it absurd? There is nothing else at all the matter. It is the same doctor as I had before, and we both smile when we get outside the door. I came here on Tuesday, but I should not think I could possibly remain longer than Saturday. She is doing Europe with her aunt. I think it is the aunt who has the money. I cost them 14 or 16 francs a day at the hotel, besides my fee which is 10 francs a day, so that soon mounts up. I shall be very glad to get some nursing to do again ...

She also joined the Reserve of Queen Alexandra's Imperial Military Nursing Service, 'in case,' she said with undercutting irony, 'my country should ever need me, but never for a moment thinking that it would! Also they paid me £2 a year as a retaining fee, very nice for doing nothing.'

Emmeline habitually took friends 'home', as she called it for many years, unworried that the terraced house in Newbridge Road carried no social cachet, and not long-standing friends only but the chance-met and potentially isolated. Such was the dilettantish Swedish girl encountered in Oxford when Emmeline attended a vacation course there, who joined her in an excursion to Abingdon and we had tea and newmade bread in a cottage and ... you in your great kindness asked me to visit your nice and interesting home! It was so different to all that I had seen in England before, that energetic family where every member of it had a work that filled the day entirely. I think I longed to be something in the same way. I believe I had rather a deal of energy but for several years I used it on piano and horseback and foreign journeys. Suddenly I decided to get a teacher and got a place at a teachers' high school ...

By accretion of experience Emmeline was learning the delicate process whereby the roles of moral guide and tutelary spirit could be reconciled with that of self-effacing midwife to freely developing personalities she later designated for headmistresses. Yet even as, in the 1940s, she insisted that 'If members of staff are to give of their best they must have scope for initiative ... be allowed to experiment ... to take individual responsibility ... to express opinions and make suggestions', she privately noted General Montgomery's definition of leadership as 'the will to dominate with the capacity to inspire trust'. Her own will to dominate cannot be in doubt. Perhaps a too intimate knowledge of the authoritarian impulse, the ease and clarity with which a strong will could enforce itself on others, impelled her by no negative reaction to distrust, even to loathe, all authoritarian politics, whether in petty institutions or at the level of the state.

In her years at Sherborne the quietly persistent propaganda for women's rights led by women like Millicent Fawcett exploded into militant rebellion and letter-bombs as Emmeline Pankhurst and others despaired of constitutional methods and demonstrated how female exclusion entailed outlaw means. Emmeline Tanner refused her backing to militant tactics by feminists, not because she lacked commitment to equality nor through any inconsistency of principle, but because she hated the politics of violence. So she was to choose the way of committees to further her causes, impatient though she was with bureaucracy, because she saw these as the basis of democracy. In committees ideas are shared, questions asked, votes taken, within a framework where alternative points of view can be heard and explained, perhaps even understood. So too in 1948 when she was in South Africa just after the election which brought the Nationalist Party to power, Emmeline questioned a prominent Nationalist MP about the racial policy soon to be known as *apartheid*, and decided that 'I don't agree with it' – almost her only unequivocal political comment in her family letters then – for 'it is ultimately based (can it be "ultimately" based?) on fear'. To express her judgment as a personal disagreement, not an absolute 'it is wrong', itself encodes her repulsion from authoritarian rule.

Yet the authority of a headmistress was what she sought in the summer of 1909. She was thirty-two, about the average age for appointment to a first headship, as indicated by a random sample of a dozen of her contemporaries, for the educational surge of the later 19th century and women's low marriage rate had thrown up a plethora of candidates of

Emmeline's age. In 1909 the *Nuneaton Chronicle* reported 'between sixty and seventy applications for the post of headmistress' for 'the new secondary school which is being built on the Leicester Road' in Nuneaton, under the aegis of Warwickshire County Council as LEA. When Emmeline went for interview there in July with the seven others on the short list the school did not exist. External organisation, of size, age range, building plans, costs and management, was determined by the conditions of the school's origin, soon made clear to Emmeline; internal organisation, of staff, curriculum, form groupings, hours, building use, was still to be decided. As Emmeline was to find, the expectations of the Governors were sometimes vague or conflicting.

Headmistress-elect, but not formally to take up duties until January 1910, Emmeline spent August in Lucerne and Mürren with Kathleen Moore. School was rarely far from her mind as she mixed her delight in 'alpine roses, all sorts of gentians, lilies, arnica montana, and very many other sorts', in 'trees, ferns, streams, waterfalls' and 'dozens of snow-clad mountains, beautiful peaks, glaciers, valleys' with the reflection that 'It is awfully instructive geographically, of course. I have given many lessons on glaciers and the effects of glaciation but it is far better to have seen them', and as they walked and used local transport she observed and investigated. She also enjoyed: 'It is lovely to walk on hard snow and on ice as much as 12 and 20 feet thick in brilliant summer sunshine and the feeling in the air is simply beautiful.' Climbing proper Emmeline did not attempt, unlike several notable schoolmistresses including the intrepid Sophie Bryant. But on a day of 'very heavy and incessant rain':

> Miss Moore had the timetable to do so we set to work on it at one o'clock, were amazed when we looked at our watches and found it was five o'clock, made some tea and continued, did not hear the dinner gong, forgot to dress [for dinner], and were visited at 7.10 by a small child of the house who was sent up to know if we did not want to eat.
> Such is the fascination of Time Tables and the advantage of a wet day!

The only letter she wrote, she said, other than those to Bath, was to her Sherborne successor. The drawback of taking school consciousness on holiday was a rare manifestation of what was conventionally deemed 'schoolmistressiness': 'I have seen so much of Lunnites this time that it would be only dire necessity that would persuade me to join one of Dr Lunn's parties on a summer tour! It is awful to travel in a herd like that.' And she hated 'the trippers' horrid sandwich papers and fruit peelings' that littered the Eiger Glacier.

The autumn was not, after all, to be free for Emmeline to find and move to a home in Nuneaton, nor for her to embark on organisation and staffing for the new secondary school there. Pneumonia incapacitated the administrator for the Sherborne House called Aldhelmsted Junior Floor, and Emmeline returned to fill a role calling for maternal rather than teaching skills. The few extra weeks brought the advantage of a fresh friend in

Margaret Skipworth, like Kathleen Moore a clergy daughter, just appointed to teach modern languages at Sherborne after experience very different from Emmeline's. Since, at seventeen in 1900, she had left the respected school of Queen Anne's, Caversham, she had travelled in France, Germany, Austria and Hungary, and gained a Sorbonne Diploma. Her stay at Sherborne proved a brief interlude, a pause before she gained a scholarship to Lady Margaret Hall, Oxford. She remained at that college as student, tutor, librarian and vice-principal for the rest of her working life, but the few weeks of overlapping tenure at Sherborne impressed on Emmeline her strong personality, independent and decided tastes, and their friendship endured.

Madge Skipworth needed no motherly care, but some of the girls discovered orphaned symptoms when Emmeline left them. 'Everything is *too* beastly for words ... everything is going wrong ... it's fearfully difficult to do things just the same when there is no one you mind seeing what you do,' one wrote tragically in the second week of November, a few days after Emmeline had said goodbye, with a farewell lantern lecture on 'The life and times of Martin Luther'. Typically she had delayed her departure to the last minute. 'We saw you running for your train from the Science Room window – it rather upset my efforts to see something weird under the microscope!'

Emmeline took from Sherborne more substantial baggage than she had brought, not only the books and stimulating friends she had collected but a seasoned blend of ideas, 'simmering in my mind', as she put it. After the four and a half years at Sherborne it was possible for Amrit Kaur, who knew Emmeline first there and better later, to judge: 'Education ... was to her a vocation.'[10] Many, probably most, of the first headmistresses of new local authority secondary schools likewise drew their images of how and to what ends a school should function not from the longstanding LEA schools, those of the elementary sector, but from their own experience gained in endowed and proprietary schools.

Chapter 8
Nuneaton

'The most important thing in my life for some ten and a half years' was Nuneaton High School. When Emmeline was appointed headmistress Nuneaton may have meant little more to her than the stage where George Eliot had depicted some of her *Scenes of Clerical Life*, 'a dingy town, surrounded by flat fields, lopped elms, and sprawling manufacturing villages, which crept on and on with their weaving-shops, till they threatened to graft themselves on the town', and the source of models for the Dodsons' lives of 'oppressive narrowness' in *The Mill on the Floss*.[1] But there Emmeline knew she was taking part in a significant change, and pioneering excited her, stimulated by what she saw as the revolutionary quality of LEA secondary schools, as far as girls were concerned, their use of public money to hack away the roots of a class-based educational system. So the Education Act of 1902 permitted.

The advantages that had been confined to girls whose parents could pay fees high enough to cover the whole cost of their education [she said in 1931] were extended to many others when schools were founded where the Government, from the taxes, and the Local Authority, from the rates, contributed to the cost ... No one knows better than I do what sacrifices parents have often made and continue to make in order to meet those lower fees, but the fact remains that they are much lower than the necessary cost of the education, and this has been made possible by the sharing of expense between taxes, rates and parents' fees.

In Emmeline's time at Nuneaton, to be specific, fees for the High School were fixed at £7/7/- per year for pupils from Warwickshire, £9/9/- for those from outside, and a constant proportion of 25 per cent paid no fees under the free place regulations for grant-earning schools introduced in 1907. These fees were inclusive of all 'subjects of instruction included in the approved curriculum, and the use of all educational equipment (including stationery)', by Board of Education rules.

This was a school for a community unused to pride in schools and respect for teachers; Emmeline took her part in that community and won respect for the High School and its headmistress. It was also part of the national system; she entered the national arena and qualified herself to speak there with authority because Nuneaton High School exemplified the LEA girls' secondary school of the next half-century in its ideals and its methods. What matters about this High School, indeed, is its very ordinariness, for this story with local variations was played out all over England.

Not least was it ordinary in its confusion of aims, of what justified spending public money on secondary education. The Board of Education was ambiguous. Although it defined such education only as 'beginning at an age not exceeding twelve ... carried on through a progressive general course of instruction up to and beyond the age of sixteen', it specified subjects of instruction intended to ensure that the 'course of education ... shall be of a generous and civilising type and neither unduly specialised nor defective in essential elements' and within these terms would 'not only permit but encourage such differentiation ... as is consistent with a broad and solid general education, and such variation of instruction towards the particular needs and capacities of the pupils as does not interfere with the function of the school as a common organism directed towards the production of trained citizens.'[2] What constituted a 'trained citizen' remained obscure; but it was clear that the school was not provided for a special type of child nor designed to direct towards a specific type of career.

For girls, the question of aims was further complicated by what Michael Sadler called the 'divided aim' of girls' uncertain futures: 'They may not eventually decide or need to earn their own living in a professional calling. Their work may lie in domestic duties at home with their parents or in a home of their own. But during their school days it is necessary in a large number of cases to prepare them, so far as may be, for either event.'[3] Again and again, openly or covertly, the question of a secondary school's aims and function remained crucial and unsettled, as will be seen.

The answer Emmeline herself affirmed repeatedly was at once human, social and professional, an attempt to negotiate this division, and based on her belief that each girl was unique. The work of the school was to discover and develop each girl's particular qualities so that she might later find where these 'might be of most use because it is that kind of work which she will do best and in which she will be of most service to the community. If the work is such that while earning the money for a living all the best that she is capable of is being starved, then it is the wrong career.' A counsel of perfection, as Emmeline knew, but this aim shows a focus not on likeness but on difference, a focus that puts in question any form of social or intellectual élitism.

Who were these girls? The 134 girls at Nuneaton in 1911 after the High School's first year of full operation ranged in age from under nine to over eighteen, with most (90) aged twelve to sixteen; in 1920-21 they numbered 395, with the same range and balance. In Emmeline's time only about half lived in Nuneaton itself, others sometimes coming considerable distances by train, from Rugby and Coventry, Atherstone and Coleshill. About a third (30 per cent) were the children of artisans, labourers, and domestic servants; rather fewer (27 per cent) those of professional families, farmers and wholesale traders; and the biggest group (42 per cent) had parents in retail trades, contracting, or public service (the Post Office or the police, for example), or who were 'clerks and commercial agents'.[4] As the Governors were to point out in 1918, fending off County Council attempts to raise fees to cope with inflation, 'the great majority' of parents had not benefited from wartime wage rises, 'being engaged either as small tradesmen or being in receipt of fixed incomes, or engaged in clerical work, the payment for which has not advanced so much'.[5] For the majority, therefore, it is likely that their parents' expectations and experience of secondary schools were as vague as had been those of Emmeline's own parents in the 1880s and 1890s.

Nuneaton was no Sherborne, not a town of beauty and history to draw visitors, though it too had its Abbey, a 'mangled, yet in parts powerful fragment', to give the 'Nun' to the Domesday name 'Etone'.[6] The town's character was inscribed in its landscape: chimneys signalled brickworks and textile factories specialising in hats or hosiery; in cramped and dirty old courts and yards large upper windows told of hand-looms above the two or three rooms where piece-working families dwelt; coal-carrying wagons on the two railways carted the products of expanding collieries in surrounding villages. The coal mines employed 30 per cent of male workers; women, one in five of the work force, were usually textile workers.

When in 1907 the Municipal Borough of Nuneaton was incorporated, to include the neighbouring villages of Attleborough, Chilvers Coton and Stockingford, farmland still enclosed these industrialising areas in pockets, but already buildings were creeping along the nine-mile road to Coventry, for though Nuneaton lay only 22 miles east of Birmingham the lie of the hills occluded links there. By the end of 1909 the new Borough Council had embarked on a 'vigorous policy, not entirely altruistic, to attract industry by cheap land and cheap electricity', and its efforts to win the planned new County Secondary School for the town were part of this expansionist drive.[7]

The borough held 30,000 people in 1911 and an estimated 49,000 in 1917, double the population of 1902. By 1917 the town's first official guide-book claimed 'as complete and dazzling a change as that effected when the insignificant caterpillar becomes the brilliant-hued butterfly' and told how a town 'small, slumbrous, obscure' in the mid-19th century had become 'alert, enterprising, successful'. The guide-book described how by 1917 a new sewage disposal works had cut mortality rates to 10 or 11 per thousand (when some inland industrial towns reckoned 14 or 18 per thousand), how a municipal electrical supply and a private gasworks powered and lit the town, new law courts kept order, public baths enabled swimming and washing. It listed a public library, two voluntary-funded hospitals, two theatres and two 'picture-palaces', and even a 'fine Aerodrome ground, with its own hangar'. Recently Councillor E. Melly JP had given the town the 15-acre Riversley park, laid it out with trees and shrubs and grassy lawns, and later built there an art gallery and museum. Finally, educationally 'Nuneaton is forging ahead, and will soon stand in the front rank of English educational centres'.[8]

The guide-book's picture was designed to attract commercial and industrial investment. The reader is not reminded of the coal and railway strikes which paralysed the town just before the outbreak of war, or of the wartime labour shortage, conscription, or the food shortage after a bitter and stormy winter had already weakened resistance to infection. No hint appears that in 1919 a housing inspection was to show that over 10 per cent of houses were deemed substandard (though overcrowding was less than in some comparably-sized towns), or that the School Medical Officer was to report that of 2,035 elementary schoolchildren inspected in 1920 a third had verminous heads and 7.1 per cent verminous bodies, 6.45 per cent suffered from 'defective nutrition' and 9.8 per cent from tonsil or adenoid problems.[9]

So new was Nuneaton High School on 1 January 1910, the day Emmeline officially became its headmistress, that girls and staff were not yet all gathered together nor the building finished. When in 1907 Warwickshire County Council's Education Committee had concluded that 'the north-eastern side of Warwickshire was sadly unprovided for as regards a proper school for the higher education of girls' they had not fixed a location; here Alderman J. K. Bourne was the pivotal figure, 'who through fair weather and foul had fought for the school', arguing to the Education Committee the convenient location and railway advantages of Nuneaton.[10]

For the town's boys a grammar school chartered by Edward VI and rescued from decay in the 1870s by reorganisation under the Endowed School Act provided secondary education, and in 1908, when one vigorous head had just been succeeded by another, it held 81 boys in some new buildings, a quarter with free places, the others paying £6 or £9 according to age, and it received various forms of grant aid. For girls the only place where non-private secondary education was available was the Pupil-Teacher Centre, and that was so cramped for space that in 1907 the Board of Education threatened to withdraw recognition. Moreover, regulations for pupil-teachers were changing, so that apprenticeship – teaching work in elementary schools alternating with five days each fortnight learning at the PT Centre – did not start until the age of sixteen. Alternatively, a bursary might now be granted for another year of full-time schooling before a year's service as a student teacher or direct entry to training college. Warwickshire preferred the latter policy but there was a snag: bursaries were tenable only at recognised secondary schools. So Nuneaton, where the Borough Council had limited authority and looked to the County Council for the town's 'higher education', feared the loss of its teacher education.

The Borough could not control but it could contribute, and its provision of £2,000 towards the estimated building costs of £8,000 for the school planned by the County Council must have been persuasive. The headmaster of the PT Centre was due to retire in December 1909; it was decided that his place would be taken by a headmistress for a secondary school. By the end of 1907 a site had been bought, just over the railway line on Nuneaton's eastern side – too close to the railway, some said, or too close to the cemetery, or too low-lying – and the County Council architect drew up plans. In the end the capital cost of site and buildings was £7956 and of equipment £900

– a total of £8,856. The constitution of the Governing Body was established in 1909, with the town appointing three members and the county eight, while two more might be co-opted by the Governors themselves. Five more sat by virtue of their offices, as Chairman and Vice-chairman of the County Education Committee, Chairman of the County Secondary and Technical Education Committee, the Mayor of Nuneaton and the Chairman of the Nuneaton Education Committee. At least three of the representative Governors (neither ex-officio nor co-opted) must be women. On the school's Opening Day Emmeline privately regretted a slight display of 'County *v.* Nuneaton' rivalry, having no wish to be drawn into a power struggle with the school at stake, but she found a strong ally and confidant in the County's Director of Education, a new position of chief permanent official in the local government department established by the new LEA after 1902 to deal with administration. Warwickshire and Emmeline were fortunate: their Director of Education was Bolton King.

Bolton King's appointment in 1904 had been controversial, his political and social views being known through his record as a founder-worker at the social-service settlement of Toynbee Hall in Whitechapel, as a rural reformer in Warwickshire, as an Alderman and as a Liberal candidate for Parliament in 1899 when his stand against the Boer War had ensured defeat. But he was not a man given to self-advertisement, and though Emmeline may already have realised that this untidily dressed man of nearly fifty was the author of *A history of Italian unity* and works on Mazzini, standard works for many years, his varied interests she learnt only gradually. From the start, however, he made clear what to her was undoubtedly welcome, his belief that if teachers were allowed responsibility they would act responsibly. The role of the LEA, in King's view, was to be 'a power behind the teacher to whom the teacher might appeal in cases of difficulty and from whom he or she might get support and encouragement'.[11] This he provided, and had in 1903, in the face of much opposition, set up a Teachers' Consultative Committee for the 238 elementary schools in his care. He sat with the Governors of Nuneaton High School holding what he called a 'watching brief' as a non-voting advisor.

The first extant minutes of a meeting record the appointment of Miss Emmeline Tanner from January 1910 at a salary of £100 per year with £1 capitation (a payment for each pupil) but a guaranteed minimum of £250 a year; her formal contract was with the County's Education Committee. The differential between Emmeline's salary and those of her assistant staff, none receiving more than half her £250 at the start, shows how important the head's work was reckoned.

Thinking over her plans Emmeline moved to Nuneaton in late 1909, finding temporary lodgings in Riversley Road. She wanted a place of her own but that had to wait. The High School was the first of Warwickshire LEA's secondary schools and even the role of the headmistress was not yet clearly defined. It had to be worked out within the school's determinative sets of relationships, involving headmistress, parents, staff, Governors and those elected councils to whom they answered, future employers, previous schools and subsequent training institutions, and the pupils themselves. Objectives, priorities, resources, constraints all pulled and pushed on each set.

The Governors themselves apparently reflected the local oligarchy: businessmen, clergy, county gentry. Their first Chairman was Alderman Bourne, who had urged the school's creation, though he was now in declining health (he died in 1917) and lived several miles away at Atherstone; Emmeline rapidly won his confidence and was soon on friendly terms with his family. Other active members included Edward Melly, in his fifties and Mayor of Nuneaton for the second time when Emmeline arrived and busy in almost every local field. He had worked as a mining engineer in Sheffield before he came to Nuneaton in 1882 to manage the Griff coalfield, and then become its managing director and chairman, but at the same time his abundant energy made him one of the chief figures, Liberal in politics, driving the 'progressive' piston of the Municipal Council. With him on the school's governing body sat his third wife Hallie, much younger than he and justifying her position by her own record of local activism, concentrated in the orthodox way of women on women's organisations, local hospitals, the NSPCC and so on. She was well liked, especially by Emmeline, for her charm and generosity, 'so kind', a friend of both once said, adding, 'That is a little woman with a great deal of tact and generosity – the way she steers through all those family relations without showing how bored she is – well, she *must* be, if you think of them.' After a particularly difficult Governors' meeting Hallie Melly invited Emmeline to a picnic lunch in the country 'to see the wild daffodils'; regularly she asked her to parties; she lent guide-books to Italy for Emmeline's use, and her gifts to the school were numerous. She demonstrated to the town, in short, that the High School's headmistress was an equal to the local élite – not the status invariably accorded to an unmarried woman living on what she earned.

Then there was Melly's Conservative counterpart, Robert Swinnerton JP, also supported by a female Governor, his sister. As Chairman of the Nuneaton Education Committee he was closely involved with the town's elementary schools and technical classes, and, like Melly, also a Governor of the Grammar School; he was as well Chairman of the Board of Guardians administering the Poor Law, a pillar of the Church of England, sitting on some diocesan lay bodies, and altogether a force to be reckoned with. From the Church itself but sitting as Chairman of Nuneaton's Higher Education Committee was Canon John Deed, Vicar of Nuneaton and incumbent of the parish church, and the Rev. William McGregor of Tamworth, further afield, again not for his vocation but for his membership of the County Education Committee. The school had no formal church links.

Emmeline admired McGregor's Turner prints, his expertise in local history and his garden, and she thought his Egyptological collection one of the finest in private hands. When in 1913 she mentioned to him that Egyptian history was included in upper school studies he promptly invited the elder girls for a visit, and to their awe led them into his steel strong-room to see and even touch glass cases of mummies, models of boats, amulets and seals, toys, beads and jewellery, even cosmetics – 'worn chiefly by women', he said. Was he *sure* men didn't use them too? asked Emmeline. They proceeded to Tamworth Castle, McGregor discoursing gently on history and architecture.

Such men and women exemplify those whose names appear regularly in the records as attending school functions and Governors' meetings. The cabinet responsibility they took for granted in dealing with the school obscures positions taken in early arguments, and their minutes record resolutions not the struggle to reach them. What can be glimpsed are the tactical principles used by Emmeline to ensure that within three or four years the Governors referred most matters to her judgment, listened to her advice and often enough rubber-stamped her decisions.

She avoided open confrontations and entrenched positions, compromising on what she reckoned lower priorities to concentrate on the maximum achievable rather than the ideal. She tried to present her case with respect for potential opponents, to see obstacles from their point of view not her own, and to adduce facts and figures where possible to show the logic on her side. She persevered, aided by an air of equable good humour and reason, conciliatory rather than aggressive in tone, practical rather than vaporous with theory, which may have soothed some fears of independent women. These were similar to methods later advocated by Eleanor Rathbone in her parliamentary work, together with the principle that policy-makers should be persuaded in the early stages of drafting rather than tackled when minds were made up – a principle Emmeline also came to recognise.

Thus Swinnerton, for example, came to respect the 'very business-like way in which she has dealt with the accounts of the School, especially in preparing the annual estimate of receipts and expenditure'; McGregor was to speak highly of her 'great breadth of view and wide-ranging sympathies'; and Deed was to praise her organisational powers and infusion of 'that tone and enthusiasm of which every good Public School is both the nursery and the guardian'.[12] One by one, each in his or her own way, they were persuaded to trust her. But it took time. Not for a year was Emmeline even told officially of the dates for Governors' meetings.

A multiplicity of details confronted her before the new buildings were ready for occupation at the beginning of the summer term of 1910. She must have moved with a brisk step that spring as she effected the conversion of Pupil-Teacher Centre to secondary school and explored the headmistress's role of internal co-ordinator. At first she coped with classes conducted in three places at once, at the PT Centre, at the Grammar School and by Grammar School staff (but not alongside boys) for certain subjects, and in rooms rented to accommodate the lowest class whose 'excessive numbers' worried the new Governors. Complicating this was the five-days-a-fortnight attendance of some girls articled as pupil-teachers to surrounding elementary schools, and Emmeline's personal teaching of history and other subjects as necessary.

Meanwhile she was responsible for the overall planning, hammering out with the staff coherent secondary school syllabuses, apt division of girls into forms, balanced use of their time, progressive advance through subject levels, entry for appropriate examinations. She held staff meetings, usually weekly, as well as freely talking – and listening – to individuals, trying to achieve, as Sara Burstall of Manchester High School urged, a balance between a centralised 'French' style of government and a locally various 'US federal' style, with local independence;[13] a year later HM Inspectors thought Emmeline's staff needed more 'supervision' than she gave. Emmeline repeatedly pondered the question 'how to rule?', concluding in 1936 that this must depend on the 'three variable factors' of 'the personality of the headmistress, the circumstances of the school, the composition and personality of the staff', but at Nuneaton in 1910 the latter two were in flux.

The core of her staff she inherited from the PT Centre. She found a right hand in Margaret Billinger, an Irishwoman in her twenties who had gained a St Andrews LLA (a diploma favoured by teachers) before two years at Homerton Training College, and who now taught English with enthusiasm and whatever else was necessary. For mathematics, some Scripture, later some geography and still later some 'commercial subjects' there was Winifred Lewis, with London Matriculation and trained for secondary teaching. She was to be a pillar of stability, stern in class but with a kindly humour outside, until she retired aged 62 in 1941. But Emmeline was not wholly lucky. Before she took up her duties she was asked to appoint an assistant to cope with the lowest class, 11-to-12 year-olds, an influx eager for the secondary school which the PT Centre could not accommodate, but after only a few weeks, in February 1910, Emmeline's choice departed precipitately. 'What a wretch...' said Bolton King sympathetically. 'I wish I could help you to find a temporary person but I know of no one.' He suggested she wire a London agency: 'You must give what salary you have to, so long as you can get somebody at once.'

In this way, and at the outset, Bolton King was endorsing the headmistress' 'freedom to select the members of her staff' urged in 1906 by the Association of Head Mistresses to governing bodies of LEA secondary schools, to secure, they argued, an harmonious co-operation between a stimulating balance of personalities, of whom they thought the headmistress the best judge, and to secure the head's authority. Uneasiness among the Governors, especially those accustomed to managing elementary schools, whose heads had no such freedom, appears to have quietened gradually. The only evidence for Nuneaton lies in a suggestive shift of practice: in April 1910 Emmeline had to obtain authorisation before she made an offer of part-time work to a qualified gymnastic mistress, but in November the Governors were approving arrangements she had already made, though technically the right to hire and fire was theirs alone.

The first of all her appointments typified the sort of woman with broad interests and secondary school background Emmeline was often to seek. To teach geography, geology and botany, and manage garden work, she chose Isobel Whitton, with a degree from Sydney University after education at Clifton Girls' High School in Bristol and with teaching experience in both Australia and South Africa before her return to the UK to join Edgbaston Church of England College, a respected high school. Others also sought such women, and Isobel Whitton stayed only until 1912 when the more prestigious St James's, Malvern, snapped her up. For though Emmeline appears to have known what she wanted she did not necessarily find it. A school with no established reputation, the ungenerous Warwickshire LEA salary rates, and a Midlands industrial town were none of them obviously attractive to candidates good enough to choose. Holidays tended to be shorter than in older secondary schools, for representatives of the ratepayers subsidising LEA schools often assumed that value for money was achieved by work not holidays. Nor in 1910 were pensions usually a secure prospect; in 1912 all Nuneaton High School staff joined 'approved societies' under the National Insurance Act of 1911; by 1917 Emmeline was checking details of a 'Pension Scheme for Mistresses', but that lay ahead still. Her only weapon in 1910 was her personality, as a head worth working under and with authority in running the school.

Then there was paperwork and parents. She had no clerical staff, though in 1913 she was allowed to buy a typewriter for the school and in 1915 install a telephone, and only in April 1910 did the Governors appoint as their Clerk a local accountant, G. R. Clay, to take over the duties of collecting fees, ordering supplies, and paying wages and salaries. It was Emmeline who visited suppliers to inspect and cost equipment and books, and painstakingly supplied information to Governors and LEA, and with Bolton King she shared the responsibility of preparing a prospectus. As administrative work grew with the school she longed for secretarial help and in 1917 persuaded the Governors to allow teaching hours to be reduced for Winifred Lewis to act as part-time secretary.

The Board of Education no longer fixed the time allowance for each subject, as it had at first, but it insisted on seeing and approving syllabuses and analyses of the time spent by each form on each subject; Emmeline supplied these. Form mistresses had to keep a daily register of attendance, but Emmeline was responsible for general records of both girls and staff, and for establishing principles for marks and reports (a 'proper system', approved the HMIs in 1911). She saw new parents, anxious parents, parents who kept daughters at home too often. Those merely unused to taking school seriously and inclined to put first even trivial social engagements were probably easier to deal with than those who called on their daughters' household services. In 1923 Emmeline contributed to a report in which it was recognised that a relatively high percentage of girl pupils, especially in Municipal Secondary Schools, did fairly heavy housework over the weekend; and a smaller, but still considerable proportion helped in preparing the daily meals, waiting on lodgers or looking after younger brothers or sisters ... it was noticeable that the least assistance in household duties was expected in boys of homes of the poorest type. In general the home always weighed more heavily on girls than on boys, and in cases of family illness, additional strain and anxiety fell on them.[14]

Emmeline learnt what she could of each girl's home circumstances and health, in order to negotiate her path through problems raised, either by pressures on health and strength or by the rigidity and subject categorisation implied by time analyses.

Very early, in February 1910, she had to confront what all headmistresses from time to time encountered and loathed: an instance of petty theft, even before she had familiarised herself with all the girls. She consulted Bolton King:

I am inclined to be hard [he told her] and advise you to expel the girl if you can prove her guilt. It is the third case that has happened and it looks as if an example were necessary. It will be very hard on the mother, but there is the school to be considered. If you think this is too harsh, I strongly advise you to suspend the girl for a week and do it publicly, and let the girls know you are reporting it to the Governors. (You have, you know, under the Articles to report an expulsion or suspension.)

Emmeline apparently did feel expulsion 'too harsh', and informed the Governors of a one-week suspension of the girl in question. No other such action appears in their minutes for Emmeline's period of office, and presumably she resorted, if it were necessary, to less formal methods.

To refresh herself she could hurry over to the new buildings to check and confer with builder and plumber, glazier and painter. So much seemed necessary, and for every individual non-standard item she must ask the Governors. Hot water was allowed for the basins in the girls' washroom and in the Art Room scullery, but not for the staff lavatories or the laboratory. No asphalt could be supplied for the playground but Emmeline could have a garden hose, a ladder, cricket sets and netball equipment. The Governors would pay for maps costing £8/3/- and the geographical and meteorological instruments Emmeline wanted (£3/15/- from Messrs Negretti and Zambra), but not for a new piano since an old one could be repaired. A grant of £20 could be made for the library. She wanted an electric lantern too, as she had used at Sherborne, and had to ask separately for the lantern sheet and blinds for black-out. And so on, endlessly, it seemed.

You won't mind my telling you [warned Bolton King] but it would not be wise to ask for too many things. Some of the Governors are getting rather restive, and I am afraid it may end in their providing less than they will otherwise do. The geography garden and frame do

not, I fear, strike any of us as very obvious needs, and it would be a
mistake to spend money on the less necessary things and have to
economise on the essentials. I am sure you won't mind my telling you
this. I am so anxious that you should have the chief hand in moulding
the school that I don't want you to do anything that would lessen your
influence. There's a sermon and I hate preaching!

So Emmeline gave up her plans for a geography garden, the latest idea
in geography teaching where a little landscape of mountains and valleys
was modelled outdoors for the girls to observe river formation or explore
communications links or settlement factors, chart contour lines and learn
mapping. And on closer inspection the clay and heavy loams of local soil
were not ideal. But she clung to the more manageable botanical garden,
useful for art as well as plant study, and enabling joint work of hands, eyes
and minds in practical gardening – but again Bolton King's quiet advice
was helpful: 'The agriculturists on the Committee were shocked to see
coltsfoot grown in the botanical garden. As a gardener I know that if it is
allowed to grow there – still more if it goes to seed – there won't be much
else there in a year or two.'

The County's Education Committee were responsible for basic furnishing,
so it was to them she wrote about preferred solutions for floor treatments –
'They decided to Ronuk [polish] the classrooms, mistresses' rooms,
cloakrooms (which we thought the most important of all) and all the rooms
upstairs,' Bolton King told her. 'The evidence as to whether it is slippery
for gymnasium is conflicting, so they left over the question of the hall.' And
Emmeline drove the local government official responsible for supplies hard,
to earn a tactful rebuke from Bolton King: 'Mr Hills ... has really put in a
tremendous amount of work into the furnishing, and I was afraid last week
he was knocking himself up. But he is all right now.'

As the daylight lengthened she worked in the garden herself, to promote
the environment both beautiful and educational of her desires, and saplings
can be seen in an early photograph. By mid-May she could write: 'Tell Jess
[Appleyard, now studying horticulture] the weather has been glorious for
my garden. Cornflowers are fully out and practically everything is living' –
and 'my' meant the school's. Areas were set aside for individual 'form
gardens' and she told the local Press she planned a tank for 'observation of
water plants'. Journalists were invited to view the school the day before
term started there in May, and they puffed its praise with all the enthusiasm
its head could have wished for the glories of the 'spacious and well-lighted
classrooms', for the laboratory, the large-windowed Art Room, the playing
field for winter hockey and summer cricket and tennis.

They stressed the school's up-to-date image: the *Midlands Counties Tribune*
reported that 'Nature study and open-air classes will be a feature of the
work', and the *Nuneaton Chronicle* that 'domestic science will command its
share of attention ... thoroughly inculcating the cardinal principles of the culinary
art'. These were fashions of the times – Sherborne opened a special wing for

Domestic Science in 1910 – and for domestic science, compulsory by Board regulation, Emmeline secured an assistant with a professional diploma, but though she never ceased to pay lip-service to the value of the subject (everyone ought to be able to manage a home, self-respect developed with the growth of capability, craft skills were part of a full education, and so on) it is difficult to find the spark which lit her feelings for the intellectual disciplines. She was proud of the laboratory for chemistry and physics, and this, though modest, was a bait by which she secured one of her few graduate assistants.

From the outside gabled roofs of varying heights broke up with angles the forthright brick, red banded with grey, of the structure itself. The design conformed to the recently issued *Building regulations for secondary schools* (1906), dealing with space, sanitation, ventilation and other needs, but its compromises with the ideals proposed by Sara Burstall's handbook on high schools or Felix Clay's *Modern school buildings* (1906) imply economy. The school was built to hold 210 girls, giving a capital cost per head of under £50, though Miss Burstall reckoned in 1907 that a 'better-class' school would cost nearer £70 a head. It was unsatisfactory, but cheaper, for the hall to double as a gymnasium, though the plan of a central hall with classrooms opening off each side facilitated clearing and filling the hall; it was cheaper to plumb a grouping of kitchen, dining-room and lavatories at the rear of the T-shaped block, but it was less convenient than a lavatory for each form-room, though the separate cloakroom entrance meant wet clothes need not be trailed through other passages. Though Emmeline once described the local builder as 'the most dilatory man' he used good local brick and his craftsmanship endured, needing few repairs through the sixty-four years of the High School's life.

On 4 May 1910 the girls gathered at the new building, and at the appointed hour assembled in the hall for Prayers, after months of 'forming wild ideas of what our school life in the future was to be', said one, before Emmeline swept in behind them, stately in her academic gown, to progress through the hall to the platform and set the morning pattern for succeeding years.[15] After the hymn, the reading, the prayers (the routine she had learnt at Sherborne) she addressed her flock on the responsibility of the founding members and on the need for earnest striving; she spoke of the motto she had chosen for the school, a tag from G. F. Watts, 'The Utmost for the Highest'. On the walls beside them hung the pictures she had given, two by G. F. Watts – 'Aspirations' and 'The Happy Warrior' – and Reynolds' 'John the Baptist'. A child could not have missed the message. But in symbol and allegory forms embody meanings indirectly, and may need thought: a subtler message.

Her audience saw her as imposing and confident, but the scores of faces below, nestlings opening trusting beaks for their mental food, provoked in her a deep anxiety. In her care, in May 1910, were 121 girls, including a score or so of pupil-teachers, and seven full-time staff, most in their twenties. At the beginning of that first term Emmeline bought a cheap exercise book, apparently to use as a commonplace book for jotting quotations of special interest, and made her first entry. She wrote out a passage from an 'Address to Teachers' given by Dorothea Beale in 1893: it dealt with the responsibility of the teacher for the child, the 'angel service to which you teachers are called', a 'mediatorial ministry'. 'We must not look at children as they *are*, but as they will be ... are becoming, as Tennyson in *In Memoriam* speaks of seeing the tree in the acorn,' urged Miss Beale, and so, at times, 'Like the disciples we must enter into the cloud on the Mount with Jesus, if we would come down and heal the suffering child.'

Her argument appealed to Emmeline's already well established sense of inner privacy and justified her personal reticence. In 1939 she was herself to transform a theme of contemplation alternating with and nurturing practical action in her presidential address to the AHM, and not only to urge the 'stilling of the mind' as a means of critical self-examination but also to re-locate development of *la vie intérieure* within the growing child. She identified such development as a mode of liberation: teachers must 'give them that inner freedom which is essential for the full development of the personality ... that inner freedom of which the peoples of the world stand today in so great need.' She did not dwell on the marked shift from the more prescriptive aim of character formation common to Beatrice Mulliner and the Board of Education's aims for elementary schools in 1904, but her introductory remarks on the need for social and economic change in Britain to avert the totalitarianism where 'individuals have not freedom to think, speak and believe as they will' established a context in which such managerial manipulation was unacceptable.

In the same 1939 speech Emmeline confessed she found 'busy busy-ness' and practical action easier than 'the quiet hour' of 'deliberately freeing the mind from its attachment to outer things', and the first stirrings of guilt may well be traced to these busy months of 1910 and her transcription of Dorothea Beale. The idea that absorption in 'multifarious duties' was culpable she repeatedly linked not only to the ambition she also implied in this speech, to take a hand in large-scale change, but to the responsibility of a headmistress for her pupils, the theme of her concluding remarks. Thus subjective autonomy, *la vie intérieure*, becomes the wellspring of social and political development. A page later in her commonplace book Emmeline quoted Liddon: 'Desire is the raw material of human life – undisciplined it leads to sin, disciplined it makes a saint.'

Sometime this first summer a snapshot caught Emmeline outside the school, after flowers planted round the edge of the walls had blossomed, and not even the staidly suitable 'coat and skirt' she wears, its hem just above the ground and the jacket over a demure high blouse, nor the absurdly large hat on her piled-up hair can disguise a springy radiance in her wide smile and briefly arrested stance. The same camera found also a dozen or so girls waiting at their entrance in a loose group, long hair tied back, all in dark stockings, unaffectedly talking and laughing together, save for one who looks shyly at the camera. Though not here earnest, otherwise they unconsciously support Bolton King's comment that 'I am always impressed by the faces of your children. They are not beauties, but they look so earnest and sensible and without the usual self-consciousness and silliness of high school girls (don't be very angry)...' They wear no uniform: as in most schools that developed only slowly through the 1920s and 1930s, except for regulation of games and gym clothes and the straw boaters which Emmeline ordained they wear outside, to unify and identify High School girls.

These straw boaters made a public group appearance only a few days after the school settled into its new home, when Edward VII died and the girls trooped into the centre of Nuneaton to flank the boys of the Grammar School at the foot of a temporary platform and hear the Mayor, gold chain round his neck, formally proclaim the accession of King George V. A change of sovereign meant little more than a new face on the postage stamps and a half-holiday next year for the Coronation but the school's showing in the town marked a new institutional presence. Emmeline intended it to participate in local affairs, and when the County decided its memorial to the late King would be an open-air tuberculosis hospital she announced the school would hold a sale of work to help raise funds, placing in meticulous order the motives – 'our sympathy for sufferers', 'our loyalty to our late Sovereign', 'our connection with the County'. Similar efforts for various causes were to take place most years, banal means concealing plural ends, for thus girls exercised creative abilities on others' behalf and at the same time showed them off, attracting public appreciation to acceptable skills.

Within school routines settled to the curriculum outlined by Board of Education regulations. Those issued in 1909 listed English language and literature, at least one language other than English, geography, history, mathematics, science, drawing, and for girls 'practical instruction in Domestic Subjects, such as Needlework, Cookery, Laundrywork, House-keeping and Household Hygiene'. No equivalent technical skills reduced for boys the time they could spend on other subjects. Also a secondary school must provide 'organised games, physical exercises, manual instruction, and singing'.[16] The most obvious departures from the curricula of elementary and the new 'higher elementary' schools were the foreign language and organised games, with the replacement of arithmetic by mathematics, and the general extension of range beyond that of the Pupil-Teacher Centre entailed fresh staff.

One foreign language seemed enough to start with, and French was the obvious choice. Judging from the HMIs' report in June 1911 it proved difficult enough to establish standards and an integrated syllabus of oral and written work with literature when the whole notion was new and strange to some and others laboured between ignorance and not necessarily helpful previous studies.[17] Matters apparently improved from 1912 when Emmeline found Gertrude Storr-Best, qualified by a diploma in French teaching from Leeds University but more vitally by her personality, 'essentially a scholar', said Emmeline, but with a lively enthusiasm for drama and current events; tall, well-dressed, dignified, she did not, it seems, awe the girls too much to prevent their enjoying her presentation of French as a living language and admiring her cosmopolitan outlook.

'One of the grandest changes,' as a girl put it for the magazine, 'appreciated by all, was the introduction of games and gymnastics.' To be outdoors and active was, it was commonly then recognised, a novelty especially to girls of the urban middle and lower middle classes, and though games were not compulsory the HMIs noted with approval 'the large proportion of girls who play them' at Nuneaton High School. The potential games field beside the school was uneven; it took two years for Emmeline to persuade the Governors to pay for drainage of the clay soil and to buy a horse-roller for maintenance. But the first cricket match was played and won in July, against the girls of Hinckley Grammar School, on a day when 'The heat is intense but the weather very brilliant,' Emmeline noted.

Singing was compulsory, the school massing in two choirs for this, and individual instrumental lessons were routinely expected, though the school was allowed to charge for these, but music developed in classwork too, with simple theory and some appreciation work, especially after Annie Bassett arrived in 1911 to take charge of general music organisation. Art developed more strikingly. In Pupil-Teacher centre days a Grammar School master had taught drawing, but for the High School Emmeline found Elizabeth Glaisyer, trained at the Birmingham School of Art and the Slade School, a young Quaker full of ideas and ideals. She encouraged imaginative drawing as well as technical expertise, formed a Sketch Club for out-of-school expeditions, and rapidly fostered so strong a reputation for Nuneaton's artwork that within a few years their productions were in demand for educational conferences and other exhibitions. When she cautiously entered girls for examinations of the Royal Drawing Society to check standards, their top placings revealed the school's to be considerably higher than the Society expected. No artist herself, Emmeline trusted Betty Glaisyer with a free hand.

The school was formally opened in June before an audience of parents and Governors, local councillors and clergy and heads of other secondary schools, including Beatrice Mulliner – all those, in short, who might wield educational influence. Emmeline had been authorised to make all the arrangements and had prepared a printed programme, its cover dignified by a blue shield holding a star and the motto 'The Utmost for the Highest'. The order of service within is flanked by a photograph of the school and a ground-plan, and in the photograph female figures can just be seen at work, gardening below the walls – did 'spadework' occur to Emmeline as a fit subtext for the proceedings?

The girls were told to wear white or cream, standard 'best clothes' for a girl of 1910, and formed a choir at the back of the hall for hymns at the start and close, with a Mendelssohn part-song after the highlight of Lilian

Faithfull's address. It was something of a coup to have secured the headmistress of Cheltenham Ladies' College, Miss Beale's successor, and a pointer to the LEA school's aspirations. In the main Miss Faithfull described in well-turned phrases the principles of the girls' secondary school as 'the development of the whole nature, physical, mental and spiritual, to the highest degree of which that nature is capable'. 'First,' she insisted, 'we must get rid of the commercial idea in education. Subjects must not be taken up or dropped because they will or will not "pay",' and she discussed the physical, intellectual and corporate means of attaining full development with stress always less on the individual in herself than on her relationships: she is to be good daughter, good citizen, good patriot.

The problem of aims was covertly central. Press reports show the good daughter preferred by the audience who applauded the words 'she should be able to make a home fit to live in'. Where the text Lilian Faithfull gave Emmeline read 'I think the best thing is to send girls home with plenty of resources or to a professional life with special equipment for it', the reporters summarised: 'after leaving school the best thing for a girl was home life (applause)'. The Chairman of the Warwickshire LEA also reserved his enthusiasm for the 'subject of household economics', especially for the 'great stream of emigration to the Colonies' he expected in the next few years.[18]

The girls had several other speeches to endure on that day of bright sunshine at Nuneaton ('symbolic sunshine', thought Beatrice Mulliner), but there was tea afterwards, and in June Emmeline always liked strawberries for tea, nor were they privy to the problem that the money allotted by the Governors did not officially include tea for all. Tea, however, like the bouquet given to Lilian Faithfull, belonged to a tradition of courteous hospitality Emmeline wished to instil. Bolton King came to the rescue again: 'I will send round the hat and think I can raise most. How would it do to raise something by giving an al fresco concert next month?' He assured Emmeline too that if the girls' singing had sounded a little flat, 'my office musician says that a crowded room generally makes singing sound a bit flat at the other end', that the observable needling of County by Town and vice versa did little 'to spoil the general result', and that 'everyone liked your speech, and you didn't *seem* a bit nervous!'

Chapter 9
Inside stories

Part of the headmistress' role was to represent the school to the outside world, to symbolise the school's values, attitudes and aims. This in itself would have justified Emmeline's desire for a home of her own, where she could entertain friends, organise domestic routine, furnish to her taste, if she needed justification, which she did not admit. Nuneaton, however, offered little to rent for a woman of limited means, and through the next decade staff accommodation was a constant headache. Sometimes two or three could find a house and share the rent, but some mistresses had to occupy the front bedroom and sitting-room of a lodger-seeking family, themselves squeezed into the kitchen and back rooms of a small house, with outside sanitation and no bath, neither comfortable nor healthy. The house belonging to the Warsops, with whom Emmeline first lodged, was apparently more commodious, but Riversley Road, on the south-west of the town, was not particularly convenient for the school, over the railway line to the east, and Emmeline could expect many late nights of dark returns.

To one side of the school a caretakers' house was being built. She asked the Governors if she could take it over, with the caretakers as tenants. No, she was told; the caretakers were to be the tenants, rent-free as part of their pay, and she could arrange to sub-rent from them. In April 1910, however, when Mr and Mrs Giddins took up their duties they disliked the idea of a tenant, especially as their wages would be reduced if they took rent. How could she 'do' for the headmistress as well as clean the school? asked Mrs Giddins. A year later Emmeline's housing problems were still unsolved, though by then she knew she would have found living with the Giddinses uncomfortable, and at Riversley Road difficulties grew:

Things are better here [she wrote in October 1911], though even yesterday Mrs Warsop had another awful fit of temper but happily not till I had gone ... On Saturday morning before I went to school she threw down the cup of tea Mr Warsop brought her and shrieked and yelled. I think she wants smacking! On Sunday she got up and got their dinner and in the afternoon was in such a rage that she broke her own bedroom grate with the poker!! However she really does seem to be getting better ... This week I am having some soup left for me at the school by Mrs Jeff [the school cook] and I go out and heat that on the gas stove and stay there till 10.30, coming home straight to bed.

She compromised on a solution that suited others as well:

There is a house to let nearly opposite the school. Miss Stevinson and Miss Pinches [two of her teaching staff] would like us to take it between us if the Governors would furnish for us and let us pay interest on the money as rent for the furniture. I don't know at all whether they would. Unfortunately I should have only one sitting-room and one bedroom, with the advantage of using one of their bedrooms (they would turn in together) when I had a visitor. They would have one sitting-room and two bedrooms and the maid one bedroom.

Of course it would be lovely to be near to school and also to be independent but it doesn't seem to me to be quite what I want. The rent is £25 [per year] and rates £8/10/-, no ground rent. There is no garden, but there are plenty of box-room and other arrangements, and there is a nice bathroom.

The next month she moved to this house, with her colleagues as sub-tenants, and symbolically she made it her own by changing its name from 'Irene' to the more dignified 'Locksbrook', a reminiscence of the stream near her parents' home. In a would-be humorous essay a friend depicted Emmeline rejecting 'all the battles and all the places on the Riviera' suggested, in favour of an 'ordinary' name – 'you won't call it castle, or manor, or hall, or court' – and portrayed Emmeline at home, pouring tea in the firelight from 'a most satisfactory little grate'. The Governors had not proved helpful about furniture so she had searched some out, bargaining for the old but good: 'Oh, E., you really have got the place *sweet*,' comments the essayist, 'just as homey and arty and bright and cheerful as yourself ... all the clever corners and angles you have contrived out of a most ordinary this-way-and-that-way sort of room.' One habit of Emmeline's caught in this scene was her strategy to exploit physical superiority. When she disagreed decisively she stood up, creating a position of dominance: it is a small but telling sign how her principle that agreement should be reached through reasoned debate conflicted with an instinct to command.

To the 130 girls and nine full-time staff assembled for Prayers in the hall on the first day of term in January 1911 she told a story. Through the Doorway of Tomorrow a dream-vision reveals the Land of the Future in dim rainbow-hued cloudiness, gradually disclosing 'shapes, some radiantly beautiful, some twisted and deformed' – yesterdays that have died – and mystical, half-veiled forms still sleeping 'in the mantle of Imagination'. In all the light and colours and sweet scents the Keeper of Tomorrow shows to the narrator the Science and Art, Knowledge and Health waiting for the world to claim them and give them life and liberty from Superstition and Ignorance. 'Power is here touching you ... Stretch out your hand, and grasp it'; the prize of Tomorrow is Love; the Secret, finally told, is 'Tomorrow is what You make it'.[1]

Emmeline retained a fondness for stories with a moral subtext but not for misty visions, later preferring traditional legends and folktales, such as 'Our Lady's Tumbler', 'Hafiz the Stone-cutter', 'St Francis and the Wolf of Gubbio', 'The Mirror of Matsuyama'. These were kept for the assemblies at beginnings and ends of terms. The daily school assembly was one of those 'influences which together promote a healthy corporate life' detected by

HM Inspectors on their first visit in June 1911, and like Emmeline's other institutions served multiple ends, of which moral propaganda was only one.[2] Wrapped in religious forms, assembly (or Prayers) not only daily renovated the 'tone' Emmeline's successor as headmistress tactfully said she found at Nuneaton, that of 'a place where strenuous endeavour was combined with a gay and cheerful spirit', but was also useful as the headmistress' review of the school as a whole and her oral notice-board. Not always was she cheerful: one ex-pupil claimed that 'Even now, although I am ninety-five years old, whenever I hear the word "appalling" I think of Miss Tanner.' On misdemeanours and disasters 'her comments after Prayers were always most emphatic!' It was the only regular time all were together; in a literal way Prayers embodied unity.

By the time the Inspectors came in June 1911 Emmeline could look back on a number of events expressive of unity and joint effort, such as the Christmas Concert of 1910 with carols and a Somerset part-song, a Dutch lullaby and a Saint-Saens double quartet, scenes from Shakespeare and a recitation of 'The Jackdaw of Rheims'. Well in hand were preparations for a sale of work in July in aid of the new hospital. Lectures had been instituted, as at Sherborne, at first relying on Emmeline's own contacts, including Kathleen Moore to speak on Dante and Beatrice Mulliner with lantern-slides to illustrate her Tennyson lecture and unaware that as she discoursed fire was beginning to lick through and destroy much of her own hall at Sherborne. (There term had not yet started and no injuries added to the devastation, but the importance of fire-drills was driven home to Emmeline.)

Later the net spread to draw in University Extension lecturers such as Hudson Shaw or Percy Scholes on musical history, and professional speakers like Mme Guérin with her costumed talks in French on Joan of Arc and Marie Antoinette, with props, and Runnels Moss who performed dramatic recitals from Dickens' works; at least twice the poet John Drinkwater read his own work; officials from various charities described their work; and Emmeline herself regularly spoke, usually on historical subjects. As the number of Old Girls grew they joined the schoolgirl audience.

The infrastructure of corporate life was laid to the HMIs' approval. No external regulations required 'Houses' or the prefect system, both elements apparently insisting on traditional forms, even forms borrowed from boys' public schools, but these situated the young LEA school in that older tradition and at her subsequent schools Emmeline was to find such institutions already operating, so much a 'normal' part of secondary schools had they become. In a day school a House system did not spring unproblematically from boarding arrangements, as at Sherborne, though Emmeline tried to ground these subdivisions in the reality of the girls' home districts, calling them Nuneaton, Atherstone, Rugby, Coventry. Their justification is best seen in the reflection of a friend of Emmeline's, teaching in India in 1915:

Nearly all the children are Anglo-Indian [of mixed blood, often despised by both British and Indian], and very different from English ones: more mannerly and easily managed in a sense than English, but lacking in energy, public spirit and trustworthiness. It is rather heartbreaking at times to look into face after face and know you cannot trust; still honour is growing, and the House system seems to be doing a great deal, but of course all that must be very slow and I am sure infinite patience is required.

'Houses', that is, were designed to emphasise the individual's public rather than private role, with loyalties attaching to supra-personal entities and not to oneself nor to private and personal objects of affection; Houses reinforced a general encouragement of obligation to the common good. Since this was one of the arguments for organised games, there the Houses had most vitality; but at Nuneaton High School they remained weak in general, mere concepts lacking physical homes and housemistresses to guide a House life.

The institution of prefects was a less artificial construct but, some headmistresses thought, more questionable in value. The Nuneaton system Emmeline founded was not a real exercise in self-government since prefects were chosen by staff, and although they might act as spokesmen for grievances their major function was as staff aids. Rules were apparently very few: silence in corridors is recorded but in general the principle held of 'always thinking of other people before yourself ... every evil can be traced to some form of selfishness', Emmeline's own summary of her mother's rule to herself as a child. Wide interpretative spaces were opened here. But the job of the prefects lay largely in administration, making lists, checking tidiness, ensuring little girls didn't lurk in the cloakrooms when they should be outside in the playground at break.

The system assumed certain pre-conditions, that deference could be expected by legally-constituted authority, for example, and that guilt and shame were viable disciplinary tools, for the appeal to conscience was the basic sanction, but uneasy headmistresses chose rather to object to the potential encouragement of priggishness, arrogance and moral bullying. Emmeline remained convinced the system could engender a sense of responsibility and develop organisational powers and intelligent judgment if (a big *if*) the staff set the example. Indirectly then, her faith in the prefect system testifies to her confidence that she could control it.

Her faith was bolstered by the County's Director of Education. Warwickshire indeed was the only County LEA where a prefect system was introduced into the elementary schools, though into only twenty-three of these, after a teachers' meeting addressed by Baden-Powell, and in evidence before a Board of Education committee in 1926 Bolton King, the Director, praised the resultant training in liberal values.[3] The key, it was agreed, was careful planning and preparation. Though hardly democratic, the system's meritocratic character subordinated claims to authority based on social or material superiority to those based on personal worth.

Considering Nuneaton's corporate life in 1911, HM Inspectors also made 'special mention' of the 'excellent' feature of dinners in which a large proportion of girls and staff shared, including Emmeline. School dinners were born of necessity where about half were 'train girls' and could not go home, paid for by a school dinner fund of 6d a head and produced by a cook (paid at first 7/6d then 10/- a week), helped by a kitchenmaid. In a touch typical of the versatility demanded by thrifty authorities, the domestic science mistress was responsible overall for the dinners, cooked in the domestic science kitchen, and she kept the accounts; moreover the meals included the dishes cooked by her fourth- and fifth-form pupils. A member of staff headed each table of girls, and it was considered, one girl remembered, 'a great honour to be asked to sit at Miss Tanner's table where, if she addressed a remark to you, she would expect a suitable and sensible reply'. Teaching what sort of remark was 'suitable' (relevant, rational, courteous) was one of the functions of the occasion, part of the school's moral economy.

Finally, after a year of the school's life, Emmeline was able to show to the HMIs the first two issues of the school's magazine. Then it was edited by herself and her English mistress Margaret Billinger, later it was passed to the care of a joint committee of staff and girls. 'When it came to College and of course was shown to the other girls they all admired it and said it was interesting, and really I have not seen among any of theirs one with so many original articles and such interesting accounts of school news,' an ex-pupil told Emmeline in 1919. *Nuneaton High School Magazine* was designed as a readable magazine rather than a record repository and, unlike Sherborne's early issues, included stories and poems by the girls in its mix of informative articles by the staff on Giotto or the life of ants, its gardening advice elicited by the annual competition for the best form garden and its lively reports of school events and societies, all pushing into decent obscurity inevitable accounts of games matches and examinations. Emmeline seized all material, sometimes ruthlessly. 'This letter is only for you – please don't put it in any magazine!' reproached Amrit Kaur after Emmeline had published her letters describing the Delhi Durbar and the Calcutta Pageant. An eye-witness view of the Durbar by an Indian woman of high rank with access to everything was not to be missed.

Like most of Emmeline's enthusiasms, the magazine had several functions: to inform entertainingly and broaden minds, to provide an outlet for the girls' literary creativity and a chance for responsible production work, and to act as a shop-window and improve public relations beyond the school. So parents and others were kept informed, or charmed into support, and the proper attitudes to forthcoming projects were demonstrated.

All were building-blocks of a 'healthy corporate life ... so many evidences of the thought and diligence with which the School has been organised', reported HM Inspectors, permeating the timetable of lessons and formal class teaching that was their chief concern. The first lesson a girl with her eyes open learnt from the staff was of devotion to duty. Only holidays gave some respite from the extensions to the school day that Emmeline, like other headmistresses, took for granted, not just for obvious preparation and correction of lesson work but because the life of the school she envisaged gave much more than lessons. Educated women from a range of backgrounds might furnish useful models to enlarge girls' horizons but they were expected to demonstrate, in action, what that meant. And if a girl needed extra help, as after illness, the staff were ready to supply it. It was not surprising that most simply assumed that secondary teaching was incompatible with married life, nor that school engrossed some in an emotionally hazardous self-identification.

Even after the remnant of the Pupil-Teacher Centre had left – Emmeline gave them a party and good advice but on separate days – teaching remained the most likely career choice, especially for less well-off girls, as a result of the system which gave bursaries for a year of full-time education followed by a student-teacher year of part-time work before training college or immediate school employment. Meeting with other headmistresses in 1916 Emmeline discussed their common misgivings. On the whole they agreed that because of its lack of continuity the student-teacher year was 'wasted and even had an adverse effect on a girl's character and education', and that they learnt little by an intermittent struggle with a wide curriculum.[4] In 1921 the bursary system was ended and the number of student-teachers fell steadily as training colleges increasingly recruited directly from secondary-school leavers, more in number now as LEA schools grew.

Girls needed bursaries less as the free place system took effect after it was introduced in 1907. Some local authorities had long given scholarships to a few promising children, usually only until they reached 14 or 16, but free place regulations provided for school life, to 18 or 19 if desired; since they might be funded either by the local authority or by the governing body out of school funds LEA scholarships counted if extended to school life, and in popular parlance free places were often called scholarships too. Three other provisos were important: first, to receive maximum grant to support its rate aid a school must award free 25 per cent of its places (calculated on the previous year's intake); second, Governors might (but need not) impose a test in English and arithmetic only when choosing recipients; and, third, all recipients must have spent the two previous years at a public elementary school.

The last condition seemed unjust to some headmistresses, especially in the case of girls. Some parents of children in the many smaller private schools were no better off than some who used the elementary schools, and many, like Emmeline's own, discriminated between sons and daughters in their early education. So, usually unwittingly, they debarred their daughters from the free secondary education their sons might win, while their incomes were too low to enable fee-paying places. With fewer schools for girls anyway, they had fewer chances: in 1907 there were 262 secondary schools for girls on the Grant List (with statutory free places) against 344 for boys and 237 mixed; in 1921 there were 450 for girls, 462 for boys, and 331 mixed. But the regulation remained in place.

A stern letter from the Board of Education reached the Nuneaton High School Governors towards the end of 1910. Their numbers were rising but their free place proportion was not keeping pace, for the Governors relied on the scholarships awarded by the town's Higher Education Committee and the County's Education Committee to fill these. As the school enlarged the Governors must select some candidates themselves and waive fees for them, and though they protested that the English and arithmetic tests they devised failed to disclose any of adequate standard in 1911, the Board stood firm. In 1912 the Governors changed policy and authorised Emmeline to fill up the number of free places beyond those supplied by LEA scholarships, and apparently she was left free to use her own methods in exercising a power of considerable significance. In 1917 she backed an AHM proposal that free places should be awarded for 'proof of mental capacity and physical fitness without reference to actual attainment', for potential not past achievement, and she seems early to have distrusted the evidence of written test papers alone. Later she consistently argued for more weight to be given to head teachers' reports on candidates and to interviews with the children, and she never showed any lack of confidence in her ability to uncover potential, at least when she knew the elementary teachers well enough to assess their point of view on candidates.

The majority of Emmeline's pupils, free or paying, came from elementary schools, 91 of the 134 girls in 1911. Secondary headmistresses were to continue to criticise the superficial, unsystematised, inaccurate foundation laid by many private schools to the disadvantage of their pupils, but ex-pupils of elementary schools also faced adjustments when they arrived at such schools as the High School at the age of 11 or 12. Generalisations are rash, but certainly many were used to large classes, sometimes exceeding the official maximum of 60, and therefore to a different, more impersonal relationship with their teacher than in a form whose maximum was 30. Accustomed to a stress on numeracy, now they found literacy at the heart; used to being 'instructed', to memorising and being drilled, now they found they were expected to enquire and to think for themselves: the idea that 'the child, not a subject, is taught' was a favourite maxim of girls' headmistresses. Discipline was conceived differently, as moral suasion without the use of force. Girls might be chastened with impositions, or deprivation of some privilege or pleasure, or be reported to the headmistress for her chiding, and in serious cases discussions with parents took place, but corporal punishment seems to have been virtually unknown, and altogether unknown in Emmeline's schools, though few boys' schools had yet followed the example of University College School in abandoning the cane, and in elementary schools it remained a potential weapon for many years. The presence of privately-educated girls helped these adjustments, just as they themselves were helped to a broader experience and often sounder work habits.

Some heads did not share the happy optimism of others that social prejudice might thus be broken down. In 1915, for example, Emmeline received a letter from Beatrice Mulliner, putting 'a few facts before you'. Miss Mulliner explained she was on a body newly formed for the purpose of establishing a new school on Headington Hill, Oxford, for 'the daughters of professional men out of refined homes'. 'These children are a very needy class,' she assured Emmeline. 'This war will necessitate their earning their own living – and there are next to no schools anywhere for them', a claim she justified with the comment: 'The very grave results of mixing elementary children with these others are beginning to be recognised.' She wanted Emmeline, with her 'great capabilities' and her 'shepherding and motherly instinct', as headmistress. Perhaps Beatrice Mulliner was unaware that Emmeline's own brothers were 'elementary children'. The offer was not taken up.

Elementary schools were not all of a muchness, as the Birmingham headmistresses had pointed out to the Bryce Commission when Emmeline was a girl in Handsworth. Some were affected when LEAs replaced the old School Boards, as in rural Warwickshire where Bolton King was using his Teachers' Consultative Committee and working on syllabus revision and building improvements, and in many places as waves of new ideas about 'play' and 'activity' and 'freedom' washed through the minds of teachers. The Board of Education's 1904 revisions to their regulations for elementary schools were generally seen as liberalising, and one of the most influential of the many books on education to condemn passively-received instruction in repressive environments was written by an ex-HM Chief Inspector, Edmond Holmes, in *What is and what might be* (1911). Such waves of ideas, however, might break on the rocks of large class sizes – free activity is hardly possible for 60 children with one teacher – or, in the worst cases, of the apathy of malnourished children, as Leah Manning found during the work in Cambridge schools that drove her on the Labour road to Parliament.[5]

Occasionally Emmeline shared in Warwickshire efforts. On a Saturday afternoon in 1912, for instance, she invited the North Warwickshire members of the NUT (the elementary teachers' union) to hold their meeting at Nuneaton High School, and after their discussion of such perennial business as aspersions cast on their 'socialistic' tendencies, the General Secretary's salary and their own low pay rates, 'Miss Tanner expressed her pleasure at meeting members and delivered an address on the teaching of historical perspective'.[6] She described her charts, outlined a syllabus for children aged nine to thirteen, and pressed for teaching of political processes with mock elections and debates – the very stuff, that is, to extend the popular participation in the political process feared by those who deplored 'socialistic' tendencies. Her words were kindly received, except for a hollow laugh at her ideal of five half-hour lessons weekly, and questions on illustrations and the use of drama showed how the wind of change blew. An ample tea, served by High School mistresses, was also well received.

But the High School entrant believed to have the most advantages was she who had been brought up in the school's ways. Local journalists, shown round in May, had been sentimentally touched by rooms 'arranged for Kindergarten teaching, the furniture adapted to the miniature sizes of the prospective pupils', in a corner of the new building with a separate entrance and cloakrooms, but contentions had raged over the planned preparatory department. Most of the GPDST high schools had junior schools, as did the proprietary Sherborne, the endowed Bedford High School and others, following the example of Cheltenham Ladies' College, and headmistresses liked such departments: they could rely on the essential grounding provided there, and they felt the presence of younger children enhanced the community or family model. The Board of Education paid no grants for junior schools but admitted that 'The education of the Secondary School may ... be advantageously begun at an age much below twelve, and in fact by means of Kindergarten and Preparatory Departments, is often made to cover education from its earliest stages'.[7] Such an admission recognised implicitly that elementary and secondary education differed qualitatively as well as in age groups handled.

At Nuneaton, however, disputes arose over the junior department apparently because it was planned to admit boys aged six to nine as well as girls. In April 1910, in what Bolton King called 'very warm proceedings', argument broke out, inflamed by other disputes over staffing policy, the caretakers' duties (and to whom they were answerable), equipment, the school's library, and possibly more. Emmeline went home 'depressed', she said, thinking that 'some of [my] cherished plans were never to materialise'. But next morning brought reassurance from Bolton King:

Thinking things over I don't think they are as bad as they seemed and I fancy good will come out of today's very warm proceedings. The difficult people are in a small minority and they saw it. I think they are only three or four – and the others realise that they must take a strong line. I walked to the station with one of the Nuneaton Governors: his language would hardly bear repetition but he was almost ready to knock down the next Governor who goes agin you.

I have practically no doubt but that the Preparatory Department will come out all right. It will no doubt take longer to make some of them see that you must reign inside the School, but I have no more doubt but that when any particular point comes before the Governors the big majority will be on your side ... One very bright spot in the position is [the Clerk to the Governors] Mr Clay's common sense and independence and wish to do the right thing.

May I make two or three suggestions? 1. Keep out of the controversies yourself as far as you can and for the sake of the School let others do the fighting. 2. Take Mr Clay into your confidence. 3.

Assume that you are mistress of the Giddins, but if they make trouble tell Mr Clay and let him deal with them ... Next term will be the difficult one, so you must make it a law not to overwork. This is horribly pedagogical, but that's my way.

So the Junior School did not open until September but among the first nine pupils were three little boys. All were under the command of Emma Stevinson, lured from Sherborne by Emmeline to fashion a modern model. For teaching reading a modified 'Dale' method was used, the elements of number were learnt by manipulating various objects and constructive exercises in measuring and cutting and modelling in cardboard, and hand-eye-brain dexterity were developed by clay-modelling, brush-drawing and other handwork: Emma Stevinson's first book, published in 1916 with illustrations by the art mistress Betty Glaisyer, was on *Handwork and social history*. Speech and language skills were trained by stories, including some from history and geography.

On such principles, which spread especially in the junior departments of girls' secondary schools, were based most of those urged for wider use by educational reformers of the next fifty years, and not by coincidence for here the secondary schools tried to lead the system, to show what could be done, as Emma Stevinson's own career illustrated. In 1919 she left Nuneaton's now thriving junior school of 101 children 'to take charge of the training of the Nursery School teachers and be responsible for the children from five to eight years old at Miss Margaret McMillan's Open Air Camp at Deptford,' Emmeline told the school.[8] 'This work is of such national importance that we could only be proud' – the words 'of national importance' tended to appear when Emmeline was excited. The wide-ranging socialist and educational concerns of Margaret McMillan had first been evident in Bradford in the 1890s but by 1919 had focused on child welfare work through nursery schools for the under-privileged; the character and functions of the 'camp school' were explained in Emma Stevinson's *The Open-Air Nursery School* in 1923. When the Rachel McMillan Training College for nursery school teachers was opened in 1930 she was appointed its Principal. Her move from the preparatory age group to nursery-age children also shows the fundamental importance educationists more and more attached to the earliest stages of experience. But after her departure from Nuneaton her chief assistant there mourned that her successor 'has swept Miss Stevinson completely out of the Preparatory, and the "home feeling" is quickly vanishing'.

Emma Stevinson shared Emmeline's house in Nuneaton, and together in the summer of 1911 they travelled to Normandy. It was Emmeline's longest holiday for two years, the whole of August: from Falaise she went on alone to meet Mai Guilloux and explore Granville, Coutances and Avranches, before a week with Mai in Fougères in 'terrific' heat. Grist for the mill of two school talks was supplied by the Bayeux Tapestry in Rouen, and by the slides she obtained ('though the stupid lantern refused to work to the end'), as well as by 'her personal adventures, some of which were distinctly amusing to us, if not to her at the time'.[9]

So the girls whose parents had applauded the notion of the 'good daughter' on the Opening Day absorbed also the image of the independent professional woman in authority over them. At the same time Emmeline's sisters were discovering other possibilities for women of their time, and two found marriage to lead in curiously opposed directions. Beatrice, like Emmeline, remained single, having established a satisfactorily full diary of private nursing, studded with maternity work and varied by attendance on expatriates in Paris or invalids cruising the Mediterranean.

By 1909 Eva had left home and found a job in London with an advertising agency, and had also found, as she informed her employer, that a single woman could hardly live respectably in London on what he paid her. Her pay rose but she had measured the discrepancy between the profits and her salary, and soon enough she left that job to set up her own business, handling publicity, programmes and advertising, often for charitable functions but acquiring also some theatrical introductions. The husband on whom she decided at about the same time also came of a Bath family, and brought a mother who lived with the couple for the rest of her life, remembered only for her headaches. Mervyn Reeves was something of an aesthete, it is said, a neat, even dapper man with an interest in poetry and art that, though genuine, seemed to his wife's more critical relations ineffectual and paltering.

He kept Eva's loyalty, to him and to his interests as she defined them, but though to the world at large she had acquired the status and greater social freedom allowed to a married woman she not only retained the management of her business, continuing to trade as 'A. Eva Tanner', but she was known in her office as 'Miss Tanner' – though Mervyn himself worked there under her. From the business point of view she was undoubtedly successful. They had no children.

Their wedding took place in Bath at the New Church in Henry Street at the end of December 1909, with a reception in the library, scene of so many tea-meetings, and her father punctiliously paid the ten-shilling fee for lighting and cleaning, as he did again for Winifred's wedding the following June. Had Win not obstinately withstood her mother, the first occasion would have been a double wedding and the expenses for catering and entertainment reduced but for once she refused to be upstaged by Eva. After several refusals she had finally agreed to marry the farmer Edwin Gauntlett, brother of Emmeline's friend Annie at the Lowes' school, but Win certainly thought this a sacrifice of independence, even from the day of her engagement in 1909 when Nettie insisted she leave her business office to learn household management at home before she gained her own.

Win clutched at the shreds of her sense of selfhood, saying desperately to Edwin: 'You know I could never have meat in the house, or cook it?' 'I love you more than meat,' he answered, though as well aware as she how unusual vegetarianism was for a Wiltshire farmer. But clinging to views widely considered eccentric was Win's only permanent gesture of rebellion and her husband was already a long-standing teetotaller. So from June 1910 she, a townbred woman, had to adapt to the different social structure of Little Bedwyn, a tiny village near the Berkshire border of Wiltshire, cut off from the amusements, freedoms and even the New Church of Bath and Bristol, in a house built for Edwin and herself all too close to her husband's alarming half-uncle and partner at the Manor.

Moreover, Win was markedly upset to discover a baby would arrive hardly more than nine months from her wedding; Edwin endured her reproaches and Nettie reminded her of her duty. As she accepted her lot and her duty and in all five children she also discovered a gift for creating a home all-comers found comfortable, unfussy and welcoming, one which came to provide a haven often taken for granted by her sisters and which furnished one of the images underlying the positive associations Emmeline brought to the word 'family', as in a nostalgic later reference to 'the friendly *family* sort of feeling we had in the early days at Nuneaton at our functions'. That Emmeline had spent only her first sixteen years in her own family's home and at others was a visitor perhaps encouraged idealisation.

She saw too how from this home base Winifred fought down her trepidation at local prominence, aided by the wartime development of Women's Institutes, and by such organisations as the Mothers' Union, with the structure these provided for non-party grass-roots practical action and public service, especially in connection with sanitation, nutrition, infant welfare and housing – the 'basis of citizenship', as the National Federation of Women's Institutes remarked in its first *Handbook* (1921).

So each sister interpreted her circumstances differently, within the existing social umbrella. The umbrella, however, was neither universally comfortable nor impervious, and part of the headmistress's role was to establish the model for the 'good citizen' of Lilian Faithfull's ideal, to set an example of community activism and public responsibility.

Chapter 10
'Finding out what it means'

Later Emmeline herself was in demand as a speaker at school ceremonies. In the first surviving address to a school other than her own she urged the girls before her to be 'intellectually honest – first, not to pass over a thing you don't understand without finding out what it means ... and secondly, by never accepting an opinion because someone else has given it to you but learn to find out as much as possible of both sides of the question, and then try to decide.' She added, 'I don't want you to accept these things because I say them ...' The girls were not to be manipulated or coerced by others; it is a step towards her concept of inner freedom.

So she explored ways to make the girls of Nuneaton High School aware of the worlds beyond their school and homes. An early experiment was her report of a visit she made in January 1912 to Spitalfields, one of the poorest districts in London and one of the most overcrowded with, for example, a four-storey tenement block of forty-eight rooms housing 240 people according to the 1911 Census, and the object of one of the urban missions Emmeline had encountered at Sherborne through the social work of Kathleen Moore's sister.

Now she met the local organiser, the Rector of Spitalfields, and became friendly with the warden of a night refuge for girls of 11 and over 'who are not able', as Emmeline put it, 'to sleep decently at home'.[1] With the warden, Miss Young, she toured 'one or two of the alleys and streets' near to 'the Nest' in Brushfield Street, to be shocked at 'slovenly women who stood gossiping outside their houses, their garments gaping and half coming off, their hair disreputably untidy and themselves dirty, leaning against the sides of doors with their arms folded'. She visited a family living in a single room and went on to the Soup Kitchen to see not only the 'enormous coppers, such as one uses for boiling clothes in' for the soup, but also the rooms where a Girls' Club was held and where girls from the Nest refuge might go for 'singing, gymnastic and dressmaking classes, and social evenings'. At the Nest itself she inspected dormitories of single beds, each with a 'pretty warm-looking rug over the bed-clothes, and there are little strips of carpet between the beds ... very clean, fresh and cheerful-looking'. This piecemeal social-rescue operation was designed to maintain family ties in that girls were encouraged to eat at home and spend there what free time they had from school or work.

Evidently Emmeline was then inclined to cast social problems in personal terms, for she noted instances where she ascribed the girls' neediness to others' self-indulgence: 'K., a child of eleven, lived with a very bad drunken mother and came to the Nest with an old coarse sacking skirt and blouse and two odd shoes as her entire stock of clothing ... A. and H., two sisters [whose] mother had ruined three good homes through drink and the man said he could not get another.' Such were the terms in which she appealed to the girls of Nuneaton High School, inciting them to adopt the Nest as a particular object of social service, construed as collecting and sewing clothing and raising money by sales of work and the like. It was an appeal directed to humanitarian sympathy with victims, an appeal that ignored or transcended sectarian divisions whether religious or political.

Here the school's interest in the Nest contrasted with the ideals of university settlements and to some extent of boys' public-school missions, for these were centred on sharing and mutual learning, not on the relationship of benefactor and beneficiary enforced by Nuneaton's physical distance from Spitalfields and the schoolgirls' immaturity. Of the principles that characterised Toynbee Hall, however, Emmeline could have heard from Bolton King, who had become the first secretary of its founding committee in 1884, his last year at Oxford, and until 1892 had lived at the settlement in Whitechapel. When Jowett, Master of Balliol, had taxed its leader, Canon Barnett, with taking Bolton King, 'the best history man of his year', away from academic life Barnett had replied he would 'show him how to *make* history', for at Toynbee Hall working-class leaders were invited to lecture and reading groups and classes were organised in an effort toward social unity.[2] In 1916 these principles of sharing were explained to the High School girls when Emmeline asked the Warden of the Birmingham Women's Settlement to speak, and added the Settlements's needs to the school's charity list. Some Labour leaders, however, saw such settlements as evading the real problems and causes of poverty, papering over cracks which ought to be exposed and destructive to working-class solidarity.

Possibly Emmeline's arm's-length strategy with the Nest was due in part to her experience of the coal strike in Nuneaton, and a recognition of how delicately the local shape of things must be presented to her pupils. Just before she first investigated the Spitalfields Mission, and after the summer of 1911 when the Home Secretary, Winston Churchill, had called in armed troops to quell riots in Llanelli and Liverpool (the outcome of transport workers' support for striking dockers), the Miners' Federation called for a national coal strike to force the adoption of a minimum wage. Miners in Nuneaton stopped work.

Only a few High School girls were directly involved on either side, and they are reported to have kept quiet at school, but an account in the school magazine cautiously skirted the rights and wrongs: 'Vague tales of minimum wage reached us, of right and wrong expressed in various terms, vague tales of suffering'; most girls noticed more immediately the shortage of coal for home fires, the late and delayed coal-fuelled trains, 'the crowds of idle men playing football in the field opposite the school, the loafers watching us at hockey, and prompted by the demon of mischief defacing our goal-posts'.[3]

Adults observed suffering: the winter brought hunger to miners' families but where feelings ran high aid to strikers was politically fraught. Undoubtedly much discussion took place behind the scenes before each form constructed a collection box for school donations so that from the school premises they might provide 'nourishing soup and half a loaf of bread to 250 starving folk in Nuneaton', though on only two occasions when the end of the strike was in sight in March 1912. Staff handled distribution in the evenings, and the fact of intervention in a local dispute between capital and labour was muffled in the manner: a Governor with local knowledge of Poor Law and other welfare work selected needy families, not all those of miners, and tickets were allocated for a dole according to family size with the emphasis on women and children.

So for this effort, as for the Nest, the school's attention was directed to victims and the need for relief, neither case encouraging complacency about the condition of England, neither accentuating economic analysis. The argument of human kindness to those in need was seen as politically neutral and widely applicable, and probably it was also more fundamental to Emmeline than ideologies of any kind other than the Christianity of the Good Samaritan; her choice of it argues her reluctance to use school as an instrument of social policy or as the vehicle of political propaganda. To her peers among the headmistresses, however, she presented socio-political issues more bluntly: 'Does the man who cannot find work enjoy personal freedom even though he has political freedom and the right to vote?' she asked in 1939, 'when,' as she said, 'democracy is being so brutally challenged ... May the rise of the totalitarian states be due in part to social failure in those democratic states where a capitalist system has tended to produce extremes of wealth and poverty?'

As an individual citizen of Nuneaton, and as she became familiar with the town, Emmeline recognised an unsatisfied demand for something other than charity and crisis aid. The miners' unified action in itself demonstrated a kindling of co-operative desire, and the torch to light it was ready to hand in the forms Emmeline most readily appreciated, of association and self-help and education, in the Workers' Educational Association (WEA).

The history of the WEA has often been told, of how it grew from Albert Mansbridge's desire that ordinary working people like himself might 'lift themselves up through higher knowledge to higher works and higher pleasures, which, if responded to, will inevitably bring about right and sound action upon municipal, national and imperial affairs', through comprehensive spare-time lectures and classes, discussion groups, excursions;[4] of how the students won the support of the universities' extension workers and from 1907 grants from the Board of Education and some local authorities but preserved intact their co-operative member-run organisation; of how, too, men like R. H. Tawney, intellectual and Christian Socialist, undertook to tutor two- or three-year courses of classes demanding regular essay work, and set university standards.

By 1914 179 local branches were at work with 11,430 individual members and 2500 affiliated societies, especially trade union branches and local co-operative societies, and among the most enthusiastic were the miners of North Staffordshire – Tawney's first tutorial classes were held at Longton there. Staffordshire borders Warwickshire; Emmeline was familiar with university extension work and was interested in the growth of such locally based groups as those of the Historical Association; and Emmeline became one of the inaugurators and early props of the Nuneaton WEA branch.

The branch secretary remembered the 'early and trying years of its existence' when he credited a large measure of its success by 1919 to Emmeline's 'consistent sympathy and support' but it was an addition to, not a substitution for, her other work. So, for example, one Wednesday in January 1914 when she arrived at Nuneaton station at 7.20 pm after a delayed journey home from Italy she had to

rush off to a WEA Council meeting which had been postponed on purpose for me, and did not get back till 10.30. I went through *piles* of correspondence and retired to bed at 1.30, very weary. I didn't attempt to unpack any but necessary things until Saturday. I had parents and people all day Thursday and then had my address and lessons to prepare for Friday. At 11.00 [on Thursday] I could stay up no longer, so I set the alarm for 4.45 am and went to bed. I got half a day's work done before school, and ...

Even Bolton King, whose heart warmed to such educational and co-operative initiatives as the WEA, was by 1916 anxious about the stress entailed by this and other irons Emmeline had in the fire:

Next you ought to accept Mr Bourne's invitation and go off for next weekend (you see Mrs Melly has been telling tales). Never mind the WEA. It would be a very tiring business, so you should avoid it on that ground alone. I know how you feel about it, but it is far and away more important that you should take care of yourself.

Nor when securely established did the branch need her so, and to recognise the time to step down was a significant lesson. But the WEA left its footprints in Emmeline's snow. It helped to open her to the points of view guiding Mansbridge and Tawney when she sat with both on the Board of Education's Consultative Committee in the 1920s; it sharpened her own belief that preferable to either totally open competition or a fully state-run system might be an associative, sharing, co-operative organisation; and probably through his WEA Presidency she came to meet and admire the Rev. William Temple, though she might have encountered him also as headmaster of Repton School from 1910 to 1914. She asked him to speak at Nuneaton High School in 1915, a choice demanding great tact and discrimination for the first wartime Commemoration service. He preached love.

For her trip to Italy in early 1914 Emmeline may have profited from the expertise on cheap travel Bolton King had gained from his organisation of mass tours on a shoestring for the 'Toynbee Travellers' Club' in the 1880s. At least she was well enough informed to apply in advance through the Italian Embassy and the Foreign Office for a free gallery permit and to locate 'about the cheapest English *pension* in Florence'. Her trip lasted just under three weeks, starting the day after Christmas 1913 with two days of travel each way and a break at Milan. She enjoyed every day of it.

There were the hillsides 'with cypresses and olives, and also a beautiful willow of which the stems are a rich reddish colour', the snowy Apennines beyond, and nearer 'masses of maidenhair fern ... still flourishing in grottoes and rocks while the icicles hang all around them', and the views of Fiesole from her bedroom window. There were the towers and red roofs of Florence itself, and the richly red trappings of the horses and mules, hung with bells, drawing the carts, and the 'earthenware or copper bowls with handles filled with hot ashes' carried by Italians in winter cold, and candles held in tri-cornered cones after dark. A train-ride away from Florence she found the walled town of Prato, many-towered and filled with the hammering of copper pans, cans and pitchers, where everyone stared after her and she concluded 'that, the Italians being a small race, they are not used to seeing women of my elephantine proportions! I was wearing my big blue coat', and fending off young men who begged to show her 'the city'.

Italy was cheap for the English:

It is astonishing how pleased [the guides] are with their pennies and twopences where in England one would never give less than 6d. Of course they live cheaply, but they are shockingly underpaid ... The boots here is a married man and he gets his food and 10 lire a month (i.e. 8/-). His wife is a housemaid at the next *pension* ... he makes something by tips but not a great deal because people stay here for a good long time and they generally come for economy's sake.

There Kathleen Moore joined her, replete with cramming of Italian language and art history: 'I could never have learnt so much or enjoyed so much if she hadn't been there to show and explain it all.' Most of her time Emmeline devoted not to the interest of the exotically foreign but to the Renaissance art her own *Renaissance and the Reformation* had placed as the 'best expression of the Renaissance spirit in Italy', central to the development of European culture. The trip was a way for Emmeline to claim an inheritance, for herself and to hand on to the girls of Nuneaton High School, and 'I long to buy photographs and photographs (especially in colour), but alas, the means are lacking' – Nettie, vicariously enjoying, sent ten shillings to pay for twenty-five large photographs.

The more recent Italy also had its symbolic value, reinforcing beliefs in progress by means of its struggle for national unity and independence from foreign tyrannies. Garibaldi had been a hero of Emmeline's youth and Mazzini's idealism fed the current in British liberal and socialist principle that elevated collective work and association above the unregulated free market.

Thus ... men have organised political society, some *solely* on respect for the rights of the individual, forgetting altogether the educational mission of society, others *solely* upon social rights, sacrificing the liberty and action of the individual. And France, after her great revolution, and England conspicuously have taught us how the first system leads only to inequality and oppression of the many; Communism, if ever it could become established fact, would show us among other things how the second condemns society to petrifaction by depriving us of all mobility and faculty of progress.

So too with the economic system, Mazzini continues, where 'unlimited freedom of competition ... has given us all the evils of anarchy' yet the 'monopoly of all the productive forces of the State to the Government ... would lead to immobility and all the evils of tyranny'.[5] For private morality he draws the lesson that 'It is not enough not to do harm; you must do good to your brothers', discovering 'the good' through constant interaction between the individual conscience and the progressively developing general conscience of Humanity, the common sense of good.

Of course Mazzini was not the sole nor even the greatest influence on the many versions of similar ideas current in the 1900s, but he was sufficiently detached (he wrote for Italians in the 1850s) to stand for the broad view, and there is no evidence Emmeline committed herself to any single 'party line' here. But such principles make sense, first, of her concurrent efforts towards reform and respect for tradition, though not the status quo of contemporary England, and, secondly, of her enthusiasm both for associations (professional and other) and for the unique value of the individual. Thirdly, they may explain how she could immerse herself in the task of transmitting to English schoolgirls a 'high' canon of European culture, and including them in it.

Such principles were much in the air she breathed, too, for example in the WEA. Its historian, Mary Stocks, detected in the WEA founders 'a widespread belief that the great heritage of human culture, its art, drama, music, literature and scholarship, should be shared by all', and that apparent apathy towards it resulted from the blunting of minds and feelings in harsh environments, and she found this belief was shared by the founders of Toynbee Hall, by F. D. Maurice and F. J. Furnivall of the Working Men's College, by university extension workers, and by the grass-roots workers of the Co-operative Movement. Of Mansbridge, in particular, Mary Stocks writes that 'it was part of his religion to bring to others that more abundant life which he himself found good'.[6] Emmeline's sympathy for such ideas may be taken as representative of many leading headmistresses of this time.

A drive towards the centre, humanity's common voice, may help account too for the step Emmeline took in November 1913. On the 15th she was confirmed into the Church of England, having resigned her membership of the Bath Society of the New Church. Her choice of the non-parochial St Paul's Cathedral for her confirmation recalls how the headmistress of Truro

High School in 1884 made the same choice, identifying the Cathedral as 'the heart of *working* London' and 'a manifestation of the Holy Church throughout the world', above local particularity.[7] Emmeline's sister Beatrice attended the ceremony, and probably Eva, for they went back to Eva's Herne Hill flat for tea. She was not, in any case, the first of her family to step outside the church of her youth. Herbert's pacific protest at the time of the Boer War had led him then to withdraw his application for adult membership, and since his marriage he had been drawn increasingly to the Society of Friends, to be by 1913 a regular attender at Quaker meetings. But probably more significant for Emmeline in relieving any feelings of disloyalty was her mother's defection.

In about 1911 an inner-ear disease had afflicted Nettie, causing dizziness, ringing in the ears, and loss of balance – 'I had another of my tumbles', Emmeline would sometimes hear. At a time when Christian Science's impact in the Bath and Bristol area was the greater for the hot controversies it aroused, Nettie was drawn to the advice of a Christian Science practitioner, and her condition improved markedly. In gratitude, she said, she turned to the teachings of Mary Baker Eddy, her ardour was aroused, and she resigned from the New Church to pursue the new faith, in many tenets not so very different.

If Sam felt any conflict of loyalties he apparently preserved an outward calm. He continued his active work in the New Church and he maintained equanimity when Nettie read aloud from *Science and Health*, eager to share its enlightenment, particularly the emphasis on Eternal Mind. She intensely admired this work, sending sheets of quotation to Emmeline, strengthening advice like 'Let the perfect model be present in your thoughts instead of the demoralised opposite', though not to the neglect of the New Testament, aided by a 'beautiful little Temple edition ... Not being in verses it is just like a book to read.'

Emmeline herself had been studying the Bible more systematically for some years, and especially since she had taken on responsibility for much of the Scripture teaching at Nuneaton. Though normal, religious education was not compulsory and if provided had legally to be kept on a broad basis of Christianity, of Bible study and historical development, impelling Emmeline to search for the central threads and to read widely. She had many Swedenborgian friends and continued to pay her dues to the Bath Society until her resignation but the occasions she could attend their services were few. Regularly she could and did worship in the local Anglican parish church, and there she encountered some of the wide range of possibility for vigorous debate a national church could permit, evident by 1913 at recent conferences. More than any sect it might be seen as potentially representative of British religious feeling. In short, the Church of England was a religious heartland Emmeline could enter on her own terms.

Some of the questions that formed in her mind she discussed with Lilian Lowe, now Mrs Eadie, on her regular visits to Scotland, and with the New

Church minister Cunnington Goldsack, and almost certainly she raised worrying issues with others, perhaps including her father. Some such worries are indicated by Goldsack's response to her confirmation:

... I believe you know me well enough to understand that I have the utmost sympathy with you in your long struggle, and although deeply deploring your attachment to what I consider an outworn ecclesiasticism, I trust you will find spiritual comfort and help and fellowship that will be eternally good. I will not attempt a controversy by letter – neither of us has time – but allow me to correct you on two points. 1. It would be better to say the Last Judgment *began* in 1757. 2. The Scripture reference about it does not refer to 'this revelation of Swedenborg', though it is true that the writings of Swedenborg refer to what is written in the Scriptures. There is an important distinction here.

What has astonished me is that you who are an expert in History, thoroughly versed in the story of the French Revolution, cannot recognise that in the middle of the 18th century some mighty change swept over the world – a New Age dawned then, and every country, family and soul since then has enjoyed increasing freedom and progress. Is there any better, or more reasonable, an explanation than that the L[ast] J[udgment] took place and cleared the world of spirits? I cannot conceive of one. Certainly the Church of England has immensely changed in the last 150 years...

However, you have followed your conscience, not hastily but calmly and prayerfully, and I trust the time will come when you will realise the 'Internal Conjunction' that will lift your whole interest above externals. We belong to the One True Invisible Church, if we are earnest disciples in our several spheres, and that *is* the great thing after all.

Whatever influenced Emmeline the decision was hers alone. The Lowes and the Eadies were regretful but dignified, appreciating her feeling of isolation and agreeing that 'One fundamental law is that man should act in freedom according to reason', in Andrew Eadie's words. They remained her friends.

Intellectual pressures and the desire to belong do not necessarily exclude arguments from professional advancement. How convenient was this conscientious move? The answer is, probably, only a little. Swedenborgianism had not obstructed Emmeline at Sherborne, under the keenest of Evangelical Anglicans, nor hindered her appointment to an LEA school, and her subsequent schools had no exclusive or explicit Church connections. Certainly Emmeline was now qualified to join the Council of Lady Margaret Hall, Oxford, on to which she was asked before 1919 when the college still required its Fellows to be members of the Church of England; and she may have avoided informal prejudices elsewhere. Largely that was a matter of intangibles and social stigmata, and Emmeline's habit in the face of these was to rely on her compelling physical presence, to which there is ample testimony. No woman who could walk into an expensive London restaurant, in the evening and where she was unknown, with a brace of schoolgirls in tow, and be greeted by waiters rushing to offer the best table could be considered to lack charisma.

The spring of 1914 saw plans for extension, literal and metaphorical. The sixth and fifth forms were taken to Coventry to hear Henry Irving lecture on *Hamlet*, and some attended university extension lectures in Nuneaton on the Puritan Revolution. Extensions in bricks and mortar were authorised by the County Council in January, since 217 girls now crowded the school, its Chairman proving 'awfully sensible, practical and nice' in Emmeline's eyes, but 'Nothing will be ready till Sept. 1915!' She saw her Halifax friend Jessie Appleyard off on the long voyage to Southern Africa to work with her brother developing Rhodesian farmlands, and from Beatrice, adventuring on the Mediterranean on a trip to Port Said with a patient, came a souvenir sheaf of photographs of SS *Orama*, nearly 19,000 tons of prim luxury. In a scribbled note Bee remarked that at Toulon she had seen 'a good many men-of-war' in the harbour, their searchlights showing at night, but recorded no ominous pangs.

Emmeline herself was putting another iron in the fire. At the earliest possible moment, as a headmistress-elect, she had joined the Association of Head Mistresses (AHM), an organisation which could justly claim to be the heartbeat of secondary headmistresses though it had cost some heart-searching for the original members, the heads of endowed and proprietary schools, to decide in 1906 that heads of LEA schools should be admitted, 'to maintain that, however different our schools and our spheres may be, our work is the same', as Sara Burstall of Manchester High School said – a reference not only to the LEA schools' inferior social status but to their management by organs of popular government.[8]

The parallel associations of headmasters, by contrast, bifurcated into the Head Masters' Conference (HMC) for heads of the heterogeneous non-profit-making group described as 'public schools', and the Incorporated Association of Head Masters (IAHM) for the rest, such as Basset Holman of Nuneaton Grammar School. Like the AHM, neither group accepted as members heads of privately-owned schools, who linked, if at all, in the Private Schools Association. But the headmistresses' voice was unified and representative, particularly as their numbers rose, from 230 in 1906 to double that by 1912 and over 700 by 1944, nor were their interests vested in conservative practices; change for them was not a risk but meant liberty and growth.

At first, as an ordinary member, Emmeline merely attended the annual conference to hear and discuss papers presented, and debate and vote on resolutions formulated by the Executive Committee. Her first real forum she developed from a meeting of a handful of headmistresses from Warwickshire, Staffordshire, Leicestershire, Worcestershire, Shropshire – the central swathe of the Midlands – at King Edward's High School,

Birmingham, on 7 March 1914. This was the birth of the Midlands
Association of Head Mistresses (MAHM).

In the chair, and probably a prime mover, was the head of King Edward's,
Edith Major, a witty Ulsterwoman who 'dispensed with all the awe and
attributes of majesty which invested Miss Buss, Miss Beale, and even her
own predecessor at King Edward's', and closed the door to her room only
when someone was with her.[9] Her style was never pompous, in private
letters or in public speeches, and when Emmeline asked her to present the
prizes at Nuneaton in 1917 she invested with comic and concrete image
and anecdote the headmistresses' standard message that the woman of the
future 'must have accuracy, concentration, respect for detail, the art of
working smoothly with all sorts of people, a deliberate judgment, and a
standard of conduct so high that she can never possibly attain to it'.[10]
Emmeline's invitation itself, and Edith Major's acceptance, signify the respect
and liking that readily sprang up between them, predating the MAHM, the
sort of informal friendship that headmistresses sought in this forum to turn
to productive account.

A certain air of cosy enjoyment permeates minutes of early MAHM
meetings, despite the constitutional formalities that enabled local
associations to affiliate to the national AHM and a local president
automatically to become a member of the AHM Executive Committee. Only
occasionally did the MAHM discuss local matters; it was more a testbed for
ideas and opinions, an intimate group who could support each other and
break down the isolation of a head in her lonely eminence within her school,
a primary vent for frustrations and problems as well as a source of advice
from the experienced. The most genteel of trade unions, it rarely fought
managements over pay or conditions, and papers given at the first full
meeting of the MAHM in October 1914 on 'Treatment of backward children
by psychoanalysis' and 'The educational value of handwork' were typical.

Never did Emmeline show any doubt of the value of such debate-and-
support groups, nor any inclination to the path of the lonely eccentric. She
preferred the centre to the margins, the common voice to the cry in the
wilderness. On the one hand this entailed compromise and a certain
pragmatism, so that at the end of her life 'I confess with shame that, while
realising the need for reform [of the curriculum], I have not in all these
years succeeded in putting any of these plans into full effect.' On the other
hand, association checked some eccentric and self-deluding errors in the
individual and gave strength to a common cause, and Emmeline trusted
enough in such fraternal co-operation as a mode of production to join in
inaugurating several more such bodies later for specialist educational
purposes and to link these and others by joint committees.

Through such channels as the AHM and MAHM, the personal
accessibility of many such as Edith Major, the previous experience of many
LEA heads like Emmeline, and the handbooks produced (such as *Public
schools for girls*, by an AHM group in 1911), the endowed and proprietary

pioneers of girls' secondary education colonised the new LEA territory, spread their gospel that education is more than instruction, and set the standards. Examinations policy provides a constant and typical example. In Emmeline's youth, examinations had been a useful tool to establish parity with boys, to set standards and do battle with sloppy vagueness, but now the problem could be re-cast in gender-free terms. A report in 1911 from the Board of Education's Consultative Committee lent weight to objections that existing written tests put 'a premium on the power of merely reproducing other people's ideas ... rewarding evanescent forms of knowledge ... favouring a somewhat passive type of mind', and so on, and found that potential good could best be achieved by 'stringent regulations as to their number, the age at which they are taken, and their general character'.[11]

Many headmistresses were also moving in this direction. Undoubtedly Emmeline took satisfaction in the rewards materialising at Nuneaton by 1912, the twelve Senior Cambridge passes, some with distinction, the awards gained in Coventry Church Council Divinity examinations and by Kindergarten student-teachers in the Froebel examinations, just as she did in the prizes won at the County exhibition at Rugby for art, geography and handwork, and at the Warwickshire Natural History Society's Exhibition. With such keen interest, indeed, had she awaited the results of the examinations for County Scholarships for university that Bolton King sent highly confidential advance notes: 'History marks still not in but unless Elsie comes down very much on them she is a safe Major. Examiner quite eloquent on her English work', and next day, 'Quite safe. Top in both subjects.' A major scholarship from Warwickshire County Council was worth £50 annually for three years, and enabled Elsie Garratt to do what her headmistress had not, to study for a degree in residence at Royal Holloway College, London University.

Yet Emmeline felt increasingly that to measure achievements only by examinations was fallacious. Noticeable in the 1912 list is the absence of external examinations for the 14- and 15-year-olds, the Preliminary and Junior Locals familiar in her Halifax days. Now even promising girls were not entered. In 1907 the AHM President, Florence Gadesden, had attacked in her presidential address the 'too often useless loading of the memory with facts [and] the reaction from the best kind of study which may follow', the stress to mind and body, and 'the agony of disappointment which accompanies so-called failure'.[12] Too many examining bodies produced too many examinations, often with different and incompatible syllabuses, some to measure attainment at various ages, some to assess potential for various universities or professional trainings, some for awarding various scholarships – and rarely did they consult teachers on what forms of test might reasonably be applied.

The Board of Education, university and other examining bodies, and the professional teachers' associations engaged from 1912 in complicated rituals of negotiation, until in 1917 the Board planted the School Certificate in a cleared jungle by establishing the Secondary Schools Examinations Council (SSEC) to co-ordinate standards set by the then seven local university examining bodies for an examination to be taken at about the age of 16. The under-16s were spared external tests, and the School Certificate was to be awarded to candidates with at least five simultaneous passes in papers taken from each of three subject groups ('English subjects', 'Languages', 'Mathematics and Science'). A fourth group for music, art, domestic and craft subjects was available but passes in these papers did not count towards the vital five. For pupils of about 18 a Higher Certificate of more specialised subject groups at a higher level was offered. So the fruit was single in form and nationally recognised, even if sour patches were later tasted.

Such is the context in which Emmeline devoted much time to discussions with fellow-headmistresses, on Board Circular 849 on secondary school examinations (1914), on qualifying examinations for teacher training candidates (in 1915), on Birmingham University's Matriculation papers (in 1916), on the form proposed for Higher Certificate (in 1917), and conferred with Oxford women tutors on entrance and scholarship examinations for their colleges (also in 1917). From the autumn of 1917 she became chairman of the AHM examinations sub-committee, and the next year started work on a standard 'school record' format, at the same time discussing allotment of free places and scholarships for entrants to secondary schools. One way or another examinations were rarely off the agenda of the AHM.

When Edith Major stepped down from her allotted two years as President of the MAHM, in October 1916, Emmeline was unanimously elected to replace her, and in the 'special circumstances' her term was extended until February 1919. *Ex officio* she sat also on the Executive Committee of the AHM, and there remained with only brief statutory breaks, for nearly thirty years, regularly attending also meetings of several sub-committees, for educational administration, scholarships, salaries and pensions, and so on. There she learnt much. From AHM members of over thirty other organisations (later more), ranging from physical training colleges to the Victoria League, from the Froebel Union to the Women's Indian Study Association, came diverse reports and news, all external links supporting the AHM's claims to be no narrow interest group.

But the 'special circumstances' which prolonged Emmeline's presidency of the MAHM were of course a euphemism. By the summer of 1914 some travellers were returning hastily from Europe. At the beginning of the summer holidays Emmeline went to Oxford for a course of Biblical study, staying at Somerville, for the first two weeks of August. Among the 150 or so other participants were several old friends, including Kathleen Moore, but Janet Lowe cancelled at the last moment because 'she considers that, under the circumstances, she ought not to spend the money. People are not likely to want doll's clothes [her trade] in any quantity for some time.' Nor while writing notes on 'Life in the Christian communities in the first and second centuries' were Emmeline's thoughts wholly on the past:

Society cannot live on strength of other people's doings [she scribbled]. It has to do them for itself, therefore modern work after crash (if it comes) to go out and see visions and dream dreams and build up again on more righteous basis. The vision is never accurate but it is the Kingdom of God and those who help on movement and further the progress [are] the true children of the Kingdom.

On 3 August the UK government said it would stand by the Treaty of London (1839) guaranteeing Belgian neutrality; on the 4th Germany invaded Belgium. That morning Beatrice, on holiday in Weston-super-Mare with her sister Win and her two children, received a letter from the War Office telling her to hold herself 'in readiness' as a member of Queen Alexandra's Imperial Military Nursing Service (Reserve); she returned at once to London and in the evening

I had a wire saying that orders had been posted ... That night I was one of the immense crowd standing silently outside Buckingham Palace waiting to know if we were at war with Germany. At last the news came, in a few minutes the King and Queen and Prince of Wales appeared on the balcony. There was a tremendous cheer and we all sang the National Anthem, and then we went quietly home. In the morning my orders arrived, telling me to report in Preston, Lancashire, on the 8th.

At first Bee kept a diary. She detailed the 'very long list of uniform and equipment to be obtained' before the 8th, for which a cheque for £20 was supplied by the War Office, with a railway warrant to Preston. Eva trudged round London with her to help buy

three cotton frocks and a mess dress. All grey with a small cape. The regular sisters had scarlet ones but ours only had scarlet bands round them. The dresses just cleared the ground. With this we wore little grey bonnets tied with ribbon bows under the chin. There were aprons, caps, etc. to be bought ... The equipment consisted of a cabin trunk, kit-bag containing camp-bed, bath, basin and chair, also a Beatrice stove and ordinary iron. We also had a large hold-all, travelling rug and sleeping bag. The £20 covered everything but the sleeping bag.

Emmeline took a day off from Oxford to visit, disturbed to find Bee had only £2/10/- in money. 'I think she will need money very much if she is abroad, and she does not get paid at all till she comes back' – an arrangement soon rescinded – so 'I tried to get her some gold just before she started because English gold is taken anywhere', but in the end she could manage only £5 and a cheque for her sister. Basic pay for the QAIMNS was £40 a year, plus a field allowance of £54/15/-, £65 to cover board and washing, and £5 for uniform. In 1914 the Service itself numbered about 300 trained nurses, and the Reserve about 200 more, all British citizens aged at least 25 and fully trained in a civil hospital.

Preston was crowded with military, and in Wakes Week shops were closed, but Bee and the forty-two nurses with her stayed only a few days before leaving 'for an unknown destination' – Southampton Docks. There their commanding officer had 'forgotten to say there were forty-three nurses in his unit', and the coal barge commandeered for transport had no space for them so 'we were left sitting on our luggage on the quay' until beds could be found, some in a 'Home for Mothers' and some in the Bugle Inn – 'no better than a doss-house,' said Bee, disgusted at dirty sheets, remains of bread and onions, and false hair on the chest-of-drawers. The next evening, the 15th, the nurses embarked on the *Cestrian* with the 11th Hussars, the 5th Dragoons and 1000 horses but neither food nor water; they sailed at 5.00 am and reached Le Havre at 4.00 pm. 'The quays were lined with people cheering and shouting "*Vive l'Angleterre*" and singing "Rule Britannia"' but Bee was more consoled by the bread and cheese a friendly steward found as they waited until 10.00 pm to disembark. A walk of two miles over 'very rough ground' took them to the railway, and Rouen was achieved at 4.00 am, No 3 Hospital having been established about three miles outside the city.

Within ten days Bee noted: 'No 7 Hospital at Amiens has been sent back and the Germans seem to be advancing rapidly. The West Kent have been almost wiped out while bathing', and two days later, as wounded men poured into Rouen, she was told to pack. They were in retreat, through Le Mans to St Nazaire where a hospital had been set up in a large boys' school 'in a great muddle. I had a ward with eighteen beds which all filled up. No serious cases but nasty shrapnel wounds in the feet, hands and arms chiefly. With great difficulty I managed to get a bucket and get them all a wash and a meal, and dressed their wounds.' By now most of her own equipment had been lost in the retreat.

Chapter 11
The Great War

So at Nuneaton High School the autumn term of 1914 started with Britain at war. At St Nazaire Bee slept in her ward, since there was nowhere else, and by 25 September

> We have had such a rush for the last ten days ... Two thousand patients passed through the hospital in three days. They come into the ward one day and are sent to England the next to make room for a fresh lot. My patients nearly all have two or three wounds and now they are in a very bad state when they get down here. There have been five or six cases of tetanus ... The horrors of war are appalling.

Tents were set up for the medical staff but work slackened, with enteric becoming a serious problem, and on 7 October Bee had time to write to Emmeline:

> Thank you very much for your letter and also for your share of the parcel which I received yesterday ... Will you please tell all the mistresses how much we appreciate it. I think sweets, chocolates and smokes are the best things to send. The men enjoy all of them. They smoke all the time they have the materials to do so, much to my annoyance as it means the beds are never clean. Matches, cigarette ends and ashes all over the place! But I suppose they must be spoilt a bit ...
>
> I do not think we need any tea at present. We get very good ration tea, and I don't think our private supplies are used yet. We are fairly well fed, but have to pay for all extras such as fruit, butter, milk, etc. I am very tired of thick bread and jam for tea which is all we get. Jam is issued to us ad lib...
>
> I had hoped the war might be over before the winter, but I fear there is no chance of that. Matters do not seem to progress at all. I should be most interested in seeing your lecture on the causes of the war. Our news is very scrappy and I have not time to study the papers very minutely.

Of Emmeline's opening address at the start of term no record remains, but the lecture she delivered a few days later was coolly analytical. She attributed the war chiefly to Prussian militarism, itself encouraged by past success with the sword and their 'quite natural' wish to extend the German coastline to the North Sea. Into this she fitted the actions of Austria after the 'pretext' of the Archduke Ferdinand's murder, the mobilisation of Russia as protector of the Balkan Slavs, and the alliance system linking Russia to France. 'All Germany's hopes now lay in getting to Paris before either France or Russia had properly mobilised. To pass through Belgium was the most direct and easiest way.' She showed the girls maps, with the help of the ever-useful lantern.

She talked in a general atmosphere of high emotion. Bolton King had prepared a leaflet, *Why are we at war?*, for circulation to schools, a leaflet defending the British entry to war but including the words 'Many of the wars we have fought have not been righteous, we have sometimes done unjust and cruel things' – to the fury of some of his Education Committee.[1] At their next meeting angry words darted. He had the misfortune to be a historian, replied Bolton King, and refused to change what he had written. On to stormy waters he threw an offer to resign. Swiftly the Committee moved to the next agenda item; he stayed Director of Education.

The war seemed all around them rapidly. As January began 3,000 Dublin Fusiliers and Royal Irish Fusiliers, brought back from India, were billeted on local families in Nuneaton. Emmeline wrote to her father:

They arrived on Monday, and already last night there were large numbers drunk. Many were helped home but twelve had to be taken to the police station. The YMCA have taken over the matter of recreation rooms, and they have sent down a man – a Mr White who tells me he was at Bath for eleven years – to superintend. I regret to say they don't allow cards and they have no billiard table, but they are thankful for dominoes and draughts, and we are getting those and things of that sort, and they are arranging for concerts, etc. for the men. I think it is a pity that they always bring some sermonising into even their concerts. It will be a pity to choke any of the men off by making it too religious on every occasion, I think ...

We really want some people to go out and fetch the men in, but it is a difficult thing for a woman to do ... Of course, these men are all regulars, and therefore more difficult than the territorials and men of the new army.

The same week Emmeline herself received a black-bordered letter from India, written before Christmas. Amrit Kaur's brother, a medical officer, had been killed in action on 23 November. 'It is too cruel – this accursed war,' wrote Amrit, and she quoted, bitterly, his last letter: 'Pray for the sorrowing, pray for the wounded and dying – pray for a speedy ending to this war, and pray for me that I may be able to perform to the utmost the task that lies before me.' Through January Amrit wrote again and again to Emmeline, as details came to light of how Indarjit had set up a dressing-station as 57th Wilde's (Indian) Rifles went into action at Ypres, how it was shelled and no search party could be sent till 4 December, how his remains were recovered and buried in Béthune Cemetery. Indarjit Singh, twice mentioned in despatches, was awarded a posthumous MC even as his sister poured out her grief, her anxiety for her 'crushed' parents and for another brother serving against the Germans in East Africa, and the 'doubts and criticisms [which] seem to have taken the place of what I once would have had no difficulty in believing'. 'I suppose one's grief is always selfish, for we mourn the loss we have suffered,' wrote Amrit, but Emmeline's letters comforted her, she said.

Dead in the first months too was the brother of the young wife Fred Tanner had married in 1912, the pretty daughter of old friends in Bath. For the next four years Emmeline needed to give much out-of-school time to what would later be called counselling, and to practical and personal support among the families of High School girls. 'Every school is a community,' later wrote Frances Gray, High Mistress of St Paul's Girls' School, 'and the sorrow that came swift and sudden to many was in some degree shared by all. The common efforts to do what was possible in relief of suffering was the best the schools could do in bearing the individual sorrows of their members', and, as for many headmistresses of her generation, Emmeline's faith in the school-as-community was confirmed in her mind.[2]

At their October meeting in 1914 the Governors of Nuneaton High School authorised Emmeline to admit 'daughters of Belgian refugees of the better class', and the first girl entered after Christmas, followed by another a few months later.[3] Remote as the Midlands town seemed from ports of refugee entry, several families arrived, Emmeline helping to prepare one house while her domestic science classes cooked soups, pies and cakes for new arrivals. This was a temporary emergency among the school's war efforts.

By cancelling their Christmas party they saved the money to add to the Belgian Relief Fund, now joining the usual payments to Dr Barnardo's Homes and for material for delaine fabric for fourth-formers to sew blouses for girls in the Nest, while others knitted 'comforts' for the 7th Battalion of the Royal Warwickshires and for the British and Foreign Sailors Society. They made cots and clothes for soldiers' families and bound books for the YMCA Naval Camp; two years into the war Emmeline had visions of 'the conversion of our piece of waste land into a useful kitchen garden', and she was 'sure that the girls will be keen to do all they can to help Miss Stephens [the games mistress] who has volunteered to be responsible' for mowing the playing field without a man.[4] The regular charity lists now ranged from funds for Disabled Soldiers' Workshops to milk for sick children in the Birmingham Women's Settlement, as well as long-standing commitments, and the school society called the French Circle had adopted a Belgian refugee child in Calais and a French prisoner of war, sending him letters and parcels every fortnight.

In the adult world women deployed their 'almost limitless adaptability' with an efficiency the AHM remarked with approval, in extractive and constructive industries, in transport and other services. In 1916 the AHM annual conference concentrated minds on 'The war and openings for girls and women', and, finding severe labour shortages in clerical and commercial work and in agriculture, resolved 'to convince the many healthy, strong young women who were still satisfied to be half-time War Supply Depot or VAD workers that they should give their whole time', leaving part-time work to the married and elderly.[5] Already the headmistresses operated a register, in effect an agency, for girls with shorthand-typing or skill at figure-work, and needs of war rather than needs of women stimulated schools (including Nuneaton) to add commercial classes to the curriculum, luke-warm though they were about encroaching on technical training fields.

'How schoolgirls can be useful in the present crisis' was the first paper Emmeline delivered for discussion by the MAHM in October 1914. When Frances Gray, with the AHM President, formed the Girls' Patriotic Union of Secondary Schools to disseminate information and co-ordinate supplies for their girls' war efforts, Nuneaton High School joined immediately. The thrust was always towards humanitarian relief, and not till 1916 did Emmeline yield to pressure to celebrate Empire Day, on 24 May, by more than flying the Union Flag from the school's flagpole (both Governors' gifts) and singing the National Anthem at Prayers.

Then, though, she elaborated a joint ceremony with Basset Holman, headmaster of the Grammar School, and ninety-nine Grammar School boys marched up the High School's gravel path, headed by cadets with shining buttons, and into the hall for the National Anthem. Emmeline read a passage from Ecclesiasticus in praise of famous men, all sang Kipling's 'Recessional', and Holman delivered an address stressing the symbolic co-operation of old grammar school and new high school, of the 'men and women of the coming generation', their 'responsibilities and their duties'. Some of the Empire 'was discovered, some bought', he told them, and some 'acquired by right of conquest, some of it by methods we do not now seek to defend ... Reparation, if due, must be made to the future. To the future and not to the past are we responsible for the present.' Then he outlined the nature of the 'trust' inherited and the need for 'duty and self-sacrifice', and for patriotism understood as 'something in the nature of *family* feeling extending in an ever-widening circle to embrace the town, the country, the Empire'.[6]

Relations between Holman and Emmeline seem to have been cordial since her arrival in Nuneaton, punctuated by invitations to meet interesting guests, discussions of history teaching, and exchange of information and ideas. Clearly she felt comfortable with his views before she agreed to this first joint ceremony, and although her under-rehearsed girls mangled their share of the final march past the flag, official hopes of more common activities were exchanged. It is difficult to find, however, that much materialised.

The propaganda aimed at the girls was consistent. At Commemoration two months later the Oxford Extension lecturer Hudson Shaw told them the purpose of education was not to obtain wealth or power or any personal or national aggrandisement but to pursue an ideal of unselfish service for others; the next year the future Archbishop Fisher looked to 'a league of nations working together, with common ideals, for the good of the whole and the protection of the weak'.[7] Emmeline chose her speakers with care. But her own was the continuing voice. 'My thoughts go back so often to war days at Nuneaton,' one ex-pupil wrote to an ex-staff member in December 1939, 'and how Miss Tanner guided our opinions during the last war. I can still see her as if it were yesterday, the morning we heard of the Battle of Jutland, and how she spoke to us that morning.'

But one perhaps under-estimated effect of the message of self-sacrificing service was, by the end of the war, to have assigned to men the moral high ground. Women had worked and endured, but the extremes of suffering and heroism belonged, in large measure, to men. Nor had women to face a choice between conscription and conscientious objection, and they felt morally diminished. So much is already perceptible in the address Mrs Graham Balfour, the lively wife of Staffordshire's Director of Education, gave for the Nuneaton prize-giving of 1916. First she exulted in a 'revolution in the lives and opportunities of women' and in their competence in manifold new roles, in munitions, in driving, on the railways. Then she said that 'we must be ready to lay down our tools and give up our places when the owners of those places, in many cases, come back and claim them'; that 'whereas some said, "A woman's place is at home" and others, "No profession should be closed to women", we now see what is a woman's true place ... wherever she is wanted.' She was wanted, Mrs Balfour argued, above all in elementary teaching, 'one of the biggest and most important things that anyone can find to do'.[8]

The life of the school, and the life for which girls were preparing, had to remain Emmeline's most immediate care. But the several thousand girls in the care of members of the AHM were, as the headmistresses well knew, a minority of their age group, and the more these girls might gain from their secondary education the wider the crevasse between them and the others, it was feared. Anecdotal evidence suggests a number of girls were prevented from taking up free places by parental opposition; they feared deracination as well as the cost of unprovided textbooks and the expense of maintaining a daughter old enough to earn for herself. Wartime conditions aggravated the unease of some heads at the divide and, feeling guilty about neglect of the majority, they detected forms of moral neglect suffered by that majority:

It is awful to think of the girls in Nuneaton [wrote Emmeline in January 1915]. I have never seen a place where they hang about the streets at night as they do here, and there are already very few girls of the factory class who are married without being obliged to if their children are to be legitimate. It is a very bad place for soldiers to come to, and although it will be largely the girls' fault it is also they who will suffer more than the men who will be going away in six weeks or so. I felt absolutely ashamed of girls I saw in the town this morning trying to attract the attention of one set of soldiers after another. They were unsuccessful for some time, but at last they got some to speak to them. Their looks were horrible! I do wish we could devise some ways of getting at girls of that sort.

Within a few days Emmeline, with several other women including Hallie Melly and Canon Deed's wife, had started a Club for Working Girls, with forty joining in the first ten days and sixty attending the Saturday social evenings. Edward Melly lent premises in Newdegate Place, until by 1917 more space was needed for the eighty-six girls now 'on the books ... many of whom are munition workers'; they paid subscriptions (about 5/- a year) but most of the funding came from donations, with High School staff and several Tanners figuring in the donor lists.

A report for 1916-17 lists classes in gymnastics, dancing, singing, needlework, and elocution, and ten years later one girl, by then married to a soldier, wrote shyly to tell Emmeline how 'My friends have often said how they like my cakes and pastries, and whenever one happens to speak of them my mind goes back to the little room at the Club where we were taught, and many other things we were taught there are still with me.' In view of Emmeline's aversion to 'sermonising' by the YMCA, no doubt she tried *not* to 'choke any ... off by making it too religious on every occasion'. The Girls' Club co-ordinated the new skills taught in dramatic performances, such as the war masque *The Empire's Honour* that the girls gave in 1916, raising £14/3/- thereby, soon after Emmeline, as Hon. Secretary, felt they were sufficiently established to join the Federation of Working Girls' Clubs and asked its Secretary to visit Nuneaton and provide suggestions and guidance.

Emmeline's revealing remark about 'some ways to get at girls' points to an ambiguity. Clubs of the Working Girls' kind encouraged skill-learning, self-respect, independence and aspiration, yet the teacher-pupil or benefactor-beneficiary relationship was maintained, a pattern of deference, and Emmeline for one deliberately wished to inculcate specific values and forms of behaviour. Parallels exist in pre-war legislation, for example for the probation of offenders which provided moral watchdogs rather than simple penalties, for regulation of child employment and child beggars, and the closer monitoring of child health through the new School Medical Service. But membership of any youth organisation was voluntary, and, as a secular and pacific crusade rather than a strategy of the thought police, was limited to its capacity to please its clientele – in competition with the new 'picture-houses' in Nuneaton.

To the generation of Emmeline's parents, alcohol had been the key symbol of degradation, and by 1915 Lloyd George was trying to combat the drunkenness he saw as a threat to the war effort with stricter licensing laws, higher duties, and the King's example of patriotic abstinence. Unsurprisingly, by 1917 Nettie was recycling for domestic correspondence unused petition forms calling for the prohibition of import, manufacture and sale of alcoholic beverages for the duration of the war. But permanent regulation was a worrying notion to many Liberals. The girls now producing munitions in Nuneaton saw their freedom to change jobs curtailed, and the Defence of the Realm Acts massively extended the potential scope of government. The militarism Emmeline had spotlighted as a cause of war now seemed to be engulfing Britain.

Conscription became the focus of such anxieties. The idea was mooted in

1915, and the reality introduced in January 1916 for unmarried men, and from May for all men aged 18 to 41. The Home Secretary, Sir John Simon, resigned in protest, and joined the Royal Flying Corps. More immediate to Emmeline than the stand of her old Sunday School teacher's son was that of her brother Herbert. He had long supported various peace movements and opposed the Dreadnought accumulation of pre-war days, and his habit was to think through issues to reach immovable decisions. Early in the war he had explained his pacifist conviction to his firm's directors. Now he prepared the necessary evidence for appeal as a conscientious objector; to his chagrin it was never used, his job being categorised as essential. Still eager to witness for peace, Herbert joined active campaigning efforts, with mass meetings in Glasgow, where he then lived, friendships with leading pacifists, and a place on a committee monitoring the workings of the local appeals tribunal, who 'appeared to have no understanding of the C.O.'s outlook,' he said contemptuously, though he himself had little sympathy with the International Socialists whose pacifism was political and not a total rejection of violence.[9]

The First World War brought into much clearer focus the complexities of commitment to peace, the possible inspirations of pacifism, and the need to choose between absolute refusal to participate in the war-making society (well-nigh impossible as the economy geared itself to the war effort) or some form of accommodation. Even medical relief work, such as that of the Friends' Ambulance Unit, could be construed as aiding the war to continue, and certainly the production that was Herbert's daily bread might be so interpretable. But conscription to fight seemed the key issue. Of the 16,500 applicants for conscientious objection nationwide, about 80 per cent received some exemption but only 350 (mostly Quakers) unconditionally, and the conditions could be semi-military or punitive. Herbert helped organise appeals from the local tribunal to the Sheriff's Court in Glasgow, and gave help and succour to families of men imprisoned, and shelter to at least one ill-treated objector, though he and Agatha found the young man's self-pity tiresome and his privations less than those of men in the trenches. They set him to some child-care, for their three small children 'did not permit a brooding silence for long'.[10]

Herbert, in short, did not keep a low profile for his views, despite the general unpopularity of his stand; even his sister Winifred, timidly defending conscientious objectors in Wiltshire on the score that 'they think it right', found herself cold-shouldered though she did not claim to share their belief. Of Emmeline's other brothers, Fred suffered only boredom as a lieutenant inspecting factories on war contract work, but Arthur was assigned to active service. Though 'Arthur was picked out to be drafted to Salonica, Mesopotamia or Egypt, but he escaped that time, I don't know how', as Nettie told Emmeline in mid-1916, he was soon sent to France, where Private Tanner could receive regular family parcels and occasionally meet his sister Beatrice. Fortunately he never required her professional services. Bee was stationed at Tréport for most of 1915, then transferred to No 4 General Hospital at Camiers. About twice a year she was allowed a week or so's leave, always spending a day or two with Emmeline at Nuneaton, and she was probably the frankest of Emmeline's informants on conditions on the Western Front.

The spring of 1916 was disturbed, however, by non-war-related problems of weather. Early mildness in Nuneaton was followed by snow and high winds, uprooting telegraph poles and disrupting trains for several days, in examination time. Only sixty of the 260 girls could struggle to school, to be sent to the hall for hot milk and Bovril while their clothes and shoes were dried; then most were sent home again. The Congregational Christian Endeavour Room in Rugby was hastily booked for the twenty-three girls there, and piles of paper, blotting paper and examination questions were manhandled by one of the staff and a couple of girls on a rare train. 'I am a gainer,' remarked Bolton King, 'as most of the schools are closed and no one has anything to write about and they can't telephone.' It was one more complication.

The headmistress and the second mistress were showing the strain, Bolton King thought: 'Mrs Melly tells me that Miss Billinger too is thoroughly overworked, and that it is your unwillingness to put things on her that is partly responsible for your tiredness,' he told Emmeline. 'Now, if Miss Billinger is given next term off, could you get a proper substitute for the time? Would you let me know about this and I will pull the strings.' So the summer term of 1916 was granted as paid sick leave to Margaret Billinger, and to replace her Emmeline, characteristically enough, demonstrated what she considered proper attitudes by selecting a woman married to a German, though British herself.

Anti-German feeling had reached a new height with the sinking of the *Lusitania* in May 1915, but even earlier Beatrice Mulliner had faced pressure to rid Sherborne's Aldhelmsted house of its long-standing housekeeper. Even as she mourned her brother's death, Amrit Kaur could still be 'glad to hear ... that Miss von Bissing was going to be kept on at Sherborne. It must be a very trying time for her – anyone less likely to be a spy it is difficult to imagine.' Nettie would have sympathised, staunchly finding and visiting 'two poor lonely German ladies. I think they have enough money, they have two maids (who won't leave them) and one huge and one small dog. Turkeys, four. They feel isolated from humanity.'

The trusted consciences of her mother and Herbert protected Emmeline, even as she sought the agreed national centre of religion and the common voice of her profession, from confusing momentary outbursts of *vox populi* with *vox Dei*. Surviving records of occasional lectures she delivered on the course of the war, conversely, do not hint that she made a virtue of dissent. Atrocity stories are suppressed altogether but not those of self-sacrificing heroism, and the wisdom of the strategy outlined is no more criticised than it is praised.

From March 1916 lighting restrictions prevented evening lectures, and the faithful audience of Old Girls was lost, but expeditions were positively stimulated. Girls taken to a performance of the wartime evergreen *Henry V* in Leicester did not allow their regret at the cutting of the voices of the common man, Pistol and his friends, to spoil all their pleasure; older girls also attended lectures of 'The British Empire and its problems' and on naval history – outside their syllabuses, unlike Shakespeare, but part of the mind-broadening endeavour of their schooling. School lectures continued to be given in afternoons, with the blinds down for the lantern's sake, but Emmeline's own delivery was becoming a struggle. She lost her voice, her essential teacher's tool.

'Emmie seedy,' observed Bee, home on leave in June, but Bolton King and Hallie Melly had diagnosed overwork months earlier. 'You are not taking care of yourself and others must therefore do it for you!' warned Bolton King. 'We can't afford to let you run down because everything at the school depends on you, and if you are tired things there are bound to suffer.'

Emmeline, it is clear, had still to learn to delegate effectively. That can be seen in her 'rout-round' as the building extensions neared completion in 1915: she returned from a trip to Birmingham to find that

I was badly needed at school to hurry things up. The furniture was coming by road tomorrow but I find the building is nothing like ready to receive it ... I have had here Mr Quick (the architect) – I telephoned to Coventry – and the builder, the decorator, the floor polisher, and the clerk of the works, and have spent many hours in the new part going into many little points and making everyone promise that as much as possibly can be done shall be set to work upon at once ... I have telephoned to Birmingham and stopped the furniture ...

Other complications too she handled herself, having still no secretary. Nearly voiceless in 1916, she consulted a doctor. Mountain air, he said. Best would be Switzerland, but failing that he recommended the Scottish Highlands. Switzerland aroused all Emmeline's longings. She had deliberately chosen the slower train home from Italy in 1914 to see the Alps by daylight; furthermore, if not consciously in her mind, to travel across France for purely private reasons was to assert the primacy of civil life over total war, to refuse to give in to war as a way of life. From Bee's visit in June she knew what she could expect of travelling conditions, and she set to work to obtain the authorisations.

But on 3 July Bee herself noted in her diary: 'Four hundred patients walked in looking so weary and exhausted'; on the 4th: 'Ward full of wounded. Miss S. sent to help'; and on the 5th: 'Very busy'. Then her diary was left blank for days. It was the first week of the Battle of the Somme. In August, Bee was transferred from the hospital at Camiers to Barge A195, to ferry patients to Abbeville at the mouth of the River Somme, for shipment to the UK.

I was not pleased at first [she wrote to Emmeline] as I thought I would rather it had been a train or [Casualty] Clearing Station. But now I feel that I would not have missed it for anything. It is such a totally different experience to anything else. I will try to give you a little idea of the life; it will probably be somewhat disjointed.

Two barges go together drawn by one tug. You will probably have heard at home where we go from and to. The interior of the barge makes a very nice ward with thirty proper beds and lockers in, and a stove at each end. At one end are the lavatories and the Medical Officer's and our cabins. I consider we are very well staffed. There is an M.O. between the two barges. He lives on mine, so feeds with us which adds to my anxieties considerably. He is a married man aged 43, and has been used to doing himself very well, I think. He has sent orders for all sorts of luxuries to Fortnum & Mason's and Harrod's, but they have not yet arrived. We get rations but have to buy eggs, milk, butter, fruit and vegetables at the different villages as we go along. Everything is frightfully dear, and it will be quite impossible to keep it to a franc a day for each, I fear, but I don't intend to worry about that.

There is a Sister and a Staff Nurse to each barge. My Staff Nurse is quite a nice fresh Glasgow girl. I think she will annoy me as little as anyone. Our cabin is 6 ft by 10 ft, with two bunks, one above the other, a small hanging cupboard and a small cupboard with shelves, and a table that lets down on which we all three have to have our meals when patients are on board. At other times we use a corner of the ward. In fine weather, when the hatches can be off, it is all right, but when they can't it is horribly stuffy.

There are three 'Inland Water Traffic' men to run the barge. These are usually recruited from the Broads or somewhere of that sort. Our Corporal is a very nice rugged old thing and looks after our comfort in a most fatherly way. Then there is a Staff Sergeant in charge of the place, a corporal who does night duty, four ward orderlies, a cook, a kitchen boy, and our servant. The latter is an extremely nice youth with a charming voice. He was a draughtsman at Waring's before the war. He calls us with tea, cleans our shoes and room, and tries to give us our meals as nicely as possible. I have never been so well looked after, I think. The orderlies are by no means perfect. They are not at all tidy or methodical but they are very good to the patients, and as they have been on the barges ever since they started it is no good my trying to reform them, so I try not to let it worry me.

We have the patients on board about thirty hours and they are always bad cases as it is the easiest mode of travelling, so then we are pretty busy. One of us stays up till 2.00 am, and the other gets up then, so we are pretty tired by the time we get to our journey's end. We take two days to get up again, though, so we have time to rest then, as we only have to get dressings, etc. ready. Flies have been our great curse, but I suppose they will gradually disappear now. We can only get letters every four or five days which is sad. We sit on the top as much as possible and take constitutionals between the locks.

I had a death on my first voyage. On the whole, though, I am sure there is less worry and strain than running a hospital ward. It is very much nicer to be only two women, too, instead of one of eighty. We hear the guns most of the time, and it seems much more like active service. The cases are heartbreaking sometimes, but it does not do to think of that. What a ghastly, senseless thing war is, to be sure.

Not unnaturally, Bee thought it 'awful waste' for Emmeline to go to Switzerland alone – 'just think how nice it would have been had I been there as well'. But Emmeline was thankful to be, for a space, no longer surrounded by eager eyes and voices, all wanting and needing something. Formalities at the Military Permit Office in London, at Southampton, at Le Havre, took several hours each; she travelled via Paris, with five hours there and a severe headache, and on to Frasnes and another long wait for passport examination, standing in a wooden shed for two and a half hours through the dawn, with further baggage examination at Vallorbes, to reach Lausanne at the start of August.

For the first few days in Glion, 'just under the hill above Territet and Montreux', she did her 'duty letters that ought to have been sent from school', but little else save sleep and gaze at 'beauty everywhere around'. From her balcony the Castle of Chillon could be seen, and the sunsets were miraculous: 'I sat out here and watched it all round the hills to the west of the lake for about an hour and a half. Even the Dent du Midi on the east seemed to have its snows tinged with the pink reflection and all the time the moon was shining over the lake too.' Then she went on to Finhaut in Valais, where she could 'sit under pine trees ... just in sight of Mont Blanc', and was strong enough to climb the Col de la Guelaz and make plans:

I am not going to climb tomorrow but shall walk to Barbaime, the French frontier, and see if it will be possible for me to pass on foot over the frontier next week. If it is, I have a great plan – to pack all my things and send them direct to the Riffelalp, then to set out very early in the morning to climb the Col de Balme, on the opposite side of the valley, and to come down to Argentière, stay the night there and walk the next day to Chamonix, stay one or possibly two nights there, walk part of the way back, then take the train to Martigny, through Finhaut from which I have a ticket, and go on to the Riffelalp next day.

On the 15th, 'Here I am, really at Chamonix!' and a week later, after a two-hour climb from Zermatt with overnight needs in a knapsack on her back, at the Hotel Riffelalp opposite the Matterhorn. Not on such postcards to her mother but privately to Bee Emmeline disclosed that headaches continued to plague her. Her voice seemed to be improving. But of what she thought about on her solitary walks in the mountains she left no record.

In 1940 she was again to seek in such mountain scenery, as near as she could find, some redemption from war for those in her charge.

Emmeline returned to Nuneaton with the school timetable prepared ('several days' work'). Term started smoothly. Then, on 29 November, after a brief illness, the art mistress Betty Glaisyer died; within two months the French mistress Gertrude Storr-Best too fell ill and died, just after her French assistant had been suddenly called home to Angers to care for her sick father. To lose these experienced staff was more than a personal severance and more than a professional difficulty, for many of the girls relied on the stability of school routine in an unstable world. Emmeline hung more Watts reproductions in memory of Betty Glaisyer – 'Love triumphant' and 'Love and life' – and pointed to the 'revelation of the kindness of our friends' in sorrow, as sisters of staff volunteered their services. One was Gertrude Storr-Best's sister-in-law Lucy, equipped with a French degree and able to enthrall her pupils with first-hand descriptions of Russia and lectures on 'European affairs' for what she called the school's 'foreign intelligence department'; at the end of 1917 she greeted the Russian Revolution with something of the hope for liberty and justice that Wordsworth had invested in the French Revolution.

So did Ann Crofts, who came to Nuneaton to replace Margaret Billinger, just appointed headmistress at Lord Digby's School, Sherborne, an old foundation now revived by Mrs Wingfield Digby to provide town girls with the secondary education few could afford at Sherborne School for Girls. If Emmeline's hand was at work here, she was giving herself another staffing problem in the loss of her second mistress and chief English teacher, for Ann Crofts' appointment was at first a temporary stopgap. Emmeline may already have encountered her when, as Ann Hony, she lectured for the WEA in the Swindon and Bristol area in 1911 to 1913, fresh from Lady Margaret Hall, Oxford; her sister Ida ran the WEA Women's Section. Or Emmeline may have met her later, as an assistant at Edgbaston High School, where the MAHM occasionally met and whose headmistress she knew well. Ann's husband John Crofts, an academic, was presently Corporal Crofts, 101st Field Ambulance, stationed in France.

Now their friendship ripened. Ann Crofts was a lively English teacher, championing unorthodox causes from vegetarianism to extreme socialism with wit and fire, and most characteristically remembered skipping from tussock to tussock on a rough fellside, talking gaily, her hands in her pockets throughout, while others panted behind. Her sister, Ida Gandy, turned to idyll their childhood roaming the Wiltshire Downs barefoot to the music of their clerical father's church bells,[11] but Ann's fury at some churchmen's bellicose greeting of war drove her from the Church, though not altogether from religious belief. To the school she brought a dynamic, maverick element that Emmeline valued to keep minds alert and ideas charged, worth the exercise of tact in managing inter-staff relationships.

Attrition of long-standing staff was joined by attrition of supplies as the submarine campaign nearly cut off imports in the winter of 1916-17 before a convoying system was devised. Worse than the handicap to teaching of a paper shortage was the dearth of food, especially wheat. Emmeline was anxious for her parents, telling Nettie:

If I were you I should get a book, *The national food economy handbook for housewives*, 2d, post-free, from 3 Woodstock Street, London W1. Of course, some of the things used are meat and fish, but there are a great many which would do for you. I have only had it today but Miss Lloyd has made 'Oatmeal sausages', p. 22, 'Dainty pudding', p. 27, 'Scotch oatcakes', p. 28, and found them very satisfactory. I have been going without bread or cake for tea, and have had oatmeal scones (very good), oatmeal biscuits and parkin (made with coarse oatmeal and dark treacle).

We are starting a Food Economy Campaign here, but people can't think *broadly* enough in organising it. I was summoned to the first meeting and I told the Mayor I saw no reason why we shouldn't do as well as Keighley if we went the right way to work about it, and I suggested a really strong Food Control Committee for the town, also an immediate meeting with all the food-supplying tradesmen in the town to arouse their interest and sympathy, and get their co-operation, but I couldn't get it done a bit satisfactorily. There is to be a meeting of all women Head Teachers and Domestic Science teachers on Monday afternoon to arrange for an exhibition and lectures, but otherwise the town committee pins its faith on handbills (worth nothing hardly!) and cinema slides.

If I were a woman of leisure I would rouse the whole town to *want* to ration itself and set to work to get in stocks of substitutes, as far as they are available, and have a shop or shops in each district where things could be explained and suggestions and advice be given, but the school needs ... to say nothing of meetings in London, etc.

Emmeline did what she could with lectures, a display at the school of foodstuffs and processes, and a cookery demonstration by Elsie Martin, the domestic science mistress, but at the High School's Commemoration the usual cookery exhibition was cancelled – 'Lord Rhondda knows why' – and the cakes at tea 'were guaranteed to be made from substitutes'.[12] 'I think most day schools did what we did,' said Frances Gray of St Paul's, 'and gave no meat after the rationing of food had begun ... It was not that we could not get enough but we could get so little variety and not enough that was nourishing.'[13] But rationing was not imposed till towards the end of 1917, when ex-pupils from Nuneaton High School helped to organise the local implementation, in elementary schools closed for their teachers to receive 'declarations' and hand out cards for allocations by family size and age, for margarine, tea, lard, cheese, meat and more. The procedure was novel and imperfect; but showed off admirably how a secondary education for girls could develop their ability to assimilate, understand and clearly present complex information, or so some headmistresses claimed.

Tighter black-out regulations dimmed the fun even at Christmas 1917, when the Sixth Form at Nuneaton stoked up a vigorous fire in their common-room hearth to make merry on roasted potatoes, only to be confronted by a Governor. The glow was visible from the road. He lectured the girls on their selfish folly, and they returned to more approved and daylight activities – the new Debating Society or the new school orchestra, for example – but when they collected their meed of certificates and awards that Christmas, Edith Major of King Edward's High School, Birmingham, addressed them in different terms.

She spoke of the good general education to instil accurate knowledge and the craftsman's love of perfection for its own sake, she spoke of the training in 'social membership' and teamwork and thoughtful independent judgement, but she spoke too of subsequent specialised training of whatever 'propensities' a girl might possess, to turn them to useful social account. She hoped that 'the girl who arranged flowers in the morning and paid calls in the afternoon, and the more active but equally useless person who gave herself up to golf and bridge' had disappeared for ever, especially because soon, she pointed out, women would have the parliamentary vote to add to their responsibilities for reconstruction.[14]

Indeed 'reconstruction' had acquired a new meaning and a new Ministry, and high hopes were aroused within the AHM by Lloyd George's imaginative choice of H. A. L. Fisher, scholar and historian, as reconstructive President of the Board of Education to formulate a new Education Bill. Already that year the AHM had sent their 'heartiest congratulations' to Millicent Fawcett 'on the successful culmination of her work for the political enfranchisement of women'; they saw visions and dreamed dreams.[15]

So the future tense was much in evidence in Edith Major's address to the girls of Nuneaton, as it had been when she and Emmeline and their colleagues on the AHM Executive Committee had issued 'Suggestions for the reform of girls' education' in the spring of 1917, and in June had discussed these in conference at St Paul's Girls' School. Some changes were already taking effect.

Chapter 12
Specialised bits of work

The Great War cut Emmeline's life in half, as years count. Once, in a Sherborne debate, she had taken peace for granted as a necessary condition for free personal and social development, but now a positive and passionate revulsion was born, so that twenty years later she could shock a protected generation with 'War is hell!' Now she kept abreast of a spate of pamphlets by H. G. Wells, Sir Edward Grey and others advocating a League of Nations, and the practical Roman-Law-based schemes put forward by Jan Christian Smuts, the South African leader. As she told some Leicester schoolgirls in 1921:

> I do think we are living in one of the great epoch-making ages in the world's history. There have been terrible happenings in the last seven and a half years. The only thing that made it possible for the world to bear them was the hope that they were going to lead to a better age in which there could never be a repetition of such evils and such tragedies ...
> The people of the world as a whole want something better – they want more friendly relationships between the different nations, they want better social conditions for the people within each nation. And if a large enough number of people *want* good things, these things can come.

She added a firm assurance that each, whatever her personal abilities or circumstances, had a 'special bit of work ... set aside for you', and lost to the world if undone or done badly, and in her own school tried to show rather than tell how to answer practical and immediate needs according to a consistent, idealistic outlook. From the snowbound winter of early 1917 a tiny vignette dramatises. In France on 30 January Beatrice, now in charge of No 25 Ambulance Train, noted: 'Arrived at Bray at 3.00 am. First A.T. here. Walked into the village. Ruins everywhere. Loaded from 2.00 to 4.30 pm.'; but in Nuneaton on 6 February, after fresh snowfall, 'Miss Tanner announced that the next day was to be a whole holiday ... girls of all sizes were to be seen gleefully dragging toboggans to the field of action, or hurrying off with merrily rattling skates to the reservoir, canal or pool.'[1]

Not for such trivial gestures of free spirit, however, did the *Journal of Education* in 1920 describe Emmeline as 'well known as a zealous educational reformer'.[2] That reputation was growing in these half-dozen years of the end of war and an unquiet peace, and derived from her laborious and undramatic efforts as President of the MAHM and on the committees of the AHM, Board of Education and others, and from her echo at local level of the principles she enunciated nationally.

As a body the AHM approved the keynote statement of the Education Act (1918) devised by H. A. L. Fisher, that 'children and young persons shall not be debarred from receiving the benefits of any form of education by which they are capable of profiting through inability to pay fees'. The large promise was as yet backed only by permission for LEAs to grant maintenance money to free-place holders in secondary schools but it spoke fair, and in the clause that LEAs should provide for 'progressive development and comprehensive reorganisation' of their area's educational facilities headmistresses detected a welcome expansive drive.

Most of the Act's important clauses were designed for the elementary sector, setting the minimum age for leaving school at 14 with no exemptions, authorising grants for nursery schools for all in need of them, planning 'day continuation' (or part-time) schooling for all under 18, enabling LEAs to grant money for physical recreation, and more. But much shrivelled in the economic frost of the early 1920s, and much disparity remained between the older elementary pupil and her coeval at secondary school. More subtly, the balance of power was shifted towards the Board by the financial lever designed to prise apart the doors of LEA initiative, a system of block government grants of 50 per cent of LEA spending on objects approved by the Board. Regulations issued by the Board were to affect secondary schools far more than any changes made by Fisher's Act.

Three local initiatives, on medical services, staff conditions and leaving scholarships, serve to show the sort of activities – the bread and butter work of headmistresses of this time – that distinguished the fully-fledged professionals from the Mrs Hoares and Miss Pannetts of Emmeline's early life, and that were the tiny but solid work of building the better world foreseen for peace. For through 1918 the war seesawed to its close. Now the Germans surged forward in a massive offensive, to break through defence lines so that Beatrice, at an Étaples base hospital, again and again tersely scribbled 'Air-raid' and dealt with new wounds inflicted on her patients and staff, scornful of some superiors who (she claimed) took refuge in the cellars. Then Ludendorff marked 8 August as a 'black day for the German army' as exhausted men were held and turned – the same day as Fisher's optimistic Education Act was passed into law.[3]

On 11 November Bee could write 'Peace!' in her diary, and two months later she heard she had been awarded the nurses' medal, the Royal Red Cross, given to 279 British nurses in that war; but during the same months influenza piled up casualties to add to the war's own, including in March 1919 Herbert and Agatha's youngest child, six-year-old George. One of Emmeline's duties, as chairman of the AHM Examinations Committee in May 1918, was to write to the various examining bodies asking for influenza problems to be taken into account, and another, as a Tanner daughter, to spend her 1919 Easter holiday caring for her ailing parents, assuring that 'It was lovely to feel I could really be of a little use and not only a visitor.' But at last her Nuneaton Governors finalised arrangements for medical inspections of the High School girls, 'lady doctor' and all, as Emmeline had pressed for years. When doctors charged fees parents often asked advice too late.

Fisher promised the betterment of teachers: one long-felt want of secondary teachers was supplied (for those in grant-earning schools) by the national system of pensions established under the Superannuation Act of 1918, and another, for national pay scales, was gradually hammered out from 1919 through the negotiating machinery of the Burnham Committees. At an MAHM meeting in December 1917 Emmeline had reported on a deputation to Fisher on disablement provisions and pension ages, and at local level she worked on her Governors. So, in early 1919, they urged to the County Council that Warwickshire salary rates were, in their view, 'totally inadequate when compared with neighbouring counties ... the salaries of their mistresses are very much lower than those paid to many of their friends and relatives teaching under other authorities'.[4] At this time graduates at Nuneaton High School were receiving about £165 to £200, and as head of the preparatory department Emma Stevinson was paid £231 in her last year.

To her Governors too Emmeline brought her staff's housing vexations, and what they could they did. A substantial house on four acres close to the school was found and the County Council persuaded to fund its cost of £3,300, and provide £1,200 for repairs and alterations, in the expectation that rent (at first £33 to £45 each) from the ten mistresses housed there might repay the investment, and the school could use the grounds for games. By 1921 the first mistresses could move into the Briars, set up a little committee to run it, and enjoy what HM Inspectors called the 'excellence of the arrangements made for their comfort', principally by Hallie Melly's dedicated efforts.[5] 'Mrs Melly and I worked very hard last Saturday hunting for things for the hostel, but the cost of furniture and of linen is simply appalling!' wrote Emmeline in February 1920, and after another such expedition 'I just feel like a bit of chewed string,' sighed Hallie Melly.

Of course not all of the Governors' generosity was disinterested, but was an investment in teaching quality answering particularly to contemporary disquiet that dingy lives in dingy lodgings bred a narrow, dull, 'spinsterish' crew. Carping at single professional women continued commonplace, assuming new forms as rationales were removed: if not dull in their lives, they were repressed in their sexuality, or if not repressed they must be 'perverted', the word of the inter-war era; they were called petty if happy with classroom work, harridans if they attempted to rise. Clemence Dane's portrayal of manipulative and unscrupulous egoism in *Regiment of women* (1917) expressed and stirred anxieties, and a generation later Ethel Strudwick of St Paul's Girls' School wryly remarked that when flattery or compliment was intended to a schoolmistress most people said that no one would ever take her for a schoolmistress. Emmeline herself cultivated her friends outside school, kept up interests outside school from gardening to politics, and as the war ended begged a sabbatical from October 1919 to February 1920, dreaming of adventure in Sicily. A paid term off for every mistress after seven years' service had been set as an objective by the MAHM in 1917, as a means to revitalise a stagnant mind.

Again she turned to her Governors to support efforts to provide scholarships to help girls go to university and other further education (in scholarship provision girls were notoriously unequal to boys), and in 1917 persuaded Edward and Hallie Melly to endow a leaving scholarship of £40 annually for three years. Soon the Governors *en masse* funded another; but any fixed sum was vulnerable to inflation. Fees at Westfield College, London University, for instance, rose from £90 to £120 a year at this time, and the Nuneaton girl awarded in 1918 a scholarship of £25 a year from the college itself, and who won too a £40 County award, still had a shortfall.

Altogether one is not astonished to find that when in late 1919 representatives of Bedford's Harpur Trust asked Emmeline 'how I got on with my Governing Body' at Nuneaton, 'I was taken by surprise and involuntarily answered, "Oh, but I have an *ideal* Governing Body!" The reply was greeted with a burst of laughter from the whole august and somewhat formidable assembly.' Forgiving and forgetting past irritations sustained Emmeline's positive optimism. Among the AHM's many 'Suggestions for reform' in 1917 had been that each school or group of schools should have its own governing body, including members experienced in secondary and university education, and on the close co-operation of Governors and Headmistress Emmeline continued always to lay much stress.

At times her notion of co-operation seems more than a little one-sided: in a press interview of 1930 she was reported as saying, 'I was allowed to organise Nuneaton High School, which was a county school, as I chose', crediting the LEA's 'sympathetic understanding' in permitting 'a free hand'.[6] But analysis of her activities throughout her career leaves no doubt that she considered a well-composed governing body, with a direct interest in the individual school, pivotal in that school's relations with the outside world – employers, the learned world, and the elected local and national governments – and that 'a free hand' did not always mean 'a high hand' or a deaf ear. Certainly 'as I chose' was broadly acceptable, measured by Nuneaton's steady rise in numbers. The traditions Emmeline honoured, those of the 19th-century pioneer headmistresses, had acquired widespread esteem; and skilful advertisement by the 'window-dressing' (Emmeline's own unashamed sales metaphor) of speech days, school events, the magazine, and the like, identified new 'needs' and persuaded the market of the worth of the goods. Sometimes opposition was eroded by slow and patient pressure, as with the right to purchase school equipment, firmly in Emmeline's hands by 1918, and sometimes she worked within constraints, especially financial constraints which she well understood, by pursuing the maximum achievable rather than an ideal.

In Emmeline's urgency for leaving scholarships can be detected her vision of careers, given form on the one hand by choice unconstrained by cost and on the other by scope for personal powers and advancement, the first harking back to limits imposed on her youth – though she never said so publicly – and the other forward to her expansive aspirations. During and through her headship of Nuneaton High School this vision clarified. With joy she greeted the inauguration of State Scholarships for universities in 1920, 200 of them for the girls and boys of England and Wales, granted by the Board of Education on the results of Higher Certificate and usually covering tuition fees plus about £80 for maintenance. So important were these to hopeful Sixth Formers and their teachers that their suspension, for economy's sake, in 1922 was reversed in 1924, and even in the economic gloom of 1930 the number granted was raised to 300.

But competition remained intense, and the many girls who sought other forms of training did not benefit. 'It is a waste to spoil the ship for a ha'porth of tar,' Emmeline told the parents of Chichester High School in 1931. 'So often, if a girl can get no specific training for her job, she is limited to a blind-alley occupation where she earns money straight away but has little chance of promotion and ... responsible work which will give scope for her powers and satisfaction for her spirit.' Congratulating them for contributing to a scholarship fund she expatiated on careers from dairy farming to factory inspection, from medical services to the retail trades, and wished that Chichester High 'had not one Leaving Scholarship but ten'.

But 'the life of a woman is so seldom exclusively professional', an AHM resolution of 1919 pointed out, and so girls especially needed certain freedoms: in 1919 because 'it is only through freedom that the personality of individuals is so developed that they can render their fullest service to the community', in 1920 because 'the true function of education is to discover the tastes and develop the capacity of the individual pupil'.[7] In both cases the bondages opposed were those of Board of Education regulations. During Emmeline's chairmanship of the AHM Examinations Committee the long campaign for 'Group IV parity' was launched, against the inflexibility of the group system for both the First and Second Examinations (also known as School Certificate and Higher Certificate). The new national examinations, organised by seven university-based examining bodies, had been devised as tests of a 16-year-old's general education and an 18-year-old's more specialised study (see p. 140) and to this end subjects were grouped. Thus to gain a School Certificate a girl must pass five papers taken from each of three groups, one covering English subjects, history and geography, another supplying papers in modern and ancient foreign languages, and the third testing mathematics and science. Tests in 'Group IV' on art and music, domestic and craft subjects, were optional extras with no certificate weight. To gain a Higher Certificate, on the other hand, she must restrict her course of study within an Arts, Sciences or Classics category.

Both the AHM's Examinations Committee and its Education Committee, on which Emmeline also sat, argued, not for the demolition of the structure but for its modification so that for School Certificate a candidate with five passes drawn from any three of the four groups should gain her Certificate – an innocent-sounding plea but one that offered some freedom of choice and placed art and music on a par with languages and science, since 'being of the highest aesthetic value [they] are consequently fundamental subjects of education'.[8] The domestic and craft subjects, it was conceded, needed as yet development on 'more educational lines'. Little sympathy was gained among headmasters, since in many boys' schools art and music were treated as trivial, but the AHM persevered, to win their way in 1937.

Emmeline had acquired more expertise in this field when in the autumn of 1918 she was asked to join the History panel for an investigation ordered by the new Secondary Schools Examinations Council (SSEC) to assess uniformity and comparative techniques between the seven examining bodies. Each examination of each examining body was itself examined and confidential reports compiled; subject reports then generalised on experience of all for publication. Critics saw a lost opportunity for inquiry into principles (such as 'Should examiners have teaching experience?' and the like) but such were not within the investigators' brief. So far as Emmeline was concerned this was the most systematic and comparative analysis she had yet undertaken of examination practices, and it no doubt contributed to her later opinion that

> Far too much stress can be laid on examinations. They ought never to be the be-all and end-all of any part of school life, though they have their part to play in forming some test of knowledge and still more in testing the qualities of perseverance and determination and the power to cope with difficulties and to make intelligent use of knowledge acquired. Yet it would be a poor thing if the aim of all our years of teaching and training were merely the passing of examinations. The danger is that pupils may look at it this way...

Such tests, she believed, assigned value to only a limited part of educational experience. In 1917-18 she chaired an AHM sub-committee working out a School Record format, inspired originally by proposals in 1916 to amend teacher training college requirements for entrants with only one Sixth Form year but eventually, in the draft Record form Emmeline produced, designed for much broader use. Her draft for the girl aged about 17 covered the entire curriculum, including physical and religious education, school offices held and activities participated in, and signalled a wish to recognise the many sides of each individual and the differing strengths between individuals, in kind and degree. Hence she hoped to provide for the girl who did not attempt the rigorously academic Higher Certificate a guarantee of personal value, and clearly, too, she was offering a bait to persuade parents that to stay on at school after the School Certificate was taken was not a waste of time for the non-university girl. The AHM in conference in 1918 approved the draft, but the scheme was largely ignored by the world beyond, though Emmeline herself retained a slightly wistful affection for the Record idea.

For those who did attempt Higher Certificate she also worked at this time, proposing to the AHM conference in 1918 that the examination should be based on subjects, two major, two subsidiary, and not on groups which restricted free choice; again the AHM agreed, and again it was a long slow battle. More immediately she joined in negotiations with individual examining bodies on such matters as syllabuses, and was the headmistresses' regular representative on the annual conference with the Oxford and Cambridge Examinations Board as well as an occasional pleader with others. Thirdly, in 1919, she proposed to the AHM that universities should be asked to accept Higher Certificate as a direct entry channel to an Honours course, by-passing the Intermediate examinations usually imposed after the first year. The Intermediate existed because most universities then accepted as equivalent to Matriculation (i.e. university entry tests) credits on certain School Certificate papers – 'She's got Matric.', ran the cant phrase for this level of School Certificate success – but to 'get Matric.' was by no means adequate for work for a university Honours degree. Heads of schools argued, however, that two years of Sixth Form work could be effectively equivalent to Intermediate work. Discussions were set up between university authorities (themselves increasingly unhappy about immature students) and the Joint Committee of Four Secondary Associations, and progress was made. This body, the Joint Four, formed to represent the AHM, the IAHM (of secondary headmasters) and the two associations for assistant masters and assistant mistresses in secondary schools, was still young and weak, but the ideas of joint action now lodged more firmly in Emmeline's mind.

There was more, Emmeline thought, to a Sixth Form than university candidates, however; to these years, indeed, she attached the greatest importance. That any headmistress has a vested interest in retaining pupils as long as possible was almost the only argument she did not openly adduce although the notion that a more mature stratum was valuable to the school as a whole must be tinged slightly with empire-building. Rather she talked of benefits to the girls and to society as a whole, of how girls might now dig deeper into some individual interests and range over others not encountered in the School Certificate course, of how they might develop co-operative and organisational abilities through school activities and responsibilities, and of how they might be trained in the techniques of thinking clearly and closely. In 1948 she diagnosed an 'age of clap-trap phrases, of second-hand opinions and machine-made ideas', but in 1918 she saw no less need for 'people who can think for themselves and express themselves clearly'. 'Do we want an educated or a matriculated community?' she asked. 'I think this period [of the Sixth Form] is even more important for those who are not going on to a university than for the prospective university candidates', a tiny minority after all.

Anxious to develop her Nuneaton Sixth Form and needing funds, Emmeline grasped at the luscious carrot offered in the provisions for Advanced Courses introduced by the Board of Education into their Regulations for Secondary Schools in 1917. A grant of £400 was dangled before the school providing one or more Advanced Courses for pupils who had passed School Certificate, but such Courses were closely defined. Three were recognised: Science and Mathematics made up one, another grouped Classical languages, literature and ancient history, and the third categorised as 'Modern Studies' two foreign languages with their literature and modern (post-1600) history. Each must last two years, occupied the major part of a pupil's time, and was planned to lead to a university Honours course; and a Course would be recognised by the Board only if it were taken by a 'reasonable number', which turned out to mean at least eight or nine pupils.

In 1918 Emmeline took the precaution of securing her Governors' promise to aid girls with bursaries to stay a second Sixth Form year, and applied for a Modern Studies course to be recognised at Nuneaton High School. The prospective grant enabled a well-qualified History specialist to be brought in, Agnes Nolting, after an interview in a Birmingham tea-shop nearly frustrated as each waited, Emmeline at a table upstairs, the applicant in the store below, before a puzzled Emmeline majestically descended the stairs, beamed a welcome, and they were friends for life.

Yet already she had scented dangers in the Advanced Courses, and at the AHM conference of 1917 opened a discussion of the new regulations. The first risk she then identified was that of rupture, between substantial schools and those with small Sixth Forms who could not guarantee the 'reasonable number' of pupils for a Course to be recognised, and who therefore might dwindle further as university hopefuls were bled away. Sometimes this happened, as in Ipswich where the head of the GPDST school secured her 'reasonable number' by offering scholarships to girls from the municipal school, thinking it 'rather a triumph to get their headmistress to agree'.[9] Second was a danger found real at Nuneaton, that the quorum requirement would bias a school which could support only one Course, because of the strength of teaching provided and because the weight of the Sixth Form would be pulled in one direction and draw the rest of the school with it; at Nuneaton an Inspection in 1922 duly observed that 'the school appears to have been somewhat unduly biased on the literary side at the cost of science'.[10]

A third possible risk was extra stress on girls who attempted to keep up subjects outside the range of their Advanced Course, perhaps in order to attempt university scholarship examinations with incompatible syllabuses. This provoked Emmeline's only recorded quarrel with visiting Inspectors, in June 1923, when a pair visited the school of which she was then headmistress solely in order to inspect the Modern Studies Advanced Course there. Their report evokes an image of Emmeline defending her young like a great mother bird, her gown lending wings as she skirmished out with express opposition to Advanced Courses: she was 'only forced to adopt them through financial pressure,'[11] she said. 'One of her objections was lack of elasticity'; the HMIs were unpersuaded. She 'stated that "Advanced Course girls are all overworked"'; again they disagreed although they conceded one case, 'of a girl who, having done French, German and Greek, was determined to pursue History as a special subject, and for university reasons had to begin Latin. She would also continue at Greek and do a little French and German "to keep them up".'

This girl's letters to Emmeline are indeed fraught with stress, surfacing as religious anxieties; Emmeline provided understanding and helpful books but deeply resented the pressure that made thoughtful questions a misery. She preferred hard work to be generated from within.

Again the mechanisms of the AHM, as pressure group and as negotiator, were called into play, and again the principle at stake was freedom: 'in order to secure complete liberty during the last two years of school life ... when it is of paramount importance to adapt the course of study to the taste and capacity of individuals, the restrictions imposed by the conditions on which Advanced Course grants are made should be removed' ran a conference resolution of 1920.[12] Negotiation won some relaxation, so that English became an alternative to the second foreign language for Modern Studies, for example, and eventually in 1935 the Board of Education accepted the whole argument and replaced Advanced Course grants with capitation grants based on Sixth Form numbers.

The next year, 1921, the AHM broadened its tack in pursuit of flexibility, variety, freedom, and resolved that the Association 'deprecates a too rigid uniformity in the enforcement of regulations ... which would prevent the authorities of schools from doing their best for particular types of pupils'. This responded to promptings, rooted in a governmental economy drive, to make all entry tests selective by intellectual merit. The 1921 AHM conference applauded when Sara Burstall 'deprecated a system of secondary education which was content to limit its provision to the comparatively few by a rigid selection of "best" applicants at the entrance examination, under the mistaken ideas (1) that secondary education should be given only to the "best", and (2) that even the "best" can be discerned by any system of selection at the age of eleven'.[13]

As the headmistresses met and voted together Emmeline stood with the majority. But she was now becoming herself a policy-maker in the AHM, and one of those who shouldered the work, and as such she herself argued both for quantitative forms of extension, such as more secondary schools, maintenance grants for the needy and abolition of fees, and also for qualitative forms, for the opening of what she called 'many windows in the mind'. The latter needed more than money and depended, she believed, on flexibility and variety within schools.

From work on her specialist subject too she was gaining a reputation, and more work. Emmeline was well placed for consultation on history teaching for, as a departmental committee of HM Inspectors observed when looking back in 1923, the development of grant-aided secondary schools like Nuneaton High School was one of the factors making for improvement in the organisation and teaching of history, with girls' schools as the leaders in experimental content and method. Another factor was the development of the Historical Association, in which Emmeline was now an active member, bringing all levels together to diffuse not only ideas but aids such as bibliographies, as Firth's letter to Beatrice Mulliner on Emmeline's book mentioned.[14]

By 1914 the notion of a connected course was commonplace but each school decided for itself between intensive 'period' treatment or the long proportioned view and identified the scope of treatment. This depended sometimes on *ad hoc* priorities, for instance the special knowledge of the teacher, but less consciously on aims, for historical study was often justified by its use for comprehending the present – it was instrumental, an explanatory tool. So interpretations of the present determined what aspects and events of the past were brought into view.

The Board of Education was aware of this. Secondary schools were guided, but specifically not governed, by the Board's Circular 599, issued in 1909 and reprinted in 1912. Where directions to teachers in elementary schools ordained a primarily moral instruction, an introduction to the 'lives of great men and women and the lessons to be learnt therefrom', with (in second place) practice in linguistic and literary expression, suggestions for the children in preparatory departments of secondary schools asked that by twelve they 'should have some idea of the nature of the great nations and stages in civilisation ... in their chronological succession', that is, a primarily intellectual goal.

But nationhood and civilisation were both notions less comfortably assumed as the events of 1914-18 publicly and dramatically demonstrated the immediacy of history. The war enlivened girls' interest in history, as Miss Noakes, history teacher at St Paul's Girls' School, pointed out in 1918, but she also judged that such interest was maimed by the battery of extreme views from parents and the Press (the use of 'Hun' to mean 'German', for example, was not helpful in the pursuit of historical understanding, she thought). Foreseeing 'proposals for changes in the curriculum' the Board had issued in autumn 1914 a supplement to Circular 599, Circular 869 on Modern European History, especially the period after 1871. It suggested, for instance, that recent events like the Balkan Wars could be linked to the origins of the Turkish Empire and the Crusades; and it hoped to build loyalty to 'British ideals'.[15]

As the war progressed attention shifted from one aspect to another – the Empire, naval history, in 1917 American history – and the Board bristled with suspicions of ideas from political sources. An internal minute by James Headlam in October 1917 stated the 'most serious objections to the Board using its influence to give any definite political bias to the teaching' of history. Aware that the franchise was likely soon to be widened, that Labour was a new and real political force, and that the pattern of world affairs was shifting, Headlam emphasised that more than a mere updating was needed. In the light of 'a thorough revision and reconsideration of our attitude towards the principles on which both the internal and external administration has been based ... [it is] clear to all thinking men that those who are to take their part as responsible members of the community must be properly equipped to give their opinions ... [by] the study of similar patterns in the past.'[16]

He asked the Historical Association to discuss at its next meeting the 'effect of the War upon the history syllabus', but little useful discussion of curricular needs emerged from the Association's meeting in January 1918, nor from a conference called in August by the headmaster of Eton. Internal memoranda flew round the Board. If the teachers could formulate no useful policy the Board must give a lead. But here it trod on eggshells, in the knowledge that 'History is a subject in respect of which some people are specially sensitive to the danger of allowing the State to exercise a direct influence'.[17]

But pressures for change grew insistently. The advent of Advanced Courses helped prompt major reports on the teaching of science and of modern languages in 1918, and inquiries into classics and English were to follow; the Historical Association drew up a memorial to the Board requesting a full inquiry into history also. In their arguments the demands of a liberal education marched hand in hand with training for citizenship, for they feared a generation of young scientists and classicists with no understanding of modern history. A group of Cambridge teachers of all levels from university to elementary school were inspired by the Franchise Act (1918), which brought the parliamentary vote not only to some women but also to many more men, to ask for a committee to evaluate a more coherent pattern for the whole educational system. And another memorial demanding curricular change was added to the Board's files by the Workers' Educational Association as WEA students uncovered in the past the roots of social and economic problems of the present.

When in autumn 1918 a deputation arrived asking for an Education Circular on the history and geography of the British Empire, the scent of 'political purposes' was smelt again, and the political danger if 'the League of Nations people ... would say that our duty was to teach not loyalty to the Empire but loyalty to humanity'.[18] The Board moved at last, and convened a confidential discussion with active teachers to discuss the situation. Invitations were sent to a select group drawn from universities, colleges, public and secondary schools, and the Regius Professor at Oxford, Charles Firth, was asked to act as chairman. A group of about twenty, including Board representatives, assembled at the Board's temporary offices at the Victoria and Albert Museum on 24 and 25 April 1919; Emmeline was the only woman.

Their agenda was crowded: teachers, the pre-secondary stage, ancient history, the ordinary secondary course, the Advanced Course in Modern Studies, the relation of history to geography and literature, university demands on candidates, all jostled each other as Firth kept an eye on his watch and a firm hand on the proceedings. Under his guidance the group considered most closely the secondary curriculum, as pivotal to the system – how it could be internally coherent and could lock on to elementary schools at one end and universities at the other, and how it could be organised to include European and Colonial history and take the whole story to the present day. The contributions of individuals are not recorded, but Emmeline's experience would have been relevant to some conclusions: first, that the elementary pupil aged 11 or 12 had only 'a vague familiarity with stories gleaned from various sources' and was 'at a disadvantage as compared with the pupil who had passed through the preparatory department of a secondary school'; secondly, that Advanced Course regulations tended to 'press hard' on girls' schools and were everywhere too rigid in their categories, encouraged undue specialisation and penalised some subject combinations; and, thirdly, that the study of history necessarily entailed geographical training.[19]

The group drew up a resolution to request a full committee of inquiry and suggested its terms of reference, composition and procedures, as Firth recorded in the minute he sent to Fisher, the Board of Education's President, on 13 May. On 15 June, however, he wrote a less official letter to point out that the real goals of the conference members were to endow history with the status of the languages and sciences, to get their views in print for the world (not the Board only), to change the organisation and methods of history teaching, and to ensure more time was allotted to history. Only a full inquiry would satisfy them, he believed, but the appointment of a substantial committee could be postponed if small expert groups cleared the ground on some specific topics.[20]

It was on this letter, not on the group's ruminations, that Fisher acted. Three small committees were chosen to deal with the topics Firth had cited as examples, and in October 1919 Emmeline's Governors at Nuneaton received a formal request for her service on two of these, 'A' on the correlation of history teaching in elementary and secondary schools, and 'B' on whether general circulars or detailed syllabuses were better instruments for improving history teaching. (The third committee studied teacher training.) Such limited terms of reference were frustrating, but for Emmeline furnished a gentle entry to the world of the Board of Education – at any rate she admitted that 'I really quite enjoyed the meetings.'

They convened in groups of five, with an HMI as secretary, in January 1920. The reports were succinct but through the various recommendations of both 'A' and 'B' groups ran the same significant thread, that teaching should be related to the age and psychological stage of the child, not to the type of school he or she attended. Unsurprisingly, they favoured co-operation between elementary and secondary teachers to achieve a broadly similar strategy for the early years, and they disliked detailed syllabuses 'which become stereotyped, would exclude exploration and initiative, and would be provided for by specially written textbooks of a uniform and narrow type' – a somewhat cynical view based on past observation. Bibliographies, suggestions on treatment, even specimen and adaptable syllabuses, might aid the non-specialist, however, and some samples were adduced.[21]

Fisher thought the conclusions of 'A' 'sketchy' but of 'B' more helpful, but these reports were intended only as preliminary to a general committee of inquiry. By July 1920, however, money was tight and a committee seemed too expensive. Instead, in April 1921, a group of HM Inspectors were asked to investigate history teaching, and in 1923 produced Education Pamphlet 37, a useful evaluation of what was going on in schools but lacking the prestige and publicity of a policy document from a full committee of inquiry.

Perhaps it was fortunate for Emmeline that the committees were so limited in their scope for she was very busy in that spring of 1920.

Chapter 13
Choosing headmistresses

In the spring of 1918 stirrings of expansive desire moved Emmeline to coax testimonials from her LEA Director of Education, Bolton King, and two of her Governors to back an application for the headship of the famously pioneering North London Collegiate School on Sophie Bryant's retirement. That post went to the head of Frances Buss' other foundation at Camden, and Emmeline waited.

The next 'plum' was advertised in September 1919. Bedford High School had been another of the flagship schools of the late 19th century, founded under the aegis of the Bedford Charity, the Trust endowed in 1566 by Sir William Harpur, and shaped from 1883 by Marian Belcher, a disciple of Dorothea Beale of Cheltenham. The Harpur Trust had originally set up, among other charities, a 'grammar' and a 'writing' school for boys; these became Bedford School and Bedford Modern School. When, 300 years later, the Endowed Schools Commission recommended adding parallel schools for girls, the Trust moved faster than some similar bodies and opened the High School in 1882, in a neo-Jacobean redbrick building designed by Basil Champneys to include a science laboratory and gymnasium and other material signs of 'progressive' ambition. Soon the Girls' Modern School, with its shorter courses for earlier leavers, was separated and moved out.

The High School was to prepare some girls to go on to 'places of liberal and professional education' after a curriculum as full in range and thorough in handling as any available elsewhere, and the Harpur Trust's endowment funds could keep fees at or below the level of GPDSC schools, initially £12 a year or less for day girls, and so enable local tradesmen and farmers, as well as the ex-army and colonial families who settled in Bedford, to send their daughters to join those of professional men.[1] By the 1890s the school held 579 girls, including several who were taking at school the London external BA degree, an indication both of the school's academic level and of the few places available within universities themselves.

So one strand woven into the school's reputation by 1919 was its intellectual distinction, and another its social breadth even as sister to Bedford School, now of public school status, so that, with the two more modest schools, the name 'Bedford' called up the idea 'education' by ingrained reputation. Adding lustre was the gold thread of Cheltenham-inspired tradition, woven by Cheltenham-trained staff and glowing with lofty abstracts of truth, service, duty, honour, and daily observances of orderly, tidy rectitude. Few headmistresses, however, conscious of their own rising costs, would have been surprised to learn that in 1918 the school's Harpur Trust Governors had applied to the Board of Education for grant aid.

The price of the grant asked was the provision of free places for about 15 per cent of pupils admitted and the reorganisation of the governing body so that, instead of being managed by its own small sub-committee devoted exclusively to its interests, the High School was to be governed as one among the many responsibilities of the full body of the Trust. Hence applicants for the post of headmistress in 1919 were asked to send no less than forty copies of their applications, and Emmeline prudently sent hers to Glasgow to be printed, far from prying Nuneaton eyes. In the last decade the school had shrunk to a size more manageable for a head who liked to know each girl, to 398 in September 1919, of whom 106 were boarders, but its status was marked by the salary offered, £800 to rise by £50 annually to £1,050 a year. For comparison, Emmeline was now earning £590 a year at Nuneaton, and her successor was to be offered £600, while in 1921 the endowed King's High School in Warwick advertised £650 for a new headmistress to oversee its 376 girls.

Perhaps, however, Emmeline had already heard the common opinion in professional circles that Bedford High School was stagnating on its laurels. The retiring headmistress, Susan Collie, had given her life to the school since she left Cheltenham to join the staff in 1885, for when she was asked to fill the breach left by Marian Belcher's premature death at the end of 1898 she had dedicated herself to maintaining the traditions and soaring ideals her mentor had established. Indeed Susan Collie developed new practices in tune with the times, such as a Field Club and a magazine, and through games, the Girl Guides and war work she deliberately subverted the restrictions on social mixing imposed by rules forbidding girls to talk or even walk home with friends without express permission. Every record shows how easily her scrupulous conscience distinguished the spirit from the letter of tradition, but, coupled with her loyal affection for old forms, her failing health and war-sickness disheartened Miss Collie for the radical challenges she foresaw for the post-war world.

Before the interviews for her successor, on 24 October 1919, she asked Emmeline to stay the night, with another of the five candidates, Ella Edghill, the headmistress of the King's High School, Warwick, who had known the school as both pupil and mistress. Susan Collie made a tour of the buildings for the stranger an occasion to open her thoughts in private. 'A dignified building outside,' Emmeline said, 'but miserable inside, old-fashioned, inadequate, and everything I should not want. She begged me not to be discouraged by it, and told me in confidence that she very, very much wanted me to be appointed, that many changes were needed and it would be best for a stranger to make them, and that she was convinced I was the right person from what she had heard of me.'

Others were more trenchant. 'It needs root-and-branch reform,' commented Bolton King briefly. The most thoughtful view came from the headmaster of St Bees, in Cumberland, whose triple vantage point impressed Emmeline enough for her to summarise his letter (she kept the original too, longer and if anything stronger):

I find sheaves of letters awaiting me, including quite a long one from the Headmaster of St Bees, who was for sixteen years Head of Bedford Modern School for Boys and a great friend of Miss Collie, and whose daughter was Head Girl at Bedford three years ago and is now up at Cambridge. He says how glad they are that it is I who have been appointed and not someone who was previously in the school. He tells me how much there is to be done and how Old Girls, while loving it better than any place in the world, deplore the lack of life in most of the school activities; he adds that it has felt the 'dead hand' of Miss Belcher – 'a very great headmistress, no doubt' – for too long! He was at Newnham the night before the election and all the Bedford Old Girls up at Cambridge had met together and were eagerly discussing the chances.

So Emmeline's reputation as a 'zealous educational reformer' was highly relevant to her application, and, as she learnt later, her allies had reinforced it. As President of the AHM Edith Major was approached by two Bedford Governors asking 'about your views on Scripture teaching, and I replied that you were very keen. I was told Miss Edghill was Miss Collie's nominee, and so – quite unasked – I gave my opinion on your relative merits!' As Director of Education for Warwickshire Bolton King was also sounded:

As I dreaded [he told Emmeline] I had a letter from one of the Bedford Governors about you and Miss Edghill. I said I could not make a direct comparison, but that you and she belonged to two different schools and I put the points as fairly as I could for both. I disliked doing it intensely – as I felt I was helping to sign our doom – but I had to do it. I only hope they preferred the other type: isn't that disgustingly selfish of me?

'The Harpur Trust that interviewed us was a very large one – about thirty, I should say, of whom four were women,' Emmeline reported to her parents. 'I had to wait nearly two hours before my turn came (my initial being T), and it was a little trying for us all to talk politely together for that long time … It was a formidable experience going in as one had to walk right across the room and all the people rose when each of us went in and when we came out.' Always happier with the specific and concrete than to articulate her larger vision whose consistency was derived from central beliefs and desires, she was taken aback too by their 'terrible questions as to what I thought about girls' education, especially in regard to modern developments! I said I really did not know!'

But after a few minutes the Clerk called her back, the Chairman made 'a nice little speech', and everyone said pretty things to everyone else, and promised to emulate the 'ideal' qualities of the Nuneaton Governors. In their minutes the Governors recorded a unanimous decision. 'Now Bedford will go forward!' said Grace Fanner, Chairman of the AHM Executive Committee, when the appointment was announced, but Emmeline herself was stimulated as much by the traditions Susan Collie loved for their spirit as by the scope for her energies. In 1929 she herself virtually echoed what

Marian Belcher had told the school and its Guild of ex-pupils in 1893: 'One of the best tests of the real worth of a school is the life and character of those who have been members ... who can always be depended on, because they do thoroughly and conscientiously whatever they take in hand.'[2] 'I myself believe,' said Emmeline, 'that the only test of a school is the type of woman it turns out, and the kind of life she leads afterwards' – the variations are as significant as the echo.

The dual stimulus was a challenge. Emmeline brooded:

Miss Moore has a Bedford Old Girl on her staff, and she says that it is quite pathetic to see how devoted she is to the school, and how fond of Miss Collie, and yet how she wants to get things altered. It is rather cheering to see how conscious everyone is of the need for change, but it is a little alarming to think of how the changes are going to be made without losing the many good things that *must* be there to arouse the devotion of such a large number of people of different types, and to give the school the great name it has.

Problems practical and emotional dogged the road out of Nuneaton, in a manner typical of Emmeline's profession. Although the Harpur Trust had accepted Susan Collie's resignation in June, their delay through the summer was 'unsettling', as Ella Edghill observed, 'and will make it difficult for the school the person selected comes from', for the new headmistress was asked to start in January, the next term. However ideal, the Nuneaton Governors could hardly appreciate so little notice. Emmeline returned to Nuneaton on the evening of 24 October, a Friday, and on Monday morning the Governors' Chairman, Robert Swinnerton, visited Bolton King's office in Warwick. King at once wrote to Emmeline:

He is very strong indeed against releasing you before the four months [of contractual notice], and others with whom he confabbed are so too. So I think you must take it for granted that they will not let you go at Christmas, and I hope that means you will stay on till Easter. They say (1) they must think of their own school first, (2) Bedford can get on better than Nuneaton, as apparently Miss Collie can stay on till you go. I must say I agree with them – I dare say it is horribly selfish but like them I care more about Nuneaton than Bedford.

But Miss Collie could not stay. She was tired and unwell, and was selling the house and large garden Emmeline had admired on her visit, to move to a smaller cottage at a tactful distance. At Emmeline's suggestion, the second mistress, Miss Lee, was appointed acting headmistress for a 'honorarium' of £105 to cover the spring term.

The second hurdle was to break the news, to staff and girls and Old Girls. 'There will be weeping and wailing at Nuneaton,' predicted Kathleen Moore, an understatement of the shock-wave Emmeline tried to control with words one assistant half-heartedly repeated back to her: 'Perhaps you are right that in order to spend one's life to the best advantage it is better to make a definite break sometimes, and the change is bound to cost us all something.'

In the school magazine the Sixth Former given the task of the school news report recorded 'words of strong cheer, calling upon us to show our love and appreciation at this moment of change by drawing closer, not by loosening, the cords of loyalty and devotion that bind us to our dear school'.[3] In Bedford Susan Collie was saying precisely the same to her Old Girls. In private, though, Emmeline confessed to Kathleen Moore that she could not feel the expected pleasure in her new appointment. Bolton King's new Assistant Director, who had just left the first headship of the re-endowed Godolphin and Latymer Girls' School, recognised how ambivalent were Emmeline's reactions: 'I know something of what it means to leave a school which has been entirely one's own; as soon as you begin to pull up your roots you will find they are planted far deeper than you thought, and I am so sorry you have all the pain of this uprooting after (or rather because of) your vitalising work at Nuneaton...' To her Old Girls Emmeline said simply, 'A part of my heart will always be in Nuneaton.'

And after the news was broken, the prospect remained of a spring term setting everything in order for her successor and overseeing from a distance affairs at Bedford. None knew better that in 1920 schools had, like the Red Queen, to run as hard as they could to stay in the same place, and to each individual girl a single term was a vital period of learning and doing. Deliberately Emmeline looked to the needs of the moment. The hoped-for Sicilian sabbatical had to be relinquished but instead she was granted leave for December, and when she stayed in Oxford the weekend after the Bedford interview for a meeting of the Council of Lady Margaret Hall the Pyrenees fired her enthusiasm. Her membership of LMH Council was a contact for the college with secondary schools, and for Emmeline not only with the university world but with friends such as Madge Skipworth, first met at Sherborne and now a college Fellow. Madge Skipworth, and the Vice-Principal, Eleanor Lodge, both expert travellers, planned a tour for Emmeline, from Pau to 'some little place, Eaux Chauds or Bagnères de Bijorre or Bagnères de Luchon, and coming back by Carcassonne and Toulouse', melodious, alluring names.

On a swift visit to Bath, however, compunction seized her for her mother. The once-unthinkable war and the tearing misery of its endurance, the death of her small grandson, her own influenza and recurrent inner-ear troubles, had tightened Nettie's lips against complaint and dug deeper lines on her face. When she heard of her daughter's new appointment 'I wept, it must have been for joy because I cannot think of one pang you ever caused me' as she recalled 'many of the chief events of your life ... from the time when you were about fourteen months old and told me to whom the things belonged on the clothes-line, to your appointment at Nuneaton'. For herself she took nothing of the credit she saw as all her daughter's. Emmeline forgot the Pyrenees, and swept her mother up to rest in the gentler Riviera, even in winter a flowery hem to a sea bluer than the waters Nettie had all her life loved to watch from the Devon cliffs.

Away from her own ground, and not speaking French, Nettie was rather amused to be, for once, her daughter's subordinate – 'Of course, it is Emmie and her Mother, and I wouldn't have it otherwise for the world. She is so unassuming and delightful.' They stayed first at the Hôtel des Anglais in Cannes, where eggs in every fashion were the French answer to vegetarianism, before moving, just after Christmas, to Antibes and more omelettes and poached eggs at the Grand Hôtel du Cap. Emmeline had not planned to spend this time off sitting knitting (her only recorded knitting) while Nettie read aloud, but Nettie's alert eye must have made her a stimulating companion.

She noticed everything, from the astonishing number of hotels in Nice ('and such huge ones! One near here took in refugees during the War, and is now too verminous to use. Many were used for the War and are not yet opened. The gardens and ground show the state they are in') to encampments round St Raphael of 'Colonial soldiers, Malays, Chinese, Algerians', not yet demobilised, as well as the fruits and flowers growing profusely and the beauties of the coastal road to Monte Carlo. There their charabanc tour stopped at the Casino, but allowed 'no time to make money!' Neither understood roulette, but simply watched, baffled, 'the counters being thrown on numbers and a man drawing them back (like people draw leaves with a hoe).'

Nettie's letters to Sam, however, for the most part were filled with ecstasy over the mountain and sea views, to assure him of her happiness although 'it seems strange to be so far away from you, dearest'. 'Your remark on coming here some day with me thrilled me through and through! It would be purgatory, though, to come with me unless you brought an interpreter – No, you must come with Emmie.' Emmeline's ability to communicate with the French impressed and satisfied her mother, for the chance to learn French was one of the reasons why she and Sam had stinted to apprentice their daughter to a private school. The years of penny-watching had justified themselves, in the scent of bunches of 'wild flowers, mimosas, heather, lavender, daisies' Emmeline brought to her and in charabanc tours through the picturesque landscape that she described minutely, as well as the hotels' carpets and hot baths. 'O, I loved it,' she assured Emmeline, 'and never worried about cost, but thought of the Good Giver.'

Emmeline knew her limits better, especially as regards the French language, admitting that 'I can always make myself understood, but I have a shockingly bad accent and do not speak well at all', that is, with the supple elegance of educated French. Leading a delegation to Paris in 1925, and received at the Sorbonne:

> I had to make a speech in reply to a very long and interesting one made to us. I did very badly indeed; if I had kept to politenesses and that sort of thing I should have been all right, but there were several questions of policy with regard to education and to girls' education raised in the original speech, and I was pining to discuss them, so I

boldly and unwisely began to do so. I did make myself understood ...
but I know that my colleagues blushed at my French, and I felt really
sorry to have shamed them in this way.

One last picture from the journey home reasserts Nettie's normal
relationship to her daughter.

... you were so annoyed at one part of the journey [Nettie later reminded
Emmeline] you thought you would get out, because they had not
reserved us corner seats as you had booked! O Emmie darling, I shall
be so glad when you can realise God can make every seat comfortable
for His children. 'Our Father who art in Heaven', that is in a Heavenly
sphere, will also make His children comfortable and happy everywhere
if they trust Him. 'Not my way but Thine, O God.' If we lose our temper
God is not there, as it isn't Heaven but hell.

In Emmeline's absence, at the end of the Christmas term, a new
headmistress was selected for Nuneaton. Over seventy applications,
including 'about fourteen headmistresses', were reduced to a short list of
six, and the girls were given a half-holiday for the interview afternoon, the
rumour put about being that they should thereby 'be at home when the end
of the world took place'. After an uncomfortable lunch with the Governors,
the second mistress Winifred Lewis had the tact to provide coffee for the
candidates in her room but to marshal the Governors into Emmeline's, from
where Bolton King could slip out for a pipe, though 'Mr McGregor had one
later *in your room* and hopes the smell will have departed before your return'.
Meanwhile the domestic scientist Elsie Martin made scones for tea after the
interviews. The mathematics teacher Agnes Lloyd showed each candidate
the school, and, like several of the interviewing group and Winifred Lewis,
returned a candid report to Emmeline. From these some grounds of decision
can be glimpsed.

Looks, manner, health all counted. Tall, dark Miss Rackham was 'very
weedy and weary-looking', 'as if she had had very heavy troubles and was
going to die the next moment – and very badly dressed, and altogether
depressing. No votes', and Miss Freer, 'tho' "essentially a gentlewoman",
as her testimonials said', appeared 'extremely nervous, poor soul, as she
was constantly twisting and untwisting somewhat shady-looking and stubby
fingers', and was dismissed as 'insignificant'. On Miss Newman opinions
divided, her 'healthy-looking' face and presentable blue coat and skirt being
in her favour but her 'complacent' manner, even 'vulgar', giving her no
advantage over Miss Franklin, 'prettily-dressed, fresh-coloured, and knew
how to walk'. But the latter was an 'artificial dolly' to one, a 'cold blanket'
to another, with 'horrible ideas about homework', 'possibly not very good-
tempered, and even possibly not quite *straight*. She had no votes.'

For ideas counted most, and the choice lay between Miss Lee and Miss
Davies. Agnes Lloyd was daunted by Miss Lee's 'perfect torrent of words'
as she was shown round, and quoted with malicious mimicry: '"A little,
little chapel, it was for that that her soul pined!" She admired the new

buildings but not the glazed windows. "The soul and the mind of a child should be without in the fresh open air and not within." I wondered how its lessons would progress but held my peace. I think she might have been amusing but was, I am sure, a self-centred crank, full no doubt of high but impossible schemes for the welfare of "the child".' The voteless but influential Bolton King thought Miss Lee had both force and humanity, and favoured her, though he also judged Miss Davies 'will develop. She is perhaps the sounder of the two', and the one he would rather lunch with; Hallie Melly thought Miss Lee 'erratic'.

By eight votes to five Muriel Davies was chosen, the youngest of them and 'rather pretty' in her tweed coat and skirt, as well as 'capable' and with warmth of manner. She pleased Agnes Lloyd 'by saying how much she had heard about you and how sad the school must be feeling that you were leaving, but otherwise I have no very clear impression of her – except that of extreme youth', and athletic health. In fact, Muriel Davies was then thirty-four; the year Emmeline sat Matriculation as a student-governess at the Lowes' school, she had been seven and entering the preparatory department of King Edward's High School, Birmingham. Ten years later she had left King Edward's for Newnham College, Cambridge, to gain Classical and Medieval-and-Modern-Language Triposes, and since 1914 had been second mistress at Edgbaston Church of England College – an impeccable pedigree for a headmistress in 1920.

When Emmeline herself met Muriel Davies she liked her, but some of her ideas were to take Nuneaton by surprise, as well as later to disturb the more conventional or staid traditionalists of the AHM. How much she disclosed to the Governors of her faith in the 'Dalton plan' of independent work in a girl's self-organised time, or of school self-government by elected Form Leaders and a discussion assembly, or how far she had yet developed her schemes for encouraging a classless society through multi-bias (or comprehensive) schooling, is unrecorded, but the general direction of her thinking must have been elicited, and – in that she was chosen – approved.

Chapter 14
Bedford High School

Susan Collie introduced Emmeline to the assembled Bedford High School in a tableau of contrast: the retiring head, as her portrait shows her, fine-boned, austere, delicate in make beside the vigorous vitality of the larger Emmeline, tall and straight and with only the first grey hairs beginning to fade the fair head Nuneaton girls remembered. At the start of her first term in January 1920 she followed exactly the established pattern for Prayers in the panelled hall. The organ in the gallery was played while girls filed silently in, to sit, form by form, on benches with their form mistress on a chair at the end. The Head Girl brought in books to lay on the headmistress' little desk, raised on a small dais, and the headmistress entered. As she stood at the desk the organ ceased and she began to read – always, at the start and end of term, the words of St Paul in his letter to the Philippians: 'Whatsoever things are good ... think on these things.' This was, and remained, one of Emmeline's own favourites.

Then followed the prayers, hymn and psalm, but, to mark the term's start and finish, Emmeline retained her Nuneaton custom and, rather than a homily or business notices, she told moral tales. For January 1920 she chose a favourite, 'Our Lady's Tumbler', and, said one listener, 'We understood what Miss Tanner wanted for the school: that we should throw ourselves heart and soul into whatever we did and do it well.'[1] From later terms others recalled 'The ship that found itself' ('It isn't what you do that matters most, nor what you think – though that matters more – but what you are') and for juniors the story of the child who helped build a cathedral by bringing hay to the tired horses, a small but useful task. Some girls were bored by the morality; others said they enjoyed the puzzle of working out what the message would be; most remembered the tale, or the teller's capacity to hold her audience. They also noticed her distinctive pronunciation of 'girls', not quite 'gels' nor yet 'gairls', but few identified it as a Victorian idiosyncrasy, or realised she had lived a quarter century under that Queen.

Seizing a moment on Sunday 15 February 1920 when 'it seems quite surprising to be at home for a whole day once more', Emmeline broke off her normal Sunday work of preparing Scripture lessons for the coming week to write, among her usual pile of correspondence, to her parents of her recent doings.

A routine was developing for visits to Bedford, usually fortnightly in this spring term but sometimes more frequent. The second mistress, Miss Lee, arranged a timetable 'and I pass rapidly from one thing to another', from staff meetings to parents, Governors to boarding-housemistresses,

Prayers to problems arising. That week Emmeline had stayed a night in Bedford with Diana Butt, a stalwart of the 'Guild', the High School's Old Girl association, and not only an early and loyal supporter of Emmeline's headship but able to pass on much of the less formal lore and tradition the new headmistress did well to take into account. Earlier in the day she had been invited to tea by a Governor, Lady Ampthill, distinguished in her own right for her wartime administration of Red Cross VADs, and now Lady-in-Waiting to Queen Mary and 'a particularly charming woman and I imagine very capable,' said Emmeline, finding her 'awfully sensible about the school and very sympathetic'.

Tall and dignified, slightly reserved for all her easy tact, Lady Ampthill was not unlike the Queen herself. As one of the four women on the Schools Committee which digested and presented to the full Harpur Trust information on their schools, and with a local home and a husband who became the Trust's Chairman, she was a significant supporter. On the whole, however, Emmeline's relationship to her new Governors seems to have been more remote than at Nuneaton, though the Rev. C. F. Farrar, Chairman of the Schools Committee and an ex-headmaster, proved approachable and humorous without patronage. But the High School and the Girls' Modern School were lower in the pecking order than the two boys' schools, or so the annual reports submitted by their heads suggest in their gradations of tone. The urbane and relaxed style of Reginald Carter of Bedford School, assuming shared attitudes, including chat about school activities, changes to business-like respect from the Boys' Modern School, and sinks to plaintive appeal from the two headmistresses, sure that explanations were necessary.

Yet Nuneaton was properly Emmeline's priority that spring term of 1920, in a long-drawn-out process of farewells and path-smoothing. Most formal and stately was the annual Commemoration service, cancelled for war and sickness in 1918 and 1919, and now brought forward to March, when all the local worthies attended to join in prayers and psalms and to hear J. L. Paton, Headmaster of Manchester Grammar School, before they turned to the worldliness of tea. Least formal was the staff tea-party when, all girls excluded, mistresses threw off the classroom to act sketches. More tea-parties followed, with the Governors, with the Old Girls, and presents were exchanged: from Emmeline to the school a Tudor refectory table, once in a Shropshire church, for the hall platform, and an oak desk and chair for the new head's use. And she had to disentangle herself from the ties of other associations, personal and professional, and long kept the chair the Girls' Club made for her and a fat file of affectionate letters.

Nor was she helped by 'my domestic situation' in Nuneaton. First her housekeeper fell sick and was replaced by a school maid, until she too developed 'an exceedingly bad throat' and 'two gathered thumbs'. For a week or more Emmeline had no one 'to do the fires and washing-up' until another school maid offered to help at weekends; more than ever she was convinced that domestic help was vital to a professional woman. Laundry could be sent out, but open fires and cleaning, with mops and brushes, meant daily chores, and Emmeline liked a neat and shining environment. One of her old Nuneaton girls, visiting her at Roedean in 1939, commented that she felt there the 'same friendly feeling' as at Nuneaton – 'even the corners of the polished boards shine and look as if they mattered' – but this was not achieved without effort, and Emmeline's share was emphatically the management and not the labour. She never showed any personal liking for domestic work, but she cared about the results.

At school the caretaker, Giddins, had given notice again – already he had left once for two years – and Clay, the Governors' Clerk, felt sour: 'Isn't he a rotter or rather Bolshevik? ... I suppose we shall have an awful job again in deciding on the new one.' Muriel Davies was anxious about a house, for herself and the five-year-old nephew she had adopted, and negotiations began, then fell through, to buy Locksbrook from Emmeline's landlord; eventually the new head was allowed what Emmeline had once sought, the caretaker's lodge. 'She turned the caretaker out of his lodge', was the girls' view, 'and moved in, sitting on the doorstep in summer evenings – a thing that Miss Tanner would never have done!' A change of style could abrade sore patches of loss, and as at Nuneaton so at Bedford.

Now Emmeline had to find herself a home in Bedford, not an easy task in a town where few houses were let and for 'moderate' houses of two reception and four bedrooms, with gas and a patch of garden, prices of £700 to £800 were quoted in 1922. For the summer she rented a furnished house in Chaucer Road, offered on the school's grapevine, and looking 'straight across the fields to the sunset – the one beautiful thing to be seen in Bedford', but during the summer holiday of 1920 she found a settled home and by the autumn term had moved into Murree Cottage, in Biddenham, a village just to the west of Bedford.

The glory of the thatched cottage was its garden, sweet-scented in the spring with purple violets she long remembered, and later heavy with fruit, greengages, plums and apples, raspberries and strawberries (92 lb in 1924); Emmeline, or more often her gardener Mortimer, grew vegetables too, to lavish seasonally on her friends and relations. From the cottage she cycled daily to the school behind a large basket crammed with books and papers, even, when evening events were in prospect, decked in the full evening dress still *de rigueur* on many occasions. Bedford was full of bicycles and many of the girls used them, indeed needed them for speed to the games field or for such expeditions with the Field Club as to the aerodrome at Cardington in December 1920, when Campbell showed a group round and explained the building and maintenance of airships. Not till 1922, though, did Emmeline secure a grant of £250 to construct bicycle sheds at the school. She encouraged cycling, an enormously liberating force, emblematic of energy and initiative, and more likely to be within a Bedford girl's means than those of a Nuneaton pupil.

Installed in Bedford after Easter 1920 Emmeline firmly took the reins from the second mistress, Miss Lee. To take over an existing school was a different project from that of establishing a new one, and much more common; Emmeline's experience typifies that of many headmistresses.

By the 1920s Bedford was far more genteelly middle-class than Nuneaton and a favourite retreat for Civil Servants home from India and the Colonies, and soldiers home from the war, as well as a convenient bedroom for London commuters. Its own industries mainly served the countryside around, supplying agricultural tools and machinery, market services, and beer from the brewery. Here the Ouse winds through meadows and meanders under Bedford's three bridges, as one of the social amenities the town offered to its families, like tennis and golf and a handsome library, and schools of repute. From 'professional people of moderate means, many of whose daughters will probably have to earn their living' were drawn the majority of the High School's pupils, according to an article written in 1922, and the journalist quoted Emmeline on the girls' futures in 'every kind of work ... some were doctors and dispensers, many were teachers – kindergarten teaching at the present time was specially attractive – while hospital nursing and secretarial work absorbed a considerable number', though she also mentioned music, insurance and 'business careers'.[2] After the war reports of HM Inspectors ceased to analyse pupils by social origin, and instead began to take more interest in university entries and in subsequent careers.

Imprisoned in Bedford in the 1660s John Bunyan sent his Christian pilgrim stumbling but persevering through the traps, deceits, frauds and betrayals of the world. The modern Bedford Prison stands next to the High School, the stern security of the one contrasting with the lofty graces of the school's trees and Champney's redbrick stone-dressed building, with a central hall topped by a cupola and winged with gabled classrooms. Pevsner praises the 'half-domed bow windows'[3] but a rebel teacher of 1920 complained that 'Air cannot enter through windows tight closed; / Clerestoried ones high up give gloom not light'; but the school of Emmeline's desires was the Interpreter's House of Bunyan's imagery, where a pageant of visions rehearsed the world's experience for Christian, training and arming him.

Among the most pressing of the Bedford tasks was the induction of new staff, the process starting even in the last term of 1919, before Emmeline was officially head. Here staff appointments had always been the head's business, but though Emmeline used her informal contacts with other heads as well as agencies (especially the Association of University Women Teachers) and advertisements, everyone admitted 'there are few candidates of outstanding merits'. Nor could she yet promise a standard scale of salaries; that was to come when the Harpur Trust revised both fees and salaries in 1921. Susan Collie stood aside, justly arguing the muddle 'if two headmistresses were to write about the same post'.

Even as Susan Collie relinquished her problems to Emmeline her gift for friendship captured her successor. Sometimes she was confiding ('I am afraid both Miss Gyde and Miss Barlow are rather ineffectual persons'),

Fig. 1: (l. to r.) Eva, Beatrice, Emmeline, the three eldest Tanners, December 1887.

Fig. 2: 1 Locksbrook Place, Weston, where Emmeline was born (photographed 1991).

Fig. 3: Fern Bank, Newbridge Road, Weston – the Tanners' home from 1880 (photographed 1991).

Fig. 4: The Tanner family, about 1890 – (l. to r. top row) Fred, Eva, Beatrice; (middle row) Emmeline, Sam, Nettie, Herbert; (front) Arthur, Winifred.

Fig. 5: Emmeline (on right), with her mother and brother Fred, about 1900.

Fig. 6: Emmeline's father, Samuel Tanner, 'Intelligently interested in everything we could tell him and in everything he saw,' said Emmeline.

Fig. 7: Beatrice (on right) at work in the early 1900s.

Fig. 8: First term at Nuneaton High School, 1910.

Fig. 9: Nuneaton, 1910: Emmeline as new headmistress.

Fig. 10: Girls waiting at the door of Nuneaton High School, first term, 1910.

Fig. 11: Bedford High School, 1922. Boarders lived in houses in neighbouring roads, separate from these school buildings.

Fig. 12: Emmeline, off duty, at Bedford, early 1920s.

Fig. 13: Roedean School, 1924. The photograph is taken from the playing-fields.

Fig. 14: Roedean
School greets
Emmeline's return
from South Africa,
1930, with a lacrosse-
stick guard of honour.

Fig. 15: Roedean: School Prefects, 1936. They wear the distinctive djibbah.

Fig. 16: 'In full cry' (Emmeline's comment on the photograph) at Roedean, March 1947. On her left is Sir Paul Lawrence and on the wall, portraits of the Lawrence sisters.

and sometimes she was consoling – 'I know too well the frigid style of letters which you will be receiving from the [Harpur Trust] office. When I was first appointed they used to make my spirits sink to zero, but it is mere officialdom, it means nothing.' Always she was unaffected and practical in priorities, from 'I am sure you will love the children. They are very responsive, though not clever', to her advice on where to buy coal and which doctor to prefer.

From the autumn of 1919, however, she resigned her right to appoint staff, and several posts needed to be filled, if not necessarily those which Emmeline would have preferred, to judge from the remarks of an uninvolved headmistress: 'What a business you will have in getting rid of the prehistoric staff, especially the masters and the two Senior French mistresses. They are sure to like you immensely and not want to go.' Nevertheless, both senior French staff inspected (with approval) in 1923 were of Emmeline's choosing, and in addition Mlle Duclos left Nuneaton for Bedford in 1923. From Nuneaton, too, came Doris Wilson for English, Elsie Hatch for mathematics, and Agnes Lloyd for lower-school modern languages. The history department was restocked, with two who were later to become headmistresses themselves, while the preparatory school presented no problem when its head retired, for the chief assistant, Miss Lockyer, was more than capable of judicious and imaginative innovation. By the autumn of 1920 the average age of the staff had dropped considerably.

But Susan Collie's final report to her Governors reinforced her emphasis on how vital was new science accommodation with the warning that the school 'has now acquired two capable and enthusiastic assistants and would like to retain them'; two years later, after Emmeline's continued pressure had resulted only in the drawing-up and shelving of plans, she took the same line: 'I cannot help thinking that it was despair as to the hope of ever having the proper Science accommodation promised to her' that caused the bright young Miss Perrott to resign.[4]

Needs of each school had to be balanced, but Bedford School's playing-fields absorbed money while High School science plans were refrigerated annually, though when in 1922 new regulations compelled the entry of whole forms, not individuals, for School Certificate subjects chemistry and physics became impossible, and, 'dreadfully handicapped by the minute size' of the laboratories, Sixth Formers were debarred from these sciences in universities and colleges which demanded School Certificate passes in the subjects. Next year Emmeline tried shame as a lever: she had been forced to explain to a party of foreigners full of 'intelligent questions' that the antiquated science, gymnasium and domestic science facilities were not typical, but a legacy of the school's forty-year start.[5]

She made no comparisons, discomforted perhaps by jostling for funds, aware the Girls' Modern School was yet worse off, and her list of needs was long, for a library, a new gymnasium and domestic science rooms as well as laboratories for natural sciences. She was granted money only for new benches in the old laboratories. Smaller sums were allowed, piecemeal, for repairs and redecoration: in the summer of 1920 the corridors and cloakrooms were painted and in the winter the gymnasium, sickroom and six classrooms, and each was fitted with electric lighting; then the hall was painted, and so by degrees the physical setting was transformed. Electric lighting was extended to the cloakrooms in January, for another £22/15/-. This was not only practical but psychologically heartening, and uncontentious, if some staff doggerel was justified: 'Cold, cheerless, complex seem to me those halls, / Hideous all decorations on their walls, / Darksome those corridors...' In 1922, £50 was squeezed out for improvements to ventilation and heating, the classrooms continuing to use the coal fires fed by the caretaker with buckets of coal and believed to be efficacious in circulating air.

Before 1924 Emmeline had renovated her person too. Gone was long hair piled beneath wide hats, and gone were long skirts with highnecked blouses, to be replaced by a short cap of hair waved back from her ears and the sight of well-shaped calves. Whether pictured hastening into her cottage garden in a loose and lightly-belted summer dress, with space at the neck to tuck in a flowering sprig, or on a platform in a well-cut coat and skirt, she presented herself as modern yet decorous, neat but not gaudy.

To the heads of the schools was given responsibility for estimates of running costs (staff salaries, 'plant and apparatus', stationery, games), but capital expenditure needed special approval. For all the schools at this time running costs exceeded income from fees and grants of public money, the High School's by the least, and like other endowed charities with grant aid for education the Harpur Trust embarked on a spirited argument with the Board of Education over responsibility for funding the required number of free places, at this time paid from Trust funds but, in their reading of the 1918 Act's provisions, properly the duty of the state. In 1922, for example, the 496 pupils at the High School included 57 'exhibitioners', or free-place girls: the proportion is almost exactly that of the ex-elementary pupils in the school. Additionally, children of fathers killed in the war qualified for fee reductions; this was a private matter for the Trust.

As Farrar, the Schools Committee Chairman, pointed out to parents in 1921, the popular view that the Trust 'kept vast sums lying at the Bank' disregarded its vast expenditure, eight-elevenths of which was tied to the four secondary schools.[6] He could have added that, since the money derived largely from property, income could fluctuate according to management and the general state of the economy, but no one needed to be reminded of inflation at this time. Thus the budget for the High School in 1920 was £8,365 but the desperately needed improvement to staff salaries the next year raised the figure to £12,052 (£10,757 for staff). Fees rose too, to vary from £12 to £24 a year according to age, plus £75 for boarding, still modest beside comparable schools.

Money, therefore, and its prudent management, were never far from

Emmeline's mind by need as well as habit. And money was not shared equally: in allocating funds the Trust reckoned three boys equal to five girls. This was realistic, since masters' salaries cost more than mistresses', and when the Burnham Scale was adopted in 1920 the salary inequality was systematised, one inequality breeding another.

If Emmeline was never as close to this Governing Body with its split attention as she had been to Nuneaton's Governors she did inherit her predecessors' wide powers within the school, of staffing, organisation and use of buildings, and she found the Governors prepared to listen, for example when she and Miss Dolby of the Girls' Modern School jointly proposed new plans for selecting free place girls from the elementary schools, with an external examiner of their choice, or when the Governors acceded to her changes to the annual examination the Trust required. As at Nuneaton, though, her freedom was limited by the Board of Education's regulations, and, as with most extensions of state activity, 'bureaucratic control' was resented by the many previously independent schools driven to seek grants. The GPDST grumbled at 'vexatious regulations', and the secondary headmasters at their 1923 conference passed a series of protesting motions: preparatory schools, entry requirements, the curriculum, examinations, all were thicketed with new brambles, and most meant at the least new paperwork, yearly returns on the timetabling of each class, for instance, or the submission of Advanced Course syllabuses.

The Board argued that its advice, disseminated in numerous circulars, set standards. They tended to elide quality and norms, coins of two sides. If narrowly interpreted 'standards' might be exclusive, as will be seen later, and normalising might, like Procrustes, chop off all individual characteristics to fit a single bed. Emmeline was not prepared, for example, to change Bedford's 'long morning' to conform to the 35-period week expected by the Board's Circular 1294 (of 1923), a response to the reports on Science, Modern Languages, Classics and English prescribing hours to be spent on these subjects. In the 1900s the AHM had argued the merits of a 9.00 am to 1.00 pm pattern of lessons, with non-compulsory afternoons given to art, music, games, needlework, or preparation, believing girls fresher for disciplined toil in the mornings and often expected to help their mothers later. It simply meant more work on the timetable jigsaw and exploitation of the actually considerable freedom allowed.

Nor, while private schools remained beyond inspection, could norm-conforming solve a problem affecting standards the High School shared with many others – as Emmeline had known since Sherborne. She summed it up to her Governors in October 1921: the overall standard of work seemed 'very fair', if not the staff's ideal, she said, but the school suffered 'very badly' from

> the large number of girls who enter the school late – between 14 and 18, often over 15 or 16 – with totally inadequate preparation. There are always among the large number of girls here some of excellent

promise and attainment, but the general standard of the school as a whole is badly pulled down by these others ... [For the first time she had rejected some on entrance tests, but] it is hard not to give girls a chance when their lack of knowledge and training is due to indifference or, much more often, lack of understanding of the importance of the earlier education on the part of the parents. There is no doubt, however, that the rest of the school suffers.[7]

In private she could cite examples, and, incidentally, demonstrate how far she had come since her years at Halifax. Miss Pannett and her sister had prospered in Seaford, their orbit crossing Emmeline's again when two of their pupils joined Bedford:

[They] had been very happy at Seaford but their Latin and Mathematics were very poor, though they were exceptionally intelligent girls. One of them is now at Oxford: we had to spend much of her time with us in slaving at her Latin and in teaching her the elements of composition, punctuation, etc., so as to get her into Oxford, though she had done a great deal of English and some French literature and was very much interested in history. I do not know quite why it is, but so many of the private schools seem to lack thoroughness and fail to give a good grounding. I don't suppose Miss Pannett can get much of a staff.

The administrative duties multiplying under the Board's umbrella Emmeline relieved by employing a secretary. Susan Collie had shared a factotum's services with music teaching and some domestic management, but into the budget for 1921-2 was built a full-time secretary's salary. At hand was tall, vigorous Miss Chomley, known for her 'cheery laugh' and good-humoured efficiency; from the time she had travelled on the Trans-Siberian Railway to the UK in 1902 after graduation from Melbourne she had taught geography at the High School and knew all its ways, but she supported all Emmeline's attempts to eradicate inefficient procedures, from complaints that 'no duplicator works, no stencil writes' to the organisation of swimming lessons. She was now also the vice-President of Bedford's branch of the National Women Citizens' Association; from 1936 she served on the Town Council for a decade.

Energy of innovation was not so apparent among all the staff. While Emmeline had been dashing over from Nuneaton in the spring of 1920 she had relied on the second mistress; and certainly no one was better equipped than Miss Lee to explain Bedford's traditional practices. Mathematics teaching there had been Miss Lee's first job in 1889, under Miss Belcher, and all accounts of her emphasise her total devotion to the school, her absorption in every detail and willing appropriation of every duty. But her bronze hair was now white and her early freshness petrified, at least in the eyes of younger staff. One who took a group of girls to the first production of Shaw's St Joan in 1924 gleefully recognised her in Courcelles: 'But the torture is customary ... It is always done ... It is the law.' On Emmeline's departure Miss Lee was still at hand to guide the able but inexperienced new head through her early days, and, sighed one assistant, 'We go in for great slowness now.'

From the start Emmeline made it plain that she was to be taken on her own terms. At the first large gathering of the Old Girls' Guild in June 1921 she tactfully opened her presidential speech with homage to the school's ideals and the Old Girls' loyalty, then challenged them: '... no two people express themselves in their work in the same way, and one's work, to be worth anything, must be spontaneous and sincere and natural to one's self, not a mere imitation of someone else.'[8] So she justified her drive.

In the school's structure the Governors were important by statute, the staff by function, the parents by social custom. A fourth group, more nebulous in its sphere of influence, was the Guild.

The name copied that of the ex-pupils' association of Cheltenham Ladies' College, as did the formal objectives 'to promote a feeling of fellowship ... and to help its members in self-improvement and in work for others', but its strategic value to a transformative project lay less in its corporate structure than in its networking facility. Old Girls spread a school's reputation as they travelled, worked, settled and socialised, as they became themselves mothers and sometimes Governors; Old Girls linked the school to further education, to careers, to the wider world, and might – if they chose – be founts of information; Old Girls might supply funds for special purposes, if sympathetic. Their President was *ex officio* the headmistress of the day, and it was she who delivered the address at the biennial weekend when Guild members took over the school for their parties, meetings, drama and worship. Hence this was the forum Emmeline chose for expounding her vision of the 'spirit of service ... often the best service one can render to one's fellows is to do one's own work as well as it can be done'.

Yet her attention was far more warm-blooded than such an analysis suggests, and greater than strategy required as well as longer-lived – for the rest of her life she kept in affectionate touch with more than those members she had known as pupils – implying that her drive was informed by sentiment, a *Gestalt*-vision of school as a community that could not be reduced to the sum of its parts, that for each individual was integral to the whole experience, good and bad, of her life, as the child makes the woman. Nor was such sentiment wholly objectified, perhaps. Years earlier, Amrit Kaur told her, with heavy irony and multiple exclamation marks, that 'Naturally I count in the number of your pupils who are going to drop you!!!!' and Emmeline's almost maternal attitude to Amrit hints at a possible source of this craving for continued links.

As a corollary to her justification by truth to self she recognised girls might march to different drums, and needed the mental space and freedom to hear their beat, each her own drummer. So among the changes suspect to the old guard was relaxation of some rules. Talking was allowed in passages and cloakrooms, for example. Homework was reduced and she urged rather its sensible organisation so that 'every girl could get her homework done ...

without becoming stupid through overwork. There was nothing that made a girl so stupid as sitting over homework hour after hour at the end of every day' and losing 'the joy of adventure in finding things out for themselves' (as well as fresh air) – so her words to the parents were reported.[9]

More responsibilities were given to prefects, more say to the girls in the choice of form prefects and games captains. When Emmeline tried to extend the day girls' House system 'many matters were brought up and discussed' with the girls themselves.[10] Not rules but 'guiding principles' were needed, she said to their parents, 'such as consideration for one's neighbour', and if parents were afraid of the decay of discipline the modern world was one where a woman 'would have to decide things on the spur of the moment, under unexpected circumstances' and everything would then depend on habits formed of deciding for oneself. School was a safe setting for practice in mistakes, she argued, even if 'I quite confess that this system is not an immediate success [and] it requires an enormous amount of patience, sympathy and understanding'.[11]

The sun to the planetary bodies of Governors and parents, staff and Guild, was the community of pupils, growing annually in numbers from the 398 of September 1919 to regain pre-war levels, with 561 in 1924 (432 day, 129 boarders). The boarding proportion was fairly constant, limited by Trust rules; a fourth boarding house was licensed in 1921. To get to know these girls, Emmeline taught them, as far as was possible, though less and less did administration of a large school – to say nothing of external commitments – permit personal teaching, nor was this necessarily easy to integrate into increasingly departmental structures.

Some history lessons for the older girls she built into her personal timetable, but, as with many other headmistresses, most of her actual classwork was now devoted to Scripture (or Religious Knowledge, or Divinity, or whatever other name was assigned, the range of names implying the vagueness that often dogged the subject). This headmistresses' custom, almost convention, partly derived from assumptions that religious instruction set the 'tone' and principles of the school and was therefore the Head's proper terrain, partly from the now-decaying tradition of ordained headmasters in public schools, and partly from the general lack of specialists in a scene where specialisation was triumphing. But Emmeline had her own interest, backed by systematic study at pre-war vacation courses.

In addition she regarded the Sixth Form as her own. Daily she talked to them in that space after Prayers before lessons started, chatting of the day's events, the news, her visits to London, whatever might awaken their minds. 'I was thinking this weekend of that phrase – I don't know who used it to describe men's ideas of the physical universe at the time of the Renaissance – "the stars fell back into illimitable space": that is the feeling we had in the Sixth Form when we faced the wider horizons you let us see'; such a response, put into words twenty years later, was the reward desired.

Quite apart from her own activities, and these were widening as will be seen, she had the whole world scene to talk about, from the heights of Mallory's and Irvine's attempts on Everest to the past revealed in Tutankhamun's tomb to the birth of broadcasting. From her brother Herbert she might hear of the Quakers who took food and medical aid to the children of starving post-war Germany, and a little later from Bolton King of the rise of Mussolini to his Italian dictatorship in 1923. (Much earlier than most, as Italian historian and lover of liberty, Bolton King recognised the dangers to Europe implicit in Fascism, publishing his perceptions in 1931 as *Fascism in Italy*, at once banned in Italy; the body of the young pilot who scattered tiny copies over Rome by air was never found.)

She could have told the girls of farm life in Rhodesia, from where Jessie Appleyard returned in 1921, now Jessie Haybittel with a husband and two small daughters, the younger Emmeline's godchild; she could have told how from India Amrit Kaur kept up her correspondence in the aftermath of the Amritsar massacre, in the light of growing reverence for Gandhi's way of life since her first meeting with him in 1915 though as yet Amrit's active public life was limited to social work in villages around Jullundur. Sixth Formers may have heard too of social work in London, for though the Spitalfields 'Nest' had limped through financial crises in the war to dwindle to smaller premises and just six girls as war changed the patterns of need and response, Emmeline had developed contact with at least two other urban missions, one with wide overseas interests. Certainly among the autumn lecturers of 1923 was included Miss Walters of the Beckenham College for Working Women, and the Sixth Form subscribed annually for a bursary for a student there.

Emmeline could have drawn for matter on her cycling holiday in Normandy in the summer of 1922, to describe the Kermesse at Caudebec with its processions and stalls decorated with 'great branches of pine', or the magnificence of Jumièges' ruined abbey, or French bitterness at spiralling food prices, and she commented too:

how much more democratic the French are in respect to the distinction between working and middle-class people. Most respectable business people, well-to-do commercial travellers and others came in and out for drinks before lunch, cheerfully shaking hands with working men with dirty hands and altogether much more soiled as to their clothes. There is no doubt that the French working men are much more courteous in their manners to each other than the English: they never meet without raising their hats, and, if they speak, shaking hands.

Then there were the implications of the 1919 Sex Disqualification (Removal) Act to discuss, and its provision that none should be debarred by sex or marriage from any public function or appointment, that, in principle, to these girls' generation were now open the highest ranks in the Civil Service, the law and local government. Not only did Emmeline talk but she listened to the girls' contributions, as she would to those of intelligent adults, and this impressed them most of all. Sometimes, apparently, she

190 / Doors of Possibility

over-egged the puddings, and, according to some, made the conscientious feel responsible for everything, the whole weight of the world on their shoulders.

Arenas for practice in their self-development, as well as windows on the world, were found in reviving moribund societies, the Sixth Form Debating Society, for instance, sometimes in debate with the boys of Bedford School, and in extending Field Club activities, an umbrella for expeditions of all kinds from printing press visits to a wireless demonstration (interrupted by thunderstorms), and in originating new groups, like the Club Molière. Drama was boosted with performances of *She Stoops to Conquer* and *The Rivals* in 1922, and the orchestra strengthened when André Mangeot joined to teach violin. An old tradition of professional chamber music recitals in the hall, preceded by a lecture, was revived when Mangeot brought Yvonne Arnaud in 1921, and Mangeot's own String Quartet, which then included John Barbirolli, was to perform frequently. By 1923 plans were ready for a Music Society to encompass the town as a whole. To provide a suitable platform in the hall for such musical and dramatic productions a fund was launched, chaired by Emmeline's ally, Diana Butt.

Musicians and Emmeline were often in harmony, despite her own lack of musicianship. Just as the pianist Frida Kindler had been a friend since Sherborne, playing at all Emmeline's schools and teaching for a while at Bedford, Mangeot too continued to bring his Quartet to play for her in later years. The pianist Clifford Curzon attributed this affinity to her uncommon appreciation that 'artists want fruits and salads after a concert to replace some of the liquid given out in toil', but she enjoyed their talk as they her hospitality, and she offered friends a post-concert party with Benjamin Britten and Peter Pears as the highpoint of a weekend in 1950. But at Bedford gentle, knowledgeable old Dr Harding was not superseded in his general guidance of the school's music.

Through the catalogue of societies and events runs a common thread, of initiative and organisational responsibility by the girls, timid enough delegation by comparison with some 'progressive' schools but, as Emmeline's care to explain her moves to parents and Old Girls shows, the contrasts were big enough gnats to swallow in some quarters. She could not innovate without convinced support.

Hence staff meetings were frequent, often lengthy too, and 'developed often into debates on educational ideas', according to Mary Millburn of the modern languages staff. A future headmistress herself, she enjoyed 'coming together to pool our ideas' – but it cost time.[12] As well as a technique of innovation such discussion was vital to Emmeline, whose ideas were rarely original, her forte lying rather in identifying and seizing what she thought best in relation to certain strongly-held principles, and she needed suggestions, reactions, other points of view to stimulate her own thinking. Few remarks in her speeches and other records cannot be traced back to others: it is their coherence and logical relation that defines her approach.

Ideas would have been useless without organisation. Before Emmeline's arrival, for example, the Art master had tried to teach all the girls above the third form, the 12-year-olds, in nine sets, sometimes groups of fifty or more. First Emmeline tried part-time assistants, then, when the juniors' Art teacher retired after thirty years at the school, she brought in a full-time, 'well-trained and zestful' young woman (by knowing Betty Glaisyer at Nuneaton she knew what to look for) and, at last, in the opinion of HM Inspectors, the Artwork could be planned on 'wide and progressive lines' by 'new and better methods'; the Inspectors added advice on stocking the Art room with examples of pottery, posters, illustrations and models of architecture, furniture and applied arts, and, a parting shot, added that the 'cast collection should be sorted out and the rubbish destroyed'.[13]

The ideal Emmeline told parents she sought, of 'a place where a large number of people are working together and where they are so keen on their life and so interested in the work that they move about quickly and quietly without fuss, and where a stranger coming in would hear noise but the pleasant hum of busy, active life', is very much on show in two articles published in 1922, in *The Graphic* and *The Queen*, especially in the sixteen photographs of the former. From the juniors absorbed in painting pottery, to Girl Guides tying knots, to upper-school scientists in a laboratory corner, to a jaunty advance on the field with lacrosse sticks (lacrosse was another novelty), all the chosen pictures depict girls happy or concentrated, or both, and bear out the desire credited to Emmeline in the article, 'to develop in the girls a sense of corporate life. If at school they have formed the habit of realising their responsibilities as members of a community they will afterwards do useful work in the world – no matter whether they be clever or dull, married or unmarried', and, she added, freedom was the key.[14]

Such was her propaganda, not just for the High School but for girls' education in general, as questions of its nature and function, in the AHM's view, entered a new phase.

Chapter 15
The Consultative Committee

In a Press interview in 1923 Emmeline was quoted as saying that she thought more attention was now paid to the 'average girl' rather than solely the intellectual, and, as often with Emmeline, 'think' was a synonym for 'hope'. Towards the 'average girl' she directed some curricular change, especially allowing greater choice among the range of subjects offered in Bedford High School's prospectus, but with her hands tied, annoyingly to her, by such regulations as the new requirement (rescinded in 1928) that whole forms be entered for School Certificate and by both Board and parental demand for examination success. She well understood the need for jobs; she did not think the School Certificate format the best preparation for all.

Yet this was now controversial: the 'average girl' had turned to a crucial issue. As an issue this should be distinguished from the problem of the badly prepared girl, a cause of distress. The curriculum of the secondary school was at stake, as it had been from the days of those models propounded by Dorothea Beale, Sophie Bryant and the others, described earlier, but with the development of publicly-funded secondary schools the nature of the fit curriculum became entangled in questions of which girls should be favoured by subsidies. Even fee-payers at such schools did not pay the whole cost of their schooling.

From the pioneering days of the later 19th century the war-cry of girls' educationists had been for extension – 'knowledge is no more a fountain sealed', trumpeted the GPDSC – and all they asked of their pupils was the desire to learn. Distinctions made, as in the endowed schools of Birmingham and Bedford, between 'High' and 'Middle' schools were primarily social, dividing those who wished and could afford to stay at school beyond 15 or so from those who could not. How to handle the 'backward girl', the 'dull girl' was a common AHM topic at the end of the First World War: none suggested getting rid of her, or ignoring her, for 'we soon found out that these girls were not "dull"; they are really different. And, as Tacitus said, "A thing is not worse because it is different."'[1]

LEA schools like Nuneaton, indebted to Bryce Commission assumptions about demand and supply, were expected to enable more to afford an education modelled on that given in such schools as King Edward's High School, Birmingham, or the GPDST high schools, and Emmeline's 1921 revision of Lilian Faithfull's 1910 role designations for a Nuneaton girl (daughter, citizen and patriot) was equally widely applicable: 'the possibility that you may become the mother of future men and women ... the certainty of playing another part in the world, too, in some profession or occupation ... the responsibility of taking part in public affairs, to the extent at any rate of using a vote both national and local'.

But by then in grant-aided schools two levels of subsidy were available, some for the fee payer, more for the free-place or scholarship girl, and because demand outstripped supply of free places qualification for one had become a competition. Thus merit measured by skill in testable subjects of English and arithmetic now mattered: in one year 8,780 candidates (both sexes), qualified by attainment and seeking free places, were turned down for lack of space, according to a Departmental Committee on Scholarships and Free Places (1920). Demand pressed, too, on fee-paying places, as was apparent at Nuneaton. With 339 pupils in 1917 Emmeline had agreed to restrict admissions on the results of an entry test, with priority for those whose parents agreed they would stay to 16; in 1918 she backed an application for building more classrooms with a report that overcrowding was forcing her not only to reject applicants but 'she has persuaded a few of the parents to take their children away, the girls not being likely to benefit by remaining longer' – the criteria for this ruthless weeding are not stated.[2] Building extension enabled Nuneaton numbers to rise to 358 in 1919-20 and 395 in 1920-1, but still demand pressed.

By 1922 public money was short. A committee under Sir Eric Geddes was appointed to advise on economies. Among a score of recommendations for education Geddes suggested limiting secondary education to 'pupils who show ability and industry'. Combining a desperate rearguard defence of educational bases, such as elementary school class sizes and teachers' pay, with a tactical assault on early leavers from secondary school, Fisher agreed to suspend further secondary development and to investigate more closely the 'quality of the entrants' to secondary schools, since, unless more stayed to 16, and took School Certificate to prove their attainments, he would concede that the cost of their support could not be justified.[3]

This directly contradicted the 1920 findings of Committee on Scholarships and Free Places. Then committee members had reckoned 75 per cent of children were 'capable of profiting' from secondary education and that therefore the 300,000 existing places in grant-aided schools in England and Wales should be increased to 2,250,000. As a first target they wanted 720,000, a recommendation endorsed by the AHM in 1921.[4] The figure of 75 per cent 'capable of profiting' was bandied about for years, and clearly did not represent an academic élite; much therefore depended on what value judgments were at work, what functions were recognised for secondary education, and hence by what criteria achievement of purpose could be evaluated.

The Regulations for Secondary Schools published in 1922-3 reflected the new approach. The Board were 'inventing ways of excluding children', exclaimed Emmeline's successor at Nuneaton. 'First "backward" pupils were doomed; then there was to be a test for those who had been admitted under the age of ten, and if "backward" they were to be turned out, no provision being made for them elsewhere; and finally in admitting new pupils preference was to be given to those who show "higher promise and capacity", which was a very difficult thing to test at an early age.'[5]

Muriel Davies spoke in the wake of the AHM's annual conference. Then the assembled headmistresses had boiled in indignation. In measured language the President, Grace Fanner of Putney County Secondary School, declared that the AHM 'always stands for greater elasticity, for individuality in schools, and for consideration of local and special circumstances', and that they could not agree that 'the standard of admission to a secondary school for all pupils should be determined by reference to the standard of a First Examination [School Certificate] taken at the normal age ... as it is impossible to guarantee the future educational capacity of girls of eleven, and it tends to the standardisation of all secondary schools to an examination level.'[6] 'Examinations,' commented the *Journal of Education*, 'are the only facts Mr Gradgrind can understand.'[7]

The following year the national economy still compelled thrift. New Board regulations prohibiting increase in secondary school accommodation, restricting grants, and limiting the percentage of free places moved Alice Stoneman of the Park School, Preston, to propose an AHM resolution on principles to determine entrance tests and pleaded 'against a too rigid insistence on uniformity of type'. Schools with grants only from the Board of Education retained more freedom than LEA schools; and as the Secretary of the GPDST told a senior civil servant at the Board in 1923:

Of course we are aware that we do not pass whole battalions of girls through Matriculation in the wonderful way that some of the best County Schools do; but their girls live mainly for that, and our girls essentially do not. Moreover, their Schools consist chiefly of picked girls from the Elementary Schools, whereas we take in the backward and stupid, in order to give them a chance in life which they deserve as much as anyone else.[8]

The Board's Inspectors carried the new policy into the classrooms. A full Inspection at Bedford in 1925, a year after Emmeline left, recorded with approval that her successor was trying to rid the school of its previous 'easy-going' character – not as regards discipline, they said, which they found very satisfactory, but for 'the allowances made in the past for backward girls'.[9] The twenty-one ex-pupils then in residence at universities, including ten at Oxford and Cambridge, were taken as a measure of value, an indication of the Board's increasing tendency to assess secondary school benefits in examination terms.

For the AHM as a whole, to restrict entry to the 'bright' and well-prepared was educationally questionable, and to do so by means of an unreliable test at 11 years old was irrational. 'Segregation of types at the school age would be a disaster in a country most of whose troubles have arisen not from ill-will but simply from the failure of one type of mind to understand another,' judged Dorothy Brock of the Mary Datchelor School in 1928.[10] For many it was also, under the present system, socially unjust. For it was very clear that if there were fewer secondary school places than children, if some of those places were fee-paying, and if family circumstances obliged many adolescents to pay their own keep, those who were excluded would be those who were poor.

In 1906 the Liberal President of the Board of Education, Augustine Birrell, had called 'detestable' and 'retrograde' the 'vulgar notion ... that elementary education was something for the children of artisans and agricultural labourers, that secondary education belonged to the children of the professional, shopkeeping and middle class, while university education was the luxury of the rich'.[11] In 1922 R. H. Tawney edited the Labour party's policy document *Secondary Education for All*, arguing that all normal children should have secondary education of some sort from 11 to 16, and that the present parallel but separate tracks on which ran the education of over-11s were based on class distinction. Like the TUC, the NUT and other groups interested in 'the workers', Tawney disliked the growth from about 1911 of Central schools, distinguished (like the Higher Elementary schools) from secondary schools not only by an upper age limit of 16 and a curriculum with some bias to employment, but by management under the Elementary regulations, with fewer facilities.

The AHM stood for the individual legacy of girls' secondary education, a legacy Emmeline wholeheartedly appropriated. Beyond her day-to-day life practising the art of the possible as a working headmistress in an imperfect society, her career may be seen as a drive to extension and inclusion; hence her focus on difference not on likeness, her oft-repeated demand for flexibility and variety to develop and discipline the varied gifts of varied women. To her, therefore, it was irrational to suppose that courses designed to lead to university – and the very term 'Matriculation' for certain credits in the School Certificate betrayed their university orientation – were suitable for all. So when 'value for money' was the cry and 'who are most likely to profit?' was the question, the curriculum was at the heart of debate.

To the 'clever' girl Emmeline evinced an ambivalence very common among headmistresses of her time. On the one hand, she testified in speech after speech to her belief that 'character' was all-important, that all girls were equally worthwhile and each had her special task, that abilities were multiple and included the practical and the nurturing and artistic; on the other, she showed a sympathy, perhaps a sense of self-recognition, identity of desire, with her university hopefuls, finding it hard even to believe that a girl capable of university might choose otherwise.

Such a tension between belief and desire fuelled her vigour at the AHM Conference of 1923, held at Newnham College, Cambridge – that unrealisable dream of her youth – and opening with a silent tribute to the pioneer Sophie Bryant, found dead in the Alps the previous summer. Then, on Saturday, Emmeline introduced seven papers grouped under the collective title 'The task of the secondary school' and based on the report just issued by the Board of Education's Consultative Committee on 'Differentiation of curriculum for boys and girls respectively in secondary schools'. 'At the outset Miss Tanner clarified our thought and determined our end by defining the problem which these preliminary investigations of the Consultative Committee have left us to solve – viz., the fit curriculum – a curriculum which may prepare a girl for full success in her life as woman, as mother, as citizen. This, Miss Tanner maintained, was the most urgent of all [the AHM's] problems today'.[12]

She had the report at her finger-tips, for she had helped to write it. Key to reformist strategy was the principle of being early in the field, influencing Ministers and civil servants before Bills and regulations were drafted rather than undergo the more exhausting and futile efforts of amending entrenched positions. Such an opportunity had opened for Emmeline in the summer of 1920 when she was asked to become a member of the Board of Education's Consultative Committee.

She knew of this body already. Its existence was written into the 1899 Act which set up the Board itself; its members were drawn from all parts of the educational network except the Board itself, and their task was to investigate topics in which the Board was interested, to inform and to recommend possible action; the Board might, if it chose, publish the Committee's reports. The Committee had no formal power to make policy, and its topics were those referred by the Board, limited in scope and specific in subject. Since 1916 activities had been suspended for the War, and the Committee had gradually dissolved as periods of membership ended, but in 1920 it was reconstituted. Emmeline was asked to serve for four years – a third of the twenty-one members were due to retire at two-year intervals, but might be reappointed – and was allowed for the usually monthly meetings her train fares (in the unaccustomed luxury of first class) and 25/- a night if she had to stay away from home; most sessions lasted two days. So, on Thursday 29 July 1920, she travelled to Whitehall, to the Board's offices in King Charles Street, for the preliminary meeting.

Round the table were some who had served on the previous Committee, including W. H. Hadow, who became Chairman, and R. H. Tawney (his reputation growing) – but the majority were new. Not all were strangers to Emmeline. There was William Vaughan of Rugby School, and the more determined innovator Joseph White, a Central school headmaster who had sat on the history committees with her; at the meeting of historians chaired by Firth she had met Ernest Barker, who had taken the scholarship route from an impoverished cottage to Oxford and was now Principal of King's College, London. Three beside herself were women: Bertha Phillpotts' experience lay in the universities, Essie Conway was headmistress of an elementary school and an ex-President of the NUT, and Freda Hawtrey came from the Training College at Feltham; Emmeline, it seemed, was to contribute the secondary-school point of view. But the role of Committee members was to hear and assess evidence, not to provide it, and in theory at least they were chosen as individuals not as representatives, though the Board later congratulated itself on the 'microcosm' or 'senate' of the educational world the choices achieved.[13]

The group rapidly got down to business at this first meeting, accepting the two new references handed down and establishing procedures. One topic, on the possible uses of 'psychological tests of educable capacity', was set aside for its technical complication and a sub-committee selected to gather and collate information on research and experimentation (Emmeline was at first a member of this sub-committee but almost immediately dropped out); the other, on differentiation of secondary-school curricula for boys and girls, was taken up first.

Some felt this was no very vitally pressing concern, not the central policy issue they craved to tackle, though it was sufficiently controversial to have been rejected by the Board as a reference in earlier days for fear of startling co-educational hares. (This Committee presented some interesting but inconclusive findings on co-education in an appendix, but recognised the subject as a red herring to the real issues.) But to women it was important. Should girls have a 'woman-centred' curriculum, answering a distinctively female nature? The pioneers had shunned such, seeing the differentiation then practised as based on assumptions of female inferiority, but that phase, thought the optimistic graduates of the 1920s, was now past. Hadow himself had once preferred separate development, when he had vigorously opposed degrees for women at Oxford years before, and years later Barker too wistfully favoured the notion of distinctively female universities to realise women's 'equal but different' intellectual capacities.

But Hadow's chairmanship was not domination, and the feeling of solidarity and amity that seems to have quickly grown, must have been due in large measure to his tactful handling of his strong-minded team. A child of the vicarage, he himself came from a family more gifted with lively intellects than money, attentive to the arts and responsive to social conscience. His intellect had been assisted by scholarships to Malvern College and Oxford, but he was now known both for the administrative flair shown first at Newcastle, then at Sheffield University, and for his efforts to lure musical appreciation from the ivory towers of professionals to the common life. Through his work for education in 1918 in the base camps of France he had developed an association with Lord Gorell, the War Office's education chief, and Gorell (administrator, minor poet and novelist) also sat at the table of the Consultative Committee.

Dates for the next meetings were fixed, and the members departed for summer – in Emmeline's case to help her parents move from Fern Bank to the house in Clifton which their son Fred's family had now left – and reconvened on 23 and 24 September 1920 to discuss categories of witnesses and draw up lists. The first job was to assess the current extent and direction of differentiation, and as the months of the next year passed they questioned in person and studied written memoranda from a variety of sources; the AHM submitted their views in December 1920, but numerous individual heads were interviewed. And they argued, not over intellectual equality or otherwise, but rather about the possible physiological, psychological and vocational differences between boys and girls.

That intellectual equality was taken for granted enormously pleased Emmeline – she described it to the MAHM as the Committee's 'absolute conviction' – especially because it enabled discussion to move beyond that point to deliberate on a possible third stage envisaged in girls' education in England. The report's introduction offers an historical pattern: first it sees, until about 1850, educational difference based on inequality, then a reaction towards assimilation to male practices to prove equality, and now perhaps there might emerge a synthesis, a 'truer and richer' equality 'founded on mutual recognition of differences'. But this neat dialectic is at once undercut by a confession that no 'clear and ascertained differences ... on which an educational policy may readily be based' could be substantiated by hard scientific evidence as opposed to 'facile generalisations' of impressionistic experience, inevitably coloured by the observer's own sex.[14] The potential third stage collapses.

The biggest handicap to the investigation was the limited breadth and depth of good evidence on psychological and emotional difference, 'good' being defined as 'by scientific method'. Under the guidance of Dr J. G. Adami the Committee drew principally on the work of Helen Thompson in Chicago, of Cyril Burt and R. L. Moore in England, and E. L. Thorndike of Columbia University, with Percy Nunn and others also contributing psychological findings. Unsatisfied, the Committee recommended more research be undertaken. Thus the report evades justification of its own primary assumption, that mental difference is based on individuality far more than on biological sex, an assumption that accounts for the report's preference for explaining evidence of, for example, girls' greater docility or lesser mathematical attainments by social and environmental influences rather than by innate qualities.

Indeed the report is as much an expression of contemporary liberal and rational attitudes as an inquiry, and with a radical bite. Decorously it is admitted that social function in adulthood may determine education in childhood; then, charged with conviction, are arguments that no subjects open to one sex should be closed to the other, that in the course of history patterns of work had constantly changed, both of the hand and of the head, and that, since 'even those employments which seem at present most unsuited to women will ... be opened to them by a change of technique or alteration of social customs', schools must 'keep open as many doors as possible ... into the world' and 'avoid any policy based on the idea that certain occupations, and certain occupations only, can be successfully undertaken by men or by women'.[15] At the AHM conference in 1923 the discussion which Emmeline led enthusiastically enshrined the phrase 'open doors of possibility' among their desiderata, though with few recorded ideas on how smaller schools could achieve this.

The radical teeth of the body of the report were camouflaged by the gentlemanly tact of the introduction, with its references to 'old and delicate graces' perhaps 'sacrificed on the austere altar of sex equality', so that sometimes historians have missed the subsequent suspicion, even disdain, of docility or eagerness to please in girls. The introduction's element of parody has often gone unrecognised, but 'we were a lively company', said Ernest Barker, and with 'a lively Chairman' in Hadow.[16] Contemporaries were rather shocked. Even the usually liberal *Journal of Education* identified the Committee's basic assumptions of school as 'what most public schoolmistresses practise, an institution in which ... any career but that afforded by home' is the objective, and an MAHM member discerned a 'subtle plea for making girls as like boys as possible' when Emmeline described the findings to a meeting in Birmingham.[17]

In one respect the report argued the reverse, in a quite unsubtle plea for the development of musical and artistic understanding (the education of 'imagination' and 'vision') for *both* sexes, though *not*, they insisted, the time-consuming and usually mediocre executive performance so popular in Emmeline's youth and after. 'Appreciation' was what Hadow called the studies he himself ardently promoted for boys as well as girls, the ardour spilling in an emotional page of this report; yet the 'apathy and neglect' he described in boys' schools of the last century were not so easily dislodged when aesthetic subjects were seen as frills to the real business of life.[18] Like the AHM the Committee recommended the parity of Group IV in the School Certificate, with music as a principal subject for Higher Certificate and an Advanced Course to include music and art.

Less radical was the Committee's unquestioning acceptance of the custom of assigning infant care to mothers. Indeed, contemporary psychologists, usually following Freud, highlighted the significance of early childhood, and the mother's status was enhanced. Hence the Committee embraced an unequal view of the sexes' social function: '... we may assume that all children have to be educated with two ends in view – (i) to earn their own living; (ii) to be useful citizens; – while girls have also to be prepared (iii) to be makers of homes'.[19]

This closely correlates with what Emmeline had long been telling her girls, and ought logically to have compelled a greater share of attention to the more burdened sex. But the troublesome factor, the relationship between the earning and home-making roles of women, was not discussed, for this lay beyond the school and was affected by local and particular circumstances – or, perhaps, because 'The views of married women are indeed notable by their absence', as one journalist noted.[20] Yet the difficulty was obliquely approached: 'it seems to us important that the determining voice ... should rest, as far as possible, with women themselves', reflected in recommendation No 24 that women should be adequately represented on all bodies dealing in any way with girls' education.[21]

That too was ignored; in fact all twenty-four recommendations were ignored by the Board of Education and other regulatory bodies, though some individual schools tried to respond to suggestions on subject treatment, or the development of initiative and independence in girls, or (occasionally) the provision of courses suited to non-academic pupils over 15, based perhaps on literature and the arts, or craft and domestic subjects, or a foreign language with geography and economics for girls interested in business.

The report's significance perhaps lies largely in this disregard. It did not fit either official policies or social prejudices, though sly footnotes suggesting boys should help more at home were less provocative than overt analysis of domestic pressures on girls from housework, childcare and social duties, or pressure from parents who saw married leisure as the highest aim, gave girls less independence than boys, thought subjects like mathematics unsuitable, and in general cabin'd, cribb'd, confin'd their growing daughters.

For Emmeline the work was significant at several levels. The investigation clarified and reinforced the direction of her existing thought and practice, and confirmed the belief she had held since the closing years of the war (and in 1949 attributed to her reading of Kenneth Richmond's works) that the curriculum was too full. The timetable was squeezed. It was a point the report made strongly, recommending more subject choice and more flexible examinations, and it was a point the AHM readily picked up at their discussion at Newnham in 1923. The opposite pitfall of over-specialisation might be avoided by 'multiplying points of contact, and in relating cognate subjects', still a favourite notion of Emmeline in 1949, though then she admitted to practical difficulties.

Secondly, her attitudes were coloured thereafter by the medical evidence heard, an array of up-to-date technical data on bone growth, blood composition, calcium metabolism, and the differing growth cycles of boys and girls, all building to two simple conclusions: girls of 11 to 16 tire more easily than boys of the same age, and for both sexes over-tiredness may be permanently damaging. Anaemia was more common in girls, for example. Nerves were raw on health in the early 20th century, after frightening claims in the early days of high schools about the stress girls suffered from intellectual exertion. Then symptoms from skeletal deformation to amenorrhea and chlorosis ('green-sickness', characterised by anaemia and lassitude) had been attributed to the draining of energy from womb to brain, for example by the influential Henry Maudsley of University College, London.[22] Emmeline herself believed anxiety about work and pressure to slog dulled and dispirited girls, and that exercise and the open air were recreative.

Gymnastics and games had developed partly in response to health worries. 'Ah, if women only recognised how much younger they would keep, how much fuller and happier their lives would be, if they studied the laws of health and lived free, untrammelled lives with plenty of physical exercise!' exclaimed Mme Bergman-Osterburg.[23] Fresh from Stockholm this physical education pioneer had been employed from 1881-7 by the London School Board; she then founded a college, from 1895 sited at Dartford, to train middle-class girls to teach in secondary schools, and the gospel spread.

Bedford High School appointed one of her students, Margaret Stansfeld, in 1887, and when she herself left to establish Bedford Physical Training College she came to a slightly unorthodox but effective arrangement with the High School that her staff should teach there and the girls be used as practice material for students. The College curriculum included anatomy, physiology and hygiene; and Emmeline saw no need to change the arrangement with Margaret Stansfeld in the light of the Consultative Committee's recommendation that common sense and caution should prevail, no girl being pushed to over-exertion by over-competition, nor forced to play vigorous games if uncomfortable through menstruation, and she showed no doubt that physical exercise justified its space in the curriculum.

To the constant concern about healthy development were added sudden crises of infection, and not till antibiotics were available from the 1940s and (ironically in view of Emmeline's stand against compulsory vaccination) inoculation was commonplace would tuberculosis, measles, whooping-cough, scarlet fever, diphtheria and the rest loosen their grip as major child-killers. The only protection was quarantine or even to close a school for weeks at a time. At least one headmistress (not Emmeline) had her classrooms swabbed twice daily with Jeyes fluid. A classic example marred a term at Nuneaton in 1919 when, according to Nuneaton's Medical Officer of Health:

> [an] outbreak of scarlet fever occurred in the autumn and was introduced into the town via the Girls' High School by a child living outside the Borough. The outbreak was not a serious one ... and no deaths resulted. It was unfortunate that a 'scare' arose in the town, and a large number of parents kept their children away from the High School. Exaggerated rumours undoubtedly caused this ... The High School was closed from October 22nd till the end of the mid-term holiday.[24]

The needs of the healthy body were used to justify headmistresses' attempts to police clothing, cleanliness, exercise, and sleep (as far as possible), drawing into the educational orbit what had been and formally remained the parents' responsibility. At a school like Bedford, both day and boarding, comparisons could be noted by an alert headmistress.

Thirdly, Emmeline adroitly turned to account the impressions of witnesses before the Consultative Committee, especially those from employers, teachers and examiners, as spine-stiffening material for girls. 'Everyone says that girls are very conscientious,' she told the girls of Lord Digby's School in Sherborne in 1922, 'but the way in which this is said is not really very complimentary to girls because the people generally mean that girls do what they think they ought but that often they do it rather stupidly and if they only thought a little more clearly they would see that their idea as to the right course was mistaken'. Examiners said girls were too diffuse, losing points in a multiplicity of words, teachers said they 'accept all details they are told without questions', and so Emmeline told the girls before her that their common 'unfortunate sex' must therefore make special efforts to learn to think for themselves and be succinct. If girls were accused of lacking a 'spirit of adventure', 'it is a very serious charge because one of the things that gives zest to life and makes the most difficult tasks impossible and interesting is the spirit of adventure' that inspires explorers, discoverers, experimenters, abstract thinkers, poetic vision: 'It would be fatal for our work and our happiness if we let the spirit of adventure ... die during our school days.' That the Committee thought the fault not necessarily that of girls themselves she did not say.

Nor was it woolly psychological testimony she brought before the headmistresses in conference at Newnham in 1923 but the practical necessities: the Committee had not found the curriculum as it stood ideal for either sex. Members had considered and found some weight in objections that the standard fare for those aged 12 to 16 of both sexes was 'too academic', 'over-burdened', 'too rigid', and required more scope for 'individual divergence of interest and ability'. Hence Emmeline emphasised as 'urgent' the problem of the 'fit curriculum', and hence the repeated complaints at the constrictive system of examinations and regulations, and the anxiety over the 'average girl'.

Altogether the AHM conference of 1923 was stimulating, and for Emmeline further gratifying in that she was elected Chairman of the Executive Committee, as by convention the nominee of the President-elect always was. When the President for 1923-5, Frances Gray of St Paul's Girls' School, initially approached Emmeline she was met with a list of 'grievous shortcomings'. In Emmeline's self-appraisal she was 'not constructive'. 'I couldn't do with a Chairman that *was*,' replied Frances Gray; 'I'm little else.' 'Not a good mind,' said Emmeline. 'That doesn't matter (if it's true) because nobody on earth would ever guess it ... Not methodical? It's [the Secretary] Miss Young's business to keep us both up to the mark in that.'

Chapter 16
To build a better world

Fortunately from Bedford to London was an easy journey. For the next two years Emmeline spent many nights at Frances Gray's flat in London before AHM committee meetings, and a solid friendship was forged between the AHM President and her Chairman of Committee. By 1925 the AHM had 537 members with 150,000 girls in their schools, and Emmeline's task was not only to steer meetings and chair some subcommittees, but to manage dealings with bodies as various as examiners, adult education organisers, parliamentary candidates, European and other foreign educationists, and to sit with Frances Gray and the leaders of the associations for secondary head-masters, assistant masters and mistresses in Joint Four meetings. During Miss Gray's presidency joint action by the Joint Four began to loom larger in AHM eyes and the matters they handled together increased in scope and range.

Professional work for the AHM and the Consultative Committee, however, was only a part of what Mary Millburn, teaching at Bedford, meant when she said that Emmeline 'belonged to the great outside world'.[1] Some of the ways in which Emmeline brought 'the great outside world' to Bedford as a town, as well as to the High School, were of course professionally shaped too: she was co-opted, for example, on to the town's Education Committee as she had been at Nuneaton to provide a professional perspective on LEA matters, and she was a founder-member of the Bedford branch of the Historical Association. There she served as President and also as a lecturer, a series on Florence being long remembered, for the Renaissance still stirred her imagination and the art of holding an audience was now second nature to her. Often her speeches, whether substantial or occasional in matter, are flat when read in print, but Emmeline's rhetoric seems to have been one of performance not of composition, and she was regularly well received.

Plenty of public speaking was needed for one of her most whole-hearted efforts. As a means to secure peace the idea of the League of Nations had gripped her from its start, along with the conviction that grass-roots support was essential so that the force of public opinion might lever governments. It was an uphill struggle. The same page of the *Bedfordshire Standard* on 9 December 1921 that carried an announcement of a forthcoming lecture-meeting chaired by Miss Tanner on 'The League of Nations at work' printed in its comment section two pieces markedly suspicious of international 'whitewashing', demanding German 'penitence' and hostile to the 'invasion' of German goods, not the vocabulary of constructive negotiation let alone of the progressive disarmament planned by the League.

Emmeline's guest speaker that December night was John Harris from the Executive Committee of the League of Nations Union, this Union (LNU) being a British organisation formed to educate the British public about the 52-member League's nature and aims. Local branches were established, and among the initiating spirits of the Bedford branch founded in 1921 was Emmeline, who became its President; Harris's talk was among the first events held in Bedford. Further meetings followed, sometimes lectures describing the League's work, for example the Humanitarian Commission's fight against international traffic in drugs and children, or efforts towards intellectual and medical co-operation, or for the development of international law through the Court at The Hague, or the work done by the International Labour Office on labour conditions, as well as work relating to the League's primary interest in peace.

Sometimes, however, crises prompted local response. One such was the Chanak Crisis of 1922. Then Emmeline called an emergency meeting at the Town Hall, and, addressing those who came with passionate urgency, proposed the motion that 'The Bedford branch of the League of Nations Union urges the Government to do all in its power to promote the intervention of the League of Nations in the crisis in the Near East in order to avert the appalling disaster of another European War'. Now her rhetoric flowered and flowed. Her arguments for co-operation and negotiation by a body too various to be accused of selfish interests she crowned with the claim that everyone had a sacred duty to perform in the cause of peace, and that everyone who stood aloof from the only body which was striving to settle disputes in a rational way was on the side of war. The habit of framing issues in moral terms was deeply ingrained in Emmeline, and to her the most compelling persuasion.

That particular crisis was in the end muddled through, and the League was able to chalk up some political successes, for instance in disputes between Sweden and Finland, between Poland and Lithuania, between Albania and Serbia when economic sanctions were threatened. Although Emmeline soon developed some scepticism about the atmosphere of such conferences as that at Lausanne in 1922, suspecting it 'depended too much upon bargaining, personality and tact which often was not guileless', she showed no doubt about the need to confer nor about the importance of demonstrating popular support. For the last popular education was required, and so in 1923 the Bedford LNU organised a week of events, imported Frederick Whelen from the LNU headquarters in London to address as many sections of the citizenry as could be reached through the network of social, religious and political societies, and finally booked the Corn Exchange for an open 'Mass Meeting'.

Whelen was kept busy with three or four meetings a day, but Emmeline herself addressed some groups and as a back-up a study circle was organised and a Schools Essay Competition held, so managed that every school, elementary and secondary, won a prize, with the best essays on the League published in the local Press. Press attention was further enticed by use of the latest technology (ironically 'of army pattern') to rig the Corn Exchange with microphones wired to amplifying apparatus outside so that proceedings at the Mass Meeting were broadcast to the street. Yet attendance was not all that was hoped; the *Bedfordshire Times* attributed this to the atrocious March weather which kept the platform party huddled in thick overcoats, but the *Bedford Record* blamed Bedford apathy and national reaction away from ideals towards 'their dancing, their beer and their sport'.[2]

Emmeline was also concerned that the essay scheme unduly exploited children. She discussed the matter with other headmistresses and in August 1923 she and Frances Gray signed a letter to *The Times* full of AHM protest at interference in education by charity organisers who distractingly called on girls for public fund-raising performances and by business-inspired competitions between schoolgirls, even 'bogus examinations', with advertisement as an ulterior object. Characteristically the liberal Emmeline preferred to rouse public support through the Press rather than demand legislation, and she herself was now more cautious in rationing school charitable efforts to those that fitted educational patterns, as the LNU essays might be deemed to do.

Within historians' circles the LNU raised a more knotty question of whether ends justified means. In May 1921 the national LNU sent a deputation headed by H. G. Wells and the historian G. P. Gooch to see Fisher at the Board of Education and ask for the overhaul of curricula and textbooks to check for militaristic propaganda, and, further, to highlight peace values and the horrors of war. But the Historical Association refused to support this request, fearful that any deliberate introduction of bias was a tactical error likely to alienate teachers and discredit historical education. Within the Association a lively debate soon moved to an elevated plane of historiography, and for classroom purposes teachers were left to work out their own procedures, but from the mid-1920s the Board of Education's handbook for elementary teachers contained a substantial appendix explaining the League of Nations as an historical development and describing its Covenant and modes of work, in a manner parallel to analyses of government structures.

In 1922 present national politics, as well as those of teaching history, came to the fore when the Coalition government dissolved and a general election was called for 15 November. A parliamentary vote was an inspiring novelty to Emmeline, and in Bedford she had both a National Liberal and an Independent Liberal candidate to consider, as well as those from the Conservative and Labour Parties. At a women's meeting called by the National Women Citizens' Association Emmeline was on the platform, supporting her secretary V. I. Chomley in the chair, and they did not limit questions to so-called women's issues as they interrogated the four candidates. Women police and divorce were among matters raised, but so too were the capital levy, the price of beer, free trade and employment.

In fact Emmeline already knew her mind: at the meeting of the Independent Liberals in the Corn Exchange she had seconded the motion to adopt Lady Lawson as the candidate, though privately Emmeline admitted 'she is not a convincing speaker'. In her speech she urged support for Lady Lawson for the sake of supplying the Commons with a majority 'which would really whole-heartedly support the League of Nations, and not only by lip service', and for the sake of free trade and of 'many social reforms about which [Emmeline] felt very strongly'.[3] According to Miss Chomley, another Liberal, 'People are ... much impressed at Miss Tanner's coming out definitely on a political platform, a thing which I believe none of the Heads of [Bedford] Schools has done before.'

It was a crowded meeting, the magnet being the widely-admired Lord Grey of Fallodon, an ardent advocate for the League of Nations – the chance to hear such men was an advantage of elections, said Emmeline once, before widespread broadcasting. 'Hundreds of people were standing, and many more were turned away,' she told her parents; the audience for Grey 'included a good many people of all parties and many working – and some very dirty – men'. Grey proved 'calm, reasoned, and I think is very good'. But she was not wholly happy:

> ... it was altogether a very fine meeting, entirely spoilt, as far as one man could do it, by the chairman, an awful man named Burridge who was once the candidate. He said such things about the broken promises of the Coalition and said them as though we wished the Coalition had hanged the Kaiser and forever forbidden aliens to enter this land that if I hadn't badly wanted to hear Lord Grey I should have got up and walked off the platform. I really did feel ashamed to be on it.

In the end the Conservative was elected, a local brewer who retained his seat through the elections of 1923 and 1924, which returned Baldwin's Conservatives to government after a brief Labour interlude. As Bedford's MP he became also a Governor of the High School. In 1922 Emmeline had characterised him to her parents:

> ... such a simple and honest young man I thought his frankness almost disarming – though I pray he won't represent us in Parliament. I think there are very few questions he would thoroughly understand. He would never speak, which, perhaps, would be a good thing, and he would vote as he was told. When asked about divorce he said, 'As a churchman I disapprove of divorce, but as a thinking man ...'!

Support for the League of Nations was the crucial factor in Emmeline's platform stand, and later she renounced active canvassing. It is impossible to situate her precisely, at this or any later time, on the map of British political thought and action. She said herself that she was 'a rather poor party politician' with 'no high regard for party politics', and seems to have been reluctant to identify herself with stereotyped positions or the formulations of others; whatever smelt of narrow sectionalism evoked unease in her. Moreover, looking back in 1952, 'I feel very doubtful whether the Liberal Party will ever recover as such, and, having been born and bred a good Liberal, I regret this fact very much and always have some resentment against Lloyd George for having broken up the Party, because I have always felt that it was he who was responsible for doing this.' By then she thought 'a reshuffling of the Parties altogether' a likelihood 'thirty years hence', as she perceived substantial shifts in all positions, though not a disappearance of 'Liberals in principle'.

She would not, to be sure, have put so much energy into the AHM or have been so ready to hold offices in the various organisations she embraced had she not agreed with the self-proclaimed Socialist William Morris that 'It is always and everywhere good that people should do their own business, and in order that they may do it well, every citizen should have some share of it, and take on his shoulders some part of the responsibility.'[4] Such a message she herself preached on numerous school speech days. Collective or co-operative action was, at the turn of the century, held to imply the left wing, but the principles of free association were variously interpreted: the Fabian Society, or at least the Fabians Sidney and Beatrice Webb, were collective in policy, but Emmeline apparently agreed with the Webbs that it was psychologically unsound for managers to be elected or dismissed by the staff they managed directly – 'to give orders all day to his staff who ... criticise his action in the evening, with the power of dismissing him if he fails to conform to their wishes'.[5] In Emmeline's schools, as in her associations, committee members were elected as representatives, not as delegates.

If her Liberalism was radical, then, allied to democratic co-operation which preferred rationality to tradition, Emmeline yet identified its framework as that of existing forms and institutions – Parliament, professional groups, conventional social structures – and these she strove to mimic in school, to naturalise them in the girls' consciousnesses. School societies and clubs were organised on the patterns familiar in the larger society, and she was rigorous in their administrative detail, with elected committees, secretaries and treasurers with defined duties, record-keeping and prepared agenda.

Collectivism, co-operation were held to be the antithesis of competition. But competition was unabashed in the award of certain school prizes (for essays, for reading, not for classwork), though leaving scholarships seem to have been granted on a combination of need and merit. If how you played mattered more than if you won, yet you must strive to win, to do well: here reward for effort was a crucial principle, justifying some competition. This contradiction was fundamental: in the rhetoric of the AHM, as of Emmeline herself, each girl's 'bent' – aptitudes and abilities became the phrase – was to be respected and developed, yet academic excellence had a special significance, symbolised by the honourable position given to scholarships to Oxford and Cambridge in speech day honours lists. However strongly headmistresses insisted that division between mental and manual labour was artificial, however ardently they urged the claims of Group IV to equality in the School Certificate, yet few of the pupils in schools run by AHM members failed to suspect that domestic science was for the 'duds' in the school hierarchy.

Like co-operation and competition, co-operation and leadership held a delicate poise both in Emmeline's notions of political activity and in the principles and structure of the institutions wherein she moved. The role of headmistress enacted such a balance; and in the 1920s and 1930s most headmistresses leant, like Emmeline herself, to the side of leadership. But although Emmeline had to be flexible to accommodate all these positions, to grant reward to excellence and initiative but to assert the value of each and every contribution, to want power to depend on consent and respond to the governed while carrying its own dynamic charge, her very lack of hard-and-fast programmes of detail was advantageous to her. She could the more easily sense the temperature of the AHM or staff meetings or committees; she could avoid alienating others by extremes and dogmas; her work could remain relevant and practical, and so be more effective.

The Bedford years which fixed these patterns were 'strenuous', she said, but she was as reluctant to submit herself to unremitting slog as to inflict it on girls, for 'the pause reinforceth the fresh onset', as the Consultative Committee had once quoted Bacon. An April holiday in Switzerland in 1923 was to be a holiday, though Emmeline took examination papers to correct and her inexhaustible curiosity noted down some effects on Swiss hoteliers of European economic woes (and that her bill was less than in more modest inns in Normandy the year before); she undertook, too, to find an English home where the proprietor's son might learn English since a job was unobtainable.

But she went there to walk in the clear air, and as she walked she watched – how the Swiss made hillside gardens, for example: 'They lift the turf, etc. off a little patch, using forks with the prongs set at right angles to the handle to pick at it first; then they turn the soil over, scatter manure over the top of it, and leave it for a little while; after that they dig it once more, and plant it.' Usually she walked alone, even when hail half-filled her pockets and 'lumps of snow melted in my hair and ran down' when she removed her hat to feel the air, but once with friends of friends on a stiff uphill expedition to achieve magnificent views from Mont Cubly over the lake towards Geneva, and then Emmeline, now aged forty-six, was rather relieved to find the others, younger and 'both hockey players and athletic', were also tired the next day.

Geneva in the end drew her, when a League of Nations official telephoned to tell her of an open Council meeting. There she found no clear arrangements for visitors to the Palais des Nations, made 'vain enquiries', and at length wandered into a garden and 'saw a long room, not unlike a dining hall, in which groups of men were chatting in window recesses or seated round a table'. She recognised none, so, unafflicted by shyness, she persuaded the English Major Buxton to draw for her a table-plan. Presiding was her own new President of the Board of Education, Fisher's replacement Edward Wood; others came from France, Belgium, Brazil, Sweden, Uruguay and Japan, and the subject was the nationality of peoples in mandated territories, specifically of the 10,000 British and 7,000 Germans in what had been German South-West Africa.

At the lunch break Emmeline left to tour the International Labour Office, escorted by another British official, and to be deeply impressed by the legal translation service and methods of investigation into labour laws worldwide. She was also impressed by the number of bicycles outside – 'worthy of Bedford' – but, lacking her own, had to leap on and off several trams and steer by her sense of direction to return to the Palais des Nations for the Council session from 4.15 to 7.15 pm, and its dispute between Hungarians and Roumanians over Transylvania. Even if the League survived the bad debating manners exhibited, she decided, 'it would break on the rock of ventilation'; she was told 'it was always the same: the English wanted the windows open and all the other people wanted them shut'.

She returned with the conviction that English Press criticism of the League's cost was unfounded in view of its research needs, and with some apprehensions. Rapidly four principles came to dominate her thinking. First, the machinery was inadequate without the will to make it work; second, the representatives sent must be 'the best' and enjoy with authority the confidence of their home nations; third, the League must be inclusive, for limited membership meant limited claim to moral authority; and, fourth, it should be permanently in session, so that trust might develop, and not be a series of *ad hoc* negotiations in which each struggled and deceived to gain advantage. The similarities between Emmeline's views on the League of Nations and her views on the English educational system are not coincidental but relate to a vision of social structures as communities of interest.

Back to Bedford then, and to a 'spotlessly clean cottage with Mrs Davis all smiling and cheerful and welcoming', to the ever-livening cycle of the school year, and to the other 'strenuous' life beyond. The autumn term of 1923 kept Emmeline well occupied, welcoming Mangeot's String Quartet for a recital and planning the Bedford Music Club, herself lecturing to the school's Field Club and encouraging the opening debate of a revived debating society, lecturing to Bedford's branch of the Historical Association and travelling to Cambridge for a conference of the British Institute of Adult Education, conferring (also on the AHM's behalf) with the Oxford and Cambridge Schools Examination Board, and in November discussing educational policy with Professor Findlay, a Labour candidate for one of the university seats in the House of Commons. And so on, and – she thought – onwards.

In the spring Emmeline had found the 13-year-old niece who stayed with her 'a very companionable little person to have in the house and very affectionate', but she had not always seemed so to her mother. For Winifred the child born just ten months after marriage could be a worry, 'vexing' in a favourite word, energetically naughty and capable of tantrums, and as a fourth pregnancy discomforted Winifred so Margaret, aged eight, was moved from the village elementary school to a small private boarding school in Gloucestershire, probably on Emmeline's advice. To Emmeline it seemed entirely natural to welcome her niece, when she outgrew this establishment, to the school she herself counted home, and Margaret became a boarder in one of Bedford High School's boarding houses, a small emblem of school as an enlarged family, a community predicated on mutual loyalty. Eight of Emmeline's nine nieces were eventually educated under her headmistress-ship.

Such a progress as Margaret's, in stages from school to school, was common to many girls who could expect secondary education. Other Bedford fee-payers might have begun in the Kindergarten attached to the Froebel Training College run by Amy Walmsley, with long-standing ties to the High School, have advanced at eight or so to the High School's own preparatory department, and moved up three years later to the High School proper. But most of the village children who had been Margaret's contemporaries at the village school both started and finished in the same building, as did many of those who spent their whole school lives within the elementary system. As the school-leaving age rose, 14 now and 15 proposed, educationists identified a problem here.

In February 1923 some members of the Consultative Committee waited on the President of the Board of Education (Edward Wood, a Conservative) to suggest he might add to their 'practical utility' and allow them to deal with 'current topics of live interest'.[6] The report on curricular differentiation between boys and girls was now complete, and the Committee chafed at having to consider the recondite problem of psychological tests when the significant question of the day was how to deal with the older elementary pupil.

Wood received the deputation with his normal affable courtesy it seems, but kept a considered response for a letter in March, among whose elaborately vague encomia of the Committee shone out a hint that he would be willing to 'receive suggestions' on future references. This softened his refusal of specific requests that the Committee might see and advise on early drafts of Board regulations and that their number might include LEA representatives to assist deliberations on the limits of 'local bureaucracy' and so perhaps 'abate the evil with which the service of education was affected or threatened by the undue extension of bureaucratic interference'.[7] The two requests showed they believed both Board and LEAs might be convicted here.

Neither within nor without the Board were Wood's mind and heart reckoned to be wholly devoted to education, nor was it to be his career. As Lord Irwin he later served as Viceroy of India, as Lord Halifax as Churchill's Foreign Secretary in 1940. He was not now prepared to disturb the civil servants of the Board by developing the Consultative Committee. Nor were other Presidents. A 1926 proposal by Gorell in the House of Lords that a small council should be constituted to advise the President of the Board of Education directly was brusquely turned down by the government spokesman.

The Committee swallowed the crumb of comfort that Wood offered, that they might initiate references. Within the Board topics were now being discussed, questions of commercial education leading the field, but within the Committee J. A. White, the Central school headmaster, proposed a motion which, after discussion, drew attention to the increasing crowding of secondary schools and similarly expanding number of entrants to Trade Schools, Junior Technical and Central schools, and to 'establishments' run by Clark's, Pitman's and others. These, the motion said, argued a 'great demand' for adolescent education. Therefore, the Committee

> desires to represent to the Board that an investigation into the possibility of providing various types of curriculum suitable to children between the ages of 11 and 16 would be welcomed by administrators, teachers, employers and parents ... to guide and encourage developments on satisfactory lines.[8]

The thrust here is towards the curriculum, Clark's and Pitman's (both private) being mentioned, as White explained, because they produced boys and girls with satisfactory shorthand, typing and book-keeping knowledge but lacking in 'general education'.

Dutifully Hadow raised 'commercial education' as a more compact subject. Too restricted, said Alderman Percy Jackson of the West Riding, when many LEAs were anxious about the education of older elementary children and needed an educationally-based study. The elementary head Essie Conway pointed out that what was taught could hardly be divorced from how and where teaching was delivered. But administration was a political issue, enmired in problems of 'dual control' – the ownership of about 11,000 elementary schools by the churches, unable to afford substantial development, unwilling to hand their pupils over to others – and of the smaller 'Part III Authorities', often also with small resources. From the start, then, the curriculum of the non-secondary older child was the object of attention and seen as a necessary and viable study; as Hadow reported to Sir Amherst Selby-Bigge, the Permanent Secretary, the Committee were 'very strongly in favour' of the subject. They were, he said, 'an extremely friendly body ... with a single-hearted desire to do something useful'.[9]

A month later, in November 1923, Hadow went with White, Jackson and Ernest Barker to see Selby-Bigge. They proposed the Committee should 'think up some alternative course of instruction for children up to 15 or 16 who would not be proceeding to secondary schools', collect evidence about various types of existing higher elementary school, and consider the 'point of junction' (Barker's phrase) between elementary and secondary education.[10] This point could have thrown open the whole question of the separate parallel lines on which the elementary and secondary systems ran for children over 16, and was one Barker felt on his pulses, for he believed that only a rare chain of chance had even entered him for the scholarship that his village elementary school and humble family saw as an exotic novelty and that had decisively shifted the course of his life.

It was, however, a point not to be handled by the Consultative Committee. As Selby-Bigge remarked, by law only an Elementary Authority could compel school attendance, and school attendance was compulsory to 14; Elementary Authorities must therefore provide free schools for children up to 14. This was the 'statutory barrier' between 'Elementary' and 'Higher' (including secondary) education, to be changed only by Parliament. In rural areas, anyway, single schools were the only practicable form. But if the Committee thought the 'path of salvation' was through advanced elementary schools, Selby-Bigge could agree – if the age-range considered were 11 to 15, not 16, a wholly unrealistic expectation since even the proposed school-leaving age of 15 was unpopular with much of the electorate.

So the discussion which had started with a rather ill-defined ambition for 'the provision for the non-secondary child of something better after 11' yielded the reference, eventually put together by Board officials and accepted by the full Committee in January 1924, that in 1926 produced *The Education of the Adolescent*, known as the Hadow Report. At first Emmeline did not expect to be involved. Her term of membership was due to expire in July 1924, with that of six others, and Selby-Bigge suggested in the spring that they should make way earlier so a new team could be in at the start. But some of these seven Hadow asked to retain, and Emmeline was one. In July she was thus re-appointed, this time for six years. White, Tawney and Albert Mansbridge were also retained, but Bertha Phillpotts was replaced by another female don, Lynda Grier, since 1921 Principal of Lady Margaret Hall, an association that strengthened Emmeline's ties with the Oxford college. Lynda Grier brought to the Committee not only her academic expertise in economics, her interest in social questions and her administrative understanding, but a quality of stillness, an inner listening ascribed to her near-total deafness as a child. Deafness had kept her from any form of school and not till she was 24, her hearing improved, did she become an 'out-student' at Newnham and rapidly make her mark.

In the spring of 1924 the old team signed the report on *Psychological Tests of Educable Capacity*, the second of the references handed down in 1920. Its keynote was caution. The theory of mental testing was not, they thought, stably advanced, and to lay down any dogmatic rules would be 'dangerous and misleading', especially since systematic experimentation in the UK had as yet provided inadequate data. Indeed, the more information they gathered, especially from work done in Germany and Austria, France and the USA, the more complex the formulation of mental tests seemed, with 'intelligence' itself defined in numerous ways. Was it, for example, the power of abstract thinking? Or the ability to act effectively under given conditions? Or the power to respond appropriately to true facts? Psychologists, it seemed, defined 'intelligence' variously because they disagreed on what it was based, whether it was the effect of a few very general 'faculties' or 'functions', the average of innumerable highly specific abilities, or a single central factor common to all intellectual processes.

Doggedly the Committee analysed the development of testing and the purposes to which it had been applied, and examined both experience in the field (in England the LEAs of Bradford and Northumberland, for instance, had adopted forms at times) and laboratory experiments with individuals and groups. The concept of 'mental age' was considered, as were the statistical techniques devised to standardise tests and work out norms. Visits to work in progress and experiments on themselves must have provided the relief of amusement. Fundamentally, the question that made the whole subject important was whether means could be developed to discriminate between innate potential and the effects of poor teaching and a disadvantageous environment.

Thus the most impassioned passage of a frequently technical report came to birth, when, turning to potential uses and starting with the most obvious, the selection of secondary school scholarship children, the Committee affirmed that 'any system of selection whatever, whether by means of psychological tests or by means of examination [of attainment], which determines at the age of eleven the educational future of children is, and must be, gravely unreliable'. Their blood up, they proceeded – irrelevantly to the actual reference – to fulminate against the shortage of secondary schools and free places, and the fact that 'a large proportion of the candidates cannot possibly, whatever their ability, be successful in winning a free place ... the whole subsequent career of many children is determined by their success or failure in the single competitive examination held at the age of eleven'. No mere improvement in methods of selection could substitute for the 'large increase in secondary school accommodation and in the supply of free places which is so urgently needed'.[11]

This is the context in which the Committee formulated the suggestion for their next reference, and the subtext of Barker's insistence on the 'point of junction' of elementary and secondary education, and it spells out the attitude the Committee brought to their consideration of the 'education of the adolescent'.

Recommendations in the report on psychological tests stressed how culture-specific existing tests were, asked for more studies of possible types (particularly less verbal ones) and for follow-up research on the later attainments of those tested, as well as correlation with school and medical records, oral interviews, and so on. Uses could be developed where innate ability needed to be discriminated from acquired skills or where internal school classifications were needed between children of similar environment and experience, but rather, it is to be inferred, because existing methods were so haphazard than because the psychology of mental processes was well understood. The principal value of the report is its comprehensive survey of work done to date, and its presentation of possible pitfalls.

Soon after the report was published, in the summer of 1924, the AHM's Executive Committee decided to experiment. Two types of 'Intelligence Quotient' test were tried, on two occasions, in fourteen schools, and the results matched against the girls' records and their teachers' opinions. When only a random correlation was found the headmistresses' doubts were strengthened, particularly as to precisely what was being measured. ('Intelligence is what is measured by intelligence tests' was a definition with many adherents.) Not proven, they decided, and Emmeline apparently agreed for she never herself depended on such tests but preferred oral interviews when scholarship candidates were chosen. She was fortunate to work where such a labour-intensive process was viable, and what was seen by some as a drawback – that interviews tend to reveal personality rather than abilities – was not necessarily so to her. Nor did she think it disadvantageous that of all methods oral interview is the least mechanical, the least susceptible to standardisation.

The report improved the Committee's appreciation of how complex was the concept called 'intelligence', and this was to affect their later work. As a working definition they adopted 'a general mental ability operating in many different ways, given as part of a child's mental endowment, as distinct from knowledge or skill acquired through teaching or experience, and more concerned with analysing and co-ordinating the data of experience than with mere passive reception of them',[12] a definition clearly more generous than one related to any bent for an 'academic' curriculum and foreshadowing the phrase that echoed through their report of 1930 on *The Primary School*, that the 'curriculum is to be thought of in terms of activity and experience rather than of knowledge to be acquired and facts to be stored'.

At the same meeting as they signed this report the Committee discussed procedures for dealing with the new reference on the schooling of older non-secondary pupils, and drew up a provisional list of witnesses. Clearly they were in a hurry to make progress.

That was in March 1924, just a month after Emmeline had told the staff of Bedford High School that she was to leave at the end of the summer term to take up the headship of Roedean School. 'It wasn't an easy day,' she said, and it was long, ending with a LNU committee meeting after school, for 'they minded more than I care to think about'. She wanted to tell Margaret that day, as her niece and the most personally affected, before the rest of the school were informed, but 'had no opportunity'. What she did not know was that somehow the Press had heard and that Roedean was 'news'. Day girls who saw their parents' newspapers told boarders with disgusted horror, as all gathered for the new day. Margaret was devastated, her loyalties riven: she knew nothing of Roedean: her friends called it a 'horrid snobby school' – how *could* Miss Tanner betray them so?

Chapter 17
Reluctantly to Roedean

Emmeline was furious to find herself pre-empted in telling the news of her move, and irritably refused the *Sketch* photographer who arrived at lunchtime, until she discovered 'the wretched man hid round a corner and snapped me as I went off on my bicycle'. Then she co-operated. 'He told me some lurid stories about the way they get photographs of people who don't want to be taken – in murder cases, for instance.' It was an early warning of how vulnerable her future school might be to popular image, the sort of image, for example, that Margaret's friends had formed.

She, of course, knew more than the schoolgirls, even before she was targeted as head-to-be and even though she had never shown any interest in Roedean School and none of the three sisters who had founded and headed it were members of the AHM (for which they became eligible only in 1920), for the Lawrence sisters ranked with the Victorian pioneers. Penelope was particularly known for developing the theory and practice of organised games, a slightly misleading distinction, for her mental bent was intellectual (in 1878 she was only the third Newnham student to pass the Natural Sciences Tripos at Cambridge) and Emmeline may have observed how regularly Roedean girls figured in lists of scholarships for the older women's colleges.

Famously, however, Roedean was the first school in England to follow the example of St Leonard's, near St Andrews, and take selected cues from the boys' public schools, including the use of prefects and a House system with teaching housemistresses. Like them, too, it had since the turn of the century been wholly non-local, the pupils coming from all parts of the UK and overseas. No leading girls' school had fees as high as the significant boys' public schools, nor were Roedean's the highest among the girls', but at Bedford High School in 1925 a senior boarder paid £99 when one at Roedean School paid £180, and since Roedean received no public grants it offered no free places to elementary pupils. All these factors gilded the school's social image; after her appointment Emmeline was asked to her first Royal Garden Party, an 'interesting' occasion if 'not what I had expected' as Royalty made a stately unconversable procession along a path between subjects.

Yet what had qualified the Lawrences as pioneers had long been adopted by others. Emmeline stood to lose as much as she might gain: she would be divorced from the state system, losing the breadth of social range of the free place quota for a grant-aided school, and all her experience had taught her to care for the extension of opportunity. She would lose the just-ripening fruits of her efforts at Bedford, and the life she had built in the town, and the ever-dearer haven of her cottage; although the salary offered was £1,200 she would lose her pension rights.

Telling Bedford was another unsatisfactory page in a chapter spattered with them, the most unsatisfactory of all being her own previous unaccustomed and uncomfortable attack of indecision. Precisely when Penelope Lawrence first approached Emmeline is not certain, but probably in late 1923 when the three sisters presented their formal resignation to the Council which was Roedean's governing body, after several months of planning arrangements for the new head's duties and housing. The official advertisements for the job of headmistress were placed in *The Times* and leading educational journals in December, attracting twenty-seven applicants.

It did not occur to Emmeline to apply, and when she was asked to do so she at first refused to consider it. Even in February 1924 she said flatly, 'I don't want to leave Bedford at all, and am sorry to be going.' But when Penelope Lawrence believed she had found the right woman she was both persistent and forceful, and perhaps artful as well. Though physically she was slowed by the bulk flowing outwards under uncorseted black silk, her mind remained strong, swift, agile, and sharpened by anxiety for her school. Faintly as yet some signs were showing that as the heads' joint vigour declined so too did the school's standards. She marked down Emmeline and hunted her. Fragments of her modes of persuasion survive from occasional remarks by Emmeline. P. L., as she was universally called, represented Roedean as 'one of the best schools in England'; she urged its peril when decapitated, and the need of its girls for leadership; she spoke, it is said, of a Providence that led her to Emmeline. In all, and backed by her sister Dorothy, she apparently developed dramatically such arguments as she perceived Emmeline responded to: standards, needs, duty.

Initial rejection softened enough for Emmeline to take the problem home to her mother, probably at Christmas when she habitually went to Bath. Nettie discarded the inverted snobbery that argued against Roedean: rich and poor were equal before God. If these girls needed help, their need was valid and their circumstances irrelevant. So a granddaughter later heard, she thought from Nettie herself; Emmeline said only that her mother persuaded her, not how.

In early January she sent her formal application to Roedean Council, attended one interview, then was recalled, with one other candidate, for a second. But immediately before that final interview P. L. and Dorothy again talked to her, without doubt of the outcome.

I found both Penelope and Dorothy Lawrence waiting for me in the lounge of the Grosvenor Hotel and then I found out that Dorothy has had a bad nervous breakdown – she can't even find the words she wants sometimes, though she was so fluent at the first meeting. I had a talk with her alone first of all and she told me all the special things in the school that she has always cherished and hoped would be continued – the scripture teaching, preparation for Confirmation, much care for music, etc. Then Penelope turned her out and said it was her turn to have me, and she said she very much wanted to see me first to ask me to be very gentle with Dorothy as her breakdown had slightly affected her mind. She herself went on to say it seemed so unnatural to be handing their life-work over to someone of whose private life they knew nothing, that she didn't know where I was born, who my father was, etc. I said that could soon be remedied ...

She asked me a good many questions and I asked her more. She told me she was really vexed about my not being allowed to see the school – that she herself really wanted me to come but that the men on the Council thought it most undesirable. She also told that the third sister, Millicent, in a nursing home at Crowborough, is most sad at not having seen me, so when I can go down to Roedean she (Penelope) will come up to town in the car to fetch me and take me down via Crowborough to call on Millicent on the way. I was really touched by these elderly women who have been great pioneers being willing to hand over to me their life-work, their child, as each of them separately called it to me. Penelope begged me to make no changes for the first year, but she said that of course she knew I should want to do things differently afterwards.

Then came the Council meeting and the interview. I went in first and was there for some time having to expound my views on many subjects. But there is one great joke against me! The chairman at the previous interview whom I thought to be a man and surmised must be the Hon. Sir P. O. Lawrence (Mr Justice Lawrence) is a woman, a Miss Abbott!! She is head of the Women Police or something of that sort. She has a deep voice and short grey hair and no hat, while all the women wore theirs. The Hon. Sir P. O. is a most distinguished, fine-looking man, quite different!

She was to tell the Bedford press that Roedean 'is an interesting kind of school'. When the Lawrence sisters called it their child they were choosing the most appropriate of metaphors. Penelope was the eldest of fourteen children of a solicitor-turned-barrister, and Roedean had been a family affair in its origin and its development. It had sprung from the little school their mother had started to educate her youngest when finances oppressed, and there in Wimbledon Dorothy and Millicent taught their siblings and a few others before they asked Penelope – the revered eldest, Newnham-educated, and a youthful Principal of a Froebel Training College – to join in a more substantial venture. Their own education, at schools in Germany and France, and Bedford College (London) for Dorothy, the Maria Grey Training College for Millicent, was all they had to live by. Their brother Paul squeezed £50 from his early earnings at the Bar to lend them. That was in 1885.

In Brighton 'schools always succeed', they heard, and to Brighton they went, other sisters coming at times to teach too. It was part of the movement to educate middle-class girls, and from the first the Lawrences aimed high. Some characteristics were defined in the prospectus drafted before the school opened in a Brighton town house with 'six [paying] pupils and four for show': for the healthy body 'two to three hours daily will be allotted to outdoor exercise and games', and for the healthy mind a 'thorough education' was to include ancient and modern languages, natural sciences, mathematics, English, history, geography, and – as extras – art and music. Academic ambition was signalled in a promise to prepare elder girls for Newnham and Girton Colleges, and the fact that the Lawrences' self-description flourished their qualifications as teachers rather than their social graces. Finally, a tradition of religious toleration was enshrined as 'The Religious Instruction of the Pupils will be in accordance with the views of their parents'.[1]

It was an act of faith – an ideological commitment – and an enactment of ideology, for thus they earned their self-respecting livings. Since the school was based financially on income from fees it was another act of faith a decade later to borrow to buy a plot of land outside the town, commission a rising architect, and build a splendid new school with space in four Houses for 200 girls, though they were fortunate in the support of numerous well-placed connections. Even before then P. L. at least was thinking in terms of a female equivalent to a great boys' public school, drawing on ideals of the 19th-century reforming headmasters, Arnold, Thring, Sanderson.

In 1897 Mrs Henry Sidgwick came from Newnham to lay the foundation stone of John Simpson's building on the cliff east of Brighton, facing the sea, and she wound up her address with the warning that 'we cannot hope to do any good in the world, nor to realise our own best happiness and the solid satisfaction of work well done, without habits of strenuous and resolute effort, and the readiness to make sacrifices for worthy ends'.[2] Earlier she had referred to the *esprit de corps,* the co-operation for common ends and subordination of private ends to the common good, which the Lawrences perceived as public school goals worthy of emulation and applied to a larger scale of the persistent Lawrence model, the family: Lawrences taught, other Lawrences sent daughters to learn; as housemistress each Lawrence kissed her charges good night. Brothers and husbands and cousins of Lawrences assisted with advice, money and professional skills. So complicated and disguised was the economic relation of a private school to education, a commodity to be bought and sold.

In the educational world Penelope, Dorothy and Millicent were considered progressive: P. L. gave evidence before the Bryce Commission of the 1890s and advised public bodies on games training; they sent candidates to universities, and especially to Newnham College, Cambridge; they counted it a triumph when Old Roedeanians gained professional qualifications. They applied to be listed as 'Efficient' in 1906 and came through Inspection with flying colours. But after the Great War the Lawrences aged, less in years than in health. They had nursed their young school to maturity, and their child outgrew them. Those who knew the school then tended to agree with the Old Roedeanian who wrote to Emmeline in 1940:

I do not wish to censure the dear Miss Lawrences, who *were* dear and wonderful people and had been, I know, as human as any, but you know yourself how the growth of the school and their increasing years had changed it, so that when they could least endure noise and numbers and so on, these things were most formidable. It became a matter of more rules, more rules ... most alarmingly mechanical.

Four hundred girls, and plenty of staff (no register was kept then to record their numbers) filled stone walls already eroding in the salt winds, when in 1920 the Lawrences decided Roedean should come of age: they negotiated the conversion of the private venture into a non-profit-making company, as in 1870 Frances Mary Buss had transferred her property of the North London Collegiate School to a similar company.

Some things did not change. Emmeline first met a Council dominated (though not packed) by Lawrences and their in-laws, and it was another act of courage for them to select as headmistress a woman of unknown origins with no Lawrence connections, no experience of this school, and a reputation for liberal reform. On her would depend much of the school's continuing prosperity where no Harpur Trust and no LEA afforded financial stability, as well as the welfare of the girls, staff and domestic staff who lived together there, for she was allotted considerable freedom of internal management.

Already the Council had planned arrangements. Applications for new pupils were to be a matter for the headmistress and the secretary she was to appoint; the long-serving member of staff who now became School Secretary would deal with routine bills, sent out or paid, and supervise repairs with responsibility to the headmistress and only through her to the Council; new staff were to be the headmistress's choice, and she would normally attend Council meetings – both points the AHM thought essential. Since, unlike the Lawrences, she would not be a housemistress, a house was being built beside the school which the new head was to use free of rent and rates, the cost of fuel and insurance borne by the school, though she must furnish it, provide her own domestic utensils, crockery, linens, and pay her own domestic staff. The salary of £1,200, rising by annual increments of £50 to £1,500, was calculated to allow for her 'to incur some cost for entertainment' there on the school's behalf. These conditions Emmeline accepted.

Not to see Roedean before her appointment was unsatisfactory; to be asked to meet the Old Roedeanians Association (ORA) but 'unfortunately ... not informed of the exact time of the meeting', as their minutes smoothly recorded, was also provoking. When she 'kindly addressed those who had remained' she told them frankly of her regret at leaving Bedford, and added that to her Roedean 'would still be the Misses Lawrence's school'.[3]

Her last term at Bedford was consoled by the temporary appointment of her friend of Nuneaton days, Ann Crofts, to cover sickness among staff, though Ann's small son was less pleased by his daily journey to nursery school, huddled on the back of the bicycle she briskly manoeuvred through the streets. So it was Ann, known and trusted by Sam and Nettie Tanner, who reported to them in early May:

Poor Emmie was taken with violent pain at the morning school on Friday, and had another still worse attack in the afternoon. [She was taken home, and the doctor] diagnosed appendicitis as well as the trouble in the gall-bladder ... he said if she were anyone else he would take her straight into Bedford and operate that afternoon. As it was, he left her to make up her own mind; but he told her that in any case she would have to lie up and keep absolutely quiet for a fortnight – with no certainty of being fit at the end of it. When I got out to see her she had already decided to have the operation and had sent in a note to Dr Nash. I went in with her in a taxi to the Nursing Home about 5.00, and they operated at 7.00. The report last night was that it had been 'a long and heavy operation but perfectly successful'.

We here are all relieved that she followed Dr Nash's advice, as it seems probable that every attack she had would have been worse than the one before, and she might have been overtaken by one in circumstances where an immediate operation would have been much more difficult. You can imagine how *very very* loth Emmie was to give in: she kept on saying that she *could not* have an operation; it was *absolutely* out of the question and so on. But she was in such pain ...

A postscript added: 'I've just seen Emmie for a minute. She is rather unhappy and full of pain, but otherwise everything is quite satisfactory.'

Emmie agonised not only over her school but her frustration in outside work, though for the AHM Frances Gray was characteristically generous:

My dear Ch. C. [she wrote], Those letters don't stand for Chairman of Committee as you might think. I have my own name for you and they happen to fit your title as well, but they really are the initial letters of the name by which I have called you in my own mind. Your name comes into the line 'And put a Cheerful Courage on'. Now you know what your name is, for you represent just exactly that for me. I won't talk business or tell you how much I miss you, but everyone is so sorry for me (as well as you) that I know they won't be hard on me if I do anything dreadful.

Certainly Emmeline returned to work before recovery was complete, however genial and robust an appearance she presented to her colleagues and girls, and the end of a final term was bound to be fraught. She could disengage herself from official positions in Bedford affairs but her references to a visit from a Nuneaton parent wanting advice on his daughter's future, and a visit to a Sherborne colleague now fatally ill with liver cancer, show how impossible she found it to shake free of past affections. At the end of July:

I was hard at work in school at the top of my speed for eleven hours a day, with only a short interval for lunch, several days at the end of term, and I have been pretty busy there ever since we broke up. I still have to sort my papers and books at school from those that are the school's but I am leaving that till I get back. Then I shall tackle that first of all before I put in ten days at the Time Table, etc., and leave only the things here at the cottage for the very end. My goods leave on September 11th.

She was departing for a brief holiday in the Lake District, a journey enlivened by a link with the past at Bletchley where 'I have just had the chance of helping Miss Wordsworth, the first Principal of Lady Margaret Hall, a great woman in the past and now very elderly, to find a seat and have established her very comfortably opposite me in a through carriage for Llanfairfechan, where she is going. She looks very frail to be journeying so far by herself, from Oxford to Llanfairfechan.' So together the women watched a 'platform full of Country Holiday Children returning to London with their arms simply full of flowers and looking pictures of happiness', a promise for an optimist of a fairer future, an assurance that Bedford High School's regular contribution to the Children's Country Holiday Fund was well used. So, herself poised between past and future, Emmeline enjoyed the journey to Keswick.

Almost every year from 1918 to the end of the 1930s Emmeline spent a week or so with Ann and John Crofts at their cottage at Stonethwaite, in the Borrowdale Fells south of Derwentwater. Well named from the stony course of the beck toppling from the valley's craggy heights to join the Derwent, and surrounded by hills once mined for their rare stores of pure graphite and for lead, the area was to be better famed in the 1930s as the scene of Hugh Walpole's popular *Herries Chronicle*. In the 1920s it was remote enough, and the cottage almost primitive, a double cottage, in fact, with an internal wall demolished and a front door blocked.

This left two rooms downstairs and four up [their son remembered]. No loo or bathroom. Some time in the early thirties a loo was installed adjacent to a 'peat'us' (peathouse) which was converted to a garage at the same time. You had to enter the garage to get to this loo, which was a prodigy of contemporary science at the time, because it was a *Water Loo* and had a flush mechanism. EMT was the first to use it – I remember my mother making a point of letting 'the lady' do us the honour of being the first. In 1937 a bathroom and upstairs loo was built, and an extra room over the garage. The whole house was solid stone built, with hefty flagstones on all ground-floor rooms.

There Emmeline could walk in the fells, the Crofts' two sons fished, and none were starved for sublime views. By the 1920s a motor bus brought travellers down the side of Derwentwater from Keswick, past the Lodore Falls, so Emmeline became familiar with Keswick Station and the sight of its neighbouring Keswick Hotel, and with the area round.

She returned to make the break, and collect her last apples and pears from her cottage garden, to send to her parents with advice on cooking the pears 'slowly in the oven in a good rich syrup preferably flavoured with a little thin lemon rind, some lemon juice, a small bit of cinnamon stick and a clove or two'. 'The leaving Murree Cottage and the garden simply won't bear thinking of,' she lamented, but had little time in either: 'I can't tell you how filled up my time was that last week ... I slept at Diana [Butt]'s the last two nights and had work to get finished before breakfast at 7.30 when I was leaving by the 8.20 train.' Before she arrived in Sussex Emmeline again saw the Lawrences, at Boxmoor in Hertfordshire where P. L. had built herself a house next to her sister, Agatha Blyth. 'They specially wanted to see me because Millicent, the invalid, had taken a furnished house next to P. L. and she wanted to tell me all sorts of things about the business side of the school before she goes abroad for the winter. Dorothy was staying at the Blyths', next door on the other side, so I was able to see them all.' All included Agatha Blyth and her husband, a leading member of Roedean Council; Millicent was credited with the business head, the eye for practical detail, while it was to gentle Dorothy, it was said, girls would turn in distress.

These brief and occasional meetings with the Lawrences, however, were no substitute for the ready help in school ways given at Bedford by Susan Collie, Diana Butt and others, leaving Emmeline vulnerable to grumbles such as 'she didn't even know that there was a head of each House at the beginning of term', used as criticism. Inner conflict may have precipitated Emmeline's collapse in May, and the illness, with its 'long and heavy' operation certainly sapped her ebullience and energy. She arrived in Sussex shortly before term started, to stay near Friston in the outlying cottage of an old farmhouse converted to a guesthouse, and displayed a strange reluctance to enter her new domain.

'I meant to go along to Roedean today to receive my belongings but I felt too tired to face anything unnecessary, so I am not going ... I go to Roedean on Saturday and only wish it were a fortnight, a month or a term ahead rather than five days.' Comfort was to be found in the 'ideal spot' where she stayed, 'in sight of the sea and in the midst of rolling downs, going right to the edge of the cliffs, which are all fine like Beachy Head, and one can walk for miles on the Downs and along the cliffs without meeting a soul'. Amusement was afforded by the other guests, a doctor's family with 'the very nicest sort of children', a colonel who nightly lit her way by torch down the rough stony lane to the cottage where both stayed and even saw her up the stairs to her room, a New Zealand Boy Scout who had made the long sea voyage for the Empire Exhibition at Wembley. Since their life histories were all at Emmeline's fingertips within a few days, her friendly openness had clearly not deserted her, though she did not enjoy the cubbing meet she attended with some of them – 'all my sympathies were with the little fox, though they say the foxes are most destructive to poultry round here. I saw one little fellow making such a gallant effort and I am thankful to say I didn't see them get him.'

At last, however, she must go to Roedean. The four senior staff appointed housemistresses in the Houses that flanked the main school entrance (two to the right, two to the left, set forward to make a three-sided quadrangle) had all been chosen by the Lawrences from their trusted colleagues, as had the head of the Junior House (located separately behind the main school) and the second mistress. Relations between staff and girls were not here close, however: the Lawrences had discouraged the intimacy of such walks and talks as Emmeline had known at Sherborne, and day-to-day discipline was largely in the hands of prefects, who ruled by moral sway and marks. Imitation of boys' public schools did not extend to any form of corporal punishment.

Instead Emmeline discovered an elaborate system of marks. One mark was imposed for 'order', one for 'punctuality', two for 'discipline', four for 'conduct', and a total of four in a week meant 'Early Bed' on Saturday evening, and hence missing the weekly dancing or occasional House play. In Emmeline's eyes such a system tended to equate moral fault with foolish errors of clothing and the like, and to imply that all were purchasable. Worse than this was the need for marks. The headmistress's new house was building slowly, so that for the first year Emmeline lived within the school itself, her sitting-room and office just east of the main door, her bedroom two floors up, her lunch and supper taken in each House by turns – for in each the catering was separately handled by its own domestic staff under the command of each housemistress. So she was peculiarly susceptible to the noise of uncontrolled voices and feet, and she had no retreat to her own space as she had once had at Murree Cottage.

Moreover, however elaborated rules had become in the Lawrences' last years, the Founders had from the start sought 'as much freedom as is compatible with safety', and at Roedean Emmeline found none of the silence in movement and courteous respect she had inherited at Bedford, so that Roedean girls seemed rowdy, unmannerly; one later admitted to 'some (probably mute) insolence', another to 'carelessness, mild disobedience and lack of self-control'. Standards were relative: in the context of the times, 'possession of sweets, except at half-term or when out with family, was a major sin; we had barely even heard of gin'. Most of all, though, girls were suspicious and resentful. The Lawrences were 'our Royal family', 'it was as though the abdicating monarch had given place to a vigorous and forward-looking Prime Minister (or President)', and the girls' attitude was likened to that towards 'a wicked stepmother'.

It was a round-the-clock life, and 'when I am in the school or grounds I constantly have people who desire to see me ... My impression is that I shall rarely have any free time worth speaking of', Emmeline told her parents. She summarised her timetable for them, from rising at 6.30 am to 'do letters' till Prayers, morning school – in early years she taught some history and religious knowledge to as many forms as possible, to get to know them – a daily housemistresses' meeting, then games, afternoon school, and supper. On Sundays there was no school but there was morning service in the school's own Chapel, taken by the Chaplain, and evening service taken by herself ('alarming experience!'), parents to see in morning and afternoon, and regularly a lecture or concert at 5.30 pm, a custom established by the Lawrences of which Emmeline throughly approved. On Tuesday evenings the weekly staff meetings were held, and on Thursdays she gave tea to senior and school prefects.

So she found the time both 'cut-up' and 'tied', and was isolated from the town life she had enjoyed earlier, though very soon she was co-opted to Brighton's Education Committee, as P. L. had earlier been, and as a member of the Higher Education Sub-Committee became a Governor of the grant-aided endowed boarding school, St Mary's Hall, and the LEA secondary school, so retaining links with the state system. But -

the minutes get filled up without my achieving much ... It takes up much more time going to one of the Houses for lunch and dinner than having it by myself. I *can* have any meal brought to my own room but it gives a good deal more trouble, and when I go to the Houses I do get to know some of the mistresses a little, and that is a great gain when there are so many people to learn ... There is no doubt that it is an entirely different kind of life. It has attractions and it has drawbacks, and there is plenty for me to do and plenty I shall probably never be able to do. With all our luxury we are *very* short of classroom accommodation ... Unfortunately the Lawrences don't realise these needs somehow or other because they haven't done much in the way of teaching or making Time Tables since the numbers increased, and of course Penelope is Chairman of the Council and must be convinced before anything can be done. However, it is no use beginning to agitate for things of that sort yet. I should like to build classrooms and also reduce numbers.

Inevitably she met clashes of expectations: early that first term the National Council of Women held its annual conference in Brighton, and 'we take about 200 girls to a great meeting of girls in the Dome – an unheard-of thing which I agreed to quite light-heartedly without having the least idea I was breaking one of the strictest laws of the Medes and Persians.' Altogether she decided in early October that 'I simply love the sea and the Downs and the air, and I quite like the school, but I now and then long to be back in my own school with my own girls, and in my own dear cottage and garden. I am very much in the midst of everything always here and I still shall be to a great extent when I am in my own house.' Reminders of the Lawrences were inwrought in the texture of the very building: above the first three houses were reliefs symbolising their Christian names, when Emmeline looked at the clock in her room she saw P. L.'s initials repeated between each number, and even the rainwater heads outside the Chapel displayed the gridiron of St Lawrence. But to look back was rare in Emmeline, and that she did so now evidences the ill-health still dogging her.

The life was indeed no more enclosed than that she had known at Sherborne in the 1900s; it was Emmeline who had changed. Yet, as at

Sherborne, compensations included some among the numerous and varied staff with wits undulled by enclosure, who knew how to live in a school without being school-girlish. A collegiate sense was assisted both by the unusually high proportion of Newnham women observed by HMIs in 1927 and by a certain detachment from the girls fostered by the Lawrences and recorded by Dorothy de Zouche. Emmeline knew Dorothy de Zouche as the headmistress of Wolverhampton High School, a colleague on the MAHM and then the AHM, but once she had been an assistant at Roedean, and when she wrote that the Founders 'omitted or postponed consideration of their relation as Heads with their Staff, their responsibility, in the bond of mutual responsibility, for promoting their interests and their professional advancement, for training them in the exercise of authority and in the technique of their work', she wrote from her personal experience and her headmistress's judgment.[4] But to those who had worked for many years with the Lawrences, and that included the powerful housemistresses, they were personal and dear friends.

So in her first few weeks Emmeline strove to establish understanding and confidence among the staff, even as she bought the school's first typewriter for her office, chafed at the spluttering gas-mantles which lit overcrowded classrooms, shut her ears to the noise, and worst of all began to suspect that, despite ample facilities for girls who wished to work, those who did not easily evaded effort. P. L.'s several visits that term made them no more inclined to settle to Emmeline's authority: 'Miss Lawrence was here again last week. She is awfully nice to me and about me but quite naturally she thinks things are all right as they are – ninety and more in houses built for fifty! – and it will be difficult to get her to agree, as Chairman of Council, to changes that will cause financial loss.'

Emmeline's speech at the start of term 'quite favourably impressed the school', said a prefect, but the prefects' vanity was annoyed to be told, in effect, they should 'be sure and go to bed at the proper time!!' Emmeline might have wooed the girls with flattery and smooth words; instead she dealt out little checks at Prayers, about 'keeping to the right of the passage, and putting our sweaters on the ground during field, and getting up quickly after Prayers'.

Then, at the start of October, when the marks handed out in the week were reported, Emmeline's patience snapped. She called the school together. Accounts of this episode recorded more than sixty years apart and without reference to each other quote how she began: 'I am *glad* this is not my school!' More than the upbraiding for 'discipline' marks P. L.'s niece Beatrice resented both the implied comparison with Bedford, summarising Emmeline's speech as 'if I don't set to work to reform [Roedean], it won't compare at all favourably with *my* school', and the implied denigration of the beloved Founders. The lower forms were then sent out, and the upper school heard 'utterly vile things ... about the whole tone of the school being wrong, put in a way which might have been solemnly calculated to put everybody's back up and make herself heartily detested ... It amazed me than anyone in her position should be so lacking in tact.'⁵

Often enough later Emmeline was angry or disappointed, and always she was frank, but this intemperance was never repeated. The reaction of the prefects, however, was illuminating. The school as a whole seethed furiously. But Beatrice Lawrence sat briefly in her study alone to collect herself before dinner, then earnestly told the table she headed how, for P. L.'s sake, they must support her successor, and she disguised how inside herself she was 'blazing with indignation'. In the afternoon the prefects kept their juniors busy with a 'scrum game', and the heads of Houses conferred, each to depart and urge her House that 'we've just *got* not to take it like that, and to realise what she said was true, and pull ourselves up'. Next day the head of the school, Joyce Handley-Seymour, addressed 'solid sense' to the assembled prefects, then to the sub-prefects, and finally to the school, and 'the outcome of it all was that there were just half the number of dishes [discipline marks] in the school next week and precisely two cons [conduct marks]'. Yet Beatrice's long account in a private letter to her mother mentions nowhere any member of staff other than the headmistress: prefect government was a real responsibility.

Probably Emmeline was not aware of all the response but she undoubtedly appreciated Joyce Handley-Seymour's level head, using her as, in Joyce's words, 'her liaison officer', and no reaction to her words could have been better calculated to reveal how beneath the careless and disobedient surface of the school the Lawrences' principle of freedom worked like yeast, how she herself might find good in Roedean. Her temper, like the gales which howled round the school in winter, blew itself out. As the senior girls learnt to know her better, so they learnt to respect and even to like what Joyce later called 'her extraordinarily strong inward integrity. I remember feeling the solution was to get her to like the school and then everything would be all right; and I think in the end this was what happened.'⁶

Nor were the girls finished with surprises. As autumn drew on Emmeline missed the trees and flowers the salt winds scorned – when she defied the gardeners' advice and instructed the planting of 4,000 wallflowers a storm blew to strip every one to the stem, and the stretch of cliff east of Brighton remains bare of trees. In mid-October:

We are having the most perfect weather ... I am going to take the whole school (450 of us) to Arundel tomorrow for a picnic if the weather holds. We aren't going to tell the girls till after Prayers at 8.30 tomorrow morning in case the weather should change but all the chars-à-banc are ordered provisionally and the housekeepers are arranging the food for us to start at 9.30. Never has the whole school gone all together before, and never have they had an unexpected holiday, but the weather is exceptional and it is such a pity for them never to see any trees in the autumn.

'It was simply heavenly,' said Beatrice Lawrence.

'The autumn colours were quite beyond words. I don't know if it was just that I hadn't seen *any* for four years or if they were exceptional, but they were perfectly glorious.... We had lunch by the lake and then we scattered till 2.45. It was sunny but not too hot, and there were some ripping old trees just made for climbing ...' Nearly twenty years later another girl told Emmeline that for her 'you are inextricably associated with autumn's loveliness and always remembered with the very warmth of the colours while my life lasts ... a breath of much-needed humanity.'

For Emmeline herself meetings of the Consultative Committee and the AHM Executive Committee provided brief breaks, and taught her of the good train service to London. After one Friday and Saturday meeting she snatched two days to spend with Hallie Melly at the farmhouse near Friston, 'a shocking thing', said Emmeline cheerfully, but her only private time. Before the end of that first Roedean term the school played lacrosse against Queen Anne's, Caversham, and Queen Anne's headmistress, Kathleen Moore, stayed the weekend. 'She was delighted with the school and the girls, but, alas, there are many weaknesses she did not see! Sometimes they almost oppress me, but one can only go on day by day and hope that as the years go on the little bits will gradually tell.' Emmeline had set her hand to the plough, and looked back no more.

Chapter 18
A headmistress of the 1920s

Some flavour of Emmeline's tactics may be sampled in a tiny episode in Avignon the following spring. Freshened by an Easter in Portofino, and on her way to Paris, where she was to head a group of headmistresses invited by French education officials to view the girls' secondary school scene, Emmeline paused. At Avignon was Herbert's daughter Barbara, now seventeen and just finishing with schooling at the Friends' school at Sidcot, staying with a French family to improve her French and work towards university entrance. Emmeline would have thought it most unnatural to pass her by, and allotted two days. On the second day she took her niece out, in a hired and 'very, very ramshackle Ford in the shape of a tiny taxi', to Nîmes, and the Pont du Gard, and Villeneuve, but on the evening of arrival she had asked some searching questions about Barbara's work.

> I was not altogether happy about her work, but after going into the whole question I made up my mind I would myself interview the Directrice of the Lycée and explain my anxiety and my difficulties. She is a very delightful woman, and she saw the point at once, so much so that she succeeded in persuading the professor of English, a French woman who took her university course at Cambridge, actually to give Barbara private lessons; this was exactly what I wanted, but I could not very well have asked for it myself because the lady refuses to give private lessons and one easily understands her reasons when one knows that she is a full-time professor at the Lycée and has a husband and two sons but no maid.

Emmeline arranged to meet the professor, and found 'a charming woman' who 'very quickly saw what Barbara needed', and agreed to give her private lessons. Quite unconscious of irony Emmeline found Barbara's host family

> a little inclined to manage everything for one. I am sure it is out of kindness, but it must become a little tiresome sometimes. I had to be very firm not to have everything planned for me, even as to what Barbara's lessons were to be and who should give them. Fortunately I find it fairly easy to be firm without offending people, and I got my own way, but I could see that Barbara would never have been able to do it for herself because Mme Renard would have thought that this professor was impossible to get, that therefore there was no more to be said, and that such and such a professor at the boys' lycée would be the right person ... However, we got it all settled, and no one was more delighted at the turn affairs had taken when it was settled than Mme Renard herself.

The simultaneous evaluation of the practical and psychological problems, and the overriding of them, the bland '*we* got it all settled', tell their own tale.

Her visit to Paris brought to the fore Emmeline's inquiring rather than decision-taking side, and provides an example of how she conceived and pursued the wider role of the modern headmistress. Principal host to the AHM group was M. Desclos, Directeur Ajoint of the Office National des Universités et Écoles Françaises, interested to promote exchanges of equivalent staff. For some years *assistantes* had worked in English schools, including Emmeline's, but these were junior women, without full status and still learning their craft. To operate an exchange system for fully-fledged teachers entailed guidelines on salaries, seniority and pension rights on return, selection, co-ordination of employing authorities – dozens of apparently bureaucratic details where vagueness could mean real difficulties for individuals. Ideas and procedures demonstrated how professionalism had developed among secondary teachers by the mid-1920s, as the Joint Four discussed the problems, and a committee drew together the four secondary associations, the Board of Education and LEA representatives. Objectives, to develop teachers and foster international understanding more systematically than by occasional sympathy-inducing visits, illustrate some postwar values.

More and more Emmeline was interesting herself in all forms of international co-operation, and as the AHM's Chairman of Committee and hence a member of the Joint Four she was the obvious leader when Desclos turned to the women's side, at a time of some Anglo-French tension after the Geneva Protocol of 1924. The ten headmistresses 'came from each of the districts of England but were not necessarily well-known people,' said Emmeline, and all could understand French, the majority speaking fluently, to the relief of their French hosts: 'I was amazed to find how few people, apart from two or three of the Directrices, spoke or even understood English. That was why it was a pity I should have been in charge of the delegation,' Emmeline added, ruefully and perhaps excessively aware of her own defects.

She reported later to the AHM, and spent some time closeted at the Board of Education with senior officials, but for her parents she provided a less technical outline of her findings in Paris. It was her first direct experience of practices outside England, and she was intent to observe.

We spent most mornings at a Lycée, that is, a public secondary school for girls, and generally went to two lessons of an hour each, 8.30 to 9.30, 9.30 to 10.30, and during the last hour watched gymnastic classes or kindergarten work or art work or heard the girls sing or inspected the building. The teaching that we heard was amazingly good. It is true that the best teachers are all appointed to schools in Paris eventually, and I do not imagine that we were given the opportunity of hearing any people that were not very good, but there is no doubt that the standard of teaching in these official girls' Lycées in Paris is very high. I think the girls are overworked, and I think they lose a great deal by having no large halls where they can assemble and no system which brings the professors into as close contact with the girls as our English system does. But they have many points which we lack. The numbers are very great, up to as many as 1,600 in one Lycée, built originally for something like 650 girls, and the ages of the girls vary from three to 19 or 20, though it is more often up to 17 or 18 ...

The actual school hours are from 8.30 to 11.30 and 1.30 to 3.30; then there are certain optional classes which girls sometimes attend out of these hours, and there are a good many hours of preparation ... All the Lycées are State schools, but the fees paid are fairly high and there are not nearly so many scholarship girls as in grant-aided schools in England. The professors are appointed by the State and the Directrice does not choose them, but I gather that most of the Directrices have a voice in the matter, because, as one said to me, 'we work beforehand'.

We went to two schools that might be called higher elementary schools, where the girls stayed from 13 to 16 or 17, and we saw the most beautiful work – art work, needlework, laundry and cookery – done there ... We also went to Sèvres to see the Training College where all women professors for the girls' Lycées of France (there are only seventy in the whole of France and seven of these are in Paris) are trained, and where they receive not only their professional training but the whole of what we should call their university course as well. The Directrice is supposed to be the most distinguished woman in all the French educational world. The College, which is called the École Normale Supérieure, is in an old palace, part of which was the original home of the manufactory of Sèvres china until that was moved to another building by Louis XV. The rooms and the gardens are beautiful. We heard there a lecture given by M. Brunot, a lecturer on French language at the Sorbonne, and M. Brunot had tea with us afterwards. I might almost say he had tea with me: one of the penalties of being, as they called it, the *présidente* of the delegation was that I was always being set aside in a place of honour with some distinguished personage.

Thursday is a whole-day holiday in French schools and there is no holiday on Saturday. It was arranged for us to go to Versailles on the Thursday and to visit the Lycée and the boarding houses connected with it there.

These four or five houses in a large park, each for 32 girls and linked to a central kitchen, were admirably organised, in Emmeline's opinion, by an ex-Directrice of several Lycées who now had charge of the boarding arrangements for all Paris and Versailles Lycées. Emmeline knew well she was viewing the élite tip of French girls' education; her sister Beatrice, for one, had been appalled at conditions in a Rouen convent school where she was temporarily billeted in 1914, at the badly ventilated attic where forty girls slept, at the still worse sanitation – 'no bathroom of any sort' and 'hardly any water to be got for any purpose' – and the English nurses had spent their nights hunting down bedbugs.

234 / Doors of Possibility

For the 'less austere occupations' promised by M. Desclos the headmistresses were given a tour of the Versailles Château and the Trianon, including normally closed apartments, a dinner with the Directrices *en masse*, a reception by the Minister for Education, another reception at the Sorbonne, and the Minister's box at the Comédie Française one night and the Opéra another. Emmeline managed a second visit to the Comédie another night, for two of Molière's shorter plays, and 'did wish that Barbara, who is taking Molière for her special subject in her examination, could have been with us. It is a revelation to see one of the plays done as they are done there.' Yet still she found time to go with a Lycée Directrice to 'a political meeting where they discussed such problems as nationalisation and all the other things they discuss in England' one evening, and, having tried and failed to deter her old friend May Guilloux from the overnight journey from Brittany to Paris, gave May and her husband dinner on another. Fortunately the thoughtful Desclos had accommodated the group in the American University Women's Club in preference to a 'banal' hotel, he said, and for the sake of its peaceful garden in a quiet spot close to the Gardens of the Luxembourg.

Officially the visit ended with a *matinée* – songs and acted scenes in French and English by girls from four Lycées, followed by a tea – after a visit to the Paris Exhibition where the Englishwomen were thoroughly ashamed of their nation's building, 'one of the blots on the landscape, very inartistic and very different from any of the others'. But Emmeline was not yet finished with inquiry. 'I stayed till the evening and crossed at night because there were a great many questions I wanted to ask about curriculum and things of that sort, and Mlle Caron, the Directrice of one of the Lycées, very kindly invited me' to her home and family dinner with 'all interesting people, themselves tremendously interested in political and other questions'.

The English establishment determined to give the French Directrices similar entertainment on their return visit two years later, and, between ministerial parties, showed off what they thought their best, the North London Collegiate School and St Paul's Girls' School, the music training at Kensington High School, Parliament Hill County School and the Barrett Street Trade School, and so on, before the visitors split into groups to travel further, some (including Mlle Caron) to Roedean. But the exchange system itself limped over the hurdles of uncertain franc values, beyond the power of educationists.

Nevertheless Emmeline found her visit worthwhile, and though the respect implied in careful attention and thoughtful inquiry was demanded by the occasion and her role, as was the enjoyment evident in her descriptions of lunch-tables 'beautifully decorated with flowers' in Paris, or their Versailles guide's 'delightful pictures in words of people whose portraits hung on the walls' of the Trianon, yet the tone and style of her letter to her parents is wholly at one with her account of her holiday in Portofino, or indeed her dealings with Barbara's affairs in Avignon. Paying attention, and finding herself happy to be so engaged, defined her approach in and out of school.

For though the Paris visit was not without consequences, school remained her priority, and her job, a job, moreover, that constituted her claim to participate elsewhere. Being a headmistress gave her an identity, and paradoxically she enlarged the headmistress's authority by refusing to immure herself in the school, finding it the prize as well as the penalty of a professional woman that work was the adventure, consuming and a consummation. As her third Roedean term started she was happier, and thought she gained ground. Five years later one housemistress, with the goodwill of recent retirement and knowing that the tact Emmeline had required had cost some concessions, took care to let her know that just before the Lawrences retired 'we constantly talked of the miracles the new headmistress was to work in clearing up on many negligences and ignorances', that 'the girls are reformed, other work is much better and all the other hoped-for changes have come', but above all that 'one thing I am very clear about and that is that no one's feelings were hurt'. 'No one's' was an exaggeration: an aging geography mistress, severely criticised by HMIs in 1927 and already humiliated by losing much of her work to a graduate newcomer, was deeply wounded by a brusque put-down in a corridor.

One concession, minor but a pang, was Emmeline's abandonment of her little moral tales told to set the key of term or holidays and disliked by some staff. Opening and closing assemblies were remembered now for practical and concrete nuggets, to be polite and considerate when dealing with overworked shop assistants at Christmas, for example. 'If the goods we had been examining were not quite what we wanted we should smile and say so, not forgetting to thank the assistant for her trouble.' Or girls should be 'helpful at home' in the holidays. More generally, an old Nuneaton quotation was revived, from George Eliot, that they should set their sights high: 'I shall not feed on doing great tasks ill, nor dull the world's sense with mediocrity.' And when, in the 1930s, the last girl left whose father had been killed in *the* war, Emmeline announced a new era. But the fables were only to be resurrected when she emerged from retirement for a locum term at another school in the 1950s.

Nor did she preach in chapel, though she took the Sunday evening service; a sermon was for the chaplain in the morning. Yet all Emmeline's work at Roedean was built on one unspoken text: 'For unto whomsoever much is given, of him shall be much required: and to whom men have committed much, of him they will ask the more' (Luke 12.48). In the Rev. Bruce Cornford, chaplain until 1938, she found an ally perfectly in accord. As a cousin to Leslie Cope Cornford, husband of another Lawrence sister, Christabel, he had been established at Roedean since the turn of the century, but it was equally typical of Lawrence management that for his not very onerous duties at school he received a stipend of £400, being the incumbent of a large and very poor Portsmouth parish for whose sake, and for his frail wife, he stinted himself. From his parish work he drew lively illustrations for school sermons, popular for brevity, audibility and lucidity, but he was remembered for his catchphrase, 'Give till it hurts!'

'Pa' Bates, the singing-master, was then 'the only other man', remarked one Old Roedeanian, ignoring more than a dozen men employed to maintain the building and grounds. To an extent impossible after 1940 most girls took for granted the hundred-odd domestic staff, many living in, who cooked, served and washed up their meals, laundered their clothes and bedlinen, stoked their fires and hot-water boilers, swept their floors, scrubbed their baths. Unobtrusiveness and presence characterised both the domestic staff and chapel. Both conformed to public-school expectations, and both could make life easier.

The staff's function was simple and obvious; a chapel on the premises was practical for the Protestant Christian Sunday worship of the majority, its organ extended musical possibilities, and within its cloistered garth quiet respite could be found. For years gifts to the school contributed to beautify with marble the columns of the nave, to furnish reading-desks, hangings, Communion vessels, and Emmeline never forgot she had promised Dorothy Lawrence to care for it. Yet rarely was the chapel the immediate image evoked by the school's name, and rarely did it loom large. Not all attended Sunday services, Jews and Roman Catholics being taken, by staff of appropriate faiths, to Brighton assemblies, and other minorities receiving instruction according to parental wishes.

This equable breadth was the more apparent when many schools either preferred a bias, as at Sherborne, rooted in the evangelical wing of the Church of England, or were committed to a church, as was St Mary's Hall, the rival Brighton boarding school endowed primarily for clergy daughters. Many schools were also believed to limit numbers of Jewish girls – proof of quotas is hard to come by, but the very belief was effectual. Roedean, however, was known to be sympathetic to Jews and to provide for their religious instruction. Other non-Christians were few but accepted: in 1927 Emmeline asked the Roedean Council if she might accept the daughter of 'a Hindu gentleman', permission was granted (only by majority vote), and she took this thereafter as policy.

So there was more to the school than met the casual eye, just as the high fees were by no means uniform. In the 1920s one entrance scholarship (of £105 a year) and several exhibitions were officially offered annually, but a bursary subcommittee more discreetly subsidised some other fees; in the mid-1920s total remissions deducted £3,000 a year from fees, showing such bursaries to be numerous.[1] Parental costs, however, were increased by non-fee needs, for games equipment, some books, the standard list of clothes and shoes – hygiene rules dictated a daily complete change after games – and on this the casual eye might pick the more easily when Roedean's distinctive 'djibbah' was familiar from *Punch* cartoons by an artist father and neatly expressed the Lawrence philosophy. This loose garment, flowing from a yoke, with short loose sleeves, and worn over a blouse, developed in the 1900s as Penelope Lawrence's answer to the imprisoning corsetry she herself had long rejected in defiance of fashion; its other merit was to treat equally the whole variety of schoolgirl shape – it equalised.

Religious policy, domestic staff, fees and uniform seemed disparate but all related to the school's boarding character and distinguished Roedean from, for example, Nuneaton High School. Internal organisation of timetables and curriculum and teaching duties, however, was hardly dissimilar to that of Bedford, and indeed Nuneaton, though the close links of Houses and school and the use of senior teachers as housemistresses more fully integrated life in and out of school.

By the school year of 1926-7 Emmeline was more assured at Roedean, of where she was, and where she was going. She was now knotting up and testing the ropes of command through which responsibilities were devolved, among the girls through prefects, games captains, committees for drama or magazine or societies, but primarily through housemistresses and department heads, second mistress and secretary. The balances shifted. So, in Emmeline's absence at the start of 1930, her secretary sighed over

a simple question Miss Child [the second mistress] and I wanted to ask at Housemistresses' meeting. We came out squashed flat as pancakes. It's really comic, but I'm afraid it hurt poor Miss Child rather a lot. We are slipping back and back into the dim ages: the second mistress is a poor nonentity – and of course the Headmistress's secretary doesn't exist at all, and will not be dreamt of for many aeons to come. Do come back quickly and rescue us!

Emmeline had told Frances Gray that she herself was 'not constructive', and indeed her materials were rarely of her own making; the architecture was.

Part derived from her conception of the headmistress' role, different in kind from the intimately detailed involvement of the three founding sisters, who were each in charge of a House, with a finger in every pie, at the height of their powers with a searching eye on each detail – 'L'école, c'est nous'. In early Nuneaton days the High School's first head was tempted to stamp her impress thus on all the school's life, but with its growth and her own enlarging view Emmeline took to heart the implications of many a presidential address at the AHM, that a school-immersed head might reduce herself, and her school, to a narrow mind and a contracted heart. Delegation developed as a skill rehearsed in professional ideal, with the division of a school into departments, so that, like a housemistress in the domestic field, a departmental head was academically a power in her own land, arranging syllabuses, responsible for their working, watching departmental staff to show beginners how to master the unruly or rearrange work in sudden sickness or soothe the anxious parent. In theory the head had only to choose her women, test them, co-ordinate, and trust them.

Such a principle was one factor that shaped Emmeline's style. Freedom, with all its variety and its acceptance of difference, was what she urged as educational policy, ever suspicious of the restrictions and central control descending in circulars from the Board of Education and proposed in the name of reform. 'Variety and flexibility', the catchwords she often repeated, were not only sociologically-based values correlating with an emphasis on the individual but a defence against politically antipathetic monopoly, mechanisation and centralisation, characteristics widely feared in the spread of films, a single radio service, a press concentrated in the hands of few owners, and from the growth of the factory assembly-line. In sheer consistency with the belief that a woman of undeveloped, unexercised spirit makes a dull teacher she had to give the same degree of freedom and trust to her staff she wanted for herself, and she did not find it always easy.

A second shaping factor was the school's boarding character. Expensive, set at a distance from a town and still more distant from most girls' homes, taking some daughters of men who neither wanted nor expected them to live independently, it still could not exist sealed in a bubble from the dust of a complex world in rapid change, though, again, to bring the outside in could be hard. Unruly modes obtruded easily enough: Emmeline may have been unaware of the Brighton College boys of the 1920s who tossed cigarettes over the boundary, by private treaty with waiting girls, but some more public manifestation of the outer world prompted school authorities to put the Metropole Hotel's *thés dansants* out of bounds in 1931.

The effort to encourage out-of-school forms of giving and not of getting was eased slightly by a third factor consolidating the policy of 'finger on the pulse, not in the pie', as one headmaster characterised the style. Emmeline *enjoyed* her own outside work, unpaid and frequently fruitless as it proved, and was happy to take it home. She met many people, and she liked people. She belonged, and there is much to hint she disliked, or feared, to be an outsider. She claimed public work to be a citizen's duty (in the idea of citizenship too is a sense of belonging), and the conscience of a Nonconformist Liberal Victorian was appeased. And she liked to be active, up and doing, even though she officially rued her 'busy busy-ness'.

The fourth shaping factor, and largest, was the changing age itself, or how change was understood. Launching a traditional attack on 'smatterings' and restless cravings for novel excitements passively enjoyed, the headmistress of Cheltenham Ladies' College in 1926 discovered three characteristics in the 'modern age'.[2] The sciences marched, to speed communications more and more, to bring ever more rush and ever more monotonous industrial processes, and ever more expectation of fresh excitement tomorrow. Organisation grew, and with it feelings of corporate responsibility and the spread of influences affecting many, and so too a belief that to be acceptable to many was a gauge for measuring these influences. Thirdly, mass movements stirred great numbers, but to each gave less need for creative, reasoning, independent thought. The assembled headmistresses listening to Beatrice Sparks recorded no disagreement on her diagnosis.

At Roedean ritual forms, like the ample blue cloaks which disguised the girls' growing figures outdoors, merely wrapped superficially round the changing meaning beneath, and few visible habits were discarded, the markers of the passing year kept intact except that in 1927 the Reunion of Old Roedeanians was detached from Speech Day, crowded enough with parents and other visitors. On Empire Day in May Roedean girls still marched past the Union Jack, hoisted on the school's flagpole, before chapel and dispersal by Houses for country picnics, despite the 1920s' increasing unease, particularly in those educational and internationalist circles Emmeline frequented, at arrogant or jingoist forms of patriotism. But little militarism clung to the line of holiday-cheered girls, and Emmeline rather enjoyed parades and spectacles: colourful dramas had been rare treats in her childhood on Bath's suburban fringe.

Within a decade of the war's end voices were raised, especially those of League of Nations supporters, to urge a Peace Day to replace Empire Day, or perhaps Armistice Day, on the grounds that the Empire's justification was its maintenance of peace; but until the end of the 1930s Roedean girls marched past the flag and called it Empire Day. Armistice Day was solemnised with a service – 'we had the chapel absolutely full,' said Emmeline in 1927, 'with about 500 people, including, in addition to our own people, the builders on the Science block, the laundrymen who happened to be delivering, the greengrocer's man, Miss Lawrence's chauffeur, etc.' For Penelope Lawrence was there too, to read the lesson ('a wonderful voice: it filled the chapel').

The rituals of Reunion filled a summer weekend, the Speech Day events another, though Speech Day itself had made its first appearance only in the Lawrences' last year, and Sir Paul Lawrence long captained cricketer fathers against the First XI. Barely noticed was the easing of timetables to give older girls more independent time, or the shortening of lessons to concentrate minds and reduce the scurry and rush from lessons to meals to games. Quietly, too, compulsory scouting was replaced by voluntary membership of a new Girl Guide company soon affiliated to the national movement, and by degrees self-expressive House play production was released into the girls' hands to make or mar as they could. Experienced staff-led drama was gradually limited to the School play, when numerous activities could be correlated to high standards, with high effort to excellence, in keeping with advice from Elsie Fogerty, Principal of the Central School of Speech and Drama who came weekly to Roedean to teach speech production. Such were the earliest of changes, each directed to what Beatrice Sparks, in her 1926 AHM speech, defined as education, 'a release of power from within rather than an imposition ... from without'.

Especially as Emmeline's personal teaching diminished, to the merely occasional by the 1930s, lower forms in the school saw for the most part mannerisms and position. Some were too daunted by the head to realise the woman, and before her physical and functional bigness shivered like the downland grass as a strong wind swept over. 'Respect' is the most frequent of all descriptions: 'we were disciplined more by the feeling that we must not fall below the standard that she expected of us than by hard-and-fast rules and regulations', 'she somehow imprinted a powerful moral sense on the atmosphere that we breathed', 'absolutely fair and just', 'downright and honest; said what she meant; you could trust her', and her aim was to make girls 'good and useful citizens – all round; she thought girls ought to *work*, whatever the nature of the work in hand, and *buckle down*'. So the coin could turn another side, and Emmeline be found 'uncomprehending of everyday human weakness', so that 'when she loomed into sight I automatically felt guilty'.

Girls watched her at assembly, 'folding her hands in front and twiddling her thumbs first one way and then the other ... quite riveting'. They noticed her thoroughgoing decorum, whether explaining to the girl who said 'gography' why the word is 'geography', or remarking on the graceless show of thighs when girls, for the first time allowed bare legs, sprawled on the grass watching games. They were happy to exploit her excursive moods in scripture lessons 'when we diverted her on to her trip to the Holy Land – a sure way of keeping off the main subject', but left limply exhausted when she took a despairing teacher's English grammar class, made them work and made them understand. They were gratified by her presence of mind on April Fools' Day when 'a silent word went round that we should go to Prayers without our hymn books ... Miss Tanner took one look. "You have no hymn books, I see." Then, with a twinkle, "Very well. We will sing 'Jerusalem'. You all know that!" And sing it we did, with great gusto.' At other times one at least particularly enjoyed her 'three rather breathless aspirates in the prayer ending "... with gallant and high-hearted happiness".' And they were calmed when the winter gales howled round the chapel to drown their voices raised on behalf of 'those in peril on the sea' by the 'firm reassuring voice saying the familiar evening prayers'.

However slight her personal contact with the girls in the middle and lower school they knew who was in control; however frequent her actual absences she was recognised by most to have 'presence'. She was recognised, too, to move in a wider world, and into that world, local, national and beyond, she went out enthusiastically, though never quite achieving the perfect delegation of the ideal head.

By mid-1925 she commanded a more satisfactory base for living and entertaining than the makeshifts in the school buildings, though the headmistress's house was notionally rather than physically detached, and linked to the school by a passage to the library. Yet though she had not planned its layout she furnished it, and though she did not own it she could use it as her own – to some extent. Without apparent conscious symbolism she hoped her parents might be her first overnight guests, but a projected stay in summer was delayed: 'Sir John Simpson [the architect] has condemned all the windows: every one has to come out, all the leaded lights have to be re-made', and when she could move in the first to stay, noted then and remembered later, was a school connection, a governor of the Johannesburg school also called Roedean and founded by one of the youngest Lawrence sisters, Theresa, and a friend. The headmistress' house was intended for school as much as for domestic use – no clear distinction was drawn between work and private life – and initially this sometimes chafed.

Work and private life also overlapped as a result of her familial drive: her niece Margaret had been taken, reluctantly, from Bedford to go instead to Roedean, on special terms. Margaret tried to be reasonable, although 'I simply loathe the idea of leaving this term. But I don't think it would be quite fair on you or Mummie and Daddy if I did stay here after all the trouble you have gone through for me ... If I take the School Cert. when I am 17 can I leave then as I don't want to stay on until I am 18. Because I do hate school so. I wish I could leave now and earn my own living; I think it would be awful fun ...'

She came resentfully to Roedean in 1925 and Roedean, and most of all the pressures of School Certificate drove her to revolt in early 1927, and to find that a girl not yet 16 was not deemed self-determinative nor could withstand her parents' combination of emotional blackmail and threats. 'I told her,' Edwin Gauntlett wrote to Emmeline, 'she had to consider that any stupidity she may do would reflect on her parents and her Auntie, and she must remember she has two sisters who would probably be coming to Roedean and if she did not do her best it would make their position on arriving at the school much more difficult.' He told Emmeline too that if his daughter continued to waste 'the fine opportunity she has got' he would 'take her away from school and not spend any more money on her education. She will then have to take the hard road to make her own way in life. She is sensitive ... but very stubborn and if she has set her mind on a thing she will drive us all to the last ditch.'

Margaret stayed, precisely the sort of girl for whose sake the AHM struggled to reform the demands of School Certificate, the sort headmistresses wanted to include and the intransigent need for five passes from three groups tended to exclude. Margaret was to take the examination repeatedly, spending time and energy for a pocketful of credits in all needed subjects – but never a full set of passes at once, as the rules required. That summer of 1927 Emmeline took her, with her brother William and a Roedean friend, to Cancale in Brittany, with intent to coach and with French lessons arranged. Years later she herself could recall her geography sessions with Margaret on the balcony, but they slipped from her pupil's mind: 'Intellectual work ... gives her no real pleasure!' Emmeline noted. 'However, she does quite recognise that she wants to pass her examination and wants to get the work done.' Yet the headmistress valued the lively enthusiasm and swift response to the human that diverted Margaret to Cancale's charms, the swimming, cycling, picnics, the expedition to Mont St Michel with four English boys from a nearby hotel, the regatta and its evening dance, and the fête that followed.

Emmeline allowed her young charges considerable freedom to rove, and did not fuss to them over her difficulties in providing the young Gauntletts with adequate vegetarian sustenance where 'the French have much more meat than we do ... The specialities of the place are oysters, lobsters and shrimps, and these are famous, but not much use to us!' But the holiday threw up another reflection of a headmistress's preoccupations: how could a sense of purposeful adventure co-exist with prudential forethought? – the question begged in the Lawrences' slogan 'as much freedom as is compatible with safety'. On the Cancale quay fishermen were preparing their boats to go to the Newfoundland cod grounds, and with them, when he could, worked Emmeline's 14-year-old nephew William. 'I am not sure that some of the words of French I learnt were quite what Em expected, but she gave a lot of thought to my request to go with them on their fishing trip. The trip was to be of three or four months' duration, and she thought I should miss too much of school.'

So Emmeline's judgment looked to the long view, with reason to know how William's father cared for schooling and regretted the brevity of his own at the Lowes' school in Handsworth. At the start of September the little party all returned to school, and Emmeline to the house she had now equipped as hers.

The first half-term in her house at Roedean had brought at once Speech Day and a full Council meeting:

On Saturday morning we have the Prize distribution, and Mr Vaughan of Rugby speaks. I then give lunch to Mr Vaughan, Miss Lawrence, Miss Theresa [visiting from South Africa to meet the new head], Sir Paul and Lady Lawrence, Miss Clough, Mrs Wharrie, Colonel Blyth and Dr Pickard [all on the Council]. I did *not* want to give so large a party but Miss Lawrence wishes it, and says that that is why the Council gave me a house with rooms of a good size. I almost retaliated, 'Then why did they give me only one bedroom for maids?' However, I must put my back into it and think out a decent menu, making the best of a poor dinner-service, with all plates chipped beyond the number of six, and rapidly buy a few more knives and a few things of that sort! It isn't really easy to see to all the domestic things *and* entertain Council and some hundreds of parents *and* make speeches, etc.! I am now trying to get a temporary daily parlourmaid for the weekend as one maid cannot wait quickly enough on a party of ten and there will always be extra people for each meal.

Blanche Clough, ex-Principal of Newnham College, and 'either Miss Theresa or Dr Pickard' were to stay in the house, so Emmeline had also 'to collect furniture to make the secretary's room a second guest room'.

Yet though the housekeeper's role irritated, she was adept at creating what several girls termed a 'civilised' atmosphere, if one penetrated by girls normally only in small weekly groups of prefects or sixth-formers for what one called 'a fabulous tea – unlike any other school meal!' and general conversation. Normal school access was to the headmistress's study in the school building, where a large window looked to the sea and let in the light, and the fire was laid in a recess like an outsized inglenook, formidably cosy. Incomers stepped on a rug patterned with Roedean's crest and punning motto '*Honneur aulx dignes*', and eyed a substantial desk for workaday business. It was in the study that a housemistress in discreet attendance on two parents discussing their daughter's future heard them sigh at Emmeline's suggestion that Oxford or Cambridge would not be *quite* suitable. 'Somewhere else is hardly the same,' they lamented. Emmeline rose, moved to the fire, and beamed sweetly down on them: '*I* have never found it a disadvantage,' she murmured.

In her house, gatherings were intended to be social though perhaps the comparisons drawn by one school-leaver in 1928 after a farewell lunch were less than wholly tactful:

It was amazing ... suddenly going into a completely different atmosphere ... a home atmosphere in the middle of school. Personally, I like living like a barbarian sometimes, but there is something about civilised life which is awfully nice to get back to. This was what we found in your house. We also thought how masterly it was for anyone in the middle of such a rushed day to be able to sit and talk of Chippendale chairs and old glass as if there was nothing else in the world to do and time was your own. I think the plans for next year's work sound most adventurous ...

Emmeline certainly wanted the 'civilisation', but not the contrast.

The context of such would-be informal gatherings was the seed-sowing Fanny Simon had enjoined on the child Emmeline in the early 1880s, a cultivating process of fertilising minds to develop ideas and values, just as the associations in which Emmeline participated were designed to link minds and activities. Thus her old Nuneaton colleague Emma Stevinson came as a personal friend from the Nursery School training centre at Deptford, but her visits could guide not only Emmeline's interest in the local Nursery Schools Association but stimulate her to lend Mansbridge's *Life of Margaret McMillan* and Emma Stevinson's own books to another visitor, staying in 1928 to speak to Roedean girls about 'Work among the Natives in South Africa'. 'I have always wanted to tell you how much I owe to that night,' wrote Dorothy Maud in 1939 from Sophiatown. 'From reading that all our nursery schools here began, and we have got two lovely ones going now, with 180 children here and 100 over in Orlando, and seventeen African girls training as Nursery School teachers.' But when Emmeline herself saw the township schools in 1948 she commented dryly, 'But what an appalling amount remains to be done!'

A base for entertaining helped more deliberate seed-sowing. One small piece that exemplified Emmeline's role as co-ordinator and nurturer of relationships between groups and individuals arose from her work on the Brighton and Hove Juvenile Welfare Council. Originally formed in 1918 as an anxious response to 'juvenile delinquency', the JWC was to act as a local authority umbrella for voluntary youth organisations, meeting common needs for concessionary fares, sports facilities, and so on, and itself to fill gaps in provision by organising the Sussex Boys' Camps, play centres, and in 1927 Brighton Girls' Club with, as prime mover and first warden, the JWC Secretary A. J. Prior.

By the mid-1930s Emmeline was Chairman of the JWC and seized the initiative offered to local authorities by the 1933 Children and Young Persons Act. The Act induced the Education Committee, whose meetings she now attended regularly, to analyse local juvenile crime, mainly petty larceny, and a positive correlation was found between non-criminal behaviour and membership of a juvenile organisation or active pursuit of (innocent) hobbies. Emmeline promptly invited not only the Mayors of both Brighton and Hove, other local councillors, the JWC members and youth leaders, but also the chairman and secretary of the Board of Education's Juvenile Organisations Committee to a conference at Roedean to discuss useful action and explain local authority powers and duties precisely. A good tea promoted good humour, and the two national officials were then given a tour of three play centres, the Girls' Club, the Boys' Club and the Sea Scouts before the party broke up at 10.00 pm, and the JWC congratulated themselves on the spotlight shone on youth problems in the hope that, as the national officials promised, the meeting might 'strengthen the links' – that is, encourage grant aid and the pooling of ideas – between the Board of Education and local voluntary youth groups.

The JWC's own initiatives were not cheap, and though the Town Council granted a favourable lease on a new site when in 1934 it demolished the entire road in which the Girls' Club stood, in the name of slum clearance, building costs for a new clubhouse, about £3,800, had to be raised by voluntary effort. But a few months after the Roedean conference Emmeline could lay the foundation stone for a hall to seat 300, a library, a kitchen, a cloakroom, and hope a substantial seed was planted with the same trowel. To publicise to Brighton girls the club's attractions the Duchess of Gloucester came to open the new building a little later, with Roedean Guides providing the guard of honour. More familiar to Roedeanians, however, was the school's own mission, developed by the Lawrences as an independent and non-local philanthropy to bring sickly London children to month-long holidays at Rottingdean. To some extent such activities kept Emmeline usefully aware that the comforts now surrounding her were not universally shared, but for her now to be the figure with the foundation trowel and not the familiar friend of club sessions as at Nuneaton underscored the reality that her school had no secure role in the town, no valid base to explore the local civic awareness earnestly promoted in many a discussion at the AHM.

Chapter 19
'Popularly known as the Hadow Report'

Seed-sowing from a national height was the function of the Consultative Committee, although reactions from the Board of Education to topics suggested by the Committee after 1926 display an increasing distrust of the nettles and puffballs among the seeds – one topic proposed might just occasion 'vague and rather angry talk', another 'moral exhortations which might also raise religious issues', a third involve administrative problems with political difficulties.[1]

Emmeline's first days at Roedean were punctuated by Committee meetings in London to discuss the new reference accepted in early 1924 with its carefully limited terms. In full this read:

(i) To consider and report upon the organisation, objective and curriculum of courses of study suitable for children who will remain in full-time attendance at schools, other than Secondary Schools, up to the age of 15, regard being had on the one hand to the requirements of a good general education and the desirability of providing a reasonable variety of curriculum, so far as is practicable, for children of varying tastes and abilities, and on the other to the probable occupations of the pupils in commerce, industry and agriculture. (ii) Incidentally thereto, to advise as to the arrangements which should be made (a) for testing the attainments of the pupils at the end of their course; (b) for facilitating in suitable cases the transfer of individual pupils to Secondary Schools at an age above the normal age of admission.[2]

The Committee therefore was to accept as a 'given' the existing division between elementary and secondary sectors, and to consider the needs of pupils who would remain technically elementary until they left school for adult work.

The Board did not wait for Committee broodings to materialise before issuing, in March 1925, a request to LEAs to prepare programmes for 1927 to 1930 or 1932 to secure provision for practical instruction in elementary schools and for advanced instruction, to extend beyond the age of 14, for older or more intelligent elementary pupils, as the 1918 Act had planned; and some LEAs had not themselves waited for such a directive. The air was thick with schemes. At the AHM Conference of 1924, for instance, a paper by Dorothy de Zouche followed Tawney's line of argument in *Secondary Education for All*, urging reorganisation into stages of primary, secondary, and higher, to provide every normal child with education up to 16 in schools various in kind but equally staffed and equipped. Every child could profit by the level of education supplied in secondary schools, she insisted. That was a teacher's view. As a member of Brighton's Education Committee

Emmeline could observe some of the considerations at work from an LEA point of view. In the course of this she became unhappy with the Brighton Education Committee, detecting 'petty political (not necessarily party-political) influences', and in 1942 declared that 'nothing would persuade me to work under the Brighton Committee, as I have told them ... I couldn't bear to have to put up with what Mr Barrow, headmaster of Brighton and Hove Grammar School, aided by four LEAs, has to put up with from the Brighton Committee. It is all so petty and often so spiteful, and I know that Brighton is not unique in that respect. I am often shocked at what other headmistresses have to bear.' For Toyne, however, the Director of Education and a local government officer not a councillor, 'I have the greatest liking and respect'.

Brighton, unlike Nuneaton, was large enough to administer both elementary and secondary sectors, and Emmeline herself was to take most interest in the latter, from her co-opted seat on the Higher Education subcommittee, though she played little active part until after 1930. Profitable as the town might be for private schools, as the Lawrence sisters had heard, in 1918 the forty-one such schools held only 800 boys and 1,100 girls, whereas (in 1925-6) 16,251 children attended elementary schools, three-quarters those 'provided' by the Council, the others 'voluntary' schools established by church bodies but maintained by LEA rates. Of these a handful might proceed to a secondary school, most probably the Varndean municipal one – at this time the boys' school held 5-600 and the girls' about 450 pupils, 68 per cent of these arriving from an elementary school (but only 25 per cent for free).[3] The GPDST High School and the Grammar School to which Emmeline referred also offered some free places to elementary pupils; a Technical College and School of Art came within the Higher Education sub-committee's purview; and the arithmetic still leaves a majority whose whole schooling was elementary. As it was, support for the two municipal secondary schools cost the LEA about £23,000 in 1925-6, in addition to repayment of capital loans for the girls' sorely needed new buildings, opened in 1926.[4]

Costs became still more contentious than usual when Board Circular 1371 in late 1925 seemed to reverse all the hopeful signs that the Geddes cuts were healing, with a change in the basis of grants made by central to local authorities from a percentage of estimated spending to a block grant calculated on budgets for 1924-5 – in effect, imposing a ceiling, and a low ceiling as widespread anger made very clear. The AHM pitched objections dramatically – economy at the expense of the children – and the Joint Four, with Emmeline on its committee, issued a memorandum in similar terms. The Brighton Education Committee uneasily reviewed its plans and their costs, and in their memorandum, submitted to the Board and circulated to other LEAs, took care to be specific. But the planners turned over ideas for further developments in unsettled and cost-conscious minds.

Their first development scheme, to include a new boys' secondary school and extensions to the Technical College, was rejected by the main

Conservative-led Council, and a second draft pruned and lopped, although the Education Committee continued to argue the case for two new 'intermediate' schools to take about 15 per cent of the over-11s. Intermediate (or 'Central') schools had been shown elsewhere to meet a definite need, explained the Education Committee, for children 'who require a curriculum on a less definitely literary basis than is provided in the Secondary School'.[5] For those selected neither for secondary nor for intermediate schools 'senior schools' or departments were envisaged, with classes smaller and more homogeneous than in existing upper elementary schools, with some scope for practical and simple laboratory work, and with a graduated curriculum looking towards an anticipated rise in the school leaving age to 15.

Such, in outline, was the plan proposed in June 1926, about six months before the Consultative Committee Report was published; other LEAs, Warwickshire for example, already had Central schools (twenty-one in Warwickshire by 1923-4), but the essential feature here was the reorganisation of all the schools for separate treatment of over-11s. That, of course, included the 'voluntary' church schools, and though the Brighton Education Committee argued their accommodation problems would thereby be eased – some were on the notorious 'Black List' of defective premises – they quite failed to suggest how the church authorities could be persuaded either to part with their senior pupils or to provide senior departments. And in fact the managers of these schools 'expressed themselves unable to agree to the Scheme'.

So the Consultative Committee deliberated in no void of ideas and about practices which varied from LEA to LEA, in a general pattern where contemporary educational theory might often be at odds with issues of finance and authority. A visit to one of their meetings in April 1925 by the Permanent Secretary, now Sir Aubrey Symonds, demonstrates the limits of the Board's appreciation of the scope of Committee thought: he saw the nation anxious about the ever-rising cost of education and wanted it shown 'it was getting something which it wanted and something for which it was well worth paying', and he saw the Committee as 'dealing with the reference concerning Central Schools', whose place in the general system puzzled him; he hoped they would clarify it.[6]

This was not as naive as it appears: it was the nub of the problem, for Central schools were controversial and yet also the basis of most reform plans. Opponents, and these included a majority of teachers, disliked what they thought a cheap and inferior substitute for secondary schools, and in a Commons debate in May 1925 an amendment favouring provision of Central schools to make up shortfalls in secondary ones won little support from any side. Supporters, including Manchester's Director of Education, Spurley Hey, argued for selective Central schools with four-year courses (i.e. to 15-16) 'definitely based upon elementary school work' and with 'regard to the fact that most pupils will pass directly into industry or commerce' as a practicable response to need now: for the hungry, ran the argument, bread-

and-scrape today is better than jam tomorrow.[7] But selective schools only would leave many pupils out. J. A. White, the Central school headmaster on the Consultative Committee, argued that a well-organised Central school did not try to imitate a secondary school, whatever the pressures from parents and employers, but could use its liberty from School Certificate demands to explore courses related to pupils' environments and experience and, not before the last year or so, allow a bias to some occupational direction.[8] Such a structure accommodated both the selective ones (preferred in Manchester) and the non-selective, more inclusive schools some LEAs were developing, because courses and methods were adapted to the pupils, not vice versa.

It is clear that educational, rather than strictly financial justifications for Central schools presupposed the 'academic' nature of secondary schools with curricula dominated by existing forms of School Certificate; the only other bases for their administrative separation were the social-class distinction Tawney opposed with more articulacy but no more passion than many, and the fees paid by just over half the children in the mid-1920s (the proportion varying by area).

The full Committee sat for 46 days from May 1924 to mid-1926, and subcommittees on extra days, examining 95 witnesses in person and studying a vast array of memoranda, statistics, questionnaire replies, specimen syllabuses, and more. In scope the material ranged from general policies to detailed activities, in area from all over England and Wales, with comparative data for Scotland and several European countries, and in source from professional organisations, LEAs and educational institutions of all kinds to commercial companies and the TUC. An enormous number of needs clamoured for attention: here were rural schools, there the Bermondsey Settlement in dockland; and numerous points of view advanced philosophies of '*how* to learn' or straightforward demands for practical sex teaching (from a girls' club organiser), and all between.[9] Soon the Committee co-opted Professor Percy Nunn, then Principal of the London Day Training College and best known for his various works of educational theory with their stress on 'securing for everyone the conditions under which individuality is most completely developed',[10] an indication of Committee distaste for standardising systems.

Briefly attention was diverted in 1924 when the Committee was asked to produce some ideas on juvenile (un)employment, though the Board was wholly unimpressed by the moral of Hadow's succinct analysis of statistics that to raise the school leaving age was the long-term answer, and that interim grants should be made now for continuing education. Since the Committee's proposal in their subsequent Report that the leaving age should rise to 15-plus was to be one of main talking-points later, an internal memorandum by E. K. Chambers, one of the senior civil servants at the Board, revealingly foreshadows the official response.[11] To raise the leaving age, he said, would be politically disadvantageous to the party responsible, because of parental opposition, lack of money (for the extra staff and buildings), the need for extra staff to be trained, and the lack of a suitable curriculum – though this last could not be argued after publication of *The Education of the Adolescent*, the Committee's Report.

The Committee worked rapidly, if the final meeting was a sample. From the Forum Club on 28 October 1926 Emmeline wrote: 'The meeting of the Consultative Committee has ended an hour and a half earlier than we expected and we have signed our report, so I have this precious time quite unexpectedly and am more than rejoiced about it. There is a very comfortable "Silence" room in the club in which it is very easy to get some writing done in warmth and comfort.' Yet included at that meeting was an account by some members, one of them Emmeline, of a joint conference with the Committee on Education and Industry the previous day, the writing of a condolence letter to Dr Adami's new-made widow and of a tribute to Adami's own Committee service to insert in the Report, renewed discussion of several sections and the confirmation of some members' reservations on specific recommendations, as well as decisions on the title and format. And Lynda Grier, the Principal of Lady Margaret Hall, found an opportunity to tell Emmeline 'that they do like Barbara so much', in her first term as the first Tanner actually to attend a university.

The Report signed that day and published the next January excited interest well beyond the little circles of educationists. Its contents are described below, on pp. 252-4. But a pointer to the future was signalled in a Commons debate in February, when the initial motion welcomed the Report and called on the Government 'at once to take all the legislative and administrative action necessary to secure a universal system of post-primary education on the lines recommended by the Committee'. Only a fundamental amendment secured a majority, however, to welcome a Report whose 'general trend ... is in accordance with the policy of HM Government and with the pro-grammes of the LEAs', and all reference to legislative change was discarded. At some points the conclusions indeed fitted such plans as Brighton's, and the Committee also showed a practical ambition to describe not a misty ideal but how actual existing conditions could be developed towards what Ernest Barker, at the North of England Conference in January 1927, called an 'educational and social revolution', one which gave dignity to the manual worker and dissolved the objection to 'secondary education for all' that the academic bias of existing secondary schools did not suit all children.

Since Barker had chaired the Drafting Subcommittee, few were more intimate with the detail of the Report, though he was no favourite with the Board of Education, if an internal description as 'inclined to be excessively meticulous, rather unpractical, and sometimes positively obstructive' was more than an individual's irritation in April 1928.[12] Emmeline, however, had found in him one of her closer friends on the Committee – he etymologised a 'natural sympathy between a Tanner and a Barker' – and the friendship ripened further when in 1927 he married as his second wife an Old Roedeanian, Olivia Horner, considerably younger and with the generosity to admit she had felt 'rather sad' at the changes to the school 'but now I've seen for myself I'm most happy and uplifted again'. That was after a visit in 1928, itself remembered by a sixth-former for 'an enthralling talk given to us by Professor Ernest Barker, who held a Cambridge Chair', and was the first of many occasions his 'large lanky figure and broad Manchester accent' (as the *DNB* put it) adorned Roedean. 'I like Roedean,' wrote Barker in thanks after that first visit, 'because I dearly like talking with *you*.' The Barkers' letters to Emmeline over the years show them unusually sensitive to her need for reassurance, for verbal caresses, where many saw simply confident strength.

Where Barker claimed revolutionary potential, then, the government refused to admit acceptance of the Report meant any change in policy. Both readings are possible. The Committee were not 'fanatics' to 'have their dreams, Wherewith they weave a paradise'; hence attention was paid to surveying just what was available to over-11s as well as to notions favoured by their witnesses. Hence too they couched conclusions in developmental not revolutionary terms, and acknowledged political and financial handicaps – for example, conclusion 29 ('We note that the existing division of education into Elementary, Secondary and Technical, is losing its rigidity, and we hope that the artificial barriers between these three divisions will rapidly disappear') is backed by the means suggested in 31 to unify local administration of elementary and higher, but 32 recognises 'difficult political issues' and 33 proposes 'an interim arrangement' of improved co-operation. Moreover, 36 failed to take by the tail the religious tiger of 'dual control' in its mere 'earnest hope that the voluntary societies ... will aid to the best of their power the development of post-primary schools' of the type suggested.

Likewise, although in the note on juvenile employment in 1924 the Committee had envisaged recommending a minimum leaving age of 15 to be followed when possible by 16, the detailed consideration in their Report's Chapter VIII (drafted by Tawney) evaluated parental reluctance, employers' reluctance, and the cost to the country, and decided the two latter were outweighed by expected benefits but the first (even with maintenance allowances) posed real difficulties, and so, as Chambers had known, political problems. So the relevant recommendation referred to the age of 15 only, though it set a date – 1932 – when energetic provision might put in place adequate staff, accommodation, and suitable curricula.

So pragmatic an approach has led to charges that the Committee were 'a well-intentioned and confused group who tried to define class and economic advantages out of education and, when that was done, found they had no clear idea of what should be substituted' and left a poisonous legacy of educational hierarchy.[13] Rather, their ideas were clear enough, but thwarted; it was the subsequent process called 'Hadow reorganisation' but ignoring Hadow recommendations that kept 'the old in the guise of the new' and led the *Journal of Education* in 1930 to conclude that 'much of the reorganisation now being carried out tends to stabilise existing standards rather than to implement the ... Hadow Report', a Report it had greeted on publication as conceived in 'the very spirit of wisdom' and careful both in its discussion of the aims of different schools and its consideration of necessary administrative changes.[14] Most trenchantly, Tawney declared: 'a different policy, described ... by the same name, was quickly substituted for it. The Committee itself [of which he was a leading member] conceived its recommendations as a step towards a universal system of secondary education. It laboured that point, indeed, with almost wearisome reiteration...'[15] For this it had recommended a break at 11. But in practice secondary education was not enlarged, though Tawney saw some 'improvement in the later stages of elementary education'.

The Welsh member Evan Davis admitted that the proposals touched many vested interests and stirred antagonisms, so that a scheme easily devised had to steer past parents, teachers, school managers and local authorities.[16] By 1931 he was himself the LEA Director of Education responsible for Chichester High School when Emmeline infused a simplified summary with still-lively hope and faith. She told how she saw:

all over the country a great movement for extending many of the benefits of secondary education to all boys and girls ... due ... to what is popularly known as the Hadow Report ... [A report lacked the force of law] but, so much were other people (local authorities, teachers, parents) in agreement with the Committee as to the desirability of widening the educational opportunities of all the children of the country that everywhere people are getting busy making arrangements to put the recommendations into effect. In cases where the boys and girls can stay at school till 16 or 18 they will pass into secondary schools, but when they are going to leave at 14, or at 15 as it is likely to be soon, arrangements are being made for separate Modern or Senior schools for boys and girls over 11, and where the population of a district is not big enough to support a separate school the authorities are collecting all the boys and girls from a number of schools into one Central school where the needs of young people of that age, 11 to 14 or 15, can be specially considered and every possible opportunity be given to them to make the best use of their varied gifts.

So Emmeline distinguished secondary schools from others purely by length of school life, and she saw the internal organisation of schools for adolescents as replete with variety to suit 'varied gifts'. Then she asked, 'Is it worth the money that is spent on it?' The rest of her speech argues yes. Within two months, however, the May Report on public spending proposed total cuts amounting to £96,578,000, of which about one-seventh (£13,850,000) were to be made on education by slowing development, reducing grants to LEAs, universities and colleges, reducing free places in grant-aided secondary schools (then 46.3 per cent of places), and cutting teachers' salaries. The Bill of 1929 to raise the school leaving age and effect some administrative changes was finally abandoned, and when the Education Act of 1936 at last set the date when 15-plus should be the minimum, that date was 1 September 1939. Waves of cuts and policy fluctuations degraded the best-planned schemes organised round a longer course than the actual school life of the majority, and disheartened teachers and LEAs. Many, and not simple, were the reasons why 'Hadow reorganisation' and Hadow hopes remained remote from each other.

What did the Report say? The phrase used within the Board of Education in 1923 summed up the objective – 'the provision for the non-Secondary child of something better after 11'. Conclusion 1 stated the problem in very similar terms. Conclusion 2 leapt a good deal further, talking of 'urgent importance', of 'allowance for the varying requirements of different pupils', an age-group of 11 to 15, and steady advance to 'a universal system of post-primary education'. In 3 to 8 the structure planned is outlined: this is the 'organisation' aspect of the reference.[17]

'Primary' education should end at 11, and 'all normal children should go forward' to a second stage, for some to close at 16, for some at 18 to 19, though most must be expected to leave when compulsion ended, that is, at 14-plus or 15-plus. This stage should 'be regarded as a single whole, within which there will be a variety of types' related (in 4) 'to the age in which the majority of children remain at school, and the different interests and abilities of the children' – 'many more children should pass to "secondary" schools, in the current sense of the term'. To these schools currently called 'secondary' with their 'predominantly literary or scientific curriculum' continuing to or beyond 16-plus (and the Junior Technical and 'Trade' schools) were to be added schools of the existing 'selective Central' type, with 'a "realistic" or practical trend' for the last two years of 'at least' a four-year course (i.e. to 15 to 16), and also non-selective Central schools and 'senior classes' or similar where specially-designed courses for over-11s were, for local reasons, impossible to separate physically from primary departments (i.e. in small rural schools and voluntary schools with tenacious managers).

So much for the organisational framework. As for the curriculum aspect of the reference, the Committee advised that the three types other than 'existing secondary' (outside their remit) should at first 'have much in common', including a foreign language, with the secondary school, though with opportunity for 'practical work' and 'living interests', and any bias to vocational work should be limited to the closing two years. Conclusions 9 to 15 reinforced the principle of broad similarity for the early years, varying only in degree of complexity as course-length compelled, of 'handwork' and work related to 'the facts of everyday life', and 'practical' or career-orientated work only towards the end. Junior Technical Schools were doing nicely as they were, with entry at about 13. Suggestions were offered for transfer mechanisms.

In the body of the Report a section of about 60 pages suggested ways to treat component subjects – a chapter of enthusiastic progressive idealism salted with occasional horse-sense – on a model that in 1931 White at least believed worked in his own Central school in Bow; a description he then gave presented a broad curriculum paying heed to the local environment and pupils' experience, a general course (English and a foreign language, mathematics and sciences, history and geography, music and art, physical training and religious knowledge, plus some handwork), and a final year with a technical or commercial bias.[18] His school selected entrants and so he saw no need to 'stream' year-groups until the final year; in a non-selective school he judged it necessary so that teaching methods could be adapted to widely varying learning rates.

Then, with conclusions 20 to 28, conditions enabling equality of all schools for adolescents were determined, that is, with regard to teacher qualifications, teacher-pupil ratios, conditions of accommodation and equipment. Authorities should work towards equality with those the Board required under the Secondary Regulations, for none was 'an inferior species ... to be hampered' by inferior conditions. But 'we fully recognise that finance is a limiting factor, and, as it is not feasible at once to establish conditions such as we have described, we must be content to recommend the establishment of the best conditions obtainable in the circumstances'.

Next to the child, in conclusions 20 to 28. Pupils should be distributed between types of school by testing, in written, oral and/or psychological ways, to uncover their fitnesses. The minimum leaving age should be raised to 15-plus by September 1932, and those not doomed to the School Certificate should be allowed – but not compelled – to take a leaving examination as the guarantee best liked by themselves, their parents and future employers, or they might opt for a report from the school itself. This proposal, the Committee admitted, was contrary to the advice of the majority of their witnesses, and it was widely criticised on publication, nor were arrangements ever made to organise such a leaving examination; but the lack of such was often believed in the 1950s and 1960s to disadvantage the children of 'secondary modern' schools.

Logically, the cumbersome definition 'post-primary' was redundant, so the whole system for over-11s should be 'secondary', were this not legally the preserve of the non-compulsory and fee-paying sector under the Board's Secondary Regulations. The Committee wanted 'existing secondary' schools to be renamed Grammar schools and the Central and senior types Modern schools, to reinforce the generally secondary nature of the scheme, but did not deal directly with the statutory complications of the relation between the types (within the Board in the 1930s was a mutter that this was a question 'too thorny to throw at the Consultative Committee').[19] Their final conclusions, however, did discuss the necessary administrative changes, treading cautiously on ground outside their competence, full of hope for unification but backing hope only with advice on co-operation.

So, by viewing the period called adolescence as a stage of mental development with its own characteristic needs, not as a tailpiece to the three

Rs, by urging ever-increasing parity of conditions with the secondary (or Grammar) schools, and by establishing curricular principles, the Committee hoped to achieve 'something better for over-11s'. But because the only part generally implemented was the split of schooling at 11 (already, as at Brighton, a strategy in many schemes), so that by 1938 about 64 per cent of elementary children had been 'reorganised' at least into senior departments, the trap of hierarchy, implicit in a selective system, opened.

The Report was essentially ambiguous about selection, using two simultaneous principles. One principle divided by situation, those expecting to leave as soon as possible being separated from those who could look forward to a four-year course or more; the other divided according to 'bent', 'academic' and 'less academic'. Of course no one supposed that the stayers, who included fee-payers at secondary schools, would be necessarily 'academic' (as headmistresses objecting to the School Certificate format frequently pointed out) but the distinction between 'Grammar' and 'Modern' tended to imply the opposite, if only because the course-length of the former made it the route to university. The principle of situation at least avoided judgment of children's essential natures, and took account of the realities of varying economic positions and parental ambitions, but the principle of 'bent' tended to elide 'academic bent' and 'ability' and was backed by the free-place system. The AHM was not alone in doggedly urging that potential could not be judged at 11. Nor, in advocating a break at that age, did the Committee argue that it could, but only that psychologists and much experienced opinion (especially that of Percy Nunn) recognised this as an age of critical change in consciousness, when new powers, new interests, new individuality emerged. That a fresh start at 11 also enabled a subsequent three-year course, the very minimum desirable, and that it matched the entry age to secondary schools, undoubtedly weighted the decision; but the Committee accepted (on p. 139) that a test at 11 was not a reliable predictor and transfer must be easy.

The TUC evidence favoured 11 as the age of change, and the TUC spoke strongly too in favour of a broad, non-vocational curriculum; so did the WEA; so did the NUT; and implicit throughout the Report, in organisational and curricular plans, is a negative, that the schools are not to be production units for the labour market: this was what Barker meant when he talked of 'dignity to the manual worker', that he was to be a man first and a worker after. Even this was ignored in some developments, for example, the school in Edgware, described by a senior assistant master in 1933, where children were divided at entry into A, B, and C groups, according to whether their 'mental age' was assessed to be above, at, or below their chronological age, and As were fed a commercial diet of book-keeping, shorthand, commercial French, commercial arithmetic, business correspondence, and so on, while Bs were taught the technical subjects of machine-drawing, geometric design, costing accounts, and the like, and Cs learnt crafts.[20] Timetables left little space for other subjects, and none for music and art. The humanistic and individualistic ideals of the Consultative Committee were not vague good intentions but a live struggle against what was seen as a live enemy, and an inheritance, too, from the definition of secondary education (in the early Regulations) as providing 'a general course'.

Such a battle had long been the terrain of the headmistresses of the AHM, and the source of Emmeline's rhetoric of 'many windows in the mind', 'open doors of possibility'. So an appropriate lens for observing developments is that of AHM responses – those of the heads of some of the schools described in the Hadow Report's introduction as 'one of the finest signs of our educational progress ... [which have] liberated a fund of latent capacity'. Though schools of the 'existing secondary' type appeared to be detached from the Report this was so only by virtue (or vice) of existing administrative rules and the terms of reference. The AHM took secondary education, not just 'secondary' schools as their province. As they thrashed out their official group response to *The Education of the Adolescent*, finalised in late 1928, they seesawed between general enthusiasm and fear lest the 'Modern'/ 'Grammar' distinction tighten yet further on them the chains of School Certificate.

So the Consultative Committee Report was joined to the struggle for a broader and more flexible examination to sweep the AHM to its high water point, in the late 1920s and early 1930s, of attack on the illiberal narrows of exclusive concentration on book-bound 'Matric.' subjects, neatly typified by a girl at Roedean from 1925-31:

> Miss Tanner did not do much teaching, but she did take the History class I attended in my School Certificate year. It was regarded as something of an honour to have her ... but our eyes were focused on getting through the exam and we felt some concern that the parallel B form were 'doing' the exam syllabus more quickly and thoroughly with the other History mistress ... Miss Tanner was at the time sitting on one of the committees or commissions on which she served. She spent a lot of time telling us about the history of education and what her committee were considering. It was interesting, and that we were privileged was evident when the other History mistress sat in on at least one of the classes, but we were worried about that exam looming ahead!

Emmeline introduced the first AHM discussion of the Report, at the 1927 Conference, outlining the Report's background; she 'spoke for what the Committee had hoped as the end of their deliberation, and made a plea for liberty and elasticity', it was reported;[21] and the discussion was the main theme of that year's Conference. From Lucy Lowe of Leeds High School, about to be elected President for 1927-9, came vigorous support for a real regrading of all post-primary education, a position she enlarged in October when asked to represent the Joint Four at a conference of the WEA and NUT. There Lucy Lowe made five points, and these became the basis of the AHM position.

The minimum leaving age should be 15-plus as soon as possible; children should proceed through primary education, in two stages (infant to 7, junior to 11) on the four parallel tracks of public elementary school, preparatory department of a secondary school, private preparatory school, or 'home tuition', and at about 11 they should move into secondary education on two tracks, one up to 15-plus, the other up to 18-plus. She disliked the names 'Grammar' and 'Modern', preferring 'Senior' and 'Middle', according to leaving age; and each of these must be various and elastic in curriculum and administration to afford both types of school a combination of academic and practical work. Finally, any external examination at 15-plus should be postponed until experiments with standardised school records had been thoroughly tried.[22]

AHM rejection of sharp curricular differentiation drew on the memorandum the headmistresses sent to the Board that same month on the subject of Group IV parity within School Certificate, and was amplified the next March: 'We are not in any way underestimating the value of an academic training, but we want to extend the educational foundation, so that school education may be a foundation not for the academic professions alone but for all kinds of citizenship and all forms of national service ... for *all* young people of the country.'[23] Letters passed back and forth between the Board and the Executive Committee of the AHM, culminating in December 1928 in a forthright charge to the Board's President (now Lord Eustace Percy) from the headmistresses:

it would appear you favour a system of the institution of a small number of schools with a definitely academic bias and a large number of schools with a practical or aesthetic bias, in short segregation of the different types of boy and girl mind; while the headmistresses would wish to see in every school a community consisting of boys and girls of varied abilities and gifts, each with something to contribute to the intellectual and social life of the school ... curriculum should in general be perceived in relation to the length of school life ... The segregation of young people in educational institutions of an acknowledged academic or practical or aesthetic nature is in their [the AHM's] opinion artificial and restrictive and is not in accordance with national interest.[24]

The Executive Committee knew themselves secure in their colleagues' backing: at the conference that year Beatrice Sparks (of Cheltenham) described the campaign to reform the School Certificate as the most far-reaching of recent AHM work, and asked those 'heart and soul' in favour to stand – 'the Conference rose as a body and stood', said the minutes – and proceeded at once to their final vote on the response to *The Education of the Adolescent*, precisely that outlined by Lucy Lowe with its emphasis on division by length of school life. Eleanor Addison Phillips kept up the pressure in a letter to *The Times* (14 December 1929), closing with 'A one-sided education produces a one-sided person, and in view of the fact that nearly all intending teachers will pass through the secondary schools [in the existing use of the term] it is essential that these schools shall not be too exclusively academic, too narrow, and too subservient to examinations ...'

By 1930 'reorganisation' schemes were well advanced in some areas, and Agnes Catnach of Wallasey High School spoke sombrely of the failure of existing 11-plus tests to pay heed to the needs of the child. The shortage and the prestige of secondary schools imposed distorting competition. When, two years later, efforts to economise yielded Circular 1421, abolishing the wholly free-place character of some secondary schools (in Bradford, for example), raising fees all round, and replacing free by means-tested 'special' places, all MPs were sent a rejection of this 'backward step' not only on educational grounds but on social ones. 'Our Secondary Day Schools,' said the London AHM, 'are democratic in the truest sense of the word. Many of them draw their pupils from all types of homes and neighbourhoods ... the professional man and the shopkeeper, the working man and the workless', but a means test would withdraw a whole linking layer, the children of poorer professionals, like the lower Civil Service grades, whose incomes were just above the line of £3 to £4 a week laid down.[25] The AHM organised a national questionnaire, with samples from all areas, eliciting comparative figures for food expenditure by parents who did and did not pay school fees for secondary-school daughters. 'If any income group [of the five groups analysed with incomes below £7 a week] is divided into those paying school fees and those not, the first definitely spends less on food than the second, showing that this is the only economy left.'[26]

Indeed the character of the secondary schools was no frivolous matter and the headmistresses related social to educational functions. In the eyes of the senior generation of the AHM, among whom Emmeline now, in her mid-fifties, belonged, it was part of the long struggle for women to be recognised as full human beings. Oppositional terms like 'struggle', 'campaign', the language of war, themselves roused suspicion in constitutionalists cast in the historiographical mould of progress and honouring Millicent Fawcett above the militant suffragettes. Women's freedoms, social, political and educational, had been won, insisted Frances Gray in 1925, not 'by pitched battles, but by a kind of peaceful penetration'; again the movement invoked is that of placing within, of inclusion.[27]

Three years later a more thorough inclusion was celebrated when the parliamentary franchise was granted to women on the same terms as to men. The members of Lady Margaret Hall made merry, and as a member of LMH Council Emmeline was included throughout – and was careful to recount to her mother the flattering remarks addressed to her by the Duchess of York, 'a very charming little person with a simple manner and a delightful smile'. But the real thrill was to stay next door to the college, as often before, with Clara Deneke, aged eighty, imbued with the intellectual and musical culture of mid 19th-century Germany, a woman of formidable verve and two daughters, both connected with the college she had made her own close concern for many years. The Deneke household was probably one of the many models for the 'civilised' atmosphere of Emmeline's own aim, for:

Dame Millicent Fawcett was staying at the Denekes' too. She told me
she was in the House of Commons when John Stuart Mill in 1867
proposed to substitute the word 'persons' for 'men' in the Reform Bill,
and she came back to London last Sunday to hear the Royal Assent
given on Monday to the Franchise Bill putting women on an equality
with men! Her sister, Elizabeth Garrett Anderson, was the first woman
doctor, you know. She is 81 now and amazingly active. She went for a
walk in the Parks each morning after breakfast. I offered to run up to
the bedroom and get her coat the first morning, but she refused and
said, 'Oh no, I cannot be "pamped". I never have been and I mustn't
begin now.' So up she ran. She has been to Palestine four times in the
last six years. It makes one realise what a long time she has been
working when she says that she remembers Brighton well, as her
husband was MP for Brighton from 1865 to 1874.

We travelled up to Paddington together on Sunday afternoon and
as we got out of the train a gentleman shook hands with her and said,
'I should like to tell you that I was in the Senate House in Cambridge
in 1892 when the Mathematical Tripos results were read out, and I can
hear now the silence and the pause when these words came: "Women.
Above the Senior Wrangler – Philippa Fawcett".'

Still on Emmeline's appointment to Roedean the *Evening Standard* had
commented: 'There are those who think that breeziness in the education of
girls has gone a little too far, and that it is time some of the qualities of the
older-fashioned fine lady were considered', and still in July 1932 'What's
wrong with girls' schools' could be the heading for a *Daily Mail* article by
Cyril Norwood, now headmaster of Harrow. In his view girls' schools erred
in imitating boys'. At his suggested course for the non-university girl, with
no mathematics, no languages other than English, none but the 'merest
elements' of physics and chemistry, the pioneers' successors stirred. Mary
Clarke, who had followed Sara Burstall as head of Manchester High School,
seized the publicity of her own school's speech day to reply, to deny any
wish to copy boys' schools in organisation, and positively to claim that girls'
aptitudes might include mental ability and that such ability should be trained
well, though not always academically. Indeed, her school's experimental
sixth-form correlation of aspects of English history, science and mathematics
was designed, she said, to prepare women to be active, forcible members of
a modern democracy – and now, she added, this was ever more necessary,
when the dangers of dictatorship were not negligible.[28]

In her presidential address to the 1936 AHM conference, Ethel Gwatkin
(of Streatham Hill High School) looked back and forward. When the AHM
was founded in 1874, 'For a girl to be obliged to earn her living, unless, of
course, she belonged to the working class, was a misfortune, if not a disgrace.'
That had changed; but had a real concept of an 'educated nation' also
developed? 'In England the fight is against class traditions, against the inertia
of indifference to education as such, and against the feeling that education

as at present offered can only be assimilated by the few' – and parents' incomes not child needs cut short or prolonged school life. She looked to an England 'in which every boy and girl receives as of right an education of a type and length determined by interest and capacity and by *nothing else*' (her italics).[29]

It was a long speech, covering much ground, and included along with personal faith that 'in girls' schools at any rate the curriculum is or can be made sufficiently wide to suit all types' and a personal liking for 'our present heterogeneous collection', a reluctant admission that schools might need to evolve to some degree of academic or practical bias in later stages – as indeed the Consultative Committee had implied when assenting to a 'bias' in the final modern-school year in the knowledge of secondary-school bias towards the academic. By 1936 Will Spens had replaced Hadow as the Committee's chairman, and Dorothy Brock, headmistress of the Mary Datchelor School, was in Emmeline's seat there; they were now considering a reference on the organisation and interrelation of schools 'other than those administered under the Elementary Code'.

The democratic mix argued in the face of Circular 1421 and the heterogeneity of ability Ethel Gwatkin enjoyed at her GPDST school had some parallel in those independent schools which, like Roedean, drew their pupils largely from the upper social ranges. The head of one of the two Francis Holland Schools in London admitted her school was unusual, in 1931, in that it included 'girls whose parents still say that they need not earn their own living. Needless to say, this view is strenuously fought by the school authorities, who teach diligently and constantly that ... no one must be content to be luggage carried by the rest.' Thus she had to frame a curriculum both 'to prepare the girls who are going to the older universities to gain a place in a sternly competitive examination, and also to instruct and develop to their utmost capacity the minds and characters of girls who enter the school perhaps ill-taught, or perhaps through circumstances of health or change of home almost untaught, or who will give up all systematic education at the age of 16 or 17 to go to a finishing school or a family abroad.' Yet, whatever the organisational problems, she believed the mixture to be invaluable, itself instructive: 'The differences in home circles are quite immense, but so long as the tone of the school is strictly simple, and riches or poverty are not allowed to assume importance in its life, these very differences may give a more interesting outlook to the whole.'[30]

Roedean's make-up and 'tone' were closely akin, but Emmeline did not accept the mixed entry standards as inevitable. In January 1933 repeated complaints of how badly prepared for secondary education were many girls from private schools and home tuition provoked her to chair a meeting between heads of preparatory schools and of secondary schools to discuss entrance conditions, particularly those of age and attainment, and in February to open a discussion of the same topic at the Association for Headmistresses of Boarding Schools, an AHM offshoot. A series of subject conferences followed and in 1934 a leaflet framed for circulation the expected attainments of a girl aged 11 to 13. Continuing complaints and the unrelenting pressure from the AHM for registration and inspection of private schools, however, suggest its influence was limited, and most heads, like Emmeline, relied on their own testing and remedial work when necessary.

At the same time as this leaflet on preparation attainments was published, the AHM, in the persons of Ethel Gwatkin, Dorothy de Zouche and Isabella Drummond, appeared before the Consultative Committee to present their views on secondary education, and argue 'with real alarm' against a standard 11-plus test as a predictive attempt to classify into 'types' and judge future attainments: prediction, they repeated, was not possible at 11. So, again, they made an opportunity to argue for secondary schools with 'pupils of a wide range of types and degrees of ability', on the grounds that 'great variety' existed among those who could 'clearly profit by secondary education'.[31] The statement, largely Ethel Gwatkin's work, uses 'secondary' in the existing sense, to mean such LEA and grant-aided and independent schools as Emmeline knew best, those that gave girls 'a general course' to 16 and beyond, as in the Board's Secondary Regulations.

The headmistresses felt misunderstood: the previous year unanimous agreement had greeted a speech of 'dismay' from Ethel Strudwick of St Paul's at the 'ignorance' of secondary school work revealed in Board Circular 1428 on staffing levels (designed to economise): it 'advocates changes in the organisation of the schools which must inevitably have a harmful effect on the education given', the AHM resolved.[32] And, although she now worked for a school run by a Council independent of public money, Emmeline was not immune to the pressures, either of educational philosophy or of economy.

Chapter 20
'Activity and experience'

On the educational philosophies of the time Emmeline drew selectively, pragmatically, appropriately to the needs and limits of Roedean, and her adjustment of current ideas to her particular vision advanced her in her profession, and the school in public eyes. By 1927, as HM Inspectors noted, Emmeline had been at Roedean long enough to assess its weak points, not yet long enough to cure them. Their own expectations prompted the despatch in June 1927 of a strong team of seniors, seven in all, including one of Emmeline's critics at Bedford.[1] Emmeline's own cheerful account for her parents summarised with fair accuracy:

> I am sure you will be interested to know that they think Roedean has a very good Headmistress!!! I don't really know what they said to the Council but when they (the Inspectors) had all gone, Miss Dorothy said, 'It was all very well for P. L. (Miss Lawrence) and me to have to sit and smile while we were all told that if there were anything to criticise in the school it wasn't Miss Tanner's fault in any way, that if the examination marks were not quite as good as they had been it certainly was not Miss Tanner's fault, etc. etc.' She said it in fun, but I rather gather it is what the Inspectors said. Sir Paul kept asking me what I had given them: they must certainly have lunched well, he said; that I knew how to get at them anyhow. As a matter of fact we found the Inspection most helpful and the suggestions the Inspectors made were very good indeed, many of them. They greatly liked the girls and found them very responsive.

The Inspectors' report ran to twenty pages of detailed analysis and another dozen of timetabling data and private notes on the meeting with the Council, plus a few candid comments for the Board's eyes only. Only games, scheduled for a later report, escaped scrutiny. Emmeline had now reduced numbers to 370 by the end of 1926 – the usual crop of springtime leavers left 350 by June 1927 – by the simplest of devices persuasive to the Council, of stiffening the entrance test and rejecting 'an appreciable number', though only a fairly basic level of attainments seems to have been demanded and special classes for easing in new entries from varied backgrounds were found. So the Inspectors could note with approval that classroom space 'seems adequate', sleeping annexes were no longer required and bedrooms designed for one or two only rarely squeezed in more. (Such individualisation reflected Lawrence standards and was not the norm: the old Brighton rival, St Mary's Hall, had dormitories for six to twenty-seven girls, divided only by curtains.) The gymnasium, dark and badly ventilated, was a black spot, but on the credit side was an 'excellent' reference library and a new science block was now rising, financed by Old Roedeanians as a tribute to the Lawrences, and opened, with panache and publicity, in 1928 by Sir William Bragge, President-elect of the British Association and one of the leading scientists of the day.

The site of Roedean, and most of the buildings, had now been occupied for thirty years, from the days of the Bryce Commission, when Emmeline had first worked for Mary Roebuck in the converted house at Halifax, and just before the birth of the Board of Education itself, and in those thirty years the Board, Emmeline and Roedean had moved towards a common ideology: Roedean Council, the headmistress and the Inspectors recognised the same aims when assessing educational provision for girls. To put it another way, by 1927 Roedean was generally recognised to be thoroughly in the public school mainstream as reinterpreted for girls, indeed with some responsibility for that reinterpretation, and expectations of public schools had, from the first Regulations for Secondary Schools in 1904, conditioned those for the secondary system as a whole.

Yet at the Speech Day a few days after the Inspection Emmeline still found it necessary to reproach parents for asking that their daughters be excused mathematics or Latin to practise tennis – 'games and work are never alternative', she told them – and the Inspectors remarked that the apparent economic advantages of some girls could actually handicap; that laziness was born where to work for a living was not expected. Unspoken comparisons were with boys' public schools, not with the national system: of the 351 girls who had left over the previous three years 32 had gone to universities and 13 to other higher education, a high proportion by national standards in the mid-1920s.

Adopting this context the Inspectors looked primarily for academic excellence, and allotted analysis of intellectual aspects considerably more space than art, housecraft, or music, polished off in a couple of approving pages qualified by regret that art, which embraced several applied arts and crafts, was an extra, taken by only about 50 per cent. In fact, the very scope of the art, with its expensive materials, hindered inclusion in basic fees till 1934. But academic excellence was found patchy. English was generally strong but particular weaknesses afflicted mathematics and classics – and indeed, though the Inspectors perhaps did not know, Emmeline had for some time been using an ex-St Paul's master to coach classicists with university aims.

Contemplating the lessons seen, the Inspectors identified some weaknesses among the staff and excessive subdivision as sources of problems, to the surprise of some of the Council. 'Setting' seemed, as they said, an 'obvious' solution where abilities and attainments varied widely, but in the Inspectors' opinion groups of less than a dozen became too easy-going, with girls failing to learn from each other, teachers relaxing without class management challenges, and at the lowest levels where girls knew themselves labelled incompetent all inspiration to try evaporating. The system of many small 'sets', said the Inspectors firmly, was the legacy of days when mathematics was believed to be the possible possession of only a chosen few, selected by a continual sifting of this kind, and those days were over.

Emmeline continued to use 'sets', but not tiny ones, for mathematics and foreign languages. However, she seems never to have made up her mind about streaming in general. The Lawrences, remembered one girl, had graded forms across a year-group as A, or B, or C 'according to ostensible intelligence and capability' but with Emmeline came mixed groups, 'a sprinkling of good, bad and indifferent ... If you had been in an A form you tended to miss at first what I suppose was the élitism, but I suspect that overall the new system was beneficial.' Though some later girls thought that, at least as they neared School Certificate, some class organisation was based on apparent capacity the record is very unclear and tends to relate to individual choices of subject combinations rather than general intelligence ratings. Possibly Emmeline was as elastic in her discretion here as she certainly was towards the entrance test, and some other staff had strong if varied views to take into account.

As a whole the Inspectors' report was shaped as a spur to prick on a promising runner, and implicitly echoed a criticism often heard of boys' public schools at that time, that a few seized on and profited by the exceptional mental repast spread before them, while the middling mass ambled past grazing now and then, in hostile accounts learning self-satisfaction. No doubt they would have approved as role model the guest Emmeline had chosen to speak and present prizes at Speech Day a few days later, the Professor of Physiology at London University, Dr Winifred Cullis, and of her message, suitably physiological in metaphor, that work was the staff of mental life as bread of physical.

Certainly, eleven years later, the next set of Inspectors considered 'not the least important' development that now over 80 per cent of leavers went on to universities, professional training, or straight into jobs of 'considerable variety', almost three times the 1927 proportion. It was with joy that Emme-line said in 1938 that 'Now it is the normal thing for almost every girl to take it for granted that she will train for a career; in my school I do not think there are five per cent who do not so train. Even if it is not a question of necessity ... they still train for a career. That gives a spaciousness and freedom to life before you, and it is a wonderful thing to live.' That proportion can probably be credited at least as much to the national climate, economic and social, as to the school's inspiration. And, as one said, 'it was assumed that most of us would end up as wives and mothers, and in the 1930s women could be full-time wives and mothers without feeling guilty, and in the '40s and '50s ... but we were expected to be intelligent and helpful women.' Motherhood was itself a career, the 'fine work' of rearing 'happy and healthy children' to Emmeline, and she herself insisted on its validity as such.

The Inspectors of 1938 assumed overall a framework of unproblematic

264 / Doors of Possibility

development on the lines implied in 1927, and they drew out comparisons with congratulations 'on the progress of the past eleven years'.[2] But the very developments charted (described below, chap. 21) sharpened, in the thinking of the 1930s, a potential strain between the school's economics, with fees its life-blood, and the values set before the girls as honourable aspirations. That a contradiction, or at least a strain, could be felt is suggested by the resignation, with continuing friendship, of one of Emmeline's most able and vital assistants, Molly Mellanby.

Among the youngest, at just over thirty, of the staff Emmeline inherited in 1924, Molly Mellanby brought English literature alive, drawing from the girls every shred of fresh intelligence her penetrating blue eyes detected – one of the school's strengths to the Inspectors of 1927. Some teaching hours were relinquished when Emmeline promoted her to housemistress in 1932 but the influence of her unsentimental compassion and diamond integrity was the more pervasive on those to whom it was channelled; members of her House remembered her as a force in their growth. In 1935, however, that very integrity persuaded her to leave Roedean, and, easily withstanding facile jokes on her qualifications, to become Governor of HM Borstal Institution at Aylesbury, telling one pupil that 'Unfortunate girls are a much more fascinating proposition than the lucky ones like you.' Thereafter she directed her sense of service to these 'unfortunates', rising to Prison Commissioner.

'Service to our fellow-men' was one of the phrases habitual to Emmeline when she talked of careers; the other was the 'fullest development' of the individual – each and every individual. As a result the concept of 'service' was very broad, encompassing almost any honest job done 'to the best of our ability', but unease about unequal opportunities for 'full development' was rising to headmistresses' consciousness fitfully then more steadily through the 1930s. It was spelt out in a debate of 1937 on 'Education and the social system desired' at the AHM Conference held in Brighton, with Roedean as a principal host. Unlike the other sessions of the Conference this one was closed to the press, but the opening paper delivered by Muriel Davies, ex-Nuneaton and now head of Streatham County Secondary School, was thought substantial enough to be one of the few reprinted for the Annual Report.

Here she slashed at a 'world organised for the benefit of a small privileged class', dismissed scholarships to secondary schools as a feeble drop in an ocean of need, and argued for a single educational system of 'multi-bias secondary schools, each [pupil] entering the course best suited to his capacity', in which:

> Public boarding schools which cater only for those with money to pay
> for them would be doomed as such: they would be filled, not with the
> rich, but with those children whose circumstances made this kind of
> school advisable. The old school tie would be gone – gone many of the
> things which we value today and which have done splendid service

in the past. But in spite of all that would be lost, something even greater would be gained – a basis of understanding and sympathy, on which a new society could be built.[3]

Beside the exotic fantasy of the Royal Pavilion, in the Dome built for a prince's horses, the headmistresses debated social revolution. At the same meeting the result of the postal ballot for the new AHM President was announced, and the badge of office handed to Emmeline. As her Chairman of Committee she nominated Agnes Catnach of Putney County Secondary School, a woman said to rise to every challenge.

The shifting shape of Roedean's activities registered by the Inspectors' report had parallels in other modernising schools and show how headmistresses like Emmeline were trying to reconcile their yearning for 'social understanding and sympathy' with an economic context where education was a commodity bought by parents and therefore implicated in the systematic inequity attacked by Muriel Davies and many others. Emmeline's own anxiety emerged in her choice of theme for the AHM's 1938 Conference, an examination of the state's role in education, with experts brought in to describe how full state systems worked in the Soviet Union and in Germany.

Such accurate, or at least informed, perception, she said, was essential to clear thought, and through the 1930s her urgency for 'understanding other people's points of view' began to lose priority in her public statements to the need 'to think clearly and independently'. She herself related this to 'a world of turmoil' in 1936, instancing horrifying events in Spain, suspicion 'to put it mildly' between Germany and Russia, strains between Russia and Japan, 'while Italy swallows Abyssinia and Japan proceeds to swallow China', and refugees poured outcast from once-civilised states. One day, she said, the girls before her would be citizens sharing the responsibility of coping with these problems 'some of which will, I fear, remain to be solved when even the youngest of you leaves school'. 'Now clear thinking is a habit that like all other habits can best be begun early,' she told more than one set of girls in 1936. 'I wonder if any of you have thought that in these days it is a very great privilege to be allowed to think for oneself ... Only a short time ago a young woman from a German university said to me, "But we are *told* what to think and it is easier."'

As a register of developing social drives and of traditional doctrines of understanding through accurately recorded observation, the Consultative Committee reports served the world of education. Invigorated by the excitement over *The Education of the Adolescent*, the Committee turned with zest to the two new references accepted in 1926, and – as in 1920 – took the smaller first.

Books in Public Elementary Schools was signed in July 1928 and published in November.[4] The report exceeded its title with discussion of the larger subject of books and library provision for children generally, rather to the annoyance of some librarians who thought their recent efforts to open access to children unappreciated. But just as Emmeline had once cheerfully urged the history teachers of North Warwickshire to burn their 'horrid little readers', the third-hand compilations given out and taken in for each lesson of exhaustive conning in elementary schools, so the Committee now rejoiced to see these disappearing and a freer use of better books, now even lent to children. A brief public interest was roused in the report, probably largely due to journalists' fascination with how 'the masses' used their leisure, for the use of leisure was a talking-point as paid holidays became commoner and work hours shorter. But the very fact that the Committee urged the establishment of school libraries, access to public libraries, and to let children retain books between lessons, suggesting that book expenditure should be a distinct item in school accounts, and so on, demonstrates how shabby the normal practices were in comparison with those of secondary schools and the assumptions of AHM discussions.

In principle the Consultative Committee's value was, as Emmeline had once told the MAHM, that it was a body of trained minds, not with a small set of vested interests, who arrived at their conclusions from hearing evidence. Apart from HM Inspectorate it was the central authority's sole link with actual practice and informed professional opinion, for the patchwork of local authority and the practical teacher-training orientation of university education departments (often seen as marginal to scholarly research) enabled ideas and even experiment to flourish but with little coherence. Trying to assess the general state of affairs for their next reference, on 'courses of study suitable for children ... up to the age of eleven in Elementary schools', the Committee found only a muddle of aims. But they found, too, a quickening sense, still unarticulated, of needs and functions undreamt of in the time of the 1870 Education Act when, as their report said (p. 91), a system 'for the children of the labouring poor' had filled the gaps of church provision with intent to inculcate definite and limited skills of basic numeracy and literacy.[5] Much had happened since.

That 'reorganisation' at 11 was now an accepted goal threw into higher relief the distinctive needs of children beyond the infant and before a secondary stage which once had been only for the better-off, children, that is, in a 'primary' stage; the Committee's reference spoke of 'Elementary schools' but they called their report of 1931 *The Primary School*. 'We do not pretend,' its introduction said, 'to have made startling discoveries or to have enunciated novel truths', but this was sugar to what in Emmeline's youth would have been a strange, perhaps distasteful draught, that 'The primary school is on the way to become *what it should be*, the common school of the whole population' (p. xxix, my italics), providing 'a primary education in the proper sense of the term – that is, one which will be a basis for all types of higher teaching and training'.

'What a wise and good parent would desire for his own children, that a nation must desire for all children,' preached the Committee (p. xxix), and filled out their sermon with advice to the state, and to parents, on the course of wisdom and goodness. In fact some criticism was levelled at the encyclopaedic fullness of the report – a simplified pamphlet version for parents would be useful, suggested the *Journal of Education*.

The primary schools' functions had been much enlarged, the Committee argued, partly as responsibilities for medical inspection and physical welfare had been channelled through them, partly as a consequence of modern urban and industrial conditions which reduced the lessons in life children had once absorbed on the farm and in the artisan's workshop – this shrinking from a mechanised industrial society was eminently characteristic of the 1920s and 1930s and one root of the pleas for 'practical' and 'hand' work heard on all sides. Equally characteristic was the notion that greater responsibilities were now loaded on the schools, and more than once at AHM Conferences were mutters that the old educative trinity of home, church and school was reducing to a unitarian fount by the abdication or failure of the first two.

To the need for the primary school to provide a substantial basis for *any* future career, and to the extension of the school's responsibility for physical, mental and moral growth, the Committee added a corollary, that growth could take place only within the terms of a child's natural development. Hence two long chapters and two long appendices of medical and psychological evidence on child growth, in all its aspects. The *imprimatur* was stamped on 'child-centred' education; the old traces of 19th-century 'standards' (tested attainment levels in the elements) gave way, and 'our main care must be to supply children with what is essential to their healthy growth – physical, intellectual and moral – during that particular stage of their development' (p. 92). It was both useless and dangerous merely to feed in 'inert ideas ...[with] no bearing upon a child's natural activities of body or mind and [which] do nothing to illuminate or guide his experience' (p. 92). Thus was kindled the catchphrase of the report, that 'the curriculum is to be thought of in terms of activity and experience rather than of knowledge to be acquired and facts to be stored' (p. 93).

The picture given of the curriculum envisaged, and the buildings, equipment and, above all, class size necessary, is remarkably akin to some practices and conditions familiar to Emmeline in the preparatory departments of some girls' secondary schools, at Nuneaton or at Bedford, for example, and at those of some AHM colleagues. But the Committee set as the maximum forty children to a class – nearly double the headmistresses' preferred number – and even this was then a rather hollow hope in some areas. Even in 1938, 2,646 classes of more than fifty children stained the record for a primary school population of 5,123,490, itself reduced in the last decade by 2.4 per cent through a fall in the birth-rate. Financial expectations curbed standards.

The main focuses are on linguistic understanding and language use, manual deftness, the 'aesthetic' subjects of handwork, art and music, literature, observational science and nature study, elementary mathematics, the beginnings of history and geography in discovering the relationship to the here and now of the distant in time and space. But much interest was excited by the Committee's endorsement of the 'project' method (traced by them as far back as William Cobbett), despite their cautious hedging of approval – the method was more suitable for younger children than those ready for more systematic work, it should not supersede special practice in the instrumental subjects of reading, writing and arithmetic, it needed skilled and imaginative handling, and so forth. The technique linked into the Committee's warmer support for a proportion of individual and co-operative group study, and in general their attitude was close to Emmeline's own towards the Dalton Plan (see pp. 281-2).

In the 1930s the line conventionally drawn between 'traditional' education and 'progressive' identified the first as seeing the subject-matter of education in the contents of a set of textbooks, and the second as causing the pupil to learn, not from ready-made texts, but from experience gradually organised. In *The Primary School* the Consultative Committee fortified the 'progressive' camp and meditated in prudent caveats on how a learner's experience might be guided, his or her freedom realised. Two incidental consequences received little publicity: first, the child's duties, as outlined in the Elementary Code of the early 20th century, disappeared from view as his needs emerged; secondly, enormous weight was thrown on the teachers who must give to their pupils 'life, and nothing less than life and the interpretation of life'. These words are not those of the Committee but from an address given in 1930 to the staff at Roedean by Ernest Campagnac, the Professor of Education at Liverpool University; Emmeline passed them on to the students training to teach at Dartford, and confessed she had felt 'a smiting of conscience'. Thus the profession justified its own dignity, its own demands: conscience and vested interests were as inseparable as the two sides of a sheet of paper.

The Primary School was widely welcomed, usually applauded on its publication in early 1931. The principle that education should be based on fundamental facts of child development rather than historical and parliamentary accident, once pointed out, seemed obvious. Hindsight criticism attended to the Committee's acceptance of innate differences in intelligence – though in fact this was listed as only one of nine sources of mental difference – and on their conclusion that the final year or so of the largest schools could well be streamed as quick, average, slow, so focusing on intellectual difference to the exclusion of other forms and turning education into a race, or musical chairs played in earnest. The widening use of 11-plus examinations for entry to an inadequate number of secondary schools could only encourage this; though the Committee themselves were more concerned for the children 'backward' for so many reasons, devoting an anxious chapter to them. How far mental difference is inborn, how far induced, is still debated, keenly because the politics of class and race are implicated. 'I believe,' said Emmeline serenely in 1949, that 'children with a high degree of innate mental ability are distributed with some approach to equality among the social classes'; then stressed how such innate ability needed active development.

At the same time as the Consultative Committee drafted its ideas a fall in admission of juniors to Roedean brought its Junior House under the private scrutiny of Roedean Council. In 1930 a subcommittee of four, including Emmeline, was set up to assess the school's provision for juniors, in the 1920s organised quite separately from the seniors and with (in 1927) 61 girls aged between eight and about 12. Was this decline due to the 'general financial depression' or were Old Roedeanians prejudiced against sending daughters by unhappy memory? Past problems were acknowledged but now no cause for complaint was seen. Hence the subcommittee.

Two drawbacks stood out: the youngest girls were a cost to the school as tiny groups with special treatment; and the subcommittee were very dubious about whether any girl ought to spend ten years, perhaps more, in the same surroundings – here echoing the Consultative Committee's arguments for a break at the age of 11. A new scheme was evolved. The Junior House would be abolished, and the building become a 'middle school' for girls aged 10 (at least) to 14, who could share some of the upper school's facilities and staff; thus the school would become wholly secondary. A new name, Number Five, was devised for the new House.

Full of the new plan, in March 1931, Emmeline appointed Elizabeth Middleton to be the new 'Head of the Middle School here from September next'. As the juniors' housemistress, Hilda Leigh, welcomed the newcomer: 'It is always rather thrilling to go out on a new adventure, and I think that we ought to be able to make this one a success.' Yet somehow, for all the optimism, Number Five remained 'Junior' in practice. In 1938 three 8-year-olds and three girls of 9 formed the lowest form; three of the next were also 9; none of the House was over 13. Ties with the upper school were indeed closer, with some sharing of staff, but a course including only the start of the standard School Certificate course began for the youngest in the hands of a Froebel-trained mistress.

Such a structure seemed anomalous, cutting across the Consultative Committee's split of primary and secondary, and more akin to boys' private preparatory schools which took boys from 8 to 13 and virtually monopolised public-school entry by their distinctive curriculum. Yet appearances misled: at Roedean girls entered the school with such varied attainments, from their mixed educational backgrounds, that a homogeneous middle school had to give way to a flexible organisation for girls aged 10 to 13 – the eldest of the Junior House and the youngest of the senior school were the same age but of different level. The presence of the youngest, however, represented a victory of pragmatism over the principles of the subcommittee, a response to revived demand. So another gap yawned between Roedean and the national system.

Not primary children alone learnt by 'activity and experience'. Usually regular in attendance at Consultative Committee meetings, and, she said, greatly enjoying them, Emmeline sent apologies for absence for those of

November 1929 to January 1930. In June 1929 Roedean looked well settled: on the 2nd 'we are already absolutely full for September' and 'the accounts have worked out all right, and we have again a balance and not a deficit, as seemed likely. It is a balance of £1,466 which is not enormous on a turnover of £60,000 odd, but it is quite satisfactory and will pay for the conversion of the old Science rooms to other purposes. Anyhow it comforts the Lawrences!!'

At the end of June, Penelope Lawrence, as Chairman, read to Roedean Council a letter inviting Roedean's headmistress to visit Roedean, Johannesburg, in order to maintain their old connection. 'Sisterly' might describe the link with the independent school Theresa Lawrence and her more scholarly friend Margaret Earle started in 1902, armed with introductions and advice from other Lawrences, but as Margaret Earle was invaded by a paralytic illness these founders looked, like Theresa's sisters, towards retirement. Lawrences and others knew 'connections' to be a practical as well as sentimental strength. The Council of the English Roedean warmly approved a visit, and granted Emmeline a term's absence and £250 for expenses.

Here was the chance of an adventure, however firmly cast in the shape of work for its justification. From the turn of the century, as Fred travelled there at the end of the Boer War and friends emigrated to farm or deal or teach, South Africa had seemed a spacious land of many-coloured excitements. Emmeline admired Smuts as an international statesman, read the 1929 autobiography in which Gandhi told of his seedbed there, taught its geography and remembered the battlefields of her young womanhood. A letter went out to Roedean parents, over P. L.'s name, to explain the importance of the South African link and reassure them that Emmeline's absence would be covered by the second mistress, the housemistresses, and the headmistress's secretary.

Emmeline set herself to work, to make the arrangements themselves work. In mid-September:

> The most important thing is that I have finished the Time Table. 'In record time, is it not, ma'am?' says Ethel [the housemaid]. I got up at 6.45 on Friday morning, did all the odds and ends I had to and then settled down in my bedroom, to which I always have a large steady table brought for the purpose from the girls' drawing-room in Number Two. I went absolutely straight on except for ten minutes for lunch and ten minutes for supper, and an interview with some parents from America, until quarter to two the next morning, by which time I had become almost incapable of either seeing or standing but I had broken the back of the job and was able to finish it off altogether by tea-time yesterday.

She booked a passage – first-class – for 18 October 1929 on the Union-Castle liner RMS *Arundel Castle*, from Southampton, and the girls saw their head off with a chorus of 'For she's a jolly good fellow' on the school terrace.

Dorothea Child, the second mistress, was slightly taken aback to be told by one girl that 'the thought of school without Miss Tanner was a nightmare', and Emmeline, though she assured them all firmly that 'everything will go all right', took some worries with her.

Among them was a Junior House child with diphtheria, too sick for the sanatorium and in hospital with doctors hovering 'very doubtful ... whether her heart would last out'. Only three years before all members of one House, mistresses, girls and maids, had had to have throats swabbed for diphtheria tests when a maid contracted the disease, and four were found to be carriers and isolated. Wireless telegraphy kept Emmeline in touch with messages compressed into three or four words. Such messages were too expensive for news of another anxiety, however. At the beginning of the year she had called it fortunate that her father was a 'strong and healthy man', able to cope when his partner retired sick, despite his nearly eighty years. Since the summer, though, increasingly distressing symptoms of Bright's Disease had troubled him, so that by October he was unable to see his daughter off at Southampton as they had both hoped.

Her mother's parting message was entirely characteristic: 'My chief message is what you know as well as I do; sometimes it is nice to be reminded. The Lord God Omnipotent reigneth. "He preserveth thee from all evil; He preserveth thy soul ..." Would not I love to see you off! But it is not to be. I would not leave Daddy if I had the chance of coming ... I am very happy doing nothing!! Farewell, dearest. I hope you will accomplish all you want to. He reigneth everywhere so of course you will.'

To experience an ocean-going liner's ways amused Emmeline for a while. She learnt the 'mysteries of deck quoits', played a few games of Bridge, and bathed each morning in the swimming pool with a Girl Guide Commander from Port Elizabeth, 'in amazingly buoyant water', shifting in the swell. In that 'great floating hotel with every luxury' innumerable staff brought food continually, first fruit in the cabin at 7.15 am before a bugle sounded for breakfast at 8.30 am, then at 11.00 am beef tea in colder latitudes or an ice after the ship called at Madeira, followed by lunch at 1.00 pm, tea at 4.00 pm, dinner at 7.00 pm, 'and if you are still up and in the lounge or smoke-room sandwiches are round at 10.00!' She eschewed much of this nourishment but loved the fresh fruit, discovering grenadillas: 'prepared in a glass with a little sugar (if desired) and some cream, they would make even Father's mouth water.' The most astonishing display celebrated the night of the Fancy Dress Ball, when the chefs elaborated 'a model of the ship and of a motor sea-plane, of R101, and of a gondola, etc. in sugar and lighted with electricity, lobsters as fishermen fishing in a pond edged with banks and shrubs made of gelatine and with real fish in it, an ostrich of tangerines etc. like the Bird's Custard Powder advertisement ... and all arranged against a background of vine leaves in a sort of trellis and with real bunches of grapes hanging from it.'

But fleshpots and swimming left the mind restless, yet 'serious reading or any thinking seems most difficult ... you wouldn't think it would be but it is a restless life'. She chatted to other passengers, mostly South African residents, elderly or middle-aged, and, encountering a member of the governing body of Roedean, Johannesburg, was able to learn more not only about the school but about 'conditions in Johannesburg and politics in South Africa generally, and I found it very interesting. He knows both Smuts and Hertzog [the Nationalist leader] and although he thinks the former in a higher plane altogether than the latter he says that Hertzog is the most charming and lovable man as a private individual. At the same time he has no vision, is very narrow in his views, and can neither think nor speak at all clearly.'

Still restless, she explored the ship's kitchens and store-rooms, and found 'all the milk is brought on at Durban for the round voyage. No wonder it isn't very pleasant to taste. It is Pasteurised and brought on in great churns and kept in the cold chamber. The cream ... is butter emulsified – butter mixed with a little milk and then very rapidly made liquid by a machine and packed in large tins'. Nor was she ever without 'duty letters' and some speeches to prepare, but 'my brain is never more than half-awake, I feel'.

After two and a half weeks Emmeline landed at Cape Town in dense fog and took her seat in the observation car of the express train to Johannesburg to watch the 'wonderful lights and shades' of mountains and valleys in the sunset. Next day, as they 'passed the Modder River and Magersfontein and all those parts, a surveyor who had fought over all that ground in the Boer War, and had afterwards surveyed it all and made the maps for *The Times History of the War*, sat by me and told me all kinds of interesting things.' So at last the journey was done, and Roedean greeted her with 'roses, honeysuckle, sweetpeas and plumbago'.

Not only from Theresa Lawrence or members of the school's Council had Emmeline heard details. For the last two years one of her Bedford staff had been teaching mathematics there, at what she summed up soon after arrival as 'a jolly, breezy family that has a very happy time and does a certain amount of work'. Elsie Hatch liked the 'not snobbish' atmosphere but found 'The whole atmosphere in Africa is a grabbing after certificates, and every form in the school seems to be taking an outside examination. Those nasty little College of Preceptors are taken, and the syllabus in mathematics is dreadful – I am writing to ask if they will alter it or set a special paper, but I don't suppose they will do either.' As for Theresa Lawrence herself, 'I don't think I've met anyone that so consistently works on the "believe-they-can-do-it" and "make-them-believe-they-can-do-it" theory as T. L. She is like a hen with chickens before exams – and we gaily cook a few test results to carry out the tenets of the theory – and I believe there's a lot in it for some children, for most perhaps. You can't help getting very fond of T. L.'

In her next letter to Emmeline she retracted previous doubts about the elaborate prefect system: 'The fact that every sort of talent gets a chance of leadership and seemingly equal valuation is rather unique, I think. The girls gain enormously in self-confidence and power of expression – I don't think the school does as much for toning down the over-assertive!'

The Johannesburg school, like its English sister, had a Junior House, and in its head, Mabel Bayley, Emmeline found 'the one person I know I can go to if I want to get information or have something done'. They had met before, when she visited England with Theresa Lawrence to see the workings of Roedean there, and the network of the New Church had created instant sympathy. Mabel Bayley was to the Tanners 'old Dr Bayley's grand-daughter', and his was a name greatly honoured in the New Church of the Tanners' early membership; she was related, too, to a family who had long ago befriended Fred, as a young man alone in a strange land. Her effusive style gushed from the warmest of hearts, so that it was Mabel Bayley who troubled to write reams in Emmeline's praise to Nettie, garnished with pictorial detail, but she was far too discreet to mention in these that, among the work assigned her, Emmeline was to compile a report for the Council on proposed changes to the Junior House.

At the school Emmeline was employed partly in building relationships and partly in informal inspection, for, as at Brighton, the imminent retirement of the two founders was expected to entail modifications. So 'I am not taking classes here but I have been in to listen to a number of lessons. I sit at the head of a table of girls at lunch, and occasionally I have the prefects to myself after supper.' She talked to and listened to as many of the school as she could, was introduced to most of the school's patrons in Johannesburg, and delivered the speech on Speech Day – adjurations to work hard, keep examinations in proportion, attempt to understand others' points of view, and by responsible service leave their great country greater than they found her: 'nothing out of the way', as she said, but widely praised. She relished unaccustomed peace in the airy precincts, so that on her return to Brighton 'some of us got rather fed up with the soft-voiced, soft-footed South Africans'.

Among the dinners, teas, receptions, schoolgirl concerts and swimming galas, she widened her view of white South African life by seeking out an old acquaintance living in more modest style than most of her official contacts, May Edwards, who had made clothes for her ten years before. Now she 'makes her living by sewing, especially by designing and making fancy dresses. I should say that it is a very precarious living and that she has a very hard struggle, but she is a plucky person and everyone who knows her likes and respects her. But it is a hard and a dull life.'

Certainly Emmeline's own education was furthered. There were geography and economics lessons: she was taken on special tours, out to the Hartebeestport Dam through farmlands of fruit and grain one day, over the Premier Diamond Mine with its open-cast techniques another, round the Rand Gold Refinery, and 4,000 feet down the rich New Modder Gold Mine. She noted down the details 'from the time the rock is mined underground till the bar gold finally leaves the refinery for the Bank of

England or the Mint or India or wherever it is going, and also all about the "compounds" where the natives live, and how they live, and how they are paid, etc.' to discuss with her father. There was an architecture lecture: to her embarrassment both the architect and the Dean of the cathedral separately offered to guide her round the new building. After one morning when an elderly man showed off the botanical treasures of his garden, followed by an afternoon with Howard Pym ('who knows almost more than anyone about the Native Question') viewing his collection of etchings, 'I couldn't help wishing that every girl and boy had a good hobby which would give them real interest to their dying day' – though she herself was dedicated to no single enthusiasm of the sort recommended.

But the industrial and labour information she never committed to paper. She returned to the school from the New Modder Mine to 'find my mail waiting for me but with it two telegrams from Roedean that make me feel that something has happened that they know and I don't.' At 4.00 pm she added a postscript:

Now Fred's cable has come and what I feared is confirmed. And yet I ought not to have *feared* because although it nearly breaks my heart to think I shall never see my darling Father again yet really God has been very good to him and to us in not letting him have a long illness. I must now go to a House Gymnastic competition. Later: I can't write a letter now. I had meant to and a tiny note to each member of the family who has been so good in writing to me but I am sure you all know what I feel, right away from you all when I just long to be with you – much love to you all.

Emmeline told no one except the two school heads and Mabel Bayley, knowing her duty lay in 'going on doing everything as it was originally arranged', and behaved in grief, it appears, as she advised girls who suffered from shyness: 'She said shyness was self-centred ... we should always think of the other person or persons to whom we were being introduced or to whom we were talking. They were probably just as shy, and we should be thinking of them and putting them at their ease, and then we should forget ourselves.' But a month later 'I still cannot realise that it has happened', and she admitted 'It seemed almost as though the bottom had gone out of the world, and I found it impossible to be as grateful as I should be to think that Father had such a comparatively short time of suffering ...' Wails sound from time to time that the information she gathered was for his sake – he was so 'intelligently interested in everything we could tell him and in everything he saw' – but in practice she did not cease to question and explore, nor to note particulars of processes.

Emmeline was very much her father's daughter, and after his death more passionately than ever noted precise distances, temperatures, quantities. Where once she had cheerfully sent him requests to find train times and routes, now she became the authority on timetables and Bradshaw's Guide to the complex system of private UK railways, the 'Bradshaw Queen' to the

irreverent. 'She really *loved* Bradshaw: "Give it to me – I'll find it in a minute"
– she was right, she *would*.' 'This is an *adorable* book,' she once exclaimed.
But now her mother dwindled from one pillar of the mighty pair of her
youth to an object of her warmly tender concern; thus obliquely Emmeline
betrayed her sense of loss. Other correspondence in South Africa she
jettisoned to lighten the luggage, but she carefully kept the descriptions of
her father's funeral and the service at the Henry Street New Church sent, in
reassuring phrases, by the most faithful of her correspondents, her brother
Herbert and her sister Winifred.

Herbert reported on practical matters also. 'Father's affairs are in the
good order we would expect. Fred, Pearce [his business partner] and I are
executors. He has left each of us seven shares which should be worth £100.
To Mother £100 and the residue after paying legacies of another £200 to
£300, including £10 to each grandchild [the rest to various charities]. We
think that Mother should have about £200 per year which will give her the
feeling of independence she will so greatly value.'

The knife-slash across Emmeline's visit to South Africa was kept out of
sight as her programme continued. The Christmas holidays began on a train
to Bulawayo, looking out at mimosa, pepper trees and the veldt's eucalyptus,
talking to a young mining engineer made redundant by mine closure and
heading north to Broken Hill to look for work. At Bulawayo Emmeline
changed trains to reach at last the Victoria Falls Hotel, dreaming through
the fitful sleep of travelling nights of her father, so that 'I woke up this
morning thinking I must tell him what a lot of things (minerals mainly)
come down on this little line (though a very long one) from the Belgian
Congo and from N. Rhodesia ... when I remember what an unknown land
the Congo was when I learnt geography at school I am amazed to realise
what changes have taken place.' No road had yet been built across the
Zambesi, and 'everything, cars included, must be trucked and come by rail',
the hotel itself being supplied with 'every single thing they use, except milk,
at least from Bulawayo, fourteen hours' journey by their fastest train, though
only 250 miles. Livingstone is really no more than a village.'

Above all it was the rain forest and the mighty Falls she had come to see,
and she embedded these in her mind with close observation, minutely noted,
wishing as elsewhere that she were 'a botanist and an entomologist, and
perhaps even more a geologist because it is a wonderful country geologically
and the rocks are full of minerals'.

Then the trains took her back through Bulawayo to Rustenburg and the
two farms owned by a Brighton Old Roedeanian, Ella Macgregor. There
she grew citrus fruit and made marmalade, while her husband worked as a
civil servant in Pretoria, returning at weekends. 'They simply could not
manage without his salary as the farms swallow up so much money and do
not make a sufficiently good return ... I do believe farming out here is even
more precarious than at home because of the many pests, some affecting
beasts and some crops, and the great risk of drought. The amount of capital

that has to be sunk in making dams and irrigating, in making dips for the cattle, etc. is enormous.' And, Emmeline realised, a tax structure by which South African sugar was sold on the world market at £13 per ton but in South Africa at £21 per ton made competitive marmalade hard to produce.

From the Macgregors' Emmeline set out through Pretoria and Pietersburg to Munnik in the northern Transvaal, to reach another farm but one where her mind turned from economics to medicine, and to race relations. Both Montgomerys were doctors – Emmeline had already met Winifred Montgomery on the platform at the school's speech day in Johannesburg – and the husband's non-farm work included twice-weekly visits to Zoukmahaar to examine recruits (mainly from Portuguese East Africa, he told Emmeline) to work at mines on the Reef. She went with him to see. 'They are never taken unless they are absolutely sound, particularly as to the lungs, and he says that they often weep when they are turned down. Directly we arrived at the village a man came running out to know if the doctor would come and attend to a man who had chopped off the top of his finger, so that had to be dealt with before we went up to the Native Labour offices.'

Since it was Christmas she was able to watch too the Montgomerys' present-giving to their

> native servants – the house ones and the farm ones, and all the boys and girls belonging to any of them ... The married farm 'boys' and the cook 'boy' (I can never get used to calling the native men 'boys' always) has each a packet of tea, a packet of sugar, sweets, cigarettes and tobacco (if they smoke), soap, a good home-made currant loaf and a present such as a good knife or something of that sort and some of them money ... [the women received] pretty cotton dress material, needles, cotton, gilt safety-pins and sweets.

In Johannesburg Emmeline had been immediately conscious of a social structure different from that she knew, and there are hints she discussed what was called 'the Native Question' wherever she thought informed judgment was available. 'Natives' was the name always used in her letters of 1929-30 for black South Africans:

> Although there is a very marked distinction here between the white man and the native, there is a very pleasant family feeling between white masters and dark servants in the nicer families, and in a place like this [Roedean]. There are very few marked social distinctions between whites here: for instance, the man whose car we had hired to take us somewhere yesterday quite naturally talked to me while I was waiting for Miss Lawrence and asked me how I was enjoying my stay, etc., and what I thought of South Africa.

Emmeline looked, listened, and for the most part kept silent on any conclusions she drew.

Durban she encountered from the perspective of Swedenborgian hosts, the Forfar family, with a family friendship cemented by their kindness to

Fred years before, like the Brabys with whom Emmeline now also enjoyed both sightseeing tours and an urban setting with the inside sanitation she had not experienced since the Victoria Falls. On 2 January she took ship at Durban, round the coast to Port Elizabeth to be driven by hired car 570 miles to Cape Town, a journey of three and a half days. Theresa Lawrence met her and took her on to her own house at Simonstown.

The Cape Peninsula seemed to Emmeline 'one of the finest things in the world'; she described its topography before claiming it for aesthetics as 'a feast of beauty'. History swung into focus at the old Dutch house of Groot Constantia, now a museum, and botany at Kirstenbosch; politics were kept in the background when Emmeline had tea at Groote Schuur with Hertzog and his wife, the first Sunday after the opening of a Parliament recomposed with the recent election victory of Hertzog's Nationalists. She found him 'charming to talk to: a very cultivated man with delightful manners', and limited her written comment there.

By the time she had been shown over the Durban factory of the paper manufacturers E. S. & A. Robinson by a colleague of her brothers, and taken by him too to a fruit farm at Simondium, 'entirely for export trade, except the grapes which are manufactured into wine', Emmeline had seen many aspects of what European settlement had meant to South Africa. Now she watched grading and packing of peaches, nectarines and late plums, she saw the wine-making machinery and the sulphur and drying rooms for drying apricots; then, the day before she boarded the RMS *Arundel Castle* again, homeward-bound, she attended a session of Parliament: 'very interesting, though when the Nationalists would speak in Afrikaans I could not understand a word. The Opposition always spoke in English ... Fortunately Hertzog made his principal speech that day in English, and it was in connection with the Mandate of S.W. Africa which I had heard discussed at the Council Meetings of the League of Nations in Geneva in April 1923.'

All was extension of experience – 'all so *interesting*' – and more had been achieved than the forging of fresh links in the two schools' friendship. For Emmeline knowledge, a function of education, was the first step to understanding, and understanding the ways and conditions of life and the ideas of others, was a step to civilised peace.

Chapter 21
Aspects of Roedean in the 1930s

In May 1938 seven men and five women Inspectors roamed Roedean School, in a week cold and wet enough to limit the games they could watch. They were not over-anxious about this: skills were evident in team records, the staff were plentiful and well qualified, the girls looked healthy and their posture was good. Their report illustrates, in all, just what was expected of a good girls' school, both in its praises and rather faint damns, in its emphases and its silences.[1]

Most developments since 1927 conformed to standard changes to meet changing standards. Hence, after the science building was completed, most structural work looked to health and safety, with more fire escapes, bathrooms and lavatories, and a filtration and chlorination plant for the swimming pool. Each House was checked by the Inspectors against a standardised questionnaire for heating, lighting, ventilation, sanitation, feeding, fire drill. Dining-rooms were used only for meals: good. Hot cupboards were available for drying wet clothes. Each girl had a daily warm bath. The sick were sent to a separate sanatorium, with a choice of man or woman doctor. And so on. 'Excellent,' said the Inspectors, though no more than the fee level demanded, and a Lawrence policy administered by housemistresses while Emmeline kept watch and ward. Sometimes the system failed, and a term's fees were remitted for a girl with temporary facial paralysis due to the draughty position of her bed.

Trying to improve the system's details, in 1926, for example, Emmeline followed up an approach from a dairy research zealot provoked (he said) by a lacrosse defeat for Roedean, with an inquiry to the Grade A (Tuberculin Tested) Milk Producers' Association. 'I doubt whether our use of it would have the effect of making us beat Wycombe Abbey at lacrosse, if we adopted it,' she told the promoter Samuel Whitley, 'and I must say the thought of eradicating tuberculosis from the herds of this country appeals to me more!' 'The ordinary retail Dairymen prefer to deal in the ordinary stuff as they have more hold over the producers and get more profit ... I quite expect you will have difficulty in getting Grade A (T. T.) but you will doing a real service to the community by *demanding* it ... at least *one thousand times* (by bacterial count) cleaner than ordinary milk,' he responded, offering to show her round the National Institute for Research in Dairying, and adding an appeal for Roedeanians with science and agricultural degrees to work there: 'We want more of that sort of girl.'

Her interest thoroughly aroused, Emmeline told him, 'It is curious that, in talking to a girl at the beginning of the term, who wants to go up to university to read science and was asking me about the possibilities of work in science other than teaching in schools, I suggested research work in food, especially milk.' So Roedean was supplied with Grade A (T. T.) milk, despite its extra cost, career contacts were opened, and the school basked in a sense of public service.

Modernisation accounted too for the pension schemes, negotiated for the teaching staff from 1927, for clerical and domestic staff from 1936. Not all the maids participated in their insurance-based scheme, nor all the mistresses in theirs, arranged under the Teachers' Superannuation Act of 1925, chief among them Emmeline herself, to her annoyance. Pensions she thought important, and for the single and childless woman desperately important. In 1932 she contemplated her own future. 'I retire in December 1936,' she told Hannah Cohen of Roedean Council. Her government pension would amount to just over £150 p.a. with a lump sum of £400; had she stayed at Bedford and on their contributory scheme, she would have received at sixty just under £400 p.a. plus the sum of £970 for contributions of £645 between 1924 and 1936, or £495 after tax, she added. But the Roedean scheme was open only to teachers under fifty on 1 January 1927, and Emmeline's fiftieth birthday had fallen four days earlier. The Council agreed that – if finances permitted – an allowance equivalent to her Bedford expectations would be made, less putative contributions, but Emmeline clearly lacked the security of state-backed arrangements.

When 1936 came, and her aches and pains were spreading from the arthritis in neck and arm to her knees, with headaches still recurrent and her sixtieth birthday approaching, Emmeline had thought of retirement, and of the travel and adventures still open were she free as she had never been. Roedean Council asked her to reconsider. She brooded, and sought out Bolton King in retirement in Buckinghamshire. As so often at Nuneaton his advice was given unemphatically, obliquely. 'One would be glad to hear of you resting and getting all the good out of life after all these strenuous years. On the other hand, one must think of the school which would be sadly orphaned. I fancy you won't go unless health drives you to it.'

To a problem framed as the conflict of duty and self-indulgence the answer was inbuilt, not least in the year of an Abdication on which Emmeline's only recorded comments held out Mrs Simpson as an example of what power a woman could wield over a man and an example of how not to use that power. She stayed at Roedean, expecting now to retire at sixty-five. New opportunities opened with the decision, primarily her election in 1937 as President of the AHM, two 'extra-busy' years, according to her secretary.

It had been new in 1924 for Roedean's headmistress to have a secretary, and the job was what Emmeline made it; she made it matter. To the 'administrative skill' praised by HM Inspectors in 1938 the headmistress's secretary was very valuable, as was the school secretary entrusted with routine financial transactions. Emmeline's first Roedean secretary 'asked me yesterday [in 1928] if I realised that I was trying to work twenty hours out of twenty-four, but it isn't really as much, though it is sometimes actually sixteen with practically no break and everything not immediately needed tends to get left', and secretaries were not spared. New ones were warned, not by Emmeline, never to admit they could tolerate early rising, unless they wished to be taking dictation before breakfast. In the later 1930s the secretary would take Emmeline 'to Brighton station in her car (so that she could dictate on the way), and I would pant after her up the platform to get down the last words before scuttling back to the car to drive back to my office and get all the letters (including all those committed to the Dictaphone before she left) typed for her to sign when I met her at the station on her return in the evening.' The car, a personal development, came with the early 1930s, just before driving tests were imposed on new drivers, and prompted a highly successful motoring tour of northern France with Madge Skipworth, punctuated with punctures but covering nearly 1500 miles.

Emmeline's files were numerous: 'To be answered', 'To be answered later', 'To be answered sometime', 'Urgent', 'Personal', and so on. Secretaries for her had to be highly qualified, with a degree as well as initiative, discretion and stamina, as she told a sixth-former of secretarial ambitions, and once settled in, a secretary was neither undervalued nor feared boredom. 'From time to time I was rebellious, exasperated, desperate, honoured by her confidence, interested, admiring – and, finally and irrevocably, her devoted and willing slave,' summed up Marian Muriel of her service from 1936-42. ('I wish I could find another Marian Muriel,' sighed Emmeline as she hunted again in 1947.)

Such were simple, if varied, forms of development. Much more striking to educationists were trends within the teaching, or rather the learning, for formal lessons were far from the whole story. Formal lessons continued to dominate treatment of the curriculum itself, especially where School Certificate set the agenda, but typical enough of how Emmeline explored professional ideas, then sifted these through the sieve of the practical and seasonable, was her attitude to the Dalton Plan. This technique excited many teachers when it had been introduced to Britain from the USA in 1921 by its originator, Helen Parkhouse, for its claims were vast: the teacher became a sought-after guide as the pupil progressed at her own rate, developing a will to learn, exercising freedom, maturing in responsible attitudes to work, independent yet co-operative. Each pupil's year's work was split into monthly 'assignments', worked out individually with advisory notes, book-lists and other resources, and for more than half her school time the untimetabled pupil worked as she chose on her assignment, asking advice at her own discretion.

Even before 1920 Dalton Plan experiments had been made at Streatham County Secondary School under Rosa Bassett, and the school became its showpiece. At Nuneaton Muriel Davies moved into action, but 'We were not ready to work on our own, and it was a good excuse for idling!' said one pupil, succinctly summarising one hazard; on the teaching side both enthusiasm and understanding of a fundamentally different style of work preparation and management were needed. When Rosa Bassett retired Muriel Davies seized the chance to apply to Streatham County, where she stayed for the rest of her teaching life.

Emmeline itched to 'give girls really big chunks of time to get on with what they are doing without interference', she said in 1949, and longed sometimes for 'a radical scrapping of the timetable ... in order that they may experience the joy of really getting their teeth into some piece of work', but she was apparently rather less sure of adolescents' ability to plan and will to do so. So she organised occasional 'Dalton Days' ('Miss Parkhouse would probably repudiate the term!') to free girls 'in a small way', when for a day no ordinary lessons were given but each girl spent the time on one or two subjects of her choice 'in any part of the school that she likes, individually or in a group', but with table or desk and chair, with a list available of where mistresses were to be found for advice if required. The staff are not recorded as brimming with enthusiasm, and response among the girls was mixed: some admitted to wasting time, surreptitiously doing their 'prep.' for other days or reading library books; others liked the chance of one-to-one coaching in problematic areas. The mixed blessing dwindled to a rarity by the end of the 1930s.

Similarly Emmeline yearned from a distance for some of the freer discipline of 'progressive' schools, and kept an eye on these through contacts with staff and parents – Ann and John Crofts sent their younger son to one of the better-known – and she paid attention to her own staff's points of view. Varied teaching backgrounds certainly assisted new mistresses' applications, as when Emmeline appointed Nina Woodcock in 1939, who for ten years had taken private pupils on the European mainland, especially Vienna, and had taught in England only at the small, 'progressive' Maltman's Green. There lessons were optional and the atmosphere free and informal, to Nina Woodcock happily so, but though, she decided, Emmeline was always open to experiment, and always eager to discuss progressive ideas, the size of Roedean inhibited her from loosening disciplinary and time patterns – in its own medium this mirrored the elementary school problem that the larger the class the more military the method.

So pupil patterns constrained parts of the model, and more was moulded by available staff. In 1949 Emmeline spoke wistfully of how, since about 1916, she had thought 'the solution of the problem of the multiplicity of subjects might lie for the lower forms of the school in the combining of cognate subjects into groups and the treating of each group as a whole', but though, for example, she sent her geography and history mistresses to a 1930s conference on combining these subjects, objections arose from specialists who feared to dissolve the distinctive characteristics of the disciplines. Another constraint was the great constant, the examination structure and the walls built by examination syllabuses. Again she compromised, encouraging staff to consult and co-operate with each other, to keep abreast of girls' progress in subjects not their own (hence the frequent staff meetings), so that, in Emmeline's ever-optimistic faith, 'all the work can be made more interesting and progress more rapid by mistresses' using one subject to illustrate another, thus throwing an idea into a new combination ...' Just as in the report on *The Primary School* approval of 'projects' was cautious and limited so 'progressive' ideas touched lightly but did not disrupt Roedean.

This cautious ardour, the general theory tailored to the problem at hand, was Emmeline's way. A fourth constraint held her, too: her scrupulous care to keep faith with the Lawrence sisters' vision, no less conscientious as the Lawrence element on Roedean Council diminished and even memory faded. When the Second World War was ended and Emmeline herself was anxious to resign her charge to a head from a younger generation, she talked to the girls unfamiliar till recently even with the Brighton buildings, of the founding sisters, their efforts, their hopes, their principles. To her Roedean was always *their* school.

So the Inspectors of 1938 watched timetabled lessons divided into examination subjects, and evaluated them by familiar standards. But these did not fill a girl's whole day. Some headmistresses of the 1930s demurred at much extra-curricular activity as a distracting frittering of energy, but the need even to register protest argues increasing enthusiasm within the profession generally. Range was one key to management, range of subject-matter from the long-habitual interest in children at the school's mission, the convalescent holiday home it ran, to History Society expeditions to Bodiam Castle or Boxgrove Priory, from Girl Guides to orchestras, from fencing with foils to fencing with words in the 'School Parliament', essentially a debating society doing double duty as constitutional training. The Parliament regularised such occasional political exploits as the mock general election of 1929, whose constitutionality impressed itself on at least one who saw 'the girls carrying out all the detail – standing as candidates for the three main parties, returning officers, registering electors, arranging the secret ballot, etc.', in the year when exaggerated fears of the 'flapper vote' were first tested in practice. Best of all, said Emmeline triumphantly, 'it was conducted without personalities' in the arguing, not here counting the naming of the school's new animals, the donkey Stanley and the kitten David. In the country Labour won; at Roedean the Conservatives.

Like the junior branch of the League of Nations Union introduced in 1929, such practices were becoming the orthodoxies of the 'good school', though the LNU, with a 'cause' as its *raison d'être*, stirred unease in some quarters as an illegitimate imposition of opinion. But, unlike the Officers' Training Corps of some boys' schools, voluntary in this case apparently meant voluntary, and the LNU interested some (particularly when a treasure hunt or social events were devised by a fertile committee, despairing of their friends' 'passivity' towards earnest lectures and debates) and was ignored by many others, in the way of the groups with musical or artistic or linguistic or historical concerns. 1937 was the first year a group of eleven

284 / Doors of Possibility

Roedeanians joined the League's Junior Summer School at Geneva, and 1939 the last.

External events of that sort, or a tour of Canada in return for a visit by Canadians (in 1937), increased, not to affect many at any one time but to open possibilities. Very likely the girls who joined a camp for public-school girls and working-club girls were handpicked as unself-conscious and open-minded 'good mixers' – though one of the Roedeanians attributed the success of this social experiment entirely to the exceptional personality of Diana Reader Harris, the organiser and a future headmistress of Sherborne – but the idea, it was hoped, inspired reflection in others.

Brooding on out-of-class activities from time to time took up sessions of AHM Conferences. In 1928, for instance, a series of papers argued the pros and cons of time taken and stress resulting, of home claims and the citizen's relation to her local community, of informal dealings with staff and ties to other schools.[2] Kathleen Moore outlined problems specific to boarding schools, and identified the chief advantages for them as teaching the use of leisure, cultivating independence, and deepening sensitive aesthetic understanding. Emmeline would have added interest in world affairs. But how to get out of school emerged as the boarding school's dilemma.

Some of Roedean's efforts were as worthy as the camp mentioned, and probably much duller. Such at least is inscribed in the lifelessly dutiful account of the Empire Rally of Youth in the Albert Hall for the Coronation of King George VI, compiled by a girl elsewhere much spritelier.[3] But Emmeline herself led a group northwards to see the total eclipse from the best (but beclouded) vantage point, in Yorkshire, and every year had its varied crop as Roedean extended itself in societies, events, and the regular weekend fare of lectures and recitals of deliberate range. Here the slump touched Roedean indirectly, maturing traditional forms of philanthropy. The 'adoption' of a Rhondda Valley primary school and gifts to it of money, clothes and Christmas presents reflected older forms, but when volunteers were encouraged for a housing reform group, the Under-40 Club, and girls allowed to attend meetings in Lewes, to watch educative films on slum clearance, to study press reports, vague benevolence was not enough: they must think as well as feel.

More significant, though, than the key of range was the principle of playing to strengths, specifically the talents and interests of a staff the Inspectors reckoned 'much stronger' in 1938 than in 1927, though slightly fewer, with 39 full-time and 15 part-time (mostly music specialists). So woodwind was introduced to the orchestra, and the excellences of the art mistress Dorothy Martin allowed to expand into, on the one hand, a long-term co-operative project of decorative tiling, on the other a life class, with the nude, for Sixth Form artists.

Greek dancing appeared when Joan Barron joined the staff in 1927, Bedford-College-trained in Physical Education but associated also with the Ginner-Mawer School of Dance and Drama, its two heads the chief English exponents of this loosely classical approach to movement to music. Roedeanians called it 'prancing'; to Ruby Ginner and her acolytes Greek dancing aimed at 'perfect mental and physical poise, serenity of thought and movement, and the power to express with simplicity the more spiritual qualities of the dance'. This summary was made in London's Scala Theatre in 1938 after a demonstration including a Roedean group by then well used to public performance. Roedeanians had danced on the school's lawns for guests at their Jubilee in 1935, and when they repeated the performance for the AHM in 1937 the Conference report flowered into uncharacteristic lyric description of the 'graceful mazes':

> girls in tunics shading from saffron through light or deep orange to an intense flame, made patterns for our delight. With the gentle breezes of a June afternoon fluttering their draperies, and ruffling peacefully the surface of the sea below, Nausicaa and her maidens might have been throwing their balls before our eyes. The eye passed from the grace of the leaping lunging figures to the poise and balance of the still forms ... wherever it turned was the satisfaction that comes from the economy and freedom of controlled movement and rhythmic interpretation of emotion.[4]

The expanding Sixth Form was both nourished by and nourished exploitation of staff strengths. From 25 in 1927 it grew to 62 in 1938, about a third to a half staying for a second, even a third year. Such a proportion was one test of a 'good school' to professional associations and the Inspectors alike, especially – in girls' schools – when plenty stayed with no university intentions. The Sixth Form's value to the girls was evangelised more often and more loudly than the girls' value to the school, in fees, as disciplinary agents, as aides to relieve staff of all that fell under the umbrella of 'corporate life'. Not only did more stay, often to find this was the time they came to know their headmistress as a person, but they had more choices open, to an extent alarming to HM Inspectors: 'whereas it is most desirable that the taste of the individual girl should be consulted, a certain moderation is necessary in this', they warned. For girls 'of academic promise' they would have preferred more intensive work.

The policy choice lay between breadth and depth. In the limited time allotted the girls' main subjects the Inspectors found the explanation of a 'not particularly striking' record of university scholarships, compared with those of similar schools. But in the breadth and often impressive approach were, they suggested, the seeds of subsequent success, the seventeen Firsts, sixteen college prizes, nineteen post-graduate scholarships and fellowships, among other academic distinctions, of the last ten years, an unusual proportion.

University was treated by the Inspectors as a natural Sixth-Form aim, and they regarded attention paid to girls with no such intentions with a sort of surprised reverence, at least where it strayed beyond the accepted literature, domestic sciences and aesthetic pursuits. Above all they admired the economics and philosophy classes of Aline Lion, and the intelligent enthusiasm she inspired. 'The one thing above all which made Roedean worthwhile to me was my two years in the Sixth Form under Mlle Lion. I had of course seen this fascinating Frenchwoman around ... her subjects – philosophy and economics – interested me as something quite different from the grind of ordinary lessons up to and including School Certificate' and the girl quoted here was speaking for many. The girls read (in English) several books of Plato's *Republic*, chapters of Aristotle's *Politics*, parts of Descartes and Locke, and so on – the sources, that is, not the 'books on books' detested by better literature teachers. Aline Lion insisted on accurate thought and statement, she put 'severe calls on the girls', the Inspectors noted, and they responded remarkably, infected with her vital intellect, so that a course 'which might easily be pretentious or fraudulent' became 'both valuable and stimulating' in the Inspectors' eyes, 'marvellous' in a girl's.

Emmeline had not waited for this strength to present itself, but had sought it out in Lady Margaret Hall, Aline Lion's base from where she drove herself to Brighton three days a week with the same erratic disregard for road conventions she showed for school norms. Not all the staff found her easy. According to Molly Mellanby, Emmeline 'positively welcomed a few freaks among [her] conventional staff, and cheerfully allowed them to have the vices of their virtues', with all that that entailed.

In groups too, Sixth Formers read and wrote on modern literature or European literature, a rather fragmented arrangement probably related to the 'distinction of mind and versatility of interests' detected in the modern languages Sixth-Form mistresses by the Inspectors, qualities to be ridden on a light rein by a well-balanced headmistress bent on utilising strength at least cost, but too light a rein, even lax in some cases, in the eyes of some young victims of boredom and perpetrators of disorder. Such a system depended, heavily, on staff qualities and abilities, and where weakness was to be found, as among the classical specialists, the school was weak.

Material facilities mattered more to scientists, who could thank the science building memorialising the Lawrences for the Inspectors' judgment in 1938 that chemistry and biology, at least, had become both more vigorous and more prominent than in most similar girls' schools. As this filtered into the school's reputation, so more embryo scientists were more attracted. But for the most part the strengths Emmeline exploited were non-material, nor is it likely that staff were attracted by money, paid as they were on the original Burnham Scale with deductions for board and lodging. Stress on the non-material might even be called principled, if her aim was to set up an example of a 'good school' – the faintest of forms of extension, although one function of Inspectors, and the chief function of the AHM, was to disseminate good practices, what was tried and how it worked. Nor should it be forgotten that of the staff who left Roedean in the eleven years between 1927 and 1938 at least ten became headmistresses themselves; during the AHM Conference held in Brighton in 1937 Emmeline gave a special tea-party for the sixteen members present who had once served under her. At the Conference of 1947 she located twenty-eight.

Hence the judgmental tone of HM Inspectors on the features described, the working parts of the machinery of a 'good school' in 1938. Some of these parts are imaged in the photographs of an *Illustrated London News* article of 1935, and when the camera was torn away from photogenic juniors cuddling rabbits, the seniors were shown in representations recalling Bolton King's comment on the Nuneaton girls of 1911: 'so earnest and sensible ... They seem really to have some idea of doing good in the world.'

Such images were approved by school authorities for public release. But so, as a corollary, Emmeline's niece Pamela, after nine years of Roedean, arrived at Cambridge in 1938 to be awed by the adult style and easy *savoir-faire* of a St Paul's girl. Roedeanians of social sophistication learnt it outside school. For one disenchanted leaver, 'War came to my rescue, and I learned far more in the WAAF for five years than at Roedean for a similar length of time. *Not* Latin, ancient history, algebra or geometry, but Life and everything connected with living.'

Some university authorities would have understood. In 1938, as the Principal of the Society of Oxford Home Students (later renamed St Anne's College), Grace Hadow observed that boarding-school products in particular wanted to throw off the community life they had left. 'There is no doubt that girls find the responsibility as prefect, and still more as head girl, something that is a strain, and occasionally there is a marked reaction ...' The mapped-out life of a school 'where even under the free and most modern methods she has been carefully guarded', the almost exclusive association with women and girls, especially girls her own age, these bred adjustment problems for ex-boarders.[5] Another Oxford Principal, Lynda Grier of Lady Margaret Hall, told Emmeline frankly in 1941:

I find it difficult to know what boarding schools give that day schools do not. I generally prefer the products of day schools. A better (less artificial) sense of values, less school-girlish, more dependable, generally more hard-working. And when I get a 'good' student from a boarding school she generally has an outstandingly good home with very strong home influences. I am all for variety. But what are we gaining from this particular form of variety?

'Could anything be more damning?' commented Emmeline, recounting this to a senior officer of the Board of Education. 'Fortunately, I honestly think that none of it is more than superficially true, except the importance of the good home.'

Boarding schools were positively disadvantageous to the national interest in some eyes, those, for example, of the headmaster of King Edward VII School, Sheffield, who in 1926 scorned public schools' claims to train for leadership. The art could not be picked up 'by intuition or chance', or by the non-prefect majority.[6] Leaders now, he insisted, must understand economic principles of production and consumption through actual acquaintance with the outlook of factory town dwellers. They must not only learn to form and stick by their own conclusions, but to get to know and sympathise with the interests and ambitions of the masses in the light of the 'new spirit' of co-operation and equal opportunities. The limitations of an enclosed youth too easily turned to complacency and reverence for conventions, a censure heard from other quarters too.

Such judgments categorised school-leavers, looking for naiveties, ignorances and faults they had in common, but Emmeline preferred to elaborate on the differences between members of any category: 'I have known thousands of girls, many intimately – and I still do not know two alike.' When compelled to generalise she stressed variety among her generalisations. So, when in 1938 she was asked to talk on 'the modern girl' for an audience of nurses – the subject was sparked off by a rash of Press disparagement of this girl's manners and morals – she described the modern girl optimistically in terms of her desire to know and argue freely, her independence, wide interest and sympathies, her sense of world responsibility.

The young, she insisted then, were 'affected by the conditions of their age and their surroundings ... really what their predecessors have made', and she talked of the changes she had seen. Significant to her were the rise in material standards of living, the faster pace and louder noise, the breakdown in formalities within and without family relationships and the girl's freer speech on freer subject-matter, the opening-up of careers to women; and she added a claim to freer attitudes in schools. 'My feeling is that the girl of today will accept discipline if she can see why. But she would not agree to the principle, "Their's not to reason why, their's but to do and die". She would think it simply silly to have to do a thing if she saw no reason for it.'

Thus liberally Emmeline generalised but extracted herself from generalisation to return to the point where she had started, to individualism and the search for unique identity. To realise such unique identity in every individual 'we must give them the right atmosphere, the right pasture, yet no one has the right to try to influence them or change them in personal qualities, as they may be going to be something, or to do something, much finer than one has ever dreamed of for them.' If this was the dilemma she recognised, that a 'right pasture' could be identified yet there must be no trespass on the individual's essence, it becomes clearer why she had no real answer to the charge that Roedean failed to prepare for life, for life, in this framework, derives from essence, an inner reality, rather than from existence, its outward terms. In this speech and her long-standing pattern of thought, analysis of environmental determinants slides towards contemplation of essences. A similar glissade from public to private, this time from the headmistress' duties to the headmistress' inner life, appeared in her presidential speech to the AHM in 1939. Here was both a strength and a weakness.

So Emmeline dedicated much of her public work to equalising opportunities without the expectation of similar attainments, from a base class-oriented theorists attacked, one which by 1935 could effortlessly be yoked by the headmistress Dorothy Brock in the quartet 'Eton and Harrow, Cheltenham and Roedean' as above the interference of the state. Here grew social prestige too, more ambiguous. Waring & Gillow named a dashing tennis outfit 'The Roedean Costume' and advertised it among cruising and beach wear; Roedean Council sent a solicitor's letter, received an apology and costs, and laughed in private over A. P. Herbert's ensuing article in *Punch*. The greater the school's pre-eminence the more the sorts of development Emmeline encouraged there appear problematic, even contradictory, expressive of conflicting claims between ideals and traditions of service ('Put others first') and their economic setting.

But no felt tension appeared on the face Emmeline presented to the world, and 'cheerfulness would keep breaking in', as for Dr Johnson's friend attempting to philosophise; the parts of her life seemed, like a happy marriage, not to clash but to sustain and endear each other, letting the 'good angels in' of a child's simplified Swedenborgianism. Looking back after their school association was over, Molly Mellanby saw Emmeline 'always smiling – I know you weren't quite always, but my mind doesn't seem to have registered that pictorially – always full of the next plan and prepared to embark on it with the utmost gusto'. Whole-hearted work was her reconciling duty, and, trying to explain to a girl how, when 'sometimes in life we are asked to do something we may not particularly have sought to do, but have come to the conclusion that we ought to do, then we may find that the task brings unanticipated rewards', she used as example her own reluctance to accept Roedean's headship.

The school had to brace itself for survival in 1931, as the slump rippled out to touch it and its peers. Numbers fell, at Harrow from 661 to 522, at Clifton (where Herbert's son Tom was a day boy) from 775 to 665, though boys' education was a better investment than girls' from the point of view of future earning power. In 1927 Roedean's finances had been stable but narrowly calculated, fee income of £67,046 just covering expenditure of £66,155 with no capital fund for repairs or for debt repayment on the debentures and mortgage on the land and buildings. By 1931 not only had applications suddenly fallen but some girls had left or given provisional notice for 'financial insecurity', the Council noted. The lowest numbers were reached in 1932 with only 285 girls, but the fall began without warning in late 1929. Emmeline's annual estimate for 1931-2 forecast a loss of £5,555, the Council set up an Economy Subcommittee, and for them she produced a succinct memorandum.

To balance the budget 340 girls were needed, at the present ratio of juniors to higher-paying seniors. Some costs – heating, lighting, water, rates, insurance, medical attendance, pensions – were fixed. Flexibility lay in salaries (staff were the chief expense of every school), food, household requisites, repairs, the grounds, and the mass of smaller outgoings on laboratory and domestic science supplies, the library, postage, interview expenses, printing, piano tuning, lecturers' fees, prizes, and so on. To cut higher salaries would be more effective than to reduce lower wages, though male wages were heavy – it took time and numbers to stoke seventeen furnaces, she said. The subcommittee worried over the figures with Emmeline, and drew up a schedule of cuts that would do least damage to 'essential efficiency'. Like the government's version for the Board of Education, a leading feature was salary cuts, 10 per cent from all those earning over £100 p.a., including the headmistress. Debenture-holders were asked to forgo some interest, not high at the best of times.

More positive proposals were aired too, and here Penelope Lawrence, her mind as fertile as ever and unhappy about the cuts, launched several ideas. Thirty years before, she said briskly, Roedean had faced much less competition – really only St Leonard's, Cheltenham and Wycombe Abbey had offered anything similar – but now girls' public schools were numerous. Propaganda was needed. P. L. suggested a two-pronged attack. A special prospectus might be drawn up to attract foreign girls who wanted a 'finishing' year in England, though 'hitherto we have not laid ourselves out for that type', interested as they were only in English and some cultural sightseeing. And pupils might be encouraged by a new supply of perhaps ten or twelve exhibitions, some granted by examination. Girls paying two-thirds of the full fee were more valuable than none since the accommodation and teaching were there.

The 'finishing' course seems never to have materialised, foreign entrants following normal courses, but the new exhibitions did, divided as scholarships, exhibitions and bursaries, the first two rewarding merit in a special annual examination, the last given to those reaching a lower level but reckoned otherwise promising and worthy. Nor did these awards disappear as the financial corner turned but instead increased, with remissions of up to £150 p.a. 'according to the financial circumstances of the parents'. The highest level of fees paid was £189 p.a. in the 1930s, now including previous extras such as art and stationery. None of the founding sisters lived to see confirmation that stability had returned, Penelope dying in 1932 and Dorothy a year later; Millicent had died in 1925. But by 1934-5 the Council now chaired by Sir Paul Lawrence could view Emmeline's estimates more cheerfully, and the Jubilee planned to celebrate fifty years of Roedean could only help, particularly as the most significant of funding devices (other than those coping with revenue) was the Jubilee Fund, a straightforward appeal directed to repayment of capital debt and thus the interest payable, in conjunction with a capital reorganisation scheme to establish a sinking fund and provide for pensioners.

For three days of July sunshine in 1935 over a thousand Roedeanians, Old Roedeanians, parents, and friends held Jubilee in Roedean's grounds, a glorified Speech Day, a festive window-dressing, with HRH Princess Alice to present prizes in a great marquee, hear tributes to the founders, and

watch 130 girls dance in Greek tunics. All had tea, and wandered through
the exhibitions of sciences and arts in a well-scrubbed and polished school.
Saturday was for sport, tennis and cricket, and for dinner for 750 in the Grand
Hotel, and Sunday was solemnised with a Thanksgiving Service in the
chapel: 'Ever fit us by service on earth for Thy service on high,' they sang.

Such was the established recipe, only the garnish of entertainments varied
to taste, already familiar to Emmeline as a guest as a generation of girls'
schools passed the age of fifty: the AHM itself had held its Jubilee Conference
in 1924. She had proposed the health of the Harpur Trust in 1932 during
the celebrations for Bedford High School but observed too another series of
birthdays. All over the country 'you will see ... constant little references in
the papers to the coming of age of various County and Municipal schools',
she told Chichester High School on its own twenty-first birthday in 1931,
just a month before she returned to Nuneaton for the 'coming of age' of
what had once been her own High School.

Not all the jubilant schools, however, were so self-conscious, even
defensive, of their non-profit-making probity and their 'good school'
qualities as to petition the Privy Council for a Royal Charter. Roedean
petitioned, with formal rather than substantial changes to its constitution
in consequence, as Roedean School Ltd was replaced by Roedean School.
No powers or privileges were conferred; the Charter awarded in December
1938 was glossed as an honour recognising Roedean's 'good school' status.

If fee remissions were inspired in part by financial needs of the school,
their survival, indeed increase, in better times indicates other motives at
work as well. In 1938 approximately one-third of the girls paid less than
full fees, at a total cost to the school of £7,815 p.a., and to the single leaving
scholarship of 1927 to assist higher education and training three or four
more had been added.[7] A handful of scholarships were for special purposes,
from 1934 for girls from Theresa Lawrence's Roedean in South Africa, from
1937 for a girl from Monticello College, Illinois, to spend a year at Roedean
to balance the equivalent offer from Monticello, and so on. After 1938 a
new wave washed in, with 'Charter Entries' of 100 guineas a year planned
for five girls from 1939 to mark the grant to Roedean of a Royal Charter. Yet
again these were no unproblematic offerings, though deliberately designed
for the less well-off with one condition a certain maximum parental income.
For Charter Entries the Council framed other conditions too, to limit entrants
to what might be considered the 'right' sort, daughters of men in certain
professions and officers in the forces.

Bursaries, the most numerous category, were given at discretion, and
with discretion, the decision apparently Emmeline's in the first instance,
with approval by the Council's subcommittee on bursaries and scholarships.
Their level was determined by parental means. As the decade wore on,
occasional refugees appeared too, at least one paying no fees at all; and in
1938 Emmeline formally asked the Council to consider 'giving help to foreign
girls who were refugees, or suffering persecution under the present political

regimes of other European countries' and was authorised to take two at a time, if their maintenance could be guaranteed from some source. So the picture was complex: not the simple 'generosity' of the Inspectors' comment in 1938, but certainly not the response of a frightened élite to pressure from below.

Chapter 22
'Even to *understand* the news'

In 1927 a joint memorandum was set before the President of the Board of Education. It asked that 'all children and young people should, before completing their formal education, learn something of the aims and work of the League of Nations, the terms of its Covenant, and the recent growth of international co-operation'.[1] Means were suggested, films and literature, speakers and study circles, junior branches of the League of Nations Union, and the use of history and geography lessons. For this Emmeline had a small but double share of responsibility, as, at that time, a member of the Joint Committee of Four Secondary Associations by virtue of her recent chairmanship of the AHM Committee, and as a member of the LNU Education Committee; other sponsors of the memorandum included the NUT and the HMC, in a rare example of teachers' unity.

LEA representatives conferred and approved, and a substantial appendix setting out the League's historical background, describing its Covenant, and noting its principal areas of work in crisis management, Mandates, welfare work and legal and medical co-operation, was added to the Board of Education's handbook of guidance for teachers in elementary schools. At once the correspondence columns of *The Times* were flooded with warnings about the perils of prostituting education to propaganda, of manipulating history lessons, of coercing LEAs, of inquisition into teachers' opinions. Though, as the LNU's own minutes for their Council meeting of 1928 remarked complacently, it was easy to show 'that the main moving force of the Union was a quite disinterested and non-party desire for the peace of the world', no responsible headmistress could forget the eggshells under her feet lest they turn to bombshells and destroy the freedoms she hoped to cherish.[2]

In July 1928 the air outside Emmeline's window was sweetened with the voices of fourteen German schoolgirls singing part-songs in thanks for sharing a weekend's life with Roedean. They came from a new co-educational school in Baden – English educationists in the 1920s followed with interest a progressive educational movement in Germany – and their visit fitted into a developing pattern of schoolgirl journeys, one flower in the garden of international co-operation Emmeline was trying to cultivate. The botanical metaphor may be extended, for here, in contrast to her work in national educational policy, she worked on grass roots, not forcing but nurturing.

That summer of 1928 she went to Switzerland again, a concatenation of interests for her – family, friends, the mountains and the League. The first few days she spent with her brother Fred, staying one night high on the Niesen 'to see the sunset and sunrise over all the great mountains of the

Bernese Oberland and down to the borders of Italy', and walking together on slopes so steep that sometimes she 'had to toboggan down in a sitting position'. After Fred went home Emmeline stayed on alone near Innertkirchen for a few days, deciding, after six hours of 'steady walking ... very steep' with 'a lady of 71, no sylph either' that neither age 'nor being stout need deter one from long and strenuous walks if one keeps fit and goes slowly and steadily'.

On her own head the grey, sometimes pure white, hairs now predominated, and from time to time she mocked her increasing girth, very noticeable on a tall woman. Her job meant many lunches, teas, dinners; at a time when fashion ordained a boyish or willowy shape, 'don't fuss' remained Emmeline's attitude to her figure. She easily walked the eight and a quarter miles, with a rise of 4,000 feet, to her hotel, leaving her luggage to come by the only other means, mule-back. From Innertkirchen she went on to Kiental to meet Kathleen Moore, in thunderstorms, and together the two women followed Emmeline's earlier route to Kandersteg to climb the Oeschinsee, a lake just under the glaciers, and 'up the Niesen ... we had a most marvellous sunset, with lights they say they sometimes do not get for years, and an excellent sunrise too'.

Then onwards alone to Lausanne, with tickets secured for a meeting of the League of Nations Assembly – two tickets, for at Lausanne Emmeline was to meet Amrit Kaur again, who had taken a villa there and would have had Emmeline to stay; she preferred independence. But most of her days she spent with Amrit, whose brother Shumshere and his family joined them for a day at the villa when 'we suddenly decided to go to Zermatt and the Gornergrat tomorrow. It means leaving here at quarter to seven in the morning and getting back at eleven at night', but the day was beautiful and the view breathtaking; it stayed in Emmeline's mind when, twenty years later, she heard of the death of Shumshere's daughter, following that of his son, the two youngest of the party that day.

At the time, as she described her holiday, she was absorbed in the present moment, giving full attention now to landscape, now to her friends who shared it, now to the two sessions of the League Assembly she watched – her second ticket was for Amrit – and to their visit to the International Labour Office and the Palais des Nations. Yet it was a time and place of prospects. By the Briand-Kellogg Pact, just signed in August that year, the French Foreign Minister and the American Secretary of State agreed to 'the renunciation of war as an instrument of national policy', and of the sixty-four states invited to subscribe only Brazil and Argentina did not: the Pact was seen as a significant commitment to peace. League enthusiasts had reservations: why, asked Gilbert Murray, was the USA apparently enthusiastic about peace when it would not join the League's development of the vital machinery of negotiation and arbitration?[3] European stability might be assisted by Germany's admission to the League two years earlier, especially as it followed the League's successful settlement of an armed dispute between

Greece and Bulgaria, and fruits of League health and welfare work were ripening in epidemic warning systems, the 'White Slave Convention' for the protection of children and women, and conventions on drug trafficking.

Amrit represented all this in microcosm. With Amrit, Emmeline could share her enthusiasm, and in her she would invest more hope than ever. By 1928 Amrit, as the first woman member of the Jullundur Municipal Committee, was working especially on local problems of education and health, but she was becoming significant too in the All-India Women's Conference, founded in 1926 to effect political and social change, particularly the ending of the caste and purdah systems and the enfranchisement of women; by 1930 she was its Chairman. In the early 1930s she was in London to be listened to by Lord Lothian on Indian issues – according to her proud friend, Lothian thought Amrit's the best evidence submitted – and then by a parliamentary Joint Select Committee as she gave evidence arguing against communal electorates for India, and on the position of women there, asking for no separate 'privileges' in the negotiations to establish a new constitution for India. From 1932 she was in close touch with Gandhi, as the campaign for civil disobedience continued; in 1934 she moved to his ashram and served as his secretary, her swift neat hand moving almost as fast as shorthand, her flawless English an advantage, her occasional arrogance fought down into humility but still she was teased by Gandhi for wanting silk underwear beneath her homespun sari.

This warmth of personal friendship across cultures, their frank but peaceful discussions of political difference were what Emmeline sought most to foster by the cultivation of grass roots and personal relationships elsewhere.

The summer of 1928 looked back as well as forward. The youngest of Amrit's brothers had been killed in the earliest days of the Great War; only in the February of 1928 died the last of Beatrice's war-gassed patients, Captain Aubrey Watson, her private patient since her demobilisation. Occasionally he and Bee had visited Emmeline at Roedean, even the most excellent tailoring failing to hide the emaciation of his frame, nor could the swagger of a moustache conceal lines of pain on his face, yet he, after all, was lucky that his parents could afford full care. To provide the outdoor interest the doctor recommended they acquired poultry and a few cows, and these Bee managed also, but even in her helper here was a reminder of war, of the sort to be found wherever war had been. In April Bee 'has had a hectic time since last Monday fortnight when Mr Adkins collapsed in a chicken run before breakfast, because she has not only had his work and her own, but also had him to nurse. It was partly acute lumbago, but complicated by the fact that, after two operations in which some has been taken out, there is still shrapnel in the bottom of his back.'

The Watsons asked Bee to stay as housekeeper after their son's death, and the mantle of her own Aunt Adelaide fell on her. From the childhood days at Sherrington Rectory Bee knew the arts of management, how to live and work with employers and domestic servants, and she stayed until Mr and Mrs Watson themselves died, more than twenty years later.

But, like her eldest sister, Bee took a holiday in the August of 1928, and hers had a specific purpose. She joined a large party bound for France – at an all-inclusive price of £4/5/- a head – whose highlight was to be a service at the Menin Gate. 'Our party was half ex-servicewomen and the other half women's section, which consisted of poor women from all over England, Scotland and Ireland.' At Roubaix 'The whole town had turned out to meet us. There were speeches and all the National Anthems and then the band marched at our head about half a mile to a large club where we had breakfast and supper each day. We had quite well-served meals and were waited on by very good-class waiters. Very nice soup, meat and veg., and sweet or cheese.'

Bee was billeted in a convent school, and found her cubicle with small bed, chair and washstand

much better than I had expected. There was also one bath with nice hot water between about a hundred of us ... We left our billets at 7.00 am and after breakfast went a two-hour train journey to Beaumont. On arrival we collected a carton containing a cardboard plate, drinking cup, a knife and fork and sprinkling box of salt, three rolls, two slices of ham or beef, a hard-boiled egg, a portion of cheese, and a tomato and banana. It was planned, of course, for a working man. Also a bottle of mineral water. We returned to the station at 4.30 and had a cup of tea and slice of cake in a sealed packet. When one thinks that 11,000 were fed like that for four days, I think it was pretty good. I cannot think how £4/5/- covered expenses of travel and everything.

Next day the party went to Vimy and on Wednesday, after a 4.30 am start, to Ypres, where they marched to the Menin Gate for the service – 'Everything went off extremely well and it was most impressive' and in the afternoon could wander round.

There are new houses everywhere and fields of corn interspersed with large British cemeteries all over the place. They are most beautifully kept. I helped a nice old Scotch nurse who was in the South African War and I knew slightly in France, to find a nephew's grave. Her sister's twin boys aged 27 had been killed within two months of each other, one a doctor and the other a minister. She stayed behind to go further south to find the other one's grave.

Bee turned to help an elderly woman 'who had been out with the YMCA throughout the war' and despite crippled knees 'insisted on doing everything although she was in agony towards the end'. As she returned, Bee judged the trip successful: 'Of course, there was a certain amount of drinking and horseplay, but considering the numbers it was a very well-behaved crowd.'

So war was not an abstract concept or a distant spectacle but personal, individual, immediate, and peace not only to be hoped for, but to be worked for, by individuals in immediate ways. Since Emmeline worked in education, her ways were educational. Hence her involvement in the LNU Education Committee (which produced films, leaflets and speakers for schools, circulated a newspaper for young people, held summer schools, youth conferences, a myriad activities to inform and encourage), while her brother Herbert sat as a 'representative employer' on the LNU Industrial Advisory Committee, chairing it in 1937.

Where Emmeline had influence, however, the League took its place in a larger context, and within school she proceeded cautiously enough. School lectures for the year 1927-8 had a decidedly international flavour but not a League-based one: between 'Equipment of a medieval house' and 'What goes on in a coal mine' and 'William Blake' were sandwiched talks on a university mission settlement in Bombay, on Turkey, on 'Problems of race in Kenya' and 'Problems of race in India', lightened with 'Shackleton's Antarctic expedition' and 'Yellowstone Park'. In trying to broaden minds Emmeline began to systematise more thoroughly, on the one hand developing lecture series (in 1930, for instance, with three talks on Italian art by an artist and four on the USA by an historian), and on the other hand focusing more precisely, so that groups of talks on 'Current events' evolved by the 1930s into regular weekly meetings for the Sixth Form usually addressed by Lieut.-Commander Elwell-Sutton. Each had a defined topic, such as the Unemployment Bill, or American elections, or the Government of India Bill, or the Pact of Rome.

Much of Emmeline's out-of-school work was devoted to the unspectacular activity of committees, unravelling for exchange and travel schemes the red tape of financial controls, administrative variations and legal restrictions, and increasingly she contemplated the significant absentee from the League of Nations, the USA. Results often seemed just as undramatic as the means. But two motifs developed. Each initiative bred more; each initiative grew, slowly but positively.

So, for example, in 1927 Emmeline represented the AHM on a committee organising schoolgirl visits to Canada, in 1928 three Roedean girls joined a party of secondary school girls to tour from Quebec to Vancouver, and so Emmeline encountered Major Ney, Secretary to the National Council of Education of Canada, based in London, and in 1935, he invited Brighton's chief education officer to visit Canada for comparative administrative studies; as a member of Brighton's Education Committee Emmeline endorsed the trip. Schoolgirl travel became fairly regular, the 1927 tour adopting a popular pattern by which the party was taken from Quebec to Halifax in Nova Scotia, then camped in Algonquin, travelled through Winnipeg and Calgary and through the Rockies to visit the fruit farms of the Okanagan Valley and the lumbermills of Vancouver; and the party mixed girls from all types of secondary school.

In another example, one of Emmeline's staff exchanged jobs for a year in 1928 with a teacher at a school in Bryn Mawr, Pennsylvania, and Emmeline herself the next year represented the AHM on a new committee for the comparative study of English and American secondary education. This interest developed into membership of a Joint Committee for the Interchange of Secondary School Teachers between Great Britain and the USA ('Joint' here encompassing the AHM, the AAM, the British Federation of University Women, and the English-Speaking Union), and by 1936 the Interchange Committee could offer fifty-nine posts in the USA in several subject specialities.

From about 1931 Emmeline was representing the AHM also at the English-Speaking Union (ESU), an organisation designed to promote Anglo-American co-operation, her concern being particularly the travel scholarships given to British women – including teachers from the elementary sector – in memory of the former Ambassador Walter Hines Page. The original four Page Scholarships increased to eight by 1937, partly funded by the teachers' associations, and enabled British women teachers to travel for two months round educational institutions in the USA, with hospitality from American families; other awards were given for women teachers to attend the Chatauqua Summer School in New York State, and American visitors were entertained in Britain. By 1937 Emmeline had been elected to the selection committee for awards, and could report to the AHM that year too on many discussions, especially a conference between teachers of all levels and administrators called to examine how British students were to get what she called 'a more accurate understanding' of US history and culture, and the place of the English-speaking countries in the world.[4] Again the fruits seemed meagre: they could agree textbooks were inadequate and that too few university history courses allowed much scope for American studies, but a lecture course for the general public, delivered the next year with the help of London University, drew disappointingly thin audiences.

With the Joint Four too, which Emmeline rejoined as President of the AHM in 1937, she pursued exchanges of secondary school pupils and gained the Board of Education's sympathetic ear in 1938 for a broad scheme open to all secondary schools. At Roedean in 1938 she could record 'many foreign visitors, including a party of five Swedish girls ... teachers from the United States, many from the Dominions, an Indian lady, ten Indian students, a Christian Arab, and a Chinese headmistress' as well as visits from two headmistresses in South Africa who had once been mistresses under Emmeline at Roedean, in addition to their private exchange scheme with Monticello College, Illinois.[5]

Travel and exchanges for teachers and students, scholarships for study abroad, hospitality to visitors from overseas, were all contacts reinforcing the lectures and books designed to increase knowledge. But in 1939 the question had to be faced: could the time and effort have been used more productively than for these sporadic contacts, limited to a few? Were all these committees, like the League itself, useful in social and intellectual ways but ineffectual as a force for peace? Emmeline was to give her answer when she addressed her school in September 1939, and by then it would be the only answer which could make coherent and positive the whole pattern of her international dealings.

For so often the picture was of dogged persistence in a task that seemed Sisyphean. Emmeline had to seek and nourish the positive in the most unlikely of situations, and it grew to be a habit even in small gestures. Thus even in one of the League's most notorious failures, its futile disarray in the face of Mussolini's invasion of Ethiopia, she would find some hope when the Emperor's young daughter Princess Tsahai, exiled in England, trained as a nurse to 'fit herself to lead a movement for a modern medical and nursing service in Ethiopia' when her country could be freed. In 1941 the Princess returned home, with the nucleus of such an organisation, but herself died almost immediately. In a tiny model of how apparent failure might yield fruit Emmeline at once joined a half-dozen doctors and academics to launch an appeal to fund an Ethiopian hospital with a medical school and ambulance service in the Princess' memory.[6]

Such school-centred activities as those so far instanced formed only one aspect of Emmeline's international dealings. Rarely did the AHM stray from strictly educational issues but from 1928 at least, resolutions to press the Government to progressive multilateral disarmament – one of the League of Nations' objectives – featured in their annual conferences, usually proposed by their current representative on the LNU. Steadily internationalism (as distinct from pacifism) gathered strength among the headmistresses, marked by formal addresses such as Lord Haldane's speech on 'East and West: the relativity of knowledge' at the 1928 AHM Conference, circular leaflets like that produced about 1930 on *World Citizenship: recommendations on the teaching of history*, and affiliations, by 1931 with the World Federation of Educational Associations which drew together in conferences 'peoples of all lands and colours and beliefs', and in 1934 with the International Federation of Secondary School Teachers (FIPESO), mainly a European body.

The *World Citizenship* suggestions set syllabus proposals into a policy framework, the authors' belief that 'true internationalism lies in the co-operation of nations, not in denationalisation ... The presentation of history should be big enough to prevent a censorious attitude and should militate against priggishness and against our thinking that our main function is to allot praise or blame: it shows that human progress is not constant and that the right of one age may be the wrong of another.'[7] It is fair to associate Emmeline with this statement. The leaflet is not signed, but she was a long-standing member of the AHM History Sub-Panel. In 1932 the Executive Committee of the AHM strengthened its reaffirmation of a resolution of 1930 that world peace demanded the progressive reduction of armaments by international agreement, with a request to members to 'prepare public opinion for a successful issue to the World Disarmament Conference' of 1932. At the AHM Conference of 1933 Emmeline seconded yet another reaffirmation, to which only one member recorded dissent.

History teachers, said *World Citizenship*, 'should stir imagination and widen sympathies', and ensure the children 'have before them facts, together with the reaction of different minds to those facts'; they should develop a sense of perspective, recognise a scientific basis to historical study, but realise that prejudice and emotion can shape even the finest historians' interpretations. To stir her own imagination, widen her own sympathies, observe her own facts, Emmeline used her holidays, sallying out eagerly every year when time and funds allowed.

Between the holidays in France and Italy and a lecture cruise to Greece and Turkey, she sandwiched more far-flung ventures, and found in her trip to Egypt in 1931 a whole litany of interests. As the guest of a wealthy Jewish family in Alexandria, parents of four Roedeanian daughters, she was fascinated as much by the international flavour and strict moral tone of the multi-lingual household as by the tour she then began, from 'Alexandria to Cairo, Luxor, Cairo, Jerusalem, Haifa, Cairo, Alexandria.'

Here was the familiar of her biblical studies made wonderful by actuality – 'the Arabs on their little donkeys (I constantly see scenes just like the pictures one knows of the Flight into Egypt, Mary and the baby on an ass and Joseph walking beside, but no one leading or guiding the beast), water-carriers, veiled women with pitchers on their heads walking beautifully, nearly all the men in Eastern robes and with turbans or tarbooshes (fez), etc.', and here the wonderful familiarised by actualities of heat and dust and mosquitoes. In Cairo she watched the 'brassworkers, beadmakers, perfume-mixers' in the Bazaar, but also visited the mosque used as a Moslem University 'to study theology, viz. the Koran', and was allowed not only to see the library with its rare manuscripts but to watch part of a lecture:

We saw the groups of students (some of them old bearded men) all sitting round in groups on the floor of the great place with a sheikh, a teacher, on a chair in the middle of each group. The complete course takes 15 years! Each group was at one stage of the Koran: students move up when they are ready. All the floor is covered with a spotlessly clean matting but they all sat on simply beautiful Turkey carpets, and we were told that King Faud presented these carpets. He is none too popular because of his British tendencies, and this is one of many things he has done to please people.

There, too, was the Delta Barrage to interest Emmeline with its engineering of dams from island to island, and in another contrast a government teacher training college, headed by one of her own ex-staff. Emmeline's driver lost his way looking for this unlikely tourist sight in Old Cairo, 'and he knew no English and I no Arabic, and neither he nor most of the people in that purely native quarter (like Petticoat Lane or any of those East End districts but with Egyptians and not Jews) could read, and therefore my written directions were of little use.' So she saw 'a bit of native life on the way and two funerals', but Miss Milvain, when at last found, was anxious to show Emmeline the whole establishment, and so, on her return through Cairo later in her tour, she spent most of a day there:

I had to go to every class in the preparatory, the secondary school, and the training college because they all knew I was coming and some had put roses on the desks, etc. One class had put a drawn threadwork afternoon tea-cloth over the teacher's desk. Miss Milvain had seen it, and remarked that it wasn't exactly the most suitable thing but they were obviously so pleased with it that she hadn't the heart to remove it! One or two of the sheikhs (Egyptian men teachers) made little speeches to me ... I found it all very interesting, though a little exhausting as there were three buildings and many stairs and the temperature was somewhere above 90° in the shade. One class acted *Bluebeard* for me in English and it seemed very right to have a little Egyptian girl as Fatima. I think they were all Egyptians but they spoke English charmingly.

With the help of the Consul-General Emmeline was able also to see several schools in Alexandria, including those for the British, but Luxor proved quite different from the great cities, a 'real little Egyptian town ... practically no regular European residents except those attached to the American Mission or possibly the Italian School', and with astonishing temples and tombs. Travelling on to Palestine by train Emmeline remarked lightly that 'it is strange to think that I shall be in Jerusalem sixteen hours from now, and it took Israelites forty years and our British Army under Allenby a good long time during the war, as they made the railway as they went', and indeed the whole trip to Egypt and Palestine exemplified more clearly than ever those formative effects of history and geography that made these subjects vital to Emmeline's ideas of understanding the present. In the fact that for her, a Westerner, to look out from a Jerusalem hotel and find a holy and solemn enchantment in the view, in the very names, lay an active historical, cultural, political significance that mattered now, in the days of the Mandate entrusted to Britain after the war and the Balfour Declaration of 1917.

Now she dashed off a postcard:

Here I am sitting in front of my open window and balcony and eating my breakfast – fresh Jaffa orange, toast, honey, roll, coffee. In front of me is Mount Zion, one of the four hills of the city of Jerusalem and part of the old city walls ... a little further away on the left is the Mount of Olives, entirely outside the city, and far away behind them all, across the Dead Sea, the long line of the mountains of Moab, misty but looking very near.

The thread of thought was to lead straight into yet another committee, so that eight years later fourteen 'individual members of the British Association for International Understanding', one of them Emmeline, sent an urgently-worded letter to the educational press advertising the Association's *British Surveys*, fortnightly informational publications 'intended to serve as the basis of lessons, lectures or study circles'.[8] The writers of the letter were provoked by war:

> The citizens of a free country ... must accustom themselves to form their opinions independently upon the available data ... more is needed to enable the intelligent man or woman, boy or girl, to form a just opinion than the day to day news which the Government issues or permits to be published. Even to *understand* the news it is often necessary to have some background of knowledge on such subjects as the following –

– and 'the following' is an unnervingly long list, of history, geography, political and religious loyalties, economic resources and needs, sources of food and raw materials, national groups within countries, hopes and fears on the issues of the war and the form of peace settlement fought, for each 'of the countries affected'. The conviction that an ignorant patriotism was not enough welded together Emmeline's personal travel, her management of school work, her dealings with the AHM and on her various committees, and her support for the League of Nations through the LNU, but not into a programme, if that means imposing a policy willy-nilly, and it made sense of the often local, scattered, even frustratingly tentative nature of the projects. As in the letter cited, the onus lay on the learner: the teacher could help with the tools and encouragement but the learner had to do the thinking for herself or himself.

Not that Emmeline's energies ought to be reduced to an educative enterprise only; the gusto and sheer enjoyment of her wide curiosity, for example as she travelled back from Palestine to Egypt, preclude merely dutiful note-taking for talks to schoolgirls. They did indeed hear much of what she saw in 'Bethany, Bethlehem, Hebron, Jericho, the Jordan and the Dead Sea ... Tiberias, on the Sea of Galilee, via Shechem and Nazareth ... Damascus ... Beyrout ... Mount Carmel', but not for broadcasting at school was her attention also to details of the household and family life of her hosts in Alexandria. The educative enterprise had its self-serving value: it was easy to justify knowledge for one who enjoyed finding out.

So 'It interested me very much to see how Jews, who are Eastern in origin, though [in this case] British by nationality and the children entirely British in birth and education, arrange these things,' she remarked in reference to the marriage arranged for one son with the schoolgirl daughter of another 'very highly respected Jewish family in Alexandria, brought up very strictly like their own girls, always with a governess, never allowed to dance with young men, etc.' – as far as Emmeline could tell, both young people were happily enthusiastic about their engagement – but this, like the more mundane domestic arrangements which fascinated her, from the duties and care of the servants to the Friday prayers, was kept for private contemplation. Throughout Emmeline's trip her Alexandria hosts had smoothed her way with great generosity, and, according to the President of the YWCA in the Eastern Mediterranean (a chance contact on a train), 'their family life is an example to all Alexandria and Mr Smouha is the salt of the earth!'

Emmeline was struck by their strict propriety, that though they 'are acceptable in any society in Alexandria, they disapprove of the sort of life lived there – young girls smoking or drinking cocktails, married men or women having "affairs", etc. – and in consequence none of the family is allowed to go out casually or to belong to the Sporting Club, the principal club in Alexandria', nor might the daughters dance with any but their own brothers. 'I don't myself believe in quite so much discipline, even though accompanied with devoted affection on both sides, among grown-up members of a family. I cannot think it is the ideal, although it seems to work with amazing success and happiness in this case,' remarked Emmeline.

When Emmeline travelled, language was her biggest handicap. In Switzerland she rued her lack of German – 'I really must learn some. It is ridiculous not to be able to talk to people and one needs German so much in this part' – and in southern Spain in 1933 she found 'their own language, though easy for us to read, is astonishingly difficult for us to speak or understand ... The curators in the Cathedral and gallery I understood easily. I knew to some extent what they were going to say and the vocabulary is a limited one. In any case, it is only words I know – no grammar and no constructions.'

So in Spain, impeded in conversation, she used her eyes as much as possible, not only in Seville and Granada but on the long bus journey between Algeçiras and these cities, deducing low wages from observable overmanning, or learning Spain's first lesson that

the distances are much greater than one realises on the map ... I no longer wonder that it is difficult to get from some places to other places in Spain. The country is full of mountains, though not many of them permanently snow-covered ... How anyone ever conquered some parts of it or moved their armies about before the roads were made (and there are very few Roman or old roads in these parts) I can't think.

From the road she watched for signs of the rural economy, cataloguing to herself the crops and livestock and the soil types revealed by vegetation patterns; in the cities she covered more ground than intended, lost among street names changed since the birth of the Spanish Republic two years before from those of the kings, dukes and saints marked on her maps.

She did not learn Spanish, or German; only in French could she really attempt rational conversation with foreigners. Quite probably, this was an important reason why she preferred to work with the ESU and the Canadian authorities rather than pursue the European connections she had established in 1925. Perhaps it was a family failing, for though she assisted some nieces and her godson Jim Crofts to spend holiday time in French households (numerous highly-educated French ladies improved straitened circumstances by such hospitality in the 1920s and 1930s), only Jim achieved fluency. Rather, a block developed in her niece Pam, wary and unusually inhibited by French notions of what was *comme il faut* for a *jeune fille*, trailing round Versailles and Chartres in hat and gloves, afraid to eat grapes because her hosts appeared to swallow the pips. Just so, hopes often outran results for Emmeline, but if she repined she did not show it.

Even brief Easter holidays like that in Spain, with its closest focus on art and architecture, enact the processes by which, as a member of the British Association for International Understanding, she sought 'to *understand* the news', and even the scrappiest of her letters home to her mother touch on all the points of the long list of subjects where a 'background of knowledge' was demanded. Such letters acknowledge no category boundaries between these subjects nor any gap between personal and professional selves: it was natural, she thought, for a holiday to be an educative experience.

Refusing to categorise entailed two significant consequences: first, when Emmeline spoke of 'education' she never reckoned this an exclusively school activity, let alone one limited to a formal curriculum, but as the term used for the growing individual's relation with the whole world beyond the self. Hence the importance she attached to the influence of a child's home and circumstances, and the urge to extend what she thought good, and hence too she insisted it was necessary to learn and practise how to live in a community and developed an increasing preference for a boarding school as a way to learn. Secondly, she was freed from categorising people, and the dogmas tied to class or race or gender, and hence too arose the urge to include – and to be included herself. The most trivial of instances illustrates: on a train through Italy in 1935 the Italian conductor struck up a conversation ('I had to labour terribly hard to make my few words of Italian go far enough'), because 'he could not understand my being in Italy alone' as a woman, and when told she was meeting a friend, asked her destination. Assisi, said Emmeline, 'and he wished to know if I were a Catholic and could not quite see why I should go to Assisi if I were not. I tried to explain to him that St Francis belongs to all Christians and that we have the same God!'

Not to be laughed off were more sinister manifestations of exclusiveness fully in Emmeline's consciousness since the previous year. Then, in 1934, her report to Roedean Council's spring meeting contained, as a *fait accompli*, the news that the school 'was giving hospitality to Miss Freidburg who had had to leave Germany', and that, as a trained librarian, this lady was engaged in cataloguing the library in return. In Oxford a fund was established for displaced academics from Germany. The 1934 *Yearbook* of the LNU put at the head of its concerns the 'revolution' in Germany, and 'the accompanying revival of militarism, and the ill-treatment of German Jews and political opponents of the revolutionary government', and urged its German counterpart to press its government 'to discontinue the oppressive measures'.

The friend Emmeline expected to meet for the Assisi visit was, as often when Italian art and the religious spirit met, Kathleen Moore, travelling more adventurously by aeroplane from Croydon, changing at Cologne for

Venice. At Bologna station she was to meet Emmeline, 'but she wasn't there so I came on alone ... I found a telegram from her from Munich to say she was arriving tomorrow'. When at last Kathleen Moore arrived, in 'a terrific storm of wind and deluging rain', Emmeline heard how

the only other passenger, a man, threw himself out of the plane. He was behind her, and she knew nothing till she felt the awful draught and saw the end of him disappearing! She tried to reach him but fortunately couldn't as it would only have meant her being pulled out too. She could not attract the pilot or the wireless man's attention for some time. Then the only thing was to go on to Frankfurt and there was much business in giving evidence in German.

Assisi in 1935 was a nest of English headmistresses – 'a place where people of my profession seem to congregate,' said Emmeline, and found she knew most of them. Twice informal parties went on expeditions beyond the town, clubbing together to pay for cars but walking back from the Carceri, 'the lonely place in a lovely grove of trees on an otherwise bare hill, where St Francis had a little cell to which he used to retreat when he wanted to be alone with God and the birds', and they found on the steep hillside 'primroses, cowslips, sweet violets, purple and pink anemones, hepatica, yellow violas and purple ones', and crocuses and scillas shone on the higher snows. Emmeline heard nightingales sing each evening in Assisi, and 'the children are the most attractive I have ever seen, clean, healthy, very bright and happy, and apparently greatly loved by their parents, and the little ones charmingly treated by their elder brothers and sisters'.

Yet by 1936 she knew why Bolton King would not talk with her of 'foreign politics ... too painful and the tangle is a terrible one. But when I lie awake at night,' he added, 'I debate whether I would rather shoot Hitler or Mussolini.' He recommended to her Salvemini's *Under the Axe of Fascism* as a 'devastating indictment of Fascism and its apologists in the English and American press', but not, he said, for 'light reading'.

Less than a year later, and a few days after his death, Emmeline again travelled to Nuneaton, as the first woman asked to preach at the High School's Commemoration service, and she spoke on 'Wisdom'. Her notes disclose unusual anxiety, with scrappy preliminary jottings and quotations to spur her own thoughts, her writing changing in size and pressure to reflect urgency, doubling back to refine and clarify. In her thinking she considered Bolton King himself, summing up 'Toynbee Hall – loyalty to principles – historian – modesty. Love of flowers, gardens and of mountains. Sympathy – personal kindness and care for a cause and for the individual. *Not* the rights of man but the duties of man', and she slipped in a quotation from Mazzini, the subject of some of his work: 'The origin of your duties is in God. The definition of your duties is found in His laws. The progressive discovery and the application of His law is the task of humanity.' She enriched and gladdened the idea, but in these notes it formed a nucleus.

The Easter idyll in Assisi ended; in May 1935 Brighton Education

Committee sent two representatives to a national conference on the teaching of international relations, and in June the AHM resolved to petition the Government to contribute to the International Committee on Intellectual Co-operation to assist educationists to travel to other countries to discuss how to train boys and girls 'in the spirit of peace and international co-operation'.[9]

The same month the Albert Hall filled for the announcement of the final totals for the great Peace Ballot. For much of 1934 thousands of volunteers had trudged from house to house with a list of five questions, the last in two parts, with dedication and persistence enough to garner replies from 38.2 per cent of the electorate, that is, from 11,640,066 adults.[10] Undoubtedly the driving force was the LNU but Lord Cecil systematically enlisted the aid of more than thirty other organisations, political parties, churches, societies and associations of various kinds, and the obvious methodological flaws in such an opinion poll were felt to be outweighed by the heftiness of the majorities. Second smallest of these was the 9,600,274 in favour to 1,699,989 against for the third question – whether national air forces should, by international agreement, be abolished – while 10,542,738 said they favoured an all-round reduction in armaments by international agreement. But the vital questions were the two parts of the last: if one nation attacked another, should other nations combine to impose economic sanctions on the aggressor? Yes, said 10,096,626. And, if economic sanctions failed to halt the aggressor, should other nations join in military measures against it?

Here lay the nub. The idea of 'collective security' had been gaining ground among 'internationalists' since 1933 when a National Peace Congress in Oxford had listened to Clifford Allen and Sir Norman Angell, both considered leaders in efforts for peace, endorse the use of (minimum) international force if necessary, and a split was opening between out-and-out pacifists – exemplified for Emmeline in her brother Herbert – and those accepting, if reluctantly, collective security; among the latter were leading members of the LNU. To the Peace Ballot question 6,833,803 answered yes, and 2,366,184 said no.

When the pacifist Dick Sheppard in 1934-5 gathered an eventual total of some 50,000 postcard replies agreeing 'We renounce war and never again, directly or indirectly, will we support or sanction another', he may have wanted to pre-empt the Peace Ballot's effort to investigate support for sanctions; when from Sheppard's Peace Movement the Peace Pledge Union developed, it began to be clearer that positions in the wide spectrum of peace politics must be defined. At least this was true for those who, like Emmeline, brought to passionate concern some intellectual alertness. The Peace Ballot of 1934 marked the British LNU's watershed between an emphasis on disarming and their acceptance of collective security, preferably without the pressure of private interests – one question had concerned private manufacture of armaments, reflecting the belief of many that the arms race before 1914, and the private profits therefrom derived, had precipitated and aggravated the Great War.

In Brighton Emmeline had been continuing the work for the LNU she had begun in Bedford, the enlightening and whipping up of local support at grass-root level on the principle that public opinion could be an effective lever on government. A tactful course had to be steered between her personal and professional lives here: Roedean seems in general to have been kept at arm's length from this work, but in 1929, when the LNU's Council held its annual general meeting in Brighton, Emmeline's desire to demolish some of the barriers between a boarding school and the world outside, to involve the school in a wider community rippling out to local, national, international, met her desire also to promote accord between the nations.

A large party of senior girls was taken to the public meeting, 'a most successful L. of N. meeting on Thursday at the Dome', said Emmeline. 'I should think there would be about 1,500 people there. Lord Cecil and Professor Gilbert Murray were very good indeed, and people liked my vote of thanks. The Bishop of Chichester came straight from his enthronement to take the chair.' The meeting prompted the birth of a junior branch of the LNU at the school, Emmeline describing to them her own recent visit to Geneva and bringing in a member of the headquarters staff to lecture the group on the work of the Tenth Assembly; a debate on the motion that 'Total disarmament is necessary for the safety of civilisation' was carried by four votes in the spring of 1930.

So the LNU was fostered but contained, a society among others, not an integral part of the curriculum except in so far as a world context was assumed in subject syllabuses. Undoubtedly, however, Emmeline tried, could not help trying, to communicate her own enthusiasm. 'Miss Tanner was very, very keen on the whole idea of the League of Nations, and we were all very imbued with the idea of the brotherhood of nations and desire for world peace ... we did have many lectures on current events and the L. of N. when we were in the Sixth Forms, and it was certainly a passionate interest of Miss Tanner', as a Roedeanian of 1932 to 1936 summed up, revealing how Emmeline tended to reply on personal example rather than impose compulsory systems, a risky method as example and influence became attenuated by distance and absence.

Her vigorous style was in local demand: 'Our two representatives who attended the LNU Teachers' Conference at Oxford last month were so impressed with your address there that at our Committee meeting this evening I was instructed to write at once and ask you if you could possibly come and speak at a Public Meeting this Branch holds annually on November 11th', was a typical plea, this one from Abingdon. But events bore down on enthusiasts. By 1938 the LNU's annual report was gloomy. The previous year, it said,

> found the League of Nations beset. It was attacked by open enemies; it was deserted by former friends ... The consequences of the League's

failure to resist the aggressor in Abyssinia continued to develop. The sequel to the earlier failure to resist the aggressor in Manchuria showed itself in the renewed attack of Japan upon China. In Spain foreign aggression under a disguise ... met with no effectual challenge ... [11]

Positive proposals in the report tended if anything to enhance the distancing between the British LNU and the League itself, urging a clear reaffirmation of the British to the principle of collective action the League was so reluctant, and too divided, to pursue.

Without doubt Emmeline endorsed the LNU's plea in the same report for closer co-operation with the USA, the significant non-League member, and it was probably with an LNU group that she herself visited America in the spring of 1937. The League of Nations Association of America welcomed the party, arranged visits to schools and colleges, to housing experiments and law courts; the Carnegie Endowment for International Peace secured even 'the privilege of being present at an important session of the Supreme Court'.[12] In Washington they also attended both Houses of Congress and influential contacts smoothed the way to the President's wife, Eleanor Roosevelt, and others of note, while initiative found a lowlier and wider range also.

In no way was Emmeline tied by the group. She took time off to ripen Roedean's friendship with the Illinois junior college of Monticello, to tour the monumental Christian Science publishing house so that she could report to her mother that it was 'probably perfect for its purpose', to meet an old Sherborne friend in Boston and lunch with Old Roedeanians in New York. Alone she braved the New York subway and ascended the Empire State Building, but rarely was she alone in those eighteen days. She enjoyed it; and she returned with at least an enhanced faith in co-operation with the USA.

The LNU meeting in the Dome at Brighton in 1929 marked Emmeline's introduction to the new Bishop of Chichester. George Bell's reputation as a forward-looking Dean of Canterbury had preceded him, and even earlier his ecumenical efforts (dating back to the 1919 meeting of World Alliance for International Friendship through the Churches) chimed sweetly with Emmeline's own views. She not only saw but declared she much enjoyed the 1928 Whitsun production of *The Coming of Christ*, especially written by John Masefield as the first post-medieval dramatic performance in an English cathedral: clad in white, massed above the screen, the singers appeared as a heavenly host above the clergy and schoolmasters, the Canterbury citizens and Oxford verse-readers who formed the cast in the great Canterbury nave. Whether it was the principle of encouraging arts to the glory of God or the grand spectacle that appealed primarily to Emmeline she did not say.

Bell's own appearance, and more his zeal, on the LNU platform was heartening. His broad, kindly face with rather prominent blue eyes was not that conventionally associated with saints and prophets, nor was Emmeline ever what was called 'a strong Churchwoman', but 'No comparison!' she reproved a girl who admitted to preferring the dignified, venerable Bishop of Lewes. As she returned from South Africa in early 1930 she collected at Madeira a letter from her secretary: 'The Bishop of Chichester has called a meeting of heads of schools in the diocese, at the Palace, to discuss the ways in which the diocese and the schools could help one another ... I said I knew you would be much interested and accepted provisionally.' Over 350 heads attended, and a plan emerged to appoint a Bishop's Chaplain for Schools, his work directed to advising teachers rather than pupils, but the real triumph for Bell's diplomacy was that the schools themselves agreed to co-operate in funding the work allotted.[13]

More such initiatives followed, lectures, study schemes, weekend groups of Sixth Formers, and so on, reflecting Bell's espousal of the 'Life and Work' movement, its emphasis on the duty of all Christian Churches to apply the Gospels in every sphere of life. 'Life means *conduct* – it means how men act,' he wrote in his *Christianity and World Order* (1940), and Emmeline wholeheartedly agreed. Most of her own contacts with the Bishop were over administrative matters, such as the appointment of a chaplain when Bruce Cornford retired, specialist teaching of religious knowledge, preparation for Confirmation, school services, and the like. But their interests overlapped – as when she sent girls from Roedean to give a Greek dancing exhibition to raise funds for the Sussex Church Builders (Bell's scheme to provide new churches where populations had grown), or when he worked in varied ways from the mid-1930s to help refugees from Germany.

So, for example, they again shared a platform on 18 March 1939 at Queen's Hall in London. The meeting was intended to celebrate obtaining 1,062,000 signatures to a petition for a new peace conference, to be presented to Chamberlain, as Prime Minister, by the platform group – George Bell, C. E. M. Joad, Vera Brittain representing writers in favour, Herbert Elvin, the trade-union official and social activist, George Lansbury, the pacifist and friend of Emmeline's brother Herbert, and Emmeline herself. This was a Saturday; the previous Wednesday Hitler had proclaimed a 'protectorate' over Bohemia, Slovakia and Moravia, and on Thursday his troops had marched into Prague. Like the other speakers, Emmeline argued these dismaying events simply made more imperative the need for a world conference, and, in an atmosphere uplifted by the Fleet Street Choir and a final mass singing of 'Jerusalem', the BBC promised to transmit overseas Bell's 'friendly message to the German *people*', as distinct from the party in power.[14]

Such was the basis of the Bishop's and Emmeline's mutual regard. Theology Emmeline left to specialists like Dorothy Batho, Divinity mistress and housemistress, a Deaconess from 1931, an Honorary Secretary to the Archbishop's Committee for the Lambeth Diploma in Theology. To the Church of England Dorothy Batho was a scholar able to relate scientific and archaeological research to theological concerns, to Emmeline she was a teacher ready with thoughtful and practical help, but to the girls of her

310 / Doors of Possibility

house – who assumed a housemistress should be available round the clock – sometimes annoyingly unavailable, her door closed while she prayed. It was awkward for the school in 1938 to be asked to release her at three weeks' notice to take over as Lady Warden of St Michael's, Bognor, just after she had been appointed Second Mistress, so that Dorothea Child had to be lured out of retirement to fill the gap, other staff asked to take extra lessons and new arrangements made for Confirmation classes, but much was outweighed by her long-standing value as the repository and fount of theological expertise at Roedean – it freed Emmeline herself from that frequent part of the headmistress's duties and left her easy in her own broad and individualistic piety. After twenty-five years' acquaintance, all Bell would say publicly of Emmeline's own faith was that it was 'simple and sincere ... She was sure that every individual had a particular part to play in fulfilling God's purpose in the world, and that each would be helped to discover and serve it through the daily habit of communing with God in prayer.'[15]

In 1936 Bell sponsored a National Christian Appeal for Refugees from Germany, and assisted the resulting International Christian Committee for German Refugees; these broadened his light as one of the few beacons of friendship for German pastors struggling and suffering for the freedom of the Confessional Church as the Nazi government imposed their preferred version on Protestants. Simultaneously the AHM was lit up with concern also, so that Ethel Gwatkin, as President, appealed for help with the education of German children now living in the UK – by February 1937, fifty-eight had been placed in secondary schools. Efforts were channelled through Save The Children's Inter-Aid Committee and the AHM's representative there, Muriel Davies, who year by year sought out places for 'non-Aryan refugee children'.

Emmeline begged Roedean Council to extend help and was allowed two refugees, but took four, approved retrospectively; evidence exists of others too, at least one wholly at the school's expense. In 1938 the influx swelled, increasingly likely to be penniless on arrival. Nine hundred secondary heads contributed £7,015 to a fund for Czech refugee children in response to a circular letter from the Joint Four, where Emmeline represented the AHM, and she wrote too to the Czechoslovak Secondary School Teachers' Association with sympathy and support. This seemed inadequate: within the Executive Committee of the AHM she spoke (as their President) of the 'great urgency' of the refugees' problems, begged the members and any women's organisations where they had a voice to join in petitioning the British government 'to act energetically', sent telegrams to the Prime Minister, Home and Foreign Secretaries, but most materially presented a scheme for school help. By this parents could 'adopt' a child, with the help of a small allowance built on pupils' donations, and refugee mothers could be assisted to find work – good residential domestic jobs would provide homes as well.[16]

Emmeline's notions of action were on a grand but pacific scale. She proposed a resolution:

Having seen in other countries the disastrous effects of modern warfare upon children, and believing that in our own country even the threat of war has already done much to destroy that sense of security without which their full development to maturity is impossible, the Executive Committee of the AHM urges the Prime Minister to call a World Conference to examine those international problems which constitute a menace to the peace of the world today.

She asked the other secondary associations to join in this, but when Chamberlain flew to Munich others were reluctant to endorse this call.[17] Emmeline sent more telegrams to ministers on specific points, dismay, for example, that the Board of Education insisted refugees pass the usual secondary school entry tests, conducted in English, or that regulations were being tightened to prevent anyone guaranteeing more than one child.

By now the LNU was sinking with the League itself. On its Education Committee the AHM representative was now Lilian Charlesworth, a GPDST head and once a member of Emmeline's staff at Roedean – in the words of Emmeline's secretary of 1930, 'a tower of strength, thorough in all she does. She has just undertaken,' she added with awe, 'to have twelve double-bass lessons.' It was Lilian Charlesworth whom Emmeline had sent in 1937 to the First National Congress of the International Peace Campaign (she was not impressed with this organisation), and it was to Emmeline that Lilian Charlesworth wrote a year later to suggest that the LNU Education Committee disinfect itself from the League by detachment, continuing its work on the study of international relations and co-operation from a new base.[18] So in 1939 the Council for Education in World Citizenship was founded, with Gilbert Murray (from the first a leader in the LNU Education Committee) as its first chairman and Lilian Charlesworth from 1953 its second. Its conferences, its summer schools, its lectures and discussion groups, drawing speakers from all over the world, were born in wartime and invigorated as prospects of peace brightened. Here Emmeline served in the ranks, chairing occasional lectures and groups.

But when, as LNU member and AHM President, in 1938 she blessed the enterprise, war was not yet declared. 'Not yet' was the keynote; anticipation kept headmistresses busy.

Chapter 23
At war again

During Emmeline's presidency of the AHM, along with and dominating the maintenance and education of refugees, and among the usual ruck of examinations, teacher training, schools broadcasting, and the emergence of new plans for the whole secondary system generated by the Spens Report of 1938, were sinister undertones of fears for Britain itself. The initials for Air Raid Precautions became familiar, and for twenty years aerial bombardment with gas had been the worst nightmare exploited by peace enthusiasts.

In May 1938, Emmeline and other representatives of women's organisations met Lady Reading to discuss development of a Women's Voluntary Service, and in July the Joint Four, Emmeline their Vice-Chairman, sent a representative to meet Sir John Anderson's Committee at the House of Commons to consider suggestions for evacuating children by schools: would parents agree to let them go? And would teachers accept the responsibility? But the summer alarm discovered inadequacies in initial plans. By November Joint Four deputations were urging co-operation between central and local ARP workers, for teachers to be included, for teachers involved in evacuation to know their destinations, transport arrangements and billeting plans, not only so that they might reassure parents but to enable them to contact and work with LEAs where they went.[1]

Often their advice went unheeded. Questions of legal responsibility for sickness and accidents, questions about what was to happen where some children went and others stayed, questions about procedures for travel to and from school during air-raid warnings, about health services in reception areas, age-related billeting allowances, railway vouchers for teachers, dozens of questions were raised with the Ministry of Health and the Board of Education, as circulars piled on to the desks of school heads.

In June 1938 Emmeline reported to Roedean Council that local ARP authorities said the school did not lie in a 'specially dangerous area'. Precautions were put in hand, however. By November 1938 trenches had been dug as shelters, and equipped with electric light, and sandbags and other materials to cope with effects of incendiary bombs acquired, at a cost so far of £1,180. The school's West Field was ploughed and planted with green vegetables (perhaps, remembering how futile had been Nuneaton's vegetable-growing plans in 1916, Emmeline was not wholly surprised that a year's production raised £30-worth of vegetables at a cost of about £80), and the East Field had already been requested by the War Office for a military camp, a worrying matter to the Council who feared this might turn Roedean into a military target. Procedures during air raids were worked out and rehearsed, the male staff trained as fire-fighters under the school's engineer, Williams, a Chief Air Raid Warden, and first aid classes started for academic staff and Sixth Formers.

In early 1939 Emmeline was asked by the authorities of the Francis Holland School, in London, if Roedean could accept girls and staff in the event of a 'National Emergency'. With the Vice-Chairman of the Council and its Secretary, respectively husband and son of Agatha Blyth (born Lawrence), she rapidly worked out details of accommodation and cost, and the Francis Holland School felt one haven was safe. At that year's Speech Day the guest was Emmeline's old friend the political historian and now Cambridge Professor Ernest Barker, to tell the girls of the individuals' concentric circles of loyalty, widening without limit. His wife, however, as she looked at Roedean's mode for 1939, pleaded to Emmeline: 'Please, *most important* (because Ernest is getting worried that I don't see to it), could we have the name and seller of the dark curtain stuff?'

That June the Ministry of Health issued a detailed Memorandum and a circular dividing England into evacuation, reception and neutral areas, and describing arrangements. Brighton was listed as 'reception', and Roedean's staff helped to survey the area for billeting, so that, according to Emmeline, 'we were able to feel ourselves part of the local educational system'. The Board of Education, however, seemed to be dragging its feet on how an education service could be maintained if evacuation took place, despite nagging from the Joint Four, particularly concerned with lack of organisation for the secondary school children above the statutory leaving age – nor, in September, did it come as a surprise that the planned raising of this age to 15-plus was postponed.

As Roedean's summer term ended, on 28 July 1939, girls departed as usual, a few to a summer camp near Cromer for public schools and girls' clubs, four to Geneva for a League summer school. When the girls reappeared on 19 September and assembled as usual next morning for their opening Prayers, Britain was at war. The party from the Francis Holland School arrived to find more space than expected, with thirty-two Roedean girls absent. Some parents of new girls had postponed or cancelled entry, some parents of girls out of England for the holidays could not or would not return them, and some found war affected finances. Likewise the loss of fees affected the school. Black-out curtains were sewn; Williams, in charge of ARP, counted 3,020 windows and set the men to make shutters for them all. Sixth Form volunteers helped the WVS, most in the Pavilion allocated to clerical work on ration cards. The school's Mission at Rottingdean filled with evacuees with special needs.

For the second time the headmistress had to open a school in war. Stamped on her words in 1939 were the memories of 1914, and of the years that followed. And when the next January her sister Winifred, beset with cares, begged her help for a presidential speech to the Bedwyn Women's Institute, Emmeline did no more than adjust a few phrases to the setting of women at home rather than girls at school, and a few to how she perceived Win's voice; no essential differences lay between the messages to Roedean girls and to the women in a corner of rural Wiltshire.

That war should come again was 'an almost unbelievable tragedy', but 'enthusiastic work done for the cause of peace' was not wasted – on this she insisted. Attitudes had changed: 'there is no glorification of war, no military bombast, but a quiet, earnest determination to see the thing through'. That was the first point of a three-point address. Second came a definition of purpose: many people – 'many very good people' – 'are sure that wars should never be fought under any circumstances', but 'the great majority of the nation' had come to believe 'that there are evils even worse than war, and that it is against those evils we are fighting, against brute force, bad faith, injustice, oppression and persecution, to use the words of the Prime Minister'. By invoking first the Prime Minister, then the King's phrase 'to free Europe from the bondage of fear', Emmeline veiled any personal opinions in an implied plea for national unity, before hinting at the corollary lurking in the abstracts, that evils might be temporarily enacted by people, but should not be wholly identified with peoples.

So she turned to her third point: what now? The girls were 'to be training ourselves so that there may be nothing within us of the spirit that leads to war ... we should say nothing against the people whom we are fighting; we should not yield to the almost irresistible temptation to pass on rumours and to repeat stories of atrocities, meannesses, brutality'. The Bedwyn women needed 'the firm determination of us all to remove from our lives and habits all things that make for war – all selfishness, all gossip, all backbiting, all thinking ill of our neighbour ... never to pass on stories of atrocities [or] spread rumours'. Now for both was the need of 'self-forgetfulness, consideration for others, hard work, and cheerfulness'. However improbable the final quotation seemed for delivery by Winifred, Emmeline refused to discard it: 'In the words of a great French writer, "Cheered by the presence of God, I will do at the moment, without anxiety, according to the strength which he shall give me, the work that his providence assigns me. I will leave the rest; it is not my affair."'

Providence had that summer assigned the task of leading the AHM to Dorothy de Zouche of Wolverhampton High School, but kept Emmeline, as past President, for two more years a member of the Joint Four and elected her as their Chairman from February 1940. Through the 1930s this committee had 'increased in interest and importance', as Agnes Catnach told the AHM in 1939, to become the significant channel to public authorities of secondary teachers male and female, head and assistant. Only the HMC, for heads of the boys' public schools, stood aloof.

So Joint Four deputations handled many of their evacuation concerns, and, true to form, Emmeline first conducted an inquiry to which 242 evacuated secondary schools replied. Of the 50,561 pupils evacuated, 11,091 had returned home by January 1940 because their billets were unsuitable, or their schools at home had reopened, or for medical reasons, or for inadequate billeting allowances, or sometimes for sheer homesickness. Equipped with facts and evidence she argued at the Ministry of Health that evacuation would fail if billeting was made too difficult, that the higher allowance of 10/6d a week should be granted at the age of 14 rather than 16 as country hosts struggled to feed their charges, and that health services and hospitals in reception areas should be staffed and equipped to cope with new needs; but she reported back to the AHM that 'the question of billeting allowances for teachers would receive attention, Sir George Chrystal said, as soon as those of civil servants had been settled'.[2]

As the months passed the nature of evacuation problems changed, so that by 1940 discussions were conducted with relevant government departments and other bodies on, for instance, how entry for 11-year-olds to split and evacuated secondary schools could be organised, on arrangements for examinations, on the lighting and ventilation of air-raid shelters, on holiday plans, on teachers' tenure as they joined schools officially conducted by one LEA but now located in another; in 1941 regulations for fire-watching prompted negotiations on teachers who found they must 'volunteer' for more than 48 hours a month, on the use of boys of 16 (better for them to join a supervised school scheme, the Joint Four believed, than volunteer at home or billet), on the division of fire-watching responsibilities between school and local ARP, on compensation for accidents. By 1941, too, bomb damage brought new work ranging from sickbay provision to an indignant protest that not only were evacuated teachers' allowances for home maintenance stopped from the date of war damage, though expenses did not cease then, but that they must themselves apply to the local authority surveyor for the certificate by which the allowance was stopped.

Such are mere examples; the work was constant and watchful. Some concerned local authorities: what of Swansea Borough Council's demand, for instance, that all their teachers take an oath pledging non-membership of the Peace Pledge Union and denying conscientious objection? The Joint Four accepted that usual freedoms might have to be limited 'for the duration' but here, they said, the only sufferers would be those both conscientious and honest. Swansea backed down and reinstated two dismissed teachers. Other work referred to professional bodies: what of the increasing tendency of medical schools to encourage entry immediately after Matriculation at about 16 rather than allow Sixth Formers to gain the First MB at school? The Joint Four argued that early total specialisation damaged the developing doctor, and that without Sixth Form work pupils lost the chance to compete for State and other scholarships. This was a question for the General Medical Council and an intangible matter of attitudes. Sustained efforts to persuade the Civil Service to reinstitute suspended entry examinations, proved fruitless.

Yet other problems related to individual schools in cases seen to have wider implications: one occurred when Blackpool Collegiate School decided their new headmistress should not attend meetings of the governing body without specific invitation and should deal with that body only through the Director of Education. Secondary heads saw a creeping dissolution of the head/governor confidence so painstakingly built, and with a head-masters' representative Emmeline called a meeting of all sides at the Board of Education. The 'value of open discussion was shown' – it was Emmeline who delivered the report on this – in a 'friendly atmosphere with points of view fairly expressed', and an acceptable solution found.[3]

Arching above all administrative details, however, issues of grand policy occupied the minds of heads. The second of the AHM annual conferences over which Emmeline presided, that of 1939, devoted itself chiefly to the latest report of the Consultative Committee, now chaired by Will Spens, on *Secondary Education with special reference to Grammar Schools and Technical High Schools*. More significant documents followed. By the time the AHM held its conference at Malvern Girls' College in April 1942 the head-mistresses' own agenda for post-war education was ready.

But as 1939 slid into 1940 to look ahead to the post-war world was a luxury. Breaks with the past were apparent, and for Emmeline acutely so. For the last three years or so her mother had settled for the most part with Winifred at Little Bedwyn, to sit up in bed enthusiastically reading Christian Science works to politely unresponsive grandchildren and to be pushed in a bath-chair along country lanes. As enthusiastically she sat propped in bed at Roedean for her eighty-ninth birthday in January 1940, more vital than her body warranted as she opened her presents and blessed the givers. Nine years later 'Mother's ninety-eighth birthday it would have been! I like to think of how happy she was on her eighty-ninth,' recalled Emmeline, 'in spite of her illness, and how her face lighted up when Win arrived unexpectedly. Not only her children but also all her grandchildren remembered her birthday and sent to her for it. It really was a very happy day.' In a wave of cold the Thames froze for the first time since 1888, curious 'frozen rain' sliced down on Sussex, and on the 27th a fierce storm blustered. Rationing was introduced on butter, sugar and some meats.

In age and sickness and the hurts of war Nettie devoted herself more than ever to her long self-investment in things of the spirit, and on 31 January died quietly, in Emmeline's house. Her children gathered for a family service in the small church at Rottingdean, and each went home to answer letter after letter as they poured in to mark Nettie's impress. To the school Emmeline appeared as usual, a serene and cheerful force.

By early January 1940 independent schools had been told to inform the Ministry of Health about evacuation plans. Emmeline was stubborn – 'how hard it was,' said one of her staff, 'to move Em over the evacuation of Roedean. She said we had survived the 1914-18 War and there was *no* reason why we should leave in 1940!' In the spring Norway was invaded, Denmark overrun, Belgium and the Netherlands assaulted; in May Winston Churchill emerged as Britain's Prime Minister and formed an all-party coalition government, and within a fortnight the Emergency Powers Act removed almost all limits on direct government control in Britain. In the first week of the summer term Roedean held a night air-raid practice, and then came an unplanned retreat to the trenches and the tunnel. Anxious parents began to remove daughters from the Sussex coast.

As May ended British forces engaged in a rearguard action on the French coast, and Emmeline wrote to all parents: 'We have not yet had an air raid or an air-raid warning, our having taken the girls to the trenches last Saturday being due to the sound of an explosion which we thought was a bomb but which was in reality the exploding of a mine on the other side of Bognor.' Officially Brighton was still a reception area, filled with evacuees. This status soon changed. As June began one of Roedean's men was among those who crossed and recrossed the Channel in 'little ships' to and from Dunkirk. On 14 June German forces entered Paris; on the 20th the French government signed terms of armistice. One of Roedean's French staff 'was *devastated*', according to an unsympathetic colleague, 'and none of us could do anything with her, but Em toiled up many flights of stairs to cheer and brace Thérèse (who was all for giving up the fight *at once*!)'

On the 19th Roedean Council's General Purposes Committee had convened and conferred with their headmistress. It was announced that the school would remain in place until 1 July, then break up early and reassemble in September at a place to be named later. Now Emmeline began to reap an unanticipated harvest from past work, first for the years of unpaid service on the Council of Lady Margaret Hall, Oxford, as the college agreed to accommodate Roedean's examination candidates until on 23 July School Certificate papers ended, at a cost of 9/- a day each. A conference on a government scheme, initiated in June, for overseas evacuation to the USA, Canada and Australia drew her attendance: it was designed to preserve a cross-section of all classes and derive from all types of school, though the children were not to go as school units. Within a month, after torpedo attacks on two ships, the scheme fell through, but Emmeline had also renewed old links with Major Ney of the National Council of Education of Canada.

Ney remembered Roedean's established friendship with Edgehill School in Nova Scotia, and on 20 June telephoned Emmeline at Roedean: Edgehill had just answered his enquiry with a brief cable – 'Gladly take about fifty Roedean girls. Cable time arrival.' He told her that the Dominions Office had given permission, limited to girls under 16; they must leave by the end of June. Immediately Emmeline despatched an urgent note to parents and the list of fifty filled rapidly. 'We would see girls crying and know that they were going; later on the crying girls were those not going,' said Winifred's youngest daughter, Ruth Gauntlett. Two places were taken by Fred Tanner's youngest daughters, but none by their cousin Ruth. 'Mother said, "Of course you are not going, we are all staying here together",' leaving Ruth resentful.

Two staff were to take charge of the party, one the domestic science specialist Barbara Briggs. 'She sent for me, late on Friday evening, and without any preliminaries said, "Barbara, can you go to Canada on Tuesday?" I was practically speechless and said that I'd rather stay and do war work. With that she beat a palm with her fist, and said, "But this *is* war work, of national importance – have you got a fur coat?"' Emmeline's secretary was set to long and exhausting hours in London to acquire the necessary papers and visas. On 26 June Emmeline saw Miss Briggs, Miss Marshall and their group of girls off from Euston Station, and on 4 July heard of their safe arrival. Still vexed, however, was the problem of payment. An embargo on sterling lay between them, and 'Edgehill is unfortunately not a rich school,' said its head apologetically, detailing the extra expenses laid out for Roedeanians to be housed and taught; for months to come Emmeline explored and attempted various means to hold and transfer funds through Major Ney's department and banks.

Difficulties of currency transfer applied to another dividend of established friendship, when the Principal of Monticello College, Illinois, offered to take Roedean girls – these must go as individuals, and anyway Emmeline thought the college more suited to over-16s, hard though it was to gain exit visas for such girls. In the end the half-dozen who went to Illinois came mainly from Edgehill in 1941.

There remained the bulk of the school, about 220 girls. The day she waved goodbye to the party bound for Nova Scotia Emmeline went on to a meeting of Roedean Council, reported, and was authorised to conclude any arrangements she thought best for the removal of the school from Sussex. Now the penalty was paid for earlier obstinacy. After the fall of France every sort of institution, business, government department was on the move, and some gave up. Among the closures reported to the AHM were those of St Mary's Hall, Brighton, and the Francis Holland School, twelve of its girls and one mistress being absorbed into Roedean itself. Dorothea Child and Hilda Leigh, the Junior House head, were sent scouting as Emmeline consulted agents and owners, and in her head simmered memories of her free and peaceful holidays with the Crofts in the fells south of Derwentwater, and the image of the 'English Alps' of the north-west.

Her later report to the Council implies that at least one set of arrangements was made only to be frustrated when 'the property was commandeered by the military'. But with Stonethwaite days the vision rose too of the hotel beside Keswick Station, at Derwentwater's northern end – too small, really, but she had put it on Hilda Leigh's list. Hardly had Hilda Leigh reached the Keswick Hotel when a telegram was delivered: 'Please hold provisionally for Roedean School.'

Soon Emmeline travelled north herself. A few days later she returned overnight, plans made, sitting up in the train calculating ahead, and as she reached King's Cross her heart almost failed her. Was she bankrupting the school? Would it be better to close 'for the duration'? She admitted these doubts much later. Instead, however, she reported to Sir Paul Lawrence, the school's Chairman, and wrote to parents again. 'We are going to the

Keswick Hotel, Cumberland ... we shall all of us benefit from having to uproot ourselves and adapt to new conditions, and we are fortunate in being able to do this in such beautiful surroundings.' As the girls left Roedean on 1 July the staff started to pack, to load into removal boxes science and art and gymnastic equipment, books and bookcases, necessaries from desks to beds, from blackboards to cloakroom-pegs.

Sir Paul heard that 220 girls and about 35 mistresses and matrons from Roedean would be accommodated in the Keswick Hotel by its owner W. D. Wivell, and in the smaller Millfield Hotel close by, which Wivell was himself buying as well as adapting and heating certain rooms above the station for classrooms. Two playing-fields were to be hired, and some use made of Keswick Football Club's fields and pavilion. Mrs Wivell would employ any school maids who wished to go. He heard that for all this, with food and laundry, the school would pay a flat fee of £20,000 a year. Emmeline had also arranged to rent another small private hotel, Shu-le-Crow, partly furnished and with light and heat supplied, at six guineas a week; the head of Keswick School was likely (at a price) to allow Roedean girls to use its laboratories for advanced chemistry and physics; offers of help had been obtained from the Urban District Council, the Cumberland Director of Education, the local clergy, and the co-operation of the railway authorities was agreed. A local doctor would act as Medical Officer. And so on. The alarming flat fee Emmeline thought preferable to separate commitments for rent, food, fuel, light, domestic staff and the rest, costs liable to unknown fluctuation, and as the war continued she proved to have judged shrewdly, enabling simpler budgeting for the rest of the tally, the normal running costs from salaries to stationery, and the extras soon found necessary. More rent had to be paid, for example, to use the Wesleyan Chapel for Prayers and Divinity lessons, and its two classrooms for other work, and to use Keswick Art Gallery for lessons twice a week.

When the packing was done and despatched, clearing and cleaning began. Furniture was stacked, curtains and china and cutlery packed into boxes and laundry-baskets, carpets and mattresses camphored against moth, rolled or piled, and moved to designated areas within the building. Only once from June to August is Emmeline recorded to have shown signs of real distress, when she called all the maids and men together in the Reference Library to give them notice. From an earlier war she knew other jobs and higher pay were likely to be available, but, unashamedly maternalist as a labour manager, she found it as painful to inflict rejection as to expose the hollow space behind the rhetoric of 'family feeling' which gilded a wage-based relation. Twelve maids chose to go to Keswick; Williams and his family were appointed caretakers, to live in the Sanatorium. So too must go some academic staff and matrons. From the Mission at Rottingdean the evacuees had now been re-evacuated, the Mission was closed 'for the duration', and staff volunteered for Dr Barnardo's. Most of those left in the school departed for a break before reassembly at Keswick on 27 August.

On Saturday 3 August the problem of what to do with the empty building was solved by the arrival, surprising Emmeline as she worked with her secretary on yet another letter to parents, of a group of officers from what she described with wartime discretion as 'Military Authorities'. She showed them round and they decided an advance guard would arrive next day and 750 men on Monday. A battalion of the Queen's Royal Regiment marched in and at church parade on Sunday saluted the headmistress as she stood on what was no longer her own quadrangle. By the time she herself left on 13 August she had received the commanding officer's assurance that they would 'bring into play what is best in Army Discipline, what is finest in Regimental Tradition, and what is most sincere in Industrial Effort', a promise they would keep Williams on, and a particular pledge of regard for the Chapel she had offered for their use as such.[4]

Then Emmeline left for London and more meetings, and a few days later took the train north.

Chapter 24
Roedean at Keswick

Roedean School, and Emmeline, spent five years in Keswick. When Emmeline talked later of 'A school in war-time' she headed sections of her notes 'accommodation', 'work', 'opportunities and thrills', 'gains', and only in subordination to these, not to be dwelt on, mentioned difficulties noted as 'underlying anxieties about parents', 'staff and their discomforts', 'few places for quiet reading' or 'no central heating'.

Her notes say nothing of herself, her own priorities or problems or objectives; the element missing from 'A school in war-time', as she told it, was the headmistress. 'This is one thing that strikes me,' said the secretary who joined her in early 1946. 'She never *said* anything about herself', and remembered how another headmistress, hearing she was to work for Miss Tanner, had commented, 'It will be a hard life but a merry one.' In a revue written by Mary Middleton and Nina Woodcock, senior and assistant housemistresses, for their House to produce on the eve of return to Brighton, the experience became a farce of bizarrely ludicrous conditions. Dispositions made life merry, and for Emmeline herself her outside work made it harder, especially for the AHM in its decisions on policy advice towards the Education Act passed in 1944, for the committee headed by Lord Fleming on the future of the public schools and the subsequent negotiations on direct grant schools. As one of her housemistresses remarked, however, 'She is the direct opposite of Jane Austen's Mr Woodhouse, who morosely declared that the sooner every party broke up the better.'

Just after mid-August 1940 the women of the uprooted staff converged on Keswick Station to find Emmeline, her secretary and the school secretary welcoming on the platform as they stumbled from the train to hot soup and bed. Next day they took stock of the foursquare Victorian hotel building of dark grey local stone that was to be their base, and eyed the life-sized models of black slave torchbearers, flanking the main staircase, setting off watercolours said to be by Turner, and the Rowlandson cartoons on the first-floor corridor, the more vulgar tucked on the stairs least used. They inspected the public rooms, few and none large, and calculated how more than 200 senior girls and 40 pianos could be fitted into the bedrooms; many of the staff themselves had to be billeted around the town. They met the hotel's owners, Mr and Mrs Wivell, responsible for their food and laundry, heating and lighting; later the strategy was adopted of mediation by a single mistress of proven tact and toughness. They identified, rimming the sparkling August-sunny lake, Latrigg and Causey Pike, Cat Bells, Maiden Moor, and 'Skiddaw's lofty height ... bronzed with a deep radiance' looming behind the hotel.[1] Always Emmeline recalled the 'sense of exhilaration' of 'walking back from Prayers facing Skiddaw golden in the morning sun' as one of her unalloyed pleasures, and the rooms designated as her study and bedroom both had magnificent views of the fells; she could pick out landmarks from Helvellyn's edge to Grisedale Pike.

They crossed the River Greta on the wooden suspension bridge that bounced at every step to the smaller Millfield Hotel and Shu-le-Crow, eventually both allotted to juniors, the Physics staff were introduced to Keswick School's laboratories and the games staff surveyed the room behind the Wesleyan Chapel in Southey Street they were to use for gym and the local football field where lacrosse might be played at certain times. They eyed the piles of equipment moved from Brighton to a promiscuous heap in the garages and for the next few days no one moved without carrying something, 'from a tape-measure to a solid wooden desk or bookcase,' wrote Nina Woodcock, describing for the magazine how 'the conservatory enshrined a wealth of semi-tropical foliage and handsome hothouse-plants one day and a forest of Bunsen burners and a series of laboratory sinks the next'.[2] Two large palm trees and a quantity of cacti remained, more battered every year, and always in the frequent rain the roof leaked, dripping on to chemistry and biology lessons already enlivened by porters wheeling through barrows of fish or baskets of laundry.

Six rooms in the station building itself became classrooms, outside which shunting trains clanged; innocent passengers still sometimes sought the old waiting-rooms, and idle girls watched through the windows the comings and goings on the platforms. Scripture lessons were allowed the dignity of the Wesleyan Chapel, and here too Prayers were held daily, the hotel having no space large enough for the whole school. A constant worry was the lack of an isolated sickbay. The garage was redesignated as the studio, and a grimy layer of oil scrubbed from the concrete floor by Dorothy Martin and the girls first to arrive, the walls whitewashed and later panelled with scenes from Cumberland legends. Already in her late fifties, Dorothy Martin worked in her artist's smock all day in this chill studio, under icicles in winter, and stayed on at night to paint delicate, accurate botanical studies, later the property of the Royal Horticultural Society.

As they set up bookcases and beds, for girls wedged four or five to a room, Emmeline worked on the timetable, intent to maintain the curriculum in its integrity and scope. From the start she determined that standards should not be lowered, and was able to announce to parents that 'although many modifications have had to be made in our organisation we are able to follow our full curriculum'.[3] In retrospect she claimed girls' work showed increased vitality and maturity, and knew her claim endorsed by external assessors. Symptomatically she had persuaded Aline Lion, with her talent for maturing young and average intellects, to accompany them, lodging in the town. Modifications to organisation included lengthening each lesson to an hour, to allow for the walks between scattered locations which girls found 'refreshing and a good time to chat', and to some syllabus reorganisation to fit three morning and three evening sessions in the day. They included exploiting the truncated staff's flexibility so that Nina Woodcock, for instance, was asked to teach German, though she regarded her real subject as English, because she had spent a decade in German-speaking countries and a German specialist had gone with the Roedean girls to Canada.

All such modifications leant heavily on the cohesion and co-operation of what Marian Muriel, then Emmeline's secretary, considered a particularly varied assortment, in personalities and interests, of staff, a spirit built in days of peace. Now, like rooms for quiet work, the old staff enjoyments had gone, the concerts and theatres of Brighton, pursuit of extra interests like Thérèse Lavauden's contributions to European news journals, trips to London or Oxford or anywhere as more bought cars, picnics on the Downs and days with friends beyond Roedean; now in war-time Keswick, petrol controlled, limitations forced them in on each other and yet the structures held. Yet modifications also allowed Emmeline to advance one dream, of greater freedom for the girls, justified because the limited space of the hotel would otherwise be intolerably restrictive, because Keswick was a safer, smaller town than Brighton for them, because organised games were limited to hours allotted on the pitches lent and the tennis courts of Fitz Park, and because before them lay Derwentwater and around them the hills.

So parents were advised to send bicycles if they could, and on Saturdays enthusiastic walkers among the staff took small groups walking and climbing on the fells. Reactions were mixed. 'At Brighton I loved playing all the games and did so whenever I could,' said Emmeline's niece Ruth. 'At Keswick I think we played games once or twice a week. On other days we had to go on compulsory walks, down to the lake ... I was a sub-prefect and in charge of these walks ... many people disappeared – I was always counting heads.' Just once she climbed Skiddaw. 'All that compulsory mountain-climbing', others reported with aggrieved exaggeration. Yet many loved the fell-walking and loved too to swim on hot summer days from a bathing-place with a diving board, in brown water with little brown fish darting in and out of the bottom weed.

Emmeline had chosen to go not merely to a place of safety but of beauty, the sublime mountains, 'lakes and sounding cataracts ... mists and winds', the 'pleasant images of trees, of sea or sky ... colours of green fields' that gave 'fair seed-time' to Wordsworth's youth and led him on 'to feel / For passions that were not my own, and think / (At random and imperfectly indeed) / On man, the heart of man, and human life'.[4] And so that 'shades of the prison-house' should not close entirely on the growing girls but they too might learn to see, to feel, to think, occasionally, when dawn promised a fair day, Emmeline announced a day off, free, and with their lunches packed on their backs or in their pockets, girls walked to Castlerigg Stone Circle, climbed Latrigg, strolled down to the lake to picnic in Brandlehow Woods along the lakeside, sketched with Dorothy Martin smoking a little pipe, cycled and explored. Such days were rare enough not to disrupt work, and, as one of the staff remarked drily, syllabuses were cut up anyway by the conditions.

But light supervision gave only rare chances for the solitary encounters with 'huge and mighty forms' that powerfully discipline and irradiate Wordsworth's *The Prelude*. Of his boyhood experiences they shared most nearly the skating scene. In two winters Derwentwater froze hard over, between leafless trees and icy crags, so that as a luminous moon rose on winter afternoons girls too might hiss along the grey crinkled surface and hear the crackling of compacting ice. 'Skating and by moonlight' Emmeline listed among 'opportunities and thrills' in her notes, below 'beauty, history, literary associations and geography of the district'.

Such days lay in the future when the girls arrived, most on 5 September, the Londoners narrowly missing the beginning of the Blitz. Still their chief pastoral guides were their housemistresses and Houses defined groups for expeditions and amusements and bedroom-sharing, but now they ate together, slept adjoining, shared more, perforce, in the congested hotel; old House rigidities relaxed. They learnt their way around as routines settled into securities, while, through the first term, night after night in city after city, sirens sounded and bombs dropped. At the end of November Churchill told the Commons the rate of deaths from air-raids was diminishing from September levels, to around three thousand a week.

Thirty or so girls could not go home that Christmas; Emmeline asked each parent to send

a home afternoon frock, reasonably warm, which she would enjoy wearing on Christmas Day [and] an ordinary tweed skirt to wear with a jumper so as to feel less 'school-y' [as well as a little pocket money, and 5/- for a Christmas present for the domestic staff]. We have been told that the Old Vic Company is coming here for one week and there are also often good and suitable films. If the weather were fine we might like to take the girls to see some other part of the district.

In the same circular she outlined the schedule of the school train, only to revise this in another a few days later, a recurring pattern with unpredictable government calls on lines and rolling-stock. At every term's start and end she arranged for a train to wind its way from Keswick to London, stopping at Preston, Wigan, Warrington, Crewe, Stafford, Nuneaton, Rugby, Bletchley, Oxford, Reading, meeting at Crewe a West Country service for Shrewsbury, Hereford, South Wales, Bristol, Exeter, Plymouth, if possible, splitting at Watford Junction for Guildford. Girls living in the North and Scotland were escorted to Carlisle for connections there. Always there were some who could not catch the train and needed *ad hoc* escorts if alone.

To Emmeline too fell the responsibility of sweetening relations with the forces occupying Roedean itself, for the first nine months a temporary halt for first the Queen's Royal Regiment, then the West Nova Scotian Regiment, Princess Patricia's Canadian Light Infantry, the 48th Highlanders of Canada, the 1st Battalion Royal Regiment, the Black Watch of Canada, and the London Scottish. To each commanding officer in turn she wrote with warm welcome, as a kind hostess temporarily absent, but they recognised what she was about. 'I know full well that – while you have not allowed even a trace of the thought to enter your letter – you must be worried about what is happening to the place during these changes in occupancy,' wrote one Canadian commander, 'My lads are not destructive. Although – as even the fondest parent must admit – they are sometimes careless.' When the faithful Williams heard rumours that HMS *Vernon*, the Royal Navy's torpedo training establishment, was relocating, word was put about and in April 1941 Roedean was transferred to the Admiralty. Emmeline kept in friendly touch, and the Navy responded: Roedean proved one of the least damaged of requisitioned schools.

What Emmeline felt about the conversion of the school where she had taught the arts of peace to instruction in torpedo and submarine warfare she never said. A pupil was certain she

abhorred war and its hideous consequences but whatever her private pacifist inclinations may have been, unlike one member of staff she kept her views strictly to herself. She spoke to us of the strain of the war on our parents, urging us to be as helpful as possible ... I don't remember hearing her comment on Hitler, Churchill or any individual. Nor do I recall her expressing views on the rights and wrongs of the war. We were simply told to do anything and everything to the best of our ability, not wasting time or materials, and being ready when the time came to do whatever was asked of us without fuss.

Another Sixth Former, who particularly enjoyed the prefects' privilege of walks with Emmeline to Prayers in the Southey Street Chapel, was enthralled by her conversation, or sometimes monologue, on current affairs of all kinds but likewise remembered no personal opinions, just a desire to broaden minds and enlarge ideas.

Such reticence underlines the potential loneliness of a head's position. Emmeline loved to hear of all the girls' doings, the hills climbed, the Literary Society, the music-making, the snowball battles, according to one of her staff; she loved to entertain visiting lecturers and 'toss the conversational ball' at an informal party with a young quartet of musicians, said another; but she was always distinct: Miss Tanner. In some ways exile relaxed formal relations between most staff and girls, as the shared climbs and boating expeditions bred closer knowledge and sympathy, and first in her catalogue of 'gains' Emmeline listed 'closer contact within school'.

The order Miss Tanner had established was strong enough to hold through her absences as regularly she travelled to London for the AHM Executive Committee and Joint Four work, until the Gordon Square office was bombed and AHM meetings were called here and there, in Leicester, Bedford, and Edgbaston in the early months of 1941, and she herself retired from the Joint Four. Perhaps she was glad to do so, for in December 1941 she reached sixty-five, and with little hope of a speedy end to war determined to retire. Though to her pupils she did not seem to belong to their grandparents' generation – not, said one, because of her clothes, always suitable to an older woman, dark, high-necked with a long back zip (they speculated on how she did it up) and sleeves always past her elbows, but because of her active mind and manner – yet she knew her age and how her body ached.

In February 1942 she wrote to Roedean's Chairman, Sir Paul Laurence. He replied at once:

> *Please* don't think or talk of retiring under present conditions. If times were normal and we were at home the reasons you advance for having a younger headmistress would require careful consideration, but as it is all these reasons are outweighed by the fact that the School is in exile and the country is undergoing a crisis unprecedented in its history. I rang up Colonel Blyth this morning and told him of your letter – he said, 'We can't let her go.' This is no doubt a selfish point of view but it expresses my sentiments and also the sentiments of the Council.

Could she not delegate more to younger staff, he asked and ease off 'undertaking personally the very many details incident to the carrying-on of the school'? Temporarily she acquiesced, overborne as usual by the hint of her moral duties, but her attempts to ease herself seem to have produced a more marked autocracy, not because she listened less or consulted less but because her will was allowed nearer the surface.

Stresses were telling, as on many heads, on those who did not evacuate as on those who did. Bedford was safe enough to receive evacuees, but devastation of its Holborn property slashed Harpur Trust income. Nuneaton High School also continued to function, and was itself spared direct bombs though it lay so close to the railway and the town suffered severely. With development of new electrical, automotive and aeronautical engineering industries the West Midlands had recovered more swiftly than most from the slump but Nuneaton's own strategic industries and its nearness to Coventry and Birmingham drew the bombers to assist, without discrimination, the slum clearance of the 1930s. The boys' Grammar School was partly destroyed and boys crammed into parts of the High School as girls cramped themselves in others. Robert Swinnerton, Emmeline's last and redoubtable Chairman of Governors, died in an air-raid of 1940; in May 1941 Emmeline heard too that Edward and Hallie Melly had died together in the ruins of their house, from a direct hit.

When she had been at Nuneaton in wartime civilian deaths had been far outweighed by those in the forces, and now at Keswick one girl at least remembered always the letter Emmeline wrote her parents when her brother was reported missing, then killed: 'it was so understanding, perceptive and full of compassion.' But now all were in danger. Several of Emmeline's own nephews and nieces served in (and survived) the forces, but one would not. Tom, Herbert's and Agatha's son, Barbara's brother, had been bred a Quaker. He had followed his sister to Oxford, gained a respectable degree and a Rugger Blue, was called to the Bar, then turned to business with his father's firm, and when war became imminent he was in his late twenties, with an unavoidable, crucial choice. He decided, his father wrote, that 'he could not join the forces and was prepared to take the consequences', and, loving action, Tom left the firm now hostile to declared pacifists of serving age to join the Friends' Ambulance Unit.[5]

Tom's work at first lay in hospitals in London's East End; he surveyed shelter provision and did battle with Ministries. Six months later he was Chairman of the FAU Executive Committee and for two years 'Tom Tanner ruled', according to the FAU's historian A. Tegla Davies.[6] The FAU's work was worldwide. Herbert and Agatha moved into a corner of their substantial house and offered the rest as a training centre for drivers and mechanics, first aid and language workers, and reckoned about 300 young men passed through altogether. In late 1942 the FAU Section in China was in difficulties, exacerbated by extraordinary communications handicaps, and a visit from headquarters was seen to be necessary, U-boats or no U-boats. Tom embarked on the *Ceramic*. Two days before 1942 ended, as Emmeline celebrated another birthday, news arrived that the *Ceramic* had been torpedoed and sunk in the South Atlantic two weeks earlier. Herbert refused to write much of Tom or his death: 'he meant so much to me ... Just one more of the dreadful sacrifices of wicked and useless wars.'[7] Every tribute to Tom's work Emmeline heard in India in 1949 she recounted to her brother, but in India in 1942 her beloved friend Amrit Kaur was starting a prison sentence for her work with Gandhi.

That Christmas her brother Fred had urged strongly she 'should fix the date for your retirement. Let me say at once I do not think you have lost any of your efficiency or that your brain is about to atrophy', but he saw no prospect that Roedean's buildings could be released to the school for at least two years and argued Emmeline's duty to her successor, who should familiarise herself so as to 'make the move when the time comes in her own way'. Emmeline sufficiently agreed to embark on a little discreet head-hunting. Confidentially she asked the advice of Francis Duckworth, the senior Chief HMI for secondary schools and a committee colleague of her own with unrivalled breadth of experience.

He supplied some names but begged to know her priorities.

I think my order would be something of this sort [she replied]: 1. A woman of character and personality who must be straight and sincere and have initiative; 2. A good mind and reasonably wide interests; 3. Varied educational experience, including, if possible, both boarding and maintained and aided schools ... The Council may not agree with me at all ... I could make a much longer list.

'Yes,' Duckworth agreed, approving her hierarchy, but he sought a closer definition of the first ranked qualities, suggesting in addition tact, poise, balance and 'sheer wiseness'.

They brooded on ideal heads, Emmeline practical, wanting 'somebody who could hold her own with Mlle Lion and Mlle Lavauden', and Duckworth speculative: his own hierarchy placed first those with a spark of 'fiery vitality', but his question of how such attributes were to be measured went unanswered.

Nor did Emmeline's fishing expeditions in the AHM net a suitable woman prepared to leave her present job. In 1943 Sir Paul himself resigned Roedean's chairmanship to Sir Robert Pickard, a research chemist knighted in 1937 when he was elected Vice-Chancellor of London University. As the war outlook improved Emmeline's efforts to retire subsided. Carrying on a school, any school, demanded much of a head's initiative in any case, as shortages grew worse and textbooks more dog-eared – publishers preferred to eke out the ream weights allotted by thinning paper on more profitable books, since light textbook papers could not be further stretched. Paper was a basic school resource; but everything dwindled or disappeared, it seemed, for laboratory science and domestic science, for art and handicrafts, and in some areas geography teachers were discouraged from local mapping by local defence authorities.

Nevertheless a new care for education was growing in the public mind, so that Sixth Form work increased generally despite the birth-rate-induced fall in adolescent numbers, and at Roedean too the Sixth Form achieved unprecedented numbers. In 1939, 80,673 candidates sat the School Certificate examinations, but in 1945, 91,853 candidates entered, Roedeanians writing their papers amid the miscellaneous curios of the Keswick Museum. Both at independent and at LEA secondary schools numbers increased, and again Roedean shared the trend so that many on the waiting list had to be told that test success could not guarantee entry. From June 1942 the Board of Education had realised that more staff were and would be needed, and from that date positively encouraged LEAs to employ married women, including qualified part-timers, and insisted teaching was war-work, for the Ministry of Labour was now adding an ever-wider range of women to its compulsory registers. 'No woman teacher should feel any doubt where her duty lies,' said Board Circular 1579 in January 1942.

So Emmeline soldiered on. For younger girls she was simply the figure leading Prayers, the ultimate but hardly known source of all authority, and typical of these was the girl to whom Emmeline 'was rather a remote figure ... I never made the Sixth Form, which was her domain. Friends in the Sixth admired her greatly', for there she functioned as form mistress, in so far as they needed one. The Sixth Form room now was the 'rather cramped Reference Library', a panelled room which had once been the hotel's smoking-room, and Emmeline would sweep in before lessons started to discourse to the girls on anything that caught her mind, discuss the contents of magazines available, relate anecdotes of incidents, enquire what they thought the most important things learned at boarding school. Sometimes she contributed to the weekend lectures and sometimes to the subject girls called 'Civilisation', run by the senior modern language mistresses, Thyra

Creyke-Clark and Thérèse Lavauden, who skilfully infused prestige to participation and dealt broadly with European culture.

Her other regular contact with girls was at lunch, the school's main meal, taken all together at assorted tables in the dining-room, each table with a mistress or prefect round whom the girls circulated to give variety, Emmeline presiding in the centre as once at Nuneaton in another war. Again they conversed: one girl 'was astonished one day when I was "sitting up" to her at lunch that she had been to see the film *Le jour s'élève*; we had the most animated discussion about Jean Gabin's performance.' But when wet weekends kept girls indoors staff checked beforehand on whether films at the local cinema were suitable, and when the cashier brightly called one 'honky-tonk' another amusement was found. Emmeline's knowledge of the girls derived partly from attentive observation as she moved around the school's varied premises, but mainly from the daily housemistresses' meetings, and she found these mother-substitutes the more forthcoming because, as they agreed, she left 'those under her to do their jobs, satisfied that they could do so. She accepted that a housemistress knew the girls in her House better than she did when any difficulty arose,' said one of her secretaries.

Second in her list of 'gains' Emmeline noted 'contacts with life and people of town', and in her notes betrayed how deep was her hunger to be a part of local life by leaping ahead of the more cautious and mundane assessments of others. Particularly at first some thought the people of Keswick reserved, a tight-knit community slightly suspicious, slightly resentful of outsiders, at least if these came trailing a name associated with social and financial advantage. The more acute recognised that much of Roedean's contact was in spasmodic bouts of co-operation for particular occasions rather than integration, though certainly a closer relation than at Brighton.

Emmeline later enlarged on how the school's artistic side developed links, surprisingly, she said, amid the general shortages and restrictions, on how the orchestra played and the choir sang for parish or YMCA entertainments, how they produced the York Nativity Play in St John's Church one Christmas or an ambitious 'Festival of Dance and Verse' outdoors in summer on the Hotel's lawn, and presented other drama, sometimes for invited audiences but in their last summer for the public, on the stage of the local cinema. She mentioned how senior girls gave dinner every week to thirty-five evacuee children, and all joined in the war-work of fruit picking, collecting sphagnum moss for wound dressing, foxgloves for digitalin and rose hips for babies' vitamin-rich syrup; she talked of the Girl Guides and Rangers and how Roedean girls became Sea Rangers on SRS *Cumberland*; she dwelt on the lectures and music as well as science shared with Keswick School, and the kindness of its head who lent a hall when needed and judged competitions with an expert eye. Meanwhile she herself drew closer to the heads of the north-west and was often asked to speak at their schools.

The clergy provided a second point of entry and so she could refer to girls who sang in the choir (the lucky alto next to the tenors was passed sweets by the local policeman, but that she did not add), or learned bell-ringing at Crosthwaite church. She organised links with two churches especially, since attendance had to be split, but the Victorian barrel-vaulted St John's in the town was much less popular with the girls than beautiful medieval Crosthwaite, where the sermons were to their taste and whither they walked along the riverside and in season watched salmon leaping up the weir. With delighted laughter Emmeline heard how some girls had been seen trying to help the valiant failures with their lacrosse sticks.

Yet she did not mention how occasional taunts of 'Rodine rat poison' – a brand name of the time – sometimes greeted them in the streets, and kept among her quotations a remark in Brogan's *English People* that 'the shopping voice of many products of Roedean or Wycombe Abbey is one of the most distressing sounds in the world'. She did not recall publicly how girls bought off-ration lemonade crystals and Horlicks tablets in the local shops, illicit addenda to the ration of murky chocolate or boiled sweets weekly doled out by housemistresses. And certainly she did not relate how she discovered some girls, in unsupervised preparation time, had been going into Keswick to buy fish and chips or how at Prayers her temper swept over them, exacerbated because taking more than their share of vital resources was the very complaint levelled at public schools in general. Every culprit should see her in her room, she announced, and a crowd of nearly a hundred eddied round the door. Emmeline hated it when girls abused their freedom, but one fierce young critic thought her too gentle with some staff, towards the end of the war, tolerating inefficiencies and excuses for lateness at lessons.

For, whatever the 'thrills and opportunities' their headmistress found, much remained to irk both staff and girls, and in congested rooms the lonely felt still lonelier and unkind teasing, cold-shouldering and other petty bullying became still more painful. Personal relationships remained central to happiness. Ruth Gauntlett summed up succinctly: 'I loved the laughter with my friends when lessons were over. I hated the food and the cold.' Food rules were repeatedly broken in ways less likely to upset delicate relations with the town. 'Being a sub-prefect,' said Ruth, 'I had to see the bedrooms were tidy: if I saw food about I would pretend I had not seen it and say I was coming back again. The food had always disappeared so no one got into trouble.' The Wivells had not chosen to reach the school's heart through its stomach, and, some said bitterly, war conditions did not account for insects in vegetables or the erratic treatment of porridge. 'Jews and vegetarians were catered for – I was the only vegetarian who did not eat fish,' said Ruth, and so avoided the kippers some liked and others grew to dread for their daily reappearance until a consignment was finished. Those who returned to Brighton in 1946 observed an immediate improvement, though rationing remained severe.

The cold was barely alleviated by the closed mica-windowed stoves and small fires that heated the hotel and station class-rooms. Usually girls resorted to 'jumpers' over pyjamas at night, with thick bedsocks, and double-folded blankets to multiply the layers. Icicles hung in the studio, ice made slippery the subway to one of the station classrooms, and walks between lesson locations kept circulations alive. In Emmeline's account such discomforts played a small role but even as she talked of the war-time school in South Africa in 1948-9 she observed with astonished enjoyment the comparative plenty of real butter, real eggs, ample fruit. In the Keswick cold her knees stiffened, worse after she tripped once at King's Cross and endured a slow journey north sitting cramped, her knee swelling, in silent pain.

The cold too at least once provoked delinquency when some girls took to augmenting the tiny buckets of coal allotted from a large pile discovered behind the hotel. Then both the Wivells and the railway authorities had to be pacified: this was railway coal and unsuitable for domestic use. To their faces girls were criticised but to outsiders they were defended with maternal loyalty. So Emmeline received in her study two ladies, strong-minded neighbouring landowners with reason for complaint. Roedean girls using a right of way across their land were entering *over* a gate locked for safety rather than *through* the slower wicket gate designed for walkers. Emmeline showed her visitors to comfortable armchairs, but habitually she talked on her feet, in sentences gathered up to her staff's admiration in long grammatical structures, and so she stood, benignly beaming, her only gestures the thumbs twirling in clasped hands, and unscrupulously cut the ground from below their feet. Girls continued to climb the gate.

Local acceptance improved with time and familiarity, it seems, but others endorsed more cautiously Emmeline's 1946 verdict that on leaving Keswick 'we should miss the consciousness of really being part of the community in which we lived'. Particularly the staff with rooms in the Hotel reckoned it 'an enclosed society with no one outside the school to talk to in free moments', for the most part, and for the girls boarding conditions enforced this.

Such were the conditions of one of Emmeline's lives, and the steady rhythm behind another, a life marked out in railway timetables and committee meetings.

Chapter 25
1944: Education Act and Fleming Report

Here is no place for a full discussion of the 1944 Education Act. Adequate accounts can be found in several of the books listed in the Bibliography. None, however, observes the processes of its shaping through the pince-nez of a secondary headmistress mindful that, though girls' secondary schools had a briefer history than boys' grammar schools, the High Schools of the later 19th century 'can claim to have played a very important role in the history of education in this country. They took part, in fact, in a notable educational experiment and, as in the case of the Grammar Schools, the Board of Education and the LEAs after 1902 built on the foundations they had laid.' For this claim, from the Fleming Committee's Interim Report on tuition fees in grant-aided secondary schools (1943), Emmeline bore partial responsibility.

As regards the Act proper Emmeline's role was that of a prominent headmistress, a representative and spokeswoman. She had been involved in its genesis when she shared in producing the Hadow Report on *The Education of the Adolescent* (1926); that report did not initiate but did enshrine in officialdom the notion that every child's education should be a sequence of stages, with secondary education of an appropriate kind for all. When in the later 1930s the Consultative Committee, now chaired by Will Spens, was asked to examine secondary education, however, the administrative framework of England still dictated that this term excluded three-quarters of the nation's children.

In 1938 the Spens Report recommended that the system should be broadened to admit all over-11s with 'parity of schools in the secondary stage' (recommendation 132), with 'three types of Secondary School, attended by children over 11, which we have named Modern Schools, Grammar Schools, and Technical High Schools to be administered under a new Code of Regulations for Secondary Schools' (134), all with the same minimum leaving age of 16 (150).[1] The report's Grammar School was based on the existing secondary schools, as embodied in Nuneaton or Bedford High Schools, and dwelt in detail on desirable curricular and examination reforms; its Modern School assumed the pattern planned in the 1926 Hadow Report, while the Technical High Schools were envisaged as an intellectually vigorous and clearly focused option developed from the junior technical schools.

When, therefore, the AHM gathered for their 1939 Conference at Bradford Grammar School for Girls the main topic chosen by their President, Emmeline, was inevitably the Spens Report. Assembled headmistresses of potential grammar schools heard Dorothy Brock, as a member of the

336 / Doors of Possibility

Consultative Committee, explain how the report tried to bring education for children over 11 into correspondence with the structure of modern society and modern economic facts in the face of a deplorable cleavage between technical and more academic types of secondary education and of a striking disparity in provision. Its main purpose, she declared, was to show the need to bring all post-primary schools into a state of 'parity' and to modify curricula to suit the needs of every pupil.[2]

Half a dozen speakers followed, dealing with various aspects from the proposed teaching establishment to the problems of sorting children into appropriate schools and syllabus changes in science, but from Muriel Davies came, subjoined to a general welcome for a step towards democracy, the observation that the Consultative Committee had made no attempt to fit private and public schools into the national secondary system envisaged. No one, and certainly not the AHM President, needed to be reminded that these wielded influence disproportionate to their numbers.

In answer to a recent Question in the House of Commons, however, the Parliamentary Secretary for Education had said that administrative reorganisation on Spens' lines was too expensive,[3] and so life went on much as before and the majority of children drifted up through elementary schools and left at 14, until a massive administrative effort evacuated city children at the outbreak of war. Though the AHM's 1940 Conference had to be cancelled, at a springtime meeting in 1941 headmistresses debated 'A Post-War Policy' with a view to achieving concerted, positive, professional policies.

Shortly afterwards, in June, a small pamphlet was received from the Board of Education, entitled 'Education after the war' and bound in green paper. This, the 'Green Book', was purportedly confidential, a discussion document for the professionally interested, but its very secrecy secured publicity and educational reform was treated to unusual public discussion. The Green Book was the work of senior civil servants at the Board at a time when, on the one hand, the upheavals of war and evacuation had provoked stronger social yearnings for equality and unity and encouraged LEAs to accept more readily central planning and control, and, on the other hand, the power of officials within the Board had been strengthened (though as a body the Board was comparatively weak) by a decade of uninterested, short-stay or frankly feeble Presidents.[4] It proposed free secondary education of some type for all children over 11, with some opportunities to continue after the minimum leaving age; it discussed such essential issues as the leaving age and the age and means of transfer to secondary schools; and it identified significant administrative stumbling-blocks.

Now Emmeline became more closely implicated, for she was on the drafting committees set up by both the AHM and the Joint Four to draft the responses requested. In July 1941, however, before these were submitted, Richard A. Butler arrived at the Board as its new President. In *The Art of the Possible* (1971) he admitted he would rather have been Viceroy of India, but, given Education by the Coalition Government, he recognised a chance to shape the future. Already he was slightly known to Emmeline, for his wife Sydney was an Old Roedeanian and he had addressed the school on its 1938 Speech Day, evincing then a proper respect for education (if no profundities of knowledge or thought inappropriate to the occasion) and a preference for the variegated 'herbaceous border' of English education over tidy greenhouses, as well as an explicit regard for public schools in the English sense of the term.[5]

More important, as President he was prepared to act, indeed determined. If he cared for it, he had Emmeline's approval. 'I have several times wanted to write a note to you,' she informed him a few months later, 'to say what a comfort it is to feel that we have a President who is giving his mind, his energy and his interest whole-heartedly to the many problems connected with education at this time, and is never content to deal with any subject superficially.'[6] It was typical of her to avoid explicit comparisons.

By then Butler had been involved in a heavy round of meetings, speeches and negotiations with as many sectors as possible, the churches (proprietors of more than half the schools affected, with slightly under half the children), the local authorities, the universities, employers, unions, bodies like the Co-operative Union and the WEA, eminent thinkers of the left like R. H. Tawney, Harold Laski and G. D. H. Cole, and his own colleagues of both right and left. In the Coalition his very able and level-headed Parliamentary Secretary was James Chuter Ede, a Labour MP and future Home Secretary, once an elementary teacher and with more educational experience than Butler, who learned to trust him. But the most eminent of all Butler's colleagues, the Prime Minister himself, was at first reluctant to countenance any new Education Bill, remembering the divisive storms over the 1902 Act. Still, 'having viewed the milk and honey from the top of Pisgah,' said Butler, 'I was damned if I was going to die in the land of Moab ... I knew that if I spared him [Churchill] the religious controversies and party political struggles of 1902, and side-tracked the public schools issue, I could win him over.'[7]

The 'religious controversies' related to the church-provided elementary schools and the changes in finance and control entailed by any scheme for redistributing post-primary pupils into any full secondary system, and, except in that the settlement entailed defining and regularising the relation of all LEA-aided schools to their LEAs, did not affect Emmeline. Recently, however, a more genuinely religious interest had been promoted, articulated most imposingly in a rare display of unity by the Archbishops of Canterbury and York, the Roman Catholic Archbishop of Westminster, and the Moderator of Free Church Federal Council when they wrote to *The Times* (21 December 1940) to urge equal educational opportunities for all and linked discovering and developing each child's particular capacity to a sense of divine vocation in daily work. This the Archbishops of Canterbury, York and Wales followed up in February 1941, again in *The Times*, with a plea for

Christian instruction for all and a daily act of worship in all schools. Neither were then required in schools provided by LEAs, and the 224 MPs who signed a similar declaration in July were perhaps justified in detecting widespread if vague apprehension at declining faith, the commonplace view that 'something ought to be done', and the standard answer that 'it ought to be taught in schools', rather as health care was channelled through them.

So, when the Joint Four delivered their thoughts on the Green Book, they included near the end the consensus opinion of secondary masters and mistresses on religious instruction, a normal feature of secondary schools but delivered with patchy expertise. Yes, it was desirable (with conscientious objection respected) but statutory compulsion was wholly undesirable, the letter killing the spirit, and teachers should be free to frame their own syllabuses. This line both the IAHM, AHM, IAAM, and AAM jointly, and the AHM separately, maintained in every subsequent policy statement before the Act, but when Butler met the secondary associations in December 1942 he insisted that the country 'was particularly interested in finding a place for religious teaching in schools', and told them that the requirement for an act of worship and instruction had been included in discussions with the churches for the reorganisation of the system.[8]

This reorganisation was the Joint Four's main concern. Their memorandum was to cover much the same ground as the AHM's (see pp. 343-4), but with a more conservative bent. Unlike the AHM individually, however, the Joint Four were not prepared to commit themselves to the policy of abolishing fees in all schools receiving public money, including those with direct grant from the Board.

Two paragraphs at least bear the signs of compromise drafting. One concerned 'multilateral' schools, then understood as broad-entry schools with two or three sides or streams and some common activities. These Spens had discouraged; others thought they deserved experimental development, and the Joint Four wording reflected both. The second Joint Four compromise concerned the schools omitted by Spens, but not, as Churchill had underlined to Butler, for their insignificance. The Joint Four recognised 'that the existence of some efficient Public and Independent schools is threatened and that their disappearance would be a loss to the nation.' They, therefore, asked for measures which would enable 'all children of suitable age, best fitted to profit' from a boarding school education to attend such schools, and they accepted that if public and independent schools were to receive some public money, some form of 'public supervision' was inevitable. Yet they asked too that such schools should retain 'a degree of independence similar to that now enjoyed by the "Direct Grant" schools'.[9]

This paragraph reflected the drafters' knowledge of negotiations on 'the public schools problem'. At the end of 1941 the Board official most deeply involved passed to Emmeline some papers summarising a series of moves since 1938 and projecting a possible policy – though no one had yet succeeded in defining limits to the term 'public school'. The HMC liked to think election to their membership identified a bona fide public-school headmaster, and the rules for membership dictated a school of considerable size, a goodly number of boys sent regularly to universities, and that schools should not be privately owned and should have a properly constituted governing body. The more nebulous matter of a school's standing also counted.

For one aspect of the schools' emergence as an issue it hardly mattered; for the 'public schools' generated most heat through their symbolic value, resting largely on the reputation of fewer than a score of boys' boarding schools for yielding massive advantage to the pupils who could afford their fees and expect to inherit a disproportionate amount of power in politics, the Diplomatic and Civil Services, the law and the Church, even bank and railway company directorships. Not, indeed, by any statutory privilege, but, on the one hand, because such schools could afford a high teacher-pupil ration, strong Sixth Forms, adequate playing-fields, libraries and laboratories, and, on the other hand, because whether their boys applied to university or for significant promotions at work they encountered authorities who had been to the same schools and 'liked the smell of the same herd', in a phrase from Aneurin Bevan's contribution to a series of papers on the subject.[10] Public schools, whatever they were and however they differed one from another, were identified as a source of inequality. This R. H. Tawney had argued since his *Equality* of 1931, and in September 1941 he told Butler in a private meeting that it was 'essential to tackle the public schools question', and a few free placers would be socially a bad solution – they 'would think themselves heaven-sent,' he said.[11] Criticisms of the schools' internal organisation and ethos were often extremely bitter, but less politically divisive.

In this aspect of the story girls were invisible. In a second aspect they were absent. Here the story tells how, fearful of falling numbers in 1938, and fearful too that the declining birth-rate and rising tax rates would erode their constituencies further, the HMC engaged in a complex dance around the Board of Education in an effort to obtain public subsidy at the least possible cost of change. Admittedly their leader, Spencer Leeson, headmaster of Winchester, preferred to stress rather their educational ideals and intellectual standards, and the sense of public duty which stirred their consciences to share more widely 'the undeniable benefits of a public boarding school education'.[12] Fortunately, details of HMC discussions, individual initiatives, area conferences with LEAs and other schools, all can be ignored, for the headmasters lent some colour to one criticism – that enclosed male communities bred disdain for women – by their efforts to ignore those girls' schools which liked to claim a similar status. Almost as soon as Butler arrived at the Board of Education, the official most involved, G. G. Williams, summarised the position in a memorandum and remarked *en passant* that it would be wiser to deal with the boys' school problem 'before considering the different and in some respects more complicated one of Girls' Boarding Schools'.[13] Earlier, with the other two authors of a report commissioned by the HMC, Williams had stated girls' schools should be omitted from the remit of the Royal Commission favoured.

But the ripples spread out. Because schools' governing bodies were necessarily party to any proceedings, those for HMC schools formed an association to discuss and propound common views; the Governing Bodies' Association (GBA) was constituted in July 1941 and chaired by Geoffrey Fisher, Bishop of London and once headmaster of Repton. In consequence governors of comparable girls' schools, in many cases the same men, began to feel they too should organise in the face of possible change, particularly as girls' schools had no equivalent to the HMC.

A second ripple was set moving when the HMC's self-definition as headmasters of 'public schools' touched the proposal to abolish fees in grant-aided schools. At present public money was granted to secondary schools in varied ways. Some schools LEAs had provided, and these they maintained and controlled; some not originally provided by LEAs had been 'municipalised' and were now wholly supported by the local authority. For others not originally provided, among them most of the ancient boys' grammar schools, LEAs granted funds on various terms, while others again had in 1926 chosen to receive funds directly from the Board of Education. For this last group, known as direct grant schools, local authorities supplied only a minority of governors and the percentage of free or special place children which was the condition of the direct grant.

The elementary system was free throughout, to the minimum leaving age; not so the secondary system, not even in LEA schools. The proportion of free and special places had risen steadily, so that by 1938, 45.8 per cent of the 470,003 pupils at aided schools paid no fees, but within individual schools none might pay, as in some LEA schools, or more than 80 per cent might, as in some direct grant schools. Fees and freedom from LEA 'interference' marched in step to some eyes; in others' eyes fees and the principle of equal access conflicted. If the secondary system was to be enlarged it was, the latter said, unfair and illogical that some parts of it could charge fees while senior elementary schools now upgraded would not.

Of the members of the HMC, 83 were heads of independent schools (with 29,729 boys in 1942) and 99 of schools aided by direct grant or LEAs (with 41,231 boys). GBA membership came from substantially the same schools, though with only 65 direct grant and other aided schools. At that time there were altogether 232 direct grant schools, including those for girls, a very miscellaneous group educationally but administratively indistinguishable from the Board of Education's point of view. In a systematic review of secondary provision the future of direct grant must come into question, and now, because of the composition of the HMC, it seemed also part of the 'public schools problem'.

Mindful of Churchill's warning, cautioned by the Parliamentary Secretary Chuter Ede that the topic of public schools was 'far more likely to be disruptive of political unity in the world of today than the religious question',[14] after three months in office Butler was telling the GBA Chairman Fisher that he was reluctant to legislate on public schools. He was 'really reaching the realisation that there is no man-made or heaven-made solution', he said to G. G. Williams; Chuter Ede recalled how 'the fiercest antagonisms were aroused on both sides' in a Commons debate the year before.[15]

On 2 December 1941 the headmistresses and governors of such girls' schools as were reckoned the equivalent to the HMC schools met to consider an equivalent to the GBA, and established a preliminary committee of four heads and four governors to organise the association and deal with matters arising. One of the heads was Emmeline, and another Osyth Potts of Liverpool Girls' College, Huyton, the current President of the AHMBS and a friend of Emmeline's since she had started a school in Switzerland in partnership with an Old Roedeanian, in 1927. Osyth Potts was keeping G. G. Williams of the Board in touch with the new association's birthpangs and to her he wrote on 29 December: 'I do not think it is any good trying to give any views about the future of girls' boarding schools until we see how the situation develops. The difficulty, of course, is that it is much easier to delimit a recognised body of boys' public schools of accepted status [he meant the HMC] than it is in the case of girls. This I am sure you will recognise, and its political implications.'[16]

At the same time he briefed Emmeline, outgoing Chairman of the Joint Four, on the problems and proposals. She replied on 6 January that the first problem was indeed

> to decide what schools are to be included. Very much against my personal wish and mainly owing to the Bishop of Southampton and the Headmaster of Winchester [in their capacity as girls' governors] the resolution that was passed at the preliminary meeting was that an Association of Governing Bodies of Independent and Direct Grant Girls' Schools should be formed. I feel that the inclusion of Direct Grant schools is a great mistake, but I believe that some of them are in such a funk (boys' perhaps more than girls') about the possibility of their fees being abolished that they want to cling to any chance of help in remaining at least semi-independent. I believe our problem is a mainly boarding-school problem which is shared also by independent schools which have a reasonable number of boarders, but St Paul's and Edgbaston High School had put in a special plea for independent day schools to be considered, and so the resolution took the form given above.[17]

The papers on the 'public schools question' were to be circulated among the committee of the AHMBS, and a meeting was due in a few days' time; meanwhile, said Emmeline, the emergency headmistress/governor committee would meet. She turned to consider the 'problem' itself:

> I am really disturbed about your main suggestion about policy in regard to public schools – the consultation with LEAs with a view to their

fitting into the regional framework, if the LEAs are to include County Boroughs, and I do not see how that is to be avoided. As you know, I have worked as a headmistress in a maintained school, a Direct Grant school and an independent school, and I have served on an Education Committee in one or other of these places for the greater part of the last thirty years. One of the things that causes me most anxiety about the future of secondary education is the deterioration in the personnel of Education Committees and the increase in them of petty political (not necessarily party-political) influences. I was ideally happy under Mr Bolton King and the Warwickshire County Council. Whether I should be happy under present administration there I do not know ...

She told Williams frankly of her unhappiness with the Brighton Committee, and the similar accounts she had heard from colleagues in the AHM, before moving to another policy suggestion and announcing herself

tremendously in favour of the use of our premises for short courses and holiday camps, and our playing fields for recreation, and for connecting us more closely with the educational and social work of the district. My experiences as an evacuated school in Keswick where we are part of the community has made me realise that it is a vital need in the life of girls from 16 to 18 or 19 in boarding schools. From the point of view of the children themselves I think it is infinitely better for them to go to a boarding school away from their own district. This will be more than ever the case during the transition period when boarders come from even more varied types of home than they do now, and when consciousness of social distinction still exists ...

Already her mind leapt ahead to grapple with the introduction of new and poorer children, tentative and embryonic as such proposals yet were. 'I did not mean to write so much,' she added, before continuing with more, recalling objections Lynda Grier had raised to boarding as a system.

The features identified in Emmeline's letter, particularly the inclusion of direct grant schools, wariness towards LEAs, and the value of boarding, define the topography she, and all those trying to cope with the 'public schools problem', explored in the next four years. Writing in her clear bold hand, she finished with the last major feature:

I ought to have said earlier in this letter that it is the fitting of the boarding schools into the national scheme and making them of most use to the country as a whole that concerns me most, far more than the financial problem, acute though that may be. If we cannot manage to exist financially we should change our character or cease to be. We have so much to give that we must not allow to be lost, but how to avoid its being spoilt by the pettiness of some LEAs and of some Directors I don't know, except by dealing directly with the Board which I have never found anything but broad-minded and helpful. Even then the most difficult part of the problem remains – how to fit us in. Yours very sincerely ...

This was the Christmas holiday of 1941-2, and Emmeline was at the Forum Club in Belgrave Square, increasingly her London base and haven, before returning to Keswick for the start of the new term and her own attempts to retire. AHM affairs swung back to the fore as preparations were made for their annual Conference to be held at Malvern on 8 and 9 April. Here the headmistresses were to discuss and vote on the policy for educational change Emmeline had helped draft.

Twelve resolutions were passed, the basis of the Memorandum concocted by the Executive Committee to edify the Board of Education. First stood the need for a national system beginning with nursery schools for all who wished, moving to infant schools for children of 5 to 7, primary schools for those of 7 to 11, and then secondary education for all to at least 16. It was equally easy to agree that infant and junior schools must have high standards of equipment and staff and smaller classes, and that LEAs should be required to provided health treatment; it had long been agreed that private schools should be inspected and registered, and that part-time day continuation should be available to all and compulsory up to the age of 18. That more women should sit on LEAs was equally uncontroversial. Some were doubtful about 11 as the transfer age to secondary education but all believed such transfer should take place, and all opposed using a competitive examination as a transfer device.

The first resolution had recommended secondary education should be of the present type (tending towards Spens' Grammar type), or with a practical bias (the Modern school of Hadow and Spens) or with a technical, commercial or trade bias, and the fourth that these forms should all be sheltered under a common secondary code as regards staffing, class size and building standards, but strong support for multilateral forms prompted the Executive Committee to add that these types of education should be either closely co-ordinated or conjoint in multilateral schools – 'we must beware of early and rigid segregation of different types of intellect, of looking upon certain schools as leading inevitably to certain types of occupation'.

Debate arose round Resolution Five, finally agreed as:

That in the opinion of this Association (a) the whole educational system of this country should embody the principles of democracy; (b) no financial or social barrier should therefore prevent any child from receiving the education best suited to his needs and abilities; (c)(i) no fees should be charged for tuition in Secondary Schools in receipt of public money, (ii) any financial loss incurred by those schools, other than private schools, which are not maintained or aided by an LEA should be made good from public funds until such time as those schools may be included in the general scheme of education, (iii) some way should be found of bringing the independent schools into relation with the national system.[18]

An amendment moved by Muriel Davies and asking that 'private, public, proprietary and independent schools should be abolished or incorporated in the national system' was lost by only 55 votes.

A second debate lit passions with religious fires, before the AHM voted in favour of 'Christian teaching and practice' in schools but against 'any statutory requirement thereof'. Finally, however, Emmeline was able to voice the vote of thanks to the President, Dorothy de Zouche, for the way she had presided over one of the longest 'and probably one of the most momentous' of AHM Conferences, and Dorothy de Zouche herself could announce the end of her emergency-extended presidency with the election of Agnes Catnach, once Emmeline's Chairman of Committee.

At the same time Butler and the Board were striving to redefine the 'public schools problem' in terms justifying omission from the Bill. To the GBA Butler said he preferred to distinguish boarding from day schools, not independent and direct grant schools from LEA-aided schools, since direct grant itself linked schools to the national system; and to the NUT – a body by no means sympathetic to the social image of public schools – that he wished to offer boarding facilities as one of the alternatives for children leaving primary schools.[19] This duly appeared in the Bill itself, in a clause dealing with the development plans demanded of all LEAs. In April a meeting was arranged between Butler and Fisher, the GBA chairman, to discuss how public schools could provide such facilities, perhaps paid for out of direct grant with some Board representatives on governing bodies.

Meanwhile G. G. Williams attacked from another angle, testing the HMC's reaction to changes in the direct grant system and the possibility of abolishing fees in such schools.[20] Headmasters fought back with a defence of both direct grant and fees as guarantors of freedom and parental choice, and implicitly suffered no split in their ranks between heads of (mainly independent) boarding schools and (mainly direct grant) day schools.

When Butler met Fisher, on 22 April, the Bishop favoured forming a committee of three governors and three headmasters to evolve a scheme to supply boarding places for state pupils, a cosy notion prompted by a meeting of the HMC and GBA earlier in April.[21] Chuter Ede at once warned Butler such a committee would stir distrust. Any such body must include 'people from origins not associated with the public school tradition ... whose views carry weight in working-class circles', and, he added, there was 'likely to be trouble unless a woman serves'.[22] So the committee idea took shape, as an exercise in bomb disposal, detaching the 'public schools problem' safely from the negotiations to reshape administration for the great mass of children.

At subsequent meetings Butler told Fisher they must avoid the impression of 'ready-made proposals hatched by the Board and the public schools', the projected committee 'would not be a tame one', and it must include a representative of organised labour.[23] When in May he met the Labour intellectuals G. D. H. Cole and Harold Laski for a broad-ranging discussion and the 'public schools problem' arose, Butler was reassured to find Cole mildly tolerant, believing that if such schools renounced any claims to train 'leaders' and focused on themselves as the boarding element in a national system they could enjoy a happy future.[24] And though exceedingly busy with other work Cole agreed a few weeks later that he would serve on the committee planned.

Formally its members would sit as individuals, so as not to commit any organisations; in practice one interest was balanced against another.[25] Some were easily selected: Cole for the intellectual left, for example, though for traditionalists A. W. Pickard-Cambridge, the recently retired Vice-Chancellor of Sheffield University, himself a classicist and brother of another, seemed '*passé*', sniffed a Board minute. Sir James Aitken, the Chairman of Lancashire Education Committee, was a favourite from the start, and a second LEA member was found in A. L. Binns, the West Riding's Director of Education and Secretary to the Association of Directors and Secretaries for Education, despite some inflammatory remarks on public schools lately reported from his Chairman. There were three headmasters. From Charterhouse (excoriated years before by Robert Graves in *Goodbye To All That*) came Robert Birley, a liberal idealist sure he was right, who had in 1926 put the strikers' case to Eton pupils and in 1931 organised relief for the unemployed of Slough; from the direct grant Nottingham High School came Cedric Reynolds, also of the HMC but said to carry weight with the IAHM; and Arthur Nichols of Hele's School, Exeter, founded by a trust but 'municipalised' in 1921, made up the score.

Teacher training and education research were embodied in M. L. Jacks, the energetic Director of the Oxford University Department of Education. The Bishop of London, Fisher himself, represented the GBA, supported by Sir Edward Crowe of the Harpur Trust and its direct grant schools. A colourful figure now in old age with a bush of white hair and a monocle, Crowe had come to the Harpur Trust since Emmeline's days at Bedford, where he himself had been educated before spending 27 years in the Far East as a commercial diplomat, to return in 1924 to direct the foreign activities of the Department of Overseas Trade. He was no scholar, any more than the choice from the employers' world, Allan Macdiarmid, public-school-educated Chairman and Managing Director of Stewarts and Lloyds Ltd. As it turned out, Macdiarmid rarely attended meetings and resigned after a year.

A trade unionist was required and Harold Clay of the TGWU was recommended as 'one of the most sensible of the trade unionists on matters of education' and a fellow of Nuffield College, the Labour establishment at Oxford. The Treasurer of the NUT, H. N. Penlington, supplied a voice from the elementary sector. The special problems of Wales were guaranteed a hearing by the inclusion of William Gruffydd, most Welsh of Welshmen, Professor of Celtic at the University College of Cardiff and the President of the Council of the National Eisteddfod of Wales – in 1909 he had himself won the Crown – as well as MP for the University of Wales.

Chuter Ede had insisted on a woman; Emmeline's name, as past Chairman of the Joint Four and headmistress of an independent boarding school, was on the earliest draft lists, soon joined by that of Dorothy Brock, also an ex-

President of the AHM, and head of the Mary Datchelor School, a day school founded by the Clothworkers' Company and now aided by the LCC. The Board knew her well, for she served on many committees, and might, if they cared, have found her views in a collection of essays published by the AHM in 1937, where her credal statement that 'I believe in variety and in a community life which mixes girls of different social background and different kinds of ability' was developed with keen analytical skill;[26] but she was no revolutionary. Ten years younger than Emmeline Dorothy Brock had seen the 'notable educational experiment' through a pupil's eyes, at a GPDST school from where she had progressed to Girton College, Cambridge. Finally, since the Governing Bodies of Girls' Schools Association (GBGSA) was now a reality, it was decided to ask its Secretary, Sir Ernest Pooley, a sturdy, genial man of Emmeline's own age, legally-trained and since 1908 the Clerk to the Drapers' Company, and a member of the London University Senate.

Only a Chairman was lacking. Rather to Butler's gratification the Lord Chancellor discreetly offered himself, telling Butler he had been a scholar at Fettes, in Scotland. 'I could never have gone to a public school if it had not been for this piece of luck – and I must add, if it had not been for my parents' sacrifice,' wrote John Simon.[27] But a member of the Government was inappropriate, they decided, and lit instead on a Scottish judge, educated at Glasgow High School and the universities of Glasgow and Edinburgh, and therefore untainted. David Fleming – Lord Fleming by virtue of Scottish legal custom – had done well since 1940, remarked Butler, on the London appeals tribunal for conscientious objectors, also emotive; he had once been, very briefly, an MP, and 'understands our ways'. He accepted. Butler thought him humourless, and certainly he preferred the lucid to the graceful, but his appointment won the widespread trust required. When the names were announced publicly in July 1942 the press generally reckoned that some decision to 'democratise' public schools had already been taken.[28]

Believing as she did in the importance of seeing from others' points of views, detaching the mind from its subjectivity as the best way to good judgment, Emmeline found such a mixed committee ideal. They met first on 28 July, and thereafter usually monthly, sitting through two consecutive days. From the meetings Emmeline would return to Keswick bright-eyed, to expound the issues to her Roedean staff, inventing imaginary examples with picturesque detail, and to listen to them, testing the women who could make or mar a girl's happiness at school – the housemistresses.

The reference given had been carefully worked out, and as usual applied only to England and Wales; Fettes, and the other half-dozen Scottish schools deemed to qualify, had been quietly sounded but held aloof. More worryingly, the Provost of Eton had already informed the Board, with cold dignity, that Eton neither wished for public money nor to be in any way an organ of the state. No design could succeed if the largest and most prestigious of public schools kept its distance.

The Fleming Committee were asked:

To consider means whereby the association between the Public Schools (by which term is meant schools which are in membership of the Governing Bodies' Association or Headmasters' Conference) and the general educational system of the country could be developed and extended; also to consider how far any measures recommended in the case of boys' Public Schools could be applied to comparable schools for girls.

Girls 'cannot be left out', the Board had decided, though its Permanent Secretary, Maurice Holmes, continued to grumble that 'there is no earthly reason for dragging them into the scheme', and preparatory discussion of the terms of reference foresaw 'special problems': 'The number of girls' schools available is much fewer and the advantages of boarding education in the case of girls by no means so widely recognised by the public at large. Further the aims of secondary education in the case of girls and the careers open to them are less obvious than in the case of boys.'[29]

'I cannot tell you how glad I am that you have remembered the girls' schools,' wrote Emmeline in reply to her invitation to serve on the committee,[30] and the yardstick for suitable girls' schools was discovered in membership of the new GBGSA, all these being reasonably large with solid Sixth Forms, either independent (80 schools) or direct grant (59 schools), and, as with the boys of HMC schools, boarders were a minority. Much of the committee's eventual report devoted itself to wrenching apart consideration of boarding from ideas for the future of the heterogeneous group of schools confronting them, and in the end they ignored the group named by the terms of reference and proposed schemes open to any schools not conducted for private profit, recognised as efficient, and approved by the Board.

Doubts about girls carried over, however, into the 'Notes for consideration' supplied to witnesses. Witnesses were adjured to 'bear in mind that there are fewer boarding schools for girls, but a considerable number of girls' Public Day Schools, the importance of which to the present enquiry may be relatively greater than that of similar boys' schools.' Specifically, witnesses should consider: '(a) whether the relative advantages of a Boarding and Day School education are necessarily the same for girls as for boys; (b) whether the general characteristics of girls' Public Schools, which are mostly comparatively recent foundations, are similar to those of the boys' Public Schools.'[31]

No doubts lodged in the evidence given by Maurice Holmes, Permanent Secretary to the Board of Education, in November 1942. Girls were irrelevant to the enquiry, he maintained, for the probable gain to a few girls of 'the education and amenities of schools such as Roedean or Wycombe Abbey' was not his primary concern. He told the Committee that he did not think it 'necessary in the national interest that the girls' Public Boarding Schools should be made available to a wider clientele'. In the case of boys, the argument rested on the schools' access to powerful positions, but 'experience has shown that, in spite of the fact that the House of Commons and the professions have been thrown open to women for a number of years, women do not in fact attain to high positions in public life to anything approaching the extent which might on purely numerical considerations be expected.'[32]

These remarks were 'heavily challenged', it was noted. Even if he correctly stated the present situation, committee members suggested, 'these were not valid reasons for excluding girls' schools ... it would be a serious thing if ... the girls' public schools remained as exclusive as they had been'. Sir Maurice insisted, however, that girls derived less advantage, and added that entry at eight, the age he suggested for boys, 'would be too early for girls'. From this long and lively session with Holmes Emmeline's notes survive: none refer to questions of gender but only to those of education (such as the advantage of high staff ratios) and class (including the TUC's angry rejection of bursary offers, as 'creaming' and 'delabourising the brightest', made in the aftermath of the Great War).

Of the other 164 witnesses, some individual, some representative of organisations, those primarily concerned with girls' education were too substantial a minority to be written off as tokens. The evidence of the GBGSA itself was inevitably accorded weight. Under the eyes of their Secretary, Pooley, and of the headmistress of a prominent member, Roedean, the GBGSA's vice-chairman, Ernest Gowers, admitted that too few girls' boarding places existed in their schools to make much contribution – the actual figure was about 10,500, and so annual admissions ran at about 2000. He thought, however, they could start with 10 per cent for children from LEA primary schools and rise gradually to 50 per cent. His colleague Ethel Steel, a Governor of the Godolphin School, Salisbury, assailed the Board's doubts on boarding value for girls. Many parents, she assured the committee, appreciated 'the regular, planned and kindly disciplined life' and 'the benefits of work done in quiet circumstances'.[33] If this were wishful thinking it functioned as a coded rebuff to pessimists.

What the Fleming Report, published as *Report of the Departmental Committee on the Public Schools and the General Educational System* (HMSO, 1944), eventually chose to quote, from the GBGSA's written memorandum, was the fighting statement of principle: 'We urge that the importance of a right education is at least as great for girls as for boys, if not greater ... If there is too great a "class consciousness", if snobbery still prevails, if "privilege" still holds too high a place, it is largely in the education and development of the minds and spirit of women that the remedy lies' (para. 240). Five years later this was glossed by Emmeline with the help of a quotation from Dr Aggrey, one of the founders of Achimote College in West Africa. '"Educate a man, and you educate an individual. Educate a woman, and you educate a family" ... Let us hope the women of West Africa will not have to wait as long as did their sisters in this country for the importance of the education of the mothers of the nation to be generally recognised,' she told the assembled heads of LEA grammar schools in 1949. Within the Fleming Committee the victory was elegantly negotiated, so that girls' schools were accorded a special chapter (as was Wales) to 'explain the differences between their history and traditions and those of Boys' Public Schools' but the recommendations explicitly 'apply equally' (para. 19) to both sexes, throughout.

The chapter on 'Girls' Schools' is tinged with virtuous triumphalism. Though places were fewer, adjustments should be easier, the committee decided, completely rejecting the initial view of the Board and the HMC. Pivotal is a passage differentiating the girls' public schools 'in the narrower sense of independent Boarding Schools' from those for boys (para. 239). First, 'A girl does not gain the same social privileges and professional advantages as a boy from the mere fact of having been educated at a Public School' – Holmes's point converted to an advantage. Secondly, staff moved more easily between types of school, and headmistresses of all types except the privately-owned mingled in the same Association. Thirdly, entrants from LEA primary schools would not be handicapped, as boys would be, by being unprepared for the curriculum they met, since in girls' schools not only was this more flexible, with a different emphasis on the individual subjects (para. 235), but habitually it was tailored more closely to the individual. Also, girls' schools were more accustomed to entrants from various educational backgrounds, not groomed to the boys' Common Entrance requirements – here was room for another quick knife-thrust at the 'often very poor' standards of small private schools. Hence the provision for preparatory bursaries envisaged for boys would be unnecessary. Girls' public schools, in short, were exclusive only because their fees limited their field of recruitment.

The committee sat for the last time in mid-June 1944, to complete the revision of the drafts. At the end Fleming told Butler that throughout 'there has been an atmosphere of complete goodwill and a desire to find a solution which can generally be regarded as satisfactory'.[34] That may be a conventional courtesy, but the Yorkshireman Binns, the West Riding Education Director, looked back 'with pleasure', he told Emmeline, 'on the spirit of co-operation which animated us' and added 'and on your forthright expression of views'.

Always Emmeline had attended, absorbedly, to the matter in hand, but now, driven as hard as she had ever been by pressure of work, she seems also to have developed a more rigorous approach to relevance, at least in her office at Roedean, her secretary of 1946 observed, and the digressive conversation she loved was rationed to her few off-duty hours. So too she kept her mind organised but only the most abbreviated and impersonal of written notes, to judge from those that survive in a small notebook filled with miscellaneous jottings on Roedean organisation, a conference agenda, references from books that interested her, and these scraps for the Fleming Committee are mere phrases, *aides-mémoire* to the inquisitor, never her own views. They may be unrepresentative. Their most prominent theme probes the demand for boarding, whether for the whole of the secondary stage for some or as an element, a year or two long, for most (an idea not favoured in the report).

Emmeline had been whole-heartedly in favour of including girls' boarding schools, and boarding departments of day schools, but dubious about the invidious inclusion of some day schools already linked to the national system by direct grant. She had opposed in vain the proposal to include them in the GBGSA, and by June 1942 had had to report to the AHM that the headmistresses of GBGSA schools were planning regular conferences. In fact this marked the birth of yet another association, roughly equating to the membership of the HMC in terms of standing, as Osyth Potts explained to Butler's Private Secretary in December. Its title was the most cumbersome yet, the Association of Head Mistresses of Independent and Direct Grant Schools (AHMIDG).

Like the HMC it did not include all direct grant schools, and so not all fell within the committee's terms of reference, but when Butler consulted Holmes on this anomaly, the Permanent Secretary advised block inclusion of direct grant schools, since these stood outside the general locally-funded system.[35] In November 1942 they dragged in on their coat-tails a large and vexed question when an urgent request came from Butler for an interim report on 'Tuition fees in grant-aided secondary schools'.

The Interim Report was ready in early 1943, though not released to the public until August, but it was divided. The Majority Report, with eleven signatures, argued no distinction should be made between maintained and aided secondary schools and that therefore fees should be abolished in all, that the direct grant list needed review and, if the system was retained, the schools should be free to the pupils, the Board making up the financial shortfall. The Minority of seven, headed by Fleming himself, believed direct grant schools, but not those maintained by LEAs, should retain the ability to charge fees as a guarantee of relative independence and as a bridge between independent schools and those in the system. Why a bridge should be needed if independent schools genuinely desired any real association with the national system is not clear. Emmeline voted with the Majority.

Into the arguments of both sides, and the careful balancing of safeguards and concessions built into the Majority Report, it is not necessary to go, for when the White Paper laying out proposals for the Bill was issued in February 1944 it excluded direct grant schools from its proposals to abandon fees. Several direct grant schools had made it clear, especially within the HMC, that they would prefer total independence to loss of fees. As bodies the HMC and GBA were strongly in favour of fees, and so too were the GBGSA, but an awkward split had already shown itself between the girls' governors and the girls' headmistresses at a meeting of their standing joint committee (one of these Emmeline) over the tuition fees question, as Osyth Potts noticed in December 1942.[36]

But the fate of direct grant as a system was now also in the hands of the Fleming Committee, and still they deliberated over their final report, even as the Bill itself was published. On 5 February 1944 the AHM Executive Committee delivered the headmistresses' reaction to the Bill. Enthusiastically they welcomed plans for a broad and comprehensive system, with provision at every stage, that the parallel tracks of elementary and secondary for children over 11 were at last to disappear, that all secondary schools were to have Articles of Government, and so on. They added caveats: regret at statutory commands to collective worship and cramping 'agreed syllabuses' for religious instruction; regret that no dates had been set for 16 to become the minimum leaving age or for the establishment of Young People's Colleges; regret that fee abolition was limited to maintained schools, and that several schools might be grouped under single governing bodies. Overall, however, if the Bill's provisions were 'rightly interpreted and generously carried out, without undue delay', and if rapid action was taken to reduce primary class sizes, then the national system might be a source of pride.[37]

Into issues of the internal nature of schools and their taxonomy, and of how children should be sorted at 11, the headmistresses did not enter now, for these were not determined by the Bill. This was deliberate. At a meeting of the Joint Four with Butler and Chuter Ede in July 1942, for example, Dorothy de Zouche had argued against segregation of 'types' as at least as damaging to the academic children as to others, backed up by H. W. Edwards of the IAHM. (In March 1944 Emmeline visited Edwards' Heckmondwike Grammar School, which he had described as successfully run on multilateral lines in three streams, and praised its standards of scholarship, values and training in community life as a model for the future.) Discussion with the Joint Four closed as the Parliamentary Secretary remarked pacifically that the most important thing was to set no formal limits but to encourage each school to develop the characteristics and organisation suited to local needs.[38]

The passage of the Bill was well advanced when, in June 1944, the Fleming Report was submitted to Butler and the Board in galley form. It was published on 26 July. Abolition or forcible incorporation of the public schools into the national system were considered and rejected. To prevent the public school hydra merely growing more heads to replace those lopped off, all private tuition would have to be banned, an unacceptably totalitarian move. At the other extreme, inaction would be intolerable. Thus the committee had had to devise a solution capable of winning voluntary acceptance by a majority of significant schools without rousing suspicions of forelock-tugging and without damage to secondary schools trying to develop within the system.

Two schemes were offered, 'A' to replace the direct grant system, 'B' to provide bursaries for boarding. Within a few months Scheme A was discarded and Scheme B so modified as to change its character, and the revised version itself soon faded to small significance. This Fleming himself did not see. He died in October 1944, aged sixty-seven. The report known by his name stands as a monument to a moment when the diverse beliefs and loyalties of the members were subsumed in a unanimous longing to 'close, in the world of schools, a social breach that follows and aggravates, if it does not actually cause, the much more serious divisions in society at large' (para. 9). Its 'Historical Sketch', with the appendix on the term 'public schools' remains one of the best-informed, most judicious and succinct of descriptions; and its discussion of the respective characteristics of boarding and day schooling illuminates contemporary attitudes and values since, devoid of the apparatus of experimental science weighting the Consultative Committee's reports, it is wholly based on examinations of a great many opinions.

Such values are not analysed; they are basic to the report's structures of thought. In the chapter on boarding the school-as-community is to the fore, and its democratising force. Hence the Co-operative Union's Education Department is quoted as recommending boarding for all, as intensive co-operative training, the County Councils Association praise boarding schools because here an adolescent may learn 'to discharge the duties' of a corporate society, and the Association of Directors and Secretaries of Education (the chief officers of local authorities) argue that non-local boarding schools mingle children from different forms of profession and industry to develop less parochial attitudes. Medical officers stress the advantages of regular sleep, diet, exercise and hygiene, reinforced by heads of day schools evacuated into residential accommodation. Character formation is significant as a consideration, and the utility of rightly-interpreted roles of Houses and prefects, but, blandly and unobtrusively, the public schools are demystified, the committee having no more time for woolly romantic attitudes than for rancorous bitterness.

The chapter opens with praise of the distinctive, and equally character-forming characteristics of day schools; and the discussion of who is better suited to which educational form may be read in two ways: either as concluding that boarding, with its advantages for pastoral work by the staff, for health, for community training, and for rooting out local insularities, should be enormously extended; or as concluding that boarding is most needed by those with inadequate homes, those who need 'the widening of experience or the extra encouragement or stimulation that would develop or strengthen their characters and release their full potentialities' (para. 137).

The political point emerged more clearly than the educational. Whether or not a child benefited more by boarding had nothing to do with the parents' income, and therefore places should be made available where benefit was possible. The committee recommended that more schools, including LEA ones, should open boarding departments, but since the present suppliers were mostly independent schools the alleged desire of these for 'association' and the problem Emmeline recognised of 'how to fit us in' dovetailed neatly into the nation's need for boarding places. It could not be claimed that the

Fleming Committee invented the need, one declared by diverse interests and written into the Education Bill, which was passed into law on 3 August 1944. By the new Act the Board of Education and its President vanished, replaced by a Ministry with a Minister.

The method of fitting independent boarding schools into the national system was Scheme B, for boarders' bursaries. The whole of Scheme B was constructed around the aim of starting by allotting 25 per cent of annual admissions to pupils from the ordinary primary schools and reviewing the position quinquennially until the schools were equally accessible to all children deemed suited to boarding on educational grounds. Suggested arrangements for funding, admissions, and changes to governing bodies were all designed, on the one hand, by checks and balances to alienate none in pursuing this aim, and, on the other hand, to mesh in course of time with the proposals of Scheme A, for certain day (or mainly day) schools. The two Schemes' merit was that they were agreed unanimously by a committee with diverse sympathies.

By October Emmeline had been 'delighted to see the keen interest in this subject shown by Old Roedeanians ... and to hear their strongly-expressed desire that Roedean should be one of the leaders in a movement of this kind. This is, I feel sure, in harmony with the spirit of our Founders.'[39] In November she formally laid Scheme B before Roedean Council. The Council contemplated the spirit of the Founders, and decided to tell the Minister they were 'in sympathy'; in any case, until the machinery was established – and the school at home again – nothing could be done.

Not on ideological rocks, like Scheme A, as will be seen, but in practical quicksands Scheme B foundered. After much internal discussion a deputation from the HMC and GBA, the AHMIDG and GBGSA, one of them Emmeline, waited on the Minister on 23 March 1945. Various modifications were sought, by the GBA especially, and only the headmistresses defended the 25 per cent initial target with progressive increase. Osyth Potts spoke in favour of simpler machinery, however, and of earlier involvement of the head in selection. In inevitable conclusion a negotiating committee (not including Emmeline) was established, chaired by Maurice Holmes of the Ministry, just the cosy establishment coterie rejected in 1942.[40] A watered-down scheme with a 10 per cent target was put together by August for the eyes of the Minister just installed by the Labour Government, Ellen Wilkinson. This too proved a sickly child, though the Ministry's Circular 120, on Boarding Education, encouraged LEAs to proceed both with their own provision and with arrangements with independent schools, and though the HMC was happier with the modified ideas. At their meeting in January 1947, indeed, John Wolfenden, a member of the 'Holmes Committee', moved a rallying-cry resolution in support of Circular 120.

By July 1947 Roedean Council, now involved in negotiations with the LCC, decided the school could offer 10 per cent of admissions. The LCC,

354 / Doors of Possibility

however, had set a ceiling on fees they would pay for their children and defined suitable candidates on a peculiarly narrow interpretation of criteria suggested in the Ministry's Administrative Memorandum 225. Refusing to be daunted, Emmeline reported she had accepted four girls from another LEA; the school was to join the Ministry's 'pool' and expected six candidates for 1948-9. As one of her housemistresses summed up, 'She thought it right in principle, but that it would be difficult – she understood all the difficulties – but she *hoped* it would work.' In the end five different LEA sources provided, in all, sixteen girls for Roedean in the four years before the scheme generally petered out, as did plans for LEAs to develop their own boarding schools.

Perhaps few were dedicated enough to generate demand where boarding was a novelty or to advertise the possibilities in primary schools, and defining suitable candidates was extraordinarily difficult if 'creaming' was to be avoided (as the Fleming Committee had insisted) without using the schools as a dump for the emotionally frail alone. Unlike the free places which from 1907 had progressively opened up the secondary schools, bursaries under this scheme were based on need and not on merit. Most of all, money followed priorities and LEAs had many more desperate priorities. Nor, as queues of fee-paying parents formed, were the public schools as hungry for public money as in 1938.

Scheme A of the Fleming Report, however, was to present Emmeline with more urgent problems, for under the Act schools not provided by LEAs but receiving LEA aid must, by 1 April 1945, choose either 'controlled' or 'maintained' status and cease to charge fees. The educational press resounded with grammar school jeremiads at LEA encroachment on their prized freedoms, for the two forms of relationship had been designed chiefly with the new secondary schools in mind by planners nervous of the ability of ex-elementary schools to sustain the freedoms of older aided secondary schools. The only life-raft in sight was direct grant from the Ministry, but enquiries about direct grant were consistently fended off as 'in the hands of the Fleming Committee', and the Fleming Committee produced Scheme A.

Before the Fleming Report's publication democracy had spoken on fees, the House of Commons deciding by 183 to 95 votes against an amendment to abolish fees in all grant-aided schools, though fees must be abandoned in those 'controlled' or 'maintained' by LEAs as well as in 'county' schools, the new name for those established by local authorities. Word had spread round that some of the most noted direct grant schools, some of which now also received LEA subsidies, would prefer to jettison all their grants and survive in independence on higher fees, and fear of this swayed many MPs. If the preference argues a somewhat skin-deep commitment to the national system it may be urged that the schools concerned believed their value to such a system lay precisely in the freedoms they thought threatened, though (as Chuter Ede pointed out) a reactionary governing body could blight an enlightened head at least as effectively as a pettifogging LEA.

'Scheme A,' announced the Fleming Report, 'would comprise schools fully accessible to all pupils and would replace the present direct grant system' (para. 173). Briefly, an agreed fee would be paid for each pupil in schools within the scheme but not necessarily by the pupil. The LEA would reserve a number of places agreed with the governing body for children of LEA choice and pay for those; the governors would choose the rest, who would pay none, or some, or all of the fee according to their parents' income, and the remissions of fees would be made up by the Ministry. Such fees should cover running costs, schools remaining free to fix staff ratios and salaries, and if a school's own endowment or capital reserve could not pay for necessary building work the LEA might grant money and reclaim it from the Ministry. The LEA would nominate (as for existing direct grant schools) one-third of the governing body. Any efficient school not privately owned nor LEA-controlled might apply to join the scheme.

At first the GBGSA and AHMIDG were cautiously welcoming, though wanting more precise details on how places were to be allocated, and on 17 November 1944 Emmeline and two other headmistresses met Butler to discuss several points relating to both Scheme A and B. A recent meeting of the AHMIDG, Emmeline reported, had discovered a substantial majority (40 to 16) of headmistresses in favour of A, but with a smaller majority (20 to 14) among the heads of existing direct grant schools taken separately. She wanted Butler to meet the GBGSA and he agreed to do so.[41]

Meanwhile the GBA and HMC were also holding meetings where the spectre of LEA purse-power brooded darkly; they clung to the capitation grant from the Ministry with a free place proportion. This Fleming had rejected as an illogical subsidy to parents with means to pay. Within the Ministry 'Scheme D' was devised, for capitation grants calculated on senior school numbers, with 25 per cent of places offered free to LEAs (and possibly more allotted by the governors) and means-tested fees for the rest. Scheme D, unlike A, would not be open to schools not presently on the direct grant list.

When the GBA and HMC met Butler, a few days after the headmistresses' visit, their unhappiness was countered with the alternative D. A few days more, and on 29 November the GBGSA arrived for their promised meeting, accompanied by four headmistresses, and announced they would accept A, without enthusiasm. Osyth Potts added that the AHM Executive Committee approved, though A 'might call for courage on the part of those schools who had to work with difficult authorities'. Even as he proffered Scheme D Butler remarked that his own inclination would have been for A but 'clearly many boys' schools were bitterly opposed'.

He was growing irritated. Should he write, he asked G. G. Williams, to offer an option between A and D in terms conveying 'that had they all had the sense to stick to one scheme it might have been easier for the future'? Williams, chief architect of D, was nakedly hostile to A in his response: it would allow new schools to enter, LEA capital grants would be eligible for Ministry grant (encouraging extravagance), and fee remission applied equally to boarders – all 'objectionable' features not found in D. Butler did not write.

The girls' authorities thought over D, and through December several letters were exchanged between Butler and Emmeline, negotiating as an AHMIDG member of the liaison committee with the GBA and familiar with – feeling partly responsible for – the Fleming schemes. Modifications to D were agreed, with most of which she professed herself 'delighted', and she passed on headmistresses' several qualms, for example that they disliked 'admission in merit order' if that entailed a hateful and unreliable competitive examination at 11 or so, and their worries for their preparatory departments, for the logic of primary and secondary now divorced these from LEA schools.

Just before Christmas Emmeline sent out a questionnaire to AHMIDG members and discovered a clear majority preferred Scheme A; at a meeting on 28 December (her sixty-eighth birthday) they decided to request an option, anxious that girls' schools should not have to forgo A despite the dislike evinced by boys' schools. 'Very few girls' schools,' Emmeline reminded Butler, 'have endowments which would help them to face the additional expenditure involved by the alternative scheme, nor do the headmistresses think a raising of school fees to be desired. Apart from this, a majority of our members believes that Scheme A is the more progressive scheme and more in key with the present trend of social thought.' She continued with another shopping list of caveats.

On 2 January 1945, however, the GBGSA chairman reported that his members liked neither scheme, for neither gave governors enough financial independence. Butler seized his chance, and on the 4th wrote to tell Emmeline that Scheme A was discarded. She replied by return:

It fills me with regret that an option between Scheme A and Scheme D cannot be given. Moreover, I am perplexed by the impression which I gather about your own estimate of the merits of Scheme A. You have written that certain features of Scheme A make it extremely difficult for the Ministry to accept it, and a little later you speak of some of its more objectionable features. I wonder whether you would be so good as to particularise the objections which you feel to be inherent in the Scheme? I am really puzzled, because on November 29th the deputation which waited on you gathered an impression so different.

She asked for another year under current direct grant regulations to enable the drastic reorganisation entailed by D; she asked for a meeting of all parties to prevent people feeling 'rushed' with consequent friction; wistfully she again hankered after Scheme A's 'more genuinely democratic' features. She sighed over disunity: 'I have myself felt it a serious difficulty, and I believe this has been your own feeling also, that boys' schools and girls' schools seem divergent in their view of this part of the new educational structure.' Finally she hinted, very gently, that any capitation grant should be generous: 'We have confidence that the Ministry will attach great importance to the maintenance of a high standard of scholarship, and will realise that this must necessarily entail a certain amount of additional expenditure.'

But she had won some modifications to D; and now the spotlight turned away to the conditions under which the schools must operate. In all their advice on the Act the secondary associations had urged a common code to promote 'parity' in the new secondary structure, and in January 1945 they saw, aghast, the draft of the new 'Regulations for Primary and Secondary Schools'. On 30 January the HMC and GBA demanded a separate, and more liberal, set for direct grant schools exclusively. Two days later the AHMIDG and GBGSA also appeared at the Ministry, bringing a list of technical questions but reluctant to detach direct grant regulations wholly from those for other secondary schools, an unappealingly divisive gesture. They wanted merely delay for 'clarification'.

In pursuit of the maximum achievable, Emmeline turned her attention to easing where the shoe pinched. 'It is true that the girls' schools did not expect the regulations for direct grant schools to be issued separately from the general regulations for secondary schools, but neither had we expected the new regulations to cover both primary and secondary schools,' she reproached Butler. That they should cover both she thought regrettable, for separate regulations 'would have emphasised the changed status of the schools that now become secondary for the first time', a change the public might anyway be slow enough to appreciate when schools remained in the same buildings, with the same amenities.

Secondly, Emmeline pointed out, 'the combining of the regulations has brought into those for secondary schools several restrictive and detailed regulations that have never before been included and that tend to take away from Governing Bodies and heads of schools that sense of individual responsibility that has been so marked a characteristic of English secondary education' – and she listed examples of new restrictions. The Harpur Trust, among others, decided not to apply for Bedford School and Bedford High School to retain direct grant status but to declare independence. Others, the schools with the new status of County, Controlled or Maintained, had no such choice. Looking one way and the other the direct grant schools worried.

February wore away in discussions and, in the upshot, some amendments were made, both to the regulations generally and to the specific conditions on which direct grant would be given. The latter were distinctive enough to raise the hackles of the radical educational press at the privileges accorded direct grant schools, and conversely to prompt a resolution by the headmistresses of GPDST schools (all direct grant schools) to express to Emmeline 'their appreciation of all the infinite trouble you have taken, with such successful results, on behalf of the direct grant schools'. 'We do realise,' added their committee chairman, 'how many long, exhausting journeys have been involved, as well as endless meetings and interruptions of your own engagements, and we feel that no one but yourself could have managed to gain so many concessions.'[42]

Yet the restriction of some of those 'concessions' to a chosen few was lamentable to Emmeline, a victory Pyrrhic if at all. The few became fewer as the Labour government drew up a new list of only 160 direct grant schools; on 9 November 1945 Ellen Wilkinson said she would have preferred Scheme A.[43] The few were also intellectually narrowed by a merit-order admission base, imposed by their official classification as 'grammar'; many headmistresses were sorry, with Lilian Charlesworth of Sutton High School GPDST, that their senior schools 'could not be multilateral in the sense that they were in the past'.[44]

To the girls of Roedean Emmeline talked, not of administrative vexations, but of the Act's generous promise, its intention 'to give to all children, irrespective of the financial position of their parents, the fullest opportunities for an education suited to their abilities and aptitudes', and impressed on her Sixth Form the fervour of her belief that no one should be held back from education for want of money.

At the AHM Conference in June 1945, however, Sybil Smith of King Edward's High School, Birmingham, cast a presidential eye over her exhausted colleagues as she spoke of the 'extraordinarily unpromising time' for a major Education Act to be implemented, of buildings destroyed, vital materials scarce, staff overburdened. Her Chairman of Committee, Lilian Charlesworth, 'spent a good deal of my time at the Conference (having a good vantage point) watching ... and looking – in vain – for personalities to follow on those who have hitherto commanded our respect and admiration ... some worthy successors should be arising and I simply do not see where they are to be found,' she told Emmeline. Perhaps they lacked the old sense of vocation, she wondered, or perhaps 'we have suffered our war casualties unnoticed' and weary women had found no time to involve themselves in AHM business.

The lack seemed particularly critical as the AHM debated whether their association should remain one for 'headmistresses of grammar schools only, or whether membership was to be extended to heads of modern and technical schools'.[45] The resolution passed at that 1945 meeting was that the AHM 'welcomes to its membership headmistresses of the new secondary schools', and was proposed by Emmeline. 'How very much moved I was by your speech,' Lilian Charlesworth told her, remembering a speech that described the new secondary schools as 'with traditions still to be made and standards differing in character but not, we hope and believe, in quality from our own'. It carried the day, and marked the end to Emmeline's formal, public activities.

May had brought VE Day, a holiday for all, and the church bells of Crosthwaite rang again, 'not in peals or changes but all together in a great burst of noise ringing out over the fields'. Keswick and Roedean went to church together, to sing 'Now thank we all our God', 'meaning every word ... all crying with relief,' as one said.[46] In the evening all save the Juniors were free to go 'on our own' to the bonfire on Latrigg, to lie on the grass eating baked potatoes, singing, straggling back late, dirty, tired, happy.

An end to war was in sight but the buildings on the cliffs by Brighton remained HMS *Vernon*. Emmeline had thoroughly enjoyed herself the year before, in September, taking the salute at the March Past at Divisions on a clear, sunny day. Two Wrens had hoisted the Colours as Emmeline stood with the Captain in the quadrangle, before her moment of glory on a small platform, her back to the sea, what had been her school before her, and, below her beaming smile, the ordered blue waves of uniforms passing by. When she departed, however, the Captain was left in no doubt of her 'great desire to get back', but his soothing sympathy was non-committal. That desire had not diminished in 1945.

Chapter 26
Retirement

To take the school home and then to retire was Emmeline's plan and her question in 1945-6. For so many years she had talked to girls leaving school in the language of opportunities that to identify these for herself, the second part of the plan, was now a test of herself. As she said to the girls of Newcastle Central High School at the end of 1944:

> when the war ends and we begin to settle down to a more regular life again we shall find that the world we knew has gone. We older people will have to adapt ourselves to new conditions ... To you girls the new world will be the natural one, but a time of transition is always difficult, even though it is also thrilling and exacting for all who love adventure.

Her 'world' was not only a metaphor for immediate personal conditions: 'when we have learnt that no country can live to itself, it is of supreme importance that we should be able to think in terms of the world,' she said, to herself as much as to the schoolgirls.

But the immediate task was to take Roedean School home – 'home', not 'back', was her word. As negotiations with the Admiralty over the release of the Roedean buildings advanced through 1945, Roedean Council established a sub-committee imposingly called 'Post-War Planning', to reconnoitre both prospective balance sheets and HMS *Vernon* itself. Officially HMS *Vernon* returned to Portsmouth in June 1945 but the phoenix Roedean was as yet an embryo among the ashes. In 1924 Emmeline had thought the school crowded with a complement, girls and all kinds of staff, of about 600, but in HMS *Vernon* 150 officers and 800 other ranks had been instructed daily in a full crew of about 2,000, or so the outgoing Captain Grace told Emmeline. Altogether, he reckoned, 6,500 officers and 25,000 men had taken courses there.

They had not lived or learned as schoolgirls had; the summer of 1945 echoed with reconstruction. The Link training aeroplane could be taken from the old music wing, and the mines and depth charges removed from Chapel cloisters; the fittings of wardroom and bar could be dismantled in the library and studio, and girls' bedrooms be divested of tiers of ratings' bunks, while the departed ratings themselves spread the happy fiction that in their temporary cabins they had found bell-pushes labelled 'In case of need ring for a mistress'. The six water tanks with attendant trailer pump houses, dotted over the grounds, the incinerators, decontamination building, and internal walls and divisions should be removed, decided the school authorities, but the solidly built Night Attack Room and Control Room could be bought, kept and converted. So too could some of the kitchen equipment and 'lavatory basins' installed by the Navy, for one objective was to reduce the number of domestic staff employed in feeding and washing arrangements in the school.

The school of 1938, as described by HM Inspectors, could not be restored. Still vital hopes of the Fleming Committee's Scheme B, even modified as it had been, energised Emmeline, and the Council looked, not to raising fees, but to economies when balancing ideal numbers against expenses. Ideal pupil numbers meant, according to Emmeline in 1945, 65 girls in each House, with 65 more in the Junior House, or 325 in all, but fees from such a total had shown only the most modest surplus over costs in pre-war years. Numbers did not seem a problem, though only 240 could be squeezed into Keswick accommodation, since applications were plentiful. Costs, however, might be difficult, if only because domestic staff were now both scarce and expensive, and their lot would almost certainly be eased by anticipated legislation on hourly rates, overtime regulations, and employers' contributions to National Insurance.

Washing reform seemed straightforward. By making a new bathroom for each floor of each House out of an old bedroom, the anachronistic practice of maids bringing hot water and removing slops could be abandoned. Feeding was more difficult. Emmeline thought the common dining of Keswick had helped general relationships and not hampered House ones – on such matters she sounded the Sixth Form – and she had in the 1930s consulted kitchen engineers on combining House kitchens in pairs, to be deterred by the expense of re-equipment. Now the planning was for a central kitchen and dining-hall, and (until building licences could be granted and funding allowed for these) for pairing House kitchens, with hatches to enable girls themselves to wait on tables. Emmeline refined these plans to co-ordinate House cleaning and supplies.

In practice some plans were discarded, others emended. The catering manager Emmeline brought in for the transition was 'a great success and everyone is delighted with the feeding', she said, but, as old habits reasserted themselves:

> I had to give up the plan of a House administrator and her assistant, though I don't think we could ever have got ready without them. The Houses are still too individualistic to allow of mobility of domestic labour and the scheme could not work well without a certain degree of that. So now [after the first term] each House has a Housekeeper as well as two Matrons ... and this plan seems to work, though it is distinctly expensive.[1]

The central kitchen and dining-rooms were twenty years in the future.

By the end of 1945 the buildings were to be in a fit state for the girls to live and work there in the new term of January 1946. So in 1945 the summer holiday lasted a mere two weeks and the Christmas break eight, so that Keswick equipment could be packed and despatched, stored goods retrieved and staff reorganised in Brighton. The captain was the last to leave her ship, settling and sorting the final details in Keswick with the help of her secretary for business and a niece with more flexible knees to bend to cases and boxes. When the school's work was done, and farewells made, and at last Emmeline settled into the southbound train she discovered an omission. She had forgotten to renew her ticket.

At Roedean she found her staff gallant but flagging. Housemistresses had entered dirty buildings, with equipment dumped in chaotic heaps, and day after day of cleaning, moving furniture and books, manhandling bedsteads, devising makeshifts for items lost or damaged, had tired the women more than Emmeline had reckoned. She refused outright, however, to delay term for another week, as one housemistress pleaded; at last she granted a four-day holiday, to go away and do and think of something completely different, and 'it made a deal of difference', they said later. Very few girls could remember pre-war Roedean and some missed Keswick and Keswick freedoms in the more fortress-like Roedean with a skirt of grounds hitched away from the living communities around, and matches and meetings with Brighton Girls' Club and Brighton schools seemed artificial encounters, a little self-conscious. Others enjoyed the wide skies over the Downs and the far horizons of the sea, and for the pursuit of the curriculum conditions were infinitely easier.

After five years some staff were strange to the buildings, others conscious of changes, and when equipment was rescued from storage in vacant houses on Brighton's sea-front they were conscious also of loss. Bomb-blasted windows had let in, as well as rain, some few recouping their own losses, and housemistresses mourned particularly the disappearance of the long velvet curtains which had once hung in their sitting-rooms. Hardly a knife or fork or spoon remained, so that for the first term girls were asked to bring their own, name-marked. For a few months even Orpen's portrait of Penelope Lawrence could not be found – 'He would have something to say on the subject!' commented his fellow-artist Oswald Birley.

These were emblematic, the velvet curtains of vanished graces, the cutlery of new self-help, and about the Lawrence sisters Emmeline made a point of talking to the girls, in the language of ideals and standards. The graces she regretted; self-help she welcomed. When she called her new domestic staff together to welcome them, the part-time daily help in assorted overalls and headscarves banished the lingering ghosts of trimly-uniformed resident maids, yet 'I reckon that we are at present paying wages at between £13,000 and £14,000 a year to men and maids at school where we only once touched £5,000 before 1940'. That the girls should bestir themselves more Emmeline thought a positive asset. 'I am sure they are better for having some domestic work to do, if only we can organise it the right way, and I long for us to find some way of getting advantages to take the place of those in Keswick in their living as ordinary members of a normal community, and not as merely part of one that exists solely for them,' she wrote to a friend, and recorded a softened version in the magazine for parents' eyes: 'I think there is no doubt that a boarding-school life which includes some domestic work is more complete than one without domestic duties.'[2] But Ethel and Kate, her own parlour-maid and cook of 1925-31, came back to her, to new wages of £2 and £2/10/- a week plus board, lodging and laundry, and with Emmeline paying 4/8d National Insurance for each.

So systems were established, new appointments made to fill gaps and retirements (in April 'I still have German with some French, and English with some good subsidiary subject, to appoint, and then I think we ought to be straight for the time being'), and in February several days were set aside for Emmeline to be closeted for the first post-war Audit. One new auditor emerged from a session to compliment the school secretary lavishly on her headmistress's financial brain; such was not among the headmistress' qualifications Emmeline listed in 1942 but to governing bodies Emmeline's business sense was undoubtedly among her endearing qualities.

For a new headmistress was at last definitely in prospect. By Easter 1946 'I have told the Council I definitely want to leave next Easter', and the Council formed an 'Exploratory Sub-committee'. This was one mark of how modes had changed since the Council's fledgling days in 1924, when Roedean was still emerging from its private-school past; another was the printed sheet of terms and conditions sent to respondents to the Press advertisement, including, not only a salary offer of £1,200 p.a., but much that Emmeline had had to negotiate step by step after her appointment, in some respects improved. Thirdly, favoured applicants were asked to visit the school and talk to Emmeline, and those short-listed for interview had to be prepared to give their views on the position Roedean's headmistress should occupy in the school and in the outside world.

What role their answers played is less sure. Though the advertisement netted a number of applicants, as in 1924 some head-hunting was indulged and several approaches were repulsed before Norah Horobin agreed to apply, prompted apparently by Emmeline herself. No other construction can be placed on a personal letter to Emmeline from the founders' sister Agatha Blyth: 'Theresa [Lawrence] has had a charming letter from Norah Horobin; one feels you must have made a good choice. What a relief it is to have that —[sic] time of choosing over! You are to be congratulated for finding a suitable candidate – yes, how safe Roedean is in your hands!'

But the interviews by the Council on 24 October were genuine acts of choice, and Norah Horobin was not the only favoured candidate, nor had Emmeline a vote to cast. But she won the majority voice: as the daughter of a Principal of Homerton Training College, Cambridge, educated at the North London Collegiate School and King's College, London, Norah Horobin had a pedigree typical of prominent headmistresses; her previous headships had been of Dulwich High School and Sunderland High School, an independent day school of the Church Schools Company (a body somewhat similar to the GPDST but with a definite church affiliation), but earlier she had lectured at St Mary's Training College and on education and public health. Moreover, she had not only shouldered some professional committee work but had known hard labour as an ARP Warden.

So Emmeline began her last term in January 1947 with the succession secured and the prospect of cheerful farewell parties and such 'state pomps' as the unveiling of her own portrait, in one of the longest, cruellest winters of the century. In January the meat ration was reduced to a shilling's worth a week, a fuel crisis restricted heating, lighting, transport, and then in February blizzards stopped all Channel shipping and the army experimented with flame-throwers to clear snowdrifts in Dorset. At Roedean, awaking dim echoes of Emmeline's last days at Nuneaton, scarlet fever broke out, to be contained, an anxiety and not an epidemic.

This, and the death of Sir Paul Lawrence's wife, delayed until 1 March the planned 'Presentation' to the school of Emmeline's portrait, commissioned from T. C. Dugdale RA by the Old Roedeanians Association, parents, past and present staff and girls; Emmeline was greatly touched that Sir Paul himself came, supported by a niece and looking all and more than his eighty-five years on the first outing of his widowhood. The elderly fragility of the several Lawrence relations and friends gathered round the luncheon table in her dining-room (a year earlier the officers' galley and its floor hard-worn) itself imaged how the old order was changing, sometimes reluctantly. A pupil of the school's earliest days caught Emmeline up on 'all you say of the way in which one looks back and sees all that one *might* have done' to grumble at 'all sorts of people with good intentions pushing on their own ideas, before things are ready for their experiments', and the design of Emmeline's portrait was palliative.

As a work of art it is undistinguished, an establishment portrait for an institution, and Emmeline's family, liking a likeness, were unsatisfied. The artist relies on the iconographic conventions of academic portraiture, a genre already in decay in schools. Seated on an upright chair with her straight back mellowed by a great soft swell of bosom – the encircling head, arms and hands make this the heart of the painting – Emmeline is draped in academic gown and hood and one ringless hand rests on a book, perhaps her own. The pose with its hint of a throne spells authority, and the gown and book establish the ideals of scholarship. Yet it is the garb of a BA (London), not of the MA to which most of Emmeline's present AHM colleagues were entitled, the lack of any ornament except an oval unjewelled brooch at her plain collar denotes workaday simplicity, and she sits not quite at rest.

Towards the end of term came a round of parties, teas and gift-giving ceremonies, most at school, down to a 'Thanks Badge' presentation from the Guides and Brownies, but also in Brighton where Emmeline described to her fellow professionals her early days in a county school, guided by Bolton King. The headmaster of the Varndean County Secondary School was one of many who urged her to write her reminiscences, 'your interpretation of things and people educational', and the rich harvest of gratefully well-wishing letters from the whole spread of her teaching days might have provoked a saint to complacency in her wisdom. But Emmeline did not look back, at least in print.

Retrospection she used instead as a tactic to respond becomingly to plaudits, to signify that she detached herself now from professional advance and to amuse with accounts of 'antediluvian days' – her phrase. So in May, at the dinner given for her by the AHM Executive Committee in London, 'I told them a few things about my early days in the Association and, arising from something Miss de Zouche said, I told them of how early and under what conditions I began teaching, and something of my earlier teaching and working history.' The headmistresses were plainly bent on a good party. They had commissioned girls of their schools to arrange posies of mixed polyanthuses for each place, as well as larger table flowers, and to inscribe calligraphic menus and place-cards, and, after they had all eaten and drunk 'temperately', as Dorothy de Zouche said, seven speakers rose in turns carefully ordered, associated with phases of Emmeline's career. One was her last Head Girl at Nuneaton, Janet Taylor, now just moving from the headship of Portsmouth Southern Secondary School to that of Talbot Heath School, Bournemouth. 'Everyone liked her immensely,' reported her loyal mother-head.

After all had said their pieces, 'I laughed, I really had to; there seemed nothing else to be done, unless it was to cry over the funeral orations. I said when I arrived at the Executive next morning that it seemed almost indecent of me to rise from the dead so soon.'

What, after all, had she achieved in thirty-seven years of headmistress-ship, years in which she had involved herself in many forms of fundamental educational change, especially for adolescent girls? The 20th century saw growing state intervention, by the establishment of maintained secondary schools and the use of central committees for analysis and advice: these she served. As a profession secondary teaching developed through maturing associations, defined standards, and training organisation: the AHM gave Emmeline a place to stand and she repaid it by furthering its ends. In curricula and standards, in doors to higher education and careers, in windows on communities and concerns outside school, girls' secondary education was enriched and extended. A comparison between the limited chances of Emmeline's youthful milieu and those of girls from the LEA secondary schools of the 1920s and 1930s, including Britain's first woman Prime Minister, tells its tale, and Emmeline set her hand to opening these 'doors of possibility' across the span of day and boarding schools, in maintained, direct grant and independent institutions.

But in educational extension she was part only of a project stretching over more than these years, involving many individuals and deriving from principles already forged. In the history of the project, moreover, 'progress' is an inadequate concept as underlying attitudes and values are seen to shift and re-focus, and is contingent on a series of historical accidents, including personalities and available models, conceptions of female function, or development resources opportunely available. Nor was Emmeline an original theorist, though she identified, articulated and propagated radical ideas in acceptable language (and paid the price of settling for the maximum achievable) and diffused many ideas through the headmistresses who learnt their craft under her.

Her contemporary appraisers circled to rest on the personal, not on hopes often deferred, diluted or adulterated in realisation. When in November 1947 Emmeline was at last granted an MA by London University, by the wry irony of an honorary degree, the Public Orator of the University spoke of how 'within our generation we have witnessed the construction of a system of democratic education' – the elation of the 1944 Act and the Fleming Report resounded still – and of how Emmeline had made 'by her faith, by the width of her experience and by her outstanding qualities of personality, a most distinguished contribution'. He spoke of 'the range of her sympathy that made her the most effective champion of broadening the path', and of the 'permanent impression upon the development of women's education in this country' she left by 'the incisive quality of her mind and the strength of her personality'.[3]

Rightly she was assessed as significant for what she was as much as for what she did, or rather the one depended on the other. She set a potent example: not rich or privileged, not beautiful or witty or artistically talented, she made the best of what she had and did not put her candle 'under a bushel, but on a candlestick' to shine before women, in the scope and standards of her activities in and out of school, with a majestic breadth of vision, practical sense, and generous equanimity. Yet, as when a French colleague spoke of '*la sphère de votre rayonnement*', this marked some limits to her achievement, and, as another friend wrote later, it seemed when she died the sun went in; without her presence her power was dimmed.

From another point of view Emmeline was equally exemplary, however, and her life a classic manifestation of a process by which the individualistic ambitions of her class clad themselves in 'respectable' values and made their own way up the ladder of material success and esteem. From a third, her career illustrated the conditions of professional achievement for a woman without private means born in the 1870s, and its constraints, limits and costs. So did those of her sisters.

None of these three views, however, uncovers the self-disciplinary rigour and compelling faith that underpinned that optimistic, edifying persona, how Emmeline enforced her habits of sense and temper by stubborn acts of will, or how she cast issues in moral terms to oblige herself to morally virtuous choices. Perhaps she repeatedly emphasised certain qualities and aspirations to distance herself from subversive fears and doubts; if so, she was successful and consistent enough to strike those who knew her as singularly well-integrated, one who laid hold on life and had it abundantly.

Not yet, however, in 1947 was the time come for 'funeral orations', as she said, and her feet were kept on the ground during the same few days of May as the AHM dinner by sessions with the dentist and the chiropodist, and a farcical dash from Baker Street to keep an appointment when the elastic of her underwear gave way so that she ran with hands clutched to her waist, intermittently retreating to quiet entries to retrieve pieces. Negotiations with Thomas Cook and banks kept her mind on the present and future.

Many of her correspondents expected her, safely retired and now seventy, to settle among pleasant civilities of books and gardens and write, if not her reminiscences, 'something on history', as one suggested. But in her closing address to the girls of Roedean, and with all the *gravitas* of parting words, Emmeline had charged them at the start to 'Remember always that education is not dull: it is an adventure that begins in our earliest days and continues through life',[4] and now that she was free as she had never been before she attended more enthusiastically to learning than to teaching, a nomad rather than a settler. In her practical way, when she had finished one thing she got on with the next.

The previous December Amrit Kaur had been in London, not now detained by His Majesty's representatives in British India, nor, as earlier in 1946, in sweepers' quarters with Gandhi in Delhi, constantly running to and fro with notes to the Cabinet Mission, but as the representative of the Central Provinces on the Legislative Council of India and a UNESCO delegate. Visiting Emmeline at Roedean then, she had talked to the Sixth Form of the Congress Party's policy for independent India, startling some of them by her Gandhian interpretation of British policies, and of difficulties with the Moslem League. In March Mountbatten sailed for India as the last Viceroy, in May the British Cabinet agreed to Partition, and in June the Congress Party endorsed Nehru's assent. British rule in India ended in August, and the Rajkumari Amrit Kaur became Minister of Health in Nehru's government. Emmeline wanted to see the shaping of India. She wanted too to go back to Southern Africa, to fill out the lacunae of the working visit of 1929, to lift the shadow cast on 1929 by her father's death, and to visit many friends.

There remained a last piece of unfinished business, arrears of tiredness, of war-weariness. Like a homing pigeon Emmeline sped to Switzerland, to Glion, her haven in 1916; by mid-May she was nested 'with a good view over the lake and the Savoy mountains'. Paying 11 francs a day for her room and board she had carefully to husband her currency through tight exchange restrictions, the Bank of England permitting her just enough for three months, to be paid through banks in monthly instalments at a rate after commission of about 17 francs to the pound. Usually she had to forgo expensive teatime cakes and meringues, for 'Food is dear in Switzerland at present but the only things that are really scarce are butter and sugar; both these rations are smaller than ours, but the cooking fat ration is very much larger', and she had to ration herself to one or at most two 2-franc baths a week. Her basin was 'large and well-shaped', however, and Emmeline had in her youth learned expertise at standing on tiny mats 'stark naked having my daily bath in the basin'. Reminders of old austerities seeped into letters home, as on a Meiringen shoe-shop trying to buy suitable laces: 'When I told the shoemaker I couldn't get those very short laces in England either he said that he could understand that because shoes like that were not worn nowadays! And they are by several years the newest of my shoes.' So too on a wet day she spent 'from 9.00 to 12.15 this morning darning my stockings. And they were all darned a fortnight ago! All except the lisle thread ones were bought before coupons came in, and most of them before the war, so perhaps it is not surprising.'

Her stockings saw increasingly hard wear. At first 'my walking powers are very much inferior to what they were', and a steep descent was 'agonising for my knees', and two hours quite long enough; instead she practised her botany with the aid of an illustrated manual, and, habitually thorough and precise, noted the 71 varieties she found. She watched men manuring fields and the harvesting of narcissi for the market, and was amused by a four-inch snail 'with its shell on the middle of its back and its horns out ... just like an illustration to one of those children's stories where the beasts are the heroes and heroines' and 'the largest hare I have ever seen, lolloping along the path'. In Montreux she encountered several friends and acquaintances, and she spent a day at the school Osyth Potts had co-founded, but the dominant image of this first phase is 'a lovely glade':

... As I sat on the felled trunk of a tree, a brown squirrel came and sat in front of me with his two little hands up to his mouth eating away at something, while he kept his bright little eyes fixed on me ... Meanwhile a butterfly had alighted and proceeded to suck honey from the flowers on my flowered frock. It continued to do this, to its apparent satisfaction, moving from one flower to another, for more than half an hour while I ate my lunch.

By the time Madge Skipworth joined her at Hohfluh in the Bernese Oberland in July, on vacation from Lady Margaret Hall, Emmeline could manage walks of six hours and more, if with 'many rests', but by then she had left Glion and spent a month in the higher, clearer air of Villars.

At Villars the secret she had brought with her was published in *The Times* of 12 June, the King's Official Birthday. *The Times* did not arrive at her hotel until the next day, but telegrams preceded it in such profusion that the proprietress was prompted to enquiry and Emmeline confessed she had been made a Dame Commander of the British Empire, then a woman's highest honour for none sat in the peers then and no life peerage was granted a woman in Emmeline's lifetime. When *The Times* arrived her photograph looked faintly incongruous, placed above two younger and much better-looking new knights, Lawrence Olivier and Malcolm Sargent, education crowning the arts.

Hotel guests fêted her with flowers and chocolates such as she had admired only from afar, and Emmeline settled down to answer 'so far 56 telegrams and 330 letters', in the first ten days. More followed. As one said cheerfully, 'Now I well remember Miss Moore's words – "I always tell Dame

Emmeline's friends: if you wish her well, *don't write* to her"', for Emmeline hated to leave a silence or a negative when a kindness was intended. She was moved, too, 'almost overwhelmed with the amount of genuine affection which the letters seem to show'. For herself – 'Many people say how much they wish Mother, and some say my parents, could have been here. It was my first thought. My second was that I was putting off a very familiar personality, "Miss Tanner", for a new and strange one.'

On arrival at Hohfluh, she took a day off letter-writing and a post-car to Brunig, a train to Alpnachstadt, a boat and another train, and from Stans a mountain railway, to go to the Stanserhorn just south of the Lake of Lucerne, for a night in a simple hotel 'just at the level where the railway ends':

The actual top of the Stanserhorn is rather more than 200 feet higher and from there you just turn yourself round and see the whole horizon with nothing in the way. Below there are all the different parts of the Lake of Lucerne and five other lakes to the north-west and south. And then there are mountains behind mountains all the way round, but especially to the west and south ... The Stanserhorn is only 6,200 or 6,300 feet high but standing alone as it does and having exceedingly steep sides you get a much better view than from many higher mountains.

Beyond the lakes and mountains of the free and peaceful republic in whose National Day celebrations Emmeline had shared just a day before, lay Germany, Austria, Italy, France and the aftermath of war. 'Let other pens dwell on guilt and misery,' wrote Jane Austen: the Europe of 1947 gave scope. The evening she arrived on the Stanserhorn Emmeline climbed the last 200 feet to see the sunset fade into darkness, and at 4.10 am again took the steeper way to the summit, joined by a Belgian family. At 5.00 am the sun touched on the horizon 'and very soon the whole brilliant rose-coloured ball had appeared; it very quickly changed from rose to gold, and the glow which had been brilliant before the sun itself showed, died down.'

The Belgians soon went back to bed, but for an hour and a half Emmeline sat on alone, watching the sunlight strengthen and spill gold to shadowed valleys. Her next family letter talked of the cowbells like musical water, of the contrast between clear-cut almost perpendicular rock and gentle green slopes, and of the buzzard circling her head and hovering 'in a most unpleasing manner, though I felt that it couldn't think that I was either an unprotected little lamb or a dead sheep'. Of what else went through her mind as she watched the mountain sunrise she told them nothing.

With her letters in July she had heard from her niece Barbara Franks that her husband 'Oliver has just departed to Paris to make a plan for Europe ... I trust he may have some slight success', and Emmeline could add now to her family letter that 'I was thrilled to see that Oliver was leading the British delegation in Paris except on the days when Bevin was there'. The British chaired the sixteen-nation negotiations for a European report towards the plan better known as Marshall Aid, a genuine instrument of Europe's peaceful reconstruction.

Chapter 27
Travelling on

Returning to England in mid-August, much stronger but without a home, Emmeline peregrinated around relations and friends and the Forum Club, keeping an important base with her sister Winifred in Wiltshire while she prepared her passage to Africa and beyond. Later she regretted some of the papers thrown away 'before I left in my effort not to leave more muddles than I could help for other people to clear up if anything should happen to me'. The news of her trip brought requests to speak here, lecture there in South Africa, and solid help from Ella LeMaitre, who had in 1934 been hastily summoned from Roedean, Brighton, to take charge of Roedean, Johannesburg, and who now passed word of Emmeline's coming to J. R. Hofmeyr, the South African Minister of Education and ally of Smuts.

> I have just heard from London [remarked a satisfied Emmeline in the summer] that the Union Government has requested the High Commissioner to give me priority, so that a single-berth cabin, possibly with shower or private bath, is certain to be available for me at some time between the middle and the end of December. Needless to say, these are not presented to me free of charge because of the honour I am doing the Union by visiting it!

Nowhere can Emmeline be found soliciting special treatment, but nor did she betray shame in accepting it, on one occasion remarking, 'What it is to have good luck and good friends!'

Nor did she fully appreciate how lucky she was until she was safely at sea at the end of December 1947, on the RMMV *Athlone Castle*, and encountered 'a little fat lady' and her small son who had stayed at a Southampton hotel 'since early October with their main luggage ready in the Customs shed, and have come down with their bags to nine Union-Castle boats (sitting in a sort of pen in the shed for the whole day of sailing, willing to take either First Class or Cabin)', until their unconfirmed tickets could secure berths. Others were in like case: 'I feel almost guilty at having a place when I think of those poor things sitting on the dock at Southampton. I noticed them as I went through the Passport Office and wondered why they were there.'

Demand for passages continued to exceed supply, so that sixteen months later, trying to return to England from India, Emmeline entered more fully into the feelings of 'those poor things' as she vainly sought a cabin on one ship after another in a steadily hotter and stickier Bombay April, wretchedly aware that however charmingly her Parsee hosts disguised it a stay prolonged from a day or two to more than three weeks must be a nuisance. When she described to her family her return voyage, in a cabin shared with a feverish toddler and his inexperienced young mother, she elaborated on the bright side, the interesting landscape of Suez and the family parties going on leave from Singapore and Penang – 'It is really impressive to see how good the fathers are, often helping with washing and ironing and always sharing in the care of the children' – and silent on the contrast with her comfortable cabin, with its own bathroom and 'a great feeling of peace and independence', on the *Athlone Castle*.

On the liner to South Africa she had amused herself, not with conscientious young fathers, but by counting peers. 'Titles are like pebbles on the beach'; seven lords she named, while 'the baronets and knights and their ladies are so numerous that I have not attempted to count them. I may have left out a few peers!' Emmeline's appreciation of the false values underpinning snobbery was as keen as Thackeray's – and, like Thackeray, had a duke offered her his arm down Bond Street she would not have refused. Nor certainly, as she settled into a chair on the boat deck, did she rebuff the simple kindness of Princess Alice in coming up to 'tuck my rug comfortably round my feet and legs. She then sat on the side of a chair next to me and talked for nearly two hours until the gong went for lunch ... As she said afterwards, our talk ranged from Waterloo to the Royal Wedding, and also went into many by-paths.'

Several times the princess paid Emmeline such attentions, in gracefully varying ways, impressing Emmeline 'by her generous point of view and her attitude to all sorts of questions', and illustrating, in fact, precisely the sort of considerate care a lady bred in the 'best' traditions would have bestowed on a superannuated governess – or on an elderly duchess – sensitively unpatronising, tactfully accommodating her conversation to the other.

> Good manners [Emmeline remarked once] are not, to my mind, something external or put on, something that can be taught by themselves; they spring from a consideration for the feelings, comfort or happiness of other people. It does not always come naturally for children to put other people first ... It is worthwhile for us to spend infinite pains in helping girls to form a habit of consideration for other people in little things as well as in big.

The *Athlone Castle* docked at Cape Town on 6 January 1948, and on 20 November Emmeline left Durban on the *Aronda*, bound for India. She had travelled round the major cities of South Africa itself with forays to smallers towns and rural sights and sites, including Basutoland (modern Lesotho) and spent a happy month in Southern Rhodesia (Zimbabwe). As the headmistress of Durban Girls' College, Emmeline's principal Durban host, summed up, headmistress-style: 'She has seen a great deal of S. Africa, and though some of it has been of necessity hurried and superficial, I think she will have gathered a fairly realistic and sound picture of the set-up.'

And indeed below the travelogue of her family letters are signs of a struggle to open-minded learning. As in 1929, South Africa's myth-making lure hooked her at times, to see and seize on every hint of post-Edenic paradise, the work-won golden age of the pioneers' heroic romance that distantly had enchanted her 1890s adolescence, on, for example, the Macgregors in Rustenburg who had made their furniture with their own hands and their home-grown timber, or the young ex-serviceman just developing a plot in the Umvukwes, 100 miles from Salisbury (Harare) 'under the government scheme for ex-servicemen ... This boy's home was only grass on poles but he introduced me to bedroom, dining-room, bathroom and kitchen – all more or less open. He has a good dog and keeps a gun beside him for leopards, etc.' She could adjust to this context the Merrimans of White River who showed her over their plantations of gum trees and their orchards of fruit and introduced her to an old man, 'one of the early Rhodesian pioneers, and he had most interesting stories to tell of the days when he was transport-driving in the Low Veld', and in the same frame she could locate the pair of English women who had driven their little car through France, across the Sahara and the then Belgian Congo and Nigeria, to coach tennis and swimming in South Africa before buying a patch of land for a smallholding and building 'their own house with direct labour, and with bricks made of their own clay with a pressing machine' and who 'work exceedingly hard'.

Most satisfying of all for this African image were the Whaleys of Ruwanga, cut off in 1929 by flooded roads, now accessible by the Beit bridges built with Sir Alfred Beit's legacy, the infrastructure engineering that followed the pioneers. Half a century earlier the Tanner family had known Josephine Whaley as Josey Rae, and she kept still the letter Nettie had written to her after the death from enteric, just a year after his emigration in 1904, of her brother, born the same day as Nettie's son Herbert. In 1913 Josey had married a veteran of Plumer's Column, they had opened a small gold mine and farmed the land nearby, and in 1926 bought 3,000 acres of 'mostly virgin forest'. Here they built their home, cleared 800 acres, established plantations of tobacco and maize, and reared four sons to be lawyer, surgeon, teacher and farmer. The early hardships and the early labours excited Emmeline and she noted in fascinated detail the processes of tobacco harvesting and drying, but what enchanted her was her diagnosis of

> one of the happiest households you can possibly imagine. I have never heard even the hint of a cross word spoken by anyone to anyone, and I often hear Josey singing at her work ... [Josey seemed to typify values Emmeline rated highly], so self-effacing in one way and yet such a power in the family and household. She has very high principles and lives up to them, but loves fun and experience and is good company ... She is simple and modest but I notice how highly she is thought of wherever we go; she is very sympathetic and people in trouble seem always to turn to her.

But the heroic romance of the pioneers was only one genre Emmeline blended into a complex narrative for her family letters (and she included here those friends, Janet Lowe, Jessie Haybittel, Ann Crofts she counted as honorary family). When she later discussed another experiential level with Ernest and Olivia Barker, the latter categorised it as 'so tragic that it's almost too much', and Emmeline's anxiety emerged in her letters as she eagerly and often searched for evidence of 'the change that has come over most of the Europeans I meet out here in their attitude to the Native Question and in their sense of responsibility about it. It is true that I meet mostly people of British origin', but for her principal tool of enquiry she drew on the diversity of those she did meet.

Through old family ties she knew emigrés of pre-1914, farmers or the Swedenborgian families of commercial Durban, or the blind Braille teacher and journalist who was cousin to her sister Beatrice's patient of the 1920s. But her working life put Emmeline in touch with others ranging from university principals and headmistresses to the wealthy businessmen and judges who interested themselves in governing schools, and ex-pupils of many destinies. So in Maritzburg she stayed with 'an Old Bedfordian', a headmistress and four-times Mayor of Maritzburg, 'the prime mover in the formation of a really delightful native village where every house is in its own garden, and the gardens round the large communal hall, the clinic, the homes for aged men, women and couples, are all kept up by the municipality so as to set a standard'. In Durban Emmeline praised warmly the excellence of the model 'Bantu nursery school' built and supported by Durban Girls' College at their head Elizabeth Middleton's instigation and with student training facilities, but for the value of its work she rated more highly the first started by Elizabeth Middleton in a church hall in one of the worst Durban slums.

From Johannesburg Emmeline reported a meeting with the woman Chairman of the Institute of Race Relations, which 'does an immense amount of excellent work, both academic and practical', and with other women who worked for the 'native blind' and the 'native deaf', and she amassed other such examples, but even as she tallied such efforts – these from the perspective of 'what is done for the natives' – she fretted that 'it only touches the fringes of the problem because the numbers are so enormous and they are increasing at a terrific pace'.

Other perspectives opened to her in her first week after arrival when Ella LeMaitre, headmistress of Roedean, Johannesburg, introduced her to Mrs Ballinger, 'one of the four members elected by the natives to represent them' in the Union Assembly, and ramified through a network of acquaintance. Among her other layers of contact Emmeline drew closer to the gentle, devout Forfars, long-standing Swedenborgian friends, and it was Jack Forfar who gave her on departure Alan Paton's recently published *Cry, the Beloved Country*, so moving to her that she later recommended it to the Sixth Form of Roedean, Brighton, and others. At Roedean, Johannesburg, she had in 1929 been satisfied to conclude her Speech Day address with a call to make South Africa 'a great nation, combining the best qualities of the two great people who form the nation' and had meant the antagonists of her youth, Boer and Briton; in 1948 she spoke there instead of 'the capacity to live successfully with other people as members of a community', of 'an active part in social and public service', of 'oases of endeavour' to make 'a good and happy world for mankind to dwell in'.

She winged the words with enthusiastic particulars and illustrations to speed their urgency, for she spoke soon after a disquieting general election on 26 May. Against expectation Smuts' United Party was defeated, Smuts himself losing his seat.

> The majority is so small, however, [said Emmeline then, ever-hopeful] that the Nationalists will hardly be able to take any very drastic measures and perhaps the responsibility of power may be good for them. It will not be to the advantage of the natives and the Coloured people to have a Nationalist government for the Nats are utterly opposed to much that has been and is being done to improve their lot and their status.

As she explored her friends' reactions she found them 'grieved', and Mrs Ballinger in particular afraid 'that native representation and native progress, as far as legislation is concerned, will soon come to an end. That will be a tragedy.' For the other point of view Emmeline questioned Albert Hertzog, the MP husband of an Old Roedeanian and one of the few Nationalists of her acquaintance, but she was not reassured by his analysis of 'native policy'.

Intermingling in a lyric thread, sometimes exotically, was woven South Africa's visual splendour, so that Emmeline herself began her Roedean Speech Day address with the striking 'contrast between the beauties that we see around us – the wild flowers at the Cape, the jacaranda trees, the loveliness of your gardens, the views from the high points in Johannesburg with the blue line of the Magaliesburg in the distance' – and the distrust and misunderstanding stalking the world. Happily she herself explored the wild flower reserve of Caledon, to learn new species and glory in the massed colours, and with equal fascination and more trepidation learnt to detect the camouflaged animals of the Kruger National park and gleefully itemise those seen. On the coast of the Cape, in the mountains of Natal, everywhere the landscape had its interest and strong beauty, but ever Emmeline returned to human affairs, to weave in a fourth element, academic at one extreme, mildly didactic at the other.

Having accepted numerous invitations to speak to audiences varying from women's lunch clubs to teachers' conferences she was compelled, it seems, to scrutinise her own role for the future, and in South Africa she seems to have questioned the gratifications of the platform. On her eventual return to England she was greeted by several requests: would she open an Oxford vacation course for secondary teachers? Would she accept nomination as the Ministry's representative on Southampton University College's Court of Governors? And so on. She was cautiously responsive, acceding usually only where she had strong previous ties. Thus she was happy to be the Vice-President, then President of Roedean School – both purely honorary positions – and she cheerfully opened a Children's Festival in Nuneaton but some approaches of more real and so more flattering significance she refused on the score of age.

South Africa encouraged her to this. Education gave Emmeline the entrée to universities and schools, which she toured with indefatigable interest born of her primary desire for the continuing adventure of her own education, and she was able to include a black high school in Orlando township for 'hundreds of boys and girls between 13 and 19' and some black primary schools, as well as meet provincial teachers. Personal meetings she enjoyed, and in several talks with J. R. Hofmeyr developed a strong respect and liking for the liberal, idealistic Deputy Prime Minister though 'he lacks the kind of personality that would make him a leader of men'; she grieved for his death soon after. A lengthy address on 'The English Education Act of 1944' for the Natal Teachers' Conference cost hard work but was rewarded with subsequent still lengthier meetings with rural headmasters for example. Such lectures, or others on 'Post-matriculation work', or 'The curriculum', even on child-rearing, drew directly on her own experience and knowledge, and 'A school in war-time' was pure enjoyment for more social gatherings.

She hated, however, to step publicly outside her expertise and was unmoved by applause of her wisdom: this was tested when a fifteen-minute chat at morning tea for the Victoria League in Durban was converted behind her back to a full evening session, with supper, 'so that the men members can attend and hear "things of importance to the Empire"!!!' Irritation at vague expectations and the subject foisted on her flashed several times at the prospect, but she did her best, collecting some notes from books, articles and reported news to use as lifelines. Eventually she took the Commonwealth with both hands, and with all her store of cheerful aplomb, identified (as she summarised) 'two challenges: to reconcile the interests of Western Europe with the interests of the Commonwealth, and the other to lead the world in the production of food and its fair distribution among the peoples of the world' – a recent report on world population and food resources painted a grim picture for the poorer nations. 'I had already explained that we are now at the beginning of what historians call "the fourth British Empire", which may not include a number of countries that were included in the third (even South Africa, perhaps), and that whether it was worthwhile for it to exist at all depended on what it stood for.'

'Judges, mayors, presidents, schoolmasters, and all and all, find her "charming", "vital", "learned", "approachable" and so on ... you might be rather astonished that the lethargic S. Africans in Durban are capable of being so moved,' reported Elizabeth Middleton, herself a headmistress whom her domestic servants called 'She who always goes quickly and says "Do"', to Emmeline's amusement – 'extraordinarily apt'. Nevertheless Emmeline had been vexed at this extension to her range, and was not to be again so trapped. Once, too, she allowed herself a sideways look, at Rhodes

University in Grahamstown, specifically at 'the small library of local history and records, and having specially interesting family and personal collections of letters and documents', and most of all at the woman with a four-year Leverhulme Scholarship to organise and develop this library: 'It is a thing I should enjoy doing.' Very rare indeed was it for Emmeline to mention a might-have-been.

If she underwent a critical self-examination she apparently concluded against the role of all-purpose pundit, and the continuing adventure of self-education was not converted to a training for the Brains Trust. In India Emmeline became disciple rather than teacher. 'I was surprised,' commented Amrit Kaur afterwards, 'to see how much knowledge she had imbibed, and how she understood India's foreign policy and her internal problems', and ascribed it to 'her amazing interest in everybody with whose work she came in contact and in everything she saw'.[1]

As the guest of a Cabinet Minister Emmeline had great advantages in India. She paid her own small coin in advance by submitting at last to vaccination before leaving South Africa, and to inoculations against yellow fever and typhoid, 'putting my principles aside ... Shame!' In the aftermath of Partition the endemic problems facing India's Health Minister were magnified and Amrit Kaur sorely pressed, but at time Emmeline could travel with her and at times explore with a retired general for escort, or the Quaker social worker Agatha Harrison.

She arrived nearly a year after she had written:

I was so shocked by the news of Gandhi's assassination that from the time I saw it when the *Cape Argus* arrived about 8.45 last night I have been able to think of little else. It is not only all that I have heard from Amrit ... but still more from reading regularly *Harijan*, the weekly paper setting forth his teaching and giving in English all the answers he gives to questions put to him after his prayer meetings ... that I have come to realise how absolutely Christ-like his teaching is ... There is no doubt that one of the most saint-like and most Christ-like people who have lived in the world has died, and that millions of people will feel the loss of his influence and his inspiration.

She remembered particularly how Amrit Kaur had been used to retreat to his *ashram* when the hours she worked ('harder and far longer than almost anyone I know') told on her physical frailty, how there she 'works hard in a different way and also for long hours, and she eventually returns entirely refreshed, physically as well as mentally and spiritually'.

A year later, in India, Gandhi's spirit was still powerful:

I do regret never having met Gandhi. When I realise what his influence has meant and the reverence and intense affection felt for him by people like the Prime Minister Nehru, the Deputy P.M. Patel, the Governor-General the scholarly Rajagopalachariar, Mrs Naidu, Amrit and millions of others I feel sure no one could be in contact with him and not be the better for it. It is curious to see the simplicity of dress and mode of life of most of the leaders in India today, and contrast it with the magnificence of the palaces, in the form of Government Houses, etc., that they have had to take over.

At the anniversary services Emmeline's emotions were touched and her intellect pursued, as she pressed a biography of the great man on her family: 'his speech after a trial, given on pp. 90 and following, seems to me to put very clearly his point of view and his reason for feeling that independence was vital for the people of India'. She herself was revising her views of the British presence:

I do feel myself the more I see of the bits of India I know a little that, in spite of the honesty and even devotion of the great majority of Englishmen who have worked in India, it is pathetic that in the last hundred years we have done so little to raise the standard of health, nutrition, and living of the mass of the people, to say nothing of their education. It seems to me that it would have been better for us to spend less of the revenue of the country on administration and on fine buildings like the various Government Houses, and more on such things as health, education and the improvement of conditions, particularly in the villages.

The Government Houses she saw each contributed. In New Delhi, she found an

amazing contrast between the magnificence of the enormous palace, Government House, and its present occupant – a tall, thin, very gentle man in white cotton hand-spun loose garments (tothi and kurta) and cream shawl, with dark glasses and stick. Yet he [C. Rajagopalachariar] is a great scholar with a very fine brain and, one feels at once, a saintly character. He is a strict vegetarian and teetotaller, and one cannot imagine him smoking.

She stayed in Government House, Calcutta, 'immense ... magnificent', and she stayed at Lucknow with the Governor of the United Provinces, the poet Mrs Sarojini Naidu, a 'very short, rather stocky, plain-faced woman of seventy ... an easy speaker and full of humour', also, Emmeline thought, with 'a good eye for colour and the gift of making any place both beautiful and home-like'.

'Home-like' was an established term of praise, as was 'simplicity', and Emmeline seems in the end to have been most open where India affirmed her most deep-held values. So Christ had been the standard by which she measured Gandhi, and so

I was very sorry indeed to leave New Delhi and it is rather strange to leave an atmosphere of Gandhian idealism, and even simplicity though in comfortable surroundings, and to find myself in the midst of the Parsee Community [in Bombay], Persian in origin, Zoroastrian in religion, well-educated, it is true, but wealthy and very disapproving of such movements as Prohibition and of the tendency for the working man to think himself as good as his neighbour.

Still living the high life, in January she had lunched with 'a Maharajah (minor) in his Palace with his Ministers' and, visiting his young Maharani in her rooms 'more or less in purdah', thought her 'something of a hothouse plant, as though a good shaking-up in a hard world might not harm her. Still she is very charming and good to look upon.' At Gwalior in February, by contrast, at the All-India Women's Conference, Emmeline reckoned the Maharani there 'a most intelligent and charming young woman': the evidence lay in her activism, her thoughtful and efficient hospitality, and a little scene when, 'as she was going across the pavement, two Gwalior women prostrated themselves to touch her feet. What a curious relic of the past! She obviously deprecated it and tried to stop them.'

Just as Emmeline tested virtues in terms familiar to her established principles, so she applied these when identifying problems at the other extreme, on visits to refugee and rehabilitation centres for 'unattached displaced women and children, i.e. those whose husbands and fathers have been killed in the communal troubles'. 'The problem,' she reported, 'of dealing with these people who have fled from their homes which are now in Pakistan is not only feeding and clothing them and giving them shelter but rehabilitating them and training them to earn their livings afterwards', maimed and mutilated as many were. Particularly Emmeline approved 'a very useful co-operative movement ... to help refugees – men, women, and families – to help themselves' in trade-based or agricultural groups.

She was as fascinated by every detail of Mira Ben's work to 'improve the cows' and her plans for model villages with rural training schools (though this farm tour involved an alarming trip on an elephant) as by Assembly debates on changes to the Hindu Code 'to do with the position of women in the matter of inheritance, adoption and divorce', and the form of both interests imply the same. The Bill in the Assembly 'comes into conflict with the old prejudices of Hindus' in some respects; Mira Ben's work was prompted by the gradual deterioration of breeding stock resulting from Hindu reverence for cows: implicitly Emmeline still adhered to standards built in the West.

But at innumerable multi-national gatherings she met many perspectives to ponder, and as she continued to write home ordering principles of any kind collapse into a tale of 'some of the things I have been doing without worrying about the chronological order'. India was, in any event, much stranger to the Tanners generally than was White South Africa; their segment of the middle classes had rarely yielded soldiers and administrators for the British raj; and the dominant images of Emmeline's letters derive from a great miscellany of thumbnail sketches to build – perhaps with deliberate intent – the picture of a great nation set to meet 'life eager and unafraid, to refuse none of its challenges, to evade none of its responsibilities, to go forth daily with a gay and adventurous heart, to encounter its risks, to overcome its difficulties and to seize its opportunities with both hands' – to adopt a unattributed quotation she herself had noted in the 1930s as an ideal of living.

So she described daily enterprise on the train to Agra, herself in a women-only compartment:

wider than our compartments but filled not only with nearly twice as many people as there was room for but apparently with most of the household goods of some of them. Everyone of every class travels with rolls of bedding in India but, in addition to tin boxes and these rolls, there were cooking stoves and sacks full of things. The space under every seat was filled and on every rack (each the width of a seat, to be used as a bed at night) and all down the middle with people sitting on them!

And she described the scene at the station as she left Gwalior in a saloon carriage with Amrit Kaur:

Amrit was told that the railway men wanted to see her (there is serious danger of a railway strike), so these men in their working clothes were allowed to come to the front of the crowd. They called out something and Amrit talked to them from the door of the saloon – in Hindi, of course. She told them something to the effect that she knew their wages were too low and the cost of living too high, that the Government would like to help them but the refugees must come first ... It would all be done in time if India were served by the honest work of all her children. We watched from the windows and saw the sullen and sad faces gradually change and light up with smiles, and they all shouted as the train went out the first words of their National Anthem, 'Hail Motherland'.

So at Agra a paragraph in her letter describing a model village being built by the voluntary after-hours effort of professional men and artisans together is followed immediately by an account of the Taj Mahal's beauty, 'soft and pearly in the dawn'. Emmeline did not, could not, tell all; she pictured and did not discuss; and in her letters unguessable reticences must play their part. Her own physical powers were tested as she noticed increasing deafness so that a softly ticking watch became inaudible and even more intense concentration was forced on her to catch all that was said, and as the April heat painfully swelled her feet and ankles, so that she did not go to 'a number of places in the Centre, and even more the South, to which I wanted to go. The South is quite different from the North.'

Still, so much was 'interesting' in Bombay, the traditional Parsee ceremonies to which she was invited by her hosts (the family of girls at Roedean under her) or the several Anglo-Indian schools and apprentice hostels in Bombay she informally inspected on behalf of the India Church Aid Committee in London, or the home life of Old Roedeanians of English origin, or of Amrit's brother, the Governor, at Government House, or at the hill station at Mahableshwar, famous for strawberries.

At last, in May, she left, draped by her farewell group 'in proper Indian fashion, with a long garland of tuberoses, pale pink rosebuds and green foliage', and her mental baggage as crammed as her trunks and cases. After an absence of almost a year and a half she was 'thrilled', she told her family, 'at the thought of seeing you all again.' Yet in a rare introspective moment she also admitted, 'I should love to sail the seas of the world and see all the lands there are to see', only to catch herself up severely: 'I dare say at bottom there may be some unconscious reluctance to take up responsibilities again and start a new life.'

India not only provided Emmeline with a great deal of information, stretching her frame to encompass the customs of 'Holi Day' ('indulged in even by the Prime Minister') and the Mission at Poona she had first heard of in letters from a teaching friend in 1915, but also perhaps clarified to her some of the moral foundations most essential to her and entailed some revisions of the resulting propositions. Yet the essentials remained unchanged, so that when at the end of that year she talked informally of girls' education to the heads of County Grammar Schools, she ended with the importance of absolute values in 'a world where there is little stability, in a changing society where standards are often slippery'. 'Fashions and tastes change, but principles stand unchanged,' she insisted then.

An initial timetable was already mapped before the *Canton* docked in England in mid-May: in May itself the ORA Reunion at Roedean, in early June the AHM Conference in Birmingham, allowing a visit to Janet and Kathleen Lowe first and afterwards to Dorothy de Zouche in Wolverhampton, then the Jubilee for Sherborne's fiftieth anniversary.

As expected, Emmeline undertook the typical business of a retired headmistress, sat on or chaired a few governing bodies for schools and colleges, and a charitable committee here and there; now she listened while a serving headmistress unburdened herself privately, now she enquired on the Indian Education Minister's behalf ('Confidential – very') about schools suitable for '(i) Indian girls coming from families of Indian Princes or aristocratic families, (ii) other Indian girls', and now she was asked to administer a special college bursary; there were interesting meetings of the Historical Association or the ESU or other long-rooted enthusiasms of Emmeline's to attend; there were innumerable old ties with individuals and institutions to keep in good repair. Such was the warp and woof for many of her age in her profession, and activities in their way all able to feed a spirit of enquiry and the need to feel useful.

Yet Emmeline constantly postponed settling down. Even before she had left England she had 'been looking at houses for me in the Newbury and Bath districts but have not yet found what I want, and the prices are fantastic – £4-5000 for very ordinary houses with four bedrooms. Domestic wages are very high too.' Repeatedly after her return her sister Winifred or brother-in-law Edwin Gauntlett or both took her to view potentially desirable properties; always she found drawbacks. Something in her seemed to jib at the finality of such a home, its closure of other possibilities. Always a sound rationale was adduced, and within a year another excuse for postponement emerged.

Would Emmeline, begged the Governors of St Felix, Southwold, act for

the autumn term of 1950 as headmistress to fill an emergency gap? She
yielded; as a well-reputed girls' boarding school St Felix was of a type
familiar to her, and indeed she had known the ex-headmistress Ella Edghill
since she had been head of King's High, Warwick, when Emmeline was at
Nuneaton. Emmeline took up the reins, found some difficulties and conflicts,
and tackled them with cheerful assurance in what one of the staff called
'the happiest term we have had, of unforgettable kindness and understanding, of security and peace, and – *and* – courage to certain of us poor
cowards!' It was Emmeline's golden autumn. On the airy coast she could
breathe freely, her mind was filled and active, her old friend Ernest Barker
came to stay a weekend and lecture, the Old Girls' function ran smoothly,
Aldeburgh had the music of Britten and Pears, and she planned an Easter
trip to Italy for some of the girls.

She stayed in Southwold for the Christmas holiday, and when finally
she drove out of the market square, steering with one hand, waving
affectionately from the window with the other, to the detriment of her
gearbox, she retained an interest there too and saw off the Italian party
with barley-sugar for all on a cold March morning at Victoria Station. The
girls responded with postcards and brought her back, with innocent
inaptness, liqueur from the monks of Certosa.

Emmeline herself returned to Switzerland with Madge Skipworth for
the summer, to Champex in Valais and flowery meadows 'full now of lovely
sulphur anemones and great trumpet gentians of the richest shade of blue',
with the 'whole range of the Dents du Midi and its surrounding mountains'
open before her hotel. She could not stay long: the exchange rate was now
12 francs to the pound sterling. But she was in good heart, emboldened,
and when, as she told the ex-secretary who from time to time helped her
still, she was indirectly approached 'and asked whether in certain
circumstances she would be willing to take over at Harrogate Ladies' College
for a term' she did not at once refuse, though 'clearly bothered'.

So in September 1952 Emmeline went north to Harrogate, and found it
neither a happy experience nor as brief as expected. At Christmas the absent
headmistress resigned 'and I had no alternative but to agree to come back
until Easter. Now [in February 1952] the new headmistress has been
appointed but cannot take up office until September, so I am here until the
end of the summer term,' she wrote to a friend, with no further comment.
Some aspects of 'the College tangle' she talked over with Ernest and Olivia
Barker as they wandered together round Fountains Abbey in the time of
snowdrops. 'These complexes ... disturb me,' owned Sir Ernest. 'They seem
so much out of the normal and take one into a sort of underworld.' Lady
Barker was brisk: 'The Governors might pull their weight a bit more.'

Moreover, influenza ambushed Emmeline's strength, and brought as its
accomplices severe bouts of arthritis in her right arm and shoulder. She
retreated for the Easter break to a health hydro to slay the disabilities and
plan how to justify the Barkers' hope that by the summer 'the ashes of the

past will be dying down, and you can be looking forward to making things straight for the new regime.' On that time in Harrogate Emmeline looked back with no pleasure, nor sense of achievement, and as soon as she was free she organised for herself another journey to Africa, to stay away from England from November 1952 until February 1954. First, however, at her brother Herbert's house, she made her will, sharing an estate eventually valued for probate at £5,500 with a careful sense of fitness round all her brothers and sisters, her nieces and nephews, their children and her godchildren. Specific gifts were bequeathed to just three old friends – Janet Lowe, Jessie Haybittel, Ann Crofts.

The happy time came again with the friends at Ruwanga, in Southern Rhodesia, 'a lovely farm and a peaceful life,' she wrote, but 'I am not thinking of settling here. It is a place for those who can go on making and developing the country – a very worthwhile thing to do.' In England the last of the Watson family died, the last of those for whom Emmeline's sister Beatrice had worked for the last thirty years, and Bee too was free and also homeless. She joined Emmeline in Durban in August 1953, and when Emmeline was engaged elsewhere saw the sights, the Victoria Falls, the Kruger National Park, the 'Garden Route', though – unlike Emmeline in 1948 – did not force her aged knees to the heights of the citadel of the Zimbabwe Ruins to endure a week's swelling as 'worth it for the experience'.

Bee frankly admitted she was bored when Emmeline took her to an Assembly debate where most of the speeches were in Afrikaans, but her sisterly presence may have been a comfort when one day Emmeline 'went for a walk after breakfast, and looking at sea and sky caught my foot in an uneven pavement, and crashed on my forehead. It was made worse by the fact that it was two and a half hours before a doctor could be found to stop the bleeding. I was fortunate not to break a limb but I had a fortnight in a nursing home and am still being doctored hard. Sickening for Bee!' What sickened Bee was the doctors' refusal to order the blood transfusion she herself thought necessary; she had encountered head wounds before, on the Western Front.

Together the sisters returned to England in March 1954 with the notion of setting up house jointly. The question arose how peaceful would be a shared life for two strong-minded old ladies, each accustomed to managing her household, but soon:

We have looked at a house two and a half miles from Winifred and six from Marlborough and we are getting an estimate for the essential alterations, after which we may make an offer for it. The rooms are smaller than we should choose but it has also some good points and it would be good to be near the Gauntletts and only a mile and a half from Bedwyn station, with its good morning and evening trains to and from London.

Nearness to family was counted an asset, reinforced by the first loss to Emmeline's generation in the death of her youngest brother Arthur in 1954.

In the end she and Bee settled near Marlborough, on the edge of Savernake Forest, choosing a pleasantly cottagey house on an untarred road, with a garden angled to fill with sun in summer, where Bee could keep a few chickens. By mid-December it was ready for them to move in, but on the 17th 'we are still in the throes,' said Emmeline, and 'I am not going to tackle books or my personal possessions until the New Year. Eva comes on Wednesday for eight days.' Eva, and Christmas, and Emmeline's seventy-eighth birthday came and went, and in early January Kathleen Moore arrived for a few days.

Snow had fallen and mornings sparkled with frost; in the afternoon of 6 January Emmeline and Kathleen Moore wrapped themselves in thick coats to walk briskly in the wintry glimmer of the whitened forest. As the winter day darkened and they turned homewards Emmeline fell, and again struck an artery in her head. In Savernake Hospital that night an operation was attempted; in the small hours before dawn on 7 January 1955 Emmeline died.

Her cremation at Oxford was private, for the family, and her staunchly pacifying, meliorative humour was missed. At the memorial service at St Martin-in-the-Fields on 24 January a crowded assembly heard George Bell, Bishop of Chichester, speak magisterially of Emmeline's work, but some missed Emmeline herself. 'Wouldn't Em have *enjoyed* it?' said one to another, after the final triumphant verse of the hymn 'Abide with me'. Where and how she had worked and lived her presence had always made a difference: she had represented, organised, guided, vitalised their best aspirations.

References

Chapter 1 First things first

1. Quotations not otherwise identified are taken from EMT Private Papers (see Sources and Bibliography) or from personal communications by numerous ex-staff, pupils and friends of EMT (see Acknowledgments).
2. H. G. Tanner, *Some recollections and reflections* (printed for private circulation, Bath, 1960), p. 8.
3. Elsie B. Sealy, *My memoirs* (Bath, n.d.), pp. 5-9.
4. F. M. L. Thompson, *The rise of respectable society* (London, 1988), p. 252. F. K. Prochaska, *Women and philanthropy in nineteenth-century England* (Oxford, 1980) gives details.

Chapter 2 'Awake our souls!'

1. Swedenborg House records: *Rules and regulations for the guidance of members of the New Church in the City of Bath* (1843-87).
2. David Chivers, *The New Church in Bath, or the history of the Bath Society from its commencement to the year 1876* (London and Bath, 1895); cf. D. Chivers, 'Memoranda and notes' (August, 1896) in Swedenborg House records.
3. Chivers, *New Church in Bath*, p. 29.
4. Information mainly derived from Swedenborg House records.
5. Swedenborg House records: Minute book, October 1903.
6. *Keene's Bath Journal*, 31 October 1901.
7. R. B. Hope, 'Educational development in the City of Bath 1830-1902; with special reference to its inter-relations with social and economic change' (unpub. dissertation for Ph.D, Bristol University, 1970), p. 262.
8. N. P. Simpson, 'A moving staircase: a study of the provision of education in the County Borough of Bath 1870-1974' (unpub. D.Phil. thesis, Hull University, 1980), pp. 13-25.
9. *Kelly's Directory of Somerset* (1889), entry on Weston.
10. Hope, 'Educational development', p. 162.
11. *Report of the Board of Education* (1902), pp. 11-12.
12. Charles E. Pascoe, *Schools for girls and colleges for women: a handbook of female education* (London, 1879), p. 14.
13. Report of the Consultative Committee, *The Education of the Adolescent* (HMSO, 1926), p. 147.
14. Hope, 'Educational development', pp. 232-4; cf. J. Kamm, *Indicative past: a hundred years of the Girls' Public Day School Trust* (London, 1971), *passim*.
15. *Report of the Schools Inquiry Commission* (Parl. Papers, 1868), vol. XIV, p. 177; vol. VII, p. 68.
16. Evidence to the Schools Inquiry Commission, 1865-8.
17. Sir William Walton, interview (1962), quoted in D. Crow, *The Edwardian woman* (London, 1978), p. 125.
18. *Report of the Royal Commission on Secondary Education* (Parl. Papers, 1895), vol. XLV, Miss Olney's evidence, p. 282.
19. D. Beale, L. Soulsby and J. F. Dove, *Work and play in girls' schools* (London, 1898), introduction by D. Beale, pp. 2, 5.

Chapter 3 Opening windows

1. *Report of the Royal Commission on Secondary Education* (Parl. Papers, 1895), vol. XLV, p. 304.
2. *Report* (1895), vol. XLIV, pp. 190-2.
3. *Report* (1895), vol. XLV, p. 304.
4. *Report* (1895), vol. XLIV, pp. 190-2.
5. Letter to Jesse Collings (26 June 1876), quoted in Denis Judd, *Radical Joe: a life of Joseph Chamberlain* (London, 1977), p. 67.
6. M. B. Rowlands, *The West Midlands from AD 1000* (Harlow, 1987), p. 289.
7. Quoted in N. Pevsner and A. Wedgwood, *Warwickshire* (Buildings of England series, Harmondsworth, 1966), p. 155.
8. Stebbing Shaw, *History of Staffordshire* (1801), quoted in Pevsner and Wedgwood, *Warwickshire*, p. 183.

9. *Report* (1895), vol. XLIV, pp. 191-2.
10. *Report* (1895), vol. XLVIII, p. 495.
11. *Report* (1895), vol. XLVI, p. 22.
12. *Report* (1895), vol. XLVIII, p. 498; p. 526.
13. *Report* (1895), vol. XLVIII, p. 527.
14. Swedenborg House records: Minute book, 1894.
15. *Report* (1895), vol. XLVIII, p. 199.
16. *Report* (1895), vol. XLV, pp. 161-2.
17. *Report* (1895), vol. XLVI, pp. 22-3.
18. Article in *Saturday Review* (14 December 1895), p. 804.
19. University Correspondence College, *The Calendar 1891-2* (1892), p. 23.
20. *Report* (1895), vol. XLIII, pp. 242-3.
21. G. Avery, *The best type of girl: a history of girls' independent schools* (London, 1991), p. 231.

Chapter 4 Halifax
1. E. Gaskell, *The life of Charlotte Brontë* (first pub. 1857), chap. 2.
2. *Report of the Royal Commission on Secondary Education* (Parl. Papers, 1895), vol. XLIX, p. 289, p. 298.
3. *Report* (1895), vol. XLIX, p. 290.
4. PRO: ED 109/7175, First Inspection of Council Secondary School (Girls), Halifax, Yorkshire, 14-17 January 1908.
5. *Report* (1895), vol. XLIX, p. 133, p. 154.
6. *Return of the pupils in public and private secondary schools in England* (Parl. Papers, 1897), vol LXX, pp. 557-665.
7. M. J. B. Baddeley, *Yorkshire*, vol. II (1890, and rev. ed. 1908), sections on Halifax and Haworth.
8. Emily Brontë, *Wuthering Heights* (first pub. 1847), chap. 24.
9. Charlotte Brontë, *Shirley* (first pub. 1849), chap. 30.
10. Penelope Lawrence, 'Games and athletics in secondary schools for girls', *Report for the Office of Special Inquiries, Department of Education* (Parl. Papers, 1898), vol. II, pp. 145-58; B. A. Clough, quoted in S. Burstall, *English high schools for girls: their aims, organisation and management* (London, 1907), pp. 99-100.
11. Quoted in G. Avery, *The best type of girl: a history of girls' independent schools* (London, 1991), p. 306.
12. Sophie Bryant, 'The curriculum of a girls' school', *Report for the Office of Special Inquiries, Department of Education* (Parl. Papers, 1898), vol. II, pp. 99-132.

Chapter 5 The turning point
1. Details from Sir H. Burdett (ed.), *The nursing profession: how and where to train* (London, 1900), pp. 154-5.
2. Phyllis Bentley, *O dreams, O destinations: an autobiography* (London, 1962), p. 81.
3. Association of Head Mistresses, 'The true cost of education for girls' (pamphlet, London, 1905); *Report of the Royal Commission on Secondary Education* (Parl. Papers, 1895), vol. XLIII, p. 187.
4. Leading article in *Journal of Education*, December 1903.
5. Leading article in *Educational Times*, December 1903.
6. PRO: ED 109/7175, First Inspection of Council Secondary School (Girls), Halifax, Yorkshire, 14-17 January 1908.
7. Bentley, *O dreams*, pp. 47-8.
8. Bentley, *O dreams*, p. 84.
9. Quoted from E. M. Tanner, *The Renaissance and the Reformation* (Oxford, 1908), pp. 23-5.

Chapter 6 Sherborne
For some material in chapters 6 and 7 I am indebted to Sherborne School for Girls records.
1. PRO: ED 109/1077, First Inspection of Sherborne School for Girls, 16-17 February 1905.
2. PRO: ED 109/1077, First Inspection, 1905; PRO ED 109/1078, Full Inspection of Sherborne School for Girls, 30 November-2 December 1910.

3. K. E. Moore, in *Sherborne School for Girls Magazine*, December 1955.
4. Penelope Lawrence, 'Games and athletics in secondary schools for girls', *Report for the Office of Special Inquiries, Department of Education* (Parl. Papers, 1898), vol. II, pp. 145-58.
5. Anon. (ed.), *Sherborne School for Girls 1899-1949* (Sherborne, Dorset, 1949), p. 94.
6. Anon. (ed.), *Sherborne School*, p. 60.
7. E. Arnot Robertson, 'Potting shed of the English rose', in Graham Greene (ed.), *The old school* (London, 1934; repr. Oxford pb, 1984), pp. 153-64.
8. Phyllis Bentley, *O dreams, O destinations: an autobiography* (London, 1962), p. 79.
9. John Ruskin, 'Of Queens' Gardens', *Sesame and lilies* (first pub. 1865).
10. B. C. Mulliner, *The application of psychology to the science of education, by Johann Friedrich Herbart* (London, 1898).
11. J. H. Badley, *Bedales: a pioneer school* (London, 1923).

Chapter 7 'An excellent chance'
1. Quoted from *Encaenia* (original title of *Sherborne School for Girls Magazine*), January 1907.
2. Quoted from *Sherborne School for Girls Magazine*, October 1910.
3. G. Battiscombe, *Reluctant pioneer: a life of Elizabeth Wordsworth* (London, 1978), p. 175.
4. D. Beale, L. Soulsby and F. Dove, *Work and play in girls' schools* (London, 1898), Part I, section 5.
5. E. H. Major, 'History', in S. Burstall and M. Douglas (eds), *Public schools for girls: a series of papers on their history, aims and schemes of study* (London, 1911), pp. 85-96.
6. Major, 'History', p. 85.
7. G. W. Kitchin to B. C. Mulliner, 11 November 1908, in EMT Private Papers.
8. C. H. Firth to B. C. Mulliner, 13 November 1908, in EMT Private Papers.
9. Board of Education, *Handbook of suggestions for the consideration of teachers and others concerned in the work of Public Elementary Schools* (HMSO, 1927), p. 113. This work replaced the previous 'Instructions to Inspectors' as guidance in curriculum and methods.
10. Rajkumari Amrit Kaur, in *Sherborne School for Girls Magazine*, December 1955.

Chapter 8 Nuneaton
For some material in chapters 8 to 13 I am indebted to Nuneaton High School records, now held by Etone School, Nuneaton, and Minutes of Governors, now in Warwickshire County Record Office.
1. George Eliot, *Scenes of Clerical Life* (first pub. 1858), 'Janet's Repentance', chap. 2; George Eliot, *The Mill on the Floss* (first pub. 1860), espec. Book IV, chap. 1.
2. Board of Education, *Regulations for Secondary Schools* (HMSO, 1909), pp. v, vi-vii.
3. Quoted in S. Burstall, *English high schools for girls* (London, 1907), pp. 14-15.
4. PRO: ED 109/6419, Full Inspection of Nuneaton High School, 19-21 June 1911.
5. Nuneaton High School Minutes of Governors, vol. I (1909-25), 26 June 1918.
6. N. Pevsner and A. Wedgwood, *Warwickshire* (Buildings of England series, Harmondsworth, 1966; repr. 1986), p. 364.
7. D. Milburn, *The growth of a town* (Nuneaton, 1963), p. 70.
8. Nuneaton Borough Council, *Nuneaton and its commercial advantages: the official guide* (Nuneaton, 1917), pp. 11-14.
9. Records of Nuneaton Borough Council Housing Committee (1920) and Education Committee (1921) held in Local Records Department, Nuneaton Public Library.
10. Quoted from speeches of J. Stratford Dugdale, Chairman of Warwickshire County Council, and the Rev. W. McGregor at Nuneaton High School, 23 June 1910.
11. R. Bolton King, J. D. Browne and E. M. H. Ibbotson, *Bolton King: practical idealist* (Warwickshire Local History Society, occasional paper no. 2, Warwick, 1978), pp. 20-21.
12. Quoted from references supplied to support EMT's application to Bedford High School, 1919.
13. Burstall, *English high schools*, pp. 170-74.
14. Report of the Consultative Committee, *Differentiation of Curriculum for boys and girls respectively in secondary schools* (HMSO, 1923), pp. 114-15.
15. Quoted from *Nuneaton High School Magazine*, October 1910.
16. Board of Education, *Regulations for Secondary Schools* (HMSO, 1909), pp. 2-3; p. vi.
17. Material drawn from HM Inspectors' Report, in PRO: ED 109/6419, Full Inspection of Nuneaton High School, 19-21 June 1911.

18. Reports in *Nuneaton Chronicle*, [Nuneaton] *Observer, Tamworth Herald*, and *Midlands Counties Tribune*, 24-9 June 1910.

Chapter 9 Inside stories
1. Quoted from *Nuneaton High School Magazine*, February 1911.
2. HM Inspectors' Report, in PRO: ED 109/6419, Full Inspection of Nuneaton High School, 19-21 June 1911.
3. PRO: ED 10/147, Committee Papers for Consultative Committee, 1924-6.
4. MAHM Minute Books, 12 February 1916.
5. Leah Manning, *A life for education* (London, 1970).
6. Reported in *Nuneaton Chronicle*, [Nuneaton] *Observer*, 1912.
7. Board of Education, *Regulations for Secondary Schools* (HMSO, 1909), p. v.
8. Quoted from *Nuneaton High School Magazine*, June 1919.
9. Quoted from *Nuneaton High School Magazine*, February 1912.

Chapter 10 'Finding out what it means'
1. Quoted from EMT's account in *Nuneaton High School Magazine*, May 1912.
2. Obituary of Bolton King, *The Times*, 18 May 1937.
3. Quoted from *Nuneaton High School Magazine*, May 1912.
4. Quoted by B. Simon, *Education and the Labour movement 1870-1920* (London, 1965), p. 304ff.
5. G. Mazzini, *The Duties of Man* (1844-58), trans. E. Noyes (Dent Everyman ed., 1907), chap. III.
6. Mary Stocks, *The Workers' Educational Association: the first fifty years* (London, 1953; repr. 1968), pp. 14-15, 20.
7. H. Deneke, *Grace Hadow* (London, 1946), p. 17.
8. M. Price and N. Glenday, *Reluctant revolutionaries* (London, 1974), p. 56.
9. Obituary of Edith Major, *The Times*, 19 March 1951.
10. Address printed in *Nuneaton High School Magazine*, February 1918.
11. J. Stuart Maclure (ed.), *Educational documents: England and Wales 1816-1963* (London, 1965), pp. 164-5.
12. Quoted by S. Burstall, *English high schools for girls* (London, 1907), pp. 181-2.

Chapter 11 The Great War
1. R. Bolton King, J. D. Browne and E. M. H. Ibbotson, *Bolton King: practical idealist*, Warwickshire Local History Society, Occas. Paper no. 2 (Warwick, 1978), p. 24.
2. Frances R. Gray, *And gladly wolde he lerne and gladly teche* (London, 1931), p. 204.
3. Nuneaton High School Minutes of Governors, vol. I (1909-25), 9 October 1914.
4. Quoted from *Nuneaton High School Magazine*, June 1916.
5. AHM Annual Report 1916-17, p. 9.
6. Quoted from *Nuneaton High School Magazine*, June 1916.
7. Quoted from *Nuneaton High School Magazine*, October 1917.
8. Quoted from *Nuneaton High School Magazine*, February 1917.
9. H. G. Tanner, *Some reminiscences and reflections* (privately printed, Bath, 1960), p. 80.
10. Tanner, *Some reminiscences*, p. 85.
11. Ida Gandy, *A Wiltshire childhood* (London, 1929; new ed., Gloucester, 1988).
12. Quoted from *Nuneaton High School Magazine*, October 1917.
13. Gray, *And gladly wolde he lerne*, p. 195.
14. Quoted from *Nuneaton High School Magazine*, February 1918.
15. AHM Annual Report 1917-18.

Chapter 12 Specialised bits of work
1. Quoted from *Nuneaton High School Magazine*, February 1917.
2. *Journal of Education*, November 1920.
3. L. C. B. Seaman, *Post-Victorian Britain 1902-1951* (London, 1966; pb 1967), p. 84.
4. Nuneaton High School Minutes of Governors, vol. I (1909-25), 12 February 1919.
5. PRO: ED 109/6420, Full Inspection of Nuneaton High School, 7-10 March 1922.
6. *Cape Argus* (South Africa), 17 January 1930.

7. AHM Annual Reports: 1920 (report of Executive Committee); 1918-19 (resolution of Education Committee); 1921 (Conference, 11-12 June 1920).
8. AHM Annual Report 1918-19 (resolution of Education Committee).
9. Josephine Kamm, *Indicative past: a hundred years of the Girls' Public Day School Trust* (London, 1971), p. 149.
10. PRO: ED 109/6420, Full Inspection of Nuneaton High School, 7-10 March 1922.
11. PRO: ED 109/13, Supplementary Inspection, Bedford High School, 20-21 June 1923.
12. AHM Annual Report 1921 (Conference, 11-12 June 1920).
13. *Journal of Education*, July 1921, report of AHM Conference, pp. 424-6.
14. PRO: ED 12/219, memoranda on Education Pamphlet no. 37 in Special Inquiries and Reports series.
15. PRO: ED 12/218, Headlam to Bruce, 14 September 1914; draft of Circular 869 (1914).
16. PRO: ED 12/218, Headlam to Bruce, 9 October 1917; Headlam to A. F. Pollard (Historical Association), 10 January 1918.
17. PRO: ED 12/218, Bruce to Permanent Secretary, 13 January 1918.
18. PRO: ED 24/1680, Headlam-Morley to Fletcher, 4 October 1918.
19. PRO: ED 24/1186, minutes of Conference on Teaching of History, 24-25 April 1919.
20. PRO: ED 24/1680, Firth to Fisher, 15 June 1919.
21. PRO: ED 12/219, reports of Committees 'A' and 'B', 1920.

Chapter 13 Choosing headmistresses
For some material in chapters 13 to 16 I am indebted to Bedford High School Minutes of Governors and to Bedford High School records.
1. The school's history is described by Joyce Godber and Isabel Hutchins, *A century of challenge: Bedford High School 1882-1982* (Bedford, 1982), K. Westaway (ed.), *Seventy-five years: the story of Bedford High School 1882-1957* (Bedford, 1957), and Joyce Godber, *The Harpur Trust 1552-1973* (Bedford, 1973).
2. Quoted in Godber and Hutchins, *A century of challenge*, p. 507.
3. Quoted from *Nuneaton High School Magazine*, June 1920.

Chapter 14 Bedford High School
1. K. Westaway (ed.), *Seventy-five years: the story of Bedford High School 1882-1957* (Bedford, 1957), p. 75.
2. *The Queen*, 23 September 1922, p. 383.
3. N. Pevsner, *Bedfordshire and the County of Huntingdon and Peterborough* (Buildings of England series, Harmondsworth, 1968), pp. 51-2.
4. Bedford High School Minutes of Governors: 30 October 1919; 27 October 1921.
5. Bedford High School Minutes of Governors: 18 September 1922; 25 September 1923.
6. Speech at Bedford High School, 5 December 1921, as reported by *Bedfordshire Standard*, 9 December 1921.
7. Bedford High School Minutes of Governors, 27 October 1921.
8. Westaway (ed.), *Seventy-five years*, p. 79.
9. Speech at Bedford High School, 5 December 1921, as reported by *Bedfordshire Standard*, 9 December 1921.
10. J. Godber and I. Hutchins, *A century of challenge: Bedford High School 1882-1982*, p. 41.
11. Speech at Bedford High School, 5 December 1921, as reported by *Bedfordshire Standard*, 9 December 1921.
12. In Westaway (ed.), *Seventy-five years*, p. 76.
13. PRO: ED 109/13, Inspection of Art, Bedford High School, 19 November 1923.
14. Article by Winifred Stephens, *The Graphic*, 21 January 1922; see also *The Queen*, 23 September 1922, p. 383.

Chapter 15 The Consultative Committee
1. D. Brock, in J. Dover Wilson (ed.), *The schools of England: a study in renaissance* (London, 1928), p. 157.
2. Nuneaton High School Minutes of Governors, 26 June 1918.

3. *Journal of Education*, April 1922, p. 197; *Journal of Education*, June 1922, p. 334.
4. Report of the Departmental Committee on Scholarships and Free Places (HMSO, 1920), Cmd 968.
5. MAHM Minute Book, 21 October 1922.
6. AHM Conference, 9-10 June 1922, reported by G. McCroben for *Journal of Education*, July 1922, p. 418.
7. *Journal of Education*, July 1922, p. 413.
8. J. Kamm, *Indicative past: a hundred years of the Girls' Public Day School Trust* (London, 1971), p. 142.
9. PRO: ED 209/14, Full Inspection of Bedford High School, 17-20 November 1925, confidential note.
10. D. Brock, in Dover Wilson (ed.), *The schools of England*, pp. 157-8.
11. Quoted in S. Burstall, *English high schools for girls* (London, 1907), p. 3.
12. AHM Conference, 22-23 June 1923, reported by E. Bancroft for *Journal of Education*, July 1923, pp. 449-50.
13. PRO: ED 24/1224, minute, 27 September 1930. Correspondence, minutes and memoranda concerning the Consultative Committee are held in PRO: ED 24/1224-27.
14. Report of the Consultative Committee, *Differentiation of Curriculum for boys and girls respectively in secondary schools* (HMSO, 1923), p. xiii.
15. *Differentiation*, p. 129.
16. E. Barker, *Age and youth* (Oxford, 1953), p. 145.
17. *Journal of Education*, March 1923, pp. 137-8; MAHM Minute Book, 10 February 1923.
18. *Differentiation*, p. 68.
19. *Differentiation*, p. 126.
20. *Journal of Education*, March 1923, p. 138.
21. *Differentiation*, pp. 131-2.
22. See P. Atkinson, 'Fitness, feminism and schooling', in S. Delamont and L. Duffin (eds), *The nineteenth-century woman: her cultural and physical world* (London, 1978), pp. 92-133.
23. Quoted from J. May, *Mme Bergman-Osterburg* (London, 1969), p. 52.
24. Nuneaton Borough records, Report of the Medical Officer of Health for 1919 (1920), p. 23.

Chapter 16 To build a better world
1. In K. Westaway (ed.), *Seventy-five years: Bedford High School 1882-1957* (Bedford, 1957), p. 75.
2. *Bedfordshire Times & Independent*, supplement, 23 March 1923; *Bedford Record*, week ending 24 March 1923, 'The Tinker's' interpretation of LNU focus on schools.
3. As reported in *Bedfordshire Times & Independent*, 10 November 1922.
4. William Morris, 'What Socialists want' (1888), quoted in P. Meier, *William Morris: the Marxist dreamer* (1972), II, pp. 311-13.
5. S. and B. Webb, *The Consumers Co-operative Movement* (1921), p. 161.
6. PRO: ED 12/1226, Wood to Hadow, 20 March 1923.
7. PRO: ED 12/1226, Wood to Hadow, 20 March 1923.
8. PRO: ED 12/1226, minutes of meeting, 25-26 October 1923.
9. PRO: ED 12/1226, Hadow to Selby-Bigge, 29 October 1923.
10. PRO: ED 12/1226, minute of meeting with Selby-Bigge, 22 November 1923.
11. Report of the Consultative Committee, *Psychological Tests of Educable Capacity* (HMSO, 1924; repr. 1928), p. 108; pp. 108-09; p. 109.
12. *Psychological Tests*, p. 71.

Chapter 17 Reluctantly to Roedean
For some material in chapters 17 to 26 I am indebted to the records of Roedean School.
1. Quoted from D. de Zouche, *Roedean School 1885-1955* (Brighton, 1955), pp. 27-8.
2. 'An address given by Mrs Sidgwick on the occasion of laying the foundation stone of Roedean School' (privately-printed pamphlet, Brighton, 1897), p. 12.
3. *Roedean School Magazine*, 1924, ORA supplement, report of meeting on 27 March 1924.
4. de Zouche, *Roedean School*, p. 85.
5. Beatrice Lawrence's letters to her mother, Mrs Roger Lawrence, 5 October and 18 October

1924, quoted by kind permission of Mrs Brenda Tyler.
6. Article by Joyce Whitehouse (born Handley-Seymour) in *Roedean School Magazine* (1947), p. 12.

Chapter 18 A headmistress of the 1920s
1. Figures in PRO: ED 109/6001, Full Inspection of Roedean School, 7-10 June 1927.
2. Speech by Beatrice Sparks at AHM Conference, 11-12 June 1926, reprinted in *Journal of Education*, July 1926, p. 488.

Chapter 19 'Popularly known as the Hadow Report'
1. PRO: ED 12/1226.
2. Report of the Consultative Committee, *The Education of the Adolescent* (HMSO, 1926), p. iv.
3. See PRO: ED 109/5995, Inspection of Brighton Municipal Secondary School for Girls, 17-20 February 1920; PRO: ED 109/5991, Inspection of Brighton Municipal Secondary School for Boys, 9-12 June 1931.
4. Records of Brighton Education Committee held by Brighton Public Library (Reference Department).
5. Draft report of Education Committee to Town Council, Brighton, June 1926.
6. PRO ED 12/1226, minutes of meeting, 23-4 April 1925.
7. Paper given at North of England Education Conference, January 1926.
8. Article in *Journal of Education*, October 1931, pp. 691-2.
9. Evidence given to Consultative Committee is held in PRO ED 10/147.
10. Percy Nunn, *Education: its data and first principles* (London, 1923), p. 5.
11. PRO: ED 12/1224, note by Chambers, 29 May 1924.
12. PRO: ED 12/1224, memorandum, 4 April 1928.
13. R. J. W. Selleck, 'The Hadow Report: a study in ambiguity', in R. J. W. Selleck (ed.), *Melbourne studies in education* (Melbourne, 1972), pp. 143-70.
14. *Journal of Education*, February 1930, p. 111; *Journal of Education*, February 1927, pp. 85-6.
15. Quoted in B. Simon, *The politics of educational reform 1920-1940* (London, 1974), p. 146.
16. Article in *Journal of Education*, February 1930, pp. 91-2.
17. Conclusions are summarised in *The Education of the Adolescent*, chapter XI.
18. Article in *Journal of Education*, October 1931, pp. 691-2.
19. Note in PRO: ED 12/1225.
20. Articles by A. B. Allen of Goldbeaters' Modern School, Edgware, in *Journal of Education*, April 1933, pp. 210-11; May 1933, pp. 270-1; June 1933, pp. 350-2.
21. AHM Report (1928) of Conference on 1-2 July 1927; see also report of Conference by E. M. Fox for *Journal of Education*, August 1927, pp. 585-6.
22. See AHM Report (1927) for L. Lowe's report to Executive Committee on conference held on 15 October 1927; AHM Report (1928) for recommendations recorded in May 1928; AHM Report (1929) for resolutions at AHM Conference, 8-9 June 1928.
23. Appendix attached to AHM Report (1928).
24. AHM Report (1929), letter to Lord Eustace Percy, signed by L. Lowe on behalf of AHM, 11 December 1928.
25. Statement on Circular 1421 by London branch of AHM printed in AHM Report for 1932.
26. Quoted from letter describing questionnaire sent to all LEAs by AHM Executive Committee, 28 November 1932.
27. Presidential address to AHM Conference, 12-13 June 1925.
28. As reported in *Journal of Education*, July and August 1933.
29. E. Gwatkin's address (13 June 1936) printed as appendix to AHM Report for 1936.
30. Article by W. E. Crapper in *Journal of Education*, August 1931, pp. 559-61.
31. Statement to Consultative Committee reported to AHM Executive Committee (23 February 1934), in AHM Minutes.
32. AHM Conference, 16-17 June 1933, reported in *Journal of Education*, July 1933, pp. 472-4.

Chapter 20 'Activity and experience'
1. PRO: ED 109/6001, Full Inspection of Roedean School, 7-10 June 1927.

2. PRO: ED 109/6002, Full Inspection of Roedean School, 16-19 May 1938.
3. AHM Report for 1937, paper read by M. Davies on 'A challenge: the relation between education and the social system desired', 12 June 1937.
4. Report of the Consultative Committee, *Books in Public Elementary Schools* (HMSO, 1928).
5. Report of the Consultative Committee, *The Primary School* (HMSO, 1931).

Chapter 21 Aspects of Roedean in the 1930s
1. PRO: ED 109/6002, Full Inspection of Roedean School, 16-19 May 1938, from which all comments by HM Inspectors (1938) are drawn.
2. AHM Report for 1938.
3. In *Roedean School Magazine*, 1937. Much information on school activities is recorded in annual issues.
4. Report of AHM Conference, 11-12 June 1937, by E. M. Fox for *Journal of Education*, July 1937, p. 444.
5. Address to Mental Health Conference, October 1936, organised by National Council of Mental Hygiene, reprinted in H. Deneke, *Grace Hadow* (London, 1946), pp. 120-6.
6. Article in *Journal of Education*, September 1926, pp. 645-7.
7. Figures drawn from PRO: ED 109/6002, Full Inspection of Roedean School, 16-19 May 1938.

Chapter 22 'Even to understand the news'
1. Annual Report of Executive Committee to General Council of League of Nations Union for year ending 31 December 1927, 'Teachers' Declaration', pp. 12-13.
2. Minutes of 9th Annual Meeting of the General Council of LNU, held at Matlock, Bath, 20-22 June 1928, remarks by Gilbert Murray in discussion on adoption of Annual Report for 1927. For LEA discussions and public comment see e.g. *Journal of Education*: July 1927, pp. 485-6; August 1927, pp. 589-90; *The Times* correspondence columns for July 1927.
3. Minutes of 9th Annual Meeting of the General Council of LNU, 20-22 June 1928, comments by Gilbert Murray on American Peace Pact, pp. 26-36.
4. AHM Report for 1937, report by EMT as AHM representative on Education Committee of English-Speaking Union; LNU *Yearbook* (1936), section on Education, p. 41.
5. *Roedean School Magazine*, 1938, EMT's report on Speech Day.
6. Letter printed in *Journal of Education*, April 1944, p. 186.
7. Paper on *World Citizenship: recommendations on the teaching of history*, printed among appendices to AHM Report for 1930 (1931).
8. Including *Journal of Education*, December 1939, p. 751.
9. Brighton Education Committee Minutes, meeting of General Purposes Committee, 14 May 1935; AHM Report for 1935, resolution at Conference, 21-22 June 1935.
10. Figures taken from LNU *Yearbook* (1936), pp. 27f; see also A. Livingstone, *The Peace Ballot* (1935).
11. LNU *Yearbook* (1938), p. 5.
12. LNU *Yearbook* (1938), p. 49 for report on visit to USA and Canada in spring, 1937.
13. See R. C. D. Jasper, *George Bell, Bishop of Chichester* (Oxford, 1967), p. 73.
14. See Vera Brittain, *Diary of the Thirties: 1932-39 Chronicle of Friendship*, ed. Alan Bishop (London, 1986), p. 346.
15. Address at memorial service for EMT at St Martin-in-the-Fields, London, 24 January 1955.
16. AHM Minute Books of Executive Committee, 8 October 1938 and 18 November 1938.
17. AHM Minute Books of Executive Committee, 18 November 1938 and 4 February 1939.
18. AHM Minute Books of Executive Committee, 18 November 1938.

Chapter 23 At war again
1. AHM Minute Books of Executive Committee, meeting with Lady Reading on 9 July 1938; evacuation discussions described in Joint Four Report for 1938.
2. My account of Joint Four activities draws principally on AHM Minute Books of Executive Committee, AHM Reports for 1939-42, and Joint Four Reports for 1939-42.
3. Meeting on 8 July 1941 described in Joint Four Report for 1941.
4. Colonel Allan Block, 50th Bn The Queen's Royal Regiment, to EMT, 14 August 1940, in EMT Private Papers.

Chapter 24 Roedean at Keswick

1. On Skiddaw: W. Wordsworth, *The Prelude* (1850 text), I, 295-6.
2. *Roedean School Magazine*, 1940, p. 64.
3. *Roedean School Magazine*, 1940, p. 5.
4. Quotations from W. Wordsworth: *The Prelude* (1850 text), I, 396-7, 301; 'Michael' (1800), 30-33.
5. H. G. Tanner, *Some recollections and reflections* (printed for private circulation, Bath, 1960), p. 160.
6. A. Tegla Davies, *The Friends' Ambulance Unit* (London, 1947), p. 35.
7. Tanner, *Some recollections*, p. 165.

Chapter 25 1944: Education Act and Fleming Report

1. Report of the Consultative Committee, *Secondary Education with special reference to Grammar Schools and Technical High Schools* (HMSO, 1938; repr. 1959)
2. AHM Report for 1939, Conference on 9-10 June 1939.
3. Hansard, vol. 343, col. 372.
4. A good discussion may be found in P. H. J. H. Gosden, *Education in the Second World War* (London, 1976), pp. 238-48.
5. *Roedean School Magazine*, 1938, pp. 19-22.
6. PRO: ED 136/601, EMT to R. A. Butler, 22 June 1942.
7. R. A. Butler, *The art of the possible* (London, 1971), p. 95.
8. PRO: ED 136/261, meeting with representatives of secondary associations, 18 December 1942.
9. Copy of Joint Four Memorandum dated 28 May 1942 in PRO: ED 136/261.
10. *Journal of Education*, February 1941, p. 47.
11. PRO: ED 136/129, meeting of R. H. Tawney and R. A. Butler, 5 September 1941.
12. Spencer Leeson, *The public schools question* (London, 1948), p. 14.
13. Memorandum, 16 August 1941, in PRO: ED 12/518 and ED 136/129.
14. PRO: ED 136/597, Chuter Ede to RAB, 13 January 1942.
15. PRO: ED 136/129, RAB to G. G. Williams, 24 October 1941; ED 136/599, Chuter Ede to RAB, 13 May 1942.
16. PRO: ED 136/667, GGW to Osyth Potts, 29 December 1941.
17. EMT's letter to GGW, 6 January 1942, filed in PRO: ED 136/597.
18. 'Resolutions passed at the Conference of the Association of Head Mistresses held at Malvern Girls' College, April 8th and 9th, 1942' and Memorandum on 'Education after the war' sent to Board of Education on 8 July 1942 in response to request by Sir Maurice Holmes, filed as TBN 20 with AHM Minute Books, etc. (see Bibliography). See also AHM Report for 1942 (report of Conference) and *Journal of Education*, May 1942, p. 224, report of AHM Conference.
19. PRO: ED 136/597, meeting of RAB with GBA Committee, 14 January 1942; *Journal of Education*, May 1942, p. 195, report of RAB's address to NUT Conference, 8-10 April 1942.
20. PRO: ED 136/597, meeting of HMC representatives with GGW, 29 January 1942.
21. PRO: ED 136/599, RAB's minute of visit from Fisher, 22 April 1942.
22. PRO: ED 136/599, Chuter Ede to RAB, 24 April 1942.
23. PRO: ED 136/599, RAB to Fisher, 29 April 1942, and RAB's minute of meeting with Fisher, 8 May 1942.
24. PRO: ED 12/518, RAB's minute of meeting with G. D. H. Cole and H. Laski, 12 May 1942.
25. Papers on selection of Fleming Committee in PRO: ED 136/599.
26. M. D. Brock, 'The creed of a head mistress', in E. Addison Phillips and others, *The head mistress speaks* (London, 1937), pp. 33-56.
27. PRO: ED 136/599, Simon to RAB, 27 May 1942.
28. See Gosden, *Education in the Second World War*, pp. 340-6.
29. PRO: ED 136/600, M. Holmes to GGW, 29 August 1942; ED 136/599, Note 7 on terms of reference, May 1942.
30. PRO: ED 136/601, EMT to RAB, 22 June 1942.
31. PRO: ED 136/604, 'Notes for ... witnesses', no. 17. Compare earlier draft, ED 136/600, 'Notes', no. 20.
32. Memorandum of evidence given by Sir M. Holmes on 10 November 1942 in PRO: ED 12/518;

minutes of MH's presentation to Committee in ED 136/604.

33. PRO: ED 12/518, evidence given by representatives of GBGSA, 29 June 1943.
34. PRO: ED 136/603, Fleming to RAB, 18 June 1944.
35. PRO: ED 136/598, RAB to MH, 14 August 1942, and MH to RAB, 18 August 1942.
36. PRO: ED 12/518, O. Potts to Heaton, 15 December 1942.
37. PRO: ED 136/470, statement by AHM Executive Committee, dated 5 February 1944.
38. PRO: ED 136/261, Joint Four meeting with President and others of Board of Education, 23 July 1942.
39. EMT's comments in *Roedean School Magazine*, 1944.
40. Minutes of meeting on 23 March 1945 in PRO: ED 12/518; list of members of negotiating committee, with copy of committee's report, in ED 136/607.
41. Papers on negotiations about Schemes for direct grant schools in PRO: ED 12/518 from which details on pp. 354-7 are drawn.
42. Copy of GPDST resolution, dated 17 March 1945, with letter from Muriel Potter, 19 March 1945, in EMT Private Papers.
43. House of Commons debate, 9 November 1945, Hansard, col. 1708.
44. See J. Kamm, *Indicative past: a hundred years of the GPDST* (London, 1971), p. 182.
45. See M. Price and N. Glenday, *Reluctant revolutionaries* (London, 1974), pp. 99-100.
46. Dr B. Evans, in *Old Roedeanians Association Magazine*, 1988, p. 17.

Chapter 26 Retirement
1. EMT to Barbara Briggs, 23 April 1946, quoted by kind permission of Miss B. Briggs.
2. *Roedean School Magazine*, 1946, p. 3.
3. *University of London Gazette*, report of ceremony for Foundation Day, 27 November 1947.
4. *Roedean School Magazine*, 1947, p. 64.

Chapter 27 Travelling on
1. Rajkumari Amrit Kaur, in *Sherborne School for Girls Magazine*, December 1955.

Sources and Bibliography

This is not an exhaustive bibliography but intended to show the sorts of material I found relevant or useful.

Principal sources of unpublished and privately-held material

EMT Private Papers: collection of material, including letters, notebooks and miscellaneous documents, originally belonging to Emmeline Tanner; reference also covers MS notes made by Beatrice Tanner and Winifred Gauntlett. All now in the possession of Mrs P. J. Kirton.

Personal communications: material deriving from correspondence and meetings with individuals, July 1990 to April 1993.

AHM Minute Books, Executive Committee Minutes, and Reports: records of Association of Head Mistresses, at Modern Records Centre, University of Warwick Library, catalogued as MS 188

Bedford High School Minutes of Governors: at offices of The Bedford Charity (Harpur Trust), Bedford

Bedford High School records: at Bedford High School, Bedford

Hope, R. B., 'Educational development in the City of Bath 1830-1902', unpub. dissertation for Ph.D., Bristol University, 1970

Joint Four Reports: records of Joint Committee of Four Secondary Associations, at Modern Records Centre, University of Warwick Library, catalogued as MSS 59/6/2

MAHM Minute Books: records of Midlands Association of Head Mistresses, at Modern Records Centre, University of Warwick Library, catalogued as MS 188

Nuneaton High School Minutes of Governors: at Warwickshire County Record Office, catalogued as CR 1589/440

Nuneaton High School records: at Etone School, Nuneaton

PRO: records at Public Record Office, Kew; Census Returns, Chancery Lane

Roedean School records: at Roedean School, Brighton

Sherborne School for Girls records: at Sherborne School for Girls, Dorset

Simpson, N. P., 'A moving staircase: a study of the provision of education in the County Borough of Bath 1870-1974', unpub. D.Phil. thesis, Hull University, 1980

Swedenborg House records: Minute Books and Accounts of Bath Society held by Library and Documents Committee, Swedenborg House, Bloomsbury Way, London

Tanner, F. W., unfinished MS memoirs in possession of his children

Tanner, H. G., *Some recollections and reflections* (printed for private circulation, Bath, 1960)

I am also indebted to the following institutions for use of material: Bath City Record Office, Guildhall, Bath; Bath Public Library (Local Records Department); Bedford Public Library (Local Records); Brighton Public Library (Reference Library); Central Library (Local Records), Halifax; Hartley Library, University of Southampton; Nuneaton Public Library (Local Records).

Official publications

Report of the Royal Commission on Secondary Education: (Parl. Papers, 1895), vols XLIII-XLIX ('Bryce Report'). C.7862

Return of the pupils in public and private secondary schools in England: (Parl. Papers, 1897), vol. LXX. C.8634

Bryant, S., 'The curriculum of a girls' school', *Report for the Office of Special Inquiries, Dept of Education* (Parl. Papers, 1898), vol. II, pp. 99-132.

Lawrence, P., 'Games and athletics in secondary schools for girls', *Report for the Office of Special Inquiries, Dept of Education* (Parl. Papers, 1898), vol. II, pp. 145-58.

Board of Education, Code of Regulations for Public Elementary Schools in England (HMSO, 1909)

Board of Education, Regulations for Secondary Schools (HMSO, 1909, 1917 *et seq.*)

Board of Education, Handbook of Suggestions for the Consideration of Teachers and Others concerned in the work of Public Elementary Schools (HMSO, 1927)

Board of Education, Circulars: see individual references

Report of the Departmental Committee on Scholarships and Free Places (HMSO, 1920)

Report of the Consultative Committee on Differentiation of Curriculum for Boys and Girls Respectively in Secondary Schools (HMSO, 1923)

Report of the Consultative Committee on Psychological Tests of Educable Capacity (HMSO, 1924)
Report of the Consultative Committee on the Education of the Adolescent (HMSO, 1926)
Report of the Consultative Committee on the Primary School (HMSO, 1931)
Report of the Consultative Committee on Secondary Education with special reference to Grammar Schools and Technical High Schools (HMSO, 1938; repr. 1959): 'Spens Report'
Report of the Committee of the Secondary Schools Examination Council on Curriculum and Examinations in Secondary Schools (HMSO, 1943): 'Norwood Report'
Report of the Departmental Committee on the Public Schools and the General Educational System (HMSO, 1944): 'Fleming Report'

Published sources

Abel-Smith, Brian, A history of the nursing profession (London, 1960; new ed., 1975)
Addison Phillips, E. and others, The head mistress speaks (London, 1937)
Ashworth, W., An economic history of England 1870-1939 (London, pb 1972)
Association of Head Mistresses, 'The true cost of education for girls' (pamphlet, London, 1905)
Atkinson, Paul, 'Fitness, feminism and schooling', in S. Delamont and L. Duffin (eds), The nineteenth-century woman: her cultural and physical world (London, 1978), pp. 92-133.
Avery, Gillian, The best type of girl: a history of girls' independent schools (London, 1991)
Baddeley, M. J. B., Yorkshire, vol. II 'The West Riding' (1890, and rev. ed., 1909)
Baker, Alfred, The life of Sir Isaac Pitman (London, 1919)
Balfour, Sir Graham, Educational administration (Oxford, 1921)
Banks, Olive, Parity and prestige in English secondary education (London, 1955)
Banks, Olive, The sociology of education (London, 3rd ed., 1976)
Barker, Sir Ernest (ed.), The character of England (Oxford, 1947)
Barker, Sir Ernest, Age and youth (Oxford, 1953)
Barnard, H. C., A history of English education from 1760 (London, 2nd ed., 1971)
Barry, C. H., and F. Tye, Running a school (London, 1972)
Battiscombe, Georgina, Reluctant pioneer: the life of Elizabeth Wordsworth (London, 1978)
Beale, Dorothea, Lucy H. M. Soulsby and Jane Frances Dove, Work and play in girls' schools (London, 1898)
Beddoe, Deirdre, Back to home and duty: women between the wars 1918-1939 (London, 1989)
Bellamy, Richard (ed.), Victorian Liberalism (London, 1990)
Bentley, Phyllis, O dreams, O destinations: an autobiography (London, 1962)
Bernbaum, Gerald, Social change and the schools 1918-1944 (London, 1967)
Berry, P., and A. Bishop (eds), Testament of a generation: the journalism of Vera Brittain and Winifred Holtby (London, 1985)
Bird, Vivian, A portrait of Birmingham (London, 1970)
Black, S. Burgoyne (ed.), A Farningham childhood (Sevenoaks, 1988)
Branson, Noreen, and Margot Heinemann, Britain in the nineteen thirties (London, 1971)
Breeden, E. H., Call back the lovely April (Kineton, 1972)
Burdett, Sir Henry (ed.), The nursing profession: how and where to train (London, 1900)
Burnett, John (ed.), Useful toil: autobiographies of working people from the 1820s to the 1920s (London, 1974)
Burnett, John, Plenty and want: a social history of diet in England from 1815 (London, rev. ed., 1979)
Burnett, John (ed.), Destiny obscure: autobiographies of childhood, education and family from the 1820s to the 1920s (London, 1982)
Burstall, Sara, English high schools for girls: their aims, organisation and management (London, 1907)
Burstall, Sara, Retrospect and prospect (London, 1933)
Burstall, Sara, and M. Douglas (eds), Public schools for girls: a series of papers on their history, aims and schemes of study (London, 1911)
Burstyn, Joan N., Victorian education and the ideal of womanhood (1980; New Brunswick, 1984)
Butler, R. A., The art of the possible (London, 1971)
Campagnac, E. T., Education in its relation to the common purpose of humanity (London, 1925)
Ceadel, Martin, Pacifism in Britain 1914-45: the defining of a faith (Oxford, 1980)
Chivers, David, The New Church in Bath, or the history of the Bath Society from its commencement to the year 1876 (London and Bath, 1895)

Clarke, A. K., A history of the Cheltenham Ladies' College 1853-1953 (London, 1953)

Clarke, F., Education and social change (London, 1940)

Cleeve, Marion, Fire kindleth fire: the professional autobiography of Marion Cleeve, headmistress of Snellham Municipal Secondary School for Girls (London, 1930)

Colls, R., and P. Dodd (eds), Englishness: politics and culture 1880-1920 (London, 1986)

Crossick, Geoffrey (ed.), The lower middle class in Britain 1870-1914 (London, 1977)

Curtis, S. J., and M. E. A. Boultwood, An introductory history of English education since 1800 (London, 2nd ed., 1962)

Delamont, S., and L. Duffin (eds), The nineteenth-century woman: her cultural and physical world (London, 1978)

Deneke, Helena, Grace Hadow (London, 1946)

Dent, H. C., The Education Act 1944 (London, 12th ed., 1968)

de Zouche, D. E., Roedean School 1885-1955 (Brighton, 1955)

Dingwall, R., A. M. Rafferty and C. Webster, An introduction to the social history of nursing (London, 1988)

Dover Wilson, J. (ed.), The schools of England: a study in renaissance (London, 1928)

Dyhouse, Carol, Girls growing up in late Victorian and Edwardian England (London, 1981)

Eaglesham, E. J. R., Foundations of twentieth-century education in England (London, 1967)

Franks, Hilda, A country child of the 1890s (Lewes, 1987)

Godber, Joyce, The Harpur Trust 1552-1973 (Bedford, 1973)

Godber, Joyce, and Isabel Hutchins, A century of challenge: Bedford High School 1882-1982 (Bedford, 1982)

Gosden, P. H. J. H., The evolution of a profession (Oxford, 1972)

Gosden, P. H. J. H., Education in the second world war (London, 1976)

Gray, Frances R., And gladly wolde he lerne and gladly teche (London, 1931)

Greene, Graham (ed.), The old school (first pub. 1934; Oxford pb, 1984)

Haddon, J., Bath (London, 1973)

Haldane, E. S., The British nurse in peace and war (London, 1923)

Halsey, A. H. (ed.), British social trends since 1900 (rev. ed., London, 1988)

Harrison, Brian, Prudent revolutionaries: portraits of British feminists between the wars (Oxford, 1987)

Harte, Negley, The University of London 1836-1986 (London, 1986)

Historical Association, The Historical Association 1906-1956 (London, 1957)

Holcombe, Lee, Victorian ladies at work: middle-class working women in England and Wales 1850-1914 (Newton Abbot, 1973)

Hollis, Patricia (ed.), Women in public: the woman's movement 1850-1900 (London, 1979)

Holtby, Winifred, Women in a changing civilisation (London, 1934)

Horn, Pamela, The Victorian and Edwardian schoolchild (Gloucester, 1989)

Hughes, M. V., A London girl of the 1880s (Oxford pb, 1978)

Hunt, Felicity (ed.), Lessons for life: the schooling of girls and women 1850-1950 (Oxford, 1987)

Jasper, R. C. D., George Bell, Bishop of Chichester (London, 1967)

John, A. V. (ed.), Unequal opportunities: women's employment in England 1800-1918 (Oxford, 1985)

Kamm, Josephine, Hope deferred: girls' education in English history (London, 1965)

Kamm, Josephine, Indicative past: a hundred years of the Girls' Public Day School Trust (London, 1971)

King, R. Bolton, J. D. Browne and E. M. H. Ibbotson, Bolton King: practical idealist, Warwickshire Local History Society, Occasional Paper no. 2 (Warwick, 1978)

Lawrence, E. S., The origin and growth of modern education (Harmondsworth, 1970)

[Lawrence, Paul], The founders of Roedean (1935)

Lawson, J., and H. Silver, A social history of education in England (London, 1973)

League of Nations Union, Annual report of the Executive Committee (London, 1927-30)

League of Nations Union, Year Book (London, 1933-8)

Leeson, Spencer, The public schools question (London, 1948)

Lewis, Jane (ed.), Labour and love: women's experience of home and family 1850-1940 (Oxford, 1986)

Lowndes, G. A. N., The silent social revolution (Oxford, 1937; rev. ed. 1969)

Macdonald, Lyn, The roses of no man's land (London, 1980)

Mack, E. C., Public schools and British opinion since 1860 (New York, 1941)

Maclure, J. Stuart (ed.), Educational documents: England and Wales 1816-1963 (London, 1965)

Maclure, J. Stuart, One hundred years of London education 1870-1970 (London, 1970)

Mais, S. P. B., All the days of my life (London, 1937)

Manning, Leah, *A life for education* (London, 1970)

Marriott, Stuart, *Extramural empires: service and self-interest in English university adult education 1873-1983* (Nottingham, 1984)

Milburn, Dennis, *The growth of a town* (Nuneaton, 1963)

Mitchell, B. R., and P. Deane, *Abstract of British historical statistics* (Cambridge, 1962)

Mitchell, J., and A. Oakley (eds), *The rights and wrongs of women* (London, 1976)

Montgomery, J., *The twenties: an informal social history* (London, 1957)

Muggeridge, M., *The thirties: 1930-40 in Great Britain* (London, 1940)

Musgrave, P. N., *Society and education in England since 1800* (London, 1968)

Nunn, T. Percy, *Education: its data and first principles* (London, 1923)

Ogg, David, *Herbert Fisher* (London, 1947)

Partington, G., *Women teachers in the twentieth century* (Slough, 1976)

Pascoe, Charles E., *Schools for girls and colleges for women: a handbook of female education, chiefly designed for the use of persons of the upper middle class, together with some chapters on the higher employment of women* (London, 1879)

Patterson, A. Temple, *The University of Southampton* (Southampton, 1962)

Patterson, A. Temple, *Southampton: a biography* (London, 1970)

Pedersen, J. S., 'Schoolmistresses and headmistresses: élites and education in 19th-century England', *Journal of British Studies*, vol. 15 (1975), pp. 135-62.

Percival, Alicia C., *The English miss yesterday and today* (London, 1939)

Price, Mary, and Nonita Glenday, *Reluctant revolutionaries: a century of headmistresses 1874-1974* (London, 1974)

Reid, Andrew (ed.), *Why I am a Liberal: definitions and personal confessions of faith by the best minds of the Liberal Party* (London, 1885)

Rowlands, Marie B., *The West Midlands from AD 1000*, Regional History of England series (London and New York, 1987)

Sanderson, Michael, *Educational opportunity and social change in England* (London, 1987)

Seaman, L. C. B., *Post-Victorian Britain 1902-51* (London, 1966)

Selby-Bigge, Sir L. A., *The Board of Education* (London, 1927)

Selleck, R. J. W., 'The Hadow report: a study in ambiguity', in R. J. W. Selleck (ed.), *Melbourne studies in education* (Melbourne, 1972)

[Sherborne School for Girls], *Sherborne School for Girls 1899-1949* (Sherborne, 1949)

Simon, Brian, *Education and the Labour movement 1870-1920* (London, 1965)

Simon, Brian, *The politics of educational reform 1920-1940* (London, 1974)

Simon, Sir John, *Portrait of my mother* (London, 1936)

Smith, W. O. Lester, *Education: an introductory survey* (Harmondsworth, rev. ed. 1966)

Spencer, F. H., *An Inspector's testament* (London, 1938)

Spencer, F. H., *Education for the people* (London, 1941)

Spender, Dale, and Elizabeth Sarah (eds), *Learning to lose: sexism and education* (London, rev. ed., 1988)

Steedman, Carolyn, *Childhood, culture and class in Britain: Margaret McMillan 1860-1931* (London, 1990)

Stevens, Frances, *The living tradition: the social and cultural assumptions of the grammar school* (London, 3rd ed. 1972)

Stevenson, John, *British Society 1914-45* (London, 1984)

Stocks, Mary, *The Workers' Educational Association: the first fifty years* (London, 1953; repr. 1968)

Stocks, Mary, *My commonplace book* (Trowbridge and London, 1970)

Strachey, Ray (ed.), *Our freedom and its results* (Letchworth, 1936)

Swanwick, Helena, *I have been young* (London, 1935)

Tawney, R. H. (ed.), *Secondary education for all: a policy for Labour* (London, 1922)

Thompson, F. M. L., *The rise of respectable society: a social history of Victorian Britain 1830-1900* (London, 1988)

Thompson, Paul, *The Edwardians: the remaking of British society* (London, 1975)

Tropp, Asher, *The school teachers* (London, 1957)

Tunstall, J., *Rambles about Bath and its neighbourhood* (Bath, rev. ed., 1889)

Turner, Barry, *Equality for some: the story of girls' education* (London, 1974)

Vicinus, Martha (ed.), *A widening sphere: changing roles of Victorian women* (Bloomington, Ind., 1977)

Westaway, K. M. (ed.), *Seventy-five years: the story of Bedford High School 1882-1957* (Bedford. 1957)

Index